CONSTRUCTING
MODERN
CANADA

Readings in Post-Confederation History

CONSTRUCTING
MODERN
CANADA

Readings in Post-Confederation History

Edited by

Chad Gaffield

University of Ottawa

Copp Clark Longman Ltd.
Toronto

ISBN: 0-7730-5253-4

Editors: Barbara Tessman, Kate Forster
Executive editor: Jeff Miller
Design: Kyle Gell
Cover illustration: Rocco Baviera
Maps and illustrations: Kyle Gell
Typesetting: B.J. Weckerle
Printing and binding: Best Book Manufacturers

Canadian Cataloguing in Publication Data

Main entry under title:

Constructing modern Canada: readings in post-Confederation history

Includes bibliographical references.

ISBN 0-7730-5253-4
1. Canada–History – 1867–   . 2. Canada – Social conditions – 1867–   .
* I. Gaffield, Chad, 1951–   .

FC500.C65 1994   971.05   C94-930110-8
F1033.C6 1994

Copp Clark Longman Ltd.
2775 Matheson Blvd. East
Mississauga, Ontario
L4W 4P7

Associated companies:
Longman Group Ltd., London
Longman Inc., New York
Longman Cheshire Pty., Melbourne
Longman Paul Pty., Auckland

Printed and bound in Canada

   3 4 5   **5253-4**   **00 99 98**

This book is dedicated to all the students in Canadian history courses who have inspired me to continue seeking an understanding of our past.

C O N T E N T S

ACKNOWLEDGMENTS

I am indebted to Jeff Miller and Barbara Tessman for all their support, encouragement, and hard work on this book. Valuable suggestions and helpful comments were generously provided by John Bonnett, Marg Conrad, Alvin Finkel, Johanna Gaffield, Pam Gaffield, Lorne Hammond, Cornelius Jaenen, Peter MacLeod, Nikki Strong-Boag, and the members of this year's doctoral seminar at the University of Ottawa.

INTRODUCTION

THE REWRITING OF POST-CONFEDERATION HISTORY

In recent years, historians have dramatically changed the ways in which we think about Canada's past. By posing different questions, employing new concepts, and developing innovative research strategies, historians have been rewriting all aspects of Canadian history. The readings in this volume illustrate some of this work, and they indicate the exciting new directions now being taken to reinterpret Canadian history since Confederation.

• Rethinking the Historical Process in Canada

The title of this book, *Constructing Modern Canada*, has two meanings related to the dynamic process of construction. The first involves the ways in which all individuals and groups, not simply those in official positions of influence and power, make history. In emphasizing that everyone was involved in constructing modern Canada, historians certainly do not mean that a single vision motivated a harmonious effort. On the contrary, historians are now analysing Canadian history in terms of distinct perspectives and action. Researchers are careful to study women as well as men, the economically disadvantaged as well as elites, minorities as well as the majority, and those living in various parts of the country. While scholars have found evidence of co-operation and consensus among such groups, recent work emphasizes the extent of conflict and contradiction, which sometimes led to violence, as various individuals and groups with different perspectives sought to pursue their own lives.[1]

Similarly, as the readings collected here illustrate, nothing about Canadian history has been inevitable except at a superficial level. Obviously, Canada is part of a larger world, and it is hard to imagine that certain developments could have been avoided. For example, the spread of daily newspapers or the arrival of television were "inevitable." But the significance and specific meaning of such developments were not fully pre-determined: newspapers and television did not affect all people and communities in the same way.

While it might be hard to imagine that our history could have unfolded very differently, recent research shows the importance of understanding how the ideas and behaviour of individuals and groups, both famous and anonymous, could have led to different outcomes. In constructing modern Canada, decisions were made, sometimes within great constraints, sometimes with significant freedom. This process was very complex. Indeed, historians now emphasize that no one succeeded in fully controlling their own destiny just as no one was a complete victim no matter how much they were victimized. Canadian historians are now just as likely to emphasize failure or unintended consequences as fulfilled ambitions, and to discover hope and integrity despite oppression and abuse. It is in this sense that more and more historians agree that everyone in Canada's past deserves to be studied as part of the historical process. The sum total of all decisions, great and small, has shaped modern Canada.

The second meaning intended by this book's title involves the ways in which Canadian historians construct interpretations of the past. Since scholars increasingly agree that the historical process is many-centred, the decision by researchers to focus on any one individual or group becomes very important. Historians stress that the "centre" of the historical process depends upon the particular point of view of the person looking back at the past. Some years ago, for example, scholars usually placed political leaders at centre stage and only examined others when they came into contact with the ideas or actions of these leaders. The result was that our history was presented as the history of only a tiny fraction of the population. Recent research has challenged this portrayal, and while the goal of "total history" remains elusive, historians have been striving to do justice to the perspectives and experiences—the stories—of all members of past societies. Rather than aiming to present a single narrative of Canadian history, scholars seek to understand and explain many narratives and their convergence in specific contexts. In this way, historians construct interpretations of how Canada was "constructed."[2]

In addition to the two meanings of *constructing*, the title of this book also specifies that the readings refer to "modern" Canada. Until recently, the word *modern* was commonly used in an approving way to mean "up-to-date," and it was juxtaposed with the negative connotations of "old-fashioned." From this perspective, history was the story of progress; the task of historians was to trace the key advances along the way. In recent years, however, Canadian historians have begun using the word to refer to the years roughly stretching from the early-to-mid-nineteenth century to the mid-to-later-twentieth century. This period is associated with social, economic, political, and cultural characteristics that are seen to distinguish it from the early periods of pre-contact, British North America, and New France (sometimes viewed as pre-modern) as well as from the more recent past, especially beginning with the 1960s (sometimes referred to as post-modern). Historians continue to debate about the characteristics of "modern Canada," but fewer and fewer judge the past in terms of ongoing "progress." Rather, they assume that judgments concerning whether or not things are getting "better" depend upon who is making that judgment and what criteria are being used.

In abandoning an exclusive focus on the leaders of the dominant society, scholars are increasingly being forced to come to grips with a diversity that reaches to the foundations of history as a discipline, even including a problematizing of the concept of time. Until recently, historians viewed time as an absolute; at least in theory, everyone's clock was considered to run at the same speed. However, historians are realizing that time, like all things, is constructed and, therefore, differs according to who is doing the construction. For example, they know now that the European-origin concept of time cannot be used to understand the ideas and behaviour of Native peoples in Canada. Clearly, different groups use different clocks in setting the pace of everyday life. Similarly, historians also now use expressions such as "family time" and "industrial time" to indicate how humans determine time according to context.

In keeping with the current rewriting of Canada's past, the ambition of this collection of readings is not to provide a single set of facts about specific aspects of our past. Indeed, as will be discussed, fewer and fewer historians believe in the possibility of establishing "facts" that reflect everyone's experience, and some doubt the existence of an objective reality that exists outside the perception and comprehension of each individual. Describing what happened is no longer considered to be a straightforward process involving the examination of as much evidence as possible. Some years ago, historians assumed that each additional piece of evidence would bring them closer to an historical truth that included everyone. Instead, they have found that new evidence can sometimes clarify the topic under study or can reveal further complexity in keeping with the diverse experiences of individuals and groups. While Canadian historians agree on a great number of facts (such as the dates of wars and the identities of political leaders), they are increasingly reluctant to offer a one-dimensional version of Canada's past. It is still important to know the facts that are currently agreed upon by historians, but gone are the days when the memorization of a single chronology of events was the central strategy for learning Canadian history. Now, historians seek to establish many chronologies and to understand how they intersect at various moments in time.

Moreover, because details are so easily forgotten, the value of this book would be quite temporary if it aimed to transfer facts from text to student. Certain dates, events, and individuals might stick in readers' minds, but most would soon be lost. Rather, the following readings offer new ways to think about Canadian history, to understand the historical process, and to view the background of contemporary life. It is hoped that these aspects of the readings will have an impact that endures long after the specific details are forgotten.

•Identities and Relationships

One way of characterizing current research on modern Canada is in terms of the study of identities and relationships. At any particular time and place, how did individuals and groups see themselves? How did others see them? How did they interact with others? What was the nature of these relationships, and how can they be explained? These questions emphasize the importance of context. They suggest that everyone in Canada's past must be situated with respect to others and that their history reflects the identities and relationships of this situation.

However, the study of identities and relationships poses serious challenges that reflect the complexity of Canada's past. How can individuals and groups be categorized for analysis? Recent research has shown that even very familiar labels must be used with great caution. For example, a number of scholars have shown that concepts of *childhood* and definitions of *children* have hardly been static. Rather, the process of growing up has varied enormously in keeping with social, economic, and cultural differences. Similarly, historians have rethought their use of words like *family* or *relative*. Not only have official definitions of such words changed over time, but they have also had very different meanings within different social and cultural settings.[3]

In the same way, recent work has begun to call into question the value and meaning of many racial and ethnic terms such as *white* or *Indian* or *Eskimo*. Whose perspectives are represented by such names? In what sense can the ambiguities of identity be boiled down to a single label? Should we think in terms of multiple identities in which individuals see themselves, and are seen, in different ways depending on the historical context?[4] The authors of the readings in this book do not all agree on the answers to such questions but, taken together, their studies provide a firm foundation for going beyond the destructive stereotypes sometimes associated with Canadian history.

In current research on Canada's past, the central aspects of identities and relationships include those of social class, gender, ethnicity, and region. The importance of social class in Canada was first actively pursued by historians in the 1970s who focussed on the men who formed the labouring classes—the marginal, the ignored, and those deprived of official power. Previous historians had left these men, along with almost all women and children, out of their analysis in the belief that they did not really count; their places in society meant that they were not considered to be among the makers of Canadian history. In contrast, scholars began to publish findings that showed how men without material advantage or formal authority had their own stories that deserved telling. Moreover, these men did affect the ideas and actions of elites; they were not simply passive victims of those in apparent control. Historians showed how poor and disadvantaged men did all they could, within the limits that enclosed them, to pursue their lives with dignity and self-respect. In certain cases, they clearly affected the course of history, perhaps most visibly in demanding better wages and working conditions.[5]

In studying the identities and relationships of the previously ignored men of Canadian history, scholars began addressing wide-ranging questions of thought and behaviour. In different times and places, did men see themselves or act as part of a working class? How unequal were the occupational structures of Canadian communities? To what extent did a working-class culture develop? What were the identities and relationships among artisans, unskilled workers, farmers, fishermen, and the many other groups of labouring men? And what were their relationships with the privileged and powerful? The importance of asking such questions is especially revealed in this collection of readings by Ian McKay's analysis of craftsmen and labourers, and Bruno Ramirez's explanation of migration from Quebec to New England.

Within a few years, scholars of women's history began re-directing the study of the anonymous of Canadian history by turning their attention to the "neglected majority." They pointed out that, along with the conventional study of elites, the study of class structure and relations was substantially, though not exclusively, based on men. Historians showed that much of the newer research on the popular classes, as well as the older research on official leaders, ignored the history of women in Canada. Initially, scholars simply aimed to add women to the established accounts of male experience but, soon, feminist theory began transforming how everything—from daily life in households to the operation of government—was viewed. New questions were posed that probed to the heart of all established versions of Canadian history. For example, to what extent are the dates of the familiar chronology of Canadian history appropriate for women? Are the key dates of our past the same for men and women?[6] Similarly, has the geography of Canadian history been notably distinct for men and women? Have certain environments been male or female? To address this question, historians use the concept of "gendered space" as illustrated in this book by Cynthia Wright's study of department store shopping and Veronica Strong-Boag's analysis of suburban sprawl.

Feminist scholarship also helped move the study of Canadian history beyond social, economic, and political themes to include the study of feelings, emotions, and the metaphysical dimensions of everyday human experience. Beyond knowing information about the type of work being done or the wages paid, for example, historians began pointing to the importance of learning how individuals felt about their work.

Furthermore, scholars challenged existing definitions of words such as *work*, which had previously been used to mean remunerated labour. Because so many women worked at home, their labour was usually not acknowledged in official records (characteristically written by men). Historians began revealing the gender-specific definition of many words commonly assumed to apply to both sexes, and they began to show the extent to which such definitions slighted or ignored the history of women in Canada.[7]

Research on the history of women in Canada has led quite recently to studies of gender, and thus, to the history of masculinity. While historical research has traditionally focussed on men, they have usually been presented as gender-neutral representatives of all humanity. Only during the past few years have questions been raised about the construction of masculinity. How have boys learned to be men? What values and characteristics have been associated with manliness? What pressures, conflicts, and contradictions have been associated with growing up male in Canada? How can we understand the violence and rage, the wife battering and child abuse, found in Canadian history? Consideration of such questions is adding considerably to our understanding of the meaning of gender in our past.[8] Excellent examples of such work are offered in the readings by Lynne Marks, Joy Parr, and Mark Rosenfeld, who explore the lives of girls and boys, women and men, in the context of work, family, and community. Similarly, Dominique Marshall relates questions of public policy to the nature of family life in her study of the emergence of the welfare state in Quebec.

Especially since the 1970s, historians have also been coming to grips with the ethnic diversity of Canada's past.[9] Rather than viewing ethnicity as a label or category, historians have been examining it as a dynamic process. Particular attention has been devoted to understanding Canada as an immigrant society that is far more complex than the common emphasis on "two founding peoples." For example, historians rarely use the expression *English Canada* anymore; not only are significant components of non-francophone Canada excluded by the adjective *English*, but even the "English" population is quite diverse, as illustrated by studies of the Irish and Scots.[10] Similarly, the expression *French Canadian* has given way to more specific adjectives such as Québécois, Franco-Ontarian, and Franco-Manitoban.[11] In his contribution to the following readings, Pierre Fortin discusses one aspect of the question of francophone identity by examining the economic dimension of recent thinking about sovereignty in Quebec.

Groups other than anglophones and francophones have also been the focus of major studies, including several works on Italian and Asian immigrants to Canada.[12] In the following readings, James W. St G. Walker and Robert F. Harney analyse aspects of the racism and ethnic prejudice that have been part of our diverse heritage.

Similarly, non-Native historians have begun to analyse the history of Native groups in Canada.[13] While Native groups have always had a strong sense of their past (communicated through oral tradition), their history has usually been neglected or misrepresented in cultures based on print. Only recently have both non-Natives and Natives begun to use these oral traditions as well as adapting the research methods of the dominant society to write Native history.[14] One important change within the work of non-

Native historians involves an interest in studying Native experiences throughout the history of Canada rather than only during certain periods (especially New France) and in specific contexts (notably, the fur trade). Striking examples of such work in this book include D.N. Sprague's re-examination of the Canadian government's dealings with Louis Riel, John Lutz's study of aboriginal labour in British Columbia, Tina Loo's analysis of Natives and the legal system of the dominant society, and Tony Hall's discussion of aboriginal "rights and wrongs."

Beyond looking at previously neglected "makers" of Canada, one of the distinguishing features of current work is a greater preference for regional history, often involving research at the level of individuals, families, and communities. The concept of *region* varies a great deal, with some historians studying a small geographic area, perhaps a town and the surrounding countryside, while other researchers examine the collective experience of a province or group of provinces. Examples of studies that focus on a region of provinces include Ernest Forbes's article on the Maritimes and Gerald Friesen's study of the Prairies. These researchers show that a central theme of Canadian history concerns the complex relationships among different parts of the country. Their approach, as well as that centring on smaller geographic areas, reflects a new sensitivity to the diversity of Canadian history across the vast lands from ocean to ocean. Scholars are now convinced that the history of Canada is not simply a larger version of the history of any one area. Only by studying the various regions on their own terms can the dynamics of Canada's past be interpreted.[15]

Beyond attention to the relationships among individuals and groups, historians are now studying the interactions between humans and the environment, including both flora and fauna and the land that sustains them. Environmental historians emphasize the interconnectedness of all components of the biosphere. In this view, humans are just one of many species on history's stage and, while it may be tempting to focus on divisions of class, gender, ethnicity, and region, such divisions need to be situated within the larger relationships of humans to animals and plants, the land and the sea. Environmental history raises new questions about familiar topics as well as suggesting completely new topics for study. For example, how would our understanding of the fur trade change if we focussed on the beavers as well as the hunters? Or if we analysed the forest economy in terms of its impact on the trees and the wildlife that the forests support? Although such questions are just beginning to be posed by Canadian historians, their importance promises that environmental history will continue its rapid growth as an emerging research area involving many disciplines from history to the natural sciences.[16] In this collection of readings, examples of recent work include Allan Smith's study of the changing attitudes towards land in the late-nineteenth century, Peter Gillis's analysis of an early controversy over water pollution, Robert Page's discussion of the far North, and Tony Hall's examination of the confrontation at Temagami.

• Rethinking the Selection and Use of Historical Evidence

In order to pursue questions of social class, gender, ethnicity, and region, historians have begun finding new ways to study familiar documents as well as to examine evidence that had previously been ignored. In terms of documents, historians have learned to "read between the lines" or decode and deconstruct written evidence. In the case of Native history, for example, historical documents generally reflect the views of "others" about Natives rather than expressing the views of Natives themselves. If taken at face value, such evidence tells us about the ambitions and actions of European-origin society rather than Native experience. However, scholars have shown that, when analysed with sensitivity, documents created by the dominant society can indeed provide insight into the actual history of Natives groups. Similar approaches have been taken to learn about the economically disadvantaged, women and children, ethnic minorities, and related groups for whom much of the written evidence was created by others.

Historians have also begun pursuing new questions through the study of well-known sources. One important example of this approach has involved the use of newspapers. Historians found that although newspapers were created by a small minority, they usually include valuable information on the activities of many different groups. Local newspapers often reported, for example, on labour disputes such as strikes and lock-outs, and on cultural events ranging from parades to baseball games, as illustrated in this book by Colin D. Howell's study of baseball as a social and cultural expression. Another innovative example involving printed sources is Keith Walden's examination of the thinking behind grocery store window displays in early-twentieth-century Canada. Not too long ago, such a topic would have been seen as marginal, if not irrelevant; however, Walden shows how such window displays tell us about basic themes in the construction of modern Canada.

The most novel evidence used to study the "anonymous" of Canadian history has come from *routinely generated sources*, an expression used to describe manuscript census returns, tax rolls, land records, parish registers of birth, marriage, and death, employment lists, and similar documents created by governments, churches, businesses, and other institutions in the course of everyday life. Such sources allow historians to learn about the lives of whole populations. Who held which occupations? Who controlled how much land? Who migrated to new communities? When did couples marry and how many children did they have? As illustrated by Bruno Ramirez's article on Quebec, the answers to these and similar questions began allowing historians to describe the changing structures of Canadian society.

Routinely generated sources usually do not provide direct information about why individuals had certain experiences, but they do indicate something about the details of their lives. For example, an employment record will not tell why a particular person ended up working in a particular factory, but it may well provide valuable information about the terms and conditions of the actual work. When many such employment records are systematically examined (and perhaps linked to other sources), a great deal can be learned about the history of work in Canada. As Joy Parr's contribution to this book shows, the same approach has been used with a wide variety of other sources to study many aspects of Canadian history.

Greater interest in the history of emotions, feelings, and personal experience, and some dissatisfaction with the limitations of routinely generated sources and documents such as newspapers, encouraged historians to look for direct expressions of ideas, perceptions, and activity. Two important sources found in this search are personal papers such as diaries and letters, and, for historians of the twentieth century, memories and recollections. The value of personal papers has long been recognized by historians of famous individuals such as prime ministers. However, such evidence was rarely used to probe emotional and personal issues. In addition, scholars have now shown that evidence like the correspondence among family members or friends, or the entries made in private diaries, can also tell a great deal about the lives of quite "ordinary" men and women. Researchers have been surprised by how many of these documents were created (even by those with little formal education), and how many that can still be found both within repositories and in private attics.[17]

The difficulties of using documents to study cultures or groups who have not left the usual types of historical evidence have encouraged historians to expand their definition of what constitutes an historical source. One important example of this expansion is the recent examination of oral traditions among Native groups. Once dismissed by non-Natives as simply fiction, such traditions are now being taken seriously as a key feature of the Native historical record.[18] In the same way, researchers have traditionally interviewed famous people to learn more about the thinking and context of their decisions. However, historians have now shown that the memories of all individuals can add insight into otherwise unrecoverable dimensions of Canadian history. The use of oral history has allowed researchers to probe into the innermost workings of life at home and in the larger society. Recollections can be combined with other types of evidence to produce rich historical analyses as evident in the work of Mark Rosenfeld, Veronica Strong-Boag, and other authors of the following readings.[19] Indeed, historians are now ready to use any type of evidence in their efforts to understand Canada's past, including the poems and paintings studied by Allan Smith in his chapter on the changing images of the land.

•New Ways of Doing Historical Research

In addition to posing new questions and using new sources, historians have developed innovative research strategies in recent years. Perhaps the most importance trend has been the emergence of *micro-history*, which involves the detailed study of individuals within specific settings such as in households, workplaces, neighbourhoods, or communities. For some scholars, such settings serve as a laboratory within which general processes can be studied in detail. In this approach, the ambition of the research is not primarily to learn about the specific setting under study; rather, the goal is to contribute to a better understanding of a historical process that is common to many similar settings. Scholars choose their laboratories according to the historical questions under examination.

Micro-history also offers the opportunity to analyse the ways in which large-scale historical change is articulated at the level of individual experience. By looking at specific populations in specific settings, historians can examine the constellation of relationships that has shaped the lives of Canadians in different parts of the country at various times in history. This approach allows the study of abstract concepts such as urbanization, industrialization, state formation, secularization, gendered space, and many others, in terms of personal experience. In this book, for example, Ester Reiter shows how a detailed study of a fast-food outlet can reveal fundamental characteristics of the global economy.

Similarly, historians use a micro-historical approach as a way of analysing the interplay of the larger forces of class, gender, ethnicity, and region. Some years ago, historians assumed that this interplay was quite similar across various communities. However, it soon became apparent that no two contexts were really identical, and the hope of general explanations gave way to the more modest ambition of understanding the range of diversity associated with specific aspects of the historical process. With each new study, historians have gained a greater appreciation of the complexity of Canadian history and the inappropriateness of reducing this history to a single narrative description based on one setting.

Canadian historians are also increasingly joining forces with other scholars in recognition that new perspectives and research strategies are needed to analyse our complex history. Interdisciplinary research has certainly been more talked about than undertaken up to this point, but increasing collaboration among scholars can be expected in future years. Perhaps the most promising area for such collaboration is in the emerging field of environmental history, which could benefit from scholars in both the arts and sciences. Thus far, most collaborators in historical research have come from the social sciences such as sociology, anthropology, archaeology, and geography.[20] Scholars from these disciplines have contributed different concepts and methods to historical research; in turn, historians have challenged the generalizations of their collaborators' disciplines by insisting on contextual specificity and change over time. Historians constantly remind social scientists that the historical process is often unpredictable and exceedingly complex, in keeping with the infinite possibilities of human existence. Despite the common saying, history never really does repeat itself.[21]

Another new approach to historical research has been the mounting of major projects involving several professors along with graduate students and research assistants. This approach departs dramatically from the traditional method in which individual historians worked on their own topics, doing their own research and coming to their own conclusions; a metaphor for this method might be the making of a jigsaw puzzle in which each researcher's goal was to contribute a piece. The launching of major research projects is generally based on quite different assumptions. Rather than each historian aiming to add a piece to a puzzle, the researchers in these projects view history as a complex and multidimensional process that can be best grasped by collective conceptual and methodological effort. This approach is still not common among Canadian historians (as reflected in the absence of multi-authored readings in this collection), with the exception of historians in Quebec who, in many cases, are members of research teams that receive collective funding for their work.[22]

As a result of posing new questions and developing new research strategies, historians have also come to see computers as helpful tools. While the image of a solitary historian carefully taking notes on index cards has not been fully replaced by the picture of research teams entering data on lap-tops or optically scanning documents, there is no doubt that historians have entered the Information Age. All aspects of the research process have been affected. Bibliographies are being compiled automatically by using key words to search vast databases, historical evidence is being transformed into machine-readable files, analyses are being word processed, and references are being checked by modem connection to remote locations. Research collaborators keep in constant touch and, indeed, are beginning to co-author without even seeing each other, as they drive the new electronic highways now connecting distant points around the world.

But computerization has raised new questions that promise to demand increasing attention in the coming years. To what extent can human experience be captured by the quantitative examination of empirical data? Can a document be usefully examined by computer-based textual analysis? Can the ambiguities and "grey zones" of the historical process be done justice in the creation of databases? Clearly, the answers to such questions are not simply negative or positive. Although computers are undoubtedly here to stay as part of research activity in Canada, historians will increasingly be forced to grapple with unprecedented issues as they strive to benefit from the new technological possibilities for probing the past.[23]

• Conclusion

Recent changes in the discipline of history are part of a larger rethinking of research throughout the arts and sciences. In fact, the ways in which historians are now conceptualizing and researching Canadian history can be compared to the new directions of the scientific disciplines. Unlike earlier years when scientific models based on empiricism and objectivity influenced the work of historians, the sciences now seem increasingly humanistic. For example, the research of physicists lends full support to the rejection of history as the linear unfolding of a chain of causes and effects. Like historians, scientists are also emphasizing the unexpected, the indeterminate, and the unpredictable. Indeed, discussions among scientists about chaos are not completely dissimilar to the debates among historians about contingency and context. Overall, researchers across the arts and sciences are gaining a new appreciation of complexity, and they are far more humble about their ability to fully understand or explain what they observe. While scientists now agree that the "laws of physics" are not one set of rules obeyed in all situations, few historians hope to achieve a general theory of change that could explain human thought and behaviour in all times and places.[24]

If recent years are any indication, the study of Canada's past will continue to take unexpected directions and to lead to unanticipated ways of thinking about the background of contemporary society. New questions, rediscovered evidence, and innovative research strategies should make the rewriting of Canadian history an ongoing process that constantly adds to the richness of our own lives. The following readings illustrate some of the exciting ways in which this process is now underway.

•Notes

[1] The changing perspectives of Canadian historians are discussed in Carl Berger, *The Writing of Canadian History*, 2nd ed. (Toronto: University of Toronto Press, 1986); M. Brook Taylor, *Promoters, Patriots and Partisans: Historiography in Nineteenth-Century English Canada* (Toronto: University of Toronto Press, 1990); Serge Gagnon, *Quebec and Its Historians, 1840–1920* (Montreal: Harvest House, 1982); and Doug Owram, ed., *Confederation to the Present* (Toronto: University of Toronto Press, 1994). For a recent example of research on historical construction, see Gérard Bouchard with Serge Courville, eds., *La construction d'une culture: Le Québec et l'Amérique française* (Sainte-Foy, PQ: Les Presses de l'Université Laval, 1993).

[2] For a general discussion of recent debate that places historians within a larger context, see Pauline Marie Rosenau, *Post-Modernism and the Social*

Sciences: Insights, Inroads, and Intrusions (Princeton, NJ: Princeton University Press, 1992).

[3] The changing views of childhood and family are reflected in Neil Sutherland, *Children in English-Canadian Society: Framing the Twentieth-Century Consensus* (Toronto: University of Toronto Press, 1976); Joy Parr, ed., *Childhood and Family in Canadian History* (Toronto: McClelland & Stewart, 1982); Bettina Bradbury, ed., *Canadian Family History* (Toronto: Copp Clark Pitman, 1992); and Joy Parr, *Labouring Children: British Immigrant Apprentices to Canada, 1869–1924* (Toronto: University of Toronto Press, 1993).

[4] Recent work on gender, race, and ethnicity emphasizes the complexities of identity; see, for example, Frances Swyripa, *Wedded to the Cause: Ukrainian Women and Ethnic Identity, 1891–1991* (Toronto: University of Toronto Press, 1993), and Suzanne Morton, "Separate

Spheres in a Separate World: African Nova-Scotia Women in Late Nineteenth-Century Halifax County," *Acadiensis* 22, 2 (Spring 1993): 61–83.

5 The most important works of the late 1970s and early 1980s include David Bercuson, *Fools and Wise Men: The Rise and Fall of the One Big Union* (Toronto: McGraw-Hill Ryerson, 1978); Michael J. Piva, *The Condition of the Working Class in Toronto, 1900–1921* (Ottawa: University of Ottawa Press, 1979); Bryan D. Palmer, *A Culture in Conflict: Skilled Workers and Industrial Capitalism in Hamilton, Ontario, 1860–1914* (Montreal: McGill-Queen's University Press, 1979); Gregory S. Kealey, *Toronto Workers Respond to Industrial Capitalism, 1867–1892* (Toronto: University of Toronto Press, 1980); Craig Heron, *Working in Steel: The Early Years in Canada, 1883–1935* (Toronto: McClelland & Stewart, 1980); and Bryan D. Palmer, *Working-Class Experience: The Rise and Reconstitution of Canadian Labour, 1880–1980* (Toronto: Butterworths, 1983).

6 The now "classic" contribution was Susan Mann Trofimenkoff and Alison Prentice, eds., *The Neglected Majority: Essays in Canadian Women's History* (Toronto: McClelland & Stewart, 1977). The results of research undertaken in the 1970s and early 1980s are synthesized in Alison Prentice et al., *Canadian Women: A History* (Toronto: Harcourt Brace Jovanovich, 1988), and Clio Collective, *Quebec Women: A History* (Toronto: Women's Press, 1987). More recent work is presented in Veronica Strong-Boag and Anita Clair Fellman, eds., *Rethinking Canada: The Promise of Women's History*, 2nd ed. (Toronto: Copp Clark Pitman, 1991).

7 An excellent example is Bettina Bradbury, *Working Families: Age, Gender, and Daily Survival in Industrializing Montreal* (Toronto: McClelland & Stewart, 1993).

8 See, for example, Thomas Dunk, *It's a Working Man's Town: Male Working-Class Culture in Northwestern Ontario* (Montreal: McGill-Queen's University

Press, 1991). The importance of studying gender as a relationship is emphasized in Karen Dubinsky, *Improper Advances: Rape and Heterosexual Conflict in Ontario, 1880–1929* (Chicago: University of Chicago Press, 1993).

9 The initial research undertaken in the 1970s and early 1980s is reviewed in Roberto Perrin, "Clio as an Ethnic: The Third Force in Canadian Historiography," *Canadian Historical Review* 64, 4 (1983): 441–67.

10 Recent research includes J.I. Little, *Crofters and Habitants: Settler Society, Economy and Culture in a Quebec Township, 1848–1881* (Montreal: McGill-Queen's University Press, 1991); Marianne McLean, *The People of Glengarry: Highlanders in Transition, 1745–1820* (Montreal: McGill-Queen's University Press, 1991); and Bruce Elliott, *Irish Migrants in the Canadas: A New Approach* (Montreal: McGill-Queen's University Press, 1988). Pauline Greenhill argues for the usefulness of the concept of "English Canada" in *Ethnicity in the Mainstream: Three Studies of English Canadian Culture in Ontario* (Montreal: McGill-Queen's University Press, 1993).

11 The changing perspectives on "French Canada" can be traced through Paul-André Linteau, René Durocher, and Jean-Claude Robert, *Quebec since 1930* (Toronto: Lorimer, 1983); John A. Dickinson and Brian Young, *Brève histoire socio-économique du Québec* (Quebec: Éditions du Septentrion, 1992); and Cornelius J. Jaenen, ed., *Les franco-ontariens* (Ottawa: University of Ottawa Press, 1993).

12 This work includes John E. Zucchi, *Italians in Toronto: Development of a National Identity, 1875–1935* (Montreal: McGill-Queen's University Press, 1990); Franca Iacovetta, *Such Hardworking People: Italian Immigrants in Postwar Toronto* (Montreal: McGill-Queen's University Press, 1992); W. Peter Ward, *White Canada Forever: Popular Attitudes and Public Policy Toward Orientals in British Columbia*, 2nd ed. (Montreal: McGill-Queen's University Press, 1990);

and Patricia E. Roy, *A White Man's Province: British Columbia Politicians and Chinese and Japanese Immigrants, 1858–1914* (Vancouver: University of British Columbia Press, 1989).

[13] The results of recent research are presented in Bruce G. Trigger, *Natives and Newcomers: Canada's "Heroic Age" Reconsidered* (Montreal: McGill-Queen's University Press, 1986); Robin Fisher and Kenneth Coates, eds., *Out of the Background: Readings on Canadian Native History* (Toronto: Copp Clark Pitman, 1988); J.R. Miller, *Skyscrapers Hide the Heavens: A History of Indian-White Relations in Canada* (Toronto: University of Toronto Press, 1989); and Olive Patricia Dickason, *Canada's First Nations: A History of Founding Peoples from Earliest Times* (Toronto: McClelland & Stewart, 1992).

[14] Georges E. Sioui, *For an Amerindian Autohistory: An Essay on the Foundations of a Social Ethic* (Montreal: McGill-Queen's University Press, 1992).

[15] Examples of the many different types of regional history include Jean Barman, *The West Beyond the West: A History of British Columbia* (Toronto: University of Toronto Press, 1991); Paul Voisey, *Vulcan: The Making of a Prairie Community* (Toronto: University of Toronto Press, 1988); Ernest Forbes, *Challenging the Regional Stereotype: Essays on the Twentieth Century Maritimes* (Fredericton: Acadiensis Press, 1989); Alvin Finkel, *The Social Credit Phenomenon in Alberta* (Toronto: University of Toronto Press, 1989); Margaret Conrad, *George Nowlan: Maritime Conservative in National Politics* (Toronto: University of Toronto Press, 1986); and René Hardy and Normand Séguin, *Forêt et société en Mauricie* (Montreal: Boréal, 1984).

[16] Michel Girard, "The New History of the Environment," *Canadian Historical Association Newsletter* 16, 3 (Summer 1990): 1–3.

[17] See, for example, Margaret Conrad, Toni Laidlaw, and Donna Smyth, eds., *No Place Like Home: Diaries and Letters of Nova Scotia Women 1771–1938* (Halifax:

Formac, 1988), and Peter Ward, *Courtship, Love and Marriage in Nineteenth-Century English Canada* (Montreal: McGill-Queen's University Press, 1990).

[18] For another example, see Joan M. Vastokas, "Native Art as Art History: Meaning and Time From Unwritten Sources," *Journal of Canadian Studies* 21, 4 (1987): 7–36.

[19] Recent work that shows the value of oral history includes Ruth A. Frager, *Sweatshop Strife: Class, Ethnicity, and Gender in the Jewish Labour Movement of Toronto 1900–1939* (Toronto: University of Toronto Press, 1992).

[20] Stephen R. Grossbart, "Quantitative and Social Science Methods for Historians: An Annotated Bibliography of Selected Books and Articles," *Historical Methods* 25, 3 (Summer 1992): 100–20.

[21] The wide range of possibilities for interdisciplinary work is suggested by the joining of history and genetics as discussed in Gérard Bouchard, "Population Studies and Genetic Epidemiology in Northeast Quebec," *Canadian Studies in Population* 16, 1 (1989): 61–86; of history and law as illustrated by Constance Backhouse, *Petticoats and Prejudice: Women and the Law in Nineteenth-Century Canada* (Toronto: Women's Press, 1991); of history and geography as shown in Graeme Wynn, ed., *People, Places, Patterns, Processes: Geographical Perspectives on the Canadian Past* (Toronto: Copp Clark Pitman, 1990); and of history and literature as evident in Carl Ballstadt, Elizabeth Hopkins, and Michael Peterman, eds., *Letters of Love and Duty: The Correspondence of Susanna and John Moodie* (Toronto: University of Toronto Press, 1993).

[22] The longest standing project in Canada produces the *Dictionary of Canadian Biography*, while the now-completed Historical Atlas of Canada Project published three volumes spanning all of Canadian history. In Quebec, several

projects have been exceedingly important including Le programme de recherche en démographie historique at the Université de Montréal, the Centre interuniversitaire de recherches sur les populations at the Université du Québec à Chicoutimi, and the Montreal Business History Group centred at McGill University. One of the most influential efforts has been the Maritime History Group based at Memorial University of Newfoundland; the results of its work include Eric Sager, *Maritime Capital: The Shipping Industry in Atlantic Canada, 1820–1914* (Montreal: McGill-Queen's University Press, 1990), and Rosemary Ommer, *Merchant Credit and Labour Strategies in Historical Perspective* (Fredericton: Acadiensis Press, 1990).

[23] Some of these complex issues are addressed in Chad Gaffield, "Machines and Minds: Historians and the Emerging Collaboration," *Histoire sociale/Social History* 21, 42 (Nov. 1988): 312–17.

[24] It should be remembered that significant differences (especially concerning the concept of *order*) still separate many humanists, social scientists, and scientists. Stephen H. Kellert analyses recent developments in the sciences in *In the Wake of Chaos: Unpredictable Order in Dynamical Systems* (Chicago: University of Chicago Press, 1993).

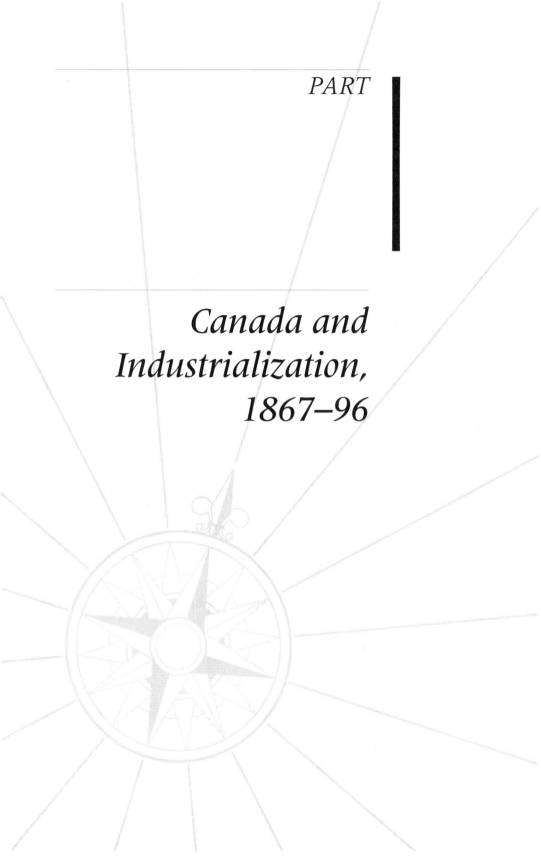

PART

Canada and Industrialization, 1867–96

The title of this section, "Canada and Industrialization," reflects a new interest in Canada's Industrial Revolution of the later nineteenth century. Without denying the continuing importance of natural resource exploitation to the economy, historians are now showing the ways in which industrialization affected all aspects of everyday experience during the decades following Confederation.

In the first article of this section, Allan Smith examines the competing rural and urban images of Canada in the late nineteenth century. His study makes an important contribution to the emerging research field of "environmental history" in which scholars focus on the changing relationship between humans and nature. In this article, Smith shows how urbanization led to a new view of the natural landscape in Ontario. In the years after Confederation, residents began altering their "mental construct" of nature; land came to be seen less as the basis of economic security and more as a factor of psychological health. By using a wide range of historical evidence, including artistic works such as poems and paintings, Smith tries to understand developments such as the building of urban "green spaces" and the increasing popularity of summer camps.

During the later nineteenth century, Canadians revised not only their views of nature but also their views of each other. Ian McKay focusses on the relationship between craftsmen and labourers in the port city of Halifax in order to explain why a united working class did not emerge during the late nineteenth century. McKay's argument is based on a careful reading of certain trade union records as well as of newspaper accounts of workers' activities. His study is an example of "micro-history" in which a general question is addressed by way of a systematic case study. McKay's main ambition is not to learn about Halifax; rather, he studied the dynamics of this city in order to better understand the general impact of economic change on the identities of craftsmen and labourers.

The question of identity is also at the heart of the changing relationship between Native peoples and the new political and economic leaders of the later nineteenth century. D.N. Sprague studied the letters exchanged among various government officials in order to understand the armed conflict of 1885 that eventually led to the hanging of Louis Riel. Sprague uses these letters to trace the connection between political considerations and Prime Minister John A. Macdonald's attitude towards the Métis land claims. His research emphasized how Riel and the Métis were increasingly seen as an obstacle to the ambitions of the Canadian Pacific Railway and, as a result, were provoked to rebel by a government anxious to get them out of the way.

The juxtaposition of Métis land claims and CPR ambition contrasts with the considerable interaction between Natives and immigrants discovered by John Lutz in British Columbia. In his analysis, aboriginal people made a significant contribution to the economic development of the province during the second half of the nineteenth century. Not only did they form the majority of the population, but they also played key roles in agriculture, fishing, trapping, and the emerging primary industries. When compared to Sprague's work on the Métis, Lutz's study illustrates the complexity of aboriginal history as well as the importance of integrating this history into general understandings of Canada's Industrial Revolution.

The great economic changes of the late nineteenth century must also be understood in terms of religion, as illustrated by Lynne Marks, and in terms of the rural changes described by Bruno Ramirez. In her study of the Knights of Labor and the Salvation Army, Marks suggests that with the growing secularization of Canadian society, recent research has tended to underestimate or altogether ignore the continuing importance of religious motivation. For his part, Bruno Ramirez examines one rural county in Quebec to study the ways in which demographic and economic change led to considerable out-migration in the late nineteenth century. Although Ramirez focusses on men, his findings should be understood in terms of family economies that are based on the productive labour of all members, including women and children. This point is important because so many New England textile mills came to depend on the labour of French-Canadian men, women, and children.

The last article of this section examines the origins of debate about pollution in Canada. Although we often assume that concern about the destruction of our environment has only been expressed in recent decades, Peter Gillis shows that this concern dates back at least to the mid-nineteenth century in the case of the forest economy. However, he also reveals the priorities of government and business leaders by analysing their views and actions with respect to the pollution of waterways such as the Ottawa River. Gillis's study provides an important lesson in the ways in which environmental issues can be appropriated by different groups for quite different purposes.

Thus, these articles emphasize that the emergence of modern Canada occurred in a changing context of industrial capitalism that affected both rural and urban areas, and that touched all social and cultural groups. By focussing on specific times and places, and by studying ideas as well as experience, historians have now provided rich reinterpretations of the early construction of modern Canada.

FARMS, FORESTS, AND CITIES:
The Image of the Land and the Rise of the Metropolis in Ontario, 1860–1914*

ALLAN SMITH

Until the era of Confederation, those who saw the Upper Canadian encounter with the landscape in positive terms tended to concentrate on the land's capacity to sustain agricultural activity.[1] Poets, publicists, politicians, land company agents, farmers, teachers, historians, geographers, novelists, journalists, and essayists—all argued that the province's abundance of good land permitted not only an important economic activity and a high material standard of living but also the emergence of a morally regenerate individual in a pure and undefiled community. "True independence"—Susanna Moodie's words were representative—"greets you here." In the fields of Canada West you "breathe a purer, freer air/ . . . Indulgent heav'n has blessed the soil,/ And plenty crowns the woodman's toil."[2] Inhabiting what Samuel Strickland called a "Garden of Eden,"[3] the farmer of that region occupied a place where "all can become the possessors of their own broad acres . . . where the invidious distinctions of rank and

*Reprinted with permission from *Old Ontario: Essays in Honour of J.M.S. Careless*, edited by David Keane and Colin Read, "Farms, Forests and Cities: The Image of the Land and the Rise of the Metropolis in Ontario, 1860–1914" by Allan Smith; Dundurn Press, Toronto, 1990: pp. 71–94. © David Keane and Colin Read, 1990.

wealth are little known."[4] As the University of Toronto's Daniel Wilson put it, thanks to the fact that the province was "dowered with the inestimable blessing of a fertile soil,"[5] its people enjoyed a truly elevated status. Alexander McLachlan, farmer and rhymster of Amarantha Township, Simcoe County, summed up the argument with wit and conviction: "He's a king upon a throne/ Who has acres of his own!"[6]

Yet, even as this view of the land was arriving at the apex of its influence, new realities were beginning to erode the foundations on which it rested. The march north towards mineral-laden and timber-rich New Ontario in the 1870s and 1880s certainly threatened the understanding of the province as an agrarian and land-based community,[7] while so far as most Ontarians were concerned, the rise of the city and the industrial and bureaucratic patterns associated with it did even more to militate against the idea that their province was a place of sturdy and independent yeoman farmers.[8]

Awareness of these trends provoked a variety of responses. Some commentators rushed to define Ontario, with the rest of the Europeanized world, as increasingly urban and industrial. "This is," proclaimed a young student of politics at the University of Toronto in 1891, "an age of great cities."[9] Others insisted that Ontario's future lay in the north. For them, "the barren north suddenly became New Ontario and the province an empire."[10] Others still remained firmly attached to what they considered the conventional wisdom concerning the province's character. This link was, paradoxically, easiest to maintain in relation to the north, for the absence of a body of experience showing that farming was not in fact practicable there left the way open for the sort of simple and direct argument which could be made by assertion. In the clay belt particularly, settlement promoters claimed, the soil was excellent, the growing season more than adequate, and the prospects for upward mobility unlimited. "The penniless pioneer of a few years ago," insisted a government pamphleteer, "is the substantial, independent, farmer of today."[11] Indeed, as a later commentator put it, "much other evidence and testimony could be adduced, all going to indicate a magnificent future for this great belt, which will some day support millions of people on the land, and prove a considerable factor, not only in Canada's development, but in meeting the world's rapidly increasing demand for food and other products of the soil."[12]

The south, however, also continued to be seen in agricultural terms, for notwithstanding the gains being made in that area by town and city, the farm remained an obvious part of its landscape. But the arguments of the farm's supporters there now betrayed a clear sense that agriculture's supremacy could no longer be taken for granted. Particularly evident in what they wrote was a distinct feeling that, in light of the ever more prominent urban reality, the farm's retention of its favoured place would require constant and unrelenting emphasis on its virtues along with an equally forceful stress on the city's many and varied defects. One of agriculture's friends thus found himself not only exalting the rural life and the "happy farm" but also putting those joyful places in explicit apposition to the rising city, where, he remarked with distaste, one lived a distressing and unpleasant life hard by "the busy hum of machinery, the regal mansion of the capitalist, and a background of squalid tenements where vice, and penury, and dirt, produce a diseased and vicious population."[13]

By the beginning of the new century some four decades of rural depopulation, with its associated migration to the United States, the Canadian Prairies and, of course, the cities of the province, had made much more acute the belief that the farm, though still society's seat of virtue, was steadily losing ground to the expanding metropolis. "Our farming community," as Ontario's deputy minister of agriculture said, might be retaining its capacity to act as a bulwark against the "decadence" being spawned by the new order. It had, however, also to be emphasized that the urban challenge was developing to the point where one could speak of the "national calamity" that would ensue "if our Ontario farms were to be deserted."[14] Indeed, thought poet and essayist William Wilfred Campbell, matters had gone so far that "the greatest cure for many of our modern ills and problems" was to be spoken of in terms of "a return to the land," a getting back to the farm-based kind of community which, he thought, had been so largely lost.[15]

These turn-of-the-century observers had no doubt that the farm retained its traditional qualities. As one 1912 commentator wrote, "the normal or natural life is living in the country. The man who does not touch the fresh-turned soil, tramp through the bush, fodder the cattle ... or watch the garden grow, has missed the great charm of existence."[16] Yet also plainly evident in what they wrote was a recognition that decreasing numbers of people were exposed to these positive and uplifting influences and that in consequence of this sad reality the farm no longer worked its magic in the comprehensive and general way it once had done.

In these circumstances, the place occupied by the farm in the task of upholding the idea that contact with the land was beneficial and regenerative steadily diminished in importance. Now plainly necessary to the preservation of that conception was something that would permit definition of the link between landscape and regeneration in terms consistent with the kind of life increasingly being lived by the most characteristic members of the new kind of society. Maintaining the integrity of the general proposition that exposure to the land was good certainly required a step of this kind, for keeping that proposition dependent on a declining institution could only serve to lessen its own strength. Meeting the specific needs of the ever more prominent city dwellers also made it necessary, for those people, enmeshed in the city, were well past the point where anything other than a massive reversal of the historical process—something akin to Campbell's "return to the land"—could restore them to the life of the farm. Forcefully struck by these developments, as much persuaded as they had ever been that the well-being of society's inhabitants required exposure to the sort of pure and uplifting influences still widely associated with the farm, believers in the importance of that sort of contact began to look about them for a kind of landscape that would allow it to be sustained.

The process of locating a landscape capable of sustaining an image of itself as a source of regeneration for the members of a society which was increasingly urban was, as it happened, greatly aided by the very circumstance which had in the first instance made that search necessary. The rise of settlement and town not only threatened the ascendancy of the farm; it also changed the character of the forest. This was of immense significance. During the province's early years only a handful of observers had perceived the forest in positive, inviting terms. The poet Adam Kidd, for example, found in the 1820s "On Huron's banks . . . that peace, that tranquil good/ which cheers the freeman of the bount'ous wood."[17] Another such early observer was Dr William "Tiger" Dunlop, who pronounced the wilderness of Upper Canada to consist of "forests abounding in game, and lakes and rivers teeming with fish."[18] But more typical were those displaying a clear tendency to describe the forest in the dreariest and most unattractive terms. Novelist John Richardson thought it had a "thick, impervious, rayless"[19] aspect; another observer characterized it as simply "wild woods";[20] in the view of Catharine Parr Traill, it contained nothing even remotely resembling any of the elements of "picturesque beauty."[21] Once, however, large portions of it had come under the axe, been cut through by roads and railways, turned into farms, or consumed by expanding towns and cities, it ceased to invite consideration of itself in language of this unpleasant kind and began to attract attention of a sort involving images of an altogether different order.

The changes which might result from this process manifested themselves with special clarity in the new view of the forest developed as a consequence of its continuing exploitation by the timber trade. Seen in the early years of the century by lumbermen and politicians alike as a virtually limitless commodity to be harvested and marketed in as great quantities as practically possible, its destruction though several decades focussed increasing attention on it as a phenomenon which, far from being inexhaustible, was finite and in need of protection. As early as the 1860s this view began to develop,[22] by the 1880s systematic concern with forest conservation was being urged,[23] and by the turn of the century argument[24] was being enforced by action.[25]

For most Ontarians, however, it was the rise of town and settlement which affected the meaning of the forest most deeply. The impact of that process can hardly be overestimated. It first vanquished the sense that the land was covered by a terrifying and impenetrable overgrowth and then replaced it with the notion that what people now confronted—if they confronted anything—was a subdued and pleasant collection of quite manageable trees. Certainly, thought two 1882 observers, the change had been dramatic in the extreme. In the space of just fifty years, they wrote, "the dense forest, the silence of whose solitudes was broken only by the bark of the wolf," had been converted by the emergence of farm and village "into the fruitful field . . . rejoicing in thousands of homesteads, filled with the bounties of a veritable promised land."[26] One observer in fact found the process of bringing the forest to heel to have been so overwhelmingly successful that memory and imagination would soon offer the only way of sustaining contact with what he called "that grand old world of woods which the nineteenth century is fast civilizing out of existence."[27] If, however, few of those contemplating these events went so far in their assessment of what was happening, there was, nevertheless, a widespread view that the forest had come to be present in the province's life in a limited, controlled, vulnerable way which was fundamentally different from the manner in which it had earlier manifested itself. Even the farmer, long its principal antagonist, began to see it in this light. Where he had once viewed trees as things to be cleared away as quickly and thoroughly as possible, he now began to perceive them as did the forester, as objects to be cultivated. "Plant some trees," the *Canada Farmer* told readers in 1868, "stock the orchard and shrubbery; line the roadside and lane. The country is far too bare and shelterless."[28] "We must," agreed a Toronto observer of farm and country life in 1891, "preserve and plant more forest in Ontario than we have been in the habit of doing, or else we shall injure the productiveness of the land as other countries have done."[29]

If these changes in the forest's estate allowed it to be seen in terms of a need for care and cultivation, they also permitted it to be given meaning within the framework of familiar romantic conventions defining it as an alternative to civilization, a place where one could find solace, uplift, repose, tranquillity, and regeneration in a withdrawal from the constraints imposed by the new urban order. That this important development could finally take place was owing directly to the delimitation of the forest by the forces of that same civilization, for it was not until this process was under way that an element essential to thinking of the woodland in these terms was actively in play. By itself, alone, untouched by the arts and techniques of man, the forest virtually compelled understanding of itself—*pace* the remarks of Richardson et al.—as a barbarizing place, withdrawal into which produced a Caliban-like state of degradation. When, however, the forces of civilization were at work, giving access to, supporting activity in, and providing a means of exit from, the forest, it could attract attention as an altogether less frightening entity. This, of course, was critical, for once it got that sort of attention, the sense of it as the venue of a terrifying encounter with an intractable force could be displaced by an understanding of it as the place where people might find a temporary, accessible, and refreshingly different alternative to the kind of life they normally lived. The new order, in sum, might have created a special need for uplift and regeneration, but it also generated conditions which made it possible to seek those things in places once thought capable of providing only their opposite. Ontarians, at last able to confront the forest with confidence instead of terror, thus moved to consider glade and tree in terms consistent with the kind of pastoral and romantic discourse which had been present in western cultural life for centuries.

That Traill reacted to the forest of the 1870s in tones far different from those she had employed earlier—"How beautiful," she wrote in 1878, "how grand are the old pine woods"[30]—was one indication of how profoundly influential the new perspective became. Equally eloquent testimony to the force of its impact can be seen in the concern shown by a variety of observers to make the link between forest and regeneration absolutely clear. The woods, insisted Alexander McLachlan, were now to be seen as a place of literal rejuvenation:

> We'll throw off our years,
> With their sorrows and tears,
> And time will not number the hours
> We'll spend in the woods,
> Where no sorrow intrudes,
> With the streams, and the birds,
> And the flowers.[31]

"These fresh forests," proclaimed one of Toronto poet Isabella Valancy Crawford's characters, "make an old man young."[32] "In this brave new world"—a fictional Upper Canadian frontiersman asked the ultimate question—"where the odour of the woods is a tonic, and the air brings healing and balm, how can death exist?"[33]

Owing, then, to changes in the province's economy and society, it became possible to conceive of wood and forest in terms formerly associated with the agricultural landscape alone. It was this important development which, finally permitting the emergence of something akin to a Wordsworthian conception of nature,[34] allowed acceptance of the farm's growing incapacity to sustain identification of itself as the place providing most of the province's people with their contact with the land. The forest, under control so far as the part of it with which most people had contact was concerned, but still wild enough to make city dwellers think they were in contact with nature uncontaminated, now stood ready to replace the farm. Having thus been taken in hand, the fundamental anxiety present in much of the commentary concerning the decline of the farm—that the loss by increasing numbers of Ontarians of their contact with it would deprive them of their access to the regenerating land—gradually grew less acute.

The simple and uncomplicated notion that the forest possessed the capacity to uplift and regenerate those exposed to it had great appeal in a society whose population was increasingly urban, since city dwellers, functioning within the framework of a highly structured system, seemed in particular need of escape from the constraints of routine and organization. This is not to say that the farm disappeared completely from the view of those concerned with these issues. It was, in fact, held by some observers to be capable of accommodating itself at least in some measure to the new and stringent requirements set by the need to flee the city. Lampman himself found respite from "the echoing city towers" in a field of timothy,[35] while a less accomplished versifier agreed that the relief provided by a sojourn on the farm was quite wonderful in its effects: "My folks, they say it's better far than paying needless doctors' bills/ So go and spend a holiday down on the farm at Uncle Will's."[36]

But if "great numbers of city families throughout Ontario spent their summers as guests on farms,"[37] those places were, nevertheless, very seriously limited in terms of what they could do for city dwellers. Their range of activities was usually narrow. More important, guests were always conscious of the farm's own routine and discipline, and of the fact that while it might not be their place of work, it nevertheless functioned as such for their host and hostess. Far, then, from giving them that measure of relief from proximity to the things of the workaday world which would allow them to feel "free at last from the city vast"[38] in some absolute sense, it left them very much in the midst of a regimen not so very different from the one they had left behind. It was, in consequence, hardly surprising that they took to the view that "one of the great pleasures of a holiday-outing is to abandon oneself to primeval nature,"[39] because in doing so they could in some real way be free and unconstrained. The requirement that there be a sense of freedom, joined with the farmer's own reluctance to risk disruption of the routine of his business and the privacy of his home, virtually ended any chance that the farm would play a significant role as a holiday destination for the urban vacationer.

As this preoccupation on the part of city dwellers with release and abandonment suggests, much emphasis was laid on the value of a forest vacation in dissipating the routine-induced nervous debilitation which was becoming all too obviously a feature of city life. "Men and women cribbed in towns/ with nerves o'er wrought and weak,"[40] the "weary, over-worked toiler of the city,"[41] and even the children of that confining place "would find their nerves being turned to healthful music" as a consequence of their time spent midst the tranquil splendours of the woods. Physical well-being, too, would be enhanced. "By leaving an atmosphere tainted with sewer gas to inhale the tonic perfume of the pine bush" they would find "their cheeks flushing with freshened tints of purified blood."[42] "The healing sunshine" and "fresh air" of the woods and forest would, in fact, "work wonders."[43]

Closely linked to this celebration of the forest's regenerative powers was a clear emphasis on the variety of ways in which city dwellers could get contact with it. Camping, noted one commentator, provided a sense of release that was almost palpable. Thanks to that activity, he continued, "the prudent man flies from all artificial conditions and yields himself to the soothing influences of nature on the shores of the lakes and rivers in the depths of our primeval forests."[44] For the growing number of city dwellers who wanted more extensive contact with the woods, the acquisition of a summer cottage, thought other observers, would provide what was needful. By 1900, noted a Toronto journalist, "the neighbourhood of each city [contains] one or more special districts where the summer cottage is in increasing evidence and where the formalism and restraint of the city can be laid aside to the benefit of mind and body."[45] So intense, claimed a visitor to Muskoka, was this rush to the woods that it was producing something close to congestion. "It is really surprising," he pointed out, "the number of tents and small cottages that dot the shores of these beautiful waters."[46]

To those to whom the delights of the woods did not encompass cooking for themselves or pitching tents, other means of gaining access to them were available. An Ottawa commentator was inspired to verse by his forest retreat—"I love this hunting lodge secluded far/ from that loud world that strives and toils in vain"[47]—while others merely turned up in ever larger numbers at such resort hotels as the Temagami region's Ronnoco, Temagami Inn, and Lady Evelyn.[48] There was, too, a particular interest in exposing children—boys especially—to the character-building influences of the woods. Joseph E. Atkinson of the Toronto *Star* established the "Fresh Air Fund" to get poor Toronto children in touch with them,[49] artist-naturalist Ernest Thompson Seton proposed the middle-class-oriented Woodcraft Indian Club for boys,[50] and Arthur Cochrane, physical training instructor at Upper Canada College, established Camp Temagami in 1903, dedicating it specifically to "character building through vigorous outdoor living and wilderness appreciation."[51] Even a simple walk in the woods, claimed some commentators, could do what was necessary. "How soothing and refreshing it is," enthused a Kingston resident, "to withdraw awhile from the toil and turmoil of life to some shady nook in a retired wood."[52] "The bush," an old pioneer informed the readers of his memoirs in 1884, "has [n]ever lost its charms for me. I still delight to escape thither; to roam at large . . . forgetting the turmoil and anxieties of the business world."[53]

If what city dwellers did received attention, where they might go also came under scrutiny. For some observers, the Thousand Islands were a favoured spot.[54] Others celebrated the attractions of Algonquin Park.[55] Still others thought the Lake Temagami area was to be preferred.[56] Above all, however, was the Muskoka region. "Here," asserted one of its partisans, "the business and professional man finds rest from care and toil; [and] the feeble, health."[57] "To the worker," insisted another, "this [vacation] life [in Muskoka] is a seduction."[58] In that happy place, as a third put it, one could spend "cool, healthy, happy days, as unlike those of busy town life as civilized men and women can devise."[59]

The woods, then, were in the view of these commentators the ideal vacation place for urban dwellers. A variety of activities, no one on hand but other vacationers or employees unobtrusively serving the holiday-takers' needs, a regimen tailored to the exigencies of the short-term visit, and an abundance of fresh air, green trees, and open skies were there before them. In these happy circumstances, how could they not find the opportunity for regeneration and uplift denied them in the midst of the city?

If some observers continued to see recreational space beyond the city as different than and distanced from the metropolis, implicit in the comment of others was a much different view. Far from seeing the forest isolated and apart, they defined it as being in the process of absorption into the metropolitan system. Subject, in their view, to the workings of urban-focussed transportation networks, the enthusiasms of planners and bureaucrats, and ultimately the imperatives created by the needs of the metropolis itself, the forest seemed in fact to be experiencing a complete loss of its identity as a place distinguishable in terms of distance, character, and function from the world of the city.

The sense that what lay beyond the city was being integrated into the city's system manifested itself in a number of different ways. Evident in one commentator's focus on the manner in which transportation technology was placing recreational space very much within the city dweller's reach— the railway, he wrote, "in half an hour . . . bears us from the stone-paved streets to quiet woods"[60]—it could also be seen in the attention another observer drew to the role the trolley might play in placing "the country, [with] its pure air, sunlight, and wholesome surroundings" so close to the "hosts of people who work in offices and shops" that they might actually be able to live there.[61]

An altered view of the land beyond the city was apparent, too, in observations which had as their thrust the notion that the forest was not something worth preserving as it stood, but a phenomenon needing the sort of improvement which could only come through the intervention of bureaucracy and system. Those who made these comments did not, of course, in any sense argue that the changes they favoured would blur the distinction between town and country so completely that it would disappear. Equally, however, their remarks betrayed a clear acceptance of the fact that the extension to the countryside of plan and organization would, in producing a triumph for the rational and systematic principles of the new order, represent a defeat for the spontaneity and distinctiveness of the old. This view of things was certainly to be seen in the remarks of one Ontario bureaucrat. Taking the province's highways as his focus, Road

Commissioner Archibald W. Campbell made it, in fact, more than clear that leaving nature on its own through failure to extend the improving hand of man to the highways, and, in particular, the countryside flanking them, had produced an exceedingly sad state of affairs. "Whatever beauty the country highways of Ontario possess has," as he put it, "been bestowed upon them by nature"—"we have been entirely deficient." Since what this gross negligence had yielded was plainly unsatisfactory, it was time to mould and reshape those highways in a manner consistent with the principles of balance, harmony, and form—to undertake, in short, "the artistic treatment of roads" in a way that would order and present them as they should be seen.[62] What, claimed another observer, had been done with relatively large tracts of land in certain parts of the province gave special cause for belief in man's capacity to render nature at once more accessible and more attractive. Queen Victoria Niagara Falls Garden Park had been in a particularly unfortunate state until the provincial government stepped in to take over and regulate its operations. Thanks to this extension of control and administration, "it has a nature setting of rare charm, one that is best realized by a comparison with the unkempt condition of the Canadian shore territory prior to government control."[63]

Even dearer evidence of the new thinking was provided by remarks which, in essence, amounted to the following: the land beyond the city was not only linked to and capable of being transformed by the metropolis; it was also a resource at the city's service. Here, too, what Road Commissioner Campbell had to say was of significance, for it offered a particularly graphic example of the manner in which this variation on the basic theme might be played. In arguing that "the artistic treatment of highways would be a constant reproach to the shiftless; neglected lawns would become fewer; ramshackle houses and barns would be less common; the eye [would not only be] refreshed [but also] educated at every point . . . ,"[64] he in fact made obvious a belief that the highway beautiful was desirable not on aesthetic grounds or as a complement to the natural charms of the countryside but because, once in being, it would act to inculcate the very values of order, discipline, and efficiency whose creature it was. Even ostensibly nature-exalting propositions conveyed the message that the good "Nature" might do was done very much in the city's interests. It might, to be sure, be showing its own power by restoring what one commentator called those "natural mechanical and inventive gifts" which had been "atrophied" by life in the city. The critical thing to note, however, was the fact that those gifts, blunted in the city and revitalized by nature though they might be, had a particular meaning for the technically oriented, machine-minded people of the town. Nature's action in restoring them could, in consequence, mean nothing other than that its powers were being directed specifically to the servicing of city dwellers' needs.[65]

The tendency to subordinate the countryside to the system, values, and requirements of the city manifested itself with absolute clarity in the treatment given by different observers to the vacationers' encounter with what they visited. Freely conceding that encounter to be finite—vacationers, after all, were by definition doing what they did for a specific and limited time and a particular and well-understood purpose—these observers placed unambiguous emphasis on the fact that the land beyond the city permitted sojourners on it only temporary contact with what it offered them. They would, indeed, be in touch only long enough to restore their flagging energies and then, at least to a point refreshed, they would return to the city, the better able to do its work. The kind of regeneration that land provided was not, in consequence, to be understood in terms of the extravagant imagery of the new beginning, but in the more restrained language appropriate to description of a process by which those who did urban society's work were revitalized. City dwellers might, to be sure, sojourn amidst "woodland sights and fragrant breezes" and get "a stock of health and strength of body and mind," but they had to keep firmly in mind that these bounties must "serve for the rest of the year."[66] Their inevitable destiny was to pursue their fate as "cogs in the wheel of that mighty machine called [urban] humanity."[67] However successful a vacationer might be in forgetting "for the term of his sojourn the common mercantile interests that yield him his subsistence," however "refreshed" he found himself upon "awakening from his reverie," he must in the end "resume his daily avocation."[68]

Thus, while the city dweller's friends might join the partisans of the farm in using the Edenic metaphor,[69] their doing so in no sense signalled the founding of what was held to be a new kind of society. Instead, their emphasis on the quite extraordinary capacity for revitalization attributed to the resort areas by those who vacationed there did no more than dramatize the reaction of these short term visitors to their temporary home. That the limited sojourn amid nature's wonders on the part of people tied firmly to the urban order had become, as an observer put it, "one of the characteristics of modern times,"[70] seemed, indeed, a proposition capable only of confirmation. So marked a feature of the new reality did it appear that, thought a contributor to a London journal, a definition of the person who best appreciated landscape and scenery now needed to be put in quite different terms from those in which it had formerly been framed. It was not, he wrote, the person in constant contact with a given terrain who best understood it. "Habitual association," it could now be seen, "dulls appreciation; a too-close focus blurs the picture." The person who would get the most out of contact with the land was the person who was always seeing it anew, whose powers of observation had been kept keen by the need to assimilate fresh sights and new information. The holidayer, the vacationer, the temporary sojourner was, it therefore followed with ineluctable force, the being to whom the land showed its most rounded face. "The picture"—nothing could now be clearer—"appears in perfection only to the thoughtful traveller."[71]

The land beyond the city thus found itself being conceived in terms that established it firmly in the city's orbit, rendered subservient to the need of the metropolis for a constantly refreshed and revitalized workforce. Put there most plainly by these commentators' emphasis on the railway, the trolley, and the planner's function, it had also been moved to that place in the much more subtle sense that commentators now defined the most fulfilling sort of contact with it in terms only the city dweller could meet. Far, then, from being perceived—as in the days of the farm's ascendancy—as the foundation of an independent order and a phenomenon best appreciated by those in constant contact with it, the land had been reduced by these observers to the status of an adjunct to the metropolis, a thing most fully understood by those who spent the bulk of their time somewhere else.

The same attitude manifested itself even more clearly in the rhetoric of those concerned with the creation of green spaces within the city itself. Enthusiasm for this activity derived, of course, from a number of sources. It was, for example, plain that many urban dwellers had neither the leisure nor the income necessary to give them contact with nature on its own ground. There was as well an increasing tendency to emphasize the role that trees, boulevards, and parks might play in making the city an aesthetically richer place, one capable of giving at least a measure of psychological satisfaction to its inhabitants. But whatever the reason for travelling in this direction, the destination was clear: an understanding of the land as a thing which worked its wonders to the benefit of, in ways permitted by, and now literally within, the metropolis.

Seeing the land in these terms did not, of course, always involve viewing it as altogether bereft of its traditional character as a place of naturalness and spontaneity. As late as the 1870s, recalled Ernest Thompson Seton, one could find more than a little of the old forest world in the mightiest Ontario city. "Not far," he remembered, "a quarter mile from our home, was Queen's Park, one hundred acres of virgin forest but little changed . . . [while] easterly was the Don Valley, a happy land of bosky hills and open meadows, abounding in bobolinks."[72] Even in the 1890s, reported clergyman and memorialist Henry Scadding, one could marvel at the noble survivors of the forest still to be seen in the midst of the metropolis.[73] The city dweller might even keep up his contact with agriculture and the farm. A 1910 observer noted, "In Toronto, there is a large club for boys called the Broadview Boys' Institute. . . . These boys have a field . . . and it is divided into farms of different sizes. . . . You mustn't think that city boys know nothing about farming, even if they have never seen a threshing, or ridden on a hay rake."[74]

Yet, as the character of this contrived and artificial enterprise suggests, the city's voracious appetite for land made it increasingly necessary to see urban green spaces as capable of establishment, maintenance, and preservation only as the result of a conscious and organized effort. Systematic activity of various kinds for the purpose of ensuring the existence of such spaces was, accordingly, advocated by a number of commentators. Tree planting, thought some, was one way in which activity of this kind could yield a positive result. Such effort was, they explained, a particularly critical undertaking for reasons concerning the physical health of the city dweller. Cities, as one put it, fouled the air, giving off "carbonic gas" and other unpleasant excrescences. Trees, by contrast, absorbed these things while releasing life-giving oxygen. The "vitiation" of the air urban dwellers breathed could thus be avoided by bringing large numbers of these wonderful objects right into the heart of the city. There was, as a result, a clear "necessity of encouraging the growth of as much vegetation as possible within the limits of the cities themselves."[75] Indeed, enthused London's Park Superintendent, trees not only fostered physical health in the direct sense; they also did it by creating an atmosphere of calm and tranquillity. "What," after all, "can be more restful and refreshing to the tired limbs and weary eyes than when refreshed with green at every point?"[76]

If a concern with health moved these observers to support an organized approach to tree planting in cities, others were stimulated to propose similar action by a blend of aesthetic concern and a related desire to see Ontario cities evolve beyond a crude materialism. As early as 1865, one commentator pointed approvingly to the presence "in very many localities" of "choice lawns, flower borders, and even conservatories" as encouraging evidence that standards of taste and refinement were beginning to show themselves. There was, of course, some way to go before "these gratifying manifestations of elevated taste, and superiority to mere money-hoarding" achieved the standard set by "the splendid grounds and conservatory at Chestnut Park on Yonge Street," but that was all. the more reason to encourage movement in the right direction.[77] By the first years of the twentieth century, reported another observer, much progress had been made. Developments had in fact become so marked, he thought—his flattery was intended to encourage its recipients to even greater efforts—that "citizenship had come to carry with it a noticeable tendency towards the pride in beautiful surroundings which brought fame to the cities of Greece for all time."[78]

The sense that a specific and planned place for trees, flowers, shrubs, and grass must be made in city life was at its clearest in the arguments for parks. Not everyone, of course, thought that their place and function could be rigidly defined in terms absolutely consistent with the character and needs of their urban progenitors. Essayist and publisher G. Mercer Adam in fact considered the urban park to be a kind of refuge, a place—here he was speaking of Toronto's Queen's Park—of "escape from the hubbub and glare of the city," a means of retaining some of the naturalness and spontaneity of the old time.[79] Others, however, were plainly of the view that these spaces could be thought of as nothing other than deliberately created devices for enhancing the aesthetic dimension of urban life within the framework of a planned environment in a way that would produce a clearly intended effect. When, therefore, a spokesman for the City Beautiful movement, which was dedicated to making cities greener, better kept, and more handsome places, called for "more park territory" for Toronto,[80] there was an expectation that it would take the form of "a great park system,"[81] a vast complex of planned spaces "integrated," as a recent student of the matter puts it, "into a system connected by parkways," all of this in its turn being done to facilitate the offering of "visual delight to vehicular traffic."[82]

The adoption by city dwellers of values consistent with the character of the new urban order—a world of planning, organization, systems, limits, and confinement—could, it was occasionally thought, be explicitly encouraged by placing them in touch with a kind of green space specifically set up for that purpose. The establishment of urban playgrounds—again a qualification is necessary—was, of course, not always seen in these terms. One of their advocates linked his argument for them directly to preindustrial times, asserting a need for a kind of "village green," "a few old-fashioned commons properly distributed within the city limits," where "growing lads and young men seeking healthful outdoor exercise near at hand" could get the sort of regenerating physical activity they needed.[83] Another, however, frankly framed his case in terms that took him far beyond this familiar kind of concern with revitalization and uplift. This was so not simply in the sense that almost all of what he said was informed by assumptions reflecting a preoccupation with system and planning; it was a reality in the far more significant respect that his argument centred on the important role of recreational activity on these spaces in encouraging the development of principles of behaviour consistent with the needs of the new order. Exposure to recreational spaces in cities, Ontario's Superintendent of Neglected Children told a Toronto meeting of the Empire Club in 1907, would not only give contact with a healthy environment; the regulated, scheduled, competitive, skill-testing activities it involved would provide an "object lesson . . . of rational enjoyment." By thus encouraging a certain kind of outlook—here was the real point—it would build up the capacities of the urban child to be "successful in business, in school, or any other line."[84]

Understanding of the circumstances under which people came into contact with the land, not to mention the result expected from that contact, had thus changed in striking ways. That understanding now involved an extraordinary stress on planned action in the midst of the urban system. By defining the encounter between citizen and land in terms of order and regimentation, it fostered a way of thinking that was absolutely compatible with the structured nature of urban life; indeed, there were even indications that some kinds of activity were to be encouraged precisely because they inculcated values that would remove any lingering capacity the city dweller might have to be rather more a natural and spontaneous than a rational and controlled being. Confined and organized within the city system, the land as viewed by these observers thus lost, literally and figuratively, all vestiges of its position as the foundation of a separate and superior estate. There was, they thought, nothing in the quality of most peoples's contact with it to warrant seeing it as anything other than wholly subordinate to the new urban reality. First outpaced by the growth of that unpleasant phenomenon, then made its servant, and finally drawn into it altogether, the land at last had lost all capacity to sustain a community with a character and purpose of its own.

A striking illustration of this point can be seen in two attempts to restore the land to its once pre-eminent position. In neither case depending on an appeal to the kind of contact with the land experienced by most Ontarians—as the source of the problem the character of that contact could hardly function as part of the solution—these efforts turned instead on the creation of mental constructs which were, in principle, independent of the circumstances defining the experience of the people in whose heads they took shape. One of them, in the event, had only a limited success; the other, by contrast, established itself almost immediately in the depths of the Ontario consciousness. In combination, however, they made it clear that, so far at least as certain observers were concerned, any attempt to establish contact between man and landscape in a way that would allow it to be invested with the sort of comprehensive and general significance it had once possessed would now have to mean using methods of a quite unprecedented kind.

The first of these two devices functioned through the medium of memory. Whatever, insisted those who deployed it, might be true in the urbanizing present, people had had purifying contact with an abundant and uplifting landscape in the pioneer past. Looking back to the province's early days, savouring the details of the settlers' existence, accompanying them on their daily rounds, would thus, it followed, involve getting in touch—in the mind's eye at least—with a society most of whose people had lived the kind of authentic, innocent, elemental life which was now so plainly gone.

The picture of the pioneer past which was built up as a result of this attitude was, needless to say, highly romanticized. Pioneer men and women, their urban descendants were told, "lived near the beginnings of society" and had "to make, invent, adapt, and bear everything."[85] Theirs was, nonetheless, a "rude abundance"—"the virgin soil brought forth plentifully, deer roamed the forest, wild fowl swarmed in marsh and mere, and the lakes and rivers teemed with the finest fish."[86] Anything could be grown, and with almost no effort: "the seeds of melons when carelessly strewed upon the ground and covered, without any further attention attained a degree of perfection in size and flavour which sounds apocryphal."[87] "We had," as a Grand River pioneer remembered it, "a beautiful garden, a great abundance [of] roses, marigolds, hollyhocks, sunflowers, bachelor's buttons, violets and pansies, and an abundance of currant bushes, gooseberries, quinces, cherries."[88] It was, recalled another commentator, "a land flowing almost literally with oil, wine and honey,"[89] "a little bit"—here spoke a third—"of Arcadia."[90]

So long as this agreeable reminiscing was related to the present only in the sense that it permitted a kind of flight from it, it did its job in an effective and uncomplicated way. When the tie that bound it to the commentator's own time became more intricate and complex, however, matters began to go awry. Those who recalled the province's beginnings in order to do more than simply stimulate a journey in the mind did, of course, concede that the happy time of which they wrote was long ago and far away. But in also going beyond that point to celebrate the pioneer's possession of virtues—mostly associated with hard work and self-help—which had a place in their own day, they established a measure of common ground, a kind of bond, between their time and the pioneer past which by definition deprived that past of its separate, distanced, pure, and innocent character. And when they went even further to imply that a full honouring of the pioneers' achievements required their descendants to be true to their sacrifice by working as they had worked, these commentators were encouraging a kind of behaviour which they considered to be fully relevant to the modern age. Thus, levered out of the past on the fulcrum of this presentist argument, lodged firmly at the centre of contemporary life, the pioneers became figures noticed for reasons precisely the opposite of those animating the commentators who had looked back to them and their time as a way of fleeing the urban order.

Emerging as early as the 1860s, when, as one Hamilton newspaper put it, "the hardy pioneers" were "now disappearing from amongst us,"[91] treatment of the pioneer past in these terms almost always involved a focus on diligence, effort, and sacrifice. Accordingly, insisted one journalist, the Huron Tract was settled by people who "with no other capital than strong arms and stout hearts" had, "single-handed," cleared land and built homes while "struggling for years amid the privations of [the] pioneer's life."[92] The land in general, another was sure, could only have been brought under cultivation "by a class of settlers of strong purpose, unceasing industry, and indomitable perseverance."[93] Whatever form these utterances took, the basic message contained in them hardly varied: any failure by the present to cultivate the virtues of the pioneer past would be doubly unfortunate; bad in itself, it would also dishonour the memory and sacrifice of the founders.

If the pioneers found themselves pulled out of their simple past and made functioning parts of the age which had supplanted their own, their privileged and innocent status was abridged in other ways as well. All those who paid tribute to pioneer society as the harbinger of "contemporary" values pointed with particular force—and an inescapable irony—to the very thing whose triumph had made recourse to the myth of the pioneer past seem necessary in the first place. Here, it should be noted, more was involved than such things as a simple stress on the farmers' role as "the forerunners of human civilization,"[94] or a general emphasis on the assertion that "the old Pioneers . . . found the country a wilderness, and by their toil and sweat have made it blossom like the rose."[95] Central to the argument was an explicit concern with the agriculturalist's place in generating what one observer of the Ontario scene called "an outburst of energy, that is building up factories, piercing the bowels of the earth, improving its cities and towns, and seeking new fields of venture."[96] It had been—the president of Toronto's National Club pressed the point home—"those lowly and obscure toilers in the midst of our trackless forest [who] laid broad and deep the foundations of Canada's position."[97] What, then, could be more obvious than that the pioneers, however tranquil and calm the existence they were held to have had in their own day, were also the first cause of the splendour, magnificence, and energy now surrounding the urban observer?

Early Upper Canadians thus emerged from these rememberings as figures surrounded by doubt and ambiguity. They might, as many observers preferred, be conceived as innocent toilers in an idyllic age. Yet they were also seen as people who, in political economist Adam Shortt's words, "laid the foundation for our present . . . life,"[98] setting in motion the play of forces which would subvert the innocence and simplicity they themselves epitomized. In sum, even in memory the unambiguous virtue of wood and farm eluded capture. Gone in reality, it was proving itself beyond the reach of remembering as well.

If a concept built on memory and recollection turned out to yield results which were at best uncertain, perhaps, thought some Ontarians, an image fabricated in different ways with other materials would give a better return. Perhaps, they suggested, the people of the province could be confronted with a visual rendering of lake, forest, wood, and rock so striking that contemplation of it would by itself excite the mind in a way which would lead directly to an apprehension of truth and beauty. This apprehension, indeed, might be so exalting and powerful that an altered state of consciousness—and, perforce, the uplift and regeneration of those experiencing it—would be produced.

The new vision of the north which began to emerge just before the Great War—culminating during and after it in the work of the Group of Seven—was, of course, the product of many influences, among which the new view of the forest, the thrust into New Ontario and the search for a uniquely Canadian landscape were central.[99] Yet it also reflected a mystical conviction, borne of a close familiarity with theosophy, transcendentalism, and the work of the Scandinavian symbolist painters,[100] that imaginative contact with the land through exposure to a properly crafted symbolic representation would allow it to work its magic even more effectively than an actual physical presence in it. That this was so, these painters argued, derived from the fact that art must not simply imitate the externals of reality as a photograph did; its purpose was rather to expose to view the inner, essential, elements of that reality. It could, however, do this only if it managed to present what painters called the accidents—line, form, mass, colour, and volume—of that reality in ways which made visible the inner truth whose existence they at once veiled and suggested. Since artists, thanks to their insight and sensitivity, had seen these accidents in the needed way, it fell to them to set them forth in a manner that permitted others to do so as well. What resulted—the work of art—thus presented the things which at once shrouded and gave access to this essential reality in a fashion that allowed viewers to see, as it were, through them so that they could have contact with what lay behind or beyond or within them. Contemplating the work, and the arrangement of line, form, mass, colour, and volume of which it consisted, thus became the principal route of access to the higher truth and the special state that knowledge of it permitted one to experience. "Art"—the Group's Arthur Lismer summed up these notions years later—came out of

> a consciousness of harmony in the universe, the perception of the divine order running through all existence. The artist, sensitive to rhythm, the beat of life, creating in space and time the image of his reception of this order, projects his vision in the eternal language of line, tone, and colour, and creates not an imitative outward appearance of the common aspects of life, but an inner, more noble life than yet we all know.[101]

The elements of this credo were, of course, only vaguely in evidence before 1914. It was not, in fact, until 1913 that J.E.H. MacDonald and Lawren Harris travelled from Toronto to Buffalo, there to find reinforcement of what they were trying to do in the painting of the Scandinavian artists on exhibit in that city. That it was a work—A.Y. Jackson's *Terre Sauvage* (1913)—done by a friend who had not been with them which first succeeded in capturing something of the "mystic north"[102] suggests, however, that ideas of this sort were already very much at work in their circle. Harris, certainly, had been reading the American transcendentalists as early as 1906.[103] And, he recalled years later, the exhibition's great contribution was not that it moved him and MacDonald in new directions but that it confronted them with "a large number of paintings which gave body to our rather nebulous ideas. . . . Our purpose became clarified and our conviction reinforced."[104]

Whatever the precise character of the painters' doctrine in this early period, there can be no doubt that those who viewed their work underwent from the beginning an experience which was in all essentials defined by the impact on their sensibility and understanding of what they saw on the plane surface in front of them. This was true not simply in the sense that those who considered such paintings as Tom Thomson's *A Northern Lake* (1912–13), MacDonald's *A Rapid in the North* (1913), or Jackson's *Terre Sauvage* might in consequence of their exposure to these works undergo the sort of mystical apprehension of an inner truth with which Harris was becoming increasingly concerned. Nor did it have merely to do with the fact that viewers would be using the power of intellect and imagination to assign their own meaning to a thing which was in itself the expression of a personal vision of the world, for they had always occupied a place of just that sort in relation to artists and their work.

What made the act of looking at these paintings so profoundly imaginative was the fact that it gave viewers their sole point of contact not only with the artist's vision but also with the thing depicted. Where gallery-goers considering a landscape by Homer Watson would be almost certain to have first-hand, and even extended, experience of Watson's settled and peaceful countryside, the same could not be said of viewers of the Group's work. Unless they were campers, cottagers, or resortgoers—and even then their contact with forest, lake, and shield would be severely limited—they would know what they were seeing thanks only to their exposure to the play of light and colour on the canvas before them. In eventually pointing out that these painters "did not live in the north . . . they lived in Toronto,"[105] the historian Frank Underhill thus managed to say only part of what needed noticing, for these were not simply paintings done by artists who themselves had little sustained contact with the land; they were—and the point is at least as important—produced for those who, having even less, were the more dependent for their sense of that land on what their minds and intellects could do with the artificial objects they found themselves confronting.

With the appearance of a device which turned on the assumption that the best link between people and landscape operated at the level of imagination rather than experience, a way of understanding that connection fundamentally different from those which had prevailed through much of the nineteenth century presented itself for the consideration of Ontarians. Distinguished from those others by its character as well as its content, in no way dependent for its validity on the fact that it reflected something of which its viewers would necessarily have sustained and close experience, the new configuration was exempt from the burden of having to be consistent with the style of life actually being lived by significant numbers of people in the present. In no way mirroring—as the imagery of farm, forest, park, and playground had tried to mirror—the point of real and tangible contact between society's members and nature, and, therefore, in no way compelled to change as the nature of that contact changed, it found itself able to breast the constraints of time and decay in a way those others had been unable to do. Much more a thing of consciousness, idea, and mind than they, it had a far larger capacity to stand forth in a fixed and permanent way, a vision projected—Lismer's phrase is worth repeating—"in the eternal language of line, tone, and colour,"[106] a phenomenon whose truth and appeal, unconnected to any sort of relationship it might have to the changing experiences of most Ontarians, could endure so long as there were minds to perceive it.

Over the course of a critical half-century a substantial number of Ontario thinkers developed a set of images to explain their society's changing relationship to, and their own understanding of, the land. Each of these had at its core the idea that the encounter with the land—a source of well-being and uplift in both a figurative and literal sense—was to be seen in positive terms. Forced by constantly shifting circumstance gradually to concede that the land as most Ontarians experienced it was being drawn into the framework of a new kind of social, economic, and geographical system, they never yielded on that central point.

With, however, the emergence of a belief that contemplation of the image rather than contact with the reality could do what was required, matters changed fundamentally. In leaving behind the nineteenth century's attempt to work out the relationship between landscape and regeneration in terms of the actual circumstances in which Ontarians lived, observers in the twentieth century would move increasingly to accomplish that goal in terms of the symbolic representation of a geographical mass which, while it made up almost all of the province, was wholly unknown to most of its people. They thus found themselves a far distance indeed from their predecessors, who had been able, albeit with difficulty, to celebrate the vitalizing power of the land on which they and their fellows actually stood.

• Notes

1 Some historians have argued that early nineteenth-century observers also saw the forest in a positive light. Challenging the argument of literary critics such as Northrop Frye, they assert that, far from seeing the wilderness as harsh, intractable, and overpowering, poets and writers were inspired by romantic modes of thinking to see it as sublime and uplifting. Some of these writers, as this study notes, did see it in these terms. A comprehensive reading of texts produced in early nineteenth-century Upper Canada suggests, however, that enthusiasm for the land was most often manifest in relation to those parts of it that were perceived to have agricultural potential. For the argument of the literary critics, see Northrop Frye, "Conclusion" in *The Literary History of Canada*, ed. C.F. Klinck et al. (Toronto, 1965); Marcia B. Kline, *Beyond the Land Itself: Views of Nature in Canada and the United States* (Cambridge, MA, 1970); Margaret Atwood, *Survival: A Thematic Guide to Canadian Literature* (Toronto, 1972);

and John Moss, *Patterns of Isolation in English-Canadian Fiction* (Toronto, 1974). For some criticism of that argument, see Edward Dahl, *"Mid Forests Wild": A Study of the Concept of Wilderness in the Writing of Susanna Moodie, J.W.D. Moodie, Catharine Parr Traill and Samuel Strickland, c. 1830–1855* (Ottawa, 1973), who claims that the Upper Canadian reaction to the forest was both positive and negative, and M.L. MacDonald, "Literature and Society in the Canadas, 1830–1850" (PhD thesis, Carleton University, 1984), 321–55, who develops the view that it was almost entirely positive.

2 Susanna Moodie, "The Backwoodsman" in *Roughing It in the Bush; or Life in Canada* (London, 1852), 1:123.

3 Samuel Strickland, *Twenty-Seven Years in Canada West*, ed. Agnes Strickland (London, 1853), 1:65.

4 *Address Delivered Before the Provincial Agricultural Association at its Twelfth Annual Exhibition at Brantford, by George Alexander, of Woodstock, C.W.* (Toronto, 1857), 16.

5 Daniel Wilson, "The President's Address," *The Canadian Journal* (March 1861), 119.

6 Alexander McLachlan, "Acres of Your Own" in his *Poems and Songs* (Toronto, 1874), 155.

7 See Morris Zaslow, *The Opening of the Canadian North 1870–1914* (Toronto, 1971), 147ff.

8 Beginning in the 1870s, "the province underwent tremendous urbanization and industrialization, developments that were promoted by considerable population movement and growth. This fundamental shift in the nature of Ontario society required major adjustments": Donald Swainson, "Introduction" in *Oliver Mowat's Ontario* (Toronto, 1972), 3.

9 Arthur H. Sinclair, *Municipal Monopolies and Their Management* (Toronto, 1891), cited in Paul Rutherford, ed., *Saving the Canadian City: The First Phase 1880–1920* (Toronto, 1974), 6.

10 H.V. Nelles, *The Politics of Development* (Hamden, CT, 1974), 51.

11 *Ontario as a Home for the British Tenant Farmer Who Desires to Become His Own Landlord* (Toronto, 1886), 3.

12 "The Clay Belt in Ontario's Northland," *Farmer's Advocate* (hereafter *FA*) (London, ON), 9 June 1910, 946; see also in *FA*: "The Ontario Pioneer Farm," 15 Sept. 1896, 370; "New Ontario Lands for Settlement," 15 Dec. 1898, 588; "The Opening of New Ontario," 1 Oct. 1901, 632; "The Golden Fleece in Canada," 8 Dec. 1904, 1661; "Northern Ontario: Is It Suitable for Successful Agriculture?" 7 Dec. 1905, 1731–32; "Agriculture in New Ontario," 29 April 1909, 720–21; and also John Sharp, "New Ontario," *Queen's Quarterly* (hereafter *QQ*) 11 (1903): 76; Frank H. Newton, "The Northern Ontario Clay Belt," *Canadian Magazine* (hereafter *CM*) 35 (1910): 530.

13 Barry Dane, "National Health," *The Week* (Toronto), 30 Oct. 1884, 760.

14 C.C. James, "The Problems of a Farmer's Wife," *FA*, 9 Dec. 1909, 1944.

15 William Wilfred Campbell, "Back to the Land," *FA*, 25 May 1905, 787.

16 "What Ails the Farm?" *FA*, 22 Feb. 1912, 313.

17 Adam Kidd, "The Huron Chief" in *The Huron Chief and Other Poems* (Montreal, 1830), 34.

18 [William Dunlop], *Statistical Sketches of Upper Canada* (London, 1832), 32.

19 [John Richardson], *Wacousta; or, the Prophecy: A Tale of the Canadas* (London, 1839), 1:7.

20 [J.L. Alexander], *Wonders of the West; Or a Day at the Falls of Niagara . . . A Poem, by A Canadian* (n.p., 1825), 23.

21 C.P. Traill, *The Backwoods of Canada* (London, 1852), 113.

22 "Forest Management," *The Canada Farmer*, 15 Jan. 1864, 1.

23 R.W. Phipps, "Forestry and the Necessity for Its Practice in Ontario," *Canadian Institute of Toronto, Proceedings*, 3rd ser., 3 (1884–85): 109–12.

24 Richard Lees, "Forestry Problems in Ontario," *QQ* 11 (1903): 110–11; Judson F. Clark, "The Forest as a National Resource," *Canadian Forestry Association, Report of the Sixth Annual Meeting, Quebec, March 9–10 1905* (Ottawa, 1905), 101. Clark was Ontario's provincial forester.

25 Nelles, *The Politics of Development*, 182–214.

26 A. Kemp and G.M. Grant, "From Toronto to Lake Huron" in *Picturesque Canada: The Country as It Was and Is*, ed. G.M. Grant (Toronto, 1882), 2:544.

27 J. Macdonald Oxley, "Through the Trackless Forest," *The Week*, 10 Oct. 1890, 713.

28 "The North," *The Canada Farmer*, 1 May 1868, 129.

29 R.W. Phipps, "Forestry," *FA*, 7 Jan. 1891, 17.

30 C.P. Traill, "Our Forest Trees," *Rose-Belford's Canadian Monthly* (July 1878): 95.

31 Alexander McLachlan, "May" in *The Oxford Book of Canadian Verse*, comp. William Wilfred Campbell (Toronto, 1913), 28.

32 Isabella Valancy Crawford, "Malcolm's Katie" in *Old Spookses Pass, Malcolm's Katie, and Other Poems* (Toronto, 1884), 86.

33 Graeme Mercer Adam and A. Ethelwyn Wetherald, *An Algonquin Maiden: A Romance of the Early Days of Upper Canada* (Montreal, 1887), 13.

34 One result of which was the fact that poet Archibald Lampman could be described by his brother-in-law as "happiest when exploring new scenes in the forest land. . . . [This] to him was the garden of nature": Rev. Ernest Voorhis, "The Ancestry of Archibald Lampman, Poet," Royal Society of Canada, *Proceedings and Transactions*, 3rd ser., vol. 15, sec. 2 (1921): 103. For another discussion of changing views of the forest and nature in this period, see George Altmeyer, "Three Ideas of Nature in Canada 1893–1914," *Journal of Canadian Studies* 11 (1976): 21–36.

35 Archibald Lampman, "Among the Timothy" in *Among the Millet* (Ottawa, 1888), 14.

36 Lilian Ruth Milner, "Down on the Farm," *FA*, 31 July 1913, 1330.

37 Roy I. Wolfe, "Ontario Summer Resorts in the Nineteenth Century," *Ontario History* 54 (1962): 159.

38 Alexander McLachlan, "The Pines" in *Poems and Songs* (Toronto, 1874), 109.

39 W.R. Bradshaw, "The Georgian Bay Archipelago," *CM* 15 (1900): 16.

40 Crowquill, "Summer Holidays," *The Dominion Illustrated*, 3 Aug. 1889, 75.

41 William B. Varley, "Tourist Attractions in Ontario," *CM* 15 (1900): 29.

42 John Hague, "Aspects of Lake Ontario," *CM* 1 (1893): 263.

43 Varley, "Tourist Attractions," 29.

44 A. Stevenson, "Camping in the Muskoka Region," *The Week*, 13 May 1886, 382.

45 [The Editor], "Canada and the Tourist," *CM* 15 (1900): 4.

46 "Muskoka as a Summer Resort," *FA*, 3 Aug. 1905, 1095.

47 W.R. Robson, "The Upper Ottawa," *The Dominion Illustrated*, 11 May 1889, 302.

48 Bruce W. Hodgins and Jamie Benedickson, "Resource Management Conflict in the Temagami Forest 1898 to 1914," *Canadian Historical Association Historical Papers* (1978): 162.

49 Ross Harkness, *J.E. Atkinson of the Star* (Toronto, 1963), 70–71.

50 Ernest Thomson Seton, *Trail of an Artist-Naturalist* (New York, 1940), 374–85.

51 Hodgins and Benedickson, "Resource Management Conflict in the Temagami Forest," 164; see also "A Boy's Camp in Temagami," *Rod and Gun* 10 (1908): 49–51.

52 K., "A Short Ramble in June," *Saturday Reader*, 14 July 1866, 289.

53 Samuel Thompson, *Reminiscences of a Canadian Pioneer* (Toronto, 1884), 108.

54 Fidelis, "The Thousand Islands," *Canadian Monthly and National Review* (July 1874): 42–47; Frederic W. Falls, "The Thousand Isles," *CM* 4 (1894): 148–63.

55 Thos. W. Gibson, "Algonquin National Park," *CM* 3 (1894): 542–55.

56 See Hodgins and Benedickson, "Resource Management Conflict in the Temagami Forest," 161.

57 "Muskoka Summer," *The Dominion Illustrated*, 15 Nov. 1890, 326.

58 W., "Lotos-Eating in Muskoka," *The Week*, 30 Aug. 1889, 618.

59 Catherine Blinfield, "Muskoka Days and Doings," *CM* 5 (1895): 486; see also E. Maurice Smith, "Muskoka, The Summer Playground of Canada," *CM* 21 (1903): 33–38; William T. James, "Midsummer in Muskoka," *CM* 11 (1898): 225; and M. Forsyth Grant, "Camping in Muskoka," *The Dominion Illustrated*, 14 June 1890, 382–83.

60 Bernard McEvoy, "Prologue" in *Away From Newspaperdom, and Other Poems* (Toronto, 1897), 9.

61 "The Eve of the Trolley Age," *FA*, 1 May 1901, 291.

62 A.W. Campbell, "Artistic Country Roads," *CM* 8 (1897): 214.

63 Frank Yeigh, "The Queen Victoria Niagara Falls Park," *CM* 39 (1912): 541.

64 Campbell, "Country Roads," 218.

65 W. Rideout Wadsworth, "With Rifle and Rod in the Moose Lands of Northern Ontario," *CM* 13 (1899): 262.

66 Fidelis, "The Thousand Islands," *Canadian Monthly and National Review* (July 1874): 44.

67 H.V.P., "A Three Weeks' Fishing Trip to Muskoka," *Rose-Belford's Canadian Monthly* (July 1880): 20.

68 Falls, "The Thousand Isles," 153.

69 Agnes Maule Machar, for example, extolled the Thousand Islands in her poem "The Happy Islands" in these terms: "Fair do they seem as Eden/ When Eden was newly made, To the weary city toilers,/ Who seek their grateful shade." See her *Days of the True North and Other Canadian Poems* (Toronto, 1902), 66.

70 Gibson, "Algonquin National Park," 543.

71 "A Holiday Jaunt: The Niagara District," *FA*, 21 June 1906, 1001.

72 Seton, *Trail of an Artist-Naturalist*, 62.

73 Henry Scadding, "Survivors of the Forest in Toronto," *The Week*, 8 Dec. 1893, 38.

74 "Farming in the City," *FA*, 31 May 1906, 897; see also Puck, "Some City Farmers," *FA*, 10 March 1910, 413.

75 "Effects of Vegetation in Cities," *FA*, 1 Jan. 1875, 10.

76 John S. Pearce, "Value of Street Trees," *FA*, 9 Aug. 1906, 1255.

77 "Hon. D.L. McPherson's Grounds and Conservatory," *The Canada Farmer*, 1 Dec. 1865, 364.

78 Horace Boultbee, "Toronto: A City of Homes," *CM* 32 (1909): 299.

79 G. Mercer Adam, "Toronto & Vicinity" in *Picturesque Canada*, 1:433.

80 Jean Graham, "The City Beautiful," *CM* 31 (1908): 177.

81 Byron E. Walker, "A Comprehensive Plan for Toronto," Canadian Club of Toronto, *Addresses 1905–06* (Toronto, 1906), 134–39, cited in Rutherford, ed., *Saving the Canadian City*, 224.

82 This was an idea developed in the Toronto Guild of Civic Art's *Report on a Comprehensive Plan for Systematic Improvement in Toronto* (Toronto, 1909); see W. Van Nus, "The Fate of City Beautiful Thoughts in Canada, 1893–1930," Canadian Historical

Association *Historical Papers* (1975): 197.

83 "A Plea for the Village Green," *The Week*, 16 Aug. 1895, 896.

84 J.J. Kelso, "The Play Spirit and Playgrounds in Toronto," Empire Club of Canada, *Addresses 1907–1908* (Toronto, 1908), 181.

85 Rev. W.W. Smith, "Backwoods Proverbs," *New Dominion Monthly* (March 1877): 220.

86 William Henry Withrow, *A History of Canada for the Use of Schools and General Readers* (Toronto, 1876), 120.

87 Robina and Kathleen M. Lizars, *In the Days of the Canada Company, 1825–1850* (Toronto, 1896), 55.

88 Charles Durand, *Reminiscences* (Toronto, 1897), 42–43.

89 C.O. Ermatinger, *The Talbot Regime, or the First Half Century of the Talbot Settlement* (St Thomas, 1904), 1.

90 William Wye Smith, "Illustrations of Canadian Life—Part II," *Rose-Belford's Canadian Monthly* (March 1882): 233.

91 "Prospectus," *Canadian Illustrated News* (Hamilton), 8 Nov. 1862; see also William Canniff, *History of the Settlement of Upper Canada (Ontario), With Special Reference to the Bay Quinté* (Toronto, 1869).

92 J.C.S., "A Summer Outing," *FA*, 28 July 1904, 1024.

93 "The Romance of Ontario's Unexampled Agricultural Progress," *FA*, 13 Dec. 1906, 1934.

94 Lizars, *In the Days of the Canada Company*, 375.

95 James Young, *Reminiscences of the Early History of Galt* (Toronto, 1880), 73.

96 J.L.S., "Sketches in Upper Canada," *New Dominion Monthly* (Dec. 1867): 140.

97 William K. McNaught, "Pioneers of the Canadian Farm" in *Canada: An Encyclopaedia of the Country*, ed. J. Castell Hopkins (Toronto, 1899), 5:19.

98 Adam Shortt, "Life of the Settler in Western Canada Before the War of 1812," *QQ* 22 (1914): 88.

99 Douglas L. Cole, "Artists, Patrons, and Public: An Enquiry Into the Success of the Group of Seven," *Journal of Canadian Studies* 13 (1978): 69–78.

100 Roald Nasgaard, "Canada: The Group of Seven, Tom Thomson, and Emily Carr" in *The Mystic North: Symbolist Landscape Painting in Northern Europe and North America 1890–1940* (Toronto, 1984), 158–202.

101 Arthur Lismer, "Canadian Art," *Canadian Theosophist*, 14 Feb. 1925, 178.

102 J.E. MacDonald, "Scandinavian Art," lecture, Art Gallery of Toronto, 17 Apr. 1931, cited in Nasgaard, *The Mystic North*, 160, and reprinted in *Northward Journal* 18/19 (1980): 9–35.

103 Dennis Reid, "Lawren Harris," *Artscanada*, 25 Dec. 1968, 13.

104 Lawren Harris, "The Group of Seven in Canadian History," Canadian Historical Association, *Annual Report* (1948): 31.

105 Frank H. Underhill, "False Hair on the Chest," *Saturday Night*, 3 Oct. 1936, 1, cited in Mary Vipond, "Ideas of Nationalism in English Canada in the 1920s" (PhD thesis, University of Toronto, 1975), 517.

106 Lismer, "Canadian Art," 178.

CLASS STRUGGLE AND MERCHANT CAPITAL: Craftsmen and Labourers on the Halifax Waterfront, 1850–1900*

IAN McKAY

They formed a powerful and worried group, the men who gathered at the Halifax YMCA on 8 May 1884.[1] Hon. A.G. Jones, Hon. L.G. Power, Messrs George E. Francklyn, F.D. Corbett, W.C. Silver, J.C. Mackintosh, George E. Boak, W.E. West: these gentlemen made up much of the Halifax merchant class and, not coincidentally, many of the city's past and future political leaders. As the city's Chamber of Commerce, they championed the port's interests in the ancient, languishing West Indies trade: and in the new and uncertain world of the National Policy, they had tried to win for Halifax a secure commercial niche as the winter port of the Dominion.[2] Neither campaign had borne fruit, and this class, now represented in this anxious forum, was in deep crisis.

Three related problems—competition of foreign steamers, the decline of the inshore fishery, and disappearing markets—coalesced in the overwhelming problem facing traditional Halifax merchants: plunging freights. Rules of trade that had guided several generations of merchants on the Halifax waterfront no longer applied. Better means of communica-

---

*Bryan D. Palmer, ed., *The Character of Class Struggle* (Toronto: McClelland & Stewart, 1986), 17–36. Reprinted by permission.

tion meant that buyers of West India produce were less at the mercy of carriers, who could now be played off one against another; the gradual triumph of the steamer upset traditional pricing mechanisms and drove sailing vessels into an ever-declining number of trades. Sail was being marginalized by steam even in those bulk trades in which it ought to have had an advantage. Internationally, sail in the late nineteenth century enjoyed advantages over steam as a cheap coal carrier. But even in this sphere, Maritime shipowners were complaining by 1888 that they were being discriminated against by coal companies: "A sailing vessel may be half or three-quarters loaded or even may only require a few tons to complete her loading," one shipowner argued, "but the moment a steamer comes in the sailing vessel has to lay off and the steamer, whatever she may be, is put in the berth and loaded."[3]

From the mid-1870s to the mid-1880s, the bourgeoisie of Halifax was squeezed between two massive consolidations of capital: one on land, as the industries based on import substitution grew under the National Policy, and one at sea, as the capitalist world-system consolidated financial power and centralized shipping in a few great centres, and, in order to provide larger and faster vessels to transport goods and raw materials to all corners of the globe, replace sail with steam. "There is no shipping in the province at the present time," exclaimed a man who had manufactured metal accessories for sailing vessels: it was hyperbole, but it drove home an obvious point.[4]

This sense of long-term structural crisis permeated the Chamber's meeting that day in 1884, but dominating the agenda was a more immediate problem: the militant eruption of the waterfront work force. Two days before, an important notice from the Laborers' Union of Halifax had appeared in the city's press threatening the "Merchants, Stevedores and Other Employers of Transient Labor in the City of Halifax" with a strike if their wage and other demands were not met.[5] Challenged from without by massive structural change in the capitalist world-system, the Halifax merchants were for the first time threatened from within their private waterfront world of wharves, sail-lofts, store-houses, shops, and ships by their own rebellious workers. It was this second, novel challenge to their power that the merchants were determined to crush when they met in May 1884.

Mr W.C. Silver, a well-known philanthropist and one of the wealthiest of the city's merchants, was perplexed that workers were not grateful for the social improvements of the past half-century: "At one time he could remember the majority of the laboring people could not read and did not know what was going on in the other centres of trade. . . . In old times mechanics and laborers used to go about in poor and patched clothing, though neat and clean, and worked for small wages, yet were happy and contented. Now they dressed in tweeds and cloths and with additional comforts in the homes and living not dearer yet they were discontented." Workers had scant appreciation for the merchants' lot in life: "They did not consider the difficulties of the merchant in successfully carrying on a business to employ men. They were too apt to consider all employers of labor as wealthy aristocrats who lived luxuriously in palatial residences. They seldom thought that men who became successful merchants had to work very hard for it."

Inspired by such sentiments, the Chamber of Commerce resolved that it learned "with regret" that the labourers and stevedores had made a demand for increased wages "at a time when all branches of trade and commerce are exceptionally dull," adding that in its opinion "any increase in wages such as is demanded will not in the end act to the advantage of the laborers themselves." Major J.C. Mackintosh—a noted financier and investor—read into this resolution a broad social program. It was vitally important to resist the union's demand, he urged, because "There was a great deal of latent communism in the city, and in his opinion it was not well to recognize the men's demands to too great an extent."[6]

The 1884 strike is important as an event, a moment of the awakening of the working class of the Maritimes in the 1880s, but it is even more important as a window on a little-explored world, that of social relations in the era of merchant capital. It brought to the level of discourse the two invisible axes of the waterfront world, its two overriding structural tendencies: technical obsolescence and casualism; and it dramatized the consequences of these two structures for the two main groups of waterfront workers: craftsmen, defending their obsolete trades as best they could in a rapidly changing world, and longshoremen, divided and immobilized by a casual labour system. Workers no less than merchants faced a huge transition as steamers replaced sail and the world trading system was centralized; but, ironically, this transition, generally so negative in its consequences for the Maritime region, enabled them to transcend a century-old tradition of fragmentation and dependence—those bitter fruits of merchant capital— and begin to organize as a class.

What follows is in three parts. In the first, the nineteenth-century waterfront craftsmen—the riggers, blockmakers, coopers, sailmakers, shipwrights, and caulkers—will be presented as a defensive "labour aristocracy" protecting their own immediate interests but structurally incapable of a more all-inclusive class consciousness. In the second, the position of the longshoremen from mid-century to 1902 will be studied as an example of the class fragmentation and dependence caused by surplus labour pools and the casual labour system. A third and concluding section will place these two intertwined stories in a more general context.

A labour aristocracy emerged among the craftsmen of the Halifax waterfront because they feared, with reason, the encroachments of other craftsmen, both rural and urban, and the competition of unskilled labourers. Confronted with large surplus labour pools, they defended their craft privileges in the only way open to them: by creating an artificial labour scarcity through the devices of the restriction of numbers and of the common rule.[7]

The transition from sail to steam was a protracted affair, and from 1850 to 1895 the two technologies co-existed, although with steam gaining inexorably on sail. The Pickford and Black registers, listing vessels calling Halifax, show sailing vessels outnumbering steamers in 1881 by two to one, but a reversal by 1901 so that steamships outnumbered sailing vessels by a ratio of approximately three to two.[8] The owners of wooden fleets did not hold a "fire sale" to sell off their depreciating vessels; they fought instead to wrench the last penny of profit from them, paying for fast passages through loss of gear, masts, spars, sails, and men.[9] This meant that until the mid-1890s traditional waterfront craftsmen found employment in Halifax repairing rather than building wooden vessels. Riggers, blockmakers, mast-makers, coopers, sailmakers, shipwrights, caulkers: such maritime crafts-men were indispensable in the building and maintenance of the large softwood fleets of the Maritimes, with their daunting repair costs.[10] Nor did sail suddenly disappear from the strategies of Halifax businessmen. Halifax dreamed of becoming the major repair port on the East Coast. Labour, businessmen urged, should not stand in the way of this important develop-ment. In 1886, two prominent ship repair firms passed along to the caulk-ers' union allegations from marine insurance companies "stating that the Port of Halifax was one of the most expensive Ports for repairing Vessels now existing," and that, as a consequence, "they were obligated to send Vessels to other places which might have been repaired in Halifax."[11] The episode suggested that the traditional craftsmen still occupied a strategic position in Halifax's tenacious struggle to survive in the new maritime world. As wooden shipbuilding virtually vanished and steamers pushed out sailing vessels from the most lucrative routes, there was continuing demand for the services of traditional waterfront craftsmen in the repair of the aging fleets.

Maritime crafts represented bodies of skilled knowledge and tech-nique that took years to acquire. Riggers, blockmakers, and mastmakers, the three smallest crafts, attended to the highly intricate work of fitting out the vessels with articles vital for their sails. Such men, few in numbers and highly specialized, were tied closely to the ship chandleries that dotted the waterfront; they were never sufficiently numerous to allow the develop-ment of an overt division between masters and journeymen.[12] Divisions did emerge in the four large crafts. Coopers played an important role through-out industrializing North America in such spheres as flour-milling, distil-ling, and oil, but in Halifax their craft had a maritime complexion and centred on two vital commodities: sugar and fish. One large cooperage, which imported its staves and hoops from Ontario, operated immediately opposite the Nova Scotia Sugar Refinery: other coopers were employed directly by sugar refineries, subcontracting for the sugar barrels and paying journeymen coopers by the piece.[13] More found work on the wharves, and the rhythm of their labour was set by the fishery, as was suggested by the journeymen coopers in a description of the trade in 1903: "The favourable season of our branch of the trade and the prevailing prosperity that should be looked for turns out to be a disappointment in the fishery which leads to a dull season also for the coopers of Halifax. The catch of bank fish is very small in quantity and the quantity of casks used is very small in comparison to former years, so some of the boys are not very busy at the present time."[14] Although manufactories had emerged in cooperage, the application of steam supplemented rather than replaced the work of the coopers.

Sailmaking was another essential craft within the mercantile economy. Often sailmakers were employed on voyages, repairing damaged sails; and of the waterfront craftsmen, they were apt to be the most peripatetic, travelling with their very portable kits up and down the coast. The making of sails required judgment and experience, as well as precision and strength. Using a roping palm or (if need be) a mallet, a sailmaker had to force large needles through tough canvas and measure expensive sail cloth exactly to the rigging plan, strengthening those parts of the canvas likely to chafe against masts, yards, and ropes; he enlarged holes in the edges of the canvas with a "fid," a cone made of wood or bone, and inside the holes sewed "grommets," rings that prevented the rope from cutting into the canvas. Once these and other tasks in the sail loft were completed, the sailmaker would deliver the sail to the master rigger, proud of his artisanal accomplishment.[15]

The two remaining groups of waterfront craftsmen, shipwrights and caulkers, also believed the skill demanded by their work separated them out from other manual labourers. Shipbuilding entailed all the skills demanded by general carpentry,[16] complicated by the need to work with a wider range of angles, to lay the plank in complex patterns requiring skill and forethought, and to use joints peculiarly adapted for shipbuilding. No matter how graceful the model, botched work by the shipwrights would ruin the vessel.[17] Caulking, the process by which the ship was made watertight, seems at first glance a far less intricate art, but it required specialized tools (the caulking-iron and caulking-mallet), physical stamina, and experienced judgment. Caulkers worked with oakum, tarred hemp, or manila fibres made from old and condemned ropes. (This is why apprentices in this trade were sometimes called "oakum-boys.") Although "picking oakum," the tedious and unpleasant job of unpicking old rope and reworking it into threads running from forty to seventy feet to the pound, was elsewhere assigned to inmates of prisons and workhouses, in Halifax it was the preserve of the caulkers. After it had been "picked," the oakum was then rammed down between the seams with the chisel-like caulking-iron and the mallet, and hot pitch was poured along the seams. A poorly caulked vessel would not be seaworthy, and marine insurance companies laid down rules governing how these tasks were to be performed, specifying that the bottom of every ship was to be caulked once in every five years. It was a musical craft: the ring of the caulkers' mallets provided the unofficial economic index of the health of the port, and the caulkers themselves required good ears to listen carefully for the sound of a solidly filled seam.[18]

Here, then, were the crafts of the waterfront, each one indispensable, each one based on time-honoured and critical skills. Together these craftsmen constituted a large and important component of the Halifax working class.[19] With the partial exception of the coopers, a minority of whom were assembled in somewhat larger groups in steam-powered manufactories, none of these craftsmen faced a change in modes of production that had prevailed for decades along the waterfront. So entrenched were the small workshop and the small master artisan along the waterfront that when the *Census of Canada* raised the qualifications of "manufactures" to a minimum of five employees in 1901, the number of Halifax County cooperages fell from ninety-six in 1891 to six in 1901, the number of sail-lofts from four to two, and the number of shipbuilders from seven to two.[20] The small, often precariously marginal producer clearly continued to dominate these trades, and they never truly became industries. Craftsmen clearly faced no revolution in production that would have suddenly undermined their status.

But together they did face two structural problems that weakened their position: competition from other workers and the obsolescence of their trades in the new world of steam. These two structures determined the outlook of the waterfront craftsmen and consequently the nature of their trade unionism.

To organize a craft means to establish boundaries, most commonly determined by apprenticeship regulations, marking the craft off from "common, unskilled labour" and from other crafts. Each one of the four major crafts felt threatened by other workers. Halifax coopers serving the fishing industry were unable to compete with rural, self-employed artisans whose costs of production were far lower. Local sailmakers found their sphere invaded by the work of merchant seamen trained in sailmaking: in a strike in 1874 these craftsmen complained that "The employers have resorted to all sorts of means to fill the places left vacant by the strike. One shop . . . has two discharged soldiers as apprentices, and merchant sailors, to do the work of sailmakers, which they are not competent to do. Merchants and Insurance Agents should notice these facts."[21] Halifax shipwrights found themselves confronted with the hundreds of rural "hatchet and saw" men who streamed out of rural Nova Scotia as the age of shipbuilding came to a close.[22] When Dartmouth shipbuilder Ebenezer Moseley attempted to replace resident shipwrights on the Chebucto Marine Railway with rural newcomers in 1874, he was denounced by one indignant worker:

> Since the large increase of Shipbuilding throughout the Province, employing as it does about 50 per cent of unskilled labour, we have

had numerous applications for admission from persons who, having acquired the alphabet of a mechanical education, attracted to the city by cash payments, travelling like birds of passage from place to place, with an abundance of assurance and a moiety of modesty, who would as readily engage to construct a locomotive or a watch, as a ship, provided they had some persons to show them how, have now taken refuge at Mr. Moseley's Shipyard, a veritable cave of adullam for them, from whence he now trots them out and introduces them to the mercantile community as Shipwrights and Caulkers.[23]

The problem of these alarmingly versatile rural craftsmen persisted into the next century, and their distinctive outlook was echoed in the words of M.L. Oliver, a crusty old shipbuilder in Digby: "I am an old ship builder, built ships in U.S.A. before the civil war & have never struck a Labour Union. *I hate the name.*"[24]

There were equally intractable problems of demarcating the turf of the shipwright from that of other crafts. The union's rulebook established, on its very first page, precise criteria for separating the work of the shipwright from that of the joiner: members were exempt from penalty while working with joiners at such work as "fitting up cabins, houses, and forecastles; planing up deck planks, putting on bulwarks, except such as requires [sic] caulking, finishing and moulding rails, &c.," but it was stressed that joiners were "to put in no piece that requires caulking." Jurisdictional friction between joiners and shipwrights became more common in the late nineteenth century, as land-based carpenters came to do an increasing amount of joiners' work on steamers and adamantly refused to accept shipwrights as members unless they left the shipwrights' association.[25] Similar patterns of competition can be found in the relationship between the shipwrights and the caulkers. Caulkers were often lumped together with the shipwrights and the two trades overlapped; when the caulkers organized to form a separate union in 1882 they spoke of their reason for creating a distinct caulkers' body: "the Secretary read a clause showing how the Caulkers feeling themselves infringed upon by Carpenters in many ways as regards their work, thought it a benifit [sic] to have a Caulkers Society and had Called this meeting for the purpose of organizing themselves into a Caulkers Association."[26] On 11 May 1885, a resolution passed stating that "no members of the Association shall work with anyone employed on the same job painting or scraping who are in the habit of doing Caulking or other wise interfering with the interest of the Association Under a penalty of $5.00 Dollars fine for each offense."[27] Sydney and Beatrice Webb argued that this spirit of "local monopoly" and the resulting fierce jurisdictional battles were especially characteristic of shipbuilding and other port trades, and E.J. Hobsbawm has underlined the intense localism of British waterside unionism, operating in ports that were competitive with each other.[28] Halifax bears out their analyses completely.

Craft unionism on the Halifax waterfront was thus profoundly marked by pressures within the labour market. The Shipwrights' and Caulkers' Association of Halifax and Dartmouth (1863–c. 1914), the Caulkers' Association of Halifax and Dartmouth (1882–1908), the Sailmakers' Union Club (1871–c. 1888), the Coopers' Union (1870–c. 1878, 1884–1901), and Local 140, the first Canadian local of the revived Coopers' International Union (1901–03), while participating in some of the general debates of the Halifax labour movement (such as denouncing the highly suspect "workingman's candidate" who sought labour support for the Tories in 1874), were never progressive, outward-looking bodies. Significantly, with the exception of the short-lived coopers' local, none was affiliated with a larger labour organization. Only rarely did any of these bodies take a clear political initiative.

What one finds, instead, is the adamant defence of craft privileges through restrictive devices, the most important of which was the limitation of numbers through skill qualifications and apprenticeship. The 1867 *Supplementary Rules* of the Shipwrights' and Caulkers' Association stated that "The term of apprenticeship shall not be less than five years or exceed seven." No member of the society was to work for any employer having more than three apprentices, and journeymen shipwrights and caulkers were forbidden to keep them. Apprentices out of their time were to pay an initiation fee of $4, which was $3 more than the initial sum.[29] Other crafts followed similar practices, often defending such limitations by strikes.[30] Restricting the number of apprentices closed the gates of the craft to the vast majority of the unskilled as well as limited the dilution of skills by the employers.

Besides apprentice restriction, such craft unions could employ other means to limit entry to crafts, including paying off rural craftsmen who came to the city. The caulkers, with a separate union after 1882, likewise survived by using the device of the limitation of numbers and the practice of the common rule. On 11 November 1884, the union simply closed entry to caulking by deciding it would receive no applications for membership for the next three months.[31] In 1886, its ability to control the hiring of caulkers was severely tested. The trouble began in mid-January when the barque *Chignecto,* carrying oil from New York to Rotterdam, put in to Halifax in distress. She was scheduled to undergo repairs at the Marine Slip in Dartmouth on 28 January, but the Dartmouth caulkers refused to work at $2.40 per day and held out for ten cents more. Country men began work on the *Chignecto* the next day, with special constables sworn in to prevent rioting; at least one caulker was arrested. But after a delegation of unionists waited on the country men most of them were "persuaded" to return to their homes with sums ranging from $5 to $20. The records of the caulkers' union report that it borrowed $135.06 (far greater than the association's total assets) to rid itself of the rural craftsmen, a cost that was supposed to be divided evenly between the shipwrights' and the caulkers' unions. It appears that the *Chignecto* was repaired slowly with a few remaining non-unionists, but such merchant revolts against the association's rule were not repeated, and shipbuilders and shipowners had learned the difficulties they would encounter in any frontal assault on its monopoly.[32]

Rivalling the importance of restricting entry to the crafts in the strategies of these unions were various controls exerted over work. Information on this topic is plentiful only for the shipwrights and caulkers. The Shipwrights' and Caulkers' Association from its inception sought control over both new (i.e., shipbuilding) and old (ship repair) work; meeting staunch resistance from the dockyard in 1864, it reduced its jurisdiction to ship repair alone. While its *public* founding documents emphasize the association's benevolent and "improving" activities,[33] its *private* documents, most notably the remarkable *Supplementary Rules,* sound like a reveille for militants. The very first rule candidly outlines what should be done when conflict breaks out in the shipyards:

> SHOULD any cause of disagreements arise between masters or employers and this association . . . the members working on the job shall then meet to consider and decide on the most desirable method of arrangement. They shall then appoint a committee from their number to carry out such instructions as may be agreed on by two-thirds of their members present, and should such persons neglect or refuse to carry out such instructions they shall be liable to a fine not exceeding five dollars . . . and any member refusing to act in accordance with the decision of the aforesaid majority of two-thirds of the members, shall be fined one dollar, unless it be clearly shown that he would violate the rules of this association by so doing.[34]

These eminently practical (and, by mid-Victorian standards, unusually candid) measures for job control soon made an impact. The stridently anti-union *Evening Express* found them outrageous:

> To give the public some idea of the effect of incorporating Trades' Unions, we may mention the fact that a few days ago one of our Merchants employed a Ship Carpenter to do some repairs to a vessel. It seems the person engaged was only a short time in business and could not afford to employ a large number of hands, so as usual with many a poor Master Mechanic, was obliged to take off his coat and work himself. But what think you reader, he worked one day, and on the next was coolly told by his employees that if he worked the second day they would quit work, and he was obliged to yield.[35]

Galled by such actions, some merchants applied pressure on the legislature to outlaw the association, and harsh criticisms were aired in the House of Assembly of the association's attempt "to create monopoly and prevent men coming to the city and engaging in work," but the effort to reverse the 1864 legalization of trade unionism came to nought. Attempts to organize a rival, more compliant union, the Dartmouth-based "Union Society of Shipwrights and Caulkers" founded by shipbuilder Ebenezer Moseley, also proved ineffectual, and the association exercised a quiet control over hiring until the turn of the century, sending for "country men" when they were required and arranging employment for its members in shipyards as distant as those of Honolulu.[36]

The Caulkers' Association was particularly noted for its tough working rules. Perhaps the most brazen and monopolistic was the constitutional provision that only oakum prepared by the caulkers themselves was to be used on any vessel. No one seriously maintained that caulkers deserved to prepare the oakum because it was "skilled work," nor that the article they produced was superior; the only rationale for such a rule was to bring under the control of the Caulkers' Association an important branch of maritime work for the relief of its underemployed members. At their anti-strike meeting in 1884 the aggrieved merchants protested that they were forced to use oakum spun by the caulkers themselves, which, at fifty cents per pound, was five times more expensive than the ready-spun article.[37] Far from being swayed by such appeals to liberal economics, the association tightened its grip. In 1886, "The Secretary asked if there could not be something done to stop one or two members from spinning Oakum when the rest of the members were walking about or not employed causing a large amount of illfeeling and Dissatisfaction," and the discussion ended by reaffirming the clause in the constitution that "no member should drive any Oakum except [of] his own spinning." On 17 July 1886, a member was charged with violating this decision by driving oakum not spun by himself; although he was not fined, the association passed the drastic resolution "That after this date no member be allowed to spin Oakum if he can be employed elsewhere at Caulking & Coopering or while any members are non employed," which meant giving the union exclusive control over the basic raw material of the craft. Even by the standards of Canadian craft unionism in the nineteenth century, the caulkers' control was remarkable.[38]

There were less contentious and "monopolist" aspects to the device of the common rule, although from an employers' viewpoint they were no less coercive. Both shipwrights and caulkers imposed conditions of hours and wages well in advance of other trades. From its foundation in 1863 to 1872, the association struggled for the $2.50 day; such was its strength that by 1872 it successfully negotiated on behalf of its eighty-eight members not only this advanced rate of wages but the nine-hour day from 1 May to 1 October. The wage rates established in 1872 seem to have held up remarkably well as the century progressed and business slowed down; even a rough sort of eight-hour day was in effect in the winter months by 1888, although this appears only to have applied to shipwrights.[39] On the basis of such conditions (which were denounced as extravagant and unusual by the merchants) the shipwrights and caulkers were able to sustain a reasonable standard of living. Michael O'Brien (1847–1912), the association's secretary from 1864 to 1894 and a native of Killarney, Ireland, told the Labour Commission in 1888 that half of the shipwrights owned their own homes; he himself, estimating his pay at $800 per year for the last seven years, had managed to accumulate a half-dozen houses, which he rented out to other working-class families. O'Brien's thirty-year stint as secretary suggests the stability, not to say immobility, of the Shipwrights' and Caulkers' Association and of waterfront craft unionism in general.[40] Unless provoked, these small unions (never totalling more than two hundred members, approximately one-fifth of the waterfront work force) defended themselves quietly, patiently, effectively. The turning point in their fortunes appears to have come in 1895—"the worst year in the history of the craft," it was remarked in Dartmouth—after which these craftsmen lapsed into a profound silence, culminating in their disappearance as an organized force, probably shortly before World War I.[41]

The achievements of these waterfront craft unions were impressive. They made the most of their difficult situation within a context of dying crafts and diminishing possibilities. But these achievements were only possible on the basis of deliberately fostered labour scarcity and monopoly control over minute details of the work process. Craft achievement demanded a policy of exclusion towards labourers and rural craftsmen. In all the published and manuscript records left by these unions, there is no mention of craftsmen making common cause with the labourers who worked on the same waterfront with them, nor of them extending their organizations to their brother craftsmen in the country. Perhaps the most telling indications of the narrow structural limits of the craftsmen's achievements and their "labour aristocratic" mentality are the symptomatic silences: the silence in 1884 when the longshore labourers struggled for their rights; the silence in 1885 when the union's battle was lost; the silence in the minute books of the caulkers' union, where the most significant of all the disturbances along the Halifax waterfront did not merit a single word.

One of Halifax's first labour historians, regrettably anonymous, summed up the history of unskilled labour on the Halifax waterfront this way: "The history of the labor movement on the Port of Halifax would make interesting reading. Its earlier record has been a succession of failures. The workmen realizing the necessity of banding themselves together for common good, would form a union, and a large amount of enthusiasm would be generated, the men crowding into line, and for a time everything would go along successfully, but the reaction would set in and the membership gradually dwindle away again."[42] This first historian of longshoremen in Halifax described the situation exactly, but the explanation for it eluded him. The relative failure of nineteenth-century Halifax longshoremen appears all the more puzzling when set beside the examples of militant ship labourers in Quebec City and Saint John, who organized massive unions and successfully struggled for better hours and wages.[43]

The answer lies in the structure of work in the port, which, unlike Saint John or Quebec City, did not have as its vital nucleus the heavy, collective, highly seasonal labour demanded by a bulky staple trade, timber, but rather the lighter, more individualized, and less seasonal tasks of an entrepôt and fishing port. Occupational structures—notably the role of the stevedore—defined quite sharply in Saint John by the 1870s, were much less so in Halifax. An 1842 visitor to Halifax from Saint John remarked upon the difference in hiring customs in the two cities: "Yesterday I passed along the head of the market wharf [Halifax], and I counted 20 labourers standing with their hands in their pockets, shoved down to the elbows. I at once recognized them as having come from your market [Saint John]—for in Halifax the labourers do not take up their position at the head of the wharf, as in Saint John. They scatter themselves about, as if ashamed to be seen in one another's company."[44] In Halifax, hiring practices varied from wharf to wharf. Some stevedores were permanently stationed on specific wharves; others managed several wharves and might specialize in various kinds of loading operations. (The loading of deals at Richmond was handled by one particular such master stevedore.) On other wharves, men who were normally considered longshoremen might contract to unload a given cargo and employ fellow workers to do the job. On West India wharves, labourers worked in good weather, drying fish and placing it in barrels by means of a "screw." Some were hired directly by the merchants; others worked under master coopers who supervised the process by which the fish was dried and secured in barrels. The most advanced wharf, Cunard's, employed clerks, a wharfinger, a timekeeper, a storekeeper, truckmen, cargo checkers, and forty-two permanent employees.[45]

Such an array of hiring practices and conditions did not give labourers the same unity they had in the timber ports, and the potential for united action was further undermined by the casual (or "transient") labour system. The distinction between permanent and casual labourers was crucial. Permanent employees worked a regular nine- or ten-hour day, were paid by the week, and were steadily employed through the year; casual employees worked the hours demanded (up to twenty at a stretch), were paid by the hour or by the day, and enjoyed no security of employment. Longshore work was frequently resorted to by other workers, even craftsmen, when times were hard, and by "foreigners" from laidup schooners, who were said to take twice as long to do the work of "skilled" longshoremen.[46] But many of the men mainly dependent on longshore work would themselves rely part-time on the fishery or take up marginal occupations (such as pawnbroking) in the city. The transient workers who prepared fish were even less secure because whenever it rained—as it is apt to do in

Halifax—they would be paid only for the number of quarters of the day they had worked. This policy of placing the unavoidable risks of fish-drying on the shoulders of the workers had aroused violent antipathy at least as early as 1856, but it was still the system in 1884.[47] Estimates in 1884 of annual earnings suggest that labourers who worked steadily could aspire to earn about $350 in the year, about half the pay of the shipwrights. Not surprisingly, the longshoremen were among the most wretched workers of the city. They were described as living in "attics and in the cheapest sort of way" and forced to place their barefoot children at work on the waterfront for fifty or sixty cents per day.[48] Sporadic strikes against such evils in 1854, the mid-1860s, 1873, and 1880 brought some short-term successes but no structural change.[49]

The steamer changed this rather desolate picture. It arrived in Halifax before any attempt had been made to alter loading or unloading techniques by using the steam winch or the donkey engine.[50] The steamer brought an entirely different tempo to longshore work. When a large steamer came into port, between 200 and 500 men might be employed in loading, discharging, or coaling. Not only was this work more collective, it was also more intensive.[51] Only if the heavy investment in the new technology was rewarded with greater speed and economy, and hence a short turnaround time in port, would it pay off. The results for labour were ambiguous. New employment was undeniably created—especially in Halifax with its advantages as a coaling centre for European steamers—and labourers were able to work in the winter to a greater extent. But in the short term, the initial consequence was the intensification of casualism, because the requirement for masses of men to be available at a moment's notice created a large surplus labour pool.[52] In the long term, nevertheless, the industrial revolution in shipping made effective trade unionism a genuine possibility, since it alone could create a sudden scarcity of labour in ports that did not otherwise have this structural characteristic.

The Laborers' Union of Halifax (often also called the "Longshore Laborers' Association") was founded on 13 April 1882, and united casual and permanent wharf labourers into a well-organized body. According to its constitution, it was open to male persons aged sixteen to sixty, "provided that they be in good health and of moral character." It provided a fund from which its members could receive assistance (based on monthly dues of twenty-five cents) and urged the necessity of a "uniform price for labour, per day and by the hour," for discharging and loading vessels and for other labour. After three months in existence the union had 325 members, an eight-man executive, and a twelve-man council. This was Halifax's first mass union. By 1883 it had 518 members and worked to give them a sense of solidarity and pride. There were marches through the streets with a fife and drum corps, picnics to McNab's Island, and an important new cohesiveness between men who worked on the wharves and those who worked on vessels.[53]

The leader of the union was John A. Mackasey (1840–1919), who for years was a commission merchant on Water Street and who represented many of the Gloucester fishing vessels when they called at Halifax.[54] A middle-class recruit to labour's cause, Mackasey became disillusioned with the impact of the National Policy on staple trades of the Maritimes and penned a compelling analysis of the regional imbalance of the tariff in a critique of federal timber policy in 1883.[55] Although one of his motivations in entering the longshoremen's struggle was his desire to wean the labourers from drink,[56] he was plainly outraged by the vast gap between the wealthy merchants and their wretched labourers. Mackasey had a well-developed critique of the Halifax merchants, who, he argued, had ignored the trading opportunities at their doorstep.[57] And, above all, he was an effective labour leader. When the merchants alleged that Halifax labourers earned more than their counterparts in Portland, Maine, Mackasey telegraphed a Portland merchant and proved the allegation false; when the merchants alleged that they provided labourers with work drying fish as a benevolent gesture, Mackasey detailed the profit margins involved in curing; when merchants argued that the labourers' living standards had improved remarkably, Mackasey simply led reporters through the hovels and attics housing the longshoremen's families. He used his contacts with the Gloucester fishing fleet to ship out some strikers for the Greenland fishery at $190 a trip, making sure to tell the merchants that, given the great demand for fishermen, they stood to lose the services of the labourers for the season. He was careful to distance himself from the militant model of Saint John trade unionism, which Halifax merchants loved to cite as a horrible example of mob rule, and he instructed union members to be respectful of their employers. In a port that had traditionally revered its merchant princes, however, Mackasey's critique and actions were genuinely radical. Workingmen, he warned, would never submit to having the city develop at their expense. The longshoremen's desire for a better life, he said sardonically, "had been taught them by the merchants themselves. The merchants of twenty years ago, mostly lived over their stores. Now they live in palaces on the banks of the North West Arm."[58]

Mackasey's efforts lay behind the 1884 demand that labourers be paid $1.50 per day for store work, seventy-five cents for a half-day, and twenty cents per hour for work after 5 PM. (This represented a 20 percent increase.) There were to be no more quarter or three-quarter days, and Sunday work was to be paid at a rate of fifty cents per hour. Stevedore work was to be paid $2 per day on sailing vessels and twenty-five cents per hour on steamships, barges, lighters, and tugboats. These demands, for all their modesty, were precisely calculated reforms, aimed at the casual labour system and low wages alike. The Laborers' Union, now representing what Mackasey called "the whole laboring class of the city," adopted new methods of mass unionism: badges were issued to identify members, marked with "L.U." for Laborers' Union, with the member's number as recorded in the union's rolls. This tactic would allow the swift identification of strikebreakers and allow permanent longshoremen not directly involved in the strike to identify and avoid non-union gangs.[59]

The strike began on 12 May 1884, a rainy day on which no fish-drying would take place in any event; many of the independent master stevedores caved in immediately. As the week progressed, they were joined by some master coopers. Everyone waited for the crucial test: the arrival of the first steamer. The unloading of the steamer *Caspian* on 16 May by union men at the union rate was a day of jubilation for the union. The remaining master coopers now gave the advanced rate and paid their labourers a full day's pay even if they had been able to work only three-quarters of the day. Union men coaling the steamer *Faraday* earned the high wage of fifty cents per hour; some cleared ten dollars each. The victory of Mackasey and the union was complete.[60]

It was also short-lived. By 27 May, merchants were planning to employ regular hands in drying fish instead of casual labour. Some employers were also insisting on removal of the badges as a condition of going to work. The return of fine fish-drying weather precipitated a crisis and the union, successful on the vessels, met defeat on the shore. By 9 July, Hart's, Butler's, and Boak's wharves were all reported to be employing non-union men exclusively. The union was forced to pass a resolution allowing union men to deliver to non-union men on the shore, provided that all gangs were "on one side and the other." These defeats paved the way for the biggest defeat of them all, in January 1885. When the *S.S. Newcastle City* was docked at Pickford and Black's, it was not unloaded by the usual labourers, who stood about demanding the union rate of twenty-five cents an hour. Instead, unemployed schooner men had taken the work away from the Halifax labourers. By 1886 casual labourers were accepting twenty cents an hour for steamer work (five cents less than the 1884 demand).[61] The Laborers' Union survived these defeats and endured until 1899 (probably largely on the strength of its death and sickness benefits). But it did not strike again for the rights of the longshoremen. Sporadic, doomed strikes for higher wages in the 1890s were without union backing.[62]

The causes of this brave failure were to be found in the structure of the port labour market. Mackasey backed away from the creation of a coercive labour monopoly on the Saint John model (and, because of Halifax's distinctively fragmented character, there were reasons to doubt such a monopoly could have been imposed). But without such power—without union domination over port hiring—the reforms wrested in 1884 were bound to be eroded by the merchants. Badges were not enough. And as the steamers called at Halifax less and less frequently, and as some lines withdrew altogether in the late 1880s and early 1890s, the structural conditions favouring united trade union action had largely dissipated.

In February 1900, the longshoremen, reorganized as the Port Workers Union of Halifax, refused en masse to work a mail steamer on Sunday unless the steamship companies guaranteed their fines for working on the Sabbath. By 1902, two locals of the International Longshoremen's Association had been formed. On 2 April, the longshoremen went on strike for a twelve-point program, which included such demands as the exclusive employment of union labour, where possible, recognized holidays, a day scale of twenty-five cents, and a night scale of thirty cents an hour. They settled for twenty cents and twenty-five cents, after a successful mediation by Mackenzie King, but their union was effectively broken in the struggle.[63]

The same cycle of failure had returned, despite the intervention of an international union and impressive support from a united Halifax labour movement. There was no mystery to this failure. Once again the inability of the men to control the labour market meant that they faced the threat of submission or replacement. As James Hall, manager of the Furness-Withy line of steamers, remarked, "There are thousands of men all along the coasts of Nova Scotia and Newfoundland seeking work. And they will be only too glad to come to Halifax and get work at twenty cents an hour." The logic of the union's demand for exclusive hiring lay precisely here as well: the building of a union could not occur in a context of uncontrolled casualism.[64] Only in 1907, in the context of an acute scarcity of labour, were the longshoremen able to build a more secure union; and a genuine structural response to waterfront casualism was left until World War II. For all its brilliance, 1884 had turned out to be a false dawn for the port workers.

Every day in the last quarter of the nineteenth century, a thousand or so men—more than would find work at one of the larger provincial coal mines—gathered for work on the Halifax waterfront. Like coal miners, they worked in a very distinctive milieu, with their own customs and traditions, taverns and neighbourhoods.[65] Unlike the coal miners, however, these workers never built large, strong unions. Craftsmen, threatened by rural migrants and urban labourers, built small, exclusivist unions that defended their particular privileges. Labourers, fragmented by the casual labour system and the diffuse character of the port, built much larger unions that failed either to change the system or to achieve a secure status on the waterfront. The indispensable coal miners wrested major political and social reforms from the government and large wage increases from the coal companies; the equally indispensable port workers won no such victories.

The difference stemmed from the stratification of waterfront labour under the aegis of merchant capital. Although nineteenth-century Canadian labour historiography has seen the struggles of skilled workers as the profoundly progressive elaboration of a "culture of control" and such men as leading a more general struggle for working-class rights, the Halifax case calls such interpretations sharply into question.[66] There is simply no evidence to suggest that skilled workers were concerned to extend their workplace controls to the unskilled, or saw their battles as parts of a more general social struggle. Had they done so, we would find them leading (or, at the very least, enthusiastically supporting) the longshoremen in 1884. They did not, and for a perfectly good reason: their whole style of trade unionism was based on excluding others from their obsolescent crafts. They were not artisans enunciating a doctrine of workers' control that could inspire all workers but labour aristocrats understandably anxious to preserve their status in a rapidly changing world. Only further research will ascertain whether this narrowly based craft unionism in Halifax or the radical, progressive, class-conscious craft unionism described in Hamilton and Toronto is the more general pattern in Canada.

With the industrialization of the port of Halifax in the twentieth century these patterns of casualism and exclusivism would change. The coming of monopoly capitalism is rightly associated with the breaking down of crafts; certainly the consolidation of world shipping capital slowly destroyed the intricate and specialized skills of the Halifax waterfront. But it should also be associated with an improvement in the conditions of labourers, for it was only within this new structure that longshoremen joined the ranks of "respectable" labour and made Halifax trade unionism a broadly based movement of workers.[67] And this was part of a regional pattern. Merchant capital was conservative. It created fragmented and fragmenting structures, from the debt bondage of the fishermen and the archaic quasi-serfdom of merchant seamen, to the isolation and pervasive paternalism of mercantile coal villages. Such fragmentation made unified opposition impossible and confined dissent to movements, which were often tremendously courageous and forceful, but which were also tragically isolated, short-lived, and non-cumulative.[68] The new possibilities opened up by the era of large-scale capital included those of linking up masses of workers in a far more aggressive search for political and social alternatives. This change would decisively mark off the eras of mercantile and competitive industrial capitalism in the Maritimes from that of monopoly capitalism. Only within this new structure could merchant capital's legacy of social fragmentation be addressed and partially overcome.

• Notes

1 This essay is a revised and rethought version of "Class Struggle and Mercantile Capitalism: Craftsmen and Labourers on the Halifax Waterfront, 1850–1902" in *Workingmen Who Got Wet*, ed. Gerald Panting and Rosemary Ommer (St John's, 1980), 289–333, and draws on trade union and other sources that surfaced after the first version was prepared. Throughout I use "Halifax" to refer to both Halifax and its suburb Dartmouth. My thanks to Judith Fingard, who first introduced me to the subject of Halifax working-class history and who has generously shared information and insights with me.

2 For an analysis of the domination of the Chamber of Commerce by the wholesaler/broker faction of the

Halifax bourgeoisie, see David A. Sutherland, "The Personnel and Policies of the Halifax Board of Trade, 1890–1914" in *The Enterprising Canadians: Entrepreneurs and Economic Development in Eastern Canada, 1820–1914*, ed. Lewis R. Fischer and Eric W. Sager (St John's, 1979), 205–10. See also Larry D. McCann, "Staples and the New Industrialism in the Growth of Post-Confederation Halifax," *Acadiensis* 8, 2 (1979): 29–64.

3 *Report of the Royal Commission on the Relations of Capital and Labour in Canada* (hereafter *RCRCL*), *Evidence— Nova Scotia* (Ottawa, 1889), 136, 325.

4 See E.J. Hobsbawm, *The Age of Capital* (New York, 1979), 59; *RCRCL, Evidence—Nova Scotia*, 154.

5 *Acadian Recorder*, 6 May 1884.

6 *Citizen and Evening Chronicle*, 9 May 1884.

7 Adopting the useful terminology of Sydney and Beatrice Webb, *Industrial Democracy* (London, 1901), although not, of course, many of their other assumptions.

8 Gerald S. Graham, "The Ascendancy of the Sailing Ship, 1850–85," *Economic History Review*, 2nd series, 19, 1 (1956): 7; Rosemary Ommer, "The Decline of the Eastern Canadian Shipping Industry, 1880–95," *Journal of Transport History* 1 (1984): 25–44; Sarah Palmer, "Experience, Experiment, and Economics: Factors in the Construction of Early Merchant Steamships" in *Ships and Shipbuilding in the North Atlantic Region*, ed. Keith Matthews and Gerald Panting (St John's, 1978), 233–49; Public Archives of Nova Scotia (hereafter PANS), MG 27, vols. 42–44, Pickford and Black registers. The printed records of the Department of Marine and Fisheries, in the *Sessional Papers*, 1890–1910, show the domination of steam vessels in the early 1890s.

9 See Eric W. Sager, "Sources of Productivity Change in the Halifax Ocean Fleet, 1863–1900" in *Volumes Not Values: Canadian Sailing Ships and World Trades*, ed. David Alexander and

Rosemary Ommer (St John's 1979), 93–115; L.R. Fischer, "The Great Mudhole Fleet: The Voyages and Productivity of the Sailing Vessels of Saint John, 1863–1912," ibid., 119–55.

10 The record of the *N.B. Lewis*, a Yarmouth vessel, suggests that heavy repair costs could wipe out much of the gross revenue from a successful trip to Java: see Clement W. Crowell, ed., *The Novascotiaman* (Halifax, 1979), ch. 8.

11 For mid-nineteenth-century repair facilities, "careening wharves," see the description of Richard Marshall in *Acadian Recorder*, 28 March 1857; and also *Herald*, 24 April 1880, 28 Aug. 1883; *Acadian Recorder*, 21 Sept. 1889; Fielding papers, PANS, MG 2, vol. 557, folder 108; and *Herald*, 20 Sept. 1920; for attacks on Halifax as a ship-repair port, see *Citizen and Evening Chronicle*, 8 May 1884, a long rebuttal of Boston attempts to discredit Halifax; and for merchant criticisms of labour for raising the price of ship repairs, see the remarks of George E. Boak in *Citizen and Evening Chronicle*, 9 May 1884; Dalhousie University Archives, MS 9 48 (microfilm), Business Book of the Caulkers' Association of Halifax & Dartmouth 1882–1895 (hereafter Caulkers' Minutes), Minutes, 11 Oct. 1886.

12 See *Steel's Elements of Mastmaking, Sailmaking and Rigging* (New York, 1932 [1794]), part 1; *RCRCL, Evidence—Nova Scotia*, 229, for comments by a Halifax rigger.

13 Franklin E. Coyne, *The Development of the Cooperage Industry in the United States, 1620–1940* (Chicago, 1940); Herbert Gutman, "La politique ouvrière de la grande entreprise américaine de 'L'âge du clinquant': le case de Standard Oil Company," *Le mouvement social* 102 (janvier–mars 1978): 67–99. For the Canadian industry, see the interesting discussion in James Delebaugh, *History of the Lumber Industry of America* (Chicago, 1906), ch. 7; *RCRCL, Evidence—Nova Scotia*, 11, 53.

14 Report from Local No. 140, Halifax, in the *Coopers' International Journal* 9 (Sept. 1903): 411.

15 Crowell, *Novascotiaman*, 286–87. One such well-worn kit, belonging to a sailmaker who travelled up and down the Atlantic seaboard, is preserved in the Dartmouth Heritage Museum. On the artisanal character of sailmaking, see Mark G. Hirsch, "Sailmakers: The Maintenance of Craft Tradition in the Age of Steam" in *Divisions of Labour: Skilled Workers and Technological Change in Nineteenth-Century Britain*, ed. Royden Harrison and Jonathan Zeitlin (Chicago, 1985), 92; and Samuel Sadler, *The Art and Science of Sailmaking* (London, 1906).

16 An important distinction was drawn between ship joiners and ship carpenters. The ship carpenters erected the structure, and their work could not be removed without affecting the strength of the structure; the work of the joiners was not intended to add to structural strength and could therefore be removed without affecting it. The ship carpenter worked with heavy materials, seldom devoting much time to the finish of surfaces; the joiner worked with light material and had constantly to bear in mind the finish and appearance of work when it was completed. In Halifax, the term *shipwright* encompassed both aspects of the work, but *joinery* was far less practised in a port devoted to ship repair than was *ship carpentry*.

17 See, for example, the discussion in Sir Wescott Abell, *The Shipwright's Trade* (Cambridge, 1948), 77.

18 Lloyd's Register of Shipping, *Rules and Regulations for the Construction and Classification of Wood Vessels* (London, 1917), 61; R.D. Culler, *Skiffs and Schooners* (Camden, ME, 1974), 9. I am indebted to Niels Jaanash of the maritime Museum of the Atlantic for this reference.

19 According to the *Census of Canada*, the number of artisans in these trades actually rose from 163 in 1871 to 207 in 1891, but this statistic is complicated by the emergence of many black, rural coopers in the community of Hammonds Plains, who made casks for fish at well under the costs of production in Halifax. (In 1891 we find in Halifax County no fewer than 87 cooperages employing only 124 men.) Of the major trades listed in 1891, 153 were coopers, 32 were in ship construction, and 22 were sailmakers. The census data underestimate considerably the number of shipwrights and caulkers.

20 Of the 64 cooperages operating in Halifax from 1872 to 1920, the average life span was 6.9 years: because of extremely low barriers to entry, the trade was chronically overcrowded and bankruptcies common. Locational factors—the need to locate right on very expensive and scarce waterfront property—probably accounted for the much greater stability of sailmaking and ship repair: 2 of the 7 shipbuilding/repairing firms lasted throughout the period, while the average life span for the 19 sail-lofts was 11.5 years. See *McAlpine's City Directory for 1871–72* (Halifax), continuing to *McAlpine's City Directory for 1920–21*.

21 *Evening Express*, 15 April 1874.

22 For this mass exodus of rural craftsmen, see Alan Brookes, "Out-Migration from the Maritime Provinces, 1860–1900: Some Preliminary Considerations" in *Atlantic Canada After Confederation*, ed. P.A. Buckner and David Frank (Fredericton, 1985), 34–63.

23 *Evening Express*, 1 Dec. 1874.

24 Public Archives of Canada, RG 27, vol. 21, file 1 (A–K), Special investigation in regard to the tendency of the Rates of Wages and Hours of Labour in Canada—The Building Trades.

25 *Supplementary Rules of the Shipwrights' and Caulkers' Association* (n.p. [Halifax], n.d. [1867]), 13; Carpenters Hall, Halifax, Records of Local 83, United Brotherhood of Carpenters and Joiners of America, Minutes, 18 July 1899.

26 Caulkers' Records, Minutes, 16 Jan. 1882.

27 Ibid., Minutes, 23 Jan. 1882, 11 May 1885. This motion was later overturned, perhaps because it was impracticable.

28 Webb, *Industrial Democracy*, 73, 517; E.J. Hobsbawm, "National Unions on the Waterside" in *Labouring Men: Studies in the History of Labour* (London, 1974 [1964]), 205.

29 *Supplementary Rules*, 15.

30 *RCRCL, Evidence—Nova Scotia*, 144, 184; *Acadian Recorder*, 15 May 1895; Minutes of Local 83, 16 July 1895; Caulkers' Minutes, 14 May 1883, 14 Jan. 1884, 27 April 1885.

31 Caulkers' Minutes, 11 Nov. 1884.

32 *Acadian Recorder*, 27 and 29 Jan. 1886; *Morning Chronicle*, 28 and 30 Jan., 2 Feb. 1886; Caulkers' Minutes, 2 March 1886.

33 PANS, RG 5, series P, vol. 126, no. 102, Petition of Shipwrights and Caulkers of the City of Halifax and Dartmouth, 15 Feb. 1864.

34 *Supplementary Rules*, 13.

35 *Evening Express*, 1 March 1865.

36 *Debates and Proceedings of the House of Assembly, Nova Scotia*, 1886, 15; *RCRCL, Evidence—Nova Scotia*, 107; for the emigration of shipwrights and caulkers, under the direction of H.I. Crandall and James Lyle, to Honolulu, see the Crandall papers, Dartmouth Heritage Museum, and *Dartmouth Times*, 16 Feb. 1884.

37 *Citizen and Evening Chronicle*, 9 May 1884.

38 Caulkers' Minutes, 12 and 17 July 1886; the Graving Dock Company subsequently opposed the union's control over oakum (Caulkers' Minutes, 7 April 1890), but evidently without success. For Toronto parallels, see Gregory S. Kealey, "'The Honest Workingman' and Workers' Control: The Experience of Toronto Skilled Workers, 1860–1892," *Labour/Le Travailleur* 1 (1976): 32–68.

39 *Morning Chronicle*, 4 June 1864; *Daily Reporter and Times*, 14 June 1870; *Morning Chronicle*, 1, 2 May 1872; *RCRCL, Evidence—Nova Scotia*, 107, 228.

40 Probate Court (Halifax), Inventory of the Estate of Michael O'Brien, 1912. The O'Brien estate was appraised at $9425; *Morning Chronicle*, 15 July 1912; *Herald*, 15 July 1912; *Acadian Recorder*, 15 July 1912. The same family names—Regan, Moseley, Devan, Hunt—recur again and again in the executive lists of the Caulkers' Association as well.

41 The only evidence I have of the association's existence after 1910 is mention of the union's floral wreath sent for the funeral of Michael O'Brien in 1912 (*Acadian Recorder*, 17 July 1912).

42 *Souvenir Booklet, Twenty-Fourth Convention of the Trades and Labor Congress of Canada* (Halifax, 1908).

43 See J.I. Cooper, "The Quebec Ship Labourers' Benevolent Society," *Canadian Historical Review* 30, 3 (1949): 336–43; James Richard Rice, "A History of Organized Labour in Saint John, New Brunswick, 1813–1890" (MA thesis, University of New Brunswick, 1968), 19–52; Judith Fingard, "The Decline of the Ship Labourer in 19th Century Timber Ports," *Labour/Le Travailleur* 2 (1977): 35–53.

44 *Morning News* (Saint John), 29 Aug. 1842.

45 *RCRCL, Evidence—Nova Scotia*, 95; *Herald*, 12 May 1884; *Acadian Recorder*, 12 May 1884; *Herald*, 2 Nov. 1880.

46 *RCRCL, Evidence—Nova Scotia*, 116, 121; *Acadian Recorder*, 24 Jan. 1885.

47 *Citizen and Evening Chronicle*, 10 May 1884; *Morning Chronicle*, 28 Oct. 1856.

48 *Herald*, 7 and 9 May 1884.

49 *Morning Chronicle*, 29 and 31 May 1873; *Citizen*, 7 June 1873; *Evening Express*, 20 June 1873; *Acadian Recorder*, 10 May 1880.

50 For interesting details on international working-class resistance to these

innovations, including machine-smashing, see Peter N. Stearns, *Lives of Labour: Work in a Maturing Industrial Society* (London, 1975), 126–27.

51 See *RCRCL, Evidence—New Brunswick*, 65, 235.

52 Gareth Stedman Jones, *Outcast London: A Study in the Relationship Between Classes in Victorian Society* (Oxford, 1971), 121.

53 *Acadian Recorder*, 8 and 14 April, 9 June, 13 July, 21 Aug. 1882; 7 and 19 April 1883; *Citizen and Evening Chronicle*, 1 Nov. 1882; PANS, vertical file, "Labour Unions—1883" (manuscript of "An Act to Incorporate Laborers' Union"); *Statutes of Nova Scotia*, 46 Vic., Cap. 77, 1883, 188–89; *Journals* of the House of Assembly, 1883, 127; PANS, RG 7, vol. 366, no. 24, Constitution of the Laborers' Union.

54 *Acadian Recorder*, 8 Oct. 1919; Probate Court, Estate of John A. Mackasey.

55 PAC, microfilm, reel C-1700, 143667–143692, John A. Macdonald Papers, John A. Mackasey to Macdonald, 23 July 1883.

56 He would later be licence inspector for the city of Halifax while leading the Laborers' Union. See *RCRCL, Evidence—Nova Scotia*, 110–12, for his comments on the Halifax Liquor Trade.

57 *Citizen and Evening Chronicle*, 10 May 1884.

58 *Herald*, 7 and 10 May 1884.

59 *Acadian Recorder*, 30 April, 6 and 10 May 1884; *Herald*, 2, 9, and 10 May 1884.

60 *Acadian Recorder*, 13, 15, 17, and 19 May 1884; *Herald*, 13 and 16 May 1884.

61 *Acadian Recorder*, 27 May, 9 July 1884; 15 July 1886.

62 *Acadian Recorder*, 6 April 1889, 4 May 1894, 10 June 1899.

63 *Herald*, 2, 3, 4, 8, and 12 April 1902.

64 *Evening Mail*, 15 March 1902; *Herald*, 3 April 1902.

65 Peter DeLottinville, "Joe Beef of Montreal: Working Class Culture and the Tavern, 1869–1889," *Labour/Le Travailleur* 8–9 (1981–82): 9–40, studies "waterfront culture" in Montreal and brings out the rifts between skilled workers and casual longshore labourers.

66 See Bryan Palmer, "Most Uncommon Common Men: Craft and Culture in Historical Perspective," *Labour/Le Travailleur* 1 (1976): 5–31; Palmer, *A Culture in Conflict: Skilled Workers and Industrial Capitalism in Hamilton, Ontario, 1860–1914* (Montreal, 1979), ch. 3; Gregory S. Kealey, *Toronto Workers Respond to Industrial Capitalism, 1867–1892* (Toronto, 1980), ch. 3–6.

67 For the subsequent history of the Halifax longshoremen, see Catherine Ann Waite, "The Longshoremen of Halifax 1900–1930: Their Living and Working Conditions" (MA thesis, Dalhousie University, 1977).

68 For studies of the social impact of merchant capital in the region, see Gary Hughes, *Two Islands, Miscou and Lamèque and their State of Bondage 1846–1861* (Saint John, [c. 1980]); Rosemary Ommer, "'All the Fish of the Post': Property, Resource Rights, and Development in a Nineteenth-Century Inshore Fishery," *Acadiensis* 10, 2 (Spring 1981): 107–23; Graham Wynn, *Timber Colony* (Toronto, 1981); I.R. Robertson, "Highlanders, Irishmen and the Land Question in Nineteenth-Century Prince Edward Island" in *Comparative Aspects of Scottish and Irish Economic and Social History, 1600–1900*, ed. C.M. Cullen and T.C. Smout (Edinburgh, 1977); David Sutherland, "The Stanyan Ropeworks of Halifax, Nova Scotia: Glimpses of a Pre-industrial Manufactory," *Labour/Le Travailleur* 6 (1980): 149–58; and Judith Fingard, *Jack in Port: Sailortowns of Eastern Canada* (Toronto, 1982). For a general interpretation of merchant capital as a conservative force, see Elizabeth Fox-Genovese and Eugene Genovese, *Fruits of Merchant Capital: Slavery and Bourgeois Property in the Rise and Expansion of Capitalism* (Oxford, 1983).

CONFRONTING RIEL AND COMPLETING THE CPR*

D.N. SPRAGUE

As the construction of [the] railway proceeded across the Prairies, the largest exodus of Red River Métis moved from Manitoba towards Saskatchewan. The most frequent destination was the district of Prince Albert, attractive because of employment by the Hudson's Bay Company (distributing freight to or from nearby Fort Carlton) and because the vacant land fronting the south branch of the Saskatchewan River closely resembled that of the old Red River colony. As positive reports from the first migrants reached discouraged relatives and former neighbours still in the large Métis parishes of St Norbert, St François Xavier, and Baie St Paul, one relative followed another with increasing frequency in 1882 and 1883.[1]

In the new colony, called St Laurent, the many settlers of the early 1880s were careful to avoid trespassing on the claims of their compatriots,[2] but normally they paid little attention to the settlement status of particular parcels as designated by the Department of the Interior. The Métis were not concerned with the grid pattern of townships, sections, and ranges, and whether the parcel on which they landed happened to fit into an even-numbered section (potentially open for homesteading) or was odd-numbered (reserved for some system of sale).[3] And even if they had been careful to settle exclusively on even-numbered sections fronting on the river, they would still have encountered difficulty with the Dominion Lands Branch because, although the basic sectional survey had been completed in 1879 (and in the normal course of events would have been open to homestead entry within one year), there was an inexplicable delay in the case of St Laurent.[4]

*From: *Canada and the Métis, 1869–1885* by D.N. Sprague (Waterloo: Wilfrid Laurier University Press, 1988), 157–77. Reprinted with the permission of the publisher.

Part of the delay is attributable to the effect of John A. Macdonald's land policy: on the south branch of the Saskatchewan, portions of several townships amounting to more than 50 000 acres had been reserved for the Prince Albert Colonization Company in April 1882; and the area underwent an inspection nearly equivalent to resurvey in 1883 before the final reservation occurred in November 1883.[5] Homestead entries became acceptable in February 1884.[6]

In the interim, almost 300 Métis families had come into the territory and settled mainly on river lots they laid out for themselves. Periodically, the Métis settlers asked George Duck, the dominion lands agent at Prince Albert, to record their claims and to recognize the emerging river-lot pattern. Of course all such requests were frustrated, at first because the land was not open to entry of any kind; then, after February 1884, the Métis found their claims were complicated by the distinction between river lots and section land, and whether the land was odd- or even-numbered in the sectional survey.[7] A few residents complied with the legal complexities; more than 90 percent of the population held out for their own pattern of settlement and for the demand for patents immediately. What made claimants all the more persistent was seeing that approximately one-fifth of the area of new settlement had been laid out as river-lots as the Métis had wanted (in 1878 to take account of the observed pattern of occupancy at the time of original survey),[8] but even the occupants of the regularly surveyed river lots were deemed to be "squatters" until they made legal entry and completed the settlement duties that would make them eligible for patents.[9]

The minister of the interior might have recommended use of the sweeping powers in section 125 of the Dominion Lands Act to cut through the complexities depicted in figure 1. He might have exempted the St Laurent Métis from the odd circumstances that made their case so complicated, but there was no political advantage to be gained by moving boldly on the matter. Sir John A. Macdonald preferred continuing doing nothing, a position he had chosen deliberately in the spring of 1879 after Métis land claims first came to his attention as the minister of the interior following the Conservatives' return to power in September 1878.

Early in 1878, the North West "half breeds" had petitioned for land, seed grain, and implements to ease their transition to farming as the extinction of the buffalo became more and more evident in the late 1870s.[10] But none of the pleas for assistance had found favour with Macdonald's predecessor, David Mills, who dismissed all such appeals with a peculiar contradiction that was frequently evident in the utterances of officials writing on the subject of "half breeds." On the one hand, they denounced the allegedly inherent aversion of the Métis to field agriculture. On the other hand (in response to explicit requests for aid to make the transition to the way of life for which priests and certain government officials seemed to have prayed so fervently), they were told that non-Indians

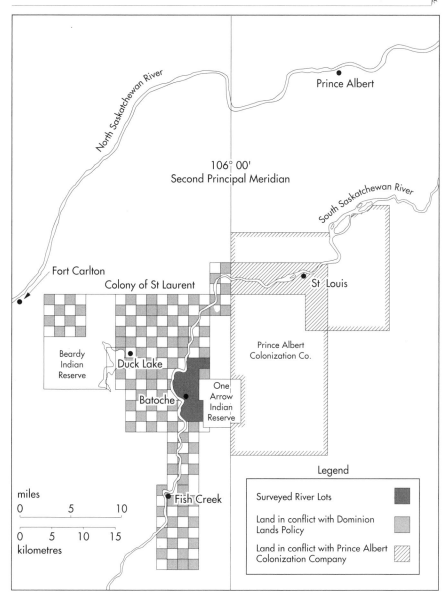

FIGURE 1: *Conflicting Claims to the Colony of St Laurent*

need not apply. In Mills's case, a letter went to the territorial governor explaining that the Métis were either Indians or not. If non-Indian, Mills could "not see upon what grounds the half breeds can claim to be treated in this particular differently from the white settlers in the territories."[11]

But the North West Territorial Council (the appointed committee advising the lieutenant governor) saw the matter rather differently. In its view, all Native people previously dependent on the buffalo were entitled to aid. Council members recommended an assistance program in August 1878 that was remarkably similar to the scheme adopted by the British for the resettlement of Loyalists in Canada after the American Revolution. They proposed that a "non-transferable location ticket" entitling the recipient to 160 acres should be issued to every "half breed" left without land in the North West. Once located on plots of their own choosing, each family could then make free use of government-supplied seed-grain and farm implements for up to three years, just as the British had resettled their displaced persons in North America a century before. Then the Métis settlements would be carefully monitored in their agricultural development. The council members recommended a ten-year period of probation for each assisted claimant of a free grant. It was not recommended that they should receive their land automatically. The "half breeds" would have to perform settlement duties in their first three years, then continue in residence for seven more years before they would be eligible to claim patents for their farms.[12]

Such was the policy recommended by the persons closest to the scene. Since the North West was a kind of Crown colony ruled from Ottawa, one delay followed another. After Sir John A. Macdonald replaced David Mills in the Interior Ministry, he neither accepted nor rejected the advice of the Territorial Council, preferring instead to refer the matter to his deputy minister, J.S. Dennis, for more study. Dennis, in his turn, did draft a broader range of alternatives, adding two other possibilities to the council's proposal late in December 1878. One was extending the provisions of the Indian treaties to the Métis and native English, to "treat them as wards of the Government . . . and look forward to their remaining for many years in their present semi-barbarous state." The other possibility was giving them an issue of scrip as had been done with the Manitoba "half breed heads of families" with the same doubtful benefit to the nominal recipients in the North West. Reluctantly, Dennis recommended the package proposed by the North West Council.[13]

Macdonald still hesitated. He disliked rewarding the Métis for what he considered their own improvidence—it was they who spoiled their opportunities in Manitoba, and they as well who killed most of the buffalo.[14] Not worrying about further delay, the prime minister instructed Dennis to send his memorandum on the subject to the three bishops most acquainted with the Métis. The two Roman Catholic consultants added their endorsements to the Territorial Council's scheme, saying, "the half breed cannot compete with the White man in the discharge of the duties of civilized life unless some steps are taken at the outset to equalize the conditions on which they start." They admitted that the appropriate affirmative action would be expensive, but the first costs were expected to be fully returned by the prosperity of future generations of Métis.[15] Later, the Anglican bishop contributed more muted approval to the growing chorus of promoters of aid, saying that he thought that the free land, seed grain, and implements would be "necessary at first." Still, because he believed that fear of starvation was God's way of teaching respect for civilization, Bishop Machray added that "the less of such gifts the better. They are apt to do mischief."[16]

The result of Macdonald's fruitless quest for a cheap and simple alternative to the proposal of the North West Council was the addition of a few phrases to the Dominion Lands Act in the spring of 1879. The new words appeared to recognize that the North West "half breeds" had a claim to a share of the Indian title to the territory and that the Cabinet was empowered to set aside land "to such extent, and on such terms and conditions, as may be deemed expedient" to satisfy such claims.[17] But in 1879, 1880, 1881, 1882, and 1883 nothing was done towards implementing the new authority to deal with the Métis. Not surprisingly, Macdonald was no more inclined to respond favourably to the new demands of the Métis reinforced in number and resolve by the large migrations from Manitoba. Consequently, the St Laurent claims underwent the same rigour of evaluation as those of any other group of complaining homesteaders. Of the more than 250 persons demanding patents in 1884, fewer than ten were considered legally entitled to what they claimed.[18] Then a new factor suddenly caused Macdonald to reassess his sense of political profit and loss in "half breed" claims. He received an alarming assessment of the situation in June 1884.

Lawrence Clarke, chief factor of Fort Carlton, had informed James Grahame (Clarke's superior officer in Winnipeg) that a pattern of escalating discontent was reaching a point of crisis; "repressive measures" were needed. Clarke explained that as "half breeds" in the District of Saskatchewan were losing freighting employment to the railway and steamboats, they were becoming poorer and poorer, and were pressing extravagant claims on the government in the hope of getting something they might readily sell for cash. As their first appeals were failing, they were on the point of taking extreme action—threatening to repeat the events of 1869–70. A delegation had gone to Montana intending to bring Louis Riel back. The repression Clarke proposed was arresting Riel at the border if he accepted the offer of leadership. Otherwise his presence among hundreds of armed Métis and native English might involve the Indians and even some of the disgruntled white settlers who resented having been bypassed by the CPR. Clarke admitted that taking Riel prisoner would anger some people, but he said a "strong detachment" of police near St Laurent could deter the most militant. The others would be calmed by judicious use of the "influence" at Clarke's disposal and that of the Catholic priests in the area.[19]

Receiving the alarm via Grahame,[20] Macdonald reacted immediately by seeking more information. On the one hand, he asked his man on the spot, Edgar Dewdney, for his assessment. The lieutenant governor replied in a matter of days that the "half breeds" had been "ventilating their grievances" in secret meetings, and Dewdney also agreed that the principal reason for their discontent was economic because the Hudson's Bay Company had drastically cut both the volume and the rate of pay for overland freighting. But Dewdney added that a little group of Prince Albert speculators (including Clarke) had suffered from the collapse of the recent land boom. They welcomed the idea of a larger police garrison for the money it would bring into the district. Indeed, Lawrence Clarke was playing a double game. Having goaded the "half breeds" to bold protest, his "very sensational" letter now played to his speculator's interest more than to a real crisis.[21]

Dewdney's reassuring letter was not confirmed by the result of the police inquiries that Macdonald requested at the same time. He wanted to know the overall number of "half breeds" in the North West, how many were disaffected Manitobans, where they lived, and their probability of following Riel in the event of his attempting to form a second provisional government. Macdonald had also asked the deputy minister in charge of the police, Fred White, to go west for his own first-hand impressions.

Before his departure, Comptroller White ordered Superintendent Crozier and Commissioner Irvine (the field officers in the North West Mounted Police with military ranks of major and colonel, respectively) to collect the statistical data. On 10 June, White ordered Irvine to make discreet inquiries while travelling from community to community under some improvised purpose—"with some object . . . other than the real one."[22] On the same day, White sent identical instructions to Crozier, ordering him to "visit the settlements and . . . form an opinion which you can communicate to me confidentially."[23]

Thus, Macdonald did not ignore Clarke's warning. He moved quickly for a comprehensive view and from diverse sources, even though he rejected the appeal for immediate "repressive measures." Riel and the delegation were not arrested when they reached the Canadian border in late June, but the police did "shadow" the progress of Riel and his entourage closely, and kept the prime minister fully informed of what followed.

While Dewdney continued to report that Riel's return was a political nuisance but no threat (not unless the Métis leader "tampered" with Indian discontents),[24] White's report was remarkably consistent with the original alarm sounded by Clarke. Canada's most senior policeman was certain that despite peaceful appearances, Louis Riel did aim for something like a second provisional government. "I am convinced that there is an illegal movement of some kind in contemplation."[25] A detailed statistical report substantiating the danger of such a development suggested that, of the 5400 "half breeds" in the North West, 4400 were Manitoba emigrants. Although they were found in twenty-one separate localities, almost half were settled near the forks of the Saskatchewan. There Riel could expect support from an estimated force of 600 men capable of bearing arms in the event of trouble. St Laurent was the true centre of "disloyalty" because its population was "chiefly from White Horse Plains, Baie St Paul, etc. in

Manitoba. A hard lot, were Riel's supporters in 1869."[26] Other communities were either too small or too far away from St Laurent to pose any serious difficulty. "They would take no steps unless Riel's party was fairly certain of being successful," or "not . . . mixed up, but if Indians were once on the warpath they would likely join them."[27]

On 10 July, Macdonald reported the disturbing news to the vacationing governor-general, Lord Lansdowne, saying that the situation was serious but manageable. He believed land was the key. "Some of the Half breeds have land claims which are in the process of adjustment. The claims are for the most part invalid, but they will be liberally treated."[28] Then, as the news continued to be "disquieting," Macdonald outlined a broader program of conciliation in more correspondence with the absent representative of the Queen. On 5 August, the prime minister repeated the idea that he was prepared to honour the land claims of Riel's followers, and something special might be offered to Riel himself:

> In his answer to the invitation sent him which was a temperate and unobjectionable paper, he spoke of some claims he had against the Gov't. I presume these refer to his land claims which he forfeited on conviction and banishment, [but] I think we shall deal liberally with him and make him a good subject again.
>
> If I don't mistake his character, he will make a good Moral Agent or Detective for the Gov't and keep the metis in order.[29]

Lansdowne replied the same day with a note stating that the idea of conciliating the leader was the key factor, and urged Macdonald to "make every endeavour to 'obtain touch'" with Riel and offer him a bribe; "it might be intimated to him that you were prepared to deal generously with him in so far as his private requirements seem concerned, and that you were ready to consider in a general conciliatory spirit the demands put forward by the half breeds."[30] In the arrangement envisioned by Lansdowne, the people would get their land, and Riel could receive at least an appointment to the North West Council if not to the Canadian Senate.

In Macdonald's opinion, the contemplated patronage for Riel was excessive. Macdonald protested that Louis Riel had "committed a cold-blooded murder in '69, which will never be forgotten by the whites either in Manitoba or Ontario."[31] A less extravagant offer was more appropriate but the rest of Macdonald's answer did make clear that he was still committed to conciliation in principle. Emissaries of good will would see Riel and his lieutenants as in 1869 and "encourage them to specify their grievances in Memorials and send them with or without delegations to Ottawa." Such a course would "allow time for the present effervescence to subside—and on the approach of winter—the climate will keep things quiet until next spring." Meanwhile officials in the Department of the Interior could use the respite bought by the promise of conciliation to go over the land claims and concede patents to any with "a semblance of foundation."[32]

Lansdowne approved. He appreciated that the problem of Riel and his people was "intricate," and Macdonald's proposed method of handling Riel would make him "understand that he has more to gain, personally and as a public man, by confining himself to the legitimate ventilation of the grievances of his clients, than by leading a disorderly movement."[33]

The first person recruited to have a private word with the Métis leader was C.B. Rouleau, a French-Canadian lawyer recently appointed to judicial responsibilities at nearby Battleford, Saskatchewan. A second, more prominent prospective emissary was Sir Hector Langevin, the minister of public works in the federal Cabinet and already committed to tour the West on other errands. Here as well the governor-general gave unqualified approval. On 13 August, he agreed that Rouleau could "gauge the situation pretty accurately"[34] and on 23 August Lansdowne expressed special satisfaction that Langevin was going on his errand to "set Riel's head the right way."[35]

All was arranged by the end of August for avoiding the political liability of Riel leading several hundred families into a second provisional government. Macdonald had reliable intelligence from diverse sources that such a development was possible, and he had a plausible plan for undercutting the basis of the "foolish plot"[36] and for buying Riel's loyalty. Should conciliation fail, the safety of the government was still assured by a planned expansion of police power. Macdonald told Lansdowne that he intended to increase the police force in the West by 30 percent with a flying column of 100 to be garrisoned at Fort Carlton.[37] If there was a second "Riel rebellion," it could be checked quickly by a mounted constabulary already on the scene. Still, timely conciliation was expected to prevent such a development.

The policy Macdonald described to the governor-general in July and August flowed from the obvious calculation that an "outbreak" in the North West was an avoidable political liability. The cost would be land that the Métis already occupied and money or patronage to be invested in Riel with the expectation of larger dividends in more general Native pacification. In this sense, Macdonald had to agree with Lansdowne that Riel's return was "anything but a misfortune."[38] Yet Macdonald appears to have decided near the end of August 1884 that an angry Riel could be even more useful in the broader field of Canadian politics. For some reason, the Langevin visit was mysteriously[39] cancelled; the land claims were handled more in conformity with the Dominion Lands Act than with what the "half breeds" demanded; and none of Riel's personal claims received favourable consideration. In the context of escalating discontent the Métis did become more militant; Riel did lead them into an illegal government; and the government of Canada did respond with force—with the mobilization of militia from as far away as Halifax, as well as with the police power already on the scene. What were the political advantages of the sequence of events as they actually occurred?

The political problem that made provocative inaction ultimately worthwhile was renewed difficulty with Stephen's railway. At the time that

Macdonald was first thinking about his program of Métis conciliation, Stephen had begun to hint that he might need more assistance from Canada.[40] Macdonald's reaction was so swift and completely discouraging on 18 July[41] that the railway president promised not to say another word on the subject, then violated his own promise in the same letter: "I will only say here that I cannot under the existing condition of affairs, any longer, look forward to the land grant as affording an available asset . . . and our 35 million capital is equally useless."[42]

Concurrent with Macdonald's corresponding with Lansdowne, Macdonald and Stephen exchanged eight letters[43] (which have survived) and held at least two meetings (mentioned in the correspondence). The prime minister fretted about the "many threads" of crisis he had to attend to personally and showed the railway president the papers documenting developments in the North West.[44] Stephen assured Macdonald that the railway construction was proceeding better than expected but continued to complain about a serious deficiency of capital for other needs. Macdonald could not agree to what Stephen thought essential, but he did agree to help in recruiting $5 million from private bankers in London and to accompany the railway president on his Atlantic crossing.

Unfortunately for Stephen, neither a letter of recommendation[45] from Canada's prime minister nor Macdonald's presence in London was sufficient to persuade Baring Brothers that the railway was a safe risk, and Stephen's need for the additional $5 million from Parliament matured before anything else to convince Macdonald's colleagues (or the country) that additional legislative assistance was warranted. Then, once Macdonald returned to Ottawa, Sir David Macpherson complained that Langevin had returned from the West as the perfect champion of "dead beats."[46]

Langevin's position even without seeing Riel was that the Métis leader was too dangerous to ignore. "We must take care not to make a martyr of him and thus increase his popularity." The solution was "good treatment of the half breeds." Langevin believed even a little would "go a long way to settle matters."[47] Macpherson tried to convince Langevin that every land claim had been "fully considered and equitably disposed of," but Sir David believed Sir Hector remained unconvinced. A meeting with Sir John was needed.[48] That appears to have ended the matter. At least there were no more memoranda advocating concessions such as Langevin had proposed early in November.

Macdonald's greater difficulty was calming Stephen. By mid-January the railway president was insisting that the survival of his company absolutely depended on aid from the government, but Macdonald insisted that the proposition was still "hopeless." A telegram from the prime minister on 20 January urged Stephen to "postpone matter to eighteen eight six can carry it in Council."[49] Stephen replied that postponement was "impossible" and begged for a meeting the next day to "decide finally on course am forced to take."[50] They did meet, but the only surviving record of what was apparently agreed to was a letter from Stephen in mid-April alluding to maturing obligations that "three months ago were postponed till now on the faith that by this time we should be in a position to meet them."[51] Further contextual evidence that something had been agreed to in late January was a more optimistic tone and shift in Stephen's correspondence on the subject in February and early March as he devoted most of his letters to the terms of the rescue he was clearly expecting.[52] Conversely, Macdonald seemed more depressed than ever. On 24 January he reported to his old friend Tupper that the situation was nearly as bad as the worst the two had imagined in the previous autumn. "Geo Stephen says the CPR must go down unless sustained," and he enumerated the key personnel in Cabinet who were adamantly opposed to any such additional aid. "How it will end I don't know."[53]

Nothing had happened to change "the thing"[54] in Ottawa. Yet the abandonment of straightforward conciliation had meant that Métis discontent was maturing into an exploitable crisis. Riel had spent the entire autumn and early winter writing—and rewriting—the draft of a comprehensive statement of grievances covering claims. The most preliminary statement specified: territorial self-government; land rights similar to the assurances in section 32 of the Manitoba Act; a two-million-acre trust (the income from which would provide long-term development capital for the Métis); 64 000 acres of "swamp lands" to be reserved for the children of Métis heads of families (to be distributed every eighteen years over seven generations); reconsideration of the land rights of the Manitoba Métis; and preferential consideration of "half breeds" for "works and contracts" in the territories.[55]

After consulting Bishops Taché and Grandin, Riel dropped some of the demands that the clerical consultants and his own close advisers considered "extravagant."[56] The petition that the St Laurent Métis finally mailed to the governor-general on 16 December was more limited in its focus upon land titles, home rule, and compensation for alleged maladministration of the Manitoba Act. Considering the last point, it was not surprising that the document was addressed to the governor-general with a covering letter requesting that the Queen's representative should forward the document directly to England in the hope that the British would compel Canada to act as in 1870.[57]

Given the direct parallel that the Métis drew between their present situation and the events of 1869, the alarms that kept streaming in from the North West might have led Macdonald to expect the formation of a provisional government at almost any moment in January. The police reports of the previous summer had indicated that delay would almost certainly result in some "illegal combination," and six months had passed without meeting any of the agitators' principal demands or taking steps to break up the agitation with police power. But nothing had happened. In late January Riel was still not acting according to prediction even as

Stephen's financial crisis reached new, more frightening proportions, and nothing had altered Macdonald's inability to deliver his partner the promised aid.

Here was the context and perhaps also the explanation for the peculiarly provocative content of an important Order in Council that was adopted on 28 January. Telegraphed to Dewdney, the news was that Canada would "investigate claims of Half Breeds and with that view [Cabinet] had decided [to make an] enumeration of those who did not participate in Grant under Manitoba Act."[58] The provocation was that only a small minority of the residents of St Laurent could benefit from awards to non-Manitobans. Moreover, the government already had the figures: 200 of 1300 potential claimants.[59] Dewdney was so stunned by the news he refused to pass on the information without alteration. Imagining the purpose of the Order in Council was conciliation rather than provocation, he changed the announcement before transmitting the telegram to St Laurent: "Government has decided to investigate claims of Half Breeds and with that view has already taken preliminary steps." Then Dewdney reminded Macdonald that "the bulk of the French Half Breeds" had "nothing to expect" from the unrevised text. The original news would "start a fresh agitation."[60]

No prime ministerial congratulation came back over the wire thanking Dewdney for his editorial intervention, and Dewdney's text was still far short of the news the Métis wanted. They demanded recognition of their aboriginal title, not additional consideration of the matter. Equally important, they wanted news that their claims to river lots were recognized. Here too the telegram from Dewdney was silent. Then on 6 February, the dominion lands agent at Prince Albert learned from the deputy minister of the Department of the Interior that the river-lot question was about to be disposed of. He could expect instructions "in the course of a few days."[61]

The claims reported to Winnipeg in June 1884 had passed from Winnipeg to Ottawa in October, and finally back from headquarters to Prince Albert near the end of February 1885. The news the lands agent was to report to the claimants was an enormous disappointment to the vast majority of the families hoping for confirmation of titles.[62] They felt they had done their part. All but a small non-co-operating group of forty-five had compromised their original demand for river lots laid out in the old Manitoba pattern. More than two hundred settlers had provided evidence of compliance with the boundaries of subdivisions as laid out in the government survey. Eight such claimants received notification that their periods of settlement, extent of cultivation, and value of improvements entitled them to patents. The others were processed as applications for "entry." Consequently, more than 60 percent of the settlers expecting patent were confronted with an infuriating contradiction: their claims were allowed; patents were denied. They would not become the owners of their land in the eyes of Canada until paying fees, performing more settlement duties, and going through another process of application, inspection, and consideration by the local agent, by the Winnipeg Lands Board, and by the Dominion Lands Branch in Ottawa. Even then they would have to pay for any acreage in excess of the 160-acre maximum allowable "free grant" (some claimants were told that the pre-emption part of their claim would cost $1 per acre, for others the price was $2). Finally, the question of trespass on the lands of the Prince Albert Colonization Company was unresolved; thirty families were excluded from "entry" as well as from patents.[63]

Canada's handling of the river-lot question was far from conciliatory, but the government could defend itself by saying that the claimants received all the consideration they were entitled to expect under the Dominion Lands Act. Indeed, in one respect—waiving the distinction between odd- and even-numbered sections (except in the vicinity of the Prince Albert Colonization Company)—the government could say that the Métis claimants were treated more liberally than the law required.

One last provocation was similarly defensible from the standpoint of rigid adherence to principle. On 20 February the prime minister informed Lieutenant Governor Dewdney that the answer to Riel's private claims was a definite no. With uncharacteristic moral outrage Macdonald declared: "We have no money to give Riel. He has a right to remain in Canada and if he conspires we must punish him. That's all."[64]

The last two provocations together—the personal disappointment of Riel and the general frustration of the land claimants—finally broke Métis patience the day after Lands Agent Duck sent out the last disturbing notification on 7 March. On 8 March, Riel announced that he thought that the time had come to form a provisional government.

Three days later, Lieutenant Governor Dewdney telegraphed the latest development to the prime minister, saying there was a possibility that the declaration was no more than a "bluff" but "if the Half breeds mean business, the sooner they are put down the better." Dewdney advised taking them by surprise. "They are like Indians. When they gather and get excited it is difficult to handle them, but if they are taken unawares there is little difficulty in arresting the leader."[65]

On the same day, 11 March, Stephen demanded bold action for the railway, complaining that his finances were "getting beyond all control." Stephen expressed sympathy for Macdonald's political problems, but the CPR president insisted that the time had come for the prime minister to do whatever was necessary to alter the current political impasse. "I know and appreciate fully the reason for delaying consideration of our matters till the proper and most favourable time arrives but I am really concerned about ways and means to carry us along in the meantime. . . . I hope you will think of this and bring things to a head as soon as possible."[66]

True to his favourite maxim, "He who waits wins,"[67] Macdonald did nothing, but not with any evident comfort. On 17 March, he informed Tupper that "Stephen asks a loan for a year of 5 millions (that Tilley [the minister of finance] can't face)" and complained that everyone was reaching the limits of endurance. "How it will end God knows—but I wish I were well out of it."[68] No doubt Stephen and Dewdney were equally perplexed. Unable to get a satisfactory answer to his letters and telegrams, Dewdney pursued his own initiative.

On 12 March, the lieutenant governor convened a meeting to consider the Riel crisis with four other people in Regina: Hayter Reed (the Indian commissioner), A.G. Irvine (the police commissioner), Hugh Richardson (the stipendiary magistrate of the district), and Lawrence Clarke (still chief factor at Fort Carlton). The primary concern was Riel's proclamation of intent: whether it was genuine or "a mere matter of bluff . . . to frighten the government into making concessions." Clarke suggested that since the total force at Riel's command was probably no more than 350 poorly armed men "with their wives and children, who must be exposed to extreme peril should they be so foolish as to resort to arms," and since the government force "already on the spot" numbered 120 well-armed police backed by artillery, the Hudson's Bay Company officer thought that the "only danger to be apprehended . . . would be in the event of Riel attempting to tamper with the loyalty of the Indians." In that event, it was agreed that they should arrest the Métis leader "no matter at what risk." And even without Riel's moving towards alliances with the Indians, it was considered that "Mr. Riel and his band of discontents should not be allowed to keep up senseless agitation, destroying all faith in the country and ruining its peaceable inhabitants." Sooner or later they would have to "settle this matter once for all." In Clarke's opinion the question was "whether this was not the time." Under the circumstances of the moment, it was agreed that Clarke should return to Fort Carlton at once, and Irvine would "start for the 'seat of war'" several days later, about the time Clarke reached Fort Carlton from Regina.[69]

Arriving at his destination on the evening of 17 March,[70] Clarke reported that Riel's movement had "apparently flattened out" but there was no doubt as to his "tampering with Indians." Clarke did not think Riel would win many over, but advised the immediate arrest of Riel to prevent any further mischief. "No better time to deal with leader and followers."[71] Dewdney responded that he had still "heard nothing from Ottawa" and reported that Irvine was departing for Fort Carlton the next day with one hundred reinforcements.[72] Then, as rather an afterthought, Dewdney sent Clarke a second telegram on 17 March advising him to make the government's intentions public. "Put in PA Times that an additional force is being sent. . . . Get paper to enlarge and state scattered that government intend to have peace in the district."[73]

Clarke passed the instruction on to his new superior officer in Winnipeg, Joseph Wrigley, who responded by telegram that he opposed the newspaper advertisement, at least as a Hudson's Bay Company announcement. Perhaps Wrigley feared that such information would be interpreted as a provocative gesture and lead to criticism of the company later. "Better for you not to act publicly but leave responsibility on Government."[74] As a result, the action that pushed Riel to take the next step was not a printed word, but verbal communication that Clarke subsequently denied he had ever spoken.

The story Lawrence Clarke later denounced as a "tissue of lies"[75] was that he had encountered a group of Métis near Fort Carlton some time before 19 March and had given them information resembling the news that Dewdney instructed him to spread through the district on 17 March. According to popular legend, the Métis asked Clarke if there was any answer yet to their petitions and protest. "His reply was that the only answer they would get would be bullets, and that, indeed, on his way northward, he had passed a camp of 500 policemen who were coming up to capture the Half breed agitators."[76] It is possible that Clarke said only that more police were on the way with the intention of arresting Riel. The rest may have been nothing more than the result of exaggeration in retelling the news at Batoche.

What is certain is that the Métis reacted to Clarke's news as the final provocation. The provisional government emerged on 19 March (with 88 percent support from the inhabitants of the colony of St Laurent).[77] Despite the risk of police intervention, Riel did not foresee any great danger because the newspapers were full of reports of the possibility of war between England and Russia. With British (and Canadian) forces occupied in a foreign war, surely Canada would dispose of a small domestic crisis peacefully as in 1870. Riel miscalculated. The mobilization for conflict overseas did not occur. Instead, Canada mobilized militia from Halifax to Winnipeg to deal with the Métis, even though Dewdney's dispatches indicated that he thought the police were competent to deal with the situation unfolding in late March.

Macdonald did not anticipate a war against the Métis. At the time of the mobilization (23 March), he cautioned the minister of militia, J.P.R.A. Caron, to "remind General Middleton that the [NWMP] Commissioner and Officers are magistrates and well acquainted with the character of the Half-breeds and Indians and must understand the best mode of dealing with them and inducing them to lay down their arms and submit to legal authority."[78] A massive show of force would compel surrender without a fight. Although Dewdney preferred resolving the problem with local resources ("I would have rather seen the trouble stopped entirely by the police"), the governor had to concede that the Métis were even less likely to resist if thousands of troops suddenly appeared on the scene, especially if the government met Riel's price and whisked him out of the country before the troops arrived. "How far can I go?" Dewdney asked on 23 March.[79]

What Macdonald seems to have envisioned was a sudden dash to the Prairies, a mysterious "escape" of Riel back to the United States, conciliatory gestures to the surrendering Métis, and aid for the railway after it played such a key role in breaking up the "outbreak" so "speedily and gallantly."[80]

On 26 March, however, the situation became unexpectedly complicated by bloodshed. Since the Métis believed five hundred police were en route to arrest Riel, they prepared to fend off the NWMP in a long siege by sending a force to seize supplies from a store at Duck Lake. Simultaneously, a party of police went to the same place to spoil the attempt. When the two groups came face to face, both sides sent out spokesmen to talk under a flag of truce, but the meeting soon deteriorated into single-champion combat with two men dead, then into general shooting with twelve fallen on the Canadian side and five Métis killed.[81]

The confrontation between police and "half breeds" was followed by sporadic Indian action and raised the spectre of war such as the Americans had fought in the 1860s and 1870s. After 26 March, greater prospects of danger and longer delays filled Macdonald with increased dread. "This insurrection is a bad business," Macdonald wrote Dewdney on 29 March, "but we must face it as best we may."[82]

Since the Americans were almost as worried as some Canadians that the "outbreak" would become a general Indian war, they offered full co-operation in the movement of troops and supplies and their own cavalry for patrolling the border.[83] Macdonald accepted the transport offer for shipping equipment, but he insisted on the CPR as the vehicle for transporting the unfortunate Canadian volunteers, the first contingent of whom left Toronto on 30 March in two separate trains. When the men reached the north shore of Lake Superior in the first week of April, they discovered that there were four gaps in the line that had to be crossed by sleigh or on foot. The worst part, however, was one section of isolated railway where the men had to ride on flat cars in the open, bitter cold.[84] Still, in less than two weeks, more than 3000 troops did reach the Territories ready to be deployed against the "half breeds" and their few Indian allies.

In the fighting that occurred here and there in late April and early May there were several encounters that could be called battles.[85] For more than fifty Canadians and a similar number of "half breeds" and Indians, death was as final as in any global conflict. And yet Macdonald did not exaggerate later when he dismissed most of the military side of the "North West Rebellion" as a "mere riot."

From Macdonald's point of view, the more important aspects of the affair were showing the flag of British authority and proving that the railway had transformed Canada into a country capable of suppressing challenges to its sovereignty in the most remote sections of habitable territory. To be sure, the opposition made searing accusations of mismanagement, but Macdonald met their charges that the war could have been avoided with countercharges that his own "half breed" policy had been far more liberal than his opponents'.[86] Indeed, on Native affairs in general he claimed to be the epitome of enlightened and progressive action, and he moved to substantiate his claim in April with a diversionary franchise bill that included proposals for nearly universal suffrage for white men and extension of the vote to certain single women and the Six Nations of Loyalist Indians in Ontario.[87]

The Liberals were triply embarrassed. Having denounced Macdonald's handling of North West matters, they seemed sympathetic to Natives; then, having posed as friends of the Indians and the Métis, they were embarrassed by their own vehement opposition to the inclusion of certain loyal Native people in the national franchise because David Mills said they were "savages." Thus, they were set up to be embarrassed the third time when they fought the aid for the railway that had saved the nation from a prolonged war with Canada's Native peoples.

The CPR did receive its aid package in July. In the same month, Louis Riel stood trial at Regina where he was held accountable for treason and sentenced to hang. Riel dropped to the end of the hangman's rope in Regina on 16 November. The railway reached its official completion almost at the same time in a last-spike ceremony on 7 November. Still jubilant over the success of his railway, Stephen wrote Macdonald just before Riel's execution to inform the prime minister of his pleasure with the rising value of CPR stock over the preceding week and to tell Sir John how "glad" he was that the "mischievous crank Riel is going to have justice meted out to him."[88] No other correspondent with Macdonald was as quick to link the two events so directly, but few people other than Stephen knew how closely the Métis loss had been joined to the railway's gain.

• Notes

1 See P.R. Mailhot and D.N. Sprague, "Persistent Settlers: The Dispersal and Resettlement of the Red River Métis, 1870–1885," *Canadian Journal of Ethnic Studies* 17 (1985): 1–30.

2 There were no "Class 16" claims (land disputes) in the detailed report upon St Laurent submitted by the Lands Board to headquarters in the autumn of 1884. See University of Alberta Archives, William Pearce papers, MG 9/2/4-4, vol. 4, 224–75.

3 For the system of sectional survey adopted by Canada see Chester Martin, *Dominion Lands Policy* (Toronto: Macmillan, 1938).

4 Thomas Flanagan, *Riel and the Rebellion: 1885 Reconsidered* (Saskatoon:

Western Producer Prairie Books, 1983), 30–33, 37–40.

5 Public Archives of Canada (hereafter PAC), RG 15, vol. 277, file 4447, 19; and House of Commons *Debates*, speech by Edward Blake, 6 July 1885, 3100.

6 The report of William Pearce, "All Claims to Land . . . on the South Saskatchewan" (University of Alberta Archives, Pearce papers, MG 9/2, series 5, vol. 1, file 6, series 4, vol. 4, 888–901) states that some of the land was open for entry as early as 1881. But in response to a question on the subject in the House of Commons on 8 June 1885, Macdonald admitted that much of the district was not open

for homestead entry until 15 February 1884 (House of Commons *Debates*, 8 June 1885, 2358).

7 PAC, Records of the Department of the Interior, RG 15, vol. 336, file 84478, George Duck to Commissioner of Dominion Lands, 15 June 1884.

8 Flanagan, *Riel and the Rebellion*, 33.

9 Pearce, "All Claims to Land," 6–8.

10 PAC, Macdonald papers, Incoming Correspondence, 42053–56, 42067–70.

11 Ibid., 42048–50, Mills to Laird, 18 March 1878. Later, Macdonald told the House of Commons that Mills had given the appropriate response. See House of Commons *Debates*, 6 July 1885, 3112.

12 PAC, Macdonald papers, Incoming Correspondence, 42067–70, Minutes of the Council of the North West Territories, 2 Aug. 1878.

13 Ibid., 138984–87, "Confidential Memorandum: Remarks on the Condition of the Half Breeds of the North West Territories, 20 December 1878."

14 See Macdonald's sketch of the history of Manitoba land claims reported to the governor-general in August 1884 (ibid., Transcripts, vol. 585, Macdonald to Lansdowne, 5 Aug. 1884).

15 Ibid., Incoming Correspondence, 42072–83, Bishop Grandin to Dennis, 18 Jan. 1879.

16 Ibid., 42084–91, Bishop Machray to Dennis, 15 Feb. 1879.

17 Statutes of Canada (1879), ch. 31: "An Act to amend and consolidate the several Acts respecting the Public lands of the Dominion," s. 125(e).

18 Pearce, "All Claims to Land," 6.

19 PAC, Macdonald papers, Incoming Correspondence, 42244–50, Clarke to Grahame, 20 May 1884.

20 Ibid., 42242–43, Grahame to Macdonald, 29 May 1884.

21 Ibid., 42767–78, Dewdney to Macdonald, 14 June 1884.

22 Ibid., 42251–53, White to Irvine, 10 June 1884.

23 Ibid., 42254–55, White to Crozier, 10 June 1884.

24 See, for example, the letter from André to Dewdney, 7 June 1884, that the governor forwarded to Macdonald (ibid., 42277–80).

25 Ibid., 134906–16, White to Macdonald, 7 July 1884.

26 Other sources tend to corroborate the police report. See "Supplement 2: The Settlers of the Colony of St Laurent" in Mailhot and Sprague, "Persistent Settlers," 18–26.

27 PAC, Macdonald papers, Incoming Correspondence, 148567, "Estimated Number of Half Breeds."

28 Ibid., Transcripts, vol. 585, Macdonald to Lansdowne, 10 July 1884.

29 Ibid., Macdonald to Lansdowne, 5 Aug. 1884.

30 Ibid., Incoming Correspondence, 32872–79, Lansdowne to Macdonald, 5 Aug. 1884.

31 Ibid., Transcripts, vol. 585, Macdonald to Lansdowne, 12 Aug. 1884.

32 Ibid.

33 Ibid., Incoming Correspondence, 32884–87, Lansdowne to Macdonald, 13 Aug. 1884.

34 Ibid.

35 Ibid., 32893–95, Lansdowne to Macdonald, 23 Aug. 1884.

36 Ibid., Letter Books, vol. 23, 33–34, Macdonald to J.C. Aikins, 28 July 1884.

37 Ibid., Transcripts, vol. 585, Macdonald to Lansdowne, 12 Aug. 1884; and Letter Book, vol. 23, 56–57, Macdonald to Donald A. Smith, 5 Sept. 1884.

38 Ibid., Incoming Correspondence, 32872–79, Lansdowne to Macdonald, 5 Aug. 1884.

39 Why Langevin failed to fulfil the mission is a problem of considerable complexity. The conventional explanation (see George F.G. Stanley, *Louis Riel* (Toronto, 1963), 285; and Bob Beal and Rod Macleod, *Prairie Fire: The 1885 North-West Rebellion* (Edmonton, 1984), 117–18) is that Langevin's change of

itinerary represented his own independent alternation of plans. Having arrived at Regina in the last week of August, he is supposed to have been so fatigued by the earlier part of his journey that he could not face travelling 200 miles over muddy cart trails to St Laurent just to suffer the harangues of political malcontents. Thus he cancelled the trip despite the consequences. Langevin proved later that he was indeed capable of foolish initiatives. But the cancellation of the Riel mission was more than foolhardy. Once Riel had been informed that Langevin was visiting in 1884—in the role Smith had played in 1869–70—and once it became known that Riel regarded the meeting as "marked proof of good will towards the North West" (Riel quoted in Beal and Macleod, *Prairie Fire*, 118), cancellation without justification or notification of regret was equivalent to provocation.

The difficulty with assigning sole responsibility to Langevin is evidence of earlier communication with Macdonald. The day of Langevin's departure from his home, 18 August, Sir Hector sent a brief note to the prime minister inviting last-minute instructions (PAC, Macdonald papers, Incoming Correspondence, 97438–43). There is no record of Macdonald's response, but on 19 August a telegram went from Langevin to Judge Rouleau at Battleford informing him that Sir Hector would not be making the digression to Batoche (Stanley, *Riel*, 285). Subsequently, Rouleau either forgot or was instructed not to report the news to Riel, with the result that the Métis continued an unsatisfying vigil, constantly watching the roadways to Batoche for some face resembling Langevin's.

If the change was Langevin's mistake, Macdonald had an opportunity to correct it on 29 August when his good-will ambassador sent him a message before leaving Manitoba for Regina (PAC, Macdonald papers, Incoming Correspondence, 97441–

42). Langevin reported that the train had taken him as far as Brandon. After a brief visit with Dewdney he expected to continue on to the end of the railway: "In a week I will have reached the end of the road and be on the return." Obviously, that itinerary precluded the errand to Batoche. If Macdonald's previous plans were still in effect, it was important to intercept Langevin before his return. No record of attempted interception has been found. Nor did Macdonald complain later about a unilateral upset of his conciliation scheme.

40 PAC, Macdonald papers, Incoming Correspondence, 122328–31. Stephen to Macdonald, 17 July 1884.

41 Ibid., Transcripts, vol. 585, Macdonald to Stephen, 18 July 1884.

42 Ibid., Incoming Correspondence, 122340–47, Stephen to Macdonald, 22 July 1884.

43 Macdonald's letters to Stephen were dated 24 and 30 July 1884 (both in ibid., Transcripts, vol. 585). Stephen's to Macdonald were 27 July, 2 Aug. (two letters), and 13, 16, and 19 Aug. (all in ibid., Incoming Correspondence, 122353–419).

44 Ibid., Transcripts, vol. 585, Macdonald to Stephen, 30 July 1884.

45 Ibid., Letter Book, vol. 23, 59–60, Macdonald to Baring Brothers, 6 Sept. 1884.

46 Ibid., Incoming Correspondence, 112802–05, Macpherson to Macdonald, 31 Dec. 1884.

47 Ibid., 97452–56, Langevin to Macdonald, 6 Nov. 1884.

48 Ibid., 112802–05, Macpherson to Macdonald, 31 Dec. 1884.

49 Ibid., Letter Book, vol. 23, 101, Macdonald cypher telegram to Stephen, 20 Jan. 1885.

50 Ibid., Incoming Correspondence, 122608, Stephen cypher telegram to Macdonald, 20 Jan. 1885.

51 Ibid., 122818–21, Stephen to Macdonald, 15 April 1885.

52 See Stephen's letters of 3, 8, 9, 12, 13, 19 Feb. and 2 March in ibid., Incoming Correspondence, 122643–704.

53 Ibid., Transcripts, vol. 585, Macdonald to Tupper, 24 Jan. 1885.

54 Ibid.

55 Ibid., Incoming Correspondence, 42935–37, Riel to Bishop Grandin, 7 Sept. 1884.

56 See Public Archives of Manitoba, Riel papers, item 414, Taché to Riel, 4 Oct. 1884.

57 Lansdowne did not forward the petition as requested. See Lansdowne to Derby, the Colonial Secretary, 21 April 1885 (PAC, Records of the governor-general, RG 7, G 10, vol. 8).

58 PAC, Macdonald papers, Incoming Correspondence, 42977–83, quoted by Dewdney to Macdonald in reply, 4 Feb. 1885.

59 Ibid., 148567, "Estimated Number of Half Breeds." Although the document is undated, contextual evidence makes clear that the numbers were determined in the summer of 1884. See also the governor-general's recital of the same figures in PAC, RG 7, G 10 (Drafts to Colonial Secretary, Secret and Confidential), vol. 8, Lansdowne to Derby, 21 April 1885.

60 Ibid., 42977–83, Dewdney to Macdonald, 4 Feb. 1885.

61 PAC, RG 15, vol. 336, file 84478, A.M. Burgess to Duck, 6 Feb. 1885.

62 See University of Alberta, William Pearce papers, MG 9/2/4-4, vol. 4, 224–75, 961–62 in relation to Pearce's published report of "All Claims to Land."

63 Their claims were taken up in the autumn of 1885 and accorded the same entry privilege as the others. See University of Alberta Archives, William Pearce papers, MG 9/2/4-4, vol. 4, 961–62.

64 PAC, Glenbow Dewdney papers, 545, Macdonald to Dewdney, 20 Feb. 1885.

65 PAC, Macdonald papers, Incoming Correspondence, 43010–13, Dewdney to Macdonald, 11 March 1885.

66 Ibid., 122735–42, Stephen to Macdonald, 11 March 1885.

67 See, for example, Macdonald to T. Robertson, in ibid., Letter Book, vol. 23, 85–86.

68 Ibid., Transcripts, vol. 585, Macdonald to Tupper, 17 March 1885.

69 Hudson's Bay Company Archives (hereafter HBCA), D.20/33, fo. 67-74, Lawrence Clarke to Joseph Wrigley, 14 March 1885.

70 HBCA, B332/b/1, vol. 1, fo. 96-121, Clarke to Wrigley, 6 July 1885.

71 Ibid., fo. 87, Clarke cypher telegram to Dewdney, 17 March 1885.

72 Ibid., fo. 82, Dewdney cypher telegram to Clarke, 17 March 1885.

73 Ibid., fo. 81, Dewdney cypher telegram to Clarke, 17 March 1885.

74 Ibid., fo. 44, Wrigley cypher telegram to Clarke, 17 March 1885.

75 Ibid., fo. 96-121, Clarke to Wrigley, 6 July 1885.

76 N.F. Black, *History of Saskatchewan and the Old North West* (Regina, 1913), 267. The same story appeared in a contemporary account of Clarke's role by James Isbister. See clipping from Winnipeg *Sun*, 19 June 1885, in PAC, Macdonald papers, Incoming Correspondence, 43861.

77 The opponents of Riel are named in Pearce's manuscript copy of "All Claims to Land" (University of Alberta Archives, Pearce papers, MG 9/2, series 4, vol. 4, 888–901).

78 PAC, Macdonald papers, Transcripts, vol. 585, Macdonald to Caron, 23 March 1885.

79 Ibid., Incoming Correspondence, 43020–23, Dewdney to Macdonald, 23 March 1885.

80 "Speedy" and "gallant" were Macdonald's adjectives in Parliament. See House of Commons *Debates*, 6 July 1885, 3117.

81 A detailed, sensational account of the conflict appears in Beal and Macleod, *Prairie Fire*, 151–59.

82 PAC, Macdonald papers, Letter Books, vol. 23, 140, Macdonald to Dewdney, 29 March 1885.

83 See Blake's questions on the matter, House of Commons *Debates*, 31 March 1885, 838; and 1 April 1885, 872.

84 Desmond Morton, *The Last War Drum* (Toronto, 1972), 40–44.

85 On the final siege, in particular, see Walter Hildebrandt, *The Battle of Batoche: British Small Warfare and the Entrenched Métis* (Ottawa, 1985).

86 See Blake's seven-hour speech and Macdonald's shorter reply in the House of Commons *Debates*, 6 July 1885, 3075–117.

87 See Malcolm Montgomery, "The Six Nations and the Macdonald Franchise," *Ontario History* 57 (1967): 13–25.

88 PAC, Macdonald papers, Incoming Correspondence, 123001–08, Stephen to Macdonald, 14 Nov. 1885.

AFTER THE FUR TRADE:
The Aboriginal Labouring Class of British Columbia, 1849–1890*

JOHN LUTZ

Aboriginal history is usually considered in isolation from mainstream Canadian history as though it were about aboriginal people and nobody else. But the major issues of Native studies—such as the appropriation of aboriginal land and resources, the denial of citizenship rights to a large segment of the Canadian population, the conditions under which aboriginal people would agree to trap, hunt or do wagework for a capitalist economy—are major issues of national development and central to Canadian history.

This paper takes up questions about aboriginal wage labour and applies them to a forty-year period on the west coast of North America from the creation of the Colony of Vancouver Island in 1849, through the gold rushes, the founding of the giant export sawmills, Confederation, the development and spread of the salmon canning industry, to just past the completion of the Canadian Pacific Railway in 1885, an event which tied the province of British Columbia to the North American continental economy. Throughout this period aboriginal people in British Columbia made up the majority of the population. Despite introduced diseases which

*Journal of the Canadian Historical Association (1992): 69–93. Reprinted with the permission of the Canadian Historical Association.

reduced the aboriginal population by approximately two-thirds, when British Columbia entered Confederation in 1871 it was in many important respects an "aboriginal province"—there were three times as many aboriginal people as all the non-aboriginals taken together.[1]

Although one might suppose historians would have turned their attention to the majority before beginning to examine minority groups, in British Columbia historiography the reverse has happened: only a few historians, notably Robin Fisher and Rolf Knight, have given their attention to the majority population in this era.[2] Most general accounts follow Fisher's pioneering work on aboriginal–non-aboriginal relations, which argued that aboriginal peoples retained control of their lives during the fur trade, and had considerable influence over the trade itself. Fisher states that, with the gold rush, the colonies which make up modern British Columbia changed from "colonies of exploitation, which made use of indigenous manpower, to colonies of settlement, where the Indians became at best, irrelevant."[3] By contrast, this paper argues that aboriginal people were not made irrelevant by the coming of settlement. In fact, they were the main labour force of the early settlement era, essential to the capitalist development of British Columbia. With other recent scholarship, this paper takes a step towards rediscovering the largest component of British Columbia's early labouring class, and highlighting one element—paid work—of the lives of the majority aboriginal population.[4]

Even in the 1860s opinion among white notables was divided about the usefulness and importance of aboriginal people to the British Columbia economy. While Charles Forbes's 1862 guide to Vancouver Island argued resolutely that "their labour cannot be depended on, and with one or two slight exceptions at present forms no point of consideration in the labour market," and A.A. Harvey described aboriginal people as "valueless in the labour market,"[5] in his 1871 report on British Columbia the federal minister of public works observed that "the Indians have been, and still are, and will long continue an important population for [British] Columbia, in the capacity of guides, porters and labourers."[6]

Who was right? Were aboriginal people "valueless in the labour market" or "an important population of . . . labourers"? How important was their labour to British Columbia's nineteenth-century economy? How important was wage and contract labour to the aboriginal economy? What motivated aboriginal people to join the early paid labour force?[7] Who, and how many, were recruited? Based on a varied sample of aboriginal voices captured in biographies, ethnographies, and letters to government and church officials, as well as the correspondence of colonial officials, fur traders, missionaries, and travellers together with the records of the Department of Indian Affairs, this paper not only attempts to answer these questions, but in doing so provides a fresh perspective from which to view the early years of capitalist development in British Columbia.

• Labourers of the Aboriginal Province

Of the 34 600 or so inhabitants of the colony of Vancouver Island and its adjacent islands and shores in 1855, all but 774 were aboriginal. Outside the colony there were probably an additional 25 000–30 000 aboriginal people living in the remainder of what became British Columbia. This vast population was extremely heterogeneous, both culturally and historically. It comprised ten distinct nations or ethnic groups, speaking twenty-six distinct, and largely mutually unintelligible, languages. Each nation had its own customary laws that defined property rights and social and gender relations, and by 1849 each village had its own history of relationships with non-aboriginal people or their trade goods.[8]

Victoria, the west coast headquarters for the Hudson's Bay Company (HBC) became the capital when the colony was established in 1849. As the largest community of non-aboriginal people north of Oregon, it became "the great emporium" for aboriginal people from all over the Pacific Northwest, from Russian America (Alaska) down. The mass migrations to Victoria began in the summer of 1853, when Governor Douglas reported a gathering of 3000 "Indians" at a potlatch hosted by the local Songhees people living across the harbour.[9] The next year aboriginal people from "all parts of the mainland coast south of Cape Spencer, in north latitude 59 degrees" dropped in on Victoria itself. Annually, from 1853 through the 1880s, 2000–4000 aboriginal people canoed their way to Victoria to trade or spend part of the year, travelling as far as 800 miles to do so.

Table 1: **ABORIGINAL AND NON-ABORIGINAL POPULATION ESTIMATES FOR BRITISH COLUMBIA, 1835–1901**

Year	Aboriginal Population	Non-aboriginal Population
1835	70 000	–
1851	65 000	–
1856	62 000	1 000
1861	60 000	13 624
1871	37 000	13 247
1881	29 000	23 798
1885	28 000	–
1891	26 000	72 173
1901	25 488	153 169

Source: Aboriginal population from Duff, *Indian History of British Columbia*, and for 1901, from the *Census of Canada*. The non-aboriginal population is taken from Douglas's census of Vancouver Island in 1854, which gave 774 whites on the island, plus an estimate for the mainland. The 1861 population estimate is from Phillips, "Confederation and the Economy of British Columbia," 59. Other estimates are from the *Census of Canada* for 1871, 1881, and 1891. Since racial information was not tabulated in 1891, the non-aboriginal population given here is the total population less Duff's estimate for the aboriginal population. See also CO 305/7, 11582, Douglas to Labouchere, 20 Oct. 1856 and CO 305/6, 10048, Douglas to Russell, 21 Aug. 1855.

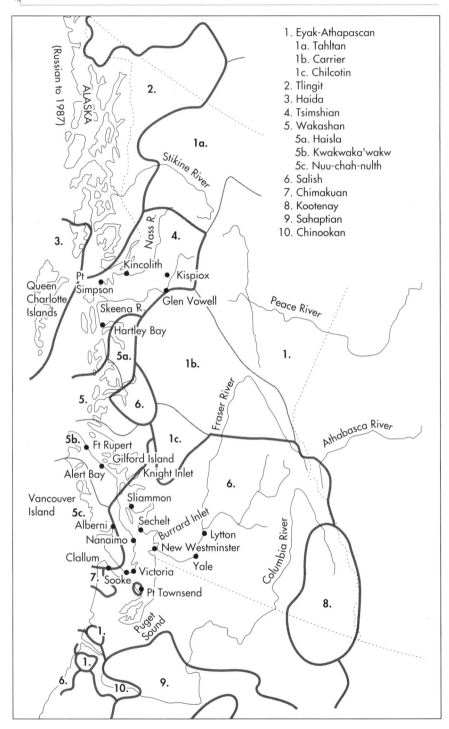

FIGURE 1: *Aboriginal Territories in the Pacific Northwest, 1849–85*

Why did thousands of aboriginal people, between 5 and 10 percent of the whole aboriginal population north of Puget Sound, paddle so far to visit a community that in 1855 numbered only 232?[10] Trading was undoubtedly a major attraction—the variety in Victoria was greater, alcohol was more easily available, and the prices of goods were perhaps better than at closer trading posts; and in the beginning at least curiosity to see this alien community was, no doubt, another factor.

There was nevertheless a third and key reason why aboriginal people returned year after year. As Governor Douglas explained in his dispatches to the Colonial Office, he was not unduly alarmed about being outnumbered ten-to-one during these seasonal visits by "ignorant and barbarous people. . . . For the object of the Indians in visiting this place is not to make War upon the White man, but to benefit by his presence, by selling their Furs and other commodities."[11]

One of the commodities aboriginal people sold was labour, a practice well established as early as 1853, when Douglas had reported that "a great part of the agricultural labour of the colony, is at present performed by means of the Natives, who though less skilled and industrious than the white men, work at a comparatively much cheaper rate, so that on the whole, they are exceedingly useful to the colonists."[12] Indeed, nearly all early accounts mention the hiring of aboriginal labour. The first bona fide colonist, W.C. Grant, hired aboriginal people on his farm and reported in 1853 that "with the proper superintendence [they] are capable of being made very useful. They all live by fishing but take kindly to any kind of rough agricultural employment, though their labour is not to be depended on for any continuous period." Similarly, colonist J.S. Helmcken used Indians "chiefly from the north" to clear land for his home, while the colony itself paid "scores of Indians" in HBC blankets to clear the land around the surveyor's office and to build roads. The Puget Sound Agricultural Company also hired aboriginal labour on their farms, and by 1857 missionary William Duncan observed that around Victoria "most of the Farm Servants employed here . . . are Chimsyan (Tsimshian) Indians— and they all give them a good character."[13]

The issue of wage labour was raised formally when, at the start of his 1856 seasonal visit, Douglas called the chiefs together and "spoke to them seriously on the subject of their relations with the whites, and their duties to the public, and after exacting a pledge for the good behaviour of their respective Tribes, *I gave them permission to hire themselves out as labourers to the white settlers, and for the public works in progress.*" He reported at the end of August that "the greater number of those people have lately departed *with their earnings* to their distant homes, and will not return to Vancouver's Island, before the spring of 1856; those who still remain about the settlements will spend the winter here."[14]

Although the economies of the aboriginal peoples varied from the coast to the interior and even within these divisions, generally they were based on a seasonal migration cycle from permanent winter villages to harvesting sites for fishing in the fall, hunting and trapping in winter, and harvesting roots and berries in the summer. From 1853 onwards, however, a spring and summer visit to Victoria became a part of the seasonal cycle, and those who could not find work in Victoria often continued south into the American territory of Puget Sound. John Fornsby, a Coast Salish living in Puget Sound, first saw these "Northern Indians" when forty to fifty of them came to work at a Puget Sound sawmill around 1858, while James Swan wrote from Port Townsend that the Northern Indians "yearly come to Victoria and whenever they get a chance, come over here to work—the men at our mills or among the farmers, where they prove themselves faithful and efficient; and the women, by their cleanly habits, their bright dresses and hoop skirts . . . winning the hearts or purses of the bachelors."[15] Others, who did not join the migration, found work closer to their own villages in the expanding activities of the Hudson's Bay Company posts, cutting shingles, spars, picking cranberries, harvesting ice, as well as gardening, fishing, preserving food, and doing general construction.[16]

While the summer migrants from the north worked on the farms and public works, some of the local Songhees people became established in year-round employment in the homes of the better-off colonists as servants and cooks. Reverend Staines wrote in 1852 that his Indian servant procured meat each day by trading with other Indians, and that he was teaching his Indian cook how to prepare beef, mutton, and venison. Other aboriginal people supplied venison, partridges, salmon, potatoes, and berries to the colonists, as well as shingles, lathes, mats, and baskets. [17]

With the 1858 gold rush and the consequent growth of Victoria came even more opportunities for work, and by 1860 whole villages might be deserted for the capital. Making for the Queen Charlotte Islands in the *Alert,* James Cooper met the entire population of Masset heading for Victoria. At Skidegate, meanwhile, Chief "Estercana" asked the officials to "tell Mr Doouglas and the man-of-war to send my people home; I wanted to build a house this summer [but] nearly all my people are away at Victoria."[18] That summer, the governor reported over 4000 visiting Indians at Victoria, double the number of non-aboriginal inhabitants in the town.[19] Despite the large gold-induced increase in the non-aboriginal population, Douglas was still not concerned about its relations with the majority. "When not under the influence of intoxication," he told the Colonial Office in 1860, "[the aboriginal people] are quiet and well conducted, make good servants and by them is executed a large proportion of the menial, agricultural, and shipping labour of the Colony. Besides their value as labourers they are of value commercially as consumers of food and clothing...."[20] He was not alone in his view. The San Francisco *Times,* for example, described the Indians around gold-rush Victoria as "industrious," which "alone establishes their superiority to the California aborigines."[21] Moreover, it was not just Victoria that felt their presence, as aboriginal people were also relocating seasonally, or even for several years, to the gold-mining communities of Fort Hope, Lytton, Yale, and New Westminster, the capital of the new colony of British Columbia.[22]

Despite claims by historians, aboriginal people were not made redundant by the influx of non-aboriginals to the gold fields, just less visible in the increasingly polyglot society of the colonies. Nor had they been bystanders as gold and coal became focal points of the economy of the Pacific Northwest between the 1840s and 1880s: in both cases, aboriginal people were the discoverers and the first miners, and they continued to work the mines throughout the century.

Coal was first discovered by aboriginal people on northern Vancouver Island. In 1846 the Royal Navy vessel *Cormorant* stopped there and "with the assistance of the Indians they collected about 60 tons."[23] The Kwakwaka'wakw (Kwakiutl) at this site told the HBC that "they would not permit us to work the coal as they were valuable to them, but that they would labor in the mines themselves and sell to us the produce of their exertions."[24] Between 1849, when the HBC established Fort Rupert at the coal mines, and 1851 when the seam was exhausted, the Kwakwaka'wakw people mined 3650 tons of coal for which they were paid the handsome price of "one blanket 2 $1/_2$ pt.s or equivalent in Grey Cotton for every two tons delivered at the Fort."[25]

Starting in 1852, the Fort Rupert experience was repeated in Nanaimo after trader Joe McKay, and then Governor Douglas, were led to various seams of coal by the local people. Douglas sent the HBC's *Cadboro* to the spot "and succeeded in procuring, with the assistance of Indians, about 50 tons of coal in one day." "The natives," he reported, "who are now indefatigable in their researches for Coal, lately discovered a magnificent seam over six feet in depth. . . . Such places are left entirely to the Indians, who work, with a surprising degree of industry, and dispose of the coal to the Agents of the Hudson's Bay Company for clothing and other articles of European manufacture."[26]

With the removal of the surface coal and the need to dig shafts and use pumps, the Hudson's Bay Company brought skilled miners from Great Britain. However, as Douglas noted in 1857, aboriginal people remained crucial to the underground operations: "The want of Indian labor is certainly a great inconvenience for the miners but really they must learn to be independent of Indians for our work will otherwise be subject to continual stoppage."[27] In the 1850s the coal mines regularly stopped production when the local people went to their seasonal fisheries, potlatched, or were attacked by illness. Although partly displaced by Chinese labour in the various coal mines that subsequently sunk shafts around Nanaimo, in 1877 it was noted that "the Nanaimo Indians . . . have hitherto been chiefly employed about the coal mines as labourers." In 1882 the Indian Agent overseeing Nanaimo noted that the aboriginal people there "find constant employment at the coal mines and wharves" and in 1888 "many Indians are again working at the coal mines at Nanaimo, taking the place of the

Chinese; the fear of accident by explosions deterred them for some time, but now the high wages paid has attracted them again to the mines."[28]

Gold, meanwhile, was first offered to the HBC in trade by the Haidas of the Queen Charlotte Islands in 1851, and in the mid-1850s by the Interior Salish of the Fraser and Thompson Valleys. In both cases white men were "obstructed by the natives in all their attempts to search for gold" and "when [the whites] did succeed in removing the surface and excavating to the depth of the auriferous stratum, they were quietly hustled and crowded by the natives who . . . proceeded to reap the fruits of their labours."[29] In 1858, however, some 30 000 non-aboriginals surged into the Fraser Valley and up the Thompson, completely overwhelming the few thousand aboriginal inhabitants, who continued to work alongside them. In 1858 James Moore reported that the "whole tribe of Yale Indians moved down from Yale and camped on Hill's bar, about three hundred men, women and children, and they also commenced to wash for gold" and Governor Douglas reported that "it is impossible to get Indian labor at present, as they are all busy mining, and make between two and three dollars a day each man."[30]

Within the decade the gold rushes had passed and while most of the aliens had abandoned the diggings, aboriginal people continued to include gold mining as part of their modified seasonal cycle. In 1871 Alfred Selwyn of the Geological Survey of Canada remarked that "nearly all the Indians of the Fraser above Yale have now become gold washers. They return to the same spot on the river year after year, at the season of lowest water, to wash the sands, and, it is asserted, can almost always earn for a day's labour from one to two dollar's worth of gold." The next year the Victoria *Colonist* reported that "$15,000–$20,000 is annually contributed to the wealth of the Province by mining on the Thompson and Fraser Rivers, which is carried on almost exclusively by the Natives at low water."[31] The Indian agents and the mining department regularly recorded the bands along the Fraser and Thompson panning gold into the twentieth century.[32] In addition to mining, many bands along the Fraser, Thompson, and Nicola rivers took up packing supplies as a vocation. Chief Justice Begbie, who travelled this circuit, recalled that "no supplies were taken in [to the gold districts] except by Indians. . . . Without them . . . the country could not have been entered or supplied in 1858–1860."[33]

Besides mining and packing, the aboriginal people of the southern interior took up farming on their own behalf and worked as farm labour for others. In 1874 the Catholic missionary C.J. Grandidier wrote from Kamloops that "The Indians in this part of the country are now quite awake to the necessity of working, of following the examples of the whites, they look to the future and are afraid for their children's sake if they do not work." Acting on behalf of the people of the Fraser Valley, Alexis, chief of Cheam, asked the Indian agent for advance warning if he visited "in order to unite our people who are now a little dispersed as they are working for the whites."[34] "Every Indian . . . who could and would work—and they were numerous," the provincial attorney general recalled in 1875,

> was employed in almost every branch of industrial and domestic life, at wages which would appear excessively high in England or in Canada. From becoming labourers, some of the Natives . . . engaged on their own account in stock breeding, in river boating, and in "packing," as it is termed, as carriers of merchandise by land and water; while others followed fishing and hunting with more vigour than formerly to supply the wants of the incoming population. The Government frequently employed those living in the interior as police, labourers, servants, and as messengers entrusted with errands of importance.[35]

Did they also engage in more industrial pursuits? Martin Robin has argued that "it was not merely the shrinking numbers . . . which accounted for the low participation of the Indians in the new industrial system. By inclination and habit, the Indian did not fit the industrial mould. His customary and casual and seasonal work schedule hardly prepared him for the discipline, pace and rhythm of industrial employment."[36] Yet the evidence shows aboriginal people were among the region's first factory workers.

The "modern" factory arrived on Vancouver Island in 1861 when Captain Stamp commenced operation of the largest sawmill on the west coast of North America, a steam-powered facility that cost $120 000 to build and was eventually capable of cutting 100 000 feet of lumber a day. For the Tseshaht people of the Alberni Inlet, where the mill was located, the industrial revolution arrived at the end of a cannon. When the white labourers arrived to set up the mill they chose the site where the local people were camped. The mill's operators were satisfied that they had "bought" the site from the local people for "some 50 blankets, muskets, molasses and food, trinkets etc." but the Tseshaht clearly had a different view of the transaction than the mill owners—they refused to leave. They were introduced to capitalist property relations when the mill managers trained their cannons on them.[37] Ultimately they agreed to move, and when they returned to the mill site it was as workers. The mill manager subsequently recorded that when he "first employed Indians at Alberni, the price of their labour was two blankets and rations of bisquits and molasses for a month's work for each man, if he worked the whole time." One source reports that over its operation, the mill paid out close to $30 000 in wages, and a considerable portion of that was likely paid to the local Tseshaht people.[38]

Two more giant export sawmills were established on Burrard Inlet between 1863 and 1867. Both rivalled the Alberni mill in size, but unlike their predecessor, they continued to operate into the next century. Together, these mills were the largest industrial operations in the colonies, each employing between 75 and 100 mill hands, exclusive of loggers and longshoremen.[39] As with other settlements around the colonies, whole aboriginal communities relocated to the sawmills, and in Burrard Inlet, most of the workers inside and outside the factory were aboriginal.

"While Europeans or at least Whites fill the responsible posts," geologist George Dawson observed in 1875, "Indians [Squa'mich], Chinamen, Negroes & Mulattoes & Half breeds & Mongrels of every pedigree abound." That year George Walkem, Attorney General of British Columbia, wrote that "our lumber mills alone pay about 130 Indian employés over $40 000 annually. Each individual receives from $20 to $30 per month and board." Recalling this period R.H. Alexander wrote: "Our mill hands were largely composed of runaway sailors and Indians and I have known the mill to shut down for several days because all the hands were engaged in an interesting poker game." By 1877 the Indian commissioner for the province found it "difficult to imagine" what "indeed in any part of the Province . . . the miner, the trader and the farmer, the manufacturer, the coast navigator, or almost any other vocation would do without the assistance of the Indian element."[40]

Inquiring into the income of the Musqueem band that worked in the Burrard Inlet, the Indian Reserve Commission reported in 1877 that from the "saw mills and other concomitant interests . . . a sum variously computed at from $80,000 to $100,000 finds its way annually into the hands of the natives. The mill owners, too, and the shipping frequenting the mills, are benefitting by a corresponding degree, by having a local source of labour constantly available." The Indian Commissioner remarked that in 1881 aboriginal sawmill workers were preferred to whites, and workers of both races earned up to $2.50 per day[41] (see table 2).

Table 2: **AVERAGE RATES OF PAY, VARIOUS PROFESSIONS IN BRITISH COLUMBIA, 1864–90 (DOLLARS PER DAY UNLESS SPECIFIED)**

Occupation	1860	1864	1883	1890
Indian agent			200/mth	
Indian Dept. constable			40/mth	
General labourers	2.50	3.00–4.00	1.75–2.00	1.25–2.50
Coal miners			3.00–4.00	
Gold miners				1.75–3.00
Colliery labourers			2.50	
Skilled tradesmen	5.00	?–4.85	3.50–4.00	4.00–6.00
Laundresses		2.10/doz shirts		10.00–18.00/mth
Longshoremen				50¢/hour
Lumbermen		48.50/mth		1.50–2.25
Millhands				2.50

Source: The 1860 wages are from Bishop Hill to the secretary, Society for the Propagation of the Gospel, 8 May 1860, in Bishop Hill Collection, text 57, box 3, file 3, Anglican Diocese of British Columbia, courtesy of Ira Chaikin; 1864 from Matthew McFie, *Vancouver Island and British Columbia* (London, 1865), 499–500; 1883 from Canada, Province of British Columbia, *Information for Intending Settlers* (Ottawa, 1883), 23; and for 1890 from Canada, *SP*, 1891 "Immigration Agents' Reports," 95–97. Longshoreman rate from Biggar, *Canadian Handbook*, 20. The figures for 1860–64 are converted to dollars at the rate of £1 to $4.85. Indian agent's salary from Indian Affairs Annual Reports.

At the same time sawmills in Puget Sound, Washington Territory, employed hundreds of British Columbia aboriginal people. William Pierce, a Tsimshian from Port Simpson, remarked that in the mid-1870s his co-workers in a Puget Sound sawmill included Haida from the Queen Charlottes, Tsimshian from the north coast, Nass and Skeena Rivers, as well as Bella Bella, Bella Coola, Kitamaat, and Kwakwaka'wakw from the central coast and Tlingit from Alaska.[42] A decade later, one of these migrants, Charles Nowell, a seventeen-year-old Kwakwaka'wakw from Fort Rupert, recalled arriving in Vancouver after returning empty-handed from seeking work in Washington State: "I was dead broke, and went over to North Vancouver in a small canoe to the sawmill and asked the manager if he could give me a job. He told me I could be a fireman in the sawmill. I says, 'I never did it before, but I will try and do my best.' He says there is another Indian there who has been working there for two years and will tell me what to do."[43] As Nowell's reference to "firemen" suggests, these mills were large factories operated by steam power. Morley Roberts worked alongside the crew of "Indians, half-breeds and Chinamen" at a New Westminster sawmill in the 1880s and his description leaves no doubt that sawmill work was among the most "industrial" in British Columbia.[44]

Some aboriginal people moved into skilled jobs but the majority of the aboriginal workers, like the non-aboriginals, were unskilled. Many aboriginal people, including the entire male population of the Sechelt band on the Sunshine Coast north of Burrard Inlet, cut wood for the mills. In addition to working for the big export mills, aboriginal people worked and ran several smaller sawmills that were scattered throughout the province, many of them first established by missionaries in order to encourage aboriginal people to adopt capitalist-Christian ethics. Not only was sawmill labour predominantly aboriginal but so were the longshoremen and -women.[45]

While the sawmills of Burrard Inlet were getting into full swing, the second major factory-based industry—salmon-canning—was in its infancy. First attempted in 1867, it was not until 1870 that continuous production started. Within a decade, however, the canneries were large, modern factories employing hundreds of people and using steam boilers and retorts to heat and cook the salmon and to seal the cans.[46] The early canneries relied almost exclusively on aboriginal men to do the fishing and a work force comprising aboriginal women and Chinese men to do most of the canning. Like the big export sawmills, they were frequently located in coastal inlets, remote from white settlement but in, or close to, aboriginal communities. One estimate suggested that the eleven canneries operating on the Fraser River in 1883 employed 1000 to 1200 aboriginal fishermen plus hundreds of aboriginal women to process the fish.[47]

By 1885 a crude estimate based on the reports of the Indian Agents suggests that of the 28 000 aboriginal people in British Columbia in 1885, over 85 percent belonged to bands that earned substantial incomes through paid labour. The remaining 15 percent, although not wage labourers, participated to a lesser degree in the economy as fur traders.[48]

More telling than the numbers are the accounts of whole villages being emptied by aboriginal people engaged in paid work. One surveyor reported, for example, that he did not know where to lay out a reserve because all the Haida were away at the canneries or the mills, while an ethnographer from the Berlin Museum was unable to trade artifacts in villages emptied by all who were mobile. One of the most interesting accounts is by Sayach'apis, a Nuu-cha-nulth, whose invitations to a potlatch in the mid-1880s were spurned by the Songhees, the Saanich, the Cowichan, and the Hikwihltaah: "You are too late," they told him; "we are going to the hop fields" to harvest the crop.[49]

Twenty-five years after the gold rush, aboriginal people had not been marginalized—rather they remained at the centre of the transformed, capitalist, economic activity. "Almost all the labour of the province is done by Indians and Chinese," the federal minister of justice reported in 1883. "All the steamboats in which we travelled were manned by Indians—the Stevedores and longshoremen and the labourers you find about the streets are for the most part Indians. All the fishing for the canneries is done by them and in all these occupations they compare favourably with the labouring classes elsewhere. . . . [T]hey get good wages, frequently $2.00 a day and over."[50]

"The stranger coming for the first time to Victoria is startled by the great number of Indians living in this town," wrote ethnologist Franz Boas in 1886. "We meet them everywhere. They dress mostly in European fashion. The men are dock workers, craftsmen or fish vendors; the women are washerwomen or working women. . . . Certain Indian tribes have already become indispensable on the labour market and without them the province would suffer great economic damage."[51] Moreover, Chinook, the *lingua franca* of the fur trade, and not English, was the language of the canneries, the docks, the sawmills, the hop-fields, and many other sites where large amounts of labour were performed.[52] At no time since have aboriginal people been so central to the province-wide capitalist economy than in the early 1880s, though they continued to be vital to specific industries long after.

• Recruitment and Composition of the Aboriginal Work Force

There is virtually no information on how aboriginal people were recruited into the preindustrial labour force for agriculture and public works, or the manifold handicraft industries sponsored by the Hudson's Bay Company and others. It seems clear, however, that with aboriginal labour abundant in and around the settlements of British Columbia, recruitment was not difficult. Moreover, in addition to the nearby bands, often whole communities moved to white settlements, some seasonally and others permanently to trade and work. The slim evidence available suggests that, in this period, chiefs acted as labour brokers for their local groups. As we have seen, Governor Douglas held chiefs responsible for the behaviour of those of their people who hired themselves out, and the Fort Rupert journals record that chiefs were paid at the same rate as labourers, to supervise. Similarly, sealing schooners would negotiate with chiefs to bring a whole crew from a single village.[53]

Recruitment became more of an issue with the advent of large sawmills and canneries—the factories—because they demanded an unfamiliar work discipline. For one thing, it was critically important to have a large, regular work force gathered at a single site for extended, and in the case of the salmon canneries, very precise periods; for another, everyone had to start and end work at the same time. In retrospect, however, it should come as no surprise that aboriginal people were recruited and employed in these factories in large numbers. They dominated the population and either lived close to the new industrial sites (since the canneries, especially, located specifically to take advantage of aboriginal labour) or had their own means of transport to and from them. In addition, aboriginal people, under some circumstances, could be paid less than "white" labour.

Yet little is known about the different methods used to bring aboriginal people into the factories or how they made the transition to factory labour discipline. At the beginning of the industrial era, chiefs were still relied upon as labour agents. We know, for example, that white recruiters visited the Sliammon chiefs on the Sunshine Coast in 1882 and told them that their people would earn $3 a day at the Fraser River canneries.[54] Evidence from the early twentieth century shows that canneries employed "Indian bosses" who would be given cash advances for themselves and others, and who would be responsible for getting a specified number of fishermen and inside workers, particularly women, to come to individual canneries. Employers also used Indian agents as informal recruiters, and large hop growers would send agents to visit bands and sign up workers in advance of the season.[55] However, it would seem from Charles Nowell's experience with the Burrard Inlet sawmill that as the number of industrial sites increased, local groups tended less to act as units; instead, individuals began to take control of their own labour and sell it independent of "Indian Bosses."[56] By the late 1880s, it was common for aboriginal women to be hired by Chinese labour contractors in the canneries on the Fraser and Skeena Rivers.[57] Whether as individuals or groups, Alfred Niblack noted in October 1886, aboriginal people were aggressive and creative about finding work:

> It was just at the end of the hop-picking season around Puget Sound, and hundreds of Indians were coming into Port Townsend en route to their villages to the north. A party of Young Haida stopped, and one of their number telegraphed over to Whidbey Island to offer the services of the party to a farmer to dig potatoes

for him. In view of the glut in the labour market, due to the presence of so many idle Indians just then, this clever bit of enterprise . . . secured them the job ahead of their rivals.[58]

The incorporation of aboriginal people into the capitalist labour force was a spatially discontinuous process that did not affect all aboriginal groups simultaneously or in the same way. Industry did not spread out gradually from the central settlements of Victoria, New Westminster, and Nanaimo; rather it arrived suddenly on inlets far removed from settlement. Moreover, many aboriginal groups opted to travel long distances to obtain employment while their neighbours did not. Those aboriginal groups that had previous exposure to working with or for non-aboriginal people were the first to take up the long migrations to find wage labour in the south.[59]

Participation also varied across generations and gender. Overall, the industrial workplace favoured younger people; agriculture, on the other hand, did not discriminate between young and old or between men and women.[60] The contrast was captured by William Lomas, the Cowichan Indian agent: "All the younger men can find employment on farms or at the sawmills and canneries, and many families are about to leave for the hop fields of Washington Territory." The elderly he saw were not faring so well:

> The very old people who formerly lived entirely on fish, berries and roots, suffer a great deal through the settling up of the country. . . . With the younger men, the loss of these kinds of foods is more than compensated by the good wages that they earn, which supplement what they produce on their allotments; but this mode of life does away with their old customs of laying in a supply of dried meat, fish and berries for winter use, and thus the old people again suffer, for Indians are often generous with the food they have taken in the chase, but begrudge what they have paid money for.[61]

The British Columbia aboriginal societies had their own gender-based division of labour which was largely appropriated into the canneries.[62] Although, generally speaking, native men would fish and women would mend nets and work in the canneries, some women also fished with their husbands (the boats required a puller and a fisher)[63] and some, particularly older, men would mend nets and work inside. The infirm would look after the infants, while even young children had work in the canneries cleaning cans. In peak cannery periods, every possible person would be brought in to work and infants were placed in a corner where they could be watched.[64]

The traditional division of labour between male hunters and female processors of the catch was generally carried over into the capitalist economy of the sealing industry as well. When the local seals were hunted-out and schooners called at west coast villages to pick up crews, as many as 870 aboriginal people were hired, most of them men, although women were sometimes employed as boat-handlers. On the other hand, "the Indian women and children are always the most eager to go to the hop fields, where they always earn considerable sums of money, and, among these Indians, the wife's purse is generally entirely separate from the husband's."[65]

In some cases, however, aboriginal gender divisions of labour could not be grafted directly onto the capitalist economy. Were women or men better suited to work on steamships, in sawmills, or to sell food in the street markets? In the era 1849–90, both men and women worked at non-industrial occupations such as gold mining, farming, agricultural labour, rendering oil, and loading coal. With regard to the service trades, men are more often mentioned as cutting and selling firewood while women are commonly recorded as bringing fish and game to urban markets. In urban areas women did domestic work such as washing clothes, taking in ironing, and cleaning house,[66] and they were also employed to make fishnets.[67] Prostitution was an additional source of income for hundreds of aboriginal women from the late 1850s through the 1880s.[68] But in keeping with the gender divisions of labour prevalent in capitalist society, I have found no mention of aboriginal women being employed in sawmills, in coal mines, and on railroad crews.

The effect on aboriginal social and familial relationships of different participation rates by age and gender deserves more scholarly attention. The one study that has been done, of the Carrier people of the Chilcotin, where there was more demand for males in wage-occupations, shows that aboriginal women carried on and even enlarged their role as providers for households in the subsistence economy. Among the Carrier people, this had the effect of increasing the social status and power of women.[69] Among the coastal people women were gaining more prominence as "title holders" or "chiefs." Further research may reveal whether this was due to depopulation, their new incomes, their increased role as providers of subsistence, or other factors.

• Why Did Aboriginal People Work for Wages?

It is noteworthy in itself that aboriginal people in British Columbia chose, in large numbers, to work for pay. Indeed, in 1852, one of the HBC agents wondered if they could get the west coast people interested in any work besides fishing: "when they can get all their wants and even a superfluity by a course congenial to them (fishing), it would be erroneous to suppose that they may be easily persuaded to follow an occupation they dislike and which is less remunerative, merely to gratify our will."[70]

Certainly in the 1840s and 1850s there was no pressure on the traditional resource base or subsistence economy which had sustained them for eons.[71] Even by the 1870s and the beginning of truly industrial labour, only a few of the aboriginal groups on southern Vancouver Island and in the Fraser and Thompson valleys were finding their traditional resource base eroded to the point that they could not have reverted to a totally subsistence economy if such was their preference. Nor did evangelism have a significant impact until the 1860s and then only in a few locations, by which time church representatives were merely reinforcing an existing desire to participate in wage labour.

Prior to the wide-scale opportunities for wage labour most of the peoples of the west coast participated in the fur trade for reasons which, according to the "enrichment thesis," were broadly based in their own culture's traditions. Moreover, the new wealth generated by the fur trade, the relocation of bands to common sites around forts, and population decimation from disease and firearms led to an enrichment of cultural activities, including, on the west coast, the potlatch.[72] "The arts and crafts, trade and technology, social and ceremonial life were all brought to new peaks of development. The climax of Indian culture was reached well after the arrival of the white man on the scene."[73]

Potlatch is a word in the Chinook jargon that refers to the different ceremonies among many nations of the Pacific Northwest that included feasting, dancing, and the giving of gifts to all in attendance. The potlatch was a central feature of the lives and economy of, especially, the coastal Indians. It was only through potlatches that one's hereditary status and rights to resources, property (including songs and dances) and names could be claimed and maintained. The more guests and the more gifts, the higher the relative status of the person giving the potlatch. High-status recipients of potlatch gifts were expected to reciprocate with potlatches in order to maintain their own relative position, and to protect their claims to traditional prerogatives.[74] All the evidence suggests that the fur trade intensified potlatching, and along with it the carving of totems and masks, the weaving of blankets, and all the other arts that were associated with the ceremony.[75]

Because of the cultural necessity to periodically distribute valuable gifts in a potlatch, the west coast people were a natural trading market. They had uses for property, possessions, and wealth which, while very different from those of the traders themselves, were nevertheless complementary. The traditional potlatch goods were valuable precisely because they were rare, or because they took much time and laborious effort to make. "On the other hand, the intrusive white civilization offered its goods for things that were relatively abundant": fur, fish, and unskilled labour.[76] Manufactured blankets and other mass-produced goods were substituted as potlatch goods for locally made, hand-produced items.

With some exceptions, aboriginal people welcomed the arrival of traders on boats and the establishment of trading posts in their territories.

They were equally jealous of trading posts in their rival's territories, or territories that they considered their hinterland.[77] Thus, in the seventy years prior to 1849, and since the first direct trading with Europeans, the society of the aboriginal people had changed so that trade with the foreigners had become an integral and largely welcome part of their culture.[78]

It appears that the same cultural forces that drew aboriginal people into the fur trade continued to operate and draw them into the wage and industrial labour force. Aboriginal people permitted, if not welcomed, initial non-aboriginal expansion into their territories to take advantage of the wealth-generating potential that the aliens offered. In 1843 the Songhees people helped the HBC build Fort Victoria.[79] In the 1850s the Haida and the Cowichan both appealed to Governor Douglas to establish a settlement among them that they might find work.[80] When he first visited them in 1881, although their village was still suffering from an unprovoked attack by the Royal Navy, the Kitamaats asked Indian Commissioner Powell if he would establish a sawmill in their community.[81] Even in the 1880s, when Port Simpson Tsimshian people refused to accept an Indian agent, refused to be administered under the Indian Act, and prevented surveyors from assigning reserves, they permitted salmon canneries into their territory. Different bands of Kwakwaka'wakw refused to allow a priest into their village yet they too permitted the canneries, sawmills, and logging camps.

Aboriginal people apparently found that these new forms of work could be used like the fur trade, to enhance their position in their own society. In 1853, for example, using the wealth they had accumulated from working around Victoria, the Songhees people hosted a potlatch. Three thousand aboriginal people, perhaps a tenth of the population of the entire coastal area, attended this feast.[82] Having seen Victoria, the wealth of the Songhees, and the opportunities for work, the steady flow of thousands of coastal people to Victoria started the following season. Wagework became another adaptation of the seasonal subsistence round that had already been modified to include an extended trapping season, when furs were the easiest route to accumulation.

White employers, government officials, and missionaries noticed that aboriginal people worked to be able to potlatch. But the non-aboriginal immigrants could not reconcile their own work ethic with the motivations that led aboriginal people into the work force. The Indian agent for Fraser Valley, James Lenihan, expressed his confusion this way:

> The Indians generally have views peculiar to the country as to the value of money. One band, numbering about fifteen families, applied to me in the spring for some agricultural implements and seeds. I questioned the Chief respecting a "potlatche" which he had held the previous winter, and ascertained that he himself and two of his headmen had given away in presents to their friends, 134 sacks of flour, 140 pairs of blankets, together with a quantity of apples

and provisions, amounting in value to about $700, for all of which they had paid in cash out of their earnings as labourers, fishermen and hunters.[83]

George Grant, who accompanied Sanford Fleming on his cross-country inspection of possible routes for the CPR, exhibited his puzzlement in describing the aboriginal work force at the Moodyville sawmill on Burrard Inlet in 1872:

> The aborigines work well till they save enough money to live on for some time, and then they go up to the boss and frankly say that they are lazy and do not want to work longer. . . . Another habit of the richer ones, which to the Anglo-saxon mind borders on insanity, is that of giving universal backshish or gifts to the whole tribe, without expecting any return save an increased popularity that may lead to their election as Tyhees or chiefs when vacancies occur.

Of particular interest was the story of "big George," who had

> worked industriously at the mill for years until he had saved $2,000. Instead of putting this in a Savings Bank, he had spent it all on stores for a grand "Potlatch." . . . Nearly a thousand assembled; the festivities lasted a week; and everyone got something, either a blanket, musket, bag of flour, box of apples, or tea and sugar. When the fun was over, "big George," now penniless, returned to the mill to carry slabs at $20 a month.

Similar comments can be found scattered throughout the accounts of missionaries, government agents, and travellers.[84]

Aboriginal accounts confirm that income from wagework was used to enhance the prestige of the labourers. Charley Nowell recollected that between 1870 and 1876 his brother had regular employment as a cook: "That's why my brother was the richest of all the Indians at Fort Rupert. Every payday he used to be paid with trade—in blankets. . . . When the people of Fort Rupert know that my brother is paid, they come and borrow blankets from him. . . . My brother keeps on loaning until he has got enough (principal and interest) to collect and give a potlatch."[85]

In addition to accumulating wealth for potlatching, many aboriginal groups had other traditional uses for wealth. James Sewid, a Kwakwaka'wakw, told the story of his great-grandfather who trapped for several winters in order to hold a potlatch needed to recruit a war party to revenge his son's life. Northern men especially paid a substantial bride price to the families of their future wives. Shamans were paid to cure illness, and compensation was often demanded as restitution for intentional or unintentional killing or wounding of another.[86]

Helen Codere, who has made an intensive study of the Kwakwaka'wakw, has noted that while fur-trade wealth increased the frequency of potlatches, wage labour increased the number of guests and the wealth distributed to an even greater extent, and to her the years between 1849 and 1921 could justifiably be called "the potlatch period."[87] Her conclusions are borne out by Kwawkewlth (Kwakwaka'wakw) district Indian agent George Blenkinsop's 1881 observation that potlatches, "of late years, increased to a very great extent." He explained that among the Kwakwaka'wakw "the custom was formerly almost entirely confined to the recognised chiefs, but that of late years it has extended to the people generally, and become very much commoner than before. . . . [The Potlatch] has spread to all classes of the community and became the recognised mode of attaining social rank and respect."[88] Codere charted the increases in the number of blankets given at Kwakwaka'wakw potlatches going back over a century, numbers which were well remembered by her informants owing to the importance of establishing relative prestige levels. The number of blankets distributed at the greatest single potlatch in the following twenty-year periods gives an indication of the striking increase in wealth available and distributed: 1829–48: 320 blankets; 1849–69: 9000 blankets; 1870–89: 7000 blankets; 1890–1909: 19 000 blankets; 1910–29: 14 000 blankets; 1930–49: 33 000 blankets. The first memories of Billy Assu, a Kwakwaka'wakw from Cape Mudge, were of his father's 1911 potlatch: "My father worked for the money to give that potlatch for many years. He gave away goods and money to the value of more than $10,000."[89]

The same phenomena appeared to be drawing other aboriginal groups into the paid labour force. In 1881 Cowichan Indian agent Lomas predicted that a significant proportion of the $15 000 earned by the Cowichan people at the canneries that season would be given away at potlatches. Similarly, in 1884 a delegation of Nuu-chah-nulth chiefs explained that they worked for their money "and like to spend it as we please, in gathering our friends together; now whenever we travel we find friends; the 'potlatch' does that." Among the Haida the number of new totems being raised with the accompanying ceremonies reached its peak in the period 1860–76. Writing generally of this period, missionary William Pierce, a converted Tsimshian, wrote: "In these days, any man of a common order may give a potlatch if he is rich enough."[90] In short, it would appear that aboriginal people were not just servants of industry but also made industrialization serve their interests as well.[91]

However, the fact that aboriginal people had their own reasons for working for wages and chose when they would both enter and leave the labour force was a source of constant frustration to white employers. Indeed, the fact that aboriginal peoples had their own agendas probably accounts for the schizophrenic comments of white employers who spoke about them as "indispensable" while condemning their "unreliability" and "laziness."

Like most other groups outside the urban area, the Kwakwaka'wakw, for example, continued to earn their own subsistence, which meant that earnings could go to the purchase of manufactured goods. Since they required only a limited amount of manufactured goods for consumption needs and since they did not hoard, any surplus could be and was used in potlatching."[92] Because of their subsistence cycle, winter was the main ceremonial season—and few aboriginal people were willing to work year-round and miss the winter festivities. In the beginning this was not a problem in labour-intensive activities like fishing, canning, harvesting, and logging, which were not conducted in the winter. Increasingly, however, the sawmills, the railways, the steamboats and other large employers were anxious to have a year-round and stable labour force so that seasonal labour, the choice of large numbers of aboriginal people, was becoming less compatible with the demands of capitalism.

It is no coincidence, then, that the federal government passed a law banning potlatch in 1884, just as aboriginal peoples reached their peak importance in the economy. Although the potlatch had drawn many aboriginal people into paid labour, by the mid-1880s it was inconsistent with the "stable" habits of industry that both missionaries and government agents saw as essential to the development of a Christian capitalist society. Seeing the potlatch as a bulwark which enabled the aboriginal people to resist acculturation since the seasonal cycle kept them mobile and away from schools and churches, missionaries and the Indian agents argued that it kept aboriginal people poor and mitigated against the accumulation of individual dwellings, land holdings, and private property.

Although the law proved ineffectual, and was not successfully enforced until 1908, it did provide government agents and missionaries with powerful suasion against potlatching.[93] Some of the bands responded to government pressure, others that had been christianized gave up the institution at the insistence of their ministers;[94] some bands in urban areas seemed to be slowly adopting the more individualistic and acquisitive ideals of the new majority. So, despite the ineffective laws, the 1880s were also the climax years of the potlatch along the coast generally.[95] Ironically, the very cultural imperative that had brought aboriginal people into the work force was outlawed because, due to changing circumstances, it was no longer sufficiently compatible with the requirements of capitalism.

• Conclusion

In the period 1849–90 the connections to the capitalist economy varied widely among the many nations and linguistic groups who were the aboriginal people of what is now British Columbia. Depending on particular circumstances, integration into the paid labour force also had different effects on the social relations between men and women, youth and elderly, and nobles and commoners. Some patterns are nevertheless emerging as research in these areas moves ahead. West coast aboriginal people joined the international economy when Captain Cook first traded sea otter pelts with the natives of Yuquat (Nootka) in 1778, but their relationship to the economy changed dramatically in the mid-nineteenth century. Before the 1850s they were largely hunters, fishermen, trappers, and gatherers who exchanged the products of the land for products of the European market. By 1890, however, the industrial revolution having arrived on many of their inlets, bays, and rivers, most aboriginal people were trading their labour for wages.

Aboriginal people were central, not marginal, to the development of new industries and the spread of capitalism in the province-to-be. Coal would not have been mined in British Columbia in the 1840s and 1850s, export sawmills would not have been able to function in the 1860s and 1870s, canneries would not have had a fishing fleet, or the necessary processors in the 1870s and 1880s, without the widespread participation of aboriginal people. The gold rush may have diverted the attention of historians, but it did not divert aboriginal people from the economy. It was the aboriginal work force that allowed the creation of a capitalist regional economy based on fur trade, then coal mining, sawmilling, and salmon canning. This was the regional economy that kept the Hudson's Bay Company on the Pacific Coast, persuaded Britain that the establishment of colonies could be profitable as well as strategic, and ultimately ensured that British Columbia would be *British* Columbia.

While the capitalist economy needed the vast pool of aboriginal labour, aboriginal people used the capitalist economy for their own cultural purposes. Wage labour was one juncture where the potlatch system and capitalism were curiously complementary. Aboriginal people fitted seasonal paid work into their own economic cycle and, in the era described, were able to maintain a level of control over their participation in both. However, the compatibility of capitalism and the aboriginal economy was breaking down by 1884, when the anti-potlatch laws were passed by the federal government: eager to participate in seasonal wage activities from spring to fall, aboriginal people were less interested in participating in the year-round employment that the economy was increasingly demanding.

By the taking of the census of 1891, British Columbia was no longer an "aboriginal province." Aboriginal populations had nearly reached their nadir and alternative pools of labour were becoming available. Since then, although aboriginal people have not made up the majority of the labour force, they have been consistently important in key sectors, namely fishing, canning, and agricultural sectors. In this way, as well as others, the aboriginal and non-aboriginal histories of British Columbia are still inextricably linked.

• Notes

[1] A fuller discussion of population estimates is taken up in table 1.

[2] Robin Fisher, *Contact and Conflict: Indian-European Relations in British Columbia 1774–1890* (Vancouver, 1977); Rolf Knight, *Indians at Work: An Informal History of Native Indian Labour in British Columbia, 1858–1930* (Vancouver, 1978).

[3] Fisher, *Contact and Conflict*, 96, 109, 111. For other statements along these lines see David McNally, "Political Economy Without a Working Class," *Labour/Le Travail* 25 (Spring 1990): 220n; Paul Phillips, "Confederation and the Economy of British Columbia" in *British Columbia and Confederation*, ed. W. George Shelton (Victoria, 1967), 59; Martin Robin, *The Rush for the Spoils: The Company Province 1871–1933* (Toronto, 1972), 30.

[4] Alicja Muszynski, "Major Processors to 1940 and the Early Labour Force: Historical Notes" in *UnCommon Property: The Fishing and Fish Processing Industries in British Columbia*, ed. Patricia Marchak et al. (Agincourt, ON, 1987), 46–65; Richard Mackie, "Colonial Land, Indian Labour, and Company Capital: The Economy of Vancouver Island, 1849–1858," (MA thesis, University of Victoria, 1985); James K. Burrows, "'A Much Needed Class of Labour': The Economy and Income of the Southern Interior Plateau Indians, 1897–1910," *BC Studies* 71 (1986): 27–46.

[5] Charles Forbes, *Vancouver Island, its Resources and Capabilities as a Colony* (London, 1862), 25; A.A. Harvey, *A Statistical Account of British Columbia* (Ottawa, 1867), 9.

[6] H.L. Langevin, *British Columbia: Report of the Hon. H.L. Langevin* (Ottawa, 1827), 28; A.C. Anderson, *Dominion on the West* (Victoria, 1872), 80.

[7] For simplicity's sake, I have combined in the term *paid labour* wagework (whether paid in kind, scrip, or cash), piecework, and independent commodity production (hand logging, for example), although each system produced its own set of social relations.

[8] For an introduction see William C. Sturtuvant, *Handbook of North American Indians* (Washington, DC), vols. 4, 6, 7. For population estimates see table 1.

[9] The Songhees, a band of the Coast Salish, were an amalgamation of several nearby villages that relocated to a site across the harbour from Fort Victoria after the latter was founded in 1843.

[10] Great Britain, Colonial Office, Original Correspondence, Vancouver Island, 1846–67, (CO) 305/6, 10048, Governor James Douglas to Russell, 21 Aug. 1855. Colonial Office correspondence (with a CO number) cited here was made available to me by James Hendrickson from his unpublished manuscript "Vancouver Island: Colonial Correspondence Dispatches."

[11] CO 305/14, 9267, Douglas to Colonial Office, 8 Aug. 1860.

[12] CO 305/4, 9499, Douglas to Newcastle, 28 July 1853.

[13] The Tsimshian were from the Skeena River area around Fort Simpson; William Duncan, "Journal," 11 July 1857, cited in Jean Usher, *William Duncan of Metlakatla: A Victorian Missionary in British Columbia* (Ottawa, 1974), 40; W.C. Grant in William Grew Hazlitt, *British Columbia and Vancouver Island* (London, 1858), 179; Dorothy B. Smith, *The Reminiscences of Doctor John Sebastian Helmcken* (Vancouver, 1975), 134.

[14] CO 305/6, 10048, Douglas to Lord Russell, 21 Aug. 1855; CO 305/4, 12345, Douglas to Newcastle, 24 Oct. 1853, emphasis mine.

[15] June Collins, "John Fornsby: The Personal Document of a Coast Salish Indian" in *Indians in the Urban Northwest*, ed. Marian Smith (New York, 1949), 301; "Northern Indians," *Evening Bulletin* (San Francisco), 4 Oct.

1860, reprinted in James Swan, *Almost Out of This World* (Tacoma, 1971), 99; CO 305/7, 3963, Douglas to Sir George Grey, 1 March 1856; and CO 305/7 5814, 10 April 1856.

16 Mackie, "Colonial Land, Indian Labour, and Company Capital."

17 CO 305/3, Rev. R.J. Staines to Thomas Boys, 6 July 1852; Smith, *Reminiscences of Doctor John Sebastian Helmcken*, 134; CO/305/3 Douglas to Earl Grey, 31 Oct. 1851.

18 British Columbia Archives and Record Services (hereafter BCARS), Colonial Correspondence, F347/26a, James Cooper, "Report by the Harbor Master at Esquimalt to the Acting Colonial Secretary"; Usher, *William Duncan of Metlakatla*, 58.

19 CO 305/14, 9267, Douglas to Colonial Office, 8 Aug. 1860.

20 CO 305/14, 8319, Douglas to Colonial Office, 7 July 1860. One major change during the gold rush was that aboriginal labour was increasingly being paid in cash instead of goods. Previously the goods most sought after as pay were blankets, which were commonly used as potlatch gifts.

21 *Times* (San Francisco), 27 Aug. 1858, in Hazlitt, *British Columbia and Vancouver Island*, 208, 215. See also Robin Fisher, "Joseph Trutch and the Indian Land Policy" in *British Columbia: Historical Readings*, ed. W.P. Ward and R.A.J. McDonald (Vancouver, 1981), 155; Sophia Cracroft, *Lady Franklin Visits the Pacific Northwest: February to April 1861 and April to July 1870* (Victoria, 1974), 79.

22 Cracroft estimates 1000 aboriginal people living at Yale in 1861 and mentions that some were engaged as servants, ibid., 53; at Lytton, the population of 250 was 80 percent aboriginal and "the Indians . . . very industrious and peaceable. Their chief employment is gold mining and packing supplies to and from the interior with their own horses of which they have in great numbers," *Lovell's*

Gazetteer 1870–73, 181; Fisher, *Contact and Conflict*, 111.

23 James Douglas to the governor and committee of the Hudson's Bay Company, 7 Dec. 1846, in Hartwell Bowsfield, *Fort Victoria Letters 1846–1851* (Winnipeg, 1979), 4.

24 E.E. Rich, ed., *The Letters of John McLoughlin from Fort Vancouver . . . , 1825–1838* (Winnipeg, 1941), 335.

25 The reference is to a blanket of $2\,1/2$ points, specifying a particular quality of blanket. Douglas to the governor and committee, 3 Sept. 1849, 3 April and 16 Nov. 1850, in Bowsfield, *Fort Victoria Letters*, 46, 84, 132; William Burrill, "Class Conflict and Colonialism: The Coal Miners of Vancouver Island During the Hudson's Bay Company Era, 1848–1862" (MA thesis, University of Victoria, 1987), 54.

26 CO 305/3, 10199, Douglas to Pakington, 28 Aug. 1852; also CO 305/3, 933, 11 Nov. 1852.

27 Douglas to Stuart, 22 Aug. 1857 in Burrill, "Class Conflict and Colonialism," 127.

28 Canada, Parliament, House of Commons, *Sessional Papers* (hereafter Canada, *SP*) 1878, 8, lx; 1883, 54; 1889, 13, 100–102. The 1877 annual report of the BC minister of mines records 51 Indians working as coal miners in the Nanaimo plus an unrecorded number working as miner's helpers. These annual reports show some aboriginal people working in the coal mines into the twentieth century. British Columbia, Legislative Assembly, *Sessional Papers* (hereafter BC, *SP*) 1877, 617.

29 Quote from CO 305/3, 3742, Douglas to Earl Grey, 29 Jan. 1852; CO 305/3, 9263, Staines to Boys, 6 July 1852; CO 305/3, Douglas to Earl Grey, 31 Oct. 1851; CO 305/3, 8866, Captain A.L. Kuper to Admiralty, 20 July 1852; CO 305/9, 5180, Douglas to Labouchere, 6 April 1858.

30 James Douglas, in T.A. Rickard, "Indian Participation in the Gold

Discoveries," *British Columbia Historical Quarterly* 2 (1938): 13, and *British Columbia Historical Quarterly* 3 (1938): 218. There are other estimates of between 200 and 500 aboriginal people mining at Hill's Bar, compared to 50–60 white miners, in Hazlitt, *British Columbia and Vancouver Island*, 137.

31 Alfred C. Selwyn, "Journal and Report of Preliminary Explorations in British Columbia," *Report of Progress for 1871–72* (Ottawa, 1872), 56; *Colonist* (Victoria), 26 Nov. 1872.

32 Canada, *SP*, 1886, 4, 87–92; BC, *SP*, 1900, 724.

33 M.B. Begbie in Langevin, *British Columbia*, 27.

34 National Archives of Canada (hereafter NAC), RG10, Dept. of Indian Affairs, vol. 1001, items 82, 186, C.J. Grandidier to I.W. Powell, 2 July 1874, and Alexis to James Lenihan, 5 Sept. 1875.

35 BC, *SP*, 1875, George Walkem, "Report of the Government of British Columbia on the Subject of Indian Reserves," 3.

36 Robin, *The Rush for the Spoils*, 30.

37 BCARS, Colonial Correspondence, file 197/5, W.E. Banfield to the Colonial Secretary, 6 Sept. 1860, from Lorne Hammond, unpublished manuscript on W.E. Banfield; James Morton, *The Enterprising Mr. Moody and the Bumptious Captain Stamp* (Vancouver, 1977), 22–23; H.C. Langely, *Pacific Coast Directory for 1867* (San Francisco, 1867), 158.

38 G.M. Sproat, *Scenes and Studies of Savage Life* (London, 1868, reprinted Victoria, 1989), 40; G.W. Taylor, *Timber: History of the Forest Industry in BC* (Vancouver, 1975), 23.

39 Morton, *Enterprising Mr. Moody*, 33–37, 59; Taylor, *Timber*, 28.

40 Douglas Cole and Bradley Lockner, eds., *The Journals of George M. Dawson: British Columbia, 1875–78* (Vancouver, 1989), 115; R.H. Alexander, "Reminiscences of the Early Days of British Columbia, Address to the Canadian Club of Vancouver," *Proceedings of the Canadian Club of Vancouver 1906–1911* (Vancouver, 1911), 111; Walkem, "Report of the Government of British Columbia," 3; James Lenihan, Canada, *SP*, 1876, 56; Powell, Canada, *SP*, 1877, 33–34.

41 Canada, *SP*, 1877, 8, "Report of the Indian Reserve Commissioners," lii; Powell, Canada, *SP*, 1884, 107.

42 J.P. Hicks, ed., *From Potlatch to Pulpit: The Autobiography of W.H. Pierce* (Vancouver, 1933), 15. In 1876, "hundreds and sometimes thousands of northern Indians congregate every spring" to trade and work at Puget Sound mills, according to J.G. Swan, "The Haida Indians of Queen Charlotte's Islands, British Columbia," *Smithsonian Contributions to Knowledge* 21 (1876): 2, 8.

43 Nowell found working as a fireman too hot so he switched to loading lumber onto the ships for $2 a day, then became a tally man for $7.50 per day. Clellan Ford, *Smoke from Their Fires: The Life of a Kwakiutl Chief* (Hamdon, CT, 1968), 134.

44 Morley Roberts, *The Western Avernus or Toil and Travel in Further North America* (London, 1887), 181–82.

45 In 1876 the 55 men of the Sechelt band cut 1 300 000 cubic feet of saw logs for the mills for which they received $3 per thousand, the same rate paid to white loggers; Canada, *SP*, 1878, 8, "Report of the Indian Reserve Commissioners," lix; Knight, *Indians at Work*, 114, 123–24. Missionary William Duncan established a sawmill and a soap factory at Metlakatla by 1871. Other mission-mills followed at Alert Bay, Glen Vowell, Hartley Bay, and Kispiox. A description of the latter can be found in Hicks, *From Potlatch to Pulpit*, 69–70.

46 Duncan Stacey, *Sockeye and Tinplate: Technological Change in the Fraser Canning Industry, 1871–1912* (Victoria, 1982).

47 "Salmon Pack for 1883, Fraser River Canneries," *Resources of British Columbia* 1 (1883): 4; aboriginal cannery labour has been considered in some detail by Muszynski and Knight.

48 This estimate subtracts the population figures of the Indian Affairs census for the bands listed as living primarily or exclusively on trapping, hunting, and fishing, from the total aboriginal population. The bands subtracted are: 239 people in Chilcotin, 600 on the coast, 300 of Kootenays, and 2000 for tribes not visited. See Wilson Duff, *The Indian History of British Columbia: The Impact of the White Man* (Victoria, 1965), 35–40, for estimates of tribes not visited.

49 J.A. Jacobsen, *Alaskan Voyage, 1881–83: An Expedition to the Northwest Coast of America*, trans. from the German text of Adrian Woldt by Erna Gunther (Chicago, 1977), 13 and passim; Canada, *SP*, 1888, 13, 109, 157–58; Edward Sapir, *Nootka Texts* (Philadelphia, 1939).

50 BCARS, A/E/Or3/C15, Alexander Campbell, "Report on the Indians of British Columbia to the Superintendent General of Indian Affairs," 19 Oct. 1883.

51 R.P. Rohner, *The Ethnography of Franz Boas* (Chicago, 1969), 6, 9; Ernst von Hesse-Wartegg, "A Visit to the Anglo-Saxon Antipodes (Chapter XVIII of *Curiosa aus der Neuen Welt*, 1893, translated by John Maass)," *BC Studies* 50 (1981): 38; Jacobsen, *Alaskan Voyage*, 5.

52 Chinook was made up of words from aboriginal languages, French and English. A provincial business directory for 1877–78 published a Chinook-English, English-Chinook dictionary for the benefit of its readers: see T.N. Hibben, *Guide to the Province of British Columbia for 1877–78* (Victoria, 1877), 222–49. Franz Boas noted in 1889 that it was impossible for someone to get around British Columbia outside the major cities without knowledge of the language. See Rohner, *Ethnography of Franz Boas*,

9, and BCARS, Add. Mss. 2305, Alfred Carmichael ("Account of a Season's Work at a Salmon Cannery, Windsor Cannery, Aberdeen, Skeena," ca. 1885, which records the widespread use of Chinook in the Skeena canneries in the mid-1880s.

53 *Post Journal* (Fort Rupert), 22 Nov. 1849, in Burrill, "Class Conflict and Colonialism," 34; for the sealing industry see C.E. Crockford, "Changing Economic Activities of the Nuu-chah-nulth of Vancouver Island, 1840–1920" (hon. thesis, University of Victoria, 1991), 58.

54 Although they went, they did not like canning. The elders "did not like to expose their young men and women to the temptations of city life," thus few Sliammon people returned the next year, Canada, *SP*, 1883, 61.

55 NAC, RG10, vol. 1349, items 85, 225, 290, 483, 501.

56 Clellan, *Smoke from Their Fires*, 134.

57 Canner F.L. Lord told the BC Fishery Commission in 1892 that Chinese contractors hired the Native women and "of course these Chinamen pay the klootchmen" in BC, *SP*, 1893, 178; "When the fishing commences the boss chinaman hires Indians to clean the fish and their squaws to fill the cans," according to Carmichael, "Account of a Season's Work."

58 A.P. Niblack, "The Coast Indians of Southern Alaska and Northern British Columbia," US National Museum *Annual Report* (1888): 339.

59 The Tsimshian who lived around the HBC post at Fort Simpson went to Victoria before other Tsimshian groups. Similarly it was the Fort Rupert Kwakwaka'wakw, and the southern Haida around Skidegate (who had exposure to white miners and whalers in addition to itinerant sea-borne fur traders) who were the first of their respective nations to begin labour migration. For the Fort Rupert people see Philip Drucker and R.F. Heizer, *To Make My Name Good: A*

Re-examination of the Southern Kwakiutl Potlatch (Berkeley, 1976), 215; for the Haida see J.H. Van Den Brink, *The Haida Indians: Cultural Change Mainly Between 1876–1970* (Leiden, 1974), 51.

60 Jacobsen, *Alaskan Voyage*, 13.

61 Lomas, in Canada, *SP*, 1888, 13, 105.

62 Jo-Anne Fiske, "Fishing is Women's Business: Changing Economic Roles of Carrier Women and Men," 186–97, and Lorraine Littlefield "Women Traders in the Fur Trade," 173–83, both in *Native People, Native Lands: Canadian Indians, Inuit and Métis*, ed. Bruce Alden Cox (Ottawa, 1988); Marjorie Mitchell and Anna Franklin, "When You Don't Know the Language, Listen to the Silence: An Historical Overview of Native Women in BC" in *A History of British Columbia: Selected Readings*, ed. P.E. Roy (Toronto, 1989), 49–68.

63 Canada, *SP*, 1883, 60, records an aboriginal husband and wife fishing team, the wife pulling the boat and the husband handling the net and making $240 in 14 days.

64 Carmichael "Account of a Season's Work."

65 Canada, *SP*, 1887, 5, 92; 1888, 13, 105. In 1913 Indian Agent Charles Cox reported that Nuu-chah-nulth men and women keep their incomes separate, in Royal Commission on Pelagic Sealing, Victoria, Indian Claims, Dec. 1913, vol. 8, 135, in Crockford, "Changing Economic Activities," 43. The Department of Fisheries Annual Reports in Canada, *SP*, record the number of aboriginal people involved in pelagic sealing, 1882–1910.

66 Canada, *SP*, 1888, 13, 106; Cracroft, *Lady Franklin Visits the Pacific Northwest*, 79, W.F. Tolmie wrote in 1883 that the aboriginal women in Victoria worked "as washerwomen, seamstresses and laundresses, earn much and spend it all in the city," BCARS A/E/Or3/C15.

67 Canada, *SP*, 1884, 106; Carmichael, "Account of a Season's Work"; Indian women "knit" nets that "will average from 120–150 fathoms [long and 16 and a half feet deep], at the cost of one dollar per fathom," *Resources of British Columbia* 1 (1 Dec. 1883).

68 By 1865 the Victoria police were writing the colonial secretary that some 200 Indian prostitutes lived "in filthy shanties owned by Chinese and rented . . . at four to five dollars a month," in Peter Baskerville, *Beyond the Island: An Illustrated History of Victoria* (Windsor, ON, 1986), 39–44. For the 1880s see John A. Macdonald, Canada, *SP*, 1885, lix. For an aboriginal account of prostitution, see Franz Boas, *Contribution to the Ethnography of the Kwakiutl* (New York, 1925), 93–94.

69 Fiske, "Fishing is Women's Business," 186–97.

70 J.M. Yale, 1852, in Mackie, "Colonial Land, Indian Labour, and Company Capital," 89.

71 J.A. McDonald, "Images of the Nineteenth–Century Economy of the Tsimshian" in *The Tsimshian: Images of the Past, Views for the Present*, ed. M. Seguin (Vancouver, 1984), 49.

72 Philip Drucker, *Cultures of the North Pacific Coast* (New York, 1965), 129; Fisher, *Contact and Conflict*, 47–48.

73 Duff, *Indian History of British Columbia*, 55.

74 There is an enormous ethnographic literature on the potlatch; a good bibliography can be found in D. Cole and I. Chaikin, *An Iron Hand upon the People* (Vancouver, 1990), 213–23.

75 Fisher, *Contact and Conflict*; Duff, *Indian History of British Columbia*; Cole and Chaikin, *An Iron Hand upon the People*; Helen Codere, *Fighting with Property: A Study of Kwakiutl Potlatching and Warfare, 1792–1930* (Seattle, 1966).

76 Drucker and Heizer, *To Make My Name Good*, 15.

77 Fisher, *Contact and Conflict*, 27–49.

78 This is particularly true of the West Coast people, and to a lesser extent, those of the interior.

79 Thomas Lowe, *Colonist* (Victoria), 29 Oct. 1897; Paul Kane, *Wanderings of an Artist* (Edmonton, 1968), 145.

80 CO 305/4, 12345, Douglas to Colonial Secretary, 24 Oct. 1853; Margaret Ormsby states that when the Haidas were unable to mine gold on the Queen Charlotte Islands for lack of tools they offered to sell their rights if the HBC would form an establishment, Bowsfield, *Fort Victoria Letters*, xci.

81 Canada, *SP*, 1881, 5, 143. This was also the wish of the Kincolith people of the Nass River, NA, RG10, vol. 11007, W.H. Collinson to the Reserve Commissioner, 10 Oct. 1887.

82 CO 305/4, 12345, Douglas to Newcastle, 24 Oct. 1853.

83 Lenihan says that on reasoning with the chief he agreed to discontinue the potlatch and was given $80 in seeds. Canada, *SP*, 1877, 38.

84 George M. Grant, *Ocean to Ocean: Sir Sanford Fleming's Expedition Through Canada in 1872* (Toronto, 1873), 319–20; Knight has a similar story from a completely different source that seems to describe a response to Big George's potlatch by a rival, *Indians at Work*, 114; Capt. C.E. Barrett-Lennard, *Travels in British Columbia With the Narrative of A Yacht Voyage Round Vancouver's Island* (London, 1862), 60.

85 Ford, *Smoke from Their Fires*, 54–55.

86 James Sewid, *Guest Never Leave Hungry: The Autobiography of a Kwakiutl Indian*, ed. James Spradley (Kingston, 1989), 27; Victoria Wyatt, "Alaskan Indian Wage Earners in the 19th Century," *Pacific Northwest Quarterly* 78 (1987): 43–49.

87 "The Kwakiutl had a potential demand for European goods in excess of any practical utility the goods might have possessed. This can be seen both as a stimulus to the Kwakiutl integration in their new economy and as a direct stimulus to the potlatch," Codere, *Fighting with Property*, 126.

88 George Blenkinsop, Indian agent, and Rev. A.J. Hall cited in G.M. Dawson, "Notes and Observations on the Kwakiool People of Vancouver Island and Adjacent Coasts made during the Summer of 1885," *Transactions of the Royal Society of Canada*, sec. 2 (1887): 17.

89 Codere, *Fighting with Property*, 124; Harry Assu with Joy Inglis, *Assu of Cape Mudge: Recollections of a Coastal Indian Chief* (Vancouver, 1989), 39.

90 Canada, *SP*, 1882, 160, 170; Canada, *SP*, 1885, 3, 101; Brink, *The Haida Indians*, 42; Hinks, *From Potlatch to Pulpit*, 126.

91 Another indication of this is that traditional raiding of enemies was performed en route to and from their seasonal wage labour until the early 1860s; see for example CO 305/7, 9708, Douglas to Labouchere, 26 Aug. 1856; CO 305/8, 7950, 13 June 1857; CO 305/10, 6949, 25 July 1859.

92 Codere, *Fighting with Property*, 126.

93 Cole and Chaikin, *An Iron Hand upon the People*, 19–20.

94 With the acceptance of Christianity, "modified potlatching" continued in some places, but the new Christians also had new imperatives to work. New houses built with milled lumber, nails, and glass windows, as well as new standards for clothing, contributions to build a church, or the purchase of musical instruments, etc., all demanded cash incomes.

95 Although the Kwakwaka'wakw proved an exception in this regard.

THE KNIGHTS OF LABOR AND THE SALVATION ARMY: Religion and Working-Class Culture in Ontario, 1882–1890*

LYNNE MARKS

In 1883 the Salvation Army marched on Kingston. Intense excitement pervaded the town, with the Army hall packed night after night. As was the case in towns and cities across Ontario, most of the men and women who flocked to the Salvation Army's tumultuous all-night meetings and rowdy parades were working-class. In Kingston, working-class involvement is seen most vividly in reports that in the town's major factories, "noon day prayer meetings amongst the working men are established . . . and conducted by the men themselves."[1] By 1887 a very different working-class movement gripped the same workplaces. Workers at Kingston's Victoria Foundry, the Locomotive Works, and the cotton mill, who had organized Salvation Army prayer meetings four years earlier, now had joined the Knights of Labor (K of L). In May 1887, they were out on strike.[2]

Both the Knights of Labor, a major working-class organization, and the Salvation Army, which in this period was an exclusively revivalistic movement, drew mass support from Ontario's working class. It is no coincidence that both movements appeared in the 1880s and saw their period of greatest strength in this decade. Industrialization first emerged in Ontario

*Reprinted with the permission of the editor of *Labour/Le Travail* 28 (Fall 1991), pp. 89–127. © Committee on Canadian Labour History.

after mid-century, but was not well established until the 1870s and, more particularly, the 1880s. In tiny villages and small towns across the province, as well as in larger centres, industrial wagework had become a way of life for many Ontarians.[3]

The existence of a class of people who sell their labour power to survive, a working class, does not necessarily mean that these people will identify themselves as a separate class. Historians have argued that when members of a class share distinct values, interests, and lifestyles—what some have termed a culture—they tend more readily to identify themselves with this class.[4] In *Dreaming of What Might Be*, the major study of the Knights of Labor in Ontario, authors Greg Kealey and Bryan Palmer have argued that the Knights, if only fleetingly, provided Ontario workers with a distinct "movement culture," which drew on working-class values and beliefs. One aspect of working-class belief that received minimal attention in their study was religion, which was central to the dominant culture of nineteenth-century Ontario. While Kealey and Palmer acknowledged that religion was not irrelevant to the Knights, they downplayed its significance.[5] The mass popularity of the Salvation Army, which provided a distinct working-class religious alternative in the 1880s, strengthens arguments regarding the existence of working-class culture, but also forces us to recognize that religion was integral to the lives of many Ontario workers.

This paper examines the role of religion within the Knights of Labor and the Salvation Army, assessing its relationship to working-class values, beliefs, and culture. Canadian historians' failure to examine religion within the Knights of Labor and their lack of interest in the Salvation Army may be linked to a broader reluctance among both religious historians and working-class historians to explore the subject of religion and the working class.[6] The majority of Canadian religious historians have focussed on either institutional histories of the development of Canadian churches, or histories of religious ideas.[7] The relationship between religion and labour has been studied only in terms of the social gospel movement, with historians focussing on the attitudes of middle-class social gospellers towards the working class, rather than on the working class itself.[8] English Canadian labour historians have also neglected the religious dimensions of male and female workers' lives, choosing instead to study workplace experience and union activism.[9] Those few historians who have examined working-class participation in non-workplace activities have focussed on leisure rather than religion.[10] The reluctance of religious historians to examine workers' religious experience can be traced to a lack of interest in class-based issues, while the explanation for labour historians' lack of interest may lie in their thoroughly secular outlook. Labour historians may also have avoided this topic from a sense that any working-class religious involvement was imposed on workers as part of a middle-class strategy of social control, and could only sully the purity of a distinct working-class culture and retard the development of class consciousness.

This paper will argue that religion was important to many Ontario workers, but that religious involvement among workers cannot in itself be viewed as evidence that workers completely accepted the dominant cultural system, in which Christian belief and practice played such a major role. Many of the same Christian beliefs professed by middle-class Canadians did appear to have been important to the workers who joined the Knights of Labor and the Salvation Army. However, as we will see through this study of religion within the two movements, these beliefs could be used by workers to help them stake out an independent respected place for themselves within an increasingly unequal society, and could also fuel a working-class critique of this society.

In examining the Knights and the Army at the local level, this study will focus particularly (but not exclusively) on small-town Ontario, since despite the significant level of industrialization in these centres, we know very little about working-class life here.[11] Historians and contemporaries alike have pointed to an apparent working-class shift away from the churches within the large cities. We have few insights, however, into the nature of religious life in smaller centres, beyond the monolithic image of dour and devout small-town Protestant Ontario.

• Origins and Membership

The Salvation Army began in London, England, in 1878, but emerged from an earlier organization known as the Christian Mission, founded in 1865 by William Booth, a former Methodist preacher. The dominant principle in Booth's life was said to be the need to convert the poorest groups in society, who were generally untouched by the churches.[12] While Booth's earliest efforts were based in traditions of Methodist revivalism, his work soon became distinctive through his willingness to use a variety of unconventional methods to reach the poor. A key method was the adoption of military organization and military trappings. Army structure was firmly hierarchical, with all members being expected to obey the orders of superior officers. Supreme power was vested in Booth, who as General commanded an Army which by the 1880s had spread around the world. The Army's military trappings included brass bands and uniforms, as well as a distinctive vocabulary in which prayer services were called "knee drills" and saying "Amen" was known as "firing a volley." Those who joined the Salvation Army after conversion were known as "soldiers"; preachers were called "officers" and congregations were "corps." In the 1880s the English Salvation Army was already involved in the social rescue work for which Booth's legions were to become famous. It must be emphasized, however, that in this decade the Canadian Salvation Army was very different from the present-day "Sally Ann" in that it remained almost exclusively a revivalistic movement, and focussed on saving souls through preaching rather than through social service.[13]

The K of L's origins are better known. This organization, which combined struggles to improve workers' conditions at the local level with a broader critique of industrial capitalist society, was founded in 1869 in Philadelphia by Uriah S. Stephens. Within the Knights, workers were organized into Local Assemblies (LAs) either by trade or as mixed assemblies. LA meetings incorporated ritual similar to that of the numerous nineteenth-century fraternal orders, while assemblies also provides various educational and social activities for their members. LAs were led by locally elected Master Workmen, while the overall leader of the Order was the Grand Master Workman, based in the United States. In the 1880s, the annual General Assembly of the Order regularly re-elected Terence V. Powderly to this position.

Although the Knights organized a secret assembly in Hamilton in 1875, both movements arrived publicly in Canada in 1882. In this year the Knights organized a number of local assemblies, including the Hamilton Painters Alliance LA 1852, and mixed assemblies like St Catharines Fidelity LA 2056 and Ingersoll's Pioneer Assembly 2416.[14] Kealey and Palmer suggest that links with the nearby United States, where the Knights already were fairly strong, help to explain the formation of the earliest Ontario LAs.[15]

A similar pattern emerges in the case of the Salvation Army. In 1882, Army services were begun in both London and Toronto by recent English immigrants, who had been converted in England. While these meetings were not officially sanctioned by Army Headquarters in England, General Booth soon sent American Army officers to Toronto to institute an official corps there and to commission those who had begun the meetings as full-time officers.[16]

It is difficult to compare the popular impact of the two movements, given their very different natures. Newspaper reports make it clear that when the Army first entered many Ontario towns, hundreds and sometimes thousands would rush to Army meetings.[17] Often the majority of the audience were curiosity seekers. But at least some of "those who came to scoff remained to pray," and the Army did make many converts. Some converts returned to the mainstream churches, but many became soldiers—the Army's equivalent of church members. The most conservative estimates of Salvation Army impact thus would be based on the number of Army soldiers. Measurement of Knights of Labor popularity have been based on membership tallies.

Membership in both organizations was extremely volatile. Although Salvation Army officers were instructed not to enroll converts as members until they were sure of the seriousness of an individual's conversion, the limited local evidence suggests that the majority of soldiers did not remain in the Army for more than three to four years, while many "backslid" much sooner, as was common in revival movements which focussed on conversion.[18] K of L membership was at least as volatile, with many remaining in the Order only during the peak 1886–87 period. Kealey and Palmer argue that in Ontario "over the course of their history the Knights organized a minimum of 21 800 members."[19] An opponent of the Army recognized that at its height in 1885–86 the Army had enrolled 25 000 soldiers, mainly in Ontario, but by 1889, it was reduced to 9000 soldiers across the country.[20] Certainly by the time of the 1891 census, just over 10 000 Ontarians are listed as Salvationists, and this, of course would include the children of adult soldiers.[21]

The basis for comparing the geographical strength of the Knights and the Army is again problematical. For an assembly of the Knights to exist in a particular centre, it required the active support of at least a core of members. The Salvation Army could claim to have a corps in a particular town simply by sending two officers there. Nevertheless, there are ways of determining the relative strength of the Army in different centres. Despite the fact that the 1891 census was taken several years after the peak of Army popularity, an analysis of the proportion of Salvationists in local communities in 1891 can provide some insights, particularly when linked to other indices of Army support.[22] As in the case of the Knights, local newspapers occasionally provide evidence of the Army's numerical strength.[23] Since Army officers were recruited from among soldiers, analysing the geographical origins of officers who joined up between 1882 and 1890 can provide further evidence of the relative enthusiasm the Army engendered in different locations.[24]

Both the Knights and the Army were successful in cities like Hamilton, Toronto, London, and Kingston. Although S.D. Clark, one of the few Canadian students of the Salvation Army, has characterized the movement primarily as a big-city phenomenon, the Army, like the K of L, was also successful in many smaller centres.[25] The Salvation Army had corps in most of the towns and villages where Knights assemblies existed (57 out of 74). The Army appears to have enjoyed considerable popularity within at least 36 of these communities.[26] The Army also established corps in many towns and villages where the Knights had no foothold. While the Army did not thrive in all of these communities, at least 32 show evidence of local support. The proportion of the population in the industrial work force tended to be as great in these communities as it was in those that welcomed both the Knights and the Army. On average, however, industrial establishments were smaller in towns which only supported the Army, suggesting that these communities were not at the forefront of industrialization. Communities that welcomed the Army but not the Knights also tended to be less populous, with more than 40 percent having fewer than 1500 inhabitants. Some small communities, like Bothwell and Dresden, reflect especially fervent support for the Salvation Army, with almost 1 percent of their populations becoming officers. Small communities which did not contain a significant number of Army supporters were not financially viable, and many of these corps were disbanded during the 1890s.[27]

In certain Knights of Labor strongholds, the Salvation Army appears to have had little success. This was the case in the Niagara area (outside of

St Catharines) and in the communities surrounding Ottawa.[28] In other areas, however, where the Knights of Labor attracted a large proportion of the town's work force, the Salvation Army also did very well. This was particularly true in the region immediately east of Toronto and in Western Ontario. In the small town of Ingersoll, the Salvation Army claimed to have converted almost 700 people in 1883, while hundreds more had attended its parades and services.[29] The Knights of Labor, which arrived in town a year earlier, also developed a significant presence over the next few years, sponsoring balls and lectures, and organizing a mass celebration on Dominion Day 1887. In the oil producing town of Petrolia crowds flocked to Salvation Army meetings in 1884; more than 200 became soldiers in the Army's first year, while only a year later 500 townspeople joined the local Knights of Labor assembly.[30] In other K of L towns—such as Woodstock, Seaforth, Chatham, Lindsay, and Belleville—the Army attracted large crowds, while in each town more than twenty soldiers were sufficiently committed to the Army to take up careers as full-time officers.[31] This compares quite favourably with the numbers of officers recruited in larger centres such as London (32), Hamilton (47), and Kingston (21).

At this point, the reader may wonder if there was any overlap between the K of L and Army memberships. This question is very difficult to answer directly, given the lack of local membership lists. Very few such lists exist for the Salvation Army, while none have been discovered for the Knights.[32] Yet less-direct evidence does suggest that the two movements' support-bases were not wholly distinct. Workers at Kingston's three largest factories became actively involved in both organizations, organizing Salvation Army prayer-meetings and Knights of Labor strikes. There is also some evidence to suggest that ironworkers belonging to a Belleville local assembly attended Army meetings.[33] A closer look at the class-bases of these movements provides further clues about the probable extent of their overlap in membership.

Although some small merchants and employers joined the Knights of Labor, the Order was primarily a working-class organization. Skilled workers appear to have dominated the leadership of the movement even at the local level, and many LAs were organized on the basis of craft skills.[34] However, the K of L was the first major labour organization that attempted to organize all workers regardless of skill level, and there were many unskilled workers within various mixed assemblies. Unlike earlier trade unions, the K of L was also open to women, who organized both within mixed assemblies and in separate women's assemblies. Kealey and Palmer have estimated that women were involved in at least 10 percent of Ontario locals.[35]

The Salvation Army was also primarily a working-class movement. Newspaper reports such as that of the *Toronto Mail* reported that Salvation Army soldiers "are chiefly working people, who give what little leisure they have to helping the cause. . . . "[36] An examination of three surviving converts' rolls for the 1887–1900 period further reinforces this evidence. In all three corps women made up slightly more than half of all converts, and over half of all women for whom an occupation was listed were servants (see tables 1 and 2). In the small towns of Petrolia and Listowel, just over half of all male converts were labourers, while most of the rest worked in a variety of skilled or semi-skilled jobs.[37] Only in rural Feversham did the Army draw a significant number of farmer converts (see table 2).

Table 1: SEX OF SALVATION ARMY CONVERTS IN SELECTED CORPS, 1887–1900*

Sex	Petrolia**		Listowel**		Feversham**	
	Number	%	Number	%	Number	%
Men	236	46	129	47	65	44
Women	274	54	144	53	84	56
Total	510	100	273	100	149	100

Source: Corps Records, Salvation Army Archives, Toronto.
*These are the only corps for which converts' rolls have survived for this period.
**Petrolia and Listowel both had populations of under 5000 in this period, while Feversham was a very small rural community.

Table 2: OCCUPATIONS OF SALVATION ARMY CONVERTS IN SELECTED CORPS, 1887–1900*

			Women			
Occupation	Petrolia		Listowel		Feversham	
	Number	%	Number	%	Number	%
At home	39	39	22	31	24	48
Dressmaker	4	4	1	1		
Servant	52	52	38	53	26	52
Other	5	5	11	15		
Total	100	100	72	100	50	100

			Men			
Occupation	Petrolia		Listowel		Feversham	
	Number	%	Number	%	Number	%
Clerk	3	2	1	1		
Skilled Worker	24	18	14	16	1	2
Semi-skilled	12	9	1	1		
Labourer**	83	60	51	59	23	41
Farmer	9	7	16	12	31	55
Other	6	4	4	5	1	2
Total	137	100	87	100	56	100

Source: Corps Records, Salvation Army Archives, Toronto.
*These are the only corps for which converts' rolls appear to have survived for this period. This table does not include those converts for whom occupation was not reported
**Including farm labourers (only in Feversham was this a significant group).

Information on the occupations of the 1228 officers who entered the Army in Ontario during the period 1882–90 provides further evidence of the class background of Army members, since officers were recruited from the membership and in the early years of the movement there appear to have been few barriers to soldiers becoming officers. As was the case with converts, over half (55 percent) of all officers were female. These women, almost all of whom were single, were far more likely to be employed than the average single woman.[38] Almost 40 percent had been domestic servants prior to entering the Army, while most of the rest were employed in traditionally feminine working-class jobs[39] (see table 3). More than 40 percent of male officers had been skilled workers prior to entering the Army. A wide range of skilled trades, traditional and more representative of the emerging industrial age, are found among male officers (see table 4). Another one-quarter of male officers had been employed in other working-class occupations, while the remaining third were primarily farmers (at 23 percent) with a small number of businessmen and a more significant representation of clerks (see table 3). The class background of officers demonstrates clearly that the Army did not simply attract working-class followers, but also had a predominantly working-class leadership.[40]

The occupational differences between converts and officers do suggest that officers may have come from a slightly higher strata within the working class than converts. Surviving converts' rolls, however, may not be representative of Army membership across Ontario. The information gleaned from the officers' roll suggests that in larger and more industrialized towns the Army attracted more skilled workers than it did in Petrolia, Listowel, or Feversham. It is also true, however, that the Army was popular in many smaller, less-industrialized communities. In such communities the Army would have attracted many non-industrial workers such as servants, labourers, and farm labourers.

The Salvation Army appears to have drawn in more of the unskilled and of the non-industrial work force than did the Knights of Labor. The Army also attracted many more women. The different composition of Salvation Army support meant that the Army was popular in many towns that remained untouched by the Knights. Even in towns that attracted both movements they would have drawn on somewhat different groups. For example, in many communities in which working-class husbands and fathers were active in the Knights, their wives and daughters may have found the Army more appealing.

While the Salvation Army and the Knights did attract somewhat different working-class populations, it is also true that both movements included skilled and unskilled workers, women and men. At the rank-and-file level, then, there may have been some overlap between the two movements. In the American context Kenneth Fones-Wolf has noted that the strong Christian faith of the majority of American workers led many to see no contradiction between union membership and even union activism, and involvement in fundamentalist Christianity.[41] It is reasonable to assume that this may also have been true in Canada.

The volatility of membership in the K of L and the Army means that even if few workers were simultaneously Knights and soldiers, many more may have been touched by both movements over the course of the 1880s. This is most likely truest in towns like Woodstock, Petrolia, and Gananoque, where the Army was strong and where Kealey and Palmer suggest that a large proportion of the work force was involved in the Knights.[42] In these small communities, many Knights (or potential Knights) probably would have been attracted to the popular Salvation Army services. At such services some may have been converted, and made the decision to join the Army.

Table 3: OCCUPATIONS OF ONTARIO SALVATION ARMY OFFICERS UPON BECOMING OFFICERS, BY SEX, 1882–90*

Women	Number	%
At home	137	28
Clerks	10	2
Nurses	7	1
Teachers	16	3
Dressmakers/tailoresses/milliners**	98	20
Factory workers	37	8
Servants	186	38
Other	2	–
Total	493	100

Men	Number	%
At home	2	–
Businessmen/professionals	14	4
Clerks	31	8
Teachers	4	1
Farmers	91	23
Skilled workers/artisans◊	164	41
Semi-skilled workers	22	6
Factory workers	30	7
Labourers/unskilled	39	10
Servants	6	2
Total	403	100

Source: Officers' Rolls, Salvation Army Archives, Toronto.
*Includes only those officers who joined up in Ontario, not those transferred from England or from elsewhere in Canada.
**Some of these women probably worked in factories, but this is impossible to determine.
◊Some of these men may have been self-employed, or even small masters, while many probably worked in factories. The roll only provided occupational titles.

Table 4:   SELECTED OCCUPATIONS OF MALE OFFICERS WHO HAD BEEN SKILLED
            WORKERS/ARTISANS*

Occupation	Number	%
Baker	9	6
Blacksmith	11	7
Butcher	6	4
Carpenter	16	10
Harness maker	6	4
Moulder	5	3
Machinist/millwright	5	3
Painter	12	7
Printer	11	7
Railwayworker**	9	6
Shoemaker	6	4
Tailor	8	5
Tinsmith	7	4
Total	164◊	

Source: Officers' Rolls, Salvation Army Archives, Toronto.
*Occupations listed are those held by five or more officers.
**Includes brakemen, engineers, and not specified.
◊Includes all male skilled workers, not just those listed above.

• Christianity and the Knights

The extent to which Knights of Labor were involved in the Salvation Army is likely to remain a fascinating but largely unanswerable question. An assessment of the role played by Christianity within the Noble and Holy Order of the Knights of Labor, however, may make any possible overlap more explicable by demonstrating the importance of Christianity both to the Order and to the workers who joined it. In *Dreaming of What Might Be,* Kealey and Palmer do note that religious zeal was part of the residual culture out of which the K of L fashioned their distinct "movement culture." However, this religious legacy merits very brief mention in their study of the Order. A closer look at this issue suggests that religion was more central both to the ideology of the Order and to the lives of individual Knights than historians have acknowledged.

Religious issues certainly were not absent from the K of L press. Newspapers were careful to avoid sectarian controversy, noting that such conflict only served to divide the working class.[43] However, the Hamilton-based *Palladium of Labor,* the Ontario K of L's principal newspaper, regularly contained reports of various sermons, both supportive of and opposed to the labour movement, with appropriate editorial commentary. The churches were not irrelevant here—their attacks were responded to while their support was applauded. The *Palladium*'s "Local News" department periodically reported on the social and religious activities of various Hamilton churches, most commonly featuring the working-class Primitive Methodist church and the Salvation Army.

In Canadian and American labour papers alike, journalists frequently expressed their hostility to the current economic system in terms of Christian belief which they obviously assumed that their readers shared. The rhetoric identified here reinforces Herbert Gutman's argument in "Protestantism and the American Labor Movement" that while many Gilded Age labour leaders had little respect for the church, their profound belief in Christianity fuelled their battles for social justice.[44] For example, a poem in the *Journal of United Labor* proclaimed: "We'll fight in this great holy war till we die/ No longer in silence we'll whimper and sigh/ No longer we'll cringe at the proud tyrant's nod/ But defy him, and fight 'neath the banner of God . . . King Labor is ruler of earth of God's word."[45] The *Palladium* is also full of the kind of religious rhetoric identified by Gutman. The editor was particularly fond of arguing that true Christianity was allied with the workers' cause. He frequently pointed out that "the doctrines of Jesus Christ, the carpenter—who would have been called a tramp and a Communist had he lived in these days—if applied to the present conditions would solve the question satisfactorily."[46] Christ was also described as "the greatest social reformer that ever lived. He had nothing but words of bitter scorn and scathing indignation for the idle and luxurious classes who oppressed the poor."[47]

In assessing similar rhetoric within the Canadian labourist tradition, Craig Heron concludes that "the crucial question remains whether working-class leaders got their politics from Christianity, or turned to a common cultural reservoir to express their politics."[48] This question could perhaps be put less starkly. The material deprivation which workers experienced and saw around them no doubt provided the primary basis for their opposition to the capitalist system. But, in the K of L's case at least, it seems that the religious imagery used did not merely reflect a routine acceptance of the dominant mode of discourse, but that it was based in fact, as Gutman suggests, on strongly held Christian beliefs. In the American context, Kenneth Fones-Wolf has argued that Christianity was at the core of the Knights' cultural system and that "a deep religious inspiration and a commitment to Christian beliefs pervaded the Order's distinctly working-class program."[49] The Knights' Christian beliefs probably did not kindle their anger against the capitalist system, but the disparity between the Christian message and nineteenth-century capitalism would have fuelled such anger.[50]

The significance of Christianity and of the churches to the Knights of Labor is also revealed through a brief look at K of L activities within certain small communities. Kealey and Palmer argue in their book that "there is evidence that in many communities the Knights of Labor usurped the traditional role of the church."[51] At the local level, no evidence has been found to substantiate the interpretation that the Knights, by acting as a kind of "secular church," came to replace the mainstream churches for small-town workers. The evidence cited by Kealey and Palmer points instead to the attendance of LA members at local ministers' special sermons on topics related to Christianity and the Knights of Labor.[52] The attendance by the Knights in a body at such sermons in towns like Ingersoll and Merritton parallels the annual attendance of fraternal orders like the Orangemen and the Oddfellows at their own special sermons.[53] On such occasions, the fraternal orders would march in a body to the church to hear a sermon that would interpret the activities of the particular order in Christian terms. This annual ritual of collective church attendance asserted these fraternal orders' position within the respectable culture of the town, which was most clearly symbolized by the institution of the church and the dominant ideology of Christianity.

The Knights' attendance at such sermons suggests that the Order was not usurping the role of the church in the local communities. The leaders of the Ingersoll Knights, who requested that the town's Presbyterian minister preach a sermon on a labour topic, probably saw that as with the fraternal associations, collective attendance at church would assert the Order's position within the respectable culture of the town.[54] Evidence for Ingersoll and Thorold (and from Kealey and Palmer's study) demonstrates that some K of L leaders also were officials in various fraternal associations, making the adoption of this ritual by the Order even more explicable. While there is still much more to learn about working-class church attendance, we do know that within some small towns, workers—particularly skilled workers—were often church members.[55] The forging of links with the churches thus may have also been viewed as a way of reassuring potential Knights that involvement with the Order would not conflict with their religious belief or involvement.

The Knights' march into the local church thus symbolizes their links to the dominant, respectable Christian culture. Like the Knights' dances, concerts, strawberry socials, and Dominion Day celebrations, which in their external form are patterned on standard components of local respectable culture, it may also mean something more. The speeches delivered at these social activities may reflect the Knights' alternative vision; what they also demonstrate are workers organizing for themselves, and in their own interests, events which in the past had been dominated by the local middle class.

Workers who were church members worshipped within churches dominated by the local elite. When they were officials within local fraternal orders, they shared such positions with local merchants and professionals. However, when they marched into church as part of the Knights of Labor contingent they were not simply members of another fraternal order. They were part of an organization of working-class townspeople who were asserting their class identity and their equal place within the dominant respectable culture. They did not want to reject Christianity, but neither did they wish to remain any longer in the galleries of the local churches.

Leon Fink has argued that the Order did not oppose many aspects of the dominant culture of respectability, but instead sought to assert working people's place within this culture, in the face of declining working-class living standards and increasing middle-class pretensions.[56] What Fink and other historians have been less interested in exploring is the extent to which this assertion of respectable "manly" equality and independence included the acceptance of an active role within the dominant religious institutions of the community.

In proclaiming themselves full and equal members of respectable Christian culture, the Knights could then go on to assert their rights on this culture's own terms, as they clearly did in the Ontario small towns of Petrolia and Thorold. In 1888 the federal government permitted the opening of the Welland Canal on Sundays for a few hours in the morning and the evening. Mountain Assembly No. 6798 of Thorold unanimously passed a resolution condemning this action, declaring "that such order will conflict with both the social and religious liberty of many of our members who are the servants of the government and as such will be compelled to perform duties which their consciences cannot approve of."[57] In Petrolia, it apparently was common for certain companies to operate their oil wells on Sundays. Soon after the Knights of Labor arrived in town they sent a letter to all offending companies requesting that they cease this practice. The grounds on which they made this demand are worth quoting. "The laws of both God and man demand the due observance of the Lord's day, and the moral sentiment of the entire community. . . . It is believed that it is only necessary to appeal to the respect and reverence which, living as you do in an enlightened and Christian community, you must feel for God's law . . . in order to secure your unhesitating consent to this reasonable request of your fellow citizens."[58] No mention was made of the men affected by this request. It was only the editorial in the *Petrolia Advertiser* (not a particularly pro-labour paper) which, in supporting the Knights' letter, pointed out that "[the] most powerful reason why this should be done is that a large number of men, greatly against their wishes, in violation of conscience and in opposition to their sense of moral right, are compelled either to violate the laws of both God and man and desecrate the Lord's day, or be discharged from their situation and thus deprived of the means of earning an honest livelihood."[59]

Why did the Knights press their demand against Sunday labour largely in religious terms? Was this simply a matter of tactics, a recognition that only an appeal to religious sentiment would be effective here? This would certainly be part of the answer. Phillips Thompson argued in the *Palladium* that "It is only that sacred character [of Sunday] which has secured to the working men the invaluable boon of a respite from toil in one day out of seven. . . . Only the religious sanction was powerful enough to interpose this barrier between the insensate greed of the money power and the rights of the toilers."[60] While tactical concerns no doubt played a role here, it is also important to recognize that at the local level most Knights probably accepted the dominant Christian values. But, in affirming that everyone had a right to the religious liberty and day of rest ordained "by God's law," they were using such values to affirm the dignity and worth of all, within the context of communities characterized by hierarchy and inequality.[61]

While ministers allied themselves with the Knights in battles over Sabbath observance, several of the sermons preached to K of L audiences, or more generally on the topic of "Capital and Labour," reinforce the popular impression that the church was not sympathetic to Knights' efforts to combat inequality. While the "large number of knights" present at the Pine Street Methodist church in the industrial village of Merritton to hear a sermon by a Rev. Mr. Snider "seemed very much pleased with the discourse,"[62] their brother and sister Knights in neighbouring Thorold had much less to be pleased about in the sermon by the Methodist minister Rev. Lanceley. Lanceley preached a strongly anti-labour sermon. "Let me warn you" he thundered "against the cry of 'our rights' it will spread like a fever. . . . It is an inflammation, a burning, that is set on fire of hell." He said that capital and labour should make common cause together and warned against discontent and covetousness, telling his listeners that "God will reward the meek and trusting spirit with its own reward."[63] Not all sermons were so extreme but few provided wholehearted support. Although the Rev. T. Atkinson of Ingersoll cautiously praised the aims of the K of L, he also talked of the interdependence of all classes and the need for capitalists not to oppress labourers and for labourers to obey their masters.[64]

Local Knights who subscribed to the *Palladium* would have pointed out to their sisters and brothers after the service that the minister preached in this way because he was under the influence of the local elite who paid his salary. One frequently saw in the labour press variations on the argument that "the paid teachers of Christianity dare not quote the Biblical denunciations of land grabbers, usurers and oppressers of the poor, and apply them personally to wealthy supporters of the church. If they did they would soon preach themselves out of their pulpit."[65]

The message of such preachers may have led some labour activists to reject not simply the church, but Christianity itself. The *Palladium* argued that "There is no cause which has contributed in greater measure to the spread of rationalistic views and the indifference to popular religionism which paves the way for full blown Secularism, than the manner in which modern so-called Christianity has become identified with wealth, position and power."[66] There clearly were freethinkers within the Order. One of the arguments put forward by T.V. Powderly in asserting that Local Assemblies should not begin or end their meetings with prayer was that "we have members who believe that the dancing of a jig would be as appropriate as the use of prayer."[67]

One must be careful, however, not to exaggerate the extent to which the Knights and labour reform generally were associated with secularism. In response to a letter asking Powderly to issue a circular stating that the word God in the Knights of Labor ritual (the Adelphon Kruptos) meant Good, Powderly responded that "the being whom God created with so little sense as to deny His existence is a fool. He may, if he chooses, have a spite against God for not furnishing him with a full stock of wit; but he should not ask others [who have] to take sides with him against their Maker."[68] Powderly may have been more conservative than many of his followers, but closer to home the *Palladium* also attacked freethought. When one member of the "Social Club" featured in *the Palladium* said that he was starting to move towards freethought, since freethinkers "are not always on the side of oppression and tyranny as religion is," Freeman, who spoke for the author, agreed that many modern ministers were self-serving hypocrites but argued that he was "confounding two different things. True religion is never on the side of tyranny."[69]

Labour activists also denied that freethought was particularly common among workers. In assessing the reasons why increasing numbers of working people were staying away from the churches, the *Palladium* recognized that "'infidelity/ . . . may have something to do with it," but argued it could be much more readily linked to the fact that "many of our places of worship have become simply Sunday Clubs or opera halls, intended to attract rich congregations, where the poor are neither invited nor welcomed."[70] A letter to the *Palladium* similarly argued that workers were not becoming freethinkers and that "the muscle and sinew of Hamilton still pins its hope of emancipation to the doctrine preached from the cross," while pointing out that if workers no longer attended church it was because the church has allied itself with capital against labour, and that ministers who dared alienate their wealthy parishioners by preaching the Bible's true pro-labour message would bring workers back into the churches.[71]

A letter from "Well Wisher" states that he had once attended church regularly but "for want of that brotherly society and sympathy fell away" and found the "human love and desire to help my fellow man" which was missing from the churches through his involvement in the Knights of Labor. Kealey and Palmer use this letter to buttress their argument that for many workers the Knights displaced the church.[72] While this is a fascinating argument and probably was true for some workers, we must be careful here. Even "Well Wisher," who had found brotherly love in the Knights, still sought something more and "would fain cry out with thousands of my fellow workmen, O for a warm kindly Christ like church, a common plane where we could all meet on an equality and be brothers in Christ in this world, even as we hope to be in the next."[73]

At the local level we have seen that the Knights did not appear to replace the churches, but used them to legitimate the Order's position within the local community. The *Palladium* also provides evidence that many Knights remained reluctant to abandon the churches. In response to a minister who preached against the labour movement that "this democratic spirit scoffs at religion," the *Palladium* responded that "this is merely an assertion without any argument whatever to bear it out. Our churches are as well attended—with perhaps one exception (the Centenary) as they were before we had any organization among our work people."[74] In describing female Knights at the Dundas Cotton Mills, the reporter noted that these women "go to make up the well dressed congregation in some of the churches."[75]

Assertions that the Knights did indeed go to church may have been intended partly to provide a respectable counter-image to the common portrayal of labour activists as Godless, bomb-throwing anarchists. However, such assertions also reflected a reality that labour historians have been reluctant to recognize. Workers were not isolated from the Christian-dominated world in which they lived. They sought an independent, respected place within it, and were as critical of churches where ministers preached the gospel of Mammon and relegated working people to the galleries as they were of the capitalist system which shaped such churches. This does not mean, however, that they abandoned Christianity, or the churches. On special occasions K of L assemblies marched in a body to local churches, asserting their equal participation within them, while many individual Knights appear to have attended church regularly. Many, and perhaps most of those who no longer attended church, still saw themselves as Christians. They shared with their middle-class contemporaries a belief in many basic Christian tenets, while also holding to distinct working-class values and beliefs, both religious and otherwise. In this context we have seen how Christian beliefs provided an important source, although certainly not the only source, of the Knights' challenge to the broader social and economic inequalities of Canadian society.

• The Salvation Army and the Working Class

The Knights of Labor was not the only working-class movement of the 1880s that used Christianity in its critique of the inequalities of contemporary society. As Engels pointed out in 1882, "the Salvation Army . . . revives the propaganda of early Christianity, appeals to the poor as the elect, fights capitalism in a religious way, and thus fosters an element of early Christian class antagonism, which one day may become troublesome to the well-to-do people who now find the ready money for it."[76] While Engels was describing the British Salvation Army, his insight is also relevant to the Salvation Army in Ontario, which in a variety of ways both promoted and fed into a certain form of class identity among Ontario Salvationists.

Like the Knights of Labor, the Salvation Army provided a very trenchant, class-based critique of the mainstream churches. The mere existence of the Salvation Army points to a belief that the churches had failed in their responsibility to minister to all classes. But many Salvationists and their supporters were much more explicit in opposing the churches. In the first few years after the Army's appearance in Ontario, local newspapers were filled with letters both attacking and defending the Army. The defence of the Army frequently included an attack on the churches as middle-class institutions which ignored Christ's true teachings. The letter from "Spectator" of Belleville is representative in this regard:

> Of all the denominations whose worship I have attended that which suffers least by comparison with the precepts and example of Christ is the Salvation Army.... As to the empty pews in the churches, they were so before the Army came to this city, and why? Because Sunday after Sunday they serve out the dry bones of sectarianism for the living truths of Christianity.... I see the haughty "Miss Shoddy" sweep up the aisle and recoil in poorly concealed discomfort lest her costly robes should touch the threadbare garments of some poor sinner who had the temerity to enter therein. I hear the doctrine of Dives preached in the name of Christ.... I see the Almighty blasphemed by the erection in His name of costly edifices, wherein are exclusive and costly people who worship in a costly style, while orphans cry for bread.[77]

"A Salvation Army Soldier" from Woodstock defended the Army which "reaches classes of people who have precious souls but whose burden of sin the clergy will not touch with even their little finger!" and attacked the "pew-renting and so-called respectable congregations of town and country, whose very respectability has crushed many a bruised reed."[78] James Smith, a London Salvationist, wrote of "the Salvation Army, who without money and without price are nobly bearing their crosses, fighting the Lord's battles; while the sluggish churches and overpaid ministry thereof have been asleep and drunken in their opulence."[79] Complaints from Ingersoll churchgoers make it clear that Captain Annie O'Leary preached a similar message, frequently attacking local ministers for being more interested in collecting their salaries than in saving the souls of the poor.[80]

The Salvation Army's class-based critique of the churches does echo in some ways that of the Knights, particularly in attacking the churches' emphasis on money and appearance to the exclusion of both the true word of God and the honest workingman. But for the Salvation Army the true sin here lies in the churches' neglect of the souls of the poor, while for the Knights it lay in the churches' refusal to speak out for workers' social and economic interests. An article by Commissioner Railton in the Army's *War Cry* makes explicit this focus on spiritual rather than temporal concerns, while at the same time drawing certain parallels between the two. Railton argued that as society is moving away from accepting "the sight of poor creatures toiling from early morning till late at night . . . for a few cents neither will religious society . . . tolerate the cold blooded existence of a Christian congregation, assembling twice or thrice a week for the worship of the Lord, and making no effort to make known His Salvation to thousands who are without it all around them."[81]

While the Ontario Salvation Army of the 1880s was largely unconcerned about the temporal welfare of the poor, its emphasis on spiritual equality and its willingness to appeal to the working class on their own ground attracted many Ontario workingmen and women. The Army's evangelical emphasis on the salvation of souls, with its assumption of spiritual equality, may have tapped into or strengthened an emerging class consciousness. The Army explicitly discouraged involvement in political movements, since its followers were to focus on the state of their own souls and the salvation of others. But, as historians such as E.P. Thompson and Bernard Semmel have argued in the case of other highly evangelical religious movements, the Army's message of spiritual equality could perhaps have spilled over into the secular realm, fuelling working-class anger at a society characterized by profound inequities.[82] At a minimum this message would have reinforced a sense of self-worth among the Army's working-class adherents, who were increasingly subordinated and devalued within the larger society.

In its focus on the equal value of all souls and in its acceptance of emotionally charged methods of bringing "the perishing" to salvation, the Army was very similar to earlier revival movements. By the 1880s, however, "emotionalism" had become anathema even among Ontario Methodists, who once had preached a "fire and brimstone" message across Upper Canada. By this period, middle-class Ontarians equated true religion with sedate church services, where they listened to rational learned sermons. Religion was respectable; indeed, was an integral element of respectability.[83] For this reason alone the intensely emotional appeal of Army services was interpreted as a class-based challenge to respectable middle-class churchgoing by middle class and working class alike.

While part of the Salvation Army's appeal to working-class people was its "blood and fire" revivalism, the Army's emotionalism was not all that distinguished it from respectable middle-class religion. Unlike earlier revivals, the Army drew explicitly on working-class popular culture as a means of attracting converts. The Army's methods included open-air meetings and parades, with colourful banners, the music of tambourines, triangles, and drums, the singing of hymns to the tunes of popular songs, and a variety of events, many of which were intended to provide a religious alternative to popular amusements, including Hallelujah Sprees, Popular Matinees, Hallelujah Picnics, Free and Easy Meetings, and Grand Tea Fights. A service in Kingston was advertised as "Superior to any show on earth" in an effort to compete with the visiting circus.[84] Some officers, like "Happy Bill" Cooper, who stood on his head and did cartwheels while preaching, clearly delivered on such advertising.

The Army's success attests to the efficacy of such methods. In pointing up the appeal of popular culture, it also suggests the distance of many Ontario workers from the more respectable culture to which the Knights' leadership sought to lay claim. In its own way, however, the Army's popularity does demonstrate a distinct class identity, a rejection of middle-class domination, and an assertion of working-class dignity and independence.

The periodic "Trades Meetings" in which all soldiers marched in their workday clothes, gives us a visual demonstration of the way in which the Salvation Army provided a space for workers to assert their distinct identity, as do the frequent advertisements that officers such as "Billy the Tinker," the "Happy Shoemaker," "Wright the Printer," and the "Hallelujah Blacksmith" would be featured at various Army events.[85] The Army's flouting of middle-class standards of respectability which marginalized the language of working-class Ontarians is seen in the comments of Captain Hall of London East:

> We are accused of being illiterate and not using the Queen's English properly. Who cares for grammar. The Devil has his grammar, so has the Salvation Army. We have just been singing that good old hymn "Better and Better Every Day" let us change it, brothers and sisters, and sing "Gooder and Gooder every day" and it was sung.[86]

The equal value of workers' language in the sight of God was also asserted by "Hallelujah Jack" of Lindsay. "It is true I have not got the best of grammar, but I have got the love of God in my heart."[87] The primacy of salvation and the resultant irrelevance of mere earthly standards and social divisions was affirmed by "Shouting Annie" who proclaimed "there are no social distinctions in Heaven."[88]

The Salvation Army's appeal as a distinct working-class space is affirmed by the prevalence of domestic servants among its adherents, both as soldiers and as officers. Servants were among the lowest on the social hierarchy, and evidence suggests that they were among the least likely to be members of the mainstream churches."[89] Rather than sitting in church where she would be treated with disdain and watched closely by her mistress, in the Salvation Army the domestic servant had freedom from such control, and a space where she would not be looked down upon, but could proclaim her equality in the context of her own distinct culture and language. The Army also provided such women with a unique opportunity to play an active leadership role, strengthening their own sense of value and self-respect in a society which devalued them.[90] Such an opportunity clearly appealed to many other workers, both women and men, skilled and unskilled.

Victor Bailey, an historian of the British Salvation Army, has noted the primarily working-class nature of Army membership, and has argued that involvement in such a distinctively working-class organization reflects the emergence of class consciousness.[91] Roland Robertson, who has also studied the Army in the British context, has suggested that for many working-class Salvationists "allegiance to the Salvation Army offered an opportunity of maintaining religiosity within the Protestant tradition but in opposition to the middle class identified denominations."[92] The evidence suggests that a similar dynamic existed within the Ontario Army. Army membership may not have implied an active opposition to the middle-class-dominated churches by all soldiers, but it would certainly reflect an alienation from class-based institutions in which workers were both subordinated and marginalized. The Salvation Army provided Ontario workers with a religious alternative which spoke to them in terms of their own cultural values, and provided a separate religious space in which they could feel comfortable and in control. The popularity of the Army points to the existence of some form of distinct culture and class identity among Ontario workers, while the Army's activities would themselves reinforce such consciousness.

It is important to remember that the Salvation Army's success points not only to working-class consciousness, but also to working-class religiosity. The Army's message was delivered in working-class cultural forms, but remained the message of evangelical Protestantism. This message was clearly a familiar one to those workers who were swept up in the Salvation Army. Some Salvation soldiers had formerly been church members, and had either drifted away from the churches or found the Army's "blood and fire" methods more appealing than sedate church services. Many other Army soldiers and officers never had been church members, but had had a Christian, very often a Methodist, upbringing.[93] Even those who had never even attended Sunday School lived within a society in which Christianity, (in particular Protestantism) was integral to the dominant culture. Anyone who had attended the public schools even briefly had been exposed to basic Christian teachings.[94] Like the workers identified by Gutman and the *Palladium,* many may have felt alienated from the churches while remaining committed to Christianity. The instant popularity of the Salvation Army certainly suggests that the basic message of evangelical Christianity was a familiar and welcome one to most workers, when presented within a culture and language with which they could identify.

The Army's message had a particular appeal to working-class women, as the gender distributions of converts and officers demonstrate. The relative overrepresentation of women within the Army is similar to that found within the mainstream denominations, suggesting at first glance a shared, cross-class feminine religiosity.[95] The behaviour expected of women in the Salvation Army was quite different, however, from the more passive, lady-like piety expected of women within the mainstream churches. Like male soldiers, female soldiers ("Hallelujah Lasses") were expected to stand up in crowded halls, testify to their faith in Jesus, and describe the sinfulness and misery of their past lives. They also marched through the streets, beating drums or tambourines to attract attention to the cause. The Army also provided many such women with the opportunity to defy more concrete, gender-based constraints. Many female soldiers challenged both the authority of husbands and fathers and their relegation to the narrow confines of the domestic sphere.[96] "Drum-Major Annie" of Petrolia proclaimed the importance of her efforts to save the souls even of unappreciative and undeserving men, defending such efforts as much more significant than "wash[ing] the crude oil out of the shirt of some dirty beast."[97]

Female soldiers who became officers posed an even greater challenge to dominant feminine roles by usurping the traditional male role of religious leader. Many such officers became Captains, and thus were in charge of local corps that could include up to several hundred soldiers and adherents. They were expected to follow the directives issued by Headquarters in Toronto, and were subject to transfer at any time. However, their work required considerable initiative and effort, not just in preaching to crowds every night of the week and three times on Sunday, but also in leading parades, visiting converts, managing the corps' finances, and planning innovative methods of drawing crowds.

As previously demonstrated, prior to becoming officers the majority of female Salvationists worked outside the home, labouring for long hours in factories, or as servants or seamstresses. Like the women who joined Knights of Labor assemblies during the same period, the image of the fragile, passive Victorian lady in the home thus may have had little relevance to the reality of female officers' lives, making them more willing to flout dominant gender roles.

Why did so many more women defy such roles through involvement in the Army than in the Knights? One reason is that while the Knights did welcome married women who worked in the home, their main female recruits were single wage earners. While this was also true of Salvation Army officers, a significant minority of female converts and soldiers appear to have been married.[98] As a result the Army had a larger pool of women to draw on.

However there is some evidence to suggest that the constraints of the dominant feminine ideology did prevent many women from joining the Knights. Certainly Leonora Barry, Organizer of Women's Work for the Knights, saw this as an issue, and cited "natural pride, timidity and the restrictions of social custom" as a barrier to women's organization.[99] Some women who did join the Knights were able to overcome such concerns, like

Katie McVicar, who organized the first woman's assembly in Canada. A female co-worker, in denying working women's ability to organize, suggests that McVicar may have been quite unusual. Her friend commented that "Organization . . . was all very well, but how were girls to accomplish it; were they to advertise mass meetings, mount platforms and make speeches? If so, the Canadian girls, at least, would never organize."[100] The fact that, upon McVicar's death, the assembly petitioned Powderly to appoint a man to chair their meetings points to the reality of such sentiments.[101]

The Knights' own ambivalence about women's sphere may not have helped here. As Karen Dubinsky has demonstrated, while welcoming women and championing suffrage, equal pay, and temperance reform, the Order often called for the family wage, and argued that in an ideal world women would not work outside the home.[102] The Knights' assertions of manly respectability, which explain their commitment to reforms such as temperance, also led them to buy into certain aspects of the dominant gender ideology. A Knights of Labor parade in St. Catharines, in which the "lady Knights" rode in carriages, while their brothers marched beside them, provides a visual reminder of such values.[103]

This image can be contrasted with Salvation Army parades, in which, as one observer commented: "there's a brave lot of lasses in the ranks, and they walk just as bravely as the men, and just take as big a step." [104] What is one to assume here? That middle-class conceptions of femininity were less relevant to the working-class women in the Salvation Army than to those in the Knights? There may be some truth to this argument, given the Army's greater willingness to reject the trappings of respectability. However, there is something else going on here. Unlike women in the Knights of Labor, Salvation Army women were not marching in parades and making speeches to improve their own lives and their own working conditions. As the Salvation Army paper the *War Cry* continually reminded them, by joining the Army they had abandoned all self-interest and dedicated their entire lives to Christ. For some women the public behaviour required of them may have been justified as part of a most appropriately feminine Christian submission to God's will.[105] However, the evident reluctance of female officers to enter social service work once it was introduced into the Canadian Army in the late 1880s shows that women preferred active public roles as preachers to more private, self-denying, and suitably feminine ones as "angels of mercy."[106] For many women, feminine self-denial provided more a justification than a motivation for their willingness to "mount platforms and make speeches."

Women's participation in the Army hints at the existence of a distinct working-class conception of femininity, which more readily acknowledged women's strength, assertiveness, and involvement in the public sphere. The willingness of many working-class women to become "Hallelujah Lasses," however, may also demonstrate the continued relevance of aspects of the dominant feminine ideal to at least some working-class women. The Army probably was more popular with working-class women than the Knights since, as a religious movement, it was a more familiar forum for feminine energies than was a trade union movement. For some, too, it may have been considered a more suitable forum.

While some female Salvationists may have viewed their involvement in the Army as demonstrating appropriate feminine piety, many middle-class observers felt otherwise. For critics like Rev. A. Wilson of Kingston "female preaching and fantastic dressing, the outrageous talk and singing of doggerel hymns" combined to render the Army completely unacceptable.[107] The Army's class-based critique of the churches was more than fully reciprocated by ministers and other middle-class observers across Ontario. These men clearly saw the respectable trappings of the mainstream churches as being integral to Christianity as they defined it. The Army was frequently accused of treating Christianity with vulgarity, levity, and frivolity, and Army activities were disparagingly compared to working-class entertainments.[108] A common, and telling, comparison identified the Army as being worse than "a negro minstrel show."[109] The adoption of the cultural forms of the marginal and the devalued, whether by class or race, placed the Army beyond the pale of true Christianity, which in the dominant discourse of the period was inextricably linked with respectable middle-class culture.

Hostility to the Army was also fuelled by fears of disorder and loss of middle-class control.[110] Common complaints about the Army included the lack of order at their meetings, and in particular their habit of marching through the streets with drums and tambourines. For example, in Ingersoll a letter to the editor complained of the "infernal drum beating and parades" that forced "ladies" off the sidewalk into the gutter, while the *Newmarket Era* attacked the "abominable nuisance of singing and howling . . . after orderly people have retired to rest" and the "drum and symball [sic] playing and singing, on the streets on Sunday."[111] Middle-class citizens frequently attempted to regain control over public space by petitioning town councils to pass by-laws prohibiting the Army from marching and beating their drums. In some cases Salvationists were arrested for refusing to comply with such laws.[112]

Outraged middle-class churchgoers and town councils were not the only Ontarians to oppose the Salvation Army. In most towns, the Army also faced considerable hostility from local young men, who appear to have been predominately working-class. This opposition took a variety of forms, from throwing rocks and rotten eggs, to putting cayenne pepper on a stove during Army meetings, to assaulting officers, to scoffing and heckling during meetings.[113] A major confrontation between the Army and these men occurred in Ingersoll in December 1883.

> During the parade of the Salvation Army on Monday evening an "indescribable" meeting took place between this and another body

headed by a brass band composed of members of our town band and others. When the Salvationist started from the market square the other body, composed principally of working men to the number of several hundreds, also started from an opposite point, the band playing vigorously . . . [when] opposite the Salvationists . . . both bodies commenced to play with renewed vigour and to emit the most hideous yells.[114]

While some of this behaviour was probably just considered "all in good fun" by the perpetrators, some of the attacks do appear to reflect real hostility to the Army. Catholic hostility to the Army's active Protestant revivalism may have been behind these activities, as it certainly was in Quebec. There is no evidence of this, however, in Ontario. It is more likely that such attacks reflect a hostility towards the Army for its efforts to transform the lifestyle of working-class men.[115] Local young men may have been particularly hostile to Army claims that through conversion they were able to transform the most hardened drinker's life to one of piety and sobriety. In this regard it is interesting to note that the behaviour of local "roughs" towards the Army parallels in certain ways the near-riots that were touched off by efforts to enforce the Scott Act in the same period.[116] Opposition to the Army also may have been grounded in a popular anti-clericalism (and perhaps anti-religiosity) among certain young working-class men that did not differentiate the Salvation Army from the churches because of its working-class composition, but for this reason saw it as more vulnerable to attack.

While many local roughs remained hostile to the Army, others were at least temporarily converted at Army meetings. Such conversions gradually transformed middle-class attitudes towards the movement. The Salvation Army was increasingly praised for its ability to bring Christianity to those who would never enter the mainstream churches.[117] Middle-class observers were no doubt genuinely pleased by the Army's ability to save the souls of "the perishing masses." However, for these middle-class supporters, "getting religion" meant considerably more than accepting Jesus Christ. The Army was praised for reducing working-class drunkenness and crime, for increasing the industriousness of workingmen, and for providing an alternative to working-class movements that sought collective salvation on earth rather than individual salvation in heaven.[118] Such middle-class support was not misplaced. The Salvation Army did in many ways bring its followers more firmly within the dominant value system. Salvationists were expected to eschew drinking, smoking, dancing, and any interest in "worldly" issues. An organization which, while denying that it provided strikebreakers, went on to say "if [we have] anything to say in reference to the strike and the strikers it would be get converted, strike against sin, and use the cash as God directs you after you have earned it," would certainly appeal to middle-class Ontarians.[119] However, the Salvation Army cannot simply be dismissed as a manifestation of working-class false consciousness and middle-class social control. The Salvation Army was a working-class organization—while it did attract a minority of farmers and middle-class converts, the vast majority of both officers and soldiers were working-class. It spoke to workers in terms of their own language and culture, and asserted the equal value of their souls to those that were ministered to in costly middle-class churches. The Army tapped into and reinforced a sense among working-class Ontarians of their own value and dignity within a society characterized by increasing inequality. The Army also provided the kind of space sought by Well Wisher in the *Palladium of Labor* where "we could all meet on an equality and be brothers in Christ in this world, even as we hope to be in the next."

• Conclusion

Neither the Knights nor the Army retained the promise of the 1880s. The Knights declined rapidly in the late 1880s as a result of poor economic conditions, external attack, and internal weakness. While the Salvation Army remains active today, it is a very different movement from the one described in these pages. By the early 1890s, the Ontario Salvation Army had been transformed into a primarily social-rescue organization along the lines of the British Salvation Army. With this change, one finds growing class divisions within the Army itself, with increasingly respectable officers ministering to the "submerged tenth." The loss of evangelical zeal which accompanied the shift to rescue-work precipitated a major schism within the Army, led by Brigadier Philpott. Philpott opposed the Army's new emphasis on social work. Most tellingly, he also attacked the appearance of class divisions within the Army. He pointed to the inconsistency of the fact that senior officers travelled first-class while local field officers often lived on less than a dollar a week, although "we have always preached so much self-sacrifice and professed to the world to have all things in common."[120]

The transformation of the Army and the decline of the Knights does not negate, however, their importance to Ontario workers of the 1880s. Thousands of Ontario workers were influenced by these movements. While each movement did have greater appeal to different strata within the working class, the popularity of both the Knights and the Army demonstrate the importance of class identity and religious belief within the Ontario working class.

Skilled working men, who had bargaining power in the workplace and often a tradition of organized resistance, more commonly turned to the Knights. Here the Christian beliefs held by many workers were used to challenge the increasingly hierarchical social order they saw around them, both within the mainstream churches and in the larger social and economic sphere. The Knights demanded the consistent application of Christian values to all Ontarians, which, by their interpretation of Christianity, would lead towards the millennium on earth.

Ontario's less powerful unskilled workers, male and female, were more likely to be attracted to the individual heavenly salvation offered by the Salvation Army. The otherworldly emphasis of the Army negated the importance of a secular world where their lot was hard, their position lowly, and the prospects of material improvement slight. In flocking to the Army, workers demonstrated the importance of Christianity to their lives. At the same time, by turning to the Salvation Army, these workers were not demonstrating simply that religion was "the opium of the masses," and that piety undermined or precluded class consciousness. In joining the Army, Ontario workers were rejecting the hierarchical mainstream churches, choosing instead a religious movement which attacked respectable middle-class Christianity, and preached the equality of all souls. The popularity of the Salvation Army, a religious movement which provided workers with their own space and spoke to them in their own language, points to the existence of distinct working-class beliefs and cultural forms among the unskilled male and female workers who made up the bulk of Salvationists.

While different strata and genders within the Ontario working class tended to find that either the Knights or the Army meshed more readily with their own values and experiences, it is also true that many Ontario skilled workers became Salvationists, and that the Knights boasted a considerable following among the unskilled. During the 1880s, some of these people may have been drawn to both movements. In small towns across Ontario as the hope of collective salvation faded with the local defeat or dissolution of the Knights, some workers may have turned to the Salvation Army. More commonly, since the Salvation Army more often preceded the Knights within Ontario communities, the Army may have contributed to the development of a sense of class identity among local workers, and when the fires of revivalism died out, certain of these workers may have turned to the social Christianity of the Knights.

While we cannot know how many workers were touched by both movements, this examination of the Salvation Army and the Knights of Labor clearly demonstrates the importance of religion to working-class life in late nineteenth-century Ontario. The religion of these workers was not totally distinct from that of their middle-class neighbours, of course, for workers did not live in a completely separate cultural world. At the same time, working-class piety did not guarantee shared values and class harmony. As Kenneth Fones-Wolf has argued, religion "was truly a contested terrain."[121] Certainly, in Ontario in the 1880s, as in many other times and places, religion did not act simply to buttress the social order, but also to challenge it.

• Notes

1 *Thorold Post*, 23 March 1883 (letter from Kingston). Also see *Daily British Whig* (Kingston) 12 March 1883.

2 Gregory S. Kealey and Bryan D. Palmer, *Dreaming of What Might Be: The Knights of Labor in Ontario, 1880–1900* (Toronto, 1982), 347–48.

3 Despite the increasing prominence of Hamilton and Toronto, manufacturing remained relatively decentralized in this period. Ibid., 27–56.

4 In some cases the existence of a distinct class culture can help lay the basis for an oppositional class consciousness, in which the members of a class see themselves as sharing common class interests opposed to those of other classes. For an exploration of working-class culture and consciousness, see for example Richard Johnson, "Three Problematics: Elements of a Theory of Working-Class Culture" in *Working-Class Culture*, ed. John Clarke et al. (London, 1979); E.P. Thompson, *The Making of the English Working Class* (New York, 1963); and Bryan D. Palmer, *A Culture in Conflict: Skilled Workers and Industrial Capitalism in Hamilton Ontario, 1860–1914* (Montreal, 1979).

5 Kealey and Palmer recognize that religion was part of the residual culture out of which the Knights forged their "movement culture." They acknowledge that "religious motivation clearly served as a vital plank in the appeal of the Hamilton Knights": *Dreaming of What Might Be*, 145. Religion, however, receives only brief mention in their study.

6 S.D. Clark's *Church and Sect in Canada* (Toronto, 1948) still provides the best scholarly discussion of the Canadian Salvation Army within a social history context, despite Clark's overly functionalist approach. Stephen M. Ashley, "The Salvation Army in Toronto, 1882–1896" (MA thesis, University of Guelph, 1969), also contributes some valuable insights, while R.G. Moyles, a Salvationist, provides a useful and fairly balanced history of the Army in *The Blood and Fire in Canada: A History of the Salvation Army in the Dominion, 1882–1976* (Toronto, 1977).

7 Two recent books are John Webster Grant, *A Profusion of Spires: Religion in Nineteenth-Century Ontario* (Toronto, 1988), and William Westfall, *Two Worlds: The Protestant Culture of Nineteenth-Century Ontario* (Montreal, 1989).

8 See, for example, Richard Allen, *The Social Passion: Religion and Social Reform in Canada, 1914–1928* (Toronto, 1973), and William H. Magney, "The Methodist Church and the National Gospel," United Church Archives, *Bulletin* 20 (1968).

9 See, for example, Craig Heron and Robert Storey, eds., *On the Job: Confronting the Labour Process in Canada* (Montreal 1986).

10 Some very recent work both in Canada and the United States does examine religion as a significant element of working-class life. See Mark Rosenfeld, "'She Was a Hard Life': Work, Family, Community and Politics in the Railway Ward of Barrie, Ontario, 1900–1960" (PhD thesis, York University, 1990); Doris Mary O'Dell, "The Class Character of Church Participation in Late Nineteenth-Century Belleville, Ontario" (PhD thesis, Queen's University, 1990; and Kenneth Fones-Wolf, *Trade Union Gospel: Christianity and Labor in Industrial Philadelphia, 1865–1915* (Philadelphia, 1989).

11 In *Dreaming of What Might Be*, Kealey and Palmer provide the best available overview of working-class activism in small-town Ontario. This study will focus particularly closely on the towns of Ingersoll, Thorold, Petrolia, and Campbellford. (Ingersoll, Thorold, and Campbellford are the focus of my PhD thesis, "Gender and Class Dimensions of Religion and Leisure in Small Town Ontario, 1882–1896").

For the Salvation Army section of this paper, information concerning other towns has also been drawn from selected Ontario newspapers. A Salvation Army officer has gone through over thirty Canadian newspapers for the first few years of the Army's presence in each town and has copied out all references to the Army in the local papers. This was the source used in references to the mainstream press, other than within the towns mentioned above.

12 Moyles, *Blood and Fire*, 5.

13 The Salvation Army founded a rescue home in Toronto in 1886, but such work did not begin in a major way in Canada until 1890.

14 Kealey and Palmer, *Dreaming of What Might Be*, 66–69.

15 Ibid., 67.

16 Moyles, *Blood and Fire*, 6–9.

17 See *Daily British Whig* (Kingston), 26 March 1883; *London Advertiser*, 27 March 1883; *Newmarket Era*, 13 June 1884; *Northern Advance* (Barrie), 22 Nov. 1883.

18 For a discussion of the short-term nature of conversion within highly revivalistic religious movements see Westfall, *Two Worlds*, 50–81. For evidence of the short-term nature of many Salvation Army conversions, see the converts' and soldiers' rolls for the towns of Listowel, Petrolia, and Chatham for the 1886–1900 period, Salvation Army Archives, Toronto.

19 Kealey and Palmer, *Dreaming of What Might Be*, 65.

20 A. Sumner, *The New Papacy: Behind the Scenes in the Salvation Army by an Ex-Staff Officer* (Toronto, 1889), 7. Sumner, who denounced the Army in this pamphlet, would have insider knowledge of Army figures, as well as no reason to make the Army look good.

21 *Census of Canada*, 1891, vol. 1, table IV. The Army stated that in 1890 over 60 000 people, the majority being non-members, attended Salvation Army services across Canada each Sunday. This figure may well be inflated, however. (Moyles, *Blood and Fire*, 11.)

22 The 10 320 Ontarians listed as Salvationists in 1891 reflects at most a fifth to a quarter of Salvationist support at its height in the mid-1880s, given the fact that the census figures include the children of Salvationists, while there appear to have been at least 20 000 adult Salvationists in Ontario in the mid-1880s (Sumner, *New Papacy*, 7).

23 Army reports regarding the number of the *War Cry*, the Army newspaper, sold in a particular location can provide further clues, but such evidence may suggest as much about the relative enthusiasm of the vendors as the buyers.

24 It must be recognized that officers recruited from a particular town may not have lived there, but may instead have lived in the surrounding countryside.

25 See Clark, *Church and Sect*, 420.

26 While there are some regional differences between K of L towns where the Army was also popular and those where it was not, there do not appear to be other significant differences. In K of L towns there does not appear to be any correlation between the proportion of population involved in the industrial work force, or the average size of industrial workplace and Army popularity.

27 See Moyles, *Blood and Fire*, 270–77.

28 In the Niagara area, the Knights organized a number of small communities (Beamsville, Chippewa, International Bridge, and Queenston) that never had Army corps. Although the Army had some initial popularity in Thorold and Welland, it died out fairly rapidly in these communities. The unpopularity of the Army in the Ottawa region can be linked to the relatively large French-Canadian Catholic population in the towns near the Quebec border, as well as to the

fact that the Army did not establish corps in these communities until relatively late, by which point the novelty of the Army may have worn off for many.

29 *Woodstock Sentinel Review*, 15 Feb. 1884.

30 *Petrolia Advertiser*, 28 June 1884, and Kealey and Palmer, *Dreaming of What Might Be*, 82.

31 See *Belleville Daily Intelligencer*, 26 Nov. 1883; *Sentinel Review*, 15 Feb. 1884 and 4 July 1884; *Canadian Post* (Lindsay), 26 Oct. 1883; and *London Advertiser*, 8 Jan. 1883. During 1882–90, 20 officers were recruited from the Belleville corps, 22 from Chatham, and 23 each from Lindsay, Seaforth, and Woodstock. (Source: "C" Roll, Salvation Army archives, Toronto).

32 A very limited amount of data of this kind is available for the western Ontario town of Petrolia, including lists of those who were Salvation Army soldiers in the late 1880s and the names of a small number of Knights of Labor leaders gleaned from the local newspaper. No overlap was discovered between these two lists. However, the K of L leadership appears to have been among the most skilled and well established workers within the order. They may have been less likely to join the Army than the rank and file Knights.

33 *Belleville Daily Intelligencer*, 15 Oct. 1883.

34 Leon Fink, *Workingmen's Democracy: The Knights of Labor and American Politics* (Urbana, 1983), 13, argues that the Knights' leaders were primarily skilled workers.

35 Kealey and Palmer, *Dreaming of What Might Be*, 323.

36 *Toronto Mail*, 17 July 1882. In a few towns both middle- and working-class people appear to have been attracted to the Army. See, for example, Kingston's *Daily British Whig*, 17 July 1883.

37 Many of the labourers in Petrolia probably worked in the dominant oil industry of the town, and an additional 6 percent of workers here are clearly identified with the industry as drillers or oil well workers.

38 In 1891 less than 11 percent of Canada's female population engaged in paid employment. Most of those who were employed were unmarried. However, although the 1891 census does not provide a breakdown of female unemployment by marital status, we can be relatively certain that less than half of the unmarried female population was employed in this period, since in 1921, when over 15 percent of the female population was gainfully employed, only 49 percent of unmarried women between the ages of 15 and 34 were employed. *Census of Canada*, 1921. Dominion Bureau of Statistics, *Occupational Trends in Canada, 1891–1931* (Ottawa 1939).

39 Many of the nurses or teachers who joined the Army may have come from working-class backgrounds, although these jobs are generally considered middle-class. Large numbers of women from working-class backgrounds were becoming teachers in this period. See Marta Danylewycz and Alison Prentice, "Teachers, Gender, and Bureaucratizing School Systems in Nineteenth-Century Montreal and Toronto," *History of Education Quarterly* 24, 1 (Spring 1984): 75–100. Nursing was only beginning to become a more professionalized middle-class occupation in Canada in this period, and most nurses came from working-class backgrounds. See Judi Coburn, "'I See and Am Silent': A Short History of Nursing in Ontario" in *Women at Work, Ontario 1850–1930* (Toronto, 1974), 127–64.

40 This was true in all Army ranks. Although women seldom were found above the rank of Captain, an examination of the 24 Ontario male officers who attained a rank higher than

Captain shows that two-thirds of these men were clearly working-class, although predominantly skilled workers.

41 Fones-Wolf argues that this may have been true at least of many rank and file unionists even in cases when fundamentalist preachers preached actively anti-union messages. See *Trade Union Gospel*, 192.

42 For a list of towns in which a high proportion of the work force became involved in the Knights of Labor see Kealey and Palmer, *Dreaming of What Might Be*, 67.

43 See, for example, *Palladium of Labor*, 18 July 1885 and 4 Dec. 1886.

44 Herbert Gutman, "Protestantism and the American Labor Movement: The Christian Spirit in the Gilded Age" in *Work, Culture and Society in Industrializing America* (New York 1966), 79–117.

45 *Journal of United Labor*, 25 May 1884.

46 *Palladium* (Toronto), 13 Feb. 1886.

47 *Palladium* (Hamilton), 27 Oct. 1883. See also 22 May 1886, 20 March 1886, 14 March 1885, 29 Dec. 1883, 8 Sept. 1883.

48 Craig Heron, "Labourism and the Canadian Working Class," *Labour/Le Travail* 13 (Spring 1984): 65.

49 Fones-Wolf, *Trade Union Gospel*, 79 and 84.

50 The disparity between the Christian message and social inequality has certainly fuelled oppositional consciousness in other contexts. See, for example, Thompson, *Making of the English Working Class*, 431, 438.

51 Kealey and Palmer, *Dreaming of What Might Be*, 311. In *Trade Union Gospel*, Fones-Wolf argues that the Knights took on the qualities of a millenarian sect. However, while he provides some fascinating arguments to buttress his assertion, he makes no effort to prove that the Knights actually usurped the role of the church among workers, in that they left the churches for the Knights. They may, however, have provided a semi-religious parallel institution for many workers that did not necessarily lead them away from the churches.

52 See for example, *Ingersoll Chronicle*, 3 June 1886, 27 May 1886. The *Stratford Beacon*, 16 April 1886, also cited by Kealey and Palmer, records a unanimous resolution of thanks by the local Knights of Labor Assembly to Rev. Gordon-Smith for his sermon on the topic of the Knights of Labor. He was thanked for "his earnest and eloquent defence of our rights, also for his effort to instruct us in our duty both to our employers and as citizens of the great commonwealth of Ontario."

53 See *Thorold Post*, 25 Nov. 1887, regarding the Merritton Knights of Labor sermon. Also see *Ingersoll Chronicle*, 20 May 1886, on the Knights of Labor sermon there. Examples of fraternal orders' annual church sermon can be found in the *Ingersoll Chronicle*, 30 April 1885, 11 June 1885, and the *Thorold Post*, 14 Dec. 1883.

54 *Ingersoll Chronicle*, 3 June 1886.

55 See O'Dell, "Class Character of Church Participation," and Marks, "Gender and Class Dimensions of Religion and Leisure."

56 Fink, *Workingmen's Democracy*, 3–15.

57 *Thorold Post*, 13 July 1888.

58 *Petrolia Advertiser*, 24 Sept. 1886.

59 Ibid.

60 *Palladium*, 10 Jan. 1885.

61 For a discussion of battles over Sunday streetcars in Toronto in the 1890s in which the labour movement at first opposed Sunday cars and later supported them, see Christopher Armstrong and H.V. Nelles, *The Revenge of the Methodist Bicycle Company* (Toronto, 1977). In *Trade Union Gospel*, Fones-Wolf demonstrates that Philadelphia workers sometimes used Sabbatarian arguments to protect workers from Sunday labour, but more often opposed Sabbatarianism as an interference in working-class leisure.

62 *Thorold Post*, 21 Oct. 1887.

63 Ibid., 21 Oct., 28 Oct. 1887.

64 *Ingersoll Chronicle*, 3 June 1886.

65 *Palladium* (Toronto), 13 Feb. 1886. Also see *Palladium*, 27 Oct. 1883, 8 Sept. 1883.

66 Ibid., 20 Dec. 1884.

67 *Journal of United Labor*, June 1883.

68 General Assembly of the Knights of Labor, *Proceedings*, 1880.

69 *Palladium*, 27 Oct. 1883.

70 Ibid., 8 Sept. 1883.

71 Ibid., 20 March 1886. In *Trade Union Gospel* Fones-Wolf argues that workers remained committed to Christianity even if they did not attend church and suggested that working-class religion was characterized by "a lack of concern for such traditional gauges of religiosity as church attendance" and demonstrated "a greater reliance on direct Scriptural inspiration," xviii.

72 Kealey and Palmer, *Dreaming of What Might Be*, 311–12.

73 *Palladium*, 28 Nov. 1885.

74 Ibid., 17 May 1884.

75 Ibid., 15 May 1886.

76 F. Engels, *Socialism, Utopian and Scientific* (London 1892), xxxi, cited in Victor Bailey, "'In Darkest England and the Way Out': The Salvation Army, Social Reform and the Labour Movement, 1885–1910," *International Review of Social History* 29, part 2 (1984): 133.

77 *Belleville Daily Intelligencer*, 5 Dec. 1883.

78 *Woodstock Sentinel Review*, 6 June 1884.

79 *London Advertiser*, 14 July 1883.

80 *Ingersoll Chronicle*, 1 Nov. 1883, 10 Jan. 1884.

81 *War Cry*, 27 Aug. 1887.

82 Semmel and Thompson make this argument for early Methodism. Thompson, *Making of the English Working Class*, 399, and Bernard Semmel, *The Methodist Revolution* (New York, 1973), 193.

83 See, for example, Neil Semple, "The Impact of Urbanization on the Methodist Church of Canada, 1854–1884," *Papers*, Canadian Society .

96 See Lynne Marks, "Working-Class Femininity and the Salvation Army: 'Hallelujah Lasses' in English Canada, 1882–1892" in *Rethinking Canada: The Promise of Women's History*, 2nd ed., ed. Veronica Strong-Boag and Anita Clair Fellman (Toronto, 1991).

97 *Petrolia Advertiser*, 8 Aug. 1884.

98 The proportion of married female converts varies from 56 percent of all female converts in Petrolia to 33 percent of female converts in Listowel.

99 Cited in Karen Dubinsky, "'The Modern Chivalry': Women and the Knights of Labor in Ontario, 1880–1981" (MA thesis, Carleton University, 1985), 151. Barry argued that the selfishness and injustice of men also played a major role in explaining the inequality of women in the workplace.

100 In a letter to the *Palladium of Labor*, Katie McVicar quotes a co-worker as making this comment. Quoted in Dubinsky, "'Modern Chivalry,'" 32.

101 Kealey and Palmer, *Dreaming of What Might Be*, 144.

102 Dubinsky, "'Modern Chivalry.'"

103 *Thorold Post*, 19 Aug. 1887.

104 *London Advertiser*, 18 April 1884.

105 This was clearly the official Salvation Army position, as illustrated by a story in the *War Cry*, 1 Dec. 1888, of an officer's wife whose refusal to preach and testify publicly is presented as evidence of disobedience to God's will and a refusal to give herself completely to God.

106 See Marks, "Working-Class Femininity and the Salvation Army," 194.

107 *Daily British Whig*, 31 Aug. 1883.

108 Comments regarding the Army's levity and vulgarity can be seen from example in the *Daily British Whig*, 30 April 1883; *London Advertiser*, 7 April 1884; *Sarnia Observer*, 16 May 1884.

109 *St Thomas Times*, 17 Aug. 1883; *Toronto World*, 5 Sept. 1884.

110 For a discussion of middle-class efforts to control working-class behaviour in this period see, for example, Graeme Decarie, "Something Old, Something New . . . Aspects of Prohibitionism in Ontario in the 1890s" in *Oliver Mowat's Ontario*, ed. D. Swainson (Toronto, 1972).

111 *Ingersoll Chronicle*, 1 Nov. 1883; *Newmarket Era*, 13 June 1884; also see *London Advertiser*, 7 April 1884.

112 For a petition to pass such a by-law see *Ingersoll Chronicle*, 27 March 1884, 10 April 1884, also see *London Advertiser*, 19 and 20 June 1884.

113 See *Daily British Whig*, 31 Jan. 1883, 3 Oct. 1883; *Northern Advance* (Barrie), 30 Aug. 1883; *Renfrew Mercury*, 15 April 1887; *Woodstock Sentinel Review*, 14 Dec. 1883; *Huron Signal* (Goderich), 13 Feb. 1885; and *Thorold Post*, 14 March 1884.

114 *Ingersoll Chronicle*, 13 Dec. 1883.

115 Victor Bailey argues that this was the primary motivation for working-class opposition to the Salvation Army in England. See "Salvation Army Riots, the 'Skeleton Army' and Legal Authority in the Provincial Town" in *Social Control in Nineteenth-Century Britain*, ed. A.P. Donajgrodzki (London, 1977), 241.

116 For opposition to the Scott Act, see *Ingersoll Chronicle*, 14 Jan. 1886, 25 Feb. 1886, 10 March 1887. In the English context, opposition to the Army was at least partially funded by tavern keepers, who perceived the Army as a threat to their business. See Bailey, "Salvation Army Riots," 239.

117 *Daily British Whig*, 7 May 1883; *London Advertiser*, 3 March 1883; *Whitby Chronicle*, 4 April 1884.

118 For comments regarding the reduction in drunkenness, see *London Advertiser*, 17 July 1883; *Belleville Daily Intelligencer*, 4 Dec. 1883; *Hamilton Spectator*, 25 Jan. 1884. For statistics pointing to a reduction in crime see *London Advertiser*, 30 Nov. 1882; *Northern Advance*, 25 Oct. 1883; *Hamilton Spectator*, 5 May 1884. For the testimony of businessmen regarding increased industriousness see *London Advertiser*, 17 July 1883; *Petrolia Advertiser*, 28 June 1884; *Toronto World*, 17 Dec. 1883. For a discussion of how the Army was preferable to revolutionary movement see *Toronto Week*, 10 Jan. 1884.

119 *War Cry*, 4 July 1885.

120 P.W. Philpott and A.W. Roffe, *New Light, Containing A Full Account of the Recent Salvation Army Troubles in Canada* (Toronto 1892), 17.

121 Fones-Wolf, *Trade Union Gospel*, xvii.

EMIGRATION AND DEVELOPMENT IN A QUEBEC RURAL COUNTY*

BRUNO RAMIREZ

Spring of 1892: turmoil and consternation in Berthier County. The *Gazette de Berthier*, the local paper that for years had reported frequently on the emigration of Berthier people to the United States, felt the time had come to pull the alarm signal as trainloads of people were leaving the county to go south of the border. Issue after issue, the *Gazette* reported mass departures from the train station of Berthierville. It gave figures on the number of families departing each time and on the number of railroad tickets sold in the area, and it depicted the other side of the picture: abandoned farms; houses closed down, their doors and windows boarded; the value of property declining rapidly—the impoverishment of the county seemed inevitable. The problem, the *Gazette* insisted, could not be more serious: "If our population keeps on abandoning the land for a few more years, the French Canadian nationality will be transported to the United States."[1]

An angry tone accompanied most of these reports as politicians were singled out as primarily responsible for letting this exodus occur and perhaps even for promoting it with their economic policies. But then the tone turned to bitterness and disappointment when the writers addressed themselves to the emigrants. All the previous warnings against the physical, moral, and political dangers awaiting those who want "to bury themselves alive in the factories [of the United States]" seemed to have gone unheeded.[2]

*From *On the Move* by Bruno Ramirez. Used by permission of the Canadian Publishers, McClelland & Stewart, Toronto.

The virtues and promises of colonization were equally ignored. The newspaper was forced to the painful realization that rural Quebeckers had lost their love for their country. "A patent fact, absolutely evident, strikes today the observers: our agricultural population is leaving, and it emigrates because it does not love our country anymore."[3]

In effect, the late 1880s and the early 1890s witnessed the crest of the emigration movement to the United States. What was observed in Berthier County seemed to be generalized throughout much of the province. Alarming reports poured in from all parts of Quebec, leading the Provincial Assembly in June 1892 to appoint a special Commission of Inquiry, and bringing, perhaps more than on previous occasions, the emigration issue to provincial and national prominence.[4]

While the official historiography has acknowledged the importance of this issue, occasionally linking it to various conjunctures of the province's economic and political history, we know little of how emigration was experienced at the local level and still less of how the phenomenon interacted with the wider process of industrialization that began to penetrate the Quebec economy, including Berthier's, during the last third of the nineteenth century.

For Berthier County, as for dozens of Quebec counties, emigration was not a new development. It was a phenomenon that had existed for a number of decades, undergoing changes in both its volume and its patterns, and constituting a permanent characteristic of the county's social and economic life. Moreover, Berthier, like many other counties, was far from being a homogeneous geoeconomic and social entity. Its landscape was marked by class differences within its population and by differences among its parishes—for instance, among its commercial centre (Berthierville) and the older or the more recently established parishes.

This article is an attempt to pierce through the thick historical screen that has given us a rather homogeneous understanding of the emigration phenomenon in the province's past and to capture some of the social and economic dynamics that made Berthier a county of exodus at the time in which one of Canada's most important poles of industrial capitalism, just fifty miles southwest, was emerging.

Berthier County is part of a wider region, known today as Lanaudière, whose natural boundaries are the Laurentian Mountains to the northwest and the St Lawrence River to the southeast.

Throughout the first half of the nineteenth century the county's population, originally settled along the river almost facing the important trading centre of Sorel, had gradually penetrated into the interior, clearing forest and establishing one parish after another. By 1871, the nearly 20 000 souls in the county—virtually all of French-Canadian stock—were spread

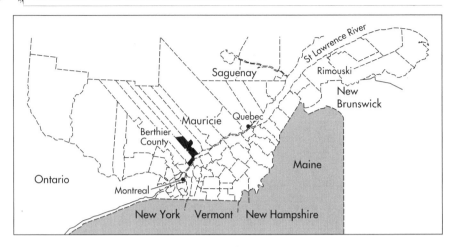

FIGURE 1: *The Province of Quebec and Berthier County*

out through a network of less than a dozen parishes ranging in size from 1000 (Île du Pads) to 3000 (St-Cuthbert).

The county's commercial seat, Berthierville, had long been an important nodal point within the Laurentian geoeconomy; as early as the mid-eighteenth century, in fact, Berthierville had become a strategic trading post along the northern "Chemin du Roi" that linked Montreal to Trois-Rivières and Quebec City; and as the region's northwestern hinterland became increasingly settled and peopled Berthierville provided the most important cross-over for travellers from *rive-nord* districts who were moving to the Eastern Townships and the United States. Throughout the second half of the nineteenth century, Berthierville continued to be the county's nerve centre. The town was quickly joined to the province's emerging railway network, reinforcing at the same time its role as a river port.[5] It was here, as we shall see, that factory production would make its uncertain and troubled beginnings.

In his pioneering investigation of the region, the distinguished French geographer Raul Blanchard was struck by the county's rich and fertile soil and by the importance of its strategic location, which, in his view, accounted for the "precocious peopling" of its inland territory. In the late eighteenth century most of Quebec's parishes lay in almost unbroken strings along the river coasts, but Berthier was one of the rare areas that could boast an agricultural parish, St-Cuthbert, well into its hinterland.[6]

Despite the importance of Berthierville for the county's geoeconomy, the overwhelming majority of the population drew their means of support from agriculture and farming-related activities. In 1871, in fact, the census listed 53 percent of the county's active work force as farmers. To this figure, however, one must add other important occupational groups—such as *forestiers* or *journaliers*—who were to varying degrees dependent on an agricultural economy, as well as farmers' wives and children, who, while not formally attached to any occupation in the census enumerations, more often than not played a central role in farming activities.[7]

If agriculture provided the base on which the county's economy rested, its structure was far from uniform. As the county moved ahead into the second half of the nineteenth century, one can detect three major interrelated dynamics at work in Berthier's socioeconomy that ultimately

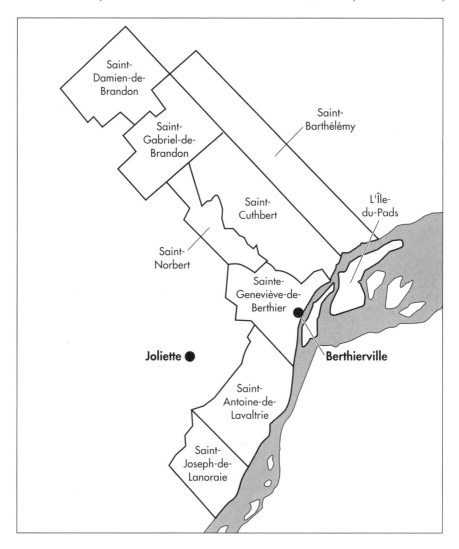

FIGURE 2: *Parishes of Berthier County, 1880*

Source: Adapted from Serge Courville et al., *Paroisses et municipalités de la région de Montréal au XIXe siècle (1825–1861)*, figure 13; Université du Québec à Montréal, Groupe de recherche sur le Renouveau religieux montréalais au 19ème siècle, "Limites paroissiales, région de Montréal, 1880."

would have a particular bearing on the process of out-migration. One was the progressive development of the commercial sector of Berthier's agriculture. The second was the reproduction of various forms of subsistence economy. And third, the proletarianization of large strata of its population was growing.

As in most of the old rural counties of the province, in Berthier economic development rested primarily on the commercial activities of the large and middle-sized farming enterprises. In 1871, 36 percent of the county's entire agricultural acreage consisted of farmholdings of 100 acres and more, and about 9.5 percent of the county's *cultivateurs* owned farms larger than 200 acres. Their value in 1861 dollars ranged from $5000 to $20 000.[8] Although essentially run as family farms, these were the units that geared their production to the market, participated in the process of agricultural mechanization, and provided seasonal wages for the growing ranks of landless labourers.

Prosper Allard symbolizes this class of prosperous farmers that constituted the backbone of agrarian development in the county. In 1871, his 210 acres of farmland were all under cultivation, except for 40 acres he used for pasturage. The report of his yields for that year shows a highly diversified use of the land with over a dozen different types of produce. At the same time, Allard, like most farmers of his rank, practised considerable agricultural specialization, having harvested 1300 bushels of oats and 7000 bales of hay. Livestock was another major activity of Allard's agricultural enterprise: seven horses, thirty-six cows, and seventy-two sheep must not only have kept his farm lively and busy but also must have required a great deal of help from hired labour. In that year he sold five head of livestock to local butchers, produced wool from half of his herd of sheep, and turned some of his milk production into 560 pounds of butter. Perhaps more importantly, Allard seems to be one of those Berthier farmers who had embraced enthusiastically the arrival of mechanization in agriculture. His mini-fleet of mechanical implements included three plows, one horse rake, one threshing machine, and one sifting machine.[9]

Of course, commercial farmers such as Allard had to contend periodically with economic trends that were national, if not continental, in scope and that inevitably affected their performance in the market. But whatever some historians may have said about the alleged backwardness of Quebec agriculture, one can hardly see the signs of economic stagnation in this stratum of farmers. All the indicators show, on the contrary, that in the ensuing decades Berthier's commercial farmers both maintained their position as the driving force of the county's economy and were able to adjust to the structural and conjunctural market changes that marked the province's agrarian universe around the turn of the century.[10]

But economic stagnation did exist in Berthier County, and one may more clearly locate it within the group of farmers who struggled to turn out crops on holdings measuring less than fifty acres. In 1871, about one-third of the county's landholdings belonged to this category. If we exclude, for the moment, the very small plots of nine acres and less (whose owners were mostly non-farmers), we are left with a small but significant group of farm properties ranging from ten to forty-nine acres. In a long-settled agricultural parish such as St-Cuthbert, 21 percent of all the holdings fell into this range. County-wide, their proportion rose to 30 percent.[11] It is very likely that on these small plots of land farming constituted more a form of subsistence activity than a commercial enterprise resulting in accumulation and growth. Small landholders belonging to this category owned on average a plot of thirty-one acres, of which twenty-one were improved, most likely used their crops to satisfy their families' immediate needs, and possibly took portions of their crops for petty local exchange. Edouard L'Ecouyer, for instance, had all his twenty-five acres under cultivation. His crop in 1871 consisted of little over one hundred bushels between grains and vegetables, such as wheat, oats, peas, corn, and potatoes. Much of the 210 bales of hay he produced that year must have been used for his own horse and the few head of livestock he raised. Similarly, the forty pounds of butter and the fifteen pounds of raw wool he reported in that year must have been destined primarily to his own household consumption. One crop that probably went to the local market was tobacco, because it was very unlikely that L'Ecouyer could smoke the twenty-eight pounds he cropped in that year.[12]

The marginal place this class of landholders occupied in the local agricultural economy is also suggested by the fact that, at least in St-Cuthbert, one out of three owners of this size was a *journalier,* namely, someone whose main source of income was wage labour. It seems, therefore, that as one moves down through the hierarchy of Berthier's agriculturalists, one not only identifies the threshold separating commercial from subsistence farming—development and growth from mere survival; one also identifies a sector of the socioeconomy where two separate occupational groups—smallholders and day labourers—seem to merge and share similar life situations.

Of course, the co-existence of commercial and subsistence agriculture was a feature of Quebec's rural society that dated from its beginnings.[13] But as the process of land accumulation became irreversible, as commercial farming became the dominant driving force of a parish economy, and as demographic pressures drastically reduced the access to land ownership for growing numbers of young people, the equilibrium that had existed between these two sectors of the socioeconomy was upset, making subsistence increasingly synonymous with proletarianization. By 1871 this process seemed to be quite advanced in Berthier County, and it was reflected in the rising number of day labourers the local economy was producing.

The presence of day labourers or *journaliers* in the rural/agricultural economy of nineteenth-century Quebec is a phenomenon that only recently has begun to be explored by some social historians. In his study of three parishes of the Lower Richelieu region, for instance, Allan Greer found that by the 1830s *journaliers* had already become a common feature of the local socioeconomic universe. What in a previous period had been a temporary condition involving mostly young people by the 1830s had become a lifelong occupation. Although *journaliers* held but a marginal place in an economic structure largely dominated by family farming, their presence is depicted by Greer as a new trend towards the proletarianization of growing sectors of the local population.[14] There is substantial documentary evidence pointing to a reinforcement of this trend as Quebec entered the well-known period of agricultural and political crises. By mid-century, day labour and landlessness, it would appear, had moved from a marginal to a central feature of the socioeconomy of many counties. In his study of a Richelieu district to the southeast of that studied by Greer, Yves Otis estimated that during the 1852–71 period from 13 to 22 percent of all the family units in the region were headed by journaliers. And although an important portion of these were young men who had recently formed a family, almost half of all *journaliers* were husbands and/or fathers aged thirty-five and upward.[15]

Our own data on Berthier County reflect a progression of the earlier trends captured by Greer and Otis and suggest that as we move into the last third of the century proletarianization had not only become an irreversible process but that the rural day-labour market had become a permanent structural feature of economic development. In Berthier, as probably in other agricultural counties, the relative weight of *journaliers* within the local active work force varied from one parish to another. Not surprisingly, *journaliers* figured most prominently in the commercial town of Berthierville. Here, river and inland transportation-related activities, as well as the concentration of artisanal and small-shop production, had long made day labour a permanent feature of the local economy, and thus it is not surprising that in some years the proportion of *journaliers* climbed as high as 26 percent. In a rural parish like St-Gabriel, located in an area of more recent settlement and where land ownership was more common, the proportion of *journaliers* fluctuated from a low of 5 percent to a high of 15 percent during the 1871–91 period. On the other hand, in the older and larger parish of St-Cuthbert, day labourers had grown to a more sizable proportion, ranging from 14 to 20 percent of the local work force. As in the Richelieu parishes studied by Otis, in Berthier County *journalier* was far from being an occupation only associated with young single people. In St-Cuthbert, for instance, a striking 57 percent of all 1871 *journaliers* were aged forty and over, and a still larger proportion was made up of family heads.[16]

In the agricultural parishes of Berthier County the existence of this stratum of the rural proletariat depended largely on the labour required during haying and harvesting seasons, when even a middle-sized family farm had to rely on the extra help of outsiders. Commercial farming could also generate a demand for day labour during the off-season in farm maintenance, hauling, and the like; and so did local public works, such as construction and maintenance of county roads. In the old parish of Kamouraska, farther northeast on the south shore of the St Lawrence River, by mid-century it was common practice for *journaliers* to be attached to a particular farmer's family through an arrangement whereby the farmer sold the *journalier* a house and a small plot of land located on the farm (payable over a ninety-nine-year period). The *journalier* and his family thereby were at hand to help year-round, as the farmer deemed it necessary.[17] We do not know how widespread this practice was in Berthier or in other rural counties. Still it is difficult to assess what level of existence intermittent wages derived from this variety of sources could provide *journaliers* and their families. It seems safe to suggest, in fact, that for many *journaliers* a great deal of their survival strategies depended on household practices typical of a subsistence economy. And here again the role of women in the production of homemade commodities (such as clothing and preserved food) was vital.[18]

This is why it was crucial for a *journalier* to own a small plot of land—an emplacement, as it was called—where he and his family could grow vegetables and raise pigs, hens, and other animals. The majority of Berthier's day labourers did. The most fortunate ones even owned ten to fifty acres, and they were probably able to complement their wage income with small cash crops. But at the same time, there was a significant proportion of *journaliers*—41 percent of them in St-Cuthbert—who owned no land at all and who had to depend entirely on the intermittent wages offered by the local labour market.[19]

These data seem to reflect the outline of a cycle of proletarianization at work in the Berthier agrarian socioeconomy that not only had transformed a growing number of farmers' sons into permanent day labourers but also had begotten a generation of *journaliers* who were themselves sons of *journaliers*. And increasingly, for many of them, breaking the cycle that only could trap them into marginality and destitution meant leaving their parishes to try their chances elsewhere. If in earlier periods geographical mobility had been predominantly associated with the fur trade or with the slow but progressive filling of vacant land within the local seigneurial confines, by mid-century this phenomenon had become increasingly associated with the physical movement of *journaliers* unable to find their means of survival in their local economy. When in 1857 a legislative committee inquired into the causes of out-migration from scores of Quebec counties, parish after parish provided testimony stressing the need for mostly young people to seek wages in distant labour markets.[20]

As the century progressed, industries such as logging and railroad construction created regional labour markets drawing surplus labour from old rural parishes and feeding the mechanisms of geographical mobility. But geographical mobility involved more than just seasonal back-and-forth movements. It also meant trying to find, in a more recently settled parish or in a nearby commercial centre, the chance for a less precarious life of subsistence. And as colonization emerged as a national project, settling into distant forests and pursuing the vision of independent farming became . . . another important motor of geographical mobility. Very little systematic research has yet been done on the phenomenon of rural depopulation in nineteenth-century Quebec. In his skilful study of this issue, Yves Otis found that between 1852 and 1871 *journalier*-headed families represented the group most responsible for the rapid population decline in the region.[21] Otis was not concerned with the geographical destination of this migrant group. But as we shall see below, in Berthier County *journaliers* became one of the two major occupational groups that swelled the ranks of the emigration movement to the United States.

A final important component of the socioeconomic landscape of Berthier County was the presence of artisans and small-shop producers. We are dealing of course with an occupational group that had long antecedents in the agrarian universe of most Quebec counties. By 1871, this group constituted 7 percent of the county's total work force, with extremes ranging from 22 percent in Berthierville to 5 percent in a more remote rural parish such as St-Gabriel.[22]

Historians have often tried to locate within this stratum of the work force the signs of a protoindustrialization, as the types of productive functions performed by these artisans/entrepreneurs made them the natural recipients of the technical and technological progress brought about by capitalism.[23] Only an in-depth historical investigation of the evolution of Berthier's socioeconomy over a long period of time could enable us to ascertain the role of Berthier's small independent producers in the transition towards industrial capitalism. The available data suggest, however, that throughout the second half of the nineteenth century, the handful of artisans to be found in the county's agricultural parishes kept on fulfilling a modest support role for the farming needs of their local clientele. And to a large extent their lot was inextricably associated with the ups and downs of the local agrarian economy. This may explain why, despite their relatively small number, artisans and small entrepreneurs were visibly represented within the ranks of those who emigrated south of the border.

The 1871 census listed 182 industrial shops for the entire Berthier County, totalling $124 165 of fixed capital. Despite the term "industrial" used by census enumerators, they were mostly artisanal shops involving an average capitalization of $682, employing on the average two workers besides the owner/craftsman, and yielding an annual average wage of $123 per worker.[24]

Twenty years later the situation appears to have changed more quantitatively than qualitatively. The number of shops, for instance, had increased considerably, due primarily to the addition of new specialized crafts, which brought the total number of hired workers to 619, from 356 twenty years earlier. One can also notice a marked increase in the average annual wages paid. But the structure had essentially remained that of a small-shop form of production, still employing an average of two workers per unit, with most of the shops dispersed in the various parishes and the few larger ones concentrated in Berthierville.[25]

The only exception to this scenario was in the county's capital, where during the 1880s a few attempts had been made to implant some small and mid-sized factories. Two small foundries, a tannery, and a sugar refinery were the larger employers and seemed to dominate the industrial configuration of the town's economy.[26]

Their history, however, was one of repeated shutdowns, prolonged inactivity, and financial difficulties. In the middle of the depression of the 1890s, the town citizenry had to intervene to keep the refinery and the tannery alive; they petitioned the City Council to vote financial grants for the two companies. After a long political tug-of-war, the grants were voted and the two factories were back in production. But as long as the depression lingered on, their activities could not but take place in a climate of stagnation, marked by repeated interruptions of production and layoffs.[27]

It was only around the turn of the century that an important infusion of capital occurred in the town's economy, producing a significant transformation of Berthier's small industrial base. Industrial census data for 1901 and 1911 clearly show this new trend. In 1901 the number of "industrial establishments" decreased to fifty-one (from 315 in 1891), and the total industrial work force had been cut in half, because only units employing five workers and more were enumerated. The presence of these larger establishments (each employing an average of seven workers) seemed now to dominate the local industrial scene, showing also the signs of a technological shift, as total capitalization had risen to nearly a half-million dollars.[28] All these indicators were doubled ten years later, showing that the process had become irreversible. However modest its performance, Berthier obviously was now partaking in the industrial revival affecting much of urban Quebec in the pre–World War I era. In 1903 the local newspaper could boast that the town's factories were in full production and even complained that it had become difficult to find a sufficient work force in the area.[29]

Clearly, when industrialization penetrated the small commercial universe of Berthierville, its agents were not the small artisans who had struggled to survive with their rudimentary tools and limited resources but financiers and industrialists who saw the potential of accumulation at the periphery of capital. By that time many of Berthier's small-shop producers had taken the path to emigration.

As we have indicated in the previous sections, intraregional and transregional geographic mobility had long been a feature of the landscape of most nineteenth-century Quebec agrarian counties. Recent research in

Quebec's rural history has begun to throw considerable light on the various patterns this mobility took within the circuits of the province's socio-economy.[30] The most dominant patterns that gave shape to the physical movement of people in their search for material security and well-being were: colonization of the county's hinterland; seasonal migration of workers attracted, for instance, by the forestry industry; interparish population transfers due to marriage; temporary or permanent migration towards urban-commercial centres. At the same time these mechanisms functioned to ensure the equilibrium among overpopulation, geographical space, and local economic resources. And these were no doubt the patterns that had been operative in Berthier for a good portion of the nineteenth century. From 1852 to 1861, evidence of these patterns is visible from the performance of the county's overall population, which grew from 16 390 to 19 608.[31] Analysis of the marriage records of some of the major Berthier parishes also shows the important extent to which marital patterns contributed to intracounty mobility; moreover, the legal boundaries of the county were constantly redrawn as new hinterland districts were settled and new parishes were added or reassigned to neighbouring counties.

But starting sometime in the 1860s and continuing through the last three decades of the century, a significant shift in the overall demographic performance of the county took place. While the above-mentioned patterns certainly continued to persist, geographical mobility increasingly took the form of depopulation. From 1871, and in each of the three subsequent census years, Berthier County registered important net losses, and by 1901 its population had declined to 18 982, an absolute decrease from its 1861 and 1871 populations. If one considers that during the same thirty-year period the population of the province as a whole experienced an increase of 38.4 percent, one gains a sense of the magnitude of the demographic decline occurring in the county and the extent to which the term "exodus," used by contemporaries to denounce the phenomenon, applied to Berthier.[32]

In these last three decades of the century, the mechanisms of demographic and economic equilibrium mentioned above had greatly enlarged their parameters of operation, with major population shifts occurring from one region of Quebec to another. As we shall see, colonization and industrialization activated the new regional poles that were taking the major share of these population shifts. During the same thirty-year period, in fact, important colonization regions such as Saguenay/Lac Saint-Jean and the Ottawa Valley experienced population increases of 61.1 percent and 65.3 percent respectively, and the Montreal Island region saw its population undergo a staggering 141.7 percent increase.[33]

Berthier County's out-migrants were certainly part of the provincial population feeding these new regional poles; but the Gazette's editorial invectives against Quebecers abandoning their county and turning its countryside into a deserted landscape had little to do with these interregional moves. These were not only tolerated but also encouraged. *L'exode* they talked about referred instead to the move that local people were making in increasing numbers out of the county and out of the province, attracted by that strong magnet that was industrial New England.

In the historiography of nineteenth-century Quebec there has long been an awareness not only of the magnitude of some of these population movements but also of their historical importance in the socioeconomic evolution of the province. Little work, however, has been done in tracing the migratory flows from a given location, in reconstituting, however approximately, the range of destinations and in putting these migration flows in their historical relationship.[34] The use of a variety of local archival sources and the elaboration of appropriate record-linkage methods have enabled us to shed new light on this complex historical issue.[35]

Despite its degree of approximation, one way of observing the range (and quantity) of destinations of the out-migrating population is through the dynamics of the marriage market. Children born in a given rural parish, when reaching adulthood, quite often found a spouse somewhere else—whether in a nearby parish or county or in some distant location. In the case of St-Cuthbert, for instance, only one in five (19.7 percent) of the spouses born in that parish during the 1845–1900 period *but marrying elsewhere* were married within the county. For four out of five, marriage was a life event that took them somewhere else in the province or, in many cases, south of the border.[36] Of course, extra-parish marriages should not be interpreted as automatically denoting out-migration. As we know well, following the established custom of the period, some of the grooms marrying outside their parishes may have subsequently returned and started a family in their native village. However, comparisons of the extra-county places of marriages give an important indication of where marriage was taking them and which marriage markets were more prominent in the parish's psychological and emotional map (table 1). At this level, what is striking is that marriage locations in the United States were equally important as those in the rest of the province—the former locations involving 146 such cases as against 149 cases of marriages occurring in the rest of the province. And although Montreal Island—just 100 kilometres southwest—figured prominently among the marriage destinations of St-Cuthbert (with 17 percent of the total marriages), the city of Woonsocket, Rhode Island, constituted the most important single outside location in which spouses were found, with 21 percent of the cases.

Analysis of notary deeds involving sales of land property throws additional light on the geographical radiation of Berthier County's population. As we have previously indicated, the centrality of land in most nineteenth-century Quebec rural parishes derives from the fact that land was a commodity owned not only by farmers but also by people belonging to other occupations. However small the plot of land owned, and whether it was the ultimate source of security for people caught in a marginal economic

Table 1: PLACES OF MARRIAGE OF PERSONS BORN IN ST-CUTHBERT, 1845–1900, BUT MARRIED ELSEWHERE

Persons Married within the Province			68%
Within Berthier County	93	29%	
Other counties	149	46%	
Montreal Island	79	25%	
Total	321	100%	
Persons Married outside the Province			32%
Rhode Island			
Woonsocket	91		
Providence	4		
Central Falls	2		
Harrisville	1		
	98	65%	
Massachusetts			
Holyoke	7		
Fall River	5		
Southbridge	5		
Other locations	13		
	30	20%	
Other US states	18	12%	
Other Canadian provinces			
Manitoba	4		
Saskatchewan	1		
	5	3%	
Total	151	100%	
TOTAL	472		100%

Source: Registres des baptêmes, Archives de la paroisse de Saint-Cuthbert, 1845–1900.

status or a source of investment or saving for people such as artisans, merchants, or widows, land constituted one of the most frequent objects of notarized transactions. A representative sample of all these transactions occurring in Berthier County from 1870 to 1910 reflects the structure of land ownership in the county, with farmers being the most frequent sellers and buyers at a rate closely paralleling their weight within the county's occupational structure. Moreover, as one would also expect, in an overwhelming majority of cases both parties of such notarized transactions were individuals residing in Berthier County.

However, in 11.8 percent of the cases, the seller resided outside the county at the time of the transaction—a pattern that strongly suggests the occurrence of extra-county out-migration. We shall comment below on the frequent practice among Quebec emigrants to maintain ownership of their holdings at the time of the emigration and subsequently to sell them once the move appeared to have become permanent. Interestingly enough, these 11.8 percent of cases suggesting extra-county out-migration parallel significantly the geography of destinations that have emerged from the marriage-market data. In this instance provincial locations actually constitute a more frequent out-of-county destination, with 6.9 percent of all cases, but American destinations follow closely with 4.8 percent of all cases, Rhode Island and Massachusetts being the dominant American residences.

Two other aspects flowing from these data have major historical and cultural-political implications, and deserve at least some brief comments. One is the virtual absence, in these out-migrating patterns, of destinations involving other Canadian provinces. Clearly, the interregional migration map originating from Berthier County had taken the form of a perimeter encompassing the provincial territory or of a north–south route linking Berthier parishes to a number of Northeast states.

The other aspect is the predominance of American destinations (taken as a whole) over the Montreal destination. Historians have long assumed the all-important role of the Montreal metropolitan region as the major pole of attraction during the province's process of urbanization. These data, while confirming that generalization, invite us to put it into a broader historical and geographical perspective. In fact, being part of Montreal's immediate hinterland, as rural Berthier was, did not automatically imply being attracted by the opportunities that the large city offered. For every group of Berthier out-migrants who moved to Montreal there was an even larger group who bypassed the city and sought their chances south of the border. Our sample of notarized land sales, moreover, allows us to put these two migration movements in temporal relationship to each other. It suggests that during the last three decades of the nineteenth century the United States consistently and progressively constituted a much more important destination than Montreal; this trend, however, seems to have reversed itself during the first decade of the twentieth century, reflecting the well-known decline of the exodus to the United States as well as the growing importance of Montreal as the major regional pole of industrialization and urbanization.

Not just buyers and sellers of land resorted to the services of a notary public. Drawing a notary deed was a widespread practice among French Canadians of all walks of life; and thus in Berthier, as in other counties, these deeds covered a wide spectrum of transactions—from the settlement of wills to the repayment of debts—and involved individuals irrespective of occupation, age, civil status, and gender. To the extent that most Berthier out-migrants who moved to the United States kept, at least initially, some kind of link with their parishes, it is not surprising that deeds would often be notarized in their county of origin, where they still had kin or relatives, and frequently property as well.

We have therefore retrieved all the Berthier deeds, for the years 1875 to 1905, involving sales of land in which the sellers resided in the United States so as to obtain a more detailed view of the United States destinations chosen by Berthier migrants. The 190 such cases we have identified confirm once more the trends discussed above. As table 2 indicates, considerations such as geographical distance or size of local labour markets were clearly not the only factors determining choice of destination. Thus, the tiny state of Rhode Island was a preferred choice over the larger and closer state of Massachusetts, and the much more distant state of Michigan seems to have attracted more Berthier migrants than several of the New England states.

Table 2: **PLACES OF RESIDENCE IN THE UNITED STATES OF MIGRANTS FROM BERTHIER COUNTY, 1875–1905***

Rhode Island	40.5%
Massachusetts	35.3
Michigan	5.8
Connecticut	4.7
New York	4.2

*The states of New Hampshire, Minnesota, Vermont, Nevada, Montana, and Illinois each received less than 3 percent of migrants from Berthier County.
Source: Notary Deeds, Berthier County, 1875–1905.

As Berthier individuals and families in increasing numbers took the road for the States, their move was part of a broader process of geographical mobility that marked not only the life of that county but also much of Quebec agrarian society during the last third of the nineteenth century. Putting the American-bound emigration movement in this broader context allows us to gain a better understanding of both its temporal and spatial dimensions, as well as to assess its special weight in the demographic and social history of the province.

At the same time, the impossibility of quantifying the population migrating to the United States from any given county—due to the nature of the existing sources—does not prevent us from identifying nominally a significant portion of that population. Just as the notary deeds lend themselves to this type of procedure, other sources may also be employed for that purpose, thus permitting us to focus the historical analysis on the emigrants themselves.[37]

The massive flow of Berthier out-migrant population into the United States (particularly New England) labour markets must be viewed as a direct result of the process of marginalization and proletarianization described earlier in this chapter. Geoeconomic factors peculiar to that county's history undoubtedly set off the movement at an earlier period than experienced in some other counties. For instance, a comparison with Rimouski County, where colonization of the region's hinterland well into the 1880s and 1890s tended to delay the development of out-migration to the United States, makes Berthier fit more clearly the profile of those older counties that by the 1860s had already undergone the process of settlement and peopling of much of their territories.[38] Thus phenomena such as demographic pressures and economic marginalization had reached a stage yet unknown in recently settled counties or in colonization regions. Moreover, the early integration of Berthierville into the provincial and continental railway network certainly had an important role in facilitating long-distance travelling, making emigration a more concrete option.

The available data show that by the 1870s emigration to the United States had become a normal occurrence in the agrarian universe of Berthier County. The movement was fed by young unmarried people, but more importantly by family units. Equally important, already in the 1870s two dominant patterns gave shape to the movement: permanent emigration and temporary emigration, the latter often engendering still another pattern, namely, repeat migration. Some of these characteristics have long been known by historians and demographers.

Some of these patterns emerge clearly from the yearly report that each parish priest was expected to send to the bishop of the local diocese, probably following his yearly pastoral visit among his parishioners. Intended primarily as an inventory of the spiritual health of a parish, the *Rapport Pastoral* contained a section that was a sort of parish census, complete with population figures, including the number of christenings, marriages, and burials occurring in any year. More importantly, the priest was also expected to report the number of new families that had joined the parish and the number of those that left the parish. More often than not, this latter information was accompanied by the name of the intended destination of each departing family. In addition, most reports indicated the number of families that returned from the United States. While these reports do not measure up in quality to an official census (due to the degree of approximation they may have contained), and despite the irregularity with which some *curés* submitted them, they provide a valuable quantitative sense of the parish's performance within the emigration movement; also, they help to chart the fluctuations marking the emigration movement during the intercensus periods.

Table 3 gives a sense of the magnitude of this movement at the parish and county level. It shows as well the extent of return migration throughout the period. And while the irregularity in the reporting prevents precise statistical analyses, one may observe in these data the marked predominance of the departures over the returns. . . .

An important component of the migration movement to the United States was represented by families who returned to their county after

Table 3:   BERTHIER COUNTY, 1878–1900:
          MOVEMENT OF FAMILIES TO AND FROM THE UNITED STATES

Year	No. reporting parishes	Departing Families Total number of families	Avg./ parish	Returning Families Total number of families	Avg./ parish
1878	2	26	13	6	3
1879	0				
1880	0				
1881	4	35	9	25	6
1882	6	64	11	39	7
1883	0				
1884	6	53	9	17	3
1885	5	20	4	23	5
1886	7	143	20	24	3
1887	6	85	14	21	4
1888	4	87	22	45	11
1889	4	48	12	18	5
1890	3	32	11	14	5
1891	8	151	19	31	4
1892	10	169	17	57	6
1893	7	67	10	36	5
1894	5	23	5	87	17
1895	2	23	12	20	10
1896	2	65	33	14	7
1897	1	7	7	3	3
1898	5	81	16	32	6
1899	0				
1900	1	4	4	5	5

having sojourned for a certain period of time south of the border. Their social and demographic profile may be clarified by adopting a procedure that allows us to identify nominally a significant portion of them. The Canadian census manuscript schedules, in fact, enable one to retrieve all those family units present in the county at a given census year and who had previously given birth to one or more children in the United States. Applying this procedure to the 1871, 1881, and 1891 census schedules shows, first of all, that this pattern was more dominant in the 1870s and 1880s, much less so in the 1860s. Moreover, in the majority of cases these families were headed by *journaliers* or *cultivateurs*—the two occupational groups most affected by the proletarianization process discussed above (table 4).

However, of the seventy-seven returnee families we have identified county-wide as of 1881, a little more than one in three (38 percent) were family units that had formed in the United States, thus unveiling another pattern at work in that migration movement: spouses who most likely had emigrated as young, unmarried adults, alone or with their families, and

Table 4:   HEADS OF RETURN-MIGRANT FAMILIES BY OCCUPATION AND MAJOR AGE
GROUPS, 1881, PARISHES OF ST-CUTHBERT AND ST-GABRIEL COMBINED

Occupation	20–29	30–39	40–49	50–59	60+	N/I	Totals
Cultivateur	5	6	11	1	1		24
Journalier	7	12	4	1			24
Voyageur	1	3					4
Forgeron		1	1				2
Menuisier		1		1			2
Médecin		1					1
Plâtrier		1					1
Maçon			1				1
Veuve				1			1
Not indicated						3	3
Totals	13	25	17	4	1	3	63

Source: *Census of Canada*, manuscript schedules, 1881, County of Berthier, St-Cuthbert and St-Gabriel
parishes.

who after marriage and childbearing in the United States had decided to
return to Quebec.

As to those cases involving emigration of family units, table 5 shows
some of their demographic characteristics at the approximate time of their
departure. Notice that this migratory pattern was practised largely by families whose head was in his prime working age (20–39 age brackets) and in
which the wife/mother was in her prime childbearing age. Also significant
is the proportion among them of couples who at the time of their departure had no children, or less than three children.[39]

One may only speculate on the precise reasons that led each one of
these families to return to their Quebec parishes after having experienced
a few years of work and life in the United States. Conjunctural economic
factors, such as the prolonged and severe depression of the mid-1870s,
undoubtedly may have played a role in convincing some of these families
to return to the rural setting of their native county. These data, coupled
with the approximate age structure of the children composing these families, however, suggest an interpretative hypothesis that will find strong
corroboration when this migrant population is set in the labour market
context of industrial New England. . . . Particularly in the textile manufacturing districts, a family unit could survive only if several members contributed to the family wage and, in most cases, if the earnings of at least
one or two children could be relied on. For the twenty-nine returnee
couples who started their families in the United States and the eight other
couples who migrated without children (which together make up almost
half the total number of return-migrant families), childbearing drastically

Table 5: DATA ON RETURN-MIGRANT FAMILIES WHO GAVE BIRTH TO ONE OR MORE CHILDREN WHILE IN THE UNITED STATES, BERTHIER COUNTY, 1881

Age range of family heads at approx. time of departure to the US	No. of children per family at approx. time of departure*														Totals
	0	1	2	3	4	5	6	7	8	9	10	11	12	13	
20–24	6	1	1												8
25–29	2	1	6	3		1									13
30–34			2	1	4	1									8
35–39			2	1	1	3			1	1					9
40–44					2	1	1	1							5
45–49							1	1						1	3
50–54				1											1
55–59		1													1
Totals	8	3	11	6	7	6	2	2	1	1	0	0	0	1	48

Children of Return Migrant Families by Age Groups
at the Approximate Time of Departure to the United States

Age groups	Number
0–4	50
5–9	48
10–14	35
15–19	21
20–24	3
Total	157

*Estimated by calculating for each couple the period between the last childbirth in Canada and the first childbirth in the United States.
Source: *Census of Canada*, 1881, schedules, County of Berthier.

changed their previous profile in the industrial labour market. Whereas the two spouses had both contributed their earnings to the family economy, now only one could do so, and his earnings had to sustain a family that had grown in size. If their previous single or childless condition had made possible their emigration from Quebec, now the arrival of children to be fed and the mother's need to rear the children made survival extremely difficult, if at all possible. Industrial America was no longer the place to be, not, at least, for the time being.

A somewhat similar scenario emerges when one focusses on those returnee families that had emigrated from Berthier with children. Their average size at the time of departure (3.9 children per family) parallels the average family size we have observed in Berthier County at this period, which shows that, despite the view perpetuated in the historical literature, the average French-Canadian rural family emigrating to the United States was not necessarily a large one. In fact, what counted most . . . was less the number of children per se and more the age of these children and their potential to contribute to the family wage once in New England. One may thus find the predominantly young age of these migrating children belonging to returnee families (62.5 percent of them aged nine and less at the time of their departure) a factor that may explain their difficulty in adapting to an industrial family economy that had to rely considerably on the earnings of children.

Still, return migration did not seem to provide the solution for these Berthier families. For the majority of them, this temporary migration to the United States turned out to be only the prelude to a subsequent migration. When one tries to locate these families ten years later in their respective parishes—in the 1891 census schedules—one finds that only 30 percent of them had become persistent residents (at least for a ten-year period) following their return from the United States. Two out of three of these families, instead, had left their parishes again, emigrating somewhere else in the province or back to the United States.

Thus, by 1891, a period that corresponds to the crest of the emigration movement towards New England, the various patterns that emigration had engendered had become clearly visible. The depopulation of countless Quebec parishes and the transformation of many rural migrants into the permanent American labour force had become an irreversible process.

We may gain an important glimpse of how some of these mechanisms of depopulation were operating in agrarian Berthier from the written observations made by the *curé* of St-Damien. In the frequent letters this *curé* wrote to his bishop, he depicted vividly the condition of rural poverty in which his parishioners lived.

Faced with an undernourished population whose material privation could be read through their rugged and often inadequate clothing, the *curé* did not even have the courage to demand the tithe. Their land was insufficient to ensure them a decent living. Many of them had been forced to spend time in the United States to make a few extra dollars: "Tired of going back and forth, and seeing that a good portion of their earnings went into travelling expenses, most of them decided to emigrate with their families."[40] What strikes a reader of these letters is the absence of any reproaching tone—something that contrasts with the condemnatory attitude *curés* usually assumed when addressing the issue of emigration directly with their parishioners.[41] Evidently the clergy knew when to yield to rhetoric and when to be realistic in governing their flocks.

St-Damien was one of the most recently settled parishes in the county, with a population made up primarily of farm labourers turned smallholders. This occupational profile of the migrant population is confirmed and enriched as one switches the focus onto the older and larger rural parishes of the county. In St-Cuthbert and in St-Gabriel de Brandon, *journaliers*, along with *cultivateurs*, were the occupations most touched by the emigration movement to the United States. In the former parish, two-thirds of the migrant family heads who in 1881 were back from the United States belonged to those two occupational categories; and in St-Gabriel the proportion was even higher (84 percent). Most of the families would disappear from their parish records in a roughly similar proportion during the ensuing ten years, the subsequent life of many of them becoming most likely part of the history of Franco-America and of the industrial miracle south of the border.

Clearly, in Berthier County emigration to the United States was a phenomenon rooted not only in the life-course of rural families but also in the marginal conditions the local agrarian economy was assigning to increasing numbers of households.

If *journaliers* of all age groups were swelling the ranks of the outmigrating population to the United States, often returning to try again in their parishes, often residing in multiple households and then disappearing again from the parish records, it is because this occupational group had emerged as the embodiment of the proletarianization engendered by the agrarian economy of late nineteenth-century Quebec. Their lack of property no doubt enhanced their propensity to move and to fill foreign labour markets; it also translated itself into an option that they could contemplate and act on more freely than those who still hoped to improve their lot betting on the evolving fortunes of their local society. For those who practised return migration, no doubt their travelling back and forth was a source of physical hardship and of financial waste—as the St-Damien *curé* observed; but it also must have functioned as a mechanism of comparison between a society that had made subsistence an impossibility for them and a society in which their most available resources (labour power) could be put to their fullest use and whose rewards foreshadowed the possibility of material and social progress.

For the mostly smallholders who made up the group of Berthier *cultivateurs* emigrating to the United States, their farm ownership gives the historian an additional clue to the dynamics that transformed them and their children into permanent labour for American industrial capitalism. Despite the insufficiency of smallholdings to ensure the material sustenance of their owners and their families, *cultivateur*-emigrants tended to hold on to their land ownership, at least for an initial period of their migrant life. Our systematic analysis of Berthier County's notary deeds involving emigrants residing in the United States shows how their land was a frequent object of transaction. And in those two rare censuses taken in the 1880s and 1890s by the *curé* of the Saint-Jean Baptiste Parish in Warren, Rhode Island, land ownership in Quebec was common among French-Canadian parishioners, many of whom were from Berthier County.[42]

There is no question that for many smallholders who resorted to emigration as a temporary means to alleviate their material hardship, a plot of land back in their parish constituted the ultimate source of security, a place where one could always return regardless of the success or failure of one's American experience. In the best of dreams, land in Quebec provided a material base enabling a returnee to start a new life with the savings brought back from the States. Only individual family biographies could tell us how many of these emigrants' dreams actually came true. Our data suggest, however, that the subsistence economy awaiting smallholders in their Berthier parishes gave little chance to start a new life by escaping those mechanisms of marginality that late nineteenth-century agrarian Quebec had increasingly engendered. It is thus not surprising if the majority of those *cultivateurs*, who by 1881 were back in their county, emigrated again in the subsequent ten years. Nor is it surprising to note, as one moves towards the end of the century, a marked progression in the sales of land by former Berthier *cultivateurs* residing in the United States.[43]

Two individual cases illustrate the type of spatial and economic itineraries that characterized the migration projects of these *cultivateurs* on the move. Ambroise Sarrasin was one of those Berthier smallholders who in the 1870s emigrated to the U.S., probably with the idea of returning one day, as he kept ownership of his plot of land in St-Barthélémy parish. His holding was a small one, measuring 2 by 17 *arpents*, but while in Woonsocket in 1876 Sarrasin saw fit to lease it to a local farmer, thereby drawing a small annual rent. Two years later, the lease was renewed for another year, perhaps an indication that a return in the not-too-distant future was being contemplated. In 1879, however, Sarrasin made a decision that no doubt helped to sever his material links with his native parish. He sold his holding, including all the farming facilities and implements. Ambroise Sarrasin had become one of the thousand French Canadians crowding the textile mills of Woonsocket—the lump sum of $770 obtained from the land sale summarizing his past as a Berthier *cultivateur* but also helping to ease his way into permanent industrial and urban life.[44]

For Norbert Dubois, the tension between a farming vocation and the promises of an immigrant life was more complex. He was born in St-Cuthbert in 1855, and his father was a small *cultivateur* who in 1871 owned eighty-seven arpents. With an elder brother already working on the family farm, Norbert probably saw little chance of drawing enough property from the family holding to become an independent farmer. Thus, in 1878, soon after his marriage in his native parish, he and his wife emigrated to the United States. One year later they had their first child, born in the United States. Norbert's move to the south, however, proved to be only a temporary one, for in 1881 he and his family were back in St-Cuthbert, where Norbert had taken up farming. We do not know whether he was farming on his father's holding or whether he had acquired some property of his own. This latter goal, however, had certainly become a reality a few years later, when Norbert signed a deed making him the owner of a plot of land measuring 1 $^{1}/_{2}$ by 20 *arpents*. When in 1891 the census enumerators asked Norbert his occupation, he declared that he was a *cultivateur patron,* to distinguish himself from tenant farmers and no doubt also from the many farm labourers who crowded the agrarian landscape of his county. But if the 1880s and 1890s had been for Norbert a decade of farming, the 1900s would see him back in industrial Rhode Island. The cession in 1904 by his father of a holding twice as large as the one he had owned previously did not seem to have attracted Norbert back to farming life; one year later he had sold the property to one of his brothers, preferring to remain in Woonsocket and use the $950 sale revenue to ease the situation of his household. For Norbert, Woonsocket had become his permanent land of adoption, until his death in 1932.[45]

Finally, if the land of a smallholder stood as symbol of the marginality of this social class, it may also have played a much more important role in the emigration process than we had previously thought. One pattern seems to emerge clearly from the notarized deeds of Berthier's emigrants to the United States. Smallholders contracted loans using their land as collateral prior to their emigration. These loans would then be repaid with their American wages while they were in the United States.

Two possible interpretations may explain this type of behaviour. The first—in line with the emphasis some Quebec historians have placed on the progressive indebtedness of smallholders—would place indebtedness and emigration into a direct causal relationship. Indebtedness would be seen here as the inevitable lot awaiting all those *cultivateurs* unable to cope with the growing monopolization of agricultural resources and the concomitant modernization of the agrarian economy. Crushed by the unbearable weight of accumulating debts, these farmers would have turned to emigration as the solution of last resort, the only means available to prevent financial and legal disaster.

The other interpretation, which is more in keeping with the analysis developed in this study, places less focus on the role of economic determinism and more on the centrality of migration in all its patterns in the everyday universe of nineteenth-century Quebec rural society. The main premise here is that migration was not something one was passively pushed into but a process involving the evaluation of one's own resources and, as our data have suggested, a decision based on a variety of strategic considerations. Moreover, emigrating as a family unit—as most French Canadians tended to do—involved a certain financial cost, from the moment a family boarded the train to the moment the family settled and started drawing wages from the local labour market. The use of one's land as collateral for obtaining loans could thus be seen as a practice whereby smallholders contemplating emigration financed their move to the south. If confirmed by more detailed and in-depth research, this hypothesis would reveal a different historical understanding from that suggested by the more conventional interpretation. We would be dealing with historical actors who, while aware of the increasing marginalization into which their agroeconomy was pushing them, overturned what for them had been a symbol of marginality and economic hardship (their plot of land) into a lever of social change.

• Notes

1 *La Gazette de Berthier*, 15 April 1892, 2. Cf. also "Où allons-nous?" 8 April 1892, 2; "Pourquoi ils s'en vont?" 22 April 1982, 2; "Pourquoi nos campagnes se depeuplent-elles?" 13 May 1892, 2. (All translations of quotations from French are the author's.)

2 Ibid., 31 May 1889, 3.

3 Ibid., 29 May 1891, 2.

4 The commission, headed by J.A. Chicoyne, presented its report to the Provincial Assembly in February 1893. See "Mémoire du Comité spécial nommé par l'Assemblée législative pour s'enquérir du mouvement d'émigration," annexe n. 1, *Journal de l'Assemblée législative de la province de Québec* (Quebec, 1983), 375–98. The Chicoyne Commission was one of several public inquiries that since the late 1840s had expressed concern for the attraction the United States exerted on Quebec rural migrants. For a brief review of the various public inquiries, see Albert Faucher, "Explication socio-économique des migrations dans l'histoire du Québec" in *Agriculture et colonisation au Québec*, ed. Normand Séguin (Montreal, 1980), 142–43.

5 Local studies on the history of the county are limited to Stanislas Moreau, *Précis d'histoire de la seigneurie, de la paroisse et du comté de Berthier* (Berthier, 1889), and to some fragmentary but useful information contained in Raoul Blanchard, *Le Centre du Canada Français* (Montreal, 1947), 65–119. For a pioneering historical study of a nearby district, see Jean-Claude Robert, "L'activité économique de Barthélémy Joliette et la fondation du Village d'Industrie (Joliette), 1822–1850" (MA thesis, Université de Montréal, 1971.)

6 Blanchard, *Le Centre du Canada Français*, 73.

7 *Census of Canada*, 1871, vol. 2, table XIII, computed by the author.

Detailed compilations of statistical data pertaining to the county's demographic, economic, and social development from 1871 to 1911 are contained in Bruno Ramirez and Jean Lamarre, "French-Canadian Emigration to the USA, 1871–1915: A Local and Comparative Analysis" (unpublished research report, Université de Montréal, 1988).

8 *Census of Canada*, 1871, vol. 3, table XXI; *Census of Canada*, 1861, manuscript schedules, St-Cuthbert, reel C-1269.

9 *Census of Canada*, 1871, manuscript schedules, St-Cuthbert, reel C-10039.

10 For a thorough discussion of Quebec's commercial farming and some of its structural characteristics in the context of the national market, see John McCallum, *Unequal Beginnings: Agriculture and Economic Development in Quebec and Ontario until 1870* (Toronto, 1980). For the transformations experienced by Quebec's commercial agriculture around the turn of the twentieth century, see, among others, Paul-André Linteau, René Durocher, and Jean-Claude Roberts, *Histoire du Québec contemporain* (Montreal, 1979), ch. 23; Robert Armstrong, *Structure and Change: An Economic History of Quebec* (Toronto, 1984), 206–19; and the various sectoral studies contained in Séguin, *Agriculture et colonisation au Québec*.

11 *Census of Canada*, 1871, vol. 3, table XXI.

12 Ibid., manuscript schedules, St-Cuthbert, reel C-10039. My classification and the ensuing discussion parallel those adopted by Normand Séguin, who considers holders of less than 10 acres as "pseudo-exploitants" and holders of 10 to 49 acres as "semi-exploitants," i.e., "those who in general farmed their smallholdings as a second activity aimed at incrementing the household revenue." Cf. his

"L'agriculture de la Mauricie et du Québec 1850–1950," *Revue d'histoire de l'Amérique française* (hereafter *RHAF*) 35, 4 (mars 1982): 541ff, where the author also discusses some of the classification problems posed by the Canadian census sources. For a recent historical survey of the place of smallholders in Quebec agriculture, see Michel Morisset, *L'agriculture familiale au Québec* (Paris, 1987).

13 Recent as well as current research on nineteenth-century Quebec shows the degree to which subsistence agriculture co-existed also with other forms of commercial activity, such as fur trading, fishing, and forestry.

14 Allan Greer, *Peasant, Lord, and Merchant: Rural Society in Three Quebec Parishes 1740–1840* (Toronto, 1985), 226–28, 184–88. See also Serge Courville, "Croissance villageoise et industries rurales dans les seigneuries du Québec (1815–1851)" in *Sociétés villageoises et rapports villes-campagnes au Québec et dans la France de l'Ouest, XVIIe–XXe siècles,* ed. F. Lebrun et N. Séguin (Trois-Rivières, 1987), 205–19. Courville's essay is an important initial attempt to study the evolving economic scene of rural Quebec in the first half of the nineteenth century and the growing differentiation between agricultural parishes, on the one hand, and, on the other, villages whose economy was dominated by small handicraft production and commercial services. The author's hypothesis of linking the *journaliers* in this latter type of villages to non-agricultural activities, although a preliminary one, is very promising.

15 Yves Otis, "Familles et exploitations agricoles: quatre paroisses de la rive sud de Montréal, 1852–1871" (MA thesis, Université du Québec à Montréal, 1985), 61, 63.

16 Computed by the author from *Census of Canada,* 1871, 1881, 1891, manuscript schedules, Berthierville, St-Cuthbert, St-Gabriel, reels C-10038, 10039, 10040, C13215, T-6387, 6388.

17 J.-P. Michaud, *Kamouraska, de mémoire . . .* (Montreal, 1981), 64–65.

18 For two pathbreaking discussions of non-wage household strategies in both rural and urban nineteenth-century contexts, see Richard L. Bushman, "Family Security in the Transition from Farm to City, 1750–1850," *Journal of Family History* 6 (Fall 1981): 238–56, and Bettina Bradbury, "Pigs, Cows, and Boarders: Non-Wage Forms of Survival among Montreal Families, 1861–91," *Labour/Le Travail* 14 (Fall 1984): 9–46. See also Bruno Ramirez, "Montreal Italians and the Socioeconomy of Settlement: Some Historical Hypotheses," *Urban History Review* 10, 1 (June 1981): 39–49. For two detailed descriptions of female domestic production in the subsistence agrarian economies of nineteenth-century New England and Ontario, respectively, see Nancy F. Cott, *The Bonds of Womanhood: "Woman's Sphere" in New England, 1780–1835* (New Haven, 1977), esp. ch. 1; and Marjorie Griffin Cohen, *Women's Work, Markets, and Economic Development in Nineteenth-Century Ontario* (Toronto, 1988), 71ff.

19 *Census of Canada,* 1871, manuscript schedules, St-Cuthbert, reel C-10039.

20 Canada, *Report of the Special Committee on Emigration, Journals of the Legislative Assembly,* 1857, appendix 47.

21 Otis, "Familles et exploitations agricoles," 63.

22 Computation based on *Census of Canada,* 1871, vol. 3, table XXI; and *Census of Canada,* manuscript schedules, Berthierville, St-Cuthbert, and St-Gabriel, reels C-10038, 10039, 10040.

23 For the growing interest among Quebec social historians on the issue of proto-industrialization, besides the above-mentioned article by Serge Courville, see also René Hardy, Pierre Lanthier, and Normand Séguin, "Les industries rurales et l'extension du réseau villageois dans la Mauricie pré-industrielle: l'exemple du comté de

Champlain durant la seconde moitié du 19e siècle," in *Sociétés villageoises*, 239–53.

24 Computation based on *Census of Canada*, 1871, vol. 3 "Industries," tables XXVII to LIV.

25 Computation based on *Census of Canada*, 1891, vol. 3 "Industries," tables I and II.

26 Moreau, *Précis d'histoire*, 113; *La Gazette de Berthier*, 6 May 1892.

27 *La Gazette de Berthier*, 20 Jan. 1893, 3; 17 March 1893, 3; 28 April 1893, 2; 8 Sept. 1893, 2; 20 Oct. 1893, 2; 1 Feb. 1895, 3; 26 April 1895, 2; 20 March 1896, 3.

28 *Census of Canada*, 1901, vol. 3, "Industries," table XIII; *Census of Canada*, 1911, vol. 3, table IX.

29 *La Gazette de Berthier*, 7 Aug. 1903, 3.

30 See, among others, Gérard Bouchard, "Family Structure and Geographic Mobility at Laterrière, 1851–1935," *Journal of Family History* 2, 4 (1977): 350–69; Christian Pouyez et al., "La mobilité géographique en milieu rural: Le Saguenay, 1852–1861," *Histoire sociale* 14 (1981): 123–55; Daniel Maisonneuve, "Structure familiale et exode rural: Le cas de Saint-Damase, 1852–1861," *Cahiers québécois de démographie* 14 (octobre 1985): 231–39; Marc St-Hilaire, "Origines et destins des familles pionnières d'une paroisse saguenayenne au XIXe siècle," *Cahiers de géographie du Québec* 32 (avril 1988): 5–26.

31 *Recensement du Bas Canada, Suivant les origines, 1851–52*, tableau I; *Recensement du Bas Canada, Suivant les origines, 1861*, tableau I.

32 *Census of Canada*, 1871, vol. I, table III; 1901, table VII; M.C. Urquhart and K. Buckley, *Historical Statistics of Canada* (Toronto, 1965), 14.

33 Paul-André Linteau et al., *Histoire du Québec contemporain* (Montreal, 1979), 1:45–46.

34 Very promising historical-demographic studies of some nineteenth-century intraprovincial migration movements are being conducted by France Gagnon and Danielle Gauvreau. See France Gagnon, "Le role de la famille dans l'adaptation des migrants de la plaine de Montréal au milieu montréalais: 1845–1875" (MA thesis, Université du Québec à Montréal, 1986), and "Parenté et migration: le cas des Canadiens français à Montréal entre 1845 et 1875," *Historical Papers* (1988): 63–85; Danielle Gauvreau, "Le peuplement de Saguenay au XIXe siècle: Mesure et caractéristiques du mouvement d'immigration jusqu'en 1911" (paper presented at the Canadian Historical Association conference, Hamilton, ON, June 1987). See also the pioneering study done by Jean-Claude Robert, "Urbanisation et population: Le cas de Montréal en 1861," *RHAF* 35 (mars 1982): 523–35.

35 See Bruno Ramirez and Jean Lamarre, "Du Québec vers les États-Unis: l'étude des lieux d'origine," *RHAF* 38 (hiver 1985): 409–22.

36 Registre des baptêmes, Archive de la Paroisse de St-Cuthbert. The systematic annotation done by the parish *curés* of the location of marriage of each St-Cuthbert-born spouse (who addressed himself/herself to that parish to obtain a birth certificate) has made these computations possible.

37 For a detailed discussion on the use of local sources and on the record-linkage methods adopted to identify nominally individuals and families emigrating to the United States, see Bruno Ramirez, with Jean Lamarre and Louise-Edith Tétreault, "The Emigration from Quebec to the USA, 1870–1915: Questions of Sources, Method, and Conceptualization" (unpublished working paper, Université de Montréal, 1988).

38 A full comparative analysis between the counties of Berthier and Rimouski in relation to the emigration movement to the United States is contained in Ramirez and Lamarre, "French Canadian Emigration."

39 The proportion of migrating childless couples could be higher. We have included only those cases for which evidence was found that they had gotten married in Quebec before emigrating (so as not to confuse them with individuals who may have migrated as single persons, got married in the United States where they also gave birth to one or more children, and in 1881 were back in Berthier County as a family unit).

40 Letter to the Bishop of Joliette, 21 April 1875, Dossier de la Paroisse de St-Damien, Archives de la Chancellerie du diocèse de Joliette. See also letters of 10 April 1872 and 15 May 1873.

41 For a skilful and updated discussion of the clergy's condemnatory attitude towards French-Canadian emigrants, see Yves Roby, "Les Canadiens français des États-Unis, 1860–1900: devoyés ou missionnaires," RHAF 41, 1 (été 1987): esp. 6–8.

42 The two census have been reproduced in Ulysse Forget, La Paroisse St-Jean Baptiste de Warren, État du Rhode Island, 1877–1952 (Montreal, 1952), 221–311. For a skilful analysis of these two censuses in the context of French-Canadian immigration to Warren, see Jean Lamarre, "Étude d'une communauté canadienne-française de la Nouvelle-Angleterre: le cas de Warren, R.I. (1880–1895)" (MA thesis, Université de Montréal, 1986).

43 Ramirez and Lamarre, "Du Québec vers les États-Unis," 420–21.

44 Notary Deed #2223 (16 Sept. 1876); Notary Deed #2836 (22 Oct. 1878); Notary Deed #2923 (25 March 1879), Files of F.E. Rouleau (Berthier County Notary Public), Palais de Justice, Ville de Joliette, Quebec.

45 Notary Deed #20526 (18 July 1889); Notary Deed #30954 (4 Aug. 1904); Notary Deed #32125 (23 Sept. 1905), Berthier County files, Bureau d'enregistrement, Hotel de Ville de Berthier, Quebec, Census of Canada, 1871, manuscript schedules, St-Cuthbert, reel C-10039, household #168; Société de généalogie de Lanaudière, Repertoire des mariages de la Paroisse Saint-Cuthbert 1770–1983 (Joliette, n.d.), 96; Census of Canada, 1881, manuscript schedules, St-Cuthbert, reel C-13215; household #91; Census of Canada, 1891, manuscript schedules, St-Cuthbert, reel T-6387, household #581; R.J. Quintin, Franco-American Burials of Rhode Island (Pawtucket, RI, n.d.).

Rivers of Sawdust:
The Battle over
Industrial Pollution in Canada,
1865–1903*

R. PETER GILLIS

Industrial pollution of rivers and lakes is a very explosive political issue in late twentieth-century North America. Fouled waterways have raised the ire of naturalists, environmentalists, recreationalists, and a host of concerned citizens as health hazards are created, recreational sites ruined, traditional fisheries destroyed, and the natural beauty of many areas reduced. These problems, however, usually are viewed as a fairly recent phenomenon, the product of an aging industrial society where manufacturing enterprises are concentrated in large, somewhat obsolete, facilities. Yet deterioration of the natural environment was an important issue for a substantial and influential group of individuals in both Canada and the United States during the late nineteenth century. Highly critical of the rapacious way in which particular business interests used natural resources, this group looked to government action and regulation to control such abuses. American historians have created a considerable literature which analyses these events in that country, but in Canada little work has been done in the field.[1] This has resulted in the oversight of a vital and interesting part of early conservationist impulse in Canada and neglect of an important perspective on controversies within the Canadian community over resource and industrial development strategies.

*Journal of Canadian Studies 21, 1 (Spring 1986): 84–103. Reprinted with the permission of the journal.

This article will attempt to shed some light on these events by focussing on one celebrated and controversial cause involving early conservationists in Canada—the dumping of sawmill refuse into rivers and lakes. Drawing on British precedents, early legislation in British North America had long contained provisions forbidding the contamination of waterways with mill waste.[2] Up until the 1850s, because the number and size of lumber-producing plants remained relatively small and the regulatory system primitive, these laws remained unenforced. The Reciprocity Treaty of 1854 dramatically changed this situation. As the United States market opened up to British North American lumbermen, there was a rapid expansion of the sawn lumber industry, especially in the Province of Canada.[3] The inevitable result was the construction of more and larger mills, the creation of a greater amount of mill waste because of increasing production, and consequently the fast deterioration of rivers and lakes where sawmills were located.

The refuse problem was particularly severe in water-powered mills which were designed, unlike their steam counterparts that used the waste for fuel, so that edgings, butts, and sawdust dropped through the floorboards into the water. Once there, this refuse was carried along by the current until it was washed into bays and other shallow areas where it sank, forming shoals of rotting material which obstructed navigation, destroyed fish spawning grounds, made the water objectionable to drink, and contributed to the formation of various gases which emitted obnoxious smells from the water and were prone to explode due to spontaneous combustion. In a few short years after large-scale lumber manufacturing began in earnest in British North America, mill refuse was perceived by a vocal and influential part of the population of these provinces as a definite nuisance to health, navigation, and recreation. It would remain so until 1902 when the largest sawdust polluter in the country, the J.R. Booth Company of Ottawa, was forced to install equipment to stop such materials entering the Ottawa River, thus paving the way for enforcement of the anti-dumping regulations.

The controversy, which brewed for almost forty years, drew into political conflict business and conservationist interests which were to marshall all the major arguments currently employed in similar, present-day disputes. The lumbermen talked of the declining quality of eastern Canadian timber, the loss of their competitive edge if forced to invest in remodelling their mills, and the economic cost to the country if they were forced to close out their businesses. These preservationists, concerned with the natural environment, charged that the mill operators were ravaging the environment to the detriment of other citizens and that they were wealthy enough to afford systems to eliminate the dumping of refuse. This, they stated, was the true test of the forest industries' public spirit and business morality.

The lines between these two groups were drawn firmly by the late 1860s and the ensuing public debate demanded from politicians an increasingly sophisticated response to the issue. Starting from a position in 1866 which largely accommodated the lumbermen, successive governments were forced by public pressure into an interventionist stance by the mid-1890s. The Department of Marine and Fisheries, the federal agency responsible for enforcing the anti-pollution regulations after 1867, responded to public sentiment against refuse dumping by actively inspecting mill sites and amassing detailed scientific data to rebut the mill operators' arguments about the negligible effects of the pollution.[4] Thus challenged, the lumbermen hired their own consultants to prove their case and experimented with new ways of using the waste. Ironically, mill owners such as W.C. Edwards, J.R. Booth, and E.H. Bronson from the Ottawa Valley were leaders of the early conservation movement in Canada. Their views were much more utilitarian, however, than those of individuals who opposed sawdust dumping; they emphasized the efficient and planned use of forest resources in support of large-scale industrial development. In this way, the "sawdust question," as it was called, became one essential catalyst which differentiated various proponents of the early Canadian conservation movement. It also helped to draw together another diverse group of interests—including sportsmen, public health advocates, individuals concerned with recreation, naturalists, scientists, and proponents of water navigation improvements—who offered a conservationist viewpoint that went beyond narrow business needs and efficiency in exploitation. They did not argue that the forest industries should be put out of business but rather that they should be carried on in a manner that respected the rights of other users of rivers and streams, preserved sanitary conditions, and protected the fish population and natural beauty of such areas. Essentially they represented a less utilitarian, more public-oriented approach to resource use which derived from an urban environment where there was some appreciation that efforts had to be made if living conditions were to be maintained and improved. Not formally organized, this collection of interests did not form a dominant strain within the Canadian population in the late nineteenth century, but was influential enough to force concerted action by the federal government against the obvious abuse of sawdust pollution. At the same time, their demand for action against the lumbermen played some part in encouraging a more scientific approach towards evaluating human beings' effect on their environment.

Canadian historians rarely have looked at the question of sawdust pollution, especially in its broader context as a crucial part of the debate over early conservationist notions,[5] mainly because there has been no detailed analysis of the impact of the sawdust question on the area which was the cockpit of the debate—the Ottawa Valley. It is to this analysis that this paper turns.

The agitation against sawdust pollution actually started among sport fishermen in the Province of Canada who were alarmed at the rapid decline in fish populations. They were particularly worried about the salmon which was suffering from deteriorating water quality as a result of more extensive settlement.[6] Lobbying by this group persuaded the legislature of the Province of Canada to pass two Fishing Acts in 1857 and 1858, providing the first means by which fishing regulations could be enforced. These remained moribund, however, until 1865 when the legislature passed another Fisheries Act. This legislation included a substantially strengthened section dealing with water pollution which brought together and expanded ideas expressed in older statutes. It read that:

> Lime, chemical substances or drugs, poisonous matter (liquid or solid), dead or decaying fish or any other deleterious substance, shall not be drawn into or allowed to pass into, be left or remain in any water frequented by any of the kinds of fish mentioned in this Act, and sawdust or mill rubbish shall not be drifted or thrown into any stream frequented by salmon, trout, pickerel or bass under penalty not exceeding one hundred dollars.[7]

The period of the early 1860s witnessed an awakening of Canadians to the decline in the quality of their natural surroundings. Immediately after passage of the new Act, Dr E. Van Cortland, officer of health for the city of Ottawa, launched a petition. In the spring of 1866 he wrote to the Department of Crown Lands, the agency responsible for fisheries until Confederation, requesting that lumber companies operating on the Ottawa River be restrained from dumping mill waste in that stream. His reasons for the ban were threefold: that refuse was a threat to public health; that it was destroying the spawning grounds for fish; and that it posed a potential threat to navigation.

Van Cortland's plea broadened the basis of support for government action on sawdust dumping beyond sport fishermen and, indeed, it set forth the exact concerns which would be espoused by anti-pollution advocates through to 1902. The letter, coming as it did from a respected local official, struck a responsive chord with the provincial Coalition ministry. On 25 August 1866, the Department of Crown Lands issued a circular which informed all mill owners in the Province of Canada that they "must adapt their premises to the disposal of waste materials in such a manner as shall obviate further injury to rivers and streams."[8] The reaction from the mill operators along the lower Ottawa River, at whom the new regulations were primarily aimed, was swift. On 8 September, the leading lumbermen of Ottawa-Hull, including Gilmour and Company, Levi Young, the Bronsons and Weston Company, Perley and Pattee, and Ezra Butler Eddy, sent a long and pointed memorial to the governor general, Lord Monck. The men involved were among the wealthiest entrepreneurs in the province and their trade in lumber products, which was oriented to both

Great Britain and the United States, was the largest non-agricultural industry in British North America. Politically, the lumbermen formed a powerful influence in both the Conservative and Reform parties. Now, they stated flatly that, as their mills were driven by water power, it was quite impossible to prevent sawdust from falling into the Ottawa River. The mills were built out over the water with wide cracks left between the floorboards precisely so that the waste would pour into the stream. To install equipment to collect this sawdust, they argued, would double the cost of producing their lumber. The only other solution, they foresaw, was to abandon their present mills and build new steam factories, but the attendant loss of business involved would be large and the operators agreed that they would rather quit the trade.[9]

Of course, the lumbermen's response was in part an elaborate bluff. Most would not abandon their lucrative trade in pine timber. Beyond a doubt their water-powered mills were cheaper to operate than many steam-mills and as a result gave these entrepreneurs some advantage in a highly competitive trade. But primarily the operators were establishing a case in hopes that the Department of Crown Lands would accept the compromise solution they had to offer.

The lumbermen seized on one aspect of the problem, the threat to navigation, with which they had considerably sympathy, given the fact that the vast majority of their product was shipped by water. They suggested that grinding machines could be installed, which would reduce mill waste to sawdust form. Boats and barges could then sail on the Ottawa River without fear of foundering on heavy and dangerous waste. In addition, the operators requested the government to appoint an arbitrator to investigate the matter and to suspend action against them until this gentleman reported.[10]

John Merril Currier, Conservative member of the provincial legislature for Ottawa and prominent lumberman, presented a copy of the memorial to the Department of Crown Lands and also met with his colleague, the Hon. Alexander Campbell, the Conservative commissioner. A conscientious and philosophical man, Campbell was a guiding spirit in securing early conservation measures.[11] He was John A. Macdonald's former law partner in Kingston, and the prime minister's good friend and political confidant. He had pushed the new Fisheries Act through the Assembly. Now, under intense pressure, Campbell suspended indefinitely all lawsuits pending against the Ottawa River lumbermen for dumping waste in the river and appointed Horace Merrill, superintendent of the Ottawa River works for the provincial Department of Public Works, as arbitrator in the matter.[12] Merrill, who had numerous private business connections with local lumbermen, produced a report on 12 December 1866 which largely adopted the mill owners' recommendations. Grinders would be installed which would reduce all waste to sawdust form; then the waste would be dumped in the river. But even Merrill could not ignore the detrimental effect mill waste was having on fish life. He candidly admitted that his recommendation was only a utilitarian compromise and not a positive solution for a grave problem.

It did, however, prove politically acceptable to the Hon. Mr Campbell. In early 1867, he ordered that all lumbermen in the Province of Canada could continue to dump mill waste in rivers as long as they installed grinders. If they did not have grinders, they would be prosecuted. Throughout 1867, mill owners on the lower Ottawa were busy installing these new machines under the watchful eye of Detective E. O'Neill of the Fisheries Service. By early 1869, O'Neill was able to report that grinders were in general use in all mills in the area, except at J.R. Booth's operations where most of the slabs were used in making lath, and at Hamilton Brothers at Hawkesbury, a firm which had secured an exemption from the regulations because it dumped its waste into a series of rapids.[13]

This grinding scheme did not, however, secure much breathing space for the lumbermen. Early in 1870 a private members' bill entitled An Act for the Better Protection of Navigable Streams and Rivers was introduced into the House of Commons. It stipulated that no sawdust or mill offal was to be thrown into any navigable stream. Its sponsor was Richard Cartwright, Liberal MP for Lennox, Ontario.[14] Although the new bill did provide for certain exemptions if they were deemed in the public interest, it attacked the lumbermen at a most vulnerable point. Good navigation was generally deemed an essential part of a sound industrial policy. If indeed the lumbermen were obstructing navigation on various streams, they were retarding, at the same time, the industrialization of the new nation.

The bill failed to pass in 1870 but it was reintroduced in both 1871 and 1872. During this time the lumbering community along the lower Ottawa galvanized its friends in Parliament to battle against the legislation. Arguments were made that lumbering, the largest non-agricultural industry in the country and a major backbone of its economy, must be given some special privileges, including the right to dump its waste in all rivers and streams. As in the previous controversy, dire threats were made about closing the mills and throwing thousands out of work. This time, as well, lumbermen from the Maritimes, who would also be affected by the new legislation, were persuaded to lend their influence against the bill.[15]

All was to no avail, however, as the act moved through the various legislative stages to become law in 1873.[16] Most MPs were inclined to agree with Cartwright's position that mill waste was an enormous and avoidable nuisance. Few were willing to deny that sawdust had had an effect on all navigable streams flowing into the Great Lakes and many were particularly incensed at the condition of the Ottawa River which was described as a "national disgrace."[17] Some felt the threat to the Ottawa River was doubly dangerous because it put in jeopardy the Georgian Bay Ship Canal—a proposed short route from Chicago, across the French River system and down the Ottawa Valley to Montreal—a route which many Canadian businessmen still felt was a key to the economic development of central Canada.

Finally, many MPs were convinced that the lumbermen had grossly inflated the cost of installing the machinery to dispose of the waste properly. Indeed, they argued that sawdust could be converted into a cheap source of fuel.[18]

The lumbermen attempted to counter these arguments with evidence about the state of the Hudson River, which they considered to be still navigable despite years of lumbering along its banks.[19] In the end, however, when the bill passed, they accepted the result and placed their trust in the Conservative federal administration of John A. Macdonald, which they hoped would be lax in enforcing a law sponsored by a Liberal private member. However, the Macdonald government fell in 1873 as a result of the Pacific scandal.[20] The new Liberal-Reform government of Alexander Mackenzie included Richard Cartwright as minister of finance. Cartwright did not move immediately but he did have his revenge. In the spring of 1875 the Department of Justice, along with the Department of Marine and Fisheries, which was responsible for administering the act, began proceedings against J.R. Booth, one of the most powerful and prominent Ottawa lumbermen.

Booth had been recalcitrant about installing the original grinders in 1867 and had constantly broken the regulations since then. Now he was the first to be convicted under the new act. His fine was not large, $20, but the threat of continued court action, escalating fines, and then finally an eventual injunction against sawdust dumping soon brought both Booth and his fellow lumbermen to heel. Having done nothing to live up to the regulations, they appealed to the governor-in-council for exemptions under the act. This suited the Department of Marine and Fisheries. It had no wish to destroy the Canadian lumber industry but rather hoped to improve upon the performance of the companies in abiding by its fisheries regulations. During 1876, because the companies had proven obstinate, the department exacted its pound of flesh. In order to be exempted from the provisions of the act, a company had to prove that the dumping of sawdust in a particular stream "was not injurious to the public interest." It declared that, along the lower Ottawa, it was readily apparent that sawdust pollution was harming the river and its tributaries. Therefore, the agency asked the lumbermen to prove that the cost involved in converting the water-powered mills so that no sawdust entered the river was prohibitive; that if the mill owners were forced to undertake these renovations they would have to close down, throwing men out of work; and, finally, whether the mill waste served other interests which had been neglected by over-concentration on the destruction of fish life and navigation.

During the early months of 1877, in order to form an opinion on these issues, the Department appointed John Mather, one of the best mill engineers in Canada, to investigate conditions in each of the sawmills along the lower Ottawa. Mather presented his report in June 1877. It was a far more critical document than that prepared by Merrill a decade before.

He stated categorically that in every mill, disposal of waste could be handled differently than at the present time. Waste burners could be installed with conveyors or tramways to carry the sawdust to them. This technology was already in use at various steam mills and could readily be applied to the water-powered facilities, though such installation would be costly. He concluded that for this reason, and the fact that the burners would push fire insurance rates up 2 percent, the lumbermen were resisting these changes. As evidence, Mather estimated that 12 300 000 cubic feet of sawdust were being dumped in the Ottawa River alone each year and that this amount was increasing annually, thus posing a serious threat to fish life and navigation. The problem had become serious enough, in Mather's view, to merit a major effort to enforce existing laws that curbed the dumping of waste, despite both the costs involved for the lumbermen and the attendant risk that they might close down their operations.

On 20 December 1877, the mill owners met with the Hon. Sir Albert James Smith, minister of marine and fisheries, and with Mather to determine if the two sides could agree on a suitable plan for limiting the dumping and to consider generally the Mather Report. W.G. Perley, prominent lumberman and Tory MP for Ottawa, acted as spokesman for the industry. The lumbermen took the same position they had held in 1866. They were of the view that slabs and other heavy waste could be kept out of the river, but argued that the sawdust was not obstructing navigation, that fish life was of negligible importance in comparison with the lumber industry, and that, therefore, the dumping of such waste should be permitted. The minister replied that he was not going to try to close the sawmills along the Ottawa River; he was, however, going to delegate Mather to supervise at each mill renovations designed to put a stop to all heavy waste entering the river and to improve the general system of disposing of all sawdust and chips. Furthermore, the owners were to institute these modifications immediately and bear their cost. The lumbermen concurred in this arrangement.[21]

Thus, during the winter and spring of 1877, each mill operator along the lower Ottawa was busy installing more chippers and grinders under various plans approved by Mather. At the same time, the Department of Marine and Fisheries received several petitions from inhabitants along the river pleading that the mill slabs not be chipped since they collected them for firewood. Such opposition did not, however, delay work on the renovations and by 15 January 1879 Mather reported that nearly every mill along the lower Ottawa was equipped in the approved fashion. The companies immediately were granted exemptions from the act, and these exceptions were officially embodied in an order-in-council on 23 June 1880.[22]

At this point, the lumbermen thought that a final arrangement on the sawdust problem had been reached. In reality, the Department of Marine and

Fisheries, despite considerable effort, had made an unsatisfactory compromise in dealing with the problem of mill offal along the Ottawa. Essentially, in the period 1866 to 1878, officials had managed only to enforce regulations which kept slabs and heavy waste out of the water, and even this was proving problematical since complaints were still being received about the dumping of heavy waste into the Ottawa. In fact, the lumbermen had managed to continue their operations in very much the way they had before the anti-dumping legislation. Thus, the condition of the Ottawa River had continued to deteriorate. In both 1866 and 1873 the mill owners had found it impossible to resist the political pressure and public outcry aroused in favour of the anti-pollution measures. After passage of the acts, however, they had managed, through negotiations with government officials, to limit the problem to the issue of navigation and then to persuade authorities that chipped waste was causing no problem. As well, the lumbermen had been sufficiently organized to present a united front through which they threatened to close all their mills and throw thousands of men out of work, a bluff the federal government was not willing to call. Finally, the operators' lawyers and agents sought support from the local population. Because no one wanted to see the mills closed down, petitioners flooded the Department of Marine and Fisheries with requests for continuance of sawdust dumping.[23] These manoeuvres demonstrated the lumbermen's effective use of their political and economic power. While appearing to negotiate earnestly with federal officials to solve a grave problem, they were actually approaching the issue in such a manner as would allow them to sidestep it. Indeed, while posing as public-spirited men, the mill owners were managing events for their own profit.

But if the lumbermen thought that their trouble over sawdust dumping had ended with the 1880 order-in-council they were sorely mistaken. True, federal authorities had lost interest in the question after the Conservatives were returned to power in 1878. Sir John A. Macdonald's government completed the arrangements started by the Liberals but then let the matter drop. However, the problem itself was too serious and obvious in nature to remain forgotten. Complaints continued to be received from boat operators and other users of the river about the dumping of not just sawdust but also heavy waste.[24] The issue was pushed to the fore when the province of Ontario passed its own fisheries act in 1885. Rumours were rife that provincial authorities would use injunctions to stop the dumping of mill offal into various streams, including the Ottawa. Once again, the lumbermen used their economic and political power to obstruct this special legislation even as they blithely assured the Ontario government that "it [the industry] was doing everything in its power to remedy the matter."[25] The Ottawa Valley mill owners felt compelled, however, to approach the federal government again for a general order-in-council insuring their right to dump sawdust into the Gatineau and Ottawa rivers. The order was granted on 17 April 1885, but its issuance once again drew attention to the abuse. Late the next year the deputy minister of fisheries, John Tilton, condemned the lumbermen's total disregard of existing regulations. Prompted by powerful renewed criticism in the Ottawa Valley of the whole mill waste problem, Tilton was particularly critical of the continued dumping of heavy waste into the Ottawa River.[26]

The issue was taken up by a long-time resident of Ottawa and Tory senator, Francis B. Clemow. Clemow was a prominent member of the Ottawa business community, manager of the Ottawa Gas Works, and frequent partner with local lumbermen in a variety of ventures.[27] He was, however, willing to risk the wrath of these entrepreneurs by championing measures to prevent the dumping of mill offal. His concern was centred on the risks that continued dumping of sawdust posed to the natural beauty of the Ottawa Valley, its fish life, its business development through navigation, and the health of its citizens. This threat was emphasized for Clemow by the growing frequency of explosions in the river resulting from concentrations of methane gas produced by the rotting refuse. Thus the senator presented the perfect combination of early preservationist and industrial promoter—he was a supporter of the Georgian Bay ship canal—which could galvanize some political action on the matter.

Clemow's interest in the sawdust question was compounded by a pressing international problem of sawdust fouling the Saint John River, its tributaries, and the waters of Maine. As a result, a select committee of the Senate was formed to study the total extent and effect of dumping refuse into Canadian streams.[28] The committee requested the government to make available Henry A. Gray, assistant chief engineer, Department of Public Works, to conduct a detailed survey of the river between the Chaudière Falls and Grenville during the summer of 1887. He took soundings and borings, and interviewed those who had lived along the river for many years. He found the sawdust to be a definite hazard to navigation, blocking channels with accumulations in some areas up to eighty feet deep. Furthermore, Gray found the substance difficult to dredge because of its loose composition and speculated that it was difficult to see how fish life could survive in such water. Finally, the engineer described the methane explosions which on occasion shook the river.[29]

Gray's official report was not released by the Department of Public Works until the spring of 1889. On the basis of his findings the Senate committee recommended, on 15 May 1888, that "the government take steps to prevent such deposits in the future."[30] The lumbermen were quick to react. The Gray Report snatched from them the main basis of their argument—that the sawdust was not obstructing navigation. They organized their own committee under E.H. Bronson, president of the Bronsons and Weston Lumber Company and Reform member of the Ontario Legislature for Ottawa. Bronson began immediately to raise money for the mill owners' own survey of the river to disprove Gray's findings. He summed up the issue succinctly to a smaller operator, W. McClymont:

This sawdust question is not as to whether we [the mill owners] shall be permitted to put a little sawdust into the river as you state you are doing, or whether we shall put in all we make, but is a question as to whether we shall be allowed to put any *at all* [emphasis his] in the river.

If the decision is that we must keep it all out, the only alternative will be for us all to make any necessary alterations in our mills to keep all the sawdust out of the river, and put in refuse burners to consume it. This would cost you and all the rest of us ten times as much every year as this examination will cost.[31]

The lumbermen were fully aware of the gravity of their situation and they wanted a prominent engineer to lend weight to their survey. After much discussion, they settled on the well-known civil engineer, inventor, and father of standard time, Sir Sanford Fleming, to organize the operation. He was not the lumbermen's first choice for the job. They had hunted in Montreal, Toronto, and the northeastern United States for a well-known and respected engineer who would prove sympathetic to the business concerns involved. Fleming appears to have become available at the eleventh hour and was considered to have the proper credentials.

Fleming undertook the survey in the summer of 1888—and reported, predictably, that, with the single exception of the mouth of the Rideau Canal, accumulations of sawdust were producing no major obstructions to navigation along the lower Ottawa River. To bolster this report, Bronson sought from various American lumbermen and politicians information on the effects of sawdust on other rivers. Most replies indicated that sawdust was not the great nuisance that some pretended it to be. With this evidence, plus the Fleming Report, Bronson was confident that the lumbermen could persuade the federal government to leave the regulations as they were. As he informed Hector Langevin, minister of public works, "[It is] our firm conviction . . . that the high water each year clears the river channel of any sawdust deposits that the slow current the preceding fall may have permitted to lodge therein."[32]

Bronson did not have to convince the prime minister, Sir John A. Macdonald. In the summer of 1889 Macdonald was an aging and tired man who was rather bewildered by the whole debate over the sawdust question. He wanted to make sure that there was "no suspension of sawmills" as a consequence of the problem and took the rather novel approach of arguing that lumbering should continue until all the trees had been cut along a river; at that point the river could be restocked with fish at government expense.[33]

In taking this stance, Macdonald was adopting the traditional view of lumbering as a transitory industry which simply removed the forests in preparation for settlement. It was an opinion that many Ottawa Valley lumbermen no longer shared. Faced with large investments in mills and declining wood stocks, they were beginning to push for more conservation-based measures regarding forest use in order to protect the pineries.[34] Now, however, in order to protect their interests, they were quite willing to abandon these recently acquired views. They told the government that logging had gone on in the Valley for ninety-five years without harm and that, since two-thirds of the merchantable timber was now gone, the lumbermen should be left to remove the last third unmolested. In such vital matters, they had little use for Clemow's preservationist ideas. Conservation for them was utilitarian and business-oriented, as witnessed by the operators' declaration that:

> As regards the beauty of the landscape . . . we admit that floating sawdust does not improve the general appearance of the river, but it must be remembered that this is a utilitarian age and that the interests of any important industry, the success of which affects the well-being of so many people, are invariably held to be paramount to the gratification of mere aesthetic taste, satisfactory and desirable as that may be under proper conditions.[35]

But others had very different views on the water pollution issue, and public pressure was placed on the government to take some action. Clemow continued to spearhead a drive to exact from the Conservative government a promise to do something about the sawdust problem. He proposed legislation which received renewed support after 15 September 1890 when it was revealed that a study by W.A. McGill, assistant analyst in the Department of Inland Revenue, revealed that the water of the Ottawa River, while not yet dangerous, was in a state which would support morbific bacteria.[36]

The battle shaped up around amendments to the Fisheries Act and whether or not the Tory administration (now without Macdonald, who had died on 6 June 1891) could be persuaded to enact tougher pollution measures. The minister of marine and fisheries was Charles Hibbert Tupper, a Nova Scotian who had little interest in any measures except those relating to commercial coastal fisheries. As he observed, the Ottawa River could continue to receive sawdust because "there are no lobsters in it."[37] In taking this stand, Tupper was reneging on what Clemow considered to be a government promise made in March 1890 to pass special clauses to protect the navigable rivers of Canada. The senator was enraged. He smelled a deal designed to protect the powerful Ottawa lumbermen at the expense of his city's health, beauty, and commercial destiny. The stench of political trading was given especial credence because the chronic offender in sawdust dumping, J.R. Booth, had just rebuilt his mills with no provision being made for the disposal of waste, except in the Ottawa River! Clemow charged publicly that the Department of Marine and Fisheries was ignoring vast amounts of information collected by government officials which documented the existence of the nuisance. Further, he launched an attack on Booth, declaring that he had come to Ottawa poor and raped the countryside to make a fortune. He concluded that the country owed the Booths of the world nothing and demanded that after 1 May 1895 all exemptions for sawdust dumping be terminated. Clemow was supported in his battle by a petition from 715 Ottawa-area residents which contended that the mill refuse in the lower Ottawa was a hazard to navigation, prevented use of river properties, and posed a menace to public health.[38] In the furor which resulted, the Senate acted on Clemow's motion to amend Tupper's Fisheries Act and the Commons moved to support the amendment.

The new provision declared that after 1 May 1895 all exemptions for sawdust dumping were to cease unless good and sufficient reasons could be given by the mill owners for continuing the practice. There was still room for some discretion in the matter but it was much narrower, especially given the fact that Colonel F.H.D. Vieth, fisheries overseer, was instructed to visit each mill to establish definitely where the offal was deposited, if it harmed spawning beds, where the sawdust came to rest, and if it was harmful to navigation. The lumbermen were notified of this arrangement on 3 August 1894. A month later William Smith, deputy minister of marine and fisheries, again wrote to operators deploring their non-co-operation with Vieth.[39] The mill owners adopted their classic stance of outright refusal to comply in preparation for another round of negotiations. Smith, however, warned them that their delay was seriously prejudicing any case that the lumbermen might be able to establish for an extension of their exemptions.

This threat brought a flood of letters of apology and justification from the lumbermen. This correspondence showed that a few operators were taking the matter more seriously. Several, including the E.B. Eddy Company and the W.C. Edwards Company, indicated that they were utilizing sawdust both for fuel and manufacturing purposes. Indeed, Eddy's was buying sawdust from other operators.[40] Such changes were not, however, particularly connected to a fit of conscience. Rather, first-class wood stocks were declining in the Ottawa Valley and there was greater need to utilize more parts of the tree, as well as to diversify into new product lines such as pulp and paper. Such measures were part of the eastern forest industry's attempt to make its basis more durable, to promote forest conservation measures, to protect standing timber, and generally to make its operations more efficient. In this sense the threat of stronger pollution regulations spurred on the diversification process. But such measures were still the exception and most mills, including the large Booth and Bronsons and Weston enterprises, had made little progress and simply stated that the delay had been occasioned by meetings among the operators to establish a common response to the department's demands.

The Ottawa Valley industry replied to Smith on 22 September 1894. It indicated that as far as navigation was concerned the operators stood by the conclusions of the Fleming Report. Further, it stated that the fishery business on the Ottawa was, at best, a very small one; if it needed to be saved, according to the lumbermen, the government should be responsible for putting in fishways and for restocking. To dwell on absolute dumping bans was to threaten what was, by contrast, a large and substantial industry. Reflecting E.H. Bronson's views, the response quoted scientists and analysts who claimed that sawdust did not harm rivers and asked pointedly why federal officials were doing nothing to stop the dumping of sewage in navigable rivers—a nuisance which really did harm the streams and posed a definite health hazard. Finally, the Valley operators reminded the government of the jobs which would be lost if the mills closed and argued that the industry had passed its peak on the Ottawa, with the consequence that smaller numbers of trees would be cut by lighter gauge saws which would automatically reduce the amount of sawdust entering the Ottawa River. As well, several lumbermen, including W.C. Edwards, informed the government that the cost of installing large burners was $13 000–15 000 per burner and that fire insurance rates would be forced up between 4 3/4 and 5 percent, both extra financial burdens on the industry.[41]

The lumbermen, while expanding the grounds of argument over their right to pollute, did not trust to chance in preserving their exemption. Booth and Hiram Robinson, a partner in the Hawkesbury Lumber Company and a known Tory, met Tupper's successor as minister of marine and fisheries, John Costigan of New Brunswick. Being from a lumbering area, Costigan was more conversant with the sawdust problem. H.K. Egan, Robinson's partner, promised to supply the minister with any data that he required to justify passage of special remedial legislation.[42] A new dimension was also introduced into these private discussions. Clemow had acquired a particularly vocal ally in R.J. Wicksteed, an Ottawa barrister who was an avid advocate not only of protecting the Ottawa River from pollution but also of ending the lumbermen's special privileges in regard to refuse dumping. Booth and Robinson now indicated to Costigan that Wicksteed was intent upon closing some of the mills through use of the fisheries regulations. This alarmed Costigan, who informed the new Conservative prime minister, Sir John Thompson, of the situation. Thompson, who was the same individual consulted by Sir John A. Macdonald on the subject, obtained directly from Smith a full appraisal of the situation.[43] The deputy minister indicated that he was pleased with the progress made by firms such as E.B. Eddy and the W.C. Edwards Co. to ease the pollution situation, but also revealed his agency's lack of resolve to push the new legislation when he stated that "he could not really justify the closing down of the other mills over the sawdust issue." He feared the impact of the closures on the Ottawa Valley and national economy and introduced the new issue of smoke pollution. The Deputy informed the prime minister that "not sufficient research has been done into the effects of smoke pollution from massive numbers of sawdust burners or the impact such burners would have on insurance rates." Sensing the political realities of the matter and the Department of Marine and Fisheries' lack of resolve, the mill owners played up the unpopularity of the waste dumping measures in the Ottawa Valley and in the Maritimes where the new regulations would also be in effect. Despite stout efforts by Clemow, particular pressure was brought by the Ottawa Board of Trade to suspend all efforts to prosecute offending mill owners under the new law and, indeed, for the Tories to seek remedial legislation to enshrine the dumping exemptions in law.[44] The two factions disputing the issue were driven almost to overt violence at Board meetings and the government simply delayed action on remedial legislation.

As the 1 May 1895 deadline approached, however, the Department of Marine and Fisheries finally revealed where the government really stood on the matter. It had continued its study of the matter with E.E. Prince, the department's leading fish specialist, reporting definitively that sawdust did affect fish spawning and did chemically foul the water. As well, other officials, including Vieth, produced evidence to refute Fleming's findings on the effect of sawdust on navigation and testimony to prove the deterioration of fish species in the Ottawa River.[45] Nevertheless, in mid-March the department, on Costigan's behalf, issued directives indicating that the government would seek remedial legislation to reinstate the dumping exemptions and that until this was passed inspectors would not enforce the existing law. Further, the directives stated that if proceedings were taken by members of the public, the department would refund any fines levied against the mill owners. The measures were justified as necessary to prevent hardship in the forest industries. News of this position on the part of the government prompted lumbermen in both the Maritimes and the Ottawa Valley to flood Marine and Fisheries with requests for exemptions which went beyond those already in place. The government, however, restricted its directives to existing exemptions. Basically, the minister indicated that no evidence had come to his attention to convince him that dumping exemptions should not be extended through remedial legislation!

The Tories were defeated in the general election of 1896 without having changed the Fisheries Act. The new Liberal government of Wilfrid Laurier appeared to be no less sympathetic to the lumbermen; W.C. Edwards was a close friend of the prime minister and other operators, such as E.H. Bronson, were powerful and influential Reformers. Nevertheless, the fact remained that the Ottawa River and its tributaries were now heavily clogged with waste. As well, public pressure for government action continued to be strong. Indeed, methane explosions were now commonplace, endangering boaters to the extent that in late 1897 a prominent Montebello area farmer was drowned when dumped in the river as a result of such a shock.[46] This deteriorating situation prompted the new deputy minister of marine and fisheries, François Gourdeau, to take action. Promoted from within the department, he was the type of public servant who was tired of seeing public research and effective regulations ham-strung by lack of political will to face down powerful business interests. Gourdeau viewed the situation along the lower Ottawa as a national disgrace and was determined to stop the dumping of sawdust. In order to meet some of the political pressure, he postponed the effective date of the new fisheries regulations until 30 June 1898, but he also officially informed the lumbermen that no exemption would be allowed beyond the extension date.[47] Basically, the operators were being given a year to alter their plants or they would be shut down.

Gourdeau might have been thwarted in achieving his objectives had he not received powerful support from his own minister, Sir Louis Davies, a P.E.I. native not vulnerable to the lumber lobby, and from the minister of public works, Joseph Israel Tarte, an ultramontanist and advocate of colonization. Tarte, in particular, was influential in Cabinet; with his reputation as a political bagman and fixer, his support at first appears somewhat strange. But the minister, like Clemow before him, had an interest in preserving the natural environment for recreational and aesthetic reasons as well as navigational purposes. In a letter to Davies on 14 August 1901, Tarte congratulated the minister on his department's strong stand against sawdust dumping and categorically declared that "there is no justification in lumber merchants and millionaires, to ruin such a magnificent highway."[48]

Only under this direct and powerful threat did the influential lumbermen on the lower Ottawa hasten to solve the sawdust problem. Mill owners, in general, began to emulate the Eddy and Edwards firms in getting rid of the waste. Some found outlets for the offal as fuel for other industries, replacing expensive American coal. Others installed pulp and paper plants and other wood products operations which utilized sawdust and chips. Still others experimented with the use of the mill waste to produce carbons and acetylene. Finally, if there was no other outlet, burners were put in the mills to dispose of the sawdust. Some of these solutions had been recommended since 1866 but stoutly resisted by business interests which wished to maximize profits while not interfering with the competitive cost advantages of their water-powered mills. Predictably, it was J.R. Booth who dragged his feet in obeying the new regulations. As the largest operator in Canada, Booth had a much more difficult problem to solve. The old entrepreneur, in a characteristically individualistic stance, refused to make piecemeal renovations to his mills but rather made plans for a new pulp plant which would utilize the sawdust as fuel.[49] This was a longer-range solution than the Department of Marine and Fisheries envisioned and tension mounted after mid-1901.

Up until 1900, Booth had shown good faith in attempting to live up to the regulations by finding buyers for his sawdust and participating in various experiments for by-products. In that year, however, a massive fire at the Chaudière wiped out many of the establishments which had bought Booth's sawdust and left him with a disposal problem. Though he had laid down plans for his pulp mill, it was not due for completion until at least 1903. Booth viewed this as the best solution because it would not only take care of the mill refuse but also employ more men. He acknowledged, however, that he was breaking the law every day in dumping the offal and the

Department of Marine and Fisheries could not ignore the situation since public complaints were now mounting. W.C. Edwards became a mediator between the firm and the government. He convinced the department to refrain from action until experiments in using sawdust to produce carbon had been completed on his assurance that Booth would then put in place "efficient measures . . . for the disposal of the sawdust."[50]

By mid-1901, the experiments had come to nothing and Booth had done little else to remedy the waste problem. The government, therefore, had little choice but to begin prosecution against the lumberman. Booth pleaded for leniency, indicating that, since his sawing season was already under way, he could not be expected to put in burners and furnaces until the coming winter. He further indicated that he would pay fines until such time as an injunction was issued; then he would close his mills, throwing 1500 to 2000 men out of work. Gourdeau and the Department of Marine and Fisheries would not be deterred, however, and instructed court proceedings to be undertaken.[51] Booth commenced to pay fines, and on 13 September 1901, Gourdeau instructed the Department of Justice to seek an injunction against sawdust dumping on behalf of the government.

The situation reached the point of confrontation; in the city of Ottawa, it was an embarrassing time for both the Liberal federal government and John Rudolphus Booth. Edwards, the local Reform fixer, intervened personally with Laurier in an attempt to reconcile the dispute. The prime minister ordered the minister, Davies, to postpone court action against Booth for one week. Then, on 24 September 1901, Laurier further indicated to Gourdeau that, "I desire you to give instructions to . . . counsel for the Department of Marine and Fisheries against Mr. Booth for putting sawdust in the Ottawa River, to have that prosecution withdrawn as Mr. Booth has undertaken, as soon as the sawing season is over, to put up a burner and to entirely stop the illegal practice complained of, at the beginning of the next season."[52] The prime minister had intervened to give Booth his extra time, but at the price of a promise to absolutely stop the dumping of sawdust. The battle over sawdust pollution finally had been won. There were still some doubts that Booth would actually keep his word. Indeed, Tarte wrote to the new minister of marine and fisheries, James Sutherland, on 8 September 1902, stating that Canada's leading lumberman "appears to have made a promise to Sir Wilfrid that he does not plan to keep."[53] But, by the spring of 1903, inspectors reported that Booth had taken care of 95 percent of the waste problem at his mills. With J.R. Booth obeying the regulations there was no reason for anyone else in Canada not to do so.

Thus, thirty-five years after the first public petition to stop the dumping of mill waste into the Ottawa River, government officials had finally been given the necessary political support to stop the abuse. It must be noted, however, that the victory was won against an Ottawa Valley sawn lumber industry which was already in decline and which was re-tooling into pulp and paper and wood by-products, procedures which demanded more efficient utilization of mill wastes. Nevertheless, the lower Ottawa had become a symbol for those who wished to end sawdust pollution. If laws could be flouted right under the windows of the Parliament buildings, then there was little hope of enforcing pollution regulations elsewhere in the nation. The battle was joined there and became the bellwether for testing the fisheries regulations. At the same time, the controversy became an important episode in defining the early conservationist impulse in Canada. The Ottawa lumber barons and associates elsewhere in eastern Canada had attempted to appropriate that movement to their own business needs by defining its precepts as solely utilitarian and oriented to efficient, planned use of the forest resource with an emphasis on preserving commercial species for full utilization. The anti-pollution proponents, however, served to challenge and widen that definition. They introduced into the pollution debate the factors of maintaining fish life, preserving natural beauty, encouraging recreation, ensuring public health, and promoting water navigation. In this way they were the early harbingers of the preservationist wing of the conservation movement, which was to have its greatest success a few years later in the expansion of wildlife sanctuaries and national parks, as well as the multiple-use concept of resources. Perhaps the most important contribution of the whole sawdust question was the use made by anti-pollution advocates of government officials and facilities to research, investigate, and regulate the dumping of waste. Once again, this was an early example of a more activist government which would regulate business activities for a politically defined public interest. In short, from the microcosm of the sawdust question emerge themes about the relationship of Canadians with their environment—natural, social, and economic—in the late nineteenth century which provide important new perspectives on the development of the country in the period of "national transformation."[54]

• Notes

1 See, for example, H. Clepper, ed., *Origins of American Conservation* (New York: Ronald Press, 1966); S. Hays, *Conservation and the Gospel of Efficiency: The Progressive Conservation Movement, 1890–1920* (New York: Atheneum, 1969); D.H. Strong, *The Conservationists* (Menlo Park, CA: Addison-Wesley, 1971); and R. Rash, *Wilderness and the American Mind* (New Haven: Yale University Press, 1967). The standard Canadian studies are R.S. Lambert and P. Pross, *Renewing Nature's Wealth: A Centennial History of the Public Management of Lands, Forests and Wildlife in Ontario, 1763–1967* (Toronto: Ontario Department of Lands and Forests, 1967); H.V. Nelles, *The Politics of Development: Forests, Mines and Hydro-electric Power in Ontario, 1849–1941* (Toronto: Macmillan, 1973); and J. Foster, *Working for Wildlife: The Beginning of Preservation in Canada* (Toronto: University of Toronto Press, 1978); as well as R.P. Gillis, "The Ottawa Lumber Barons and the Conservation Movement, 1880–1914," *Journal of Canadian Studies* 18 (Feb. 1974): 14–30; and R.P Gillis, B. Hodgins, and J. Benidickson, "The

Ontario and Quebec Experiments in Forest Reserves, 1883–1930," *Journal of Forest History* 26, 1 (Jan. 1982): 20–33.

2 Statutes of Lower Canada, 6 Vict., Cap. 17, An Act for Better Preventing the Obstruction of Rivers and Rivulets in Canada East, 1843; and Statutes of Upper Canada, 7 Vict., Cap. 36, An Act to Prevent Obstruction in Rivers and Rivulets in Upper Canada, 9 Dec. 1843.

3 The best discussion of the development of the North American lumber free trade is found in A.R.M. Lower, *The North American Assault on the Canadian Forest* (Toronto: Ryerson, 1938).

4 The details of these activities and, therefore, many of the documents for this article are drawn from Public Archives of Canada (hereafter PAC), Dept. of Fisheries, record group 23, file 1669, vols. 1–3.

5 See, for instance, P. Mitchell, "Déjà Vu: Refuse in Rivers and Harbours," *Nature Canada* 7 (Oct.–Dec. 1978): 33–34; and G. Allardyce, "The Vexed Question of Sawdust: River Pollution in Nineteenth-Century New Brunswick," *Dalhousie Review* 52 (1972): 177–90.

6 Lambert and Pross, *Renewing Nature's Wealth*, 151–54.

7 Province of Canada, Statutes, 29 Vict., Cap. 11, An Act to Amend Cap 62 of the Consolidated Statutes of Canada and to Provide for the Better Regulation of Fishing and Protection of Fisheries.

8 PAC, RG23, file 1669, Digest of Papers on the Sawdust Question, 1866–1918.

9 Ibid.

10 Ibid., Record of Transmittal and Interview, J.M. Currier and Hon. A. Campbell, 12 Sept. 1866.

11 Lambert and Pross, *Renewing Nature's Wealth*, 151–54 and 178.

12 PAC, RG23, file 1669, Report of Horace Merrill, 12 Dec. 1866.

13 Ibid., Plan submitted by Merrill, 4 Mar. 1867; Report on ability of Victoria Foundry and Machine Shops to provide slab cutters, 18 Apr. 1867; Report by Detective E. O'Neill that mills taking steps to install machinery, 19 Nov. 1867; and Final Reports by O'Neill, 19–20 Aug. 1868. It is worth noting that in line with the political morality of the time Merrill was a leading shareholder in the Victoria Foundry, the company that made the chipping equipment.

14 Canada, House of Commons, *Debates*, 1871, 171.

15 PAC, RG23, file 1669, Various Requests for Exemption, 1871–76.

16 Canada, Statutes, 36 Vict., Cap. 65, An Act for the Better Protection of Navigable Streams and Rivers.

17 Canada, *Debates*, 1871–72.

18 Ibid.

19 Ibid., see Currier's statement, 1871.

20 Details given in D.G. Creighton, *John A. Macdonald: The Old Chieftain* (Toronto: Macmillan, 1965), 158–60.

21 PAC, RG23, file 1669, Various petitions from mill owners and Conviction of J.R. Booth under act, 22 June 1875; Report of John Mather, June 1877; Summation of Meeting with Smith, 20 Dec. 1877.

22 Ibid., Representation of Ottawa mill owners for Formal Exemption, 3 Feb. 1880, and Official Order-in-Council, 23 June 1880.

23 Ibid., Circular Letter to all Mill Owners as Result of Complaint by Capt. Bowie of Steamship *Peerless*, 2 Nov. 1886; and Petition from Residents of Counties Bordering the Ottawa River, 29 Jan. 1878, 19 Feb. 1878, and 7 Mar. 1878.

24 Ibid., Complaint by Capt. Bowie of *Peerless*, 2 Nov. 1886; and *Antoine Rattee vs. Booth, Perley and Bronson*, Ontario Appeal Reports, vol. 14, L.R. 15, 188. Rattee was a boat owner below the Chaudière Falls in Ottawa. He contended in court and eventually won a claim that mill waste in the river prevented him from properly operating his boats and detracted from the value

of his property. The mill owners considered him a shyster who lived off the damages collected from them. The Ontario appeal court thought otherwise, however, and decided in Rattee's favour. He petitioned frequently against the waste problem.

25 PAC, Bronsons and Weston Company Records, MG28III37, vol. 106, Bronsons and Weston to Thomas Murray MPP, 19 Mar. 1885; and RG23, file 1669, Ottawa Committee of Lumbermen to Minister of Marine and Fisheries, 22 Sept. 1894, recalling Ontario situation.

26 PAC, MC28III37, J. Tilton, Deputy Minister of Fisheries to Bronsons and Weston Co., 3 Nov. 1886; and RG23, file 1669, Bowie Complaint.

27 J.K. Johnson, ed., *The Canadian Directory of Parliament* (Ottawa: Public Archives, 1968), 124.

28 Canada, Senate, *Sessional Paper*, no. 43C, submitted 16 Dec. 1890; and RG23, file 1669, Notation, 15 May 1888.

29 Canada, Department of Public Works, Report of Chief Engineer's Office, Ottawa, 1888.

30 Canada, Senate, *Debates*, 1891, Senator Clemow on background to the Sawdust Bill, which he is sponsoring.

31 PAC, MG28III37, E.H. Bronson to Messrs W. McClymont and Co., 26 May 1888.

32 PAC, RG23, file 1669, Summation of Fleming Report, 30 Jan. 1889; MG28III37, E.H. Bronson to Judge Brown, Glen Falls, NY, 12 June 1888; Bronson to T. Pringle, Montreal, 29 Nov. 1888; Bronson to City Clerk, Muskegon and Bay City, MI, 4 Feb. 1890; and Bronson to Hector Langevin, Minister of Public Works, 22 May 1888.

33 PAC, Sir John A. Macdonald papers, MG26A, Macdonald to A.W. McLelan, Lieutenant Governor of Nova Scotia, 4 July 1889; Macdonald to John Thompson, Minister of Justice, 4 July 1889.

34 For a full discussion of these issues see Gillis, "The Ottawa Lumber Barons."

35 PAC, RG23, file 1669, Ottawa Committee of Lumbermen to Minister of Marine and Fisheries, 22 Sept. 1894.

36 Ibid. There is no doubt that the state of the river in this respect resulted from the dumping of human waste in it, but there was a feeling at the time that sawdust was also a contributing factor.

37 Canada, House of Commons, *Debates*, Sir Charles Hibbert Tupper on amendments to Fisheries Act, 4557–66.

38 Canada, Senate, *Debates*, 1894, 720–25; and PAC, RG23, file 1669, Petition A. Rattee, W.R. Bell MD, F.X. Valade MD, P. St Jean MD, and 715 others.

39 Canada, Statutes, 58–59 Vict., Cap. 27, An Act Further to Amend the Fisheries Act; and PAC, RG23, file 1669, Marine and Fisheries Circular to Mill Owners, 3 Aug. 1894.

40 PAC, RG23, file 1669, Ottawa Committee of Lumbermen to Minister of Marine and Fisheries, 22 Sept. 1894; Report from W.C. Edwards on his mills, 19 Sept. 1894; Buell, Hurdman and Co. to Deputy Minister of Marine and Fisheries, 21 Sept. 1894; Bronsons and Weston Co. to Deputy Minister of Marine and Fisheries, 22 Sept. 1894; E.B. Eddy Co. to Deputy Minister of Marine and Fisheries, 22 Sept. 1894; and MG28III37, vol. 115, E.H. Bronson to A.M. Low, Secretary, International Sulphide, 18 Nov. 1890, 17 Dec. 1890, 12 Jan. 1891, and to Geo. M. Fletcher, President, International Sulphide, 28 May 1891.

41 PAC, RG23, file 1669, Ottawa Committee to Minister, 22 Sept. 1894, and W.C. Edwards to Charles Hibbert Tupper, 24 Sept. 1894.

42 Ibid., Hiram Robinson to Charles Hibbert Tupper, 10 Aug. 1894.

43 Ibid., H.K. Egan (partner in the Hawkesbury Lumber Co.) to John

Costigan, 5 Apr. 1895; Deputy Minister of Marine and Fisheries to Sir John Thompson, 27 Sept. 1894.

44 Ibid., Resolutions passed by Citizens of Hawkesbury, 19 Nov. 1894; Ottawa Board of Trade to Minister of Marine and Fisheries, 26 Feb. 1895; Departmental Memorandum by John Hardie, Acting Deputy Minister of Marine and Fisheries, 11 March 1895.

45 Ibid., E.E. Prince, Report Regarding Sawdust Question on the Ottawa River, [July] 1894; W. Wakeham, Report on Ottawa River Sawdust Nuisance, 11 July 1894; Note from Minister of Marine and Fisheries to Samuel Wilmot, 25 July 1894; Survey by F. Vieth of Quebec, New Brunswick, and Nova Scotia mills, Oct. 1894; Report by F. Vieth on Navigation of Ottawa River, [Autumn] 1894; Departmental Memorandum, John Hardie, Acting Deputy Minister of Marine and Fisheries, 11 March 1895; and MG28III37, vol. 123, E.H. Bronson to Sen. Sanford, 4 July 1895.

46 *Citizen* (Ottawa), 12 Nov. 1897, Report on death of John Kemp.

47 PAC, RG23, file 1669, Circular from F. Gourdeau, deputy minister of fisheries, 27 Sept. 1897.

48 Ibid., see Hon. I. Tarte, minister of public works, to Hon. Sir L. Davies, minister of marine and fisheries, 14 Aug. 1901.

49 Ibid., J.R. Booth to F. Gourdeau, Deputy Minister of Marine and Fisheries, 13 Aug. 1901.

50 Ibid.

51 Ibid., Gourdeau to Booth, 14 Aug. 1901; Report of Fisheries Overseer, R.C. MacQuaig, Conversation with J.R. Booth, 17 Aug. 1901; Gourdeau to Booth, 23 Aug. 1901; Gourdeau to E.L. Newcombe, Deputy Minister of Justice, 24 Aug. 1901; Newcombe to Gourdeau, 26 Aug. 1901; and Gourdeau to Newcombe, 13 Sept. 1901.

52 Ibid., Sir Wilfrid Laurier to Sir Louis Davies, 17 Sept. 1901; PAC, Sir Wilfrid Laurier papers, MG26G, Laurier to F. Gourdeau, 24 Sept. 1901.

53 PAC, RG23, file 1669, Hon. I. Tarte to James Sutherland, Minister of Marine and Fisheries, 8 Sept. 1902.

54 The term *nation transformed* has been fastened on the late nineteenth and early twentieth centuries by two leading scholars in the field, R.C. Brown and R. Cook, in *Canada 1896–1921: A Nation Transformed* (Toronto: McClelland & Stewart, 1974).

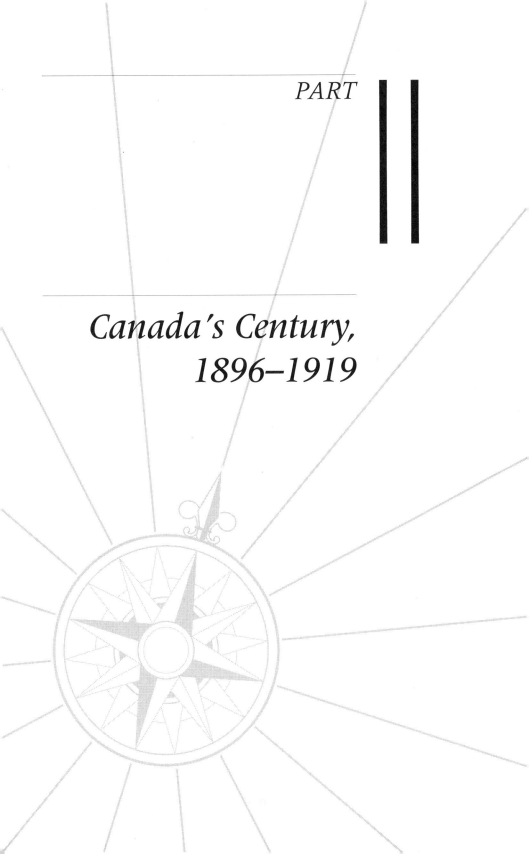

PART

Canada's Century, 1896–1919

Not too long ago, it would have been unthinkable for a historian to conduct serious research on topics such as grocery store window displays or baseball. What relevance could such topics have for "national history?" Historians also largely ignored the history of Natives, women, visible minorities, and the working class. What role could such "powerless" groups have played in affecting the course of history? New research provides convincing answers to these questions and helps to explain why historians are now interested in all dimensions of Canada's past.

Keith Walden's article offers an example of how historians are now using linguistic theory to understand the emerging urban, industrial culture of the late nineteenth and early twentieth centuries. Walden examines the purpose and content of grocery store window displays in order to probe the ways in which Canadians learned to "speak modern." In his study, window displays represent the emerging consumer culture, and his detailed analysis illustrates how language and visual images began to restructure everyday thought and belief at the turn of the century.

Tina Loo also examines one specific historical topic in order to address general questions about the role of law in society, especially with respect to white-Native relations. By focussing on the federal government's banning of the potlatch (a ritual practised by Natives on the West Coast to strengthen social links and exchange goods), Loo seeks to understand the power inherent in the law. She concludes that law should be viewed as a "system of rhetoric" rather than simply as a coercive or symbolic force. Like Walden, Loo stresses the power of language both in terms of the rules of the legal system and in the arguments used by lawyers defending Native groups. Her study contributes to a quite recent reinterpretation of legal history as well as to a better understanding of Native-white relations.

In its own way, baseball also has "laws," as Colin Howell suggests in his study of the Maritimes at the turn of the century. Like Tina Loo, Howell emphasizes the ways in which different groups strove to make these laws work to their own advantage. In this analysis, the history of baseball involves "the social relations of cultural production," in which reformers, entrepreneurs, gamblers, working people, athletes, and spectators tried to shape the game to meet their own needs. While the late nineteenth-century Maritimes are far removed from Toronto's Skydome or Montreal's Olympic Stadium, Howell's discussion relates directly to the ways in which Canadian culture has evolved in the changing context of class, gender, and regional identity.

The final article in this section focusses on World War I, showing the ways in which visible minorities maintained their dignity and resisted final defeat by the racism of official Canadian attitudes and policy. James W. St G. Walker not only exposes the discriminatory practices and racist prejudices inherent in Canada's war effort, but he also shows how Natives, blacks, and those of Chinese and Japanese ancestry reacted to official policy both before their recruitment and once in service. Walker's study illustrates why research on the history of Canada's visible minorities is necessary both for an appreciation of the groups themselves and for a better understanding of racism in the dominant society.

Taken together, the range of approaches and topics represented in this group of readings indicates some of the ways in which historians are now analysing the construction of modern Canada. By focussing on the subtle but powerful roles of language, symbols, rituals, and games, and by examining the question of power in the context of gender, class, ethnicity, and race, historians are rewriting the history of Canada of this period.

SPEAKING MODERN:
Language, Culture, and Hegemony in Grocery Window Displays, 1887–1920*

KEITH WALDEN

Historians are beginning to acknowledge the crucial role of language in cementing social and political hegemony. An understanding that meaning emerges through language is hardly profound. What is new is a recognition of the complexity of meaning, and, by extension, of the agents which embody it. Part of this complexity stems from the fact that meaning is never self-evident. It is an ideological construct continually debated by different groups, each striving to impose a mental attitude towards the world by shaping and inventing appropriate texts. Language is a contested terrain. It is a ritual process which can be understood only in the context of specific frameworks of power relations. Dialogue exists, however, not simply among the parties in an ongoing discourse but within each utterance. Any communication contains traces left by previous speakers and any particular text, therefore, represents an accommodation between existing structures of meaning imposed on or accepted by the speaker and what it is that she or he ideally tries to say.[1]

As well, recognition of the complexity of meaning has grown with an understanding that texts encompass many things besides words. Language is only one kind of sign system and many different media can contribute to

*Canadian Historical Review 70, 3 (Sept. 1989): 285–310. Reprinted with the permission of University of Toronto Press.

the same discourse. Even human behaviour, according to anthropologist Clifford Geertz, should be understood as symbolic action which attempts to communicate. The analysis of cultural forms, he has argued, should be thought of in terms of penetrating a literary text. Not what is being done but what is being said through it is the important thing to establish. As meaning—its creation, dissemination, and deciphering—has become the central preoccupation of many scholars, its intricacies have become boggling.[2] The text, as semioticians are wont to say, is infinite.

All this, at first glance, seems dense and remote, more appropriate to a few elite productions than the experience of ordinary people in the workaday world. Yet here, too, linguistic theory provides insight. Change occurs across the whole spectrum of human activity; people at every social level are faced with consequent adjustments of meaning. This kind of analysis is particularly useful because it demonstrates that response to change is not monolithic; that different groups generate different strategies to accommodate the same developments; and that the creation of meaning is rooted in concrete situations, not abstract possibilities. While it encourages historians to recognize that not everyone understands the world the same way, it can also help them glean new perspectives on their own discipline by knitting together a variety of approaches to the past that often remain quite separate.

An example of a struggle for meaning and hegemony which joins business and social history with intellectual and cultural history can be found in the grocery trade in Canada in the late nineteenth and early twentieth centuries. Though not as spectacular as the large urban department stores which have tended to preoccupy historians,[3] groceries too were culturally influential, not least because they were so numerous and close to home. At the end of the nineteenth century, Eaton's and Simpson's may have dominated their commercial horizon but Torontonians were far more likely to patronize on a day-to-day basis one or more of their city's nine hundred food stores. As with department stores, what people saw and did there established, defined, and conditioned an acceptance of modern life.[4]

Those sights and actions are extraordinarily difficult to recapture. The existence of these marts—usually small, with few employees, often short-lived—was taken for granted. Customers did not confide to diaries or share with correspondents the pleasures of buying a pound of cheese or a jar of pickles. Surviving account ledgers reveal little about human activities in and perceptions of the stores. One source, however, does shed some light on food shops in Canada—the weekly trade paper, the *Canadian Grocer.* Founded in 1887 by John Maclean to keep merchants abreast of availabilities and prices of commodities, it also tried to foster all aspects of the business. To a large extent it was a repository of platitudes about successful merchandising but it frequently carried descriptions, photographs, and critiques of real establishments, especially those in Toronto where it was published. In the absence of other records, the *Grocer is* invaluable.

It indicates that from the 1880s to the First World War and well beyond, food-store window displays had considerable significance. Subscribers were continually admonished to mount well-thought-out trims, and many did. Since any form of human organization reflects an effort to impose meaning on existence, its study can suggest a lot about whoever spawns it. What this article tries to do, then, is explore why the grocery window was emphasized so much and what it communicated. Window displays constituted a series of texts in a discourse about the character of modern life. Like any sign system, they were shaped by previous constructions and were a ground of contention. The displays represented in effect, a language of modernity—a language promoted by merchandise producers, trade journalists, and some grocers, though not necessarily for entirely the same reasons. These groups used this language to mould an understanding of industrial society and, with different degrees of success, to buttress their authority within that system. Displays are worthy of consideration because they suggest not just what changed in the modern era but how particular versions of reality were made credible and how the contest for meaning was actually fought.

This article describes the *Grocer*'s advice about window display, often lifted or abstracted from American and British trade publications. It then attempts to assess whether Canadian merchants followed this advice, to indicate what they did put in their windows, and to explain something of what these efforts said. Naturally, the number of trims put up was vast, each one a symbolic tableau which contained endless possibilities of interpretation. To delineate the entire range of messages would be impossible and any attempt exceedingly tedious. The analysis here, which can only be suggestive, emphasizes what displays said about order, abundance, new standards and expectations of industrial capitalist society, and, most importantly, changes in the definition of fundamental categories of culture. Finally, the paper suggests why the window was used so much as a locus of discourse and why, as grocers became de-skilled, its significance faded. Trimming, in the food business, was a transitional strategy in the adjustment of power relations among merchants, manufacturers, and the trade press.

The origins of deliberate window display are obscure. Dorothy Davis suggests some English shopkeepers took advantage of the introduction of plate glass in the mid-eighteenth century to beguile passersby with choice goods. Leonard Marcus argues it began in the northeast of the United States around 1840, spreading to Europe in the 1860s and 1870s. Nonetheless, late nineteenth-century commentators regarded trimming as a recent inspiration. Through most of the Victorian era, windows were valued primarily as light sources, essential in typically long, narrow, dark stores. However, by the time the *Canadian Grocer* started publishing, improved interior lighting allowed consideration of other uses, while new construction techniques had begun to expand dramatically the scale of window space. In the 1850s and 1860s architects started to design fronts composed almost exclusively of iron and glass. This trend intensified in the 1880s, when it was not uncommon to see panes of glass extended upwards to the second floor and beyond. By the turn of the century a large plate-glass front was considered one of the distinguishing characteristics of a modern store, and the *Grocer* was advising owners that an attractive facade with two 7-by-7-foot sheets facing the street and two 5-by-7-foot sheets bevelled towards the doorway could be installed in an existing structure in any eastern Canadian town for about a hundred dollars, an investment which would quickly pay for itself if weekly sales increased by as little as seventy-five cents.[5]

The importance of window display was signalled by the appearance of professional decorators. Their emergence was formalized in 1898 with the founding in the United States of the National Association of Window Trimmers and its journal, the *Show Window*, edited by L. Frank Baum, who later became more famous for his Oz books.[6] Probably few Canadian grocers subscribed, but snippets from it and a plethora of other sources appeared regularly in their own trade paper.

In fact, the *Grocer* did much more than plagiarize occasionally from other periodicals. It harped on the subject continually, often castigating itself for not doing more.[7] It offered ideas for designs, hints about construction, critiques of displays. It pleaded with owners and clerks to submit photographs of effective designs, promising to publish them. After 1903, it sponsored an annual contest with cash prizes for the best Christmas installation. Well before, it had instituted a weekly feature on window and interior display. Put together, this material constituted a substantial body of advice on the why and how of showing goods.

The fundamental premise was that windows were essential to the art of selling. Of course, display transcended mere economic considerations. To one commentator, the well-decorated store front provided a "great free spectacle which offers to the multitude almost the only diversion in their narrow, confined lives." To another, it stimulated aesthetic sensibilities, especially those of middle-class women. But the impulse to public service aside, a merchant's commercial well-being was rooted in trimming. The owner who did not realize his window was "the biggest thing in his business," proclaimed Frank Baum, might as well put on his coat and wait for the sheriff.[8]

Display encouraged impulse buying by regular customers but it also attracted new clients. In this "pushing, bustling, hurried age," asserted the *Grocer*, the consumer "will do his business where the windows show him he can get what he wants without waste of time or words." In a more general way, as well, a store's welfare depended on its windows, which were a per-petual announcement of an establishment's taste and quality. "As a man's face is generally an index to his character, so is the front of a shop."[9] Grocers who believed the staple nature of their merchandise made display irrelevant needed to open their eyes. To encourage these laggards the trade press took pains to emphasize that, with advances in package labelling, no other kind of store could compete in either assortment or attractiveness of goods.[10]

Since the quality of exhibits mattered, competent designers were an absolute necessity. To some, the authentic trimmer, "like the true genius in the purer realms of art," was born not made. Majority opinion, however, held that while some innate qualities were needed—a sense of colour and proportion, facility with language, knowledge of the value of goods—neces-sary skills could be cultivated through study and practice.[11] All were agreed that a specific individual should take on the responsibility, preferably not the owner who would have to ignore other tasks to do the job properly. If a professional could not be hired, a talented clerk should be assigned the job and given a relatively free hand:

> His work is more of an irregular nature: at the best it should be subjected to but little orders even from the proprietor. . . . If the window dresser is merely a salesman who is supposed to crowd in window dressing with waiting on customers, he is nevertheless allowed latitude not accorded to the other clerks. He must have time to plan windows, to forage around and discover stock that is "sticking" and to arrange the display upon which he has decided. He should not be disturbed when building the window, and should be allowed as far as possible to adopt his own ideas.[12]

This strategy enhanced simultaneously the prospects of both clerk and owner while deflecting the attention of an ambitious employee away from account ledgers which might have inspired higher wage demands or out-right competition.

The *Grocer* rightly assumed that most decorators were not professional and proffered a great deal of information about how to make windows effective. Technical aspects were often addressed, especially lighting. Besides using proper equipment such as reflectors, shades, and movable lamps, the main ideas here were to keep the windows bright at night and during the darker seasons of the year and to ensure that illumination fell inside the case rather than on the street beyond. Background materials, display apparatus, colour harmonics, among other things, were discussed as well.[13]

More important than such technical considerations were general principles which supposedly underlay successful display. Effective installa-tions, in theory, were sales oriented, preplanned, immediately comprehen-sible, sensibly augmented with show cards, and original. The fundamental premise was dressing the window to sell goods. The goal was not just to attract attention but to stimulate buying. The window "must tell a story that will take the mind of the observer across the threshold. It must create a desire that the inside of the store alone can gratify. It should be a magnet that halts the passerby and ultimately pulls him to the counter." Mere artistry did not make a successful trim. Fancy designs with no relation to goods carried inside might be used occasionally for variety but "airy frippery" should not remain for long. Customers must be shown the articles they were expected to purchase.[14]

A second imperative was working out features in advance. Some decorators approached the showcase with no ideas, pinning up goods first in one section, then another, letting the structure work itself out by chance. They were unwise. "Good window-trimming," stressed the *Grocer*, "cannot be obtained by trying to work on the inspiration of the moment, any more than an architect can build a house without first making out his plans." Prearranging meant more effective design but also speedier, more efficient installation and hence quicker realization of a display's selling potential.[15]

Coherent planning was an essential precondition for a third principle: intent should be readable at a glance. As "Rambler," a regular *Grocer* contributor, pointed out, "people don't stay looking long at a window." They scan in passing. The human eye could not absorb everything in a quick glimpse. The exhibit, therefore, had to provide "an instant comprehension of the goods shown."[16] Some considerations here were matters of common sense, such as ensuring that the glass was clean and unencumbered with extraneous notices, and placing materials high enough to be read from a distance. Eliminating frost and flies were equally obvious though not as easy to control, despite numerous hints about coping with them.[17]

Beyond mere visibility, though, two related maxims had to be respected. First, in the words of a merchant from Carberry, Manitoba, "never crowd your window. Do not give it the appearance that you have all your stock in the window and may have some in the store." Trimmers had to accept space limitations of their windows and cognitive limitations of their viewers. Not everything could be shown at once. Instead, and this was the second key to quick comprehension, a display should feature a single line or class of goods at a time. In the words of the *San Francisco Advocate*, it was better "to force one single idea into the heads of the passersby than to excite their curiosity about a dozen things without interesting them particularly in any." This did not mean that only one product should be featured, but rather that everything in the window should fit a common theme. Putting "canned tomatoes, canned peas, canned salmon, canned everything" together was perfectly acceptable: "that's one class." Combining soap and tea was folly. A few experts maintained that, with careful planning, large assortment in a display could be effective, but even they emphasized that sight lines had to be arranged to concentrate the gaze on a featured item. Most recommended that to show a variety of things, window space should be divided.[18]

A fourth principle of display was the necessity of showcards. Catchy phrases, suggestions about use or value, cute observations—these called attention to goods that otherwise went unnoticed. The *Grocer*, which claimed cards were more effective than the human voice, described them as assistant clerks and continually advocated their use. The striking pile of nuts in a Toronto store window in 1900, it noted, would have been even more effective with a sign reading: "Bushels of them; we have everything you want for Christmas." Cards could not be composed hurriedly. They had to be brief and simple, yet calculated to excite interest and inquiry. Trimmers were well advised to keep a notebook close by to jot down sudden inspirations for future use.[19]

Price tickets were far more controversial. Some experts believed higher-class stores should talk only of the quality of their merchandise. The *Grocer*, while acknowledging this view, was heavily on the side of clearly marked costs. "Now-a-days," it insisted, "all wide-awake merchants make it a rule to ticket everything." Consumers were spared the embarrassment of having to pester clerks about things which might be too expensive. Alternatively, they might be surprised at what could be afforded. Moreover, tickets confirmed a single price for everyone, reassuring buyers and facilitating the work of sellers. Admitting periodically that some stores did very well without them, the *Grocer* still maintained for the most part that unticketed trim was "almost useless." Whether or not prices were marked, cards had to be attractive. If they were poorly painted or ragged, too large or too numerous, the eye was repelled. Common sense was required but the *Grocer* offered practical help as well, publishing step-by-step charts showing how to draw every letter and number in a variety of scripts. If professional painters were too expensive, any diligent clerk could produce adequate cards with a bit of practice.[20]

A fifth tenet, the most important to some, was the need for originality. Novelty almost always paid off. "Only by introducing something out of the ordinary can the majority of people be made to stop to examine a window display." Especially in the "hurry, bustle and crowd of a large city," oddities and startling effects were necessary to capture attention and sustain ongoing interest in a store. The *Grocer* was full of suggestions. Most made use of regular merchandise—canned peaches set beside a peach tree, cigar boxes formed into a castle, tins of meat next to a mock cannon. Some proposals—farm and beach scenes, special lighting effects, mechanical toys and live animals—had at best a tenuous link to store goods, and readers may have been confused by contradictory injunctions to create striking effects yet display only what was actually being sold.[21]

One extraneous element which could unobtrusively enhance a window's appeal was plants. In a store interior, they provided a fragrant respite from summer heat or winter drab; in the display case, they added a sprightly touch of green and diffused overly symmetrical lines. The trade press warmly endorsed their use, pointing out the many advantages of artificials.[22]

Unusualness of design was not the only novelty to be considered. Longevity of display was important as well. "The handsomest of windows will become stale in time; people like new things as well as pretty things, and so to attract people's attention, a window should be changed as frequently as possible." Recommendations varied as to how long a display should sit, ranging mostly from three days to a week, with two weeks as the outside limit. Summer arrangements might require daily changes to counter the fly menace. It was not necessary to introduce completely new materials with every shift: altering the arrangement or making a different colour more prominent would satisfy those on the lookout for evidence of change.[23]

As much as how, experts were eager to suggest what, and what not, to display. The first consideration here, in keeping with advice about novelty, was not to feature bulk and standard goods. Little was gained by exhibiting enormous quantities of sugar, coffee, tea, or flour: everyone knew grocers carried them. Besides, once exposed, these goods might have to be sold at a loss or thrown out. Even then customers might worry their purchases had been adulterated with shoddy leavings. Now and then, the impression of abundance created by the massing of bulk goods in a window might be justified, but this could be achieved just as effectively with packages. What should be emphasized were specialty items that would never be asked for without advertising, and slow-moving goods that had to be sold quickly.[24]

The most emphatic advice, however, was to align displays with the calendar. "Seasonal windows are essential to active retailing," counselled the *Grocer:* "in a careful study of this point exists much of the profit of window dressing. Lines should be displayed in advance of the best selling period and then brought out more prominently during the proper season. In this way not only will customers be shown goods when they are needed, but they will be prepared beforehand for the needs of the season and know where to get the required articles." Besides beating competition to the punch, it would keep the shop looking progressive, attracting custom for things not on show. The easiest way to emphasize seasonality was to construct displays around appropriate themes. Not all theme window suggestions were time specific. Laundry products shown around a wash tub and board were always suitable, as were breakfast articles displayed in front of a large menu card. Most motifs, however, had to be synchronized with the yearly round. Cleaning windows, with brushes, brooms, pails, soaps, and detergents, were most effective in spring. So, obviously, were Easter and Lenten windows. Camping and vegetable windows suited the summer. In fall, pickling and preserving could be featured, along with hunting and the Thanksgiving holiday. In early winter, grocers could begin to work with the most important theme of all—Christmas. Nuts, candies, dried fruit, bottled delectables, and fat poultry lured the patronage of many families who made a point of touring window attractions at this time of year.[25] Theme displays, designed to train and reinforce consuming habits, were never more effective than in the festive season, especially because of their presumed impact on children.

Plan the window, keeping in mind its purpose was to sell goods by making a quick impression. Change the display frequently using imaginative arrangements of seasonable goods to keep the public's attention. In a nutshell, this was the *Grocer*'s prescription. It was conventional wisdom, reiterated constantly in the North American trade press. Advice offered is not necessarily advice taken. To what extent did real Canadian grocers conform to these ideals? What did they actually do with their windows? Because the *Grocer* was preoccupied with these matters, it reported fairly frequently on what it saw. These observations allow at least an impressionistic answer to the questions.

What it saw was predictable. Many merchants, perhaps a majority, neglected their windows. Most shops encountered on a fall tour of downtown Toronto in 1895 "presented a very unattractive appearance." More than a decade later the same conclusion emerged from a survey of about 200 stores in thirty cities. The closest the *Grocer* came to distinguishing between those who did and those who did not decorate was after a stroll along Queen Street in 1899. Almost none of the stores in the downtown and working-class neighbourhoods from Yonge to Bathurst, all of which catered to the transient trade, paid any attention to the window. They used it as a storage space, usually obstructing the view with bins and barrels on the sidewalk in front. Further west, in upscale Parkdale, showcases done up to appeal to stable neighbourhood patrons were the norm. It demonstrated, concluded the observer, that grocers dressed their windows to suit their trade. This was as far as the paper would go in admitting what was obvious to most merchants: effective display had to be geared to a specific clientele, and the character of a clientele probably was determined largely by a store's location. No amount of preaching that "a good window display attracts a higher class of customer" was likely to impress shopkeepers in the Ward, Toronto's notorious slum. They survived, more likely, through a willingness to extend credit.[26]

More than just a different social reality was at work here; there was a different social vision. What the *Grocer* insisted was laziness and indifference was, consciously or otherwise, a challenge to its own ideological disposition. An undecorated window asserted that success was not simply a matter of human will, that community was founded on relationships of people with people, not people with goods, that trust and mutual aid should prevail over the cash nexus, that traditional ways were more comfortable than innovation. In the discourse of windows, the undressed spoke just as eloquently as the dressed. The display case was terrain contested by competing value systems, which helps to account for the *Grocer*'s intense interest in it.

While many merchants did not bother with display, an increasing number probably did. The *Grocer* was convinced this was true. After an inspection of Montreal stores in 1901, for example, impressed by high, well-lighted, well-painted plate-glass cases, the editor ventured to suggest it was no longer necessary to persuade owners to use their windows. What he did lament, voicing a common complaint, was the lack of originality in design. "There is that sameness wherever one looks."[27] At the same time, by the turn of the century, his journal seemed to have little trouble finding trims worthy of comment.

Some of these displays originated with manufacturers. Baker's Cocoa equipped a model kitchen which was loaned without charge for periods of two weeks. It could be set up in the store or in the window. All the user had to do was hire someone to mix and serve the chocolate. The N.K. Fairbank Company provided display paraphernalia and gave $5 worth of its soaps for a month's use of a window. Gillette hired its own designers who travelled around putting in custom installations.[28] With large companies knocking at their doors, trade papers harping on the theme, and a whole culture more attuned to display, it is not surprising that increasing numbers of grocers made at least an effort to use their windows.

A few, striving for the unusual, went to considerable trouble. Scale models were the most common novelty. A window in British Columbia's mining district featured a locomotive made of groceries. In Stratford, a suspension bridge made of cereal boxes was put on view; in Peterborough, the lift-lock was reproduced with tea packages. Occasionally, demonstrations were mounted. In a Kingston window, two boys took turns shampooing each other while a girl did washing at a tub. Between, constructed from bars of soap, was a model of the factory where the featured product was made. A Toronto store offered an exhibition of maple-syrup making in a mock forest setting, complete with a live rabbit. Some ploys bore no relation to the grocer's merchandise. The simulated smashed window in Toronto in 1899 was just a startling visual joke. Such scenes and devices were sure to attract attention, especially if some animation was involved. The owner of a small Toronto store off the main thoroughfare claimed there were regularly fifteen or twenty spectators examining a miniature flour mill in operation.[29]

More common were various types of theme windows, the designs of which ranged along a broad spectrum. At one end, they overlapped with novelty productions, as with the soap and maple-syrup windows mentioned above. This approach was especially popular for summer vacation promotions. Lockhart's, at King and York streets in Toronto, spread camping delicacies on a table which could be seen through the folds of a tent. A decade later, in 1903, a Montreal store created a miniature resort complete with lake, rocks, bushes, boats, docks, canoes, hotel, wigwams, and human figures. Typical of the other end of the spectrum was a cleaning window, put up in a Queen Street store in 1899:

This window is a wide one, but only about three feet deep. In the center of the background are a number of washtubs of various sizes. At either side of these are brooms, washboards, pails, and clotheslines. In front of these, package goods, such as starch, soap, washing compounds, polishes, etc., are arranged in neatly-built piles Scattered along the full length of the front of the window are scouring brushes of every description.

Here, related goods were grouped tastefully but without any attempt to create out-of-the-ordinary effects. Between these extremes could be found baking windows, preserving windows, laundry, Lent, and Easter windows—in fact, all the types recommended by the trade press including the de rigueur Christmas windows.[30]

In many displays, however, thematic unity was not an important consideration. A 1902 window containing, among other things, canned salmon, breakfast cereal, sugar boxes, canned peaches, and sardines was not at all unusual. Even the *Grocer* passed a favourable judgment on it.[31] As long as an arrangement was orderly, as long as mismatches like molasses and coal oil were avoided, many merchants did not worry about what goods were juxtaposed.

Some commodities, especially vegetables, eggs, nuts, and dried fruit, were simply laid out on the floor, but more common were terrace effects made by stacking cans, bottles, jars, and boxes on shelves, crates, or each other. Critics, like the *Grocer* editor after his 1901 inspection of Montreal, railed against their triteness, but trimmers obviously appreciated how little effort it took to build these displays.[32]

The favourite shape in these arrangements was the pyramid. Rectangles, squares, rings, and concave and convex arcs were by no means rare, but photos and verbal comments confirm the prevalence of triangular forms. Goods were piled into pyramid shapes, or different sized boxes were used as platforms. Sometimes a display laid out on the floor at the front receded into a pinnacle of goods at the back.[33] The pyramid shape created useful sight lines, raised the height of displays, and gave an illusion of quantity with relatively limited amounts of merchandise. It was frequently used as well for interior displays both on the floor and in the space between shelf top and ceiling.

Evidence from the *Grocer* suggests then that a substantial number of merchants did make an effort to put up passable displays, and a few, if perhaps only periodically, went well beyond. Collectively, they were not as imaginative as the experts wished; their constructions were not always carefully planned, logical selling tools which unfailingly pricked consumer desire at a glance. While the wisdom of seasonal display prevailed, probably few shops changed their designs on a bi-weekly or weekly basis. Some larger stores catering to the carriage trade did, but most shops, especially those that made a serious effort, left displays of non-perishables in for considerably longer. The model flour mill which drew large crowds, for example, was to be exhibited "for some time."[34] Still, if the *Grocer* had few votaries who followed all its precepts religiously, it was not preaching in a vacuum.

Given that many grocery windows were deliberately arranged, what did they attempt to communicate? The range of messages was vast and, as with most materials of popular culture, it is difficult to state categorically what designers intended or what viewers understood. Still, something of the import of these displays may be reasonably posited.

For one thing, they affirmed the existence of social order. Stocking windows with seasonal goods indicated, perhaps especially to city people, that human culture was linked to a regular, predictable progression in nature. Hunting windows and cleaning windows defined gender role expectations; Christmas confectionery windows reinforced ideas about the nature of children and childhood; patriotic windows with flags, bunting, and pictures of the king and queen buttressed concepts of nation and race. Besides delineating traditional categories, windows provided more general reassurances about the actuality of order. Sometimes they contained specific allusions to the sacred. By the turn of the century, figs and dates in Christmas trims probably came from California, but the Mediterranean and biblical associations of the fruit connected everyday existence to the well springs of a variety of faiths. Rectangular terraces often bore a striking resemblance to church altars. Pyramid-shaped displays not only alluded to some of the oldest symbols of stability and persistence in the Western world, but also echoed the popular Gothic motif of Victorian architecture. The elaborate detail and heaven-soaring pinnacles of many nineteenth-century buildings, which helped to reconcile spiritual longings with material aspirations, were imitated in many a neighbourhood shop front.[35] In subtle ways, the display window aligned religious values with capitalist products, hinting that the road to salvation lay in consumption.

Even without these references to formal religion, the very act of deliberate arrangement provided reassurance to a society deeply worried about the possibilities of order that it could be made to exist. An 1897 window containing honey, canned goods, jams, catsup, worcester sauce, and pickles arranged in symmetrical order, though not limited to a single line or class of goods, appealed to the "Rambler" probably for this very reason. These objects embodied not just rational organization but also a solidity and bulk which assuaged feelings of "weightlessness" that accompanied the erosion of longstanding sources of authority.[36]

If displays provided reassurances about what was traditional, they also demonstrated the availability of new kinds of merchandise. As the *American Grocer* pointed out in 1889, three decades earlier canned goods had not been in use; variety in crackers, tea, and coffee was extremely limited; and many foods, such as preserves, soups, mincemeat, and catsup, had to be made at home. The commercially prepared bottles, cans, jars, and boxes which changed this situation had to be shown to the public, not just to advertise their existence but to break down consumer resistance to innovation.[37] Windows stimulated curiosity and conditioned familiarity. Moreover, they helped to define new standards and expectations of industrial capitalist society. The cleaning display drove home to women the imperative to maintain a spotless home. If they lacked any substance or utensil on view, deficiencies in their homemaking would have to be considered. The summer window indicated what was available in the way of camping supplies but also induced people to take outings and vacations,[38] suggesting as well what they should do on them. Even monotonous masses of packaged goods taught about the possibilities of abundance in modern society and of consistency in mass production.

Windows helped to create new aesthetic standards. Trimming intensified expectations about colour and design in everyday life but also changed ideas about perception. The *Michigan Tradesman* insisted that decorators study all the conditions governing light and its effect on objects in the window. Those who did would discover "what changes of colour, light and shadow are visible to the critical eye at different times of the day." The lessons of impressionism were disseminated far more broadly in the corner store than the art gallery. So were the lessons of cubism. Mirrors were commonly placed in the window to amplify light and space but also to provide simultaneously a host of different views of objects on display. This effort to allow observers to see different sides of three-dimensional objects at the same time was developed in shop windows well before Picasso and Braque latched on to the idea.[39] Merchants kept apace of some of the fundamental advances of modern art but did so in response to their own needs. Who is to say their creations were any less central to the development of modern sensibilities than those of more illustrious artists?

Perhaps the most significant message of grocery window displays involved the redefinition of fundamental cultural concepts. Every human society divides the world into categories that make everyday experience comprehensible. They distinguish what is alive from what is inanimate, what is good to eat from what is not, what is acceptable behaviour and what is taboo. They distinguish the fragrant from the foul, the clean from the dirty, the wild from the tame. These dichotomies, to mention just a few, are so built into the fabric of a culture that their rightness is usually accepted without question. The values derived from them are an inextricable part of the myths, institutions, and relationships of society, conveyed and reinforced in all the acts and processes of life. Naturally these divisions were articulated in grocery displays. Soap windows, for example, were part of a larger discourse about the clean and the dirty. Comestibles spoke to differences between what was good to eat and what was not. A potent instrument of socialization, the display window would be worthy of consideration at any time, but in the late nineteenth and early twentieth centuries it was especially important because it helped to illuminate shifts within one of the most basic social dichotomies—the distinction between nature and culture.

Culture exists by definition as a counterpoint to nature. "If a culture is to refer to itself," suggests advertising critic Judith Williamson, "it can only do so by the representation of its transformation of nature—it has meaning in terms of what it has changed." Well-known anthropologist Claude Lévi-Strauss described this polarity in terms of the raw and the cooked. Just as the raw materials of diet are processed to make them edible, so all raw elements of nature are "cooked" to make them part of culture.[40] What the grocery window did was present a substantial discourse on the relationship between these two categories, informing people of new boundaries between them while reassuring them that the change posed no threat to human well-being. These messages would have been cumbersome to articulate in words.

Consider the simple "coconut window" recommended by J.B. Richardson in *Grocery World*. On each side of the window was a pyramid of whole coconuts and between them, at roughly the same height, a pile of shredded coconut. In the back, a heap of packages of shredded coconut showed plainly above the three piles. The idea, he noted for the more obtuse, "is to show in three exhibits the evolution of the coconut—first in the shell, then in shredded form, but unpacked, and finally in the regular package shape, as it is sold."[41] The display effectively demonstrated that for the coconut, a new degree of "cooking" existed. Formerly, bulk shredded material was the most refined product carried by the store; now it was the raw material for more highly processed boxes. The coconut itself had not changed but packaging created a different context, one which diminished the cultural accomplishment involved in shredding, making the bulk shredded product seem, therefore, more natural.

The new degree of cooking was not limited to putting bulk goods into containers. It also involved qualitatively different commodities. Toronto merchant R.H. Stewart's "cereal window" contained several small sheaths of wheat, various sized bags of flour, and some piles of biscuit. While many housewives continued to do much of their own baking, the display called attention to ready-to-eat crackers, breads, and cakes available at the grocery. To cap the point, Stewart's other window contained a display of Swiss Food, a prepared breakfast cereal which could not be duplicated easily in the home. Increasingly, flour was seen not as an end product of processing sold in the store but as a raw ingredient of more highly finished items which consumers were expected to buy. Bulk bags could still be purchased, but they existed in a new system of relationships which put them closer to nature. In coffee windows containing green beans, bags of roasted beans, and cans of ground coffee; in marmalade windows containing oranges, white sugar, and jars of the finished product; in preserving windows with piles of spices, barrels of vinegar, and bottles of pickles, similar messages were driven home.[42] Industrial capitalism had changed and was changing not just the economic system and human relationships within it but also fundamental categories of cultural meaning. Grocery windows helped explain what that change involved.

Displays demonstrated changing conceptions of the raw and the cooked, but they also attempted to provide reassurance that higher degrees of culture were not unnatural. In the food business, this was an important point to make. Claims that overrefining destroyed nutritional value and did positive harm to the human system had been voiced since the early decades of the nineteenth century.[43] They fit into a broader pattern of concern, prevalent throughout the modern age, that nature and the beneficence it embodied were being eroded unrelentingly by what boosters called progress. Making explicit the connection between whole coconuts and packages of the shredded product, or between shocks of grain and boxes of breakfast cereal indicated that nature and culture remained united as parts of a single spectrum. The same message was perhaps intended by the inclusion of plants and ferns in window arrangements. As well as lending variety of line and colour to displays, they suggested a harmony between inanimate processed goods and the living, organic world from which they originated.[44]

These brief examples of how the grocery window communicated basic cultural distinctions can only be suggestive. It is important to re-emphasize the broad range of its discourse. However, it is also important to recognize that because it featured items essential to human survival, the grocery was a significant venue for transmitting this kind of information. Its windows were not as striking as those of the department store, yet their very mundaneness created authority. Impressions penetrated slowly and thoroughly, convincing people by their seeming mediocrity.

It is all very well to decipher the meaning of displays, but it remains something of a puzzle why the window became their venue. Why were many grocers willing to invest so much time and money on showcases? Why not rely on newspaper advertisements or interior displays? Alternatively, if grocery windows were considered so important in the late nineteenth and early twentieth centuries, why did their significance fade, especially when trimming continued to be done in other sorts of stores?

The influence of department stores was a factor. While their growth terrified many small shopkeepers, there is no doubt that by the late nineteenth century large urban emporiums were the most glamorous of merchandising establishments. Other ambitious merchants, encouraged by trade publications, naturally sought to emulate what had made them successful. Because department stores emphasized window display, many provisioners followed suit, lifting not just the general imperative to show goods but also specific display ideas. Indeed, grocers were often warned that while big stores were a useful source of inspiration, the smaller windows of their own premises dictated a much reduced scale.[45]

Imitation was rooted in economic logic. Those who took the trouble to dress showcases were convinced "there is money in a well-trimmed window": "No grocer needs to be told that the average shopper comes to his store with a list prepared of the articles required, and that it rests with the grocer to swell that list to just the extent that his ingenuity allows." Display encouraged impulse buying and, perhaps more importantly, provided an approach to competitive merchandising that did not involve cutting prices.[46]

To understand fully the significance of the window, however, it is necessary to look beyond merchandising strategies and economic incentives. Window display, consciously or unconsciously, was part of a broader project of adaptation to emerging industrial capitalist society. Creating modern culture involved more than developing new technologies, new institutions, new goods. The meaning of these things had to be formulated and disseminated. Conveying meaning in the mass age involved new sorts of problems, such as coping with rapidity of change, greater distances, and larger numbers of people of more diverse backgrounds. To deal effectively with these problems, new forms of communication—for example, advertising—had to be devised. However, to articulate new meanings, not just new media but new language was required.

As those who study structuralism have emphasized, members of a speech community use many things besides spoken language to communicate: "The clothes we wear, the food we eat, the houses we live in, and so on, all convey information to those who understand the 'codes' in question . . . these codes are 'languages' in the same sense (or very nearly the same sense) as spoken languages."[47] Grocery display was such a language. Like any language, its utterances contained traces left by previous speakers. The centrality of seasonal themes testifies to this relationship, as does the reliance on pyramid and altar shapes. Like any language, it was connected to other channels of discourse, as the parallels with modern painting suggest. Like any language, it was an arena of contestation. The fact that many grocers refused to decorate their windows is just one indication of different values.

Language is a form of ritual. It is not innate in humans but develops slowly with the assimilation of vocabulary and grammatical structure in the process of socialization. It matures with constant practice and repetition. Anthropologist Victor Turner has pointed out that the essence of ritual is liminality, a concept derived from Arnold van Gennep's analysis of rites of passage. Liminality is a period or area of ambiguity, betwixt and between, which possesses few of the characteristics of the state which precedes or follows. In liminal time or space, anything might or even should happen, which means cultural elements are free to combine and recombine in any possible pattern.[48]

This is the essence of language. Messages represent experiments in meaning floating between the intentions of the sender and the understanding of the receiver. They are composed from an infinite variety of possible combinations of words, tones, and constructions, and susceptible to an infinite variety of interpretations. Language, at least that aspect of it which Ferdinand de Saussure defined as *parole*, is a classic instance of liminality.[49] If language, or the use of language, is a ritual act, it is most effectively performed in a liminal space. For grocery display, the window represented just such a place.

Physically, its position was ambiguous—intruding into the street without being part of it, attached to the store yet somehow separate. It was betwixt and between. It could be viewed as a discrete entity, complete in itself, or one element in the larger architectural composition of a facade. The primary material which created the window-glass contributed to the ambiguity by confusing the nature and extent of boundaries. As Daniel Boorstin has noted, the transparency of glass transformed the meaning of indoors and outdoors, and the relation between them.[50] In the day, exterior sunlight penetrated into dim interiors, while at night artificial illumination produced inside flooded into the darkness beyond. The window was private space arranged to suit the whims of its owner, but also public space available to the scrutiny of whoever wandered by. The eye could trespass inside but the hand could not. For all its transparency the window was unclear and indeterminate, a space where the designs of the sellers could interact with the imaginations of consumers.

The shop window was a liminal space but one that the merchant could control. He or she could protect it from the far more chaotic situation outside and impose a logical order within. If display was a language, the window was a place where discordant and competing sounds could be reduced. This was precisely the thrust of much of the advice about trimming. When experts urged the elimination of frost, dirt, and obstructing notices, when they recommended strutless sheets of plate glass, when they advised that only one line of goods be shown at a time and that the window be readable at a glance, in effect they were telling grocers how to articulate comprehensible messages and how to turn their windows into "noiseless" boxes where a language of modernity could be heard clearly.[51] Those who recommended that the window be partitioned off completely from the rest of the store merely took this logic to its ultimate conclusion.[52]

Dressing the window, for the grocer, would be a ritual activity which taught a new syntax and vocabulary. Examining the window would be a ritual activity for the consumer, teaching the same things. This accounts for the emphasis on frequent change of display. Constant novelty would accustom people to look—to hear what was being said—and would permit the expression of a wide range of messages. No single display could transmit an entire vocabulary. Change, as advisers pointed out, created an ongoing discourse which over time would build towards a more comprehensive degree of understanding.[53]

When the *Canadian Grocer* advocated window decoration it was arguing for the adoption of a new language. Just as trimmers, from their own necessities, grappled with the same problems as impressionist painters, so they moved towards modern understandings of communications independent of linguistic theorists. Well before semioticians arrived on the scene,

Harry Harmon, a professional designer, was telling merchants that the store window addressed customers "as forcefully as your words."[54]

Still, the language of modernity germinated slowly. As with any cultural change there were many continuities with earlier forms and meanings. Recognition of what window display was and how it could speak was not immediately obvious. It had to evolve, which explains the frequent exhortations to produce "crisp and fascinating" show cards. While shoppers today might understand why a ticket proclaiming "unique cheapness" was considered ill-advised, they would probably wonder why ones advising "Your house and clothing will be improved if you buy a broom and wisk," "For best results in baking use So-and-so's flour," and "Try Ludella Tea. It is good" were so highly recommended. What these cards did, however, was harken back to the older language of merchandising when grocers themselves had talked. "The dealer must remember," cautioned the *Grocer* as late as 1910, "that it is he who is talking when he uses cards."[55]

Alas, that voice was less and less compelling, and this helps explain the decline of grocery window display. When food was sold from anonymous bulk containers, consumers relied on grocers for information about its qualities. They depended on a merchant's abilities to explain the difference between various oils, the usage of unfamiliar spices, the proportion of fruit to sugar in jam. They relied on his or her skill in blending tea and coffee. The grocer's knowledge was a vital component in the production of a successful meal.

With the advent of brand names, standard packages, and product guarantees, goods themselves talked. Grocers did not need to speak. This was a deliberate strategy of manufacturers eager to gain control over their markets. The more authority they invested in their labels, the less their success depended on local shopkeepers whose bins might be dirty, scales inaccurate, and sales persuasiveness deficient. Manufacturers, in effect, set about to de-skill neighbourhood merchants. Many tradesmen and women, while cognizant that packages saved them time and money, resented what was happening. John McAree's uncle, who prided himself on an ability to blend, was not enthusiastic about the appearance of packaged teas: "he perceived that one of his arts was becoming outmoded."[56]

As the packaging revolution intensified, as advertising became more extensive, as food advice appeared more frequently in mass media, decorating the store window became one way individual grocers could try to assert their own voices, to maintain individual identities. Decorating, in part, compensated for the loss of authority in other areas. It was a different skill which could salvage occupational status. It is important to recognize, of course, that other groups had different reasons for promoting display. For the *Canadian Grocer*, persuading merchants to compete on the basis of the presentation of goods rather than cost meant an avoidance of price wars, hence a decline in business failures and the maintenance of a healthy subscription rate, especially since the trade paper was an essential source of information about design ideas. For manufacturers, window display put their products in the forefront of consumers' attention. The interests of the three groups overlapped but only partly. As each sought to advance its own interests, the show window became a field of contestation.

It was an uneven struggle. Every trim which featured packaged goods reinforced the authority of brand names. While the producer could speak on labels and in advertisements without alluding to individual merchants, the reverse was not true. As messages embedded in the language of display became more familiar and as the manufacturers' hegemony solidified, the impulse to decorate declined. At the same time, chain stores and super-markets appeared, based on a strategy of selling high volumes at bargain rates.[57] For these establishments, tarting up windows was an expensive, unnecessary frill. Customers were drawn by low prices. These developments were not uniform in all retail sectors. In areas such as fashion, where cultural standards and categories continued to change dramatically and consumers had to be convinced about matters of taste at the point of purchase, window display remained important.

The language of modernity was not restricted to grocery windows. To understand fully the modern discourse, messages conveyed through other vehicles, other kinds of stores, other activities beside retailing will have to be explored, and all of them considered in relation to each other. It is a big task. This article makes no pretense of having deciphered all the codes. Rather, it has tried to demonstrate that the codes exist, that food-store trims were more than simply merchandising devices to indicate the availability of goods. They were a language which helped people adapt to the dynamic flux of industrial capitalism. That language was used to stanch traditional values as well as to elucidate at a manageable human level new cultural standards and meanings. It was also used by different groups—grocers, manufacturers, trade journalists—to assert their interests and their identities. The utility of that language has largely faded, at least in the food sector, but that is not to say its role in the evolution of the culture of consumption should be underestimated. Only by grasping the significance of the sights and sounds of everyday life is it possible to comprehend how the profound technological, economic, intellectual, and social changes of the modern era came to be accepted.

• Notes

1 T.J. Jackson Lears, "The Concept of Cultural Hegemony: Problems and Possibilities," *American Historical Review* 90 (June 1985): 589–93; John E. Toews, "Intellectual History After the Linguistic Turn: The Autonomy of Meaning and the Irreducibility of Experience," *American Historical Review* 92 (Oct. 1987): 881–82, 885; Dominick La Capra, *Rethinking Intellectual History: Texts, Contexts, Language* (Ithaca, 1983), 292–324.

2 William J. Bowsma, "Intellectual History in the 1980s: From History of

Ideas to History of Meaning," *Journal of Interdisciplinary History* 12 (Autumn 1981): 279–91; Clifford Geertz, *The Interpretation of Cultures* (New York, 1973), 10, 448; Bernice Martin, *A Sociology of Contemporary Cultural Change* (Oxford, 1981), 27–52.

3 See, for example, William R. Leach, "Transformations in a Culture of Consumption: Women and Department Stores, 1890–1925," *Journal of American History* 71 (Sept. 1984): 319–42; Susan Porter Benson, *Counter Cultures: Saleswomen, Managers and Customers in American Department Stores, 1890–1940* (Urbana, 1986); Michael B. Miller, *The Bon Marché: Bourgeois Culture and the Department Store, 1869–1920* (Princeton, 1981); Gunter Barth, *City People: The Rise of Modern City Culture in Nineteenth-Century America* (New York, 1982), 110–47; Rachel Bowlby, *Just Looking: Consumer Culture in Dreiser, Gissing and Zola* (New York, 1985); Rosalind H. Williams, *Dream Worlds: Mass Consumption in Late Nineteenth-Century France* (Berkeley, 1982); Elizabeth Ewen and Stuart Ewen, *Channels of Desire: Mass Images and the Shaping of American Consciousness* (New York, 1982), 57–71.

4 The figure comes from the *Canadian Grocer* (hereafter *CG*), 22 Feb. 1895, 32. Very little has been written about the history of the grocery store, especially in the nineteenth century. See J.M. Blackman, "The Corner Shop: The Development of the Grocery and General Provisions Trade" in *The Making of the Modern British Diet*, ed. Derek Oddy and Derek Miller (London, 1976), 148–60; Michael J. Winstanley, *The Shopkeeper's World, 1830–1914* (Manchester, 1983); Gerald Carson, *The Old Country Store* (New York, 1954); Dorothy Davis, *Fairs, Shops and Supermarkets: A History of English Shopping* (Toronto, 1966); Chester H. Liebs, *Main Street to Miracle Mile: American Roadside Architecture* (Boston, 1985), 117–35; W.I. Walsh, *The Rise and Decline of the Great Atlantic*

& Pacific Tea Company (Secaucus, 1986); Michael Bliss, *A Canadian Millionaire: The Life and Business Times of Sir Joseph Flavelle* (Toronto, 1978). Literature on European stores is often concerned with defining the class status of the small grocer. See, for example, Alain Faure, "The Grocery Trade in Nineteenth-Century Paris: A Fragmented Corporation" in *Shopkeepers and Master Artisans in Nineteenth-Century Europe*, ed. Geoffrey Crossick and Heintz-Gerhard Haupt (London, 1984), 155–74.

5 Davis, *Fairs, Shops and Supermarkets*, 192; Leonard S. Marcus, *The American Store Window* (New York, 1978); 15; Kelly Crossman, *Architecture in Transition: From Art to Practice, 1885–1906* (Montreal, 1987), 68; *CG*, 2 June 1899, 32, and 26 Oct. 1900, 23. One establishment that redesigned its facade was Allen, Taylor & Co. in Waterloo, Quebec. See *CG*, 8 Oct. 1909, 35. On the development of plate glass see Daniel J. Boorstin, *The Americans: The Democratic Experience* (New York, 1974), 336–45, and Warren C. Scoville, *Revolution in Glassmaking* (Cambridge, MA, 1948). On changing lighting technology see Wolfgang Schivelbusch, *Disenchanted Night: The Industrialization of Light in the Nineteenth Century* (Berkeley, 1988).

6 Marcus, *American Store Window*, 12.

7 See, for example, *CG*, 25 Jan. 1895, 32, and 16 March 1900, 12.

8 Ibid., 25 Dec. 1896, 34; 3 March 1893, 4; 18 May 1900, 34.

9 Ibid., 30 Jan. 1903, 38; 18 Oct. 1895, 84. See also 29 Nov. 1901, 8; 8 May 1896, 8.

10 Ibid., 3 Jan. 1896, 28; 16 June 1905, 62; 16 June 1899, 14.

11 Ibid., 25 Dec. 1896, 34; 25 June 1897, 10; 15 June 1900, 6; 13 Sept. 1907, 58.

12 Ibid., 27 Feb. 1903, 50; 7 Oct. 1904, 47. See also 12 Oct. 1900, 4; 1 Jan. 1904, 11.

13 See, for example, ibid., 27 March 1896, 33; 13 April 1900, 5; 6 Dec.

1889, 2–3; 11 May 1906, 25; 16 March 1900, 12; 26 Oct. 1900, 24. See also Schivelbusch, *Disenchanted Night*, 137–54.

14 *CG*, 5 June 1896, 15; 26 May 1905, 62; 6 Nov. 1903, 44; 23 Dec. 1892, 12.

15 Ibid., 7 Oct. 1904, 47; 30 May 1902, 14; 6 March 1903, 20; 9 July 1897, 5.

16 Ibid., 30 July 1897, 6; 14 Oct. 1898, 24; 2 March 1900, 40; 6 July 1900, 32.

17 See, for example, ibid., 12 Aug. 1898, 5; 29 July 1904, 44; 11 May 1906, 25; 12 May 1893, 8; 12 April 1901, 18; 3 May 1889, 4.

18 Ibid., 4 Dec. 1896, 12; 10 Nov. 1899, 38; 6 July 1900, 6; 16 Jan. 1903, 46; 29 May 1896, 17.

19 Ibid., 31 Oct. 1902, 54; 14 Dec. 1900, 12; 22 May 1896, 10.

20 Ibid., 21 Oct. 1898, 38; 15 June 1900, 5; 3 Nov. 1893, 6; 25 Oct. 1901, 52; 26 June 1901, 34; 22 May 1903, 13; 14 July 1899, 7.

21 Ibid., 27 Oct. 1905, 61; 23 Feb. 1894, 6; 24 July 1903, 40; 15 June 1900, 5; 10 May 1895, 8; 20 Oct. 1893, 16.

22 Ibid., 8 July 1898, 34; 8 May 1891, 4; 1 May 1903, 22.

23 Ibid., 12 June 1903, 29; 3 April 1891, 3; 2 Oct. 1891, 28; 26 Aug. 1892, 8; 3 Sept. 1903, 50; 21 Aug. 1896, 19.

24 Ibid., 11 Oct. 1901, 40; 20 Nov. 1891, 4; 16 Dec. 1892, 3–4; 30 Sept. 1910, 33; 17 March 1899, 33; 25 June 1897, 10. The *Grocer* frequently gave hints about how to avoid wasting stock in window displays. See, for example, 20 April 1900, 34; 7 June 1901, 38.

25 Ibid., 31 Oct. 1902, 52; 7 Oct. 1904, 47; 25 Sept. 1891, 2; 6 Oct. 1893, 29; 12 Oct. 1906, 25; 9 July 1897, 5; 14 Oct. 1898, 24; 19 Dec. 1902, 25; 9 Dec. 1892, 4.

26 Ibid., 18 Oct. 1895, 84; 18 May 1906, 102; 24 Nov. 1899, 12; 28 Aug. 1903, 52. The store owned by the family of J.V. McAree was one that survived on credit. See *Cabbagetown Store* (Toronto, 1953), 8.

27 *CG*, 25 Oct. 1901, 50. See also 6 April 1906, 23; 16 March 1900, 12.

28 *CG*, 26 Aug. 1898, 10; 18 Sept. 1903, 10; 21 Dec. 1906, 22; 20 Sept. 1907, 33. When this practice began is uncertain. In 1910 the *Grocer* published an 1893 photo which it described as "one of the first made for Salada Tea." See 23 Dec., 31.

29 Ibid., 19 Oct. 1900, 30; 6 Nov. 1903, 44; 23 Aug. 1907, 36; 25 April 1902, 7; 30 Oct. 1903, 44; 26 Jan. 1900, 31; 21 Dec. 1906, 22.

30 Ibid., 13 Oct. 1893, 8; 23 Oct. 1903, 92; 24 Nov. 1899, 12; 18 Oct. 1895, 84; 14 Dec. 1900, 12; 10 Nov. 1899, 38; 21 Nov. 1902, 38; 14 Dec. 1906, 23; 7 April 1899, 11.

31 Ibid., 11 July 1902, 7.

32 Ibid., 10 Nov. 1899, 38; 7 April 1899, 11; 18 Oct. 1895, 84; 15 June 1900, 5; 22 April 1904, 5.

33 See, for example, ibid., 30 Dec. 1892, 22; 18 May 1906, 103; 18 Oct. 1895, 84; 14 Dec. 1906, 23; 19 Dec. 1902, 25.

34 Ibid., 21 Dec. 1906, 22.

35 See William Westfall, "The Dominion of the Lord: An Introduction to the Cultural History of Protestant Ontario in the Victorian Period," *Queen's Quarterly* 83 (Spring 1976): 47–70.

36 *CG*, 22 Oct. 1897, 14. On the sensation of "weightlessness" see T. Jackson Lears, *No Place of Grace: Antimodernism and the Transformation of American Culture, 1880–1920* (New York, 1981), 32, 41–47.

37 *CG*, 5 July 1889, 3. As late as 1928, for example, only 10 percent of household sugar in the United States was sold in package form. Boorstin, *The Americans*, 441. See also Ruth Schwartz Cowan, *More Work for Mother: The Ironies of Household Technology from the Open Hearth to the Microwave* (New York, 1983), 71–73.

38 This was said explicitly of a display in the window of Mitchie & Co. in Toronto. *CG*, 6 July 1900, 6.

39 Ibid., 12 Oct. 1900, 5; 24 April 1903, 20; 28 Aug. 1891, 8; 26 Oct. 1900, 22. On the connection between the world of art and the culture of consumption see Bowlby, *Just Looking*, 8; Remy G. Saisselin, *Bricabracomania: The Bourgeois and the Bibelot* (London, 1985); Jackson Lears, "Uneasy Courtship: Modern Art and Modern Advertising," *American Quarterly* 39 (Spring 1987): 133–54.

40 Judith Williamson, *Decoding Advertisements: Ideology and Meaning in Advertising* (London, 1978), 103; Claude Lévi-Strauss, *The Raw and the Cooked* (London, 1970). See also Bowlby, *Just Looking*, 25, 29.

41 *CG*, 1 Oct. 1897, 5.

42 Ibid., 23 Oct. 1903, 10. See also 6 July 1900, 5; 10 Feb. 1899, 28; 18 Oct. 1895, 84; 20 Aug. 1897, 15. This is not to say that other messages were not also intended. For example, such windows helped to quell fears of adulteration.

43 See James C. Whorton, *Crusaders for Fitness: The History of American Health Reformers* (Princeton, 1982), and Stephen Nissenbaum, *Sex, Diet and Debility in Jacksonian America* (Westport, CT, 1980).

44 Elizabeth Ewen and Stuart Ewen have argued that "a consumptionist ideology required a world-view in which people and nature were not merely separate but at odds with one another." However, in the food business, it was important to emphasize the essential continuity between nature and culture. The link was especially obvious in Christmas displays, which often featured natural products such as raisins, currants, prunes, oranges, lemons, grapes, cranberries, and nuts, demonstrating that the primary religious festival in Western culture was firmly linked to the natural realm. The popularity of these foods, traditional Christmas treats, also indicates the continuing strength of festival customs. See Ewen and Ewen, *Channels of Desire*, 58.

45 *CG*, 23 Sept. 1898, 12; 25 June 1897, 10; 25 Dec. 1896, 34; 25 May 1900, 34; 15 June 1900, 6; 13 April 1900, 5; 24 Aug. 1900, 6; 8 Jan. 1904, 24.

46 Ibid., 20 April 1900, 34; 21 April 1905, 64; 25 Sept. 1891, 1. A store on Spadina Avenue in Toronto calculated that a mechanical novelty display of a rescue at sea brought in $400 of extra business. *CG*, 27 Dec. 1907, 66.

47 Edmund Leach, "Structuralism in Social Anthropology" in *Structuralism: An Introduction*, ed. David Robey (Oxford, 1973), 39.

48 See Victor Turner, *The Ritual Process: Structure and Antistructure* (Ithaca, 1969).

49 Saussure made a distinction in the phenomenon of language between *langue*, the theoretical system or structure of language, its system of rules, and *parole*, the actual day-to-day use made of the system by individual speakers. See John Sturrock, *Structuralism and Since: From Lévi-Strauss to Derrida* (Oxford, 1979), 8.

50 Boorstein, *The Americans*, 337.

51 The term is borrowed from Paul Bouissac, *Circus and Culture: A Semiotic Approach* (Bloomington, 1976), 98.

52 See, for example, *CG*, 1 May 1896, 30; 18 Oct. 1907, 91.

53 Ibid., 1 June 1900, 40; 25 Sept. 1891, 2.

54 Ibid., 8 May 1896, 8.

55 Ibid., 28 June 1895, 16; 25 June 1897, 10; 11 Dec. 1896, 14; 1 June 1900, 42; 4 Jan. 1907, 12.

56 McAree, *Cabbagetown Store*, 18; *CG*, 3 April 1891, 1. It is no coincidence that only after this process occurred, only after the expertise of clerks was reduced to restocking shelves, adding bills, and making change, were large numbers of women given employment in grocery stores. The opportunity to speak with authority had passed. On changing relationships between merchants and manufacturers see Glenn Porter and Harold C. Livesay, *Merchants and*

Manufacturers: Studies in the Changing Structure of Nineteenth-Century Marketing (Baltimore, 1971).

57 On the appearance of chain stores and supermarkets see Liebs, *Main Street to Miracle Mile*, 116–35; Bliss, *A Canadian Millionaire*, 111–14. For reactions to their establishment in Canada see, for example, *CG*, 17 Dec. 1920, 26; 20 Feb. 1925, 14; 13 March 1925, 15; 20 March 1925, 15; 7 Aug. 1925, 15.

DAN CRANMER'S POTLATCH:
Law as Coercion, Symbol, and Rhetoric in British Columbia, 1884–1951*

TINA LOO

At the beginning of January [1922] I learnt that a large "Potlatch" had taken place at Village Island on Christmas day and the three days preceding that day.

I at once commenced investigations, but for some time could not obtain any definite information as to who had taken part in the "Potlatch."

On Jan 5th I obtained the services of one David Shaughnessy an Indian to act as interpreter, and from then till the end of January interviewed a large number of Indians throughout the district. By that time I had obtained sufficient information to prove that the following facts took place.

During December one Dan Cranmer, Indian of Alert Bay, sent out word to the Indians throughout the Kwawkewlth Agency to gather together at Village Island, and on the 22nd December the proceedings started. On that day Jim Hall paid back canoes, and Kawkute spoke thanking Hall (the first proceedings of a "Potlach" [sic] is usually the paying back of old "Potlatch" debts . . .). No more was done that day as some of the tribes had not yet arrived.

*Canadian Historical Review, 73, 2 (June 1992): 125–65. Reprinted with the permission of University of Toronto Press.

On the 23rd Dec. Billy Asu paid back $2000.00 in blankets. Sam Charlie paid back canoes. Abraham spoke for Sam Charlie. Harry Hanus paid a copper back. This copper was then sold back to Hanus by Cranmer for $3000.00. Hanus then paid Cranmer furniture, canoes, blankets, etc. in this transaction he was acting for Mrs. Dan Cranmer who was paying back to her husband, as a woman cannot speak at a "Potlatch" a man has to transact the business for her. At the time Hanus paid the copper to Cranmer, Spruce Martin spoke thanking Hanus. Jumbo paid back sewing machines. Sam Poulgash paid back bracelets and jewellery. Billy Highakus paid back money. At all the different paying back either Komkute or Abraham spoke. After the paying back was completed, Herbert Martin danced the "Hamitsa" (commonly known as the "Wild Man dance") and Jas. Knox danced the "Kamongenis." The giving away then commenced, the canoes and some gas boats were given away that evening. Sam Scow was the caller. (The caller is the man who announces to whom the various articles are to be given.) After this the "Galeklalath" dance was given by Amos Dawson to Cranmer, this was danced by Mrs. Moses Alfred. (These dances are personal property, and what might be termed copyright is given away by the one person to another.) On the following day the furniture was given away. Sam Scow was the caller, and Peter Knox, Kenneth Hunt, Moses Alfred & Johnson Cook carried the various articles to the recipients. Later pool tables were given away. Johnny Drabble was caller and Kenneth Hunt carried a cue to each of the recipients to signify that each had received a pool table. Then Jewellery was given away. Sam Scow was the caller, the jewellery was tied on sticks and Nahok cut them off as they were given away, and they were carried to the recipients by Johnson Cook. The "Quiaque" dance was then given by Billy Asu to Cranmer. This was a masked dance, danced by four men but I was unable to learn who they were. Three women, Mrs. Peter Knox, Mrs. Johnny Warnock & Mrs. Nahok also danced at the same time. This finished the proceedings on the 24th December. On Christmas day the flour was given away, Monaquilla was caller. Peter Knox, Jas. Knox, Kenneth Hunt & Johnson Cook carried it to the recipients. Moses Alfred was on the pile of flour (about 400 sacks) handing it down to the aforementioned carriers. Money was given away, Sam Scow was caller, and the same carriers acted for this as did for the flour. A "Feast Song" was then sung, this was conducted by Joe Nadone. The Potlatch was then concluded by Kweemqlas bringing out a wooden image supposed to represent the enemy, which he knocked down and jumped on as if he were the winner of a fight.

On 1st February I laid informations before W.M. Halliday, Indian Agent under Section 149 Indian Act against all of the aforementioned active participants of this "Potlach" [sic] and summonses were issued. . . . [1]

They arrested us. That is what Angermann did. That was because Kenneth Hunt had given the list to Angermann. They brought us to the old day school. They were questioning us. Asking us things. They were calling out our names and what we did at there [the Potlatch]. We were all questioned. All of us got two months. We all got two months. They kept us in prison at the day school. We found out that Gah-uk-sta-lus (Jane Cook) was working together with Kenneth Hunt and also Dave Shaughnessy . . . they really wanted to put an end to the Potlatch. . . . We were in prison at the Day School. We were all there. We went to sleep that night. All we had was blankets, no mattress. Daylight came and Zoh-la-lee-tless-louq (Emma Cranmer) came to give us breakfast. She fed us. She fed us lunch. She fed us supper. It was getting late. At dusk they were shipping us to Vancouver. They made all of us form a line. All our relatives were weeping as they marched us down in line. We got on the "Beatrice" a C.P.R. boat. We went southward. We got to Vancouver.

The police had two transporting wagons. Two trucks. They were both full. They did not have room for me in one. I got angry at Angermann. "What do you think we are," I said, "That you should want to arrest us when we have not done anything wrong." All the white people were staring because I just about hit him. Angermann got scared. I wanted to jump into the wagon and beat him up. He just left. We started off for Oakalla. . . . [T]hey packed the people into these trucks that they could hardly breathe. . . . We suffered so.[2]

That was not the end of the matter. When the prosecutions arising from the Village Island gathering were completed, some fifty-eight informations had been laid, resulting in nine dismissals and forty-nine convictions. Of those convicted, twenty-two were sentenced to two months' imprisonment, four got six months, and twenty-three received suspended sentences. The suspended sentences were awarded after each of the recipients signed affirmations to stop potlatching and agreed to turn in their ceremonial regalia, which consisted mainly of elaborately carved cedar masks, to the Indian agent.[3]

Dan Cranmer's potlatch and the ensuing arrests loom large in Kwakiutl[4] consciousness. Even today—some seventy years later—the incarcerations are still talked about by young Natives.[5] While the event is emblematic of their oppression, it has also come to represent a triumph.[6] For the Alert Bay Kwakiutl, the outlawing of the potlatch and the "confiscation" of their masks mark the beginnings of a political consciousness that has led them into the courts to resist the incursions of white society and to recover their land and cultural identity.[7] The 450 pieces of potlatch regalia that were turned into the Alert Bay Indian agent in return for suspended sentences ended up in the Victoria Museum (now the Museum of Civilization) in Ottawa and the Royal Ontario Museum in Toronto, where they made up a significant portion of the Northwest Coast collection—that is, until 1963, when two Alert Bay Indians appeared in Ottawa, asked to see the "confiscated" material, and announced they were there to reclaim what was rightfully theirs.[8] The episode sparked a debate about museums and the ownership of culture that led to the return of the last of the masks to Alert Bay and Cape Mudge in 1987, where they sit housed in a Native-run museum.

For non-Native historians, the criminalization of the potlatch, the resistance on the part of aboriginal peoples to the law's enforcement, and the recent renaissance of the practice illustrate the contact experience in microcosm.[9] For many white British Columbians in the late nineteenth and early twentieth centuries, the ritual was symbolic of the savagery and depravity of Indians. As a result, the potlatch became a lightning rod for the efforts of Christian missionaries bent on civilizing the province's Native peoples. When they failed to convince Indians to give up their practice, both Protestant and Catholic clerics, sometimes supported by Indian converts, turned to the federal government, asking it to assist their efforts by outlawing the potlatch. The government complied, and in 1884 the apparatus of white domination was further reinforced when the Indian Act was amended to meet the wishes of British Columbia's missionaries. The efforts to suppress the potlatch were part of a larger attempt on the part of white society to use the law, as well as other institutions like schools, to assimilate Native peoples into a Western, capitalist culture. For missionaries and Department of Indian Affairs administrators alike, moral improvement was not only necessary for the continued survival of Indians, but it was also the prerequisite to humanity. According to the Indian Act, an Indian was not considered a "person" until he or she demonstrated to the superintendent-general of Indian Affairs "the degree of civilization to which he or she has attained, and the character for integrity, morality and sobriety."[10] At that time, Indians could be enfranchised. When they were, however, they "ceased to be Indians."[11] Despite these invidious distinctions and the harm inflicted as a result, Native peoples managed to resist the assimilationist efforts of white society to a degree and, in the case of the law against the potlatch, to witness the triumph of their own customary law (as they saw the potlatch) over the "Queen's law" in 1951, when the provision against potlatching was left out of the revised Indian Act.

Although it is impossible to separate issues relating to Indian–white relations from a study of the potlatch, I want to try to do so. Like scholars of Native history, I also consider the potlatch "a site of struggle"; however, I am interested in this struggle less for what it can reveal about the relations between Native and non-Native peoples per se, and more for what it can tell us about how the law works. For if nothing else, the potlatch provision of the Indian Act was a law, and its enforcement history can show us the nature of the power invested in statute law and the courts as well as the consequences of its exercise.

There has been considerable interest from scholars working in a variety of disciplines, including history, in exploring the nature of the law's power. The historical literature focusses on two particular aspects of the law's power: its coercive and its symbolic or ideological dimensions. Because the coercive power of the law flows from the monopoly the state has on the use of legitimate force, some historians contend that those whose interests are represented by the state have those interests reinforced by and through statute and common law. Thus, despite the law's pretensions to neutrality, it creates and imposes a certain kind of order: it represents and reinforces the interests of whites, Anglo-Saxons, heterosexuals, the propertied, the married, and men—or any combination of these groups.[12] People who do not fit these categories are labelled "other," and are subject to legal regulation and sanctions aimed at reinforcing a particular social, economic, and political order. For instance, Constance Backhouse has shown that despite the passage of legislation that could be considered liberal in terms of women's rights in marriage, divorce, property, and custody, (male) judges routinely interpreted these statutes as narrowly as possible and prevented women from reaping their intended benefits.[13] Similarly, her work on rape law and that of Mary Jane Mossman on decision making in the courtroom reveal the hidden gender of the law, demonstrating, as feminist legal theorist Catharine MacKinnon argues, that the "law sees and treats women the way men see and treat women."[14]

Other historians have shifted the focus away from the interests upheld and furthered by the law to how the law manages to compromise its neutrality but still retain its legitimacy. These scholars, while acknowledging the coercive dimension of the law, point to its symbolic and ideological dimensions as the key to understanding the nature of its power. Douglas Hay and E.P. Thompson, two of the most influential writers taking this line, argue that the power of the law cannot rest on naked force because obedience to the law depends on a continued belief in its legitimacy.[15] People must believe that despite their condition they will be treated equally before the law, and that those who administer it as well as the laws they enforce are reasonably fair. Belief in the rule of law is achieved and maintained by the theatrical and ritualistic features of courtroom procedure that mask the interests upheld by the law. However, as Thompson points out, the rule of law cannot be a complete fiction: there has to be some substance to it. In fact, he argues, the ruling class in eighteenth-century England were forced to trade some of their power for the legitimacy that underpinned their continuing right to govern. Thus, though the law was biased, the fact that its power depended on maintaining a belief in its neutrality meant there were very real limits to its being used to further ruling-class interests. Ultimately, the law's ideological nature tempered its power and the potential for abuse.[16]

Coercion and ideology, however, do not completely explain the power of the law or how it works. Focussing on the law's coercive dimension can reduce those who are the subjects of regulation to mere objects or victims who possess little agency. What little they do have is limited to resistance: reacting to the actions and agenda of the powerful, whoever they may be. While it is important to take notice of resistance on the part of the so-called "powerless," it is also important to recognize that they have the capacity to act as well as react. Similarly, while it is necessary and important to acknowledge the symbolic and ideological dimensions of the law, we should not make too much of them. People do not have to believe in the rule of law to obey it or use it; nor should their obedience or willingness to participate in the legal process be interpreted as an indication of their belief in the rule of law and the legitimacy of the larger system of authority of which it is a part. How else can we explain why people who are oppressed by the law, like women for instance, or people for whom the common law is culturally alien, like Indians, use it?

False consciousness and Gramsci's concept of hegemony take us a certain distance in understanding why and how people can be the authors of their own oppression, but they do not explain why people participate in a system of law that is alien to them. Perhaps there may be a simpler answer to both questions: people obey and use the law because it is in their interest to do so. While this is hardly a revelation, it seems a point worth noting because it has been lost in the debate over the nature of the power of the law and how it works. Because an individual's interests shift constantly and are contingent on a set of equally shifting, immediate, and fairly narrow circumstances, it is possible for that person simultaneously to maintain a belief in something as fuzzy and abstract as the rule of law (or any other ideology for that matter, like democracy, socialism, or equality, for instance) while acting in a manner that is completely inconsistent with that belief. Thus, there can be a dichotomy between belief and action that is sustained and explained by interest.

I want to explore the nature of the law's power and how it works from a perspective different from those discussed, but which take them into account while, I hope, avoiding their shortcomings. Using the potlatch provision of the Indian Act as an example, I argue that although this statute had coercive as well as symbolic and ideological dimensions, its enforcement revealed that the law and the legal process can be profitably viewed as a system of rhetoric or a way of arguing. The potlatch law certainly was an attempt to impose a certain kind of order on Native peoples, and the reaction to its problematic enforcement by the province's missionaries and Indian agents certainly revealed the law's symbolic and ideological dimensions. However, the manner in which both the prosecution and the prosecuted argued the cases arising from law's enforcement illustrated that argument or rhetoric is central to an understanding of how the law works and the nature of its power. While this notion of the law as rhetoric or a system of argument will be explored further in the body of the paper, it might be worthwhile to spell out in broad terms what this means, for understanding how the law works requires an understanding of how arguments work and what gives them power.[17]

To understand how the law is a way of arguing, we need first to understand what arguing is. Arguing is a way of organizing our experience; it is a way of understanding the world. More importantly, arguments are also made so that we can make a decision about our experience and act accordingly—or, more precisely, arguments are made to convince others to see things as we do and to act in certain ways. But how do we argue? What makes an argument effective? How do arguments motivate people to act? What, in short, gives an argument power?

In answering these questions, it is useful to make a distinction between arguing in life and in the law. In life, the arguments we find convincing are those in which the teller makes her point of view and actions seem commonsensical, natural, and rational. Strong arguments have the effect of resonating with the listener so that, if placed in the same situation, the listener would see the situation similarly and act similarly to the teller. But what is involved in making arguments resonate? Primarily, arguments are made; they are self-consciously created by the teller. Making an effective argument requires understanding the audience to which the argument will be presented and manipulating the story so that it evokes certain sensibilities in the audience that forge a connection between it and the teller. Good arguments, like good literature or poetry, make the listeners see and feel what the teller saw and felt. They make the alien—the world and life of the teller—familiar. To evoke the sensibilities that connect the teller to the listener, the teller emphasizes certain aspects of the story and not others. For instance, depending on my reading of the audience, depending on whom I am talking to, I emphasize different aspects of my work: I can tell my colleagues about my research using a certain kind of language and an implicit frame of reference, but when my friends' children ask me what I do, my story changes—I tell them I teach. In neither case am I being untruthful; but in both I have adjusted my story in accordance with what I think will resonate with them.

Arguments are central to the law, and in the law, as in life, powerful arguments depend on the teller's ability to play to members of the audience and to evoke certain sensibilities in them. But arguing in the law is different in one very important respect: in framing legal arguments, the teller has to abide by rules of legal rhetoric. Legal arguments involve using a particular language, working within a set of rules of evidence and procedure that determine what can be said and how and when it can be said, as well as determining what value and meaning can be placed on those facts that are put forward.[18] Equally importantly, and the point I will focus on, legal arguments must address the issues raised by the laws that govern the actions in question: Do the actions of the defendant match the description of the behaviour outlined by the law? What was the defendant's state of mind when she committed the act in question? What did the defendant think she was doing? What was the intent? In addressing these questions, legal arguments implicitly accept the terms of debate imposed by the law. There is no discussion of whether the law in question is just—that is deemed a political question, and outside the realm of the law—nor does a discussion of the larger social, political, or economic injustice of the situation that led both parties to get into the situation before the court occupy a central place. Trial courts are courts of law, not courts of justice. To a certain extent, then, the rules of legal rhetoric (the rules that spell out how we must argue in the law) result in removing actions from their social context. Though decontextualizing the actions of the contesting parties is done to clarify the issues, it has other implications: it shapes the questions that are asked and, in so doing, shapes the picture of the relationship between the two parties and the possibilities for the resolution of their dispute.

Sexual assault trials are a good example of how the law sets the terms of debate.[19] According to the law, the consent of the victim is what separates sex from rape.[20] Because the law has determined that consent is the central issue, trials for sexual assault revolve around determining whether there was consent: Did the victim agree to having sex with the accused, and did the accused believe there was consent? If the answers are yes, then the act in question was sex, and the accused is not guilty of sexual assault; if the answer is no, then the accused is guilty. Thus, the outcome of the trial is determined by a series of questions and yes/no responses that in no way capture the ambiguity of sexual relations. What did the parties consent to? Having a drink? A dance? A date? A kiss? Does consent to any of these things create a reasonable expectation on the part of the accused that the victim also consented to sex? Added to this ambiguity surrounding consent is a problematic assumption about the nature of consent. "Consent" assumes an equality between the victim and the accused, and that if it is given it is given freely. Again, in making this assumption, the courts ignore both the ambiguity of sexual relations, their possible inequities, and the complex pressures imposed by sex roles and expectations which, taken together, raise questions about how freely consent is given by either party. Instead, the law deems that sexual assault centres on the presence or absence of consent. In setting the terms of debate in this way, the system of argument characterized by the law shapes the questions asked as well as determines the "truth" that emerges in the courtroom.

The necessity of adhering to the rules of legal rhetoric—adopting legal conventions and addressing the questions the law deems relevant— involves adopting something classicist, linguist, and lawyer James Boyd White calls a "culture of argument."[21] This culture of argument, like any other culture, creates a particular way of seeing the world that makes certain choices for action appear reasonable and thus possible and others not. We usually call the way of seeing the world that emerges from the legal process the "truth," but given the conventions that shape it, it would appear that "truth" is constructed in the courtroom and is partial at best— just like my responses to the question of what I do. That, however, is the point: as sociologist Carol Smart notes, "the power of the law lies in its claim to the truth."[22] Even though the construction of events on which a legal decision is made is partial, we still label that construction as the "truth" and the means of reaching it (the rules of legal rhetoric) truth-finding rather than truth-making. What we are convinced by in the court-room—what makes a powerful legal argument—is still that which is reasonable and commonsensical; but it is the process by which arguments are framed, the way we argue, that we should look at to understand how the law works and where the power of the law lies.

Because the power of argument is creative, because it is all about making a case, seeing the law in this way opens up the possibility that people who are the subject of legal regulation can act as well as react. As will be discussed, the potlatch law was certainly oppressive (it had a coercive dimension) and symbolized white values, but the Indians who practised the ritual not only had success at avoiding prosecution, they also were successful in arguing their cases before the court.

As Herbert Martin told the judge at his trial, potlatch derives from the Chinook jargon, the language of trade along the coast that was an amalgam of English and a variety of Indian languages, and simply means "to give."[23] A potlatch is a ceremony given by a family or extended family to display its hereditary possessions such as dances, songs, and carvings. Potlatches are usually given on the occasion of a birth, marriage, or death, but because a social debt is incurred by the attending guests, potlatches can be given simply to fulfil a social obligation. Dan Cranmer held his potlatch to celebrate Emma Cranmer's "repurchase." He distributed goods to his wife's family and her relatives.[24] During the ceremony, the hosts might relate the genealogy of their hereditary privileges, introducing members of their family in the process, and perhaps bestowing new names (the equivalent of social ranks) on them. The formal display of those privileges follows: dances are performed and songs sung. The affair ends with the host distributing gifts to the guests. Guests are important to the ceremony because they validate the rights to the privileges displayed by the hosts and, ultimately, to the status associated with those privileges.[25]

According to anthropologists, the ceremony is a mechanism for social integration.[26] It publicly identifies people as belonging to a certain social group and defines each of their positions within that group. As well, the social order of the guests is recognized as gifts are distributed in proportion to social status. The potlatch did not, however, create social status; it was simply a way of proving and acknowledging existing status and changes in status (the giving of names, births, marriages, and deaths).[27] No matter how many potlatches a person gave, he could not alter his status beyond what he acquired through marriage or inheritance.[28] Having acquired a certain social rank, however, a person was expected to behave in a manner commensurate with his position or to risk embarrassment. Thus, a person stood to lose, but not to gain rank through potlatching.

Of course, the ceremony did change as a result of European contact.[29] Because the potlatch was a social ceremony that relied on material goods, important modifications came about in response to new economic conditions. In the late eighteenth century, Northwest Coast Indians began to participate in a European commercial economy, and the Kwakiutl potlatch reflected this change. There was an influx of new consumer goods that largely replaced many of the traditional gifts that were given away in the pre-contact potlatch. Most notably, woollen blankets became a chief item of exchange. But in the early twentieth century things like sacks of flour, mass-produced bolts of fabric, outboard motors, and fishing skiffs were also commonly distributed.[30]

Not only did the kinds of goods change, but their volume increased.[31] The new economy that Northwest Coast Natives participated in was resource-based: trapping, sealing, and fishing were the main occupations for both Indians and non-Indians alike. Though these tasks were tied to a larger commercial capitalist economy, and in that sense were quite different from what existed prior to European contact, trapping, sealing, and fishing were all fields of Native expertise. So Indians prospered—at least initially.[32] Because of their economic success, they were able to buy more goods—more blankets, more bolts of cloth, more flour, and more canoes. The potlatch expanded.

It was this expanded version of the potlatch that caught the attention of missionaries, some Christianized Indians, and Indian agents, who lobbied the federal government in the 1880s to put an end to the ceremony. Though the federal government believed a proclamation "discountenancing the custom of 'potlaches' [sic]" would be sufficient, I.W. Powell, British Columbia's superintendent of Indian affairs, disagreed. Acquainting Christian Indians "with the 'Queen's objection' to the potlatch [sic] . . . no doubt had a good effect," he told his Ottawa superiors, "but this class forms a small part of the whole Indian population, and to be effective in reaching all, I think some legislative enactment preventing the practice of the 'potlach' [sic] will be necessary. Otherwise, the proclamation will, really, have little effect on putting a stop to the custom."[33] Gustave Donckele, the Roman Catholic missionary at Cowichan, agreed. "Stringent measures" were necessary to put an end to the "heathen practice."[34] His secular counterpart at Cowichan, Indian agent William Lomas, believed that while some of his Native charges opposed the potlatch, without a law they lacked the "moral courage" to refuse to participate outright.[35]

Powell, Donckele, and Lomas each considered the law and its sanctions a prerequisite to the progress and civilization of the Native population. Their comments resonated with the same Victorian faith in the transformative capacity of the law that underlay other social reform agendas. If their confidence in the law as an instrument of reform reflected part of the progressive spirit, so too was the object of their energies. What the province's missionaries and Indian agents found so reprehensible about the potlatch was its singular combination of profligacy, debauchery, and squalor. "Individuals . . . in accordance with the well-known custom of giving away absolutely all they happen to possess . . . reduce themselves to beggery [sic] and distress," wrote Methodist missionary Cornelius Bryant in 1884:

> but beyond a mere impoverishment, and what is much worse, [are] the physical misery and evils resulting from exposure of the elements in travelling to and from these "potlatches," which they do in their canoes in all kinds of weather, and the debauchery produced by intoxication, in which they often indulge upon such occasions leaves no doubt as to the personal demoralization which follows these Native feasts.

"Hapless children and aged people" were denied the "comforts of convenient homes and wholesome food, owing to [the] reckless and spendthrift customs which are maintained at the potlatches," he concluded.[36]

Furthermore, Native hosts often resorted to illegal means—either theft or prostitution—to procure the goods they could not afford. "A man will say to his wife," argued British Columbia reserve commissioner Gilbert Malcolm Sproat, "nay to his maiden daughter, that before the spring or other appointed time he must have so many dollars for his proposed 'Potlach' [sic] and they in this way, and I believe more than from licentious desire, are forced into prostitution."[37] Moreover, the large groups of Indians that participated in the ceremony were themselves a threat to order. There were about 300 guests at Dan Cranmer's potlatch, but figures four, five, and six times that number were not unheard of—numbers that could be greater than the surrounding white population. Missionaries like Bryant and agents like Lomas contended these potlatches quickly turned into drunken orgies that lasted for days, or riots in which valuable property was destroyed. There were even reports of cannibalism and of the participants biting the flesh of their all-too-alive fellows. All told, the potlatch was "the parent of numerous vices which eat out the heart of the people"[38]—a "worse than useless custom."[39]

The lobbying efforts of British Columbia's missionaries and Indian agents were successful. In 1884 the federal government passed an amendment to the Indian Act making the potlatch an indictable criminal offence. The relevant section read as follows:

> Every Indian or other person who engages in or assists in celebrating the Indian festival known as the "Potlatch" or the Indian dance known as the "Tamanawas" is guilty of misdemeanor, and shall be liable to imprisonment of a term not more than six months nor less than two months in any gaol or place of confinement; and any Indian or other person who encourages, either directly or indirectly, an Indian or other Indians to get up such a festival or dance, or to celebrate the same, shall be guilty of a like offence, and shall be liable to the same punishment.[40]

Unfortunately, no one had bothered to define what a "potlatch" was. This ambiguity turned out to be the grounds for an appeal in 1889. Charged with potlatching by Kwawkewlth Agency agent Reginald Pidcock, Hemasak pleaded guilty and was sentenced to six months' imprisonment in August 1889. Matthew Baillie Begbie's Supreme Court quashed the conviction on appeal, however, citing the ambiguity in the statute as the reason. "A plea of guilty means guilty of the Act forbidden by the Statute," the chief justice reasoned.

> It is by no means clear that it was fully explained to the defendant what the Statute forbids. It would seem that the Statute should set out what acts constitute the forbidden festival. Until a defendant knows what those forbidden Acts are, how can he say whether he committed them or not? . . . It is easy to suppose a man might plead guilty to swearing being conscious he had used such an aspersion as "Adzookers," which is no oath, or plead guilty to gaming meaning to admit to have played at cribbage without stakes.

"I think," he concluded, "that these considerations show that there would be some difficulty in convicting at all under the Statute."[41]

It was not until 1895 that the Indian Act was amended again to address Begbie's critique. It read:

> Every Indian or other person who engages in, or assists in celebrating or encourages either directly or indirectly another to celebrate any Indian festival, dance or ceremony of which the giving away or paying back of money, goods or articles takes place before, at or after the celebration of the same, or who engages in or assists in any celebration or dance of which the wounding or mutilation of the dead or living body of any human being or animal forms a part or is a feature of is guilty of an indictable offence and is liable to imprisonment for a term not exceeding six months and not less than two months. Provided that nothing in this section shall be construed to prevent the holding of any agricultural show or exhibition or giving of prizes thereat.[42]

The amended statute appeared straightforward enough. The illegal acts consisted of giving away goods or money in association with a festival, dance, or ceremony, or the wounding of the dead or living body of a human or other animal. As will be discussed, those charged with enforcing the act did not find the amended version any easier to administer.

There were two other amendments. The first, made in 1914, was an additional attempt to restrict potlatching by outlawing the wearing of aboriginal costume (unless expressly permitted by the superintendent of Indian affairs or his official representative) and by making dancing off an Indian's home reserve illegal.[43] The second and more significant attempt came four years later, in 1918, when wartime exigencies made Ottawa even more sensitive to what it considered the improvident aspects of the potlatch and the need to eliminate it. In a circular distributed to all agents in British Columbia, Duncan Campbell Scott reminded his field officers of "the urgent need for conservation in all directions . . . no wasteful practice or mode of life can be countenanced." To this end, the department expected its agents to exercise to the full the powers given to them under the newly amended act—powers that made potlatching a summary, instead of an indictable, offence. Each agent in his concurrent capacity as a justice of the peace could now try to convict Indians for violations of the potlatch provision instead of simply committing them for trial.[44]

Of the many troubling aspects of Native culture, the potlatch seemed to offend European sensibilities most deeply. The ceremony provoked an astonishingly emotional and protracted response that filled thousands of pages of correspondence and was manifested in a series of restrictive laws that remained in force for more than half a century. This action reflected and was rooted in the deep play of anxieties about the essential order of things in white society that were brought to the surface by the close juxtaposition of another seemingly alien culture.

For whites, the ceremony united and challenged two central ideas around and through which they constituted themselves: economics and law. The argument presented by those who lobbied for legislation outlawing the potlatch was primarily an economic one, though in characteristic Victorian fashion economics and morality were intertwined and mutually reinforcing standards of behaviour. As LaViolette argues, potlatching appeared wasteful and excessive—the antithesis to the twin pillars of the Protestant work ethic: industry and sobriety.[45]

But was it? It appears that few Indians were reduced to complete penury through their participation. In fact, the potlatch was a far more ambiguous ceremony than the self-confident Victorian language of the missionaries and agents would have us believe. If the ritual were as decadent, debilitating, and demoralizing as its opponents charged, it is hard to imagine the practice continuing for long, for in short order few could afford to participate. But the potlatch did continue and, even more significantly, among the Kwakiutl it expanded. The reasons for this lay, as I noted, in their successful participation in the province's resource economy. Indians prospered, and the increased accumulations of goods that preceded Kwakiutl potlatches were not a sign of savage profligacy but, in many ways, of their successful accommodation and embodiment of LaViolette's Protestant work ethic—or at least a capitalist one. The anthropologists certainly thought so. People like Edward Sapir, Harlan Smith, and Franz Boas protested against the potlatch provisions of the Indian Act. In their opinion, the law was flawed in part not because it was ethnocentric, but because its architects failed to appreciate the broad similarities between the potlatch and modern Western economic behaviour. If Indians were economic people just like whites and their potlatch was a central economic institution, then neither they nor their culture was in need of reform through the law. In fact, the law against the potlatch stood as an obstacle to the integration of Native peoples into white society. Sapir referred to the potlatch as a "system of credit" and a "business transaction." "Bankruptcy" would be the result of enforcing the law. "The abolition of the potlatch and the consequent inability of the owner of a copper to utilize his wealth works the same sort of havoc that the wanton destruction of a white man's checks [and] drafts [would]," he told Duncan Campbell Scott.[46] Harlan Smith was even more struck by the capitalist aspects of the potlatch. "It is said to be more blessed to give than to receive," he wrote. "Mr. Carnegie is honored for what he gives away. Many have made investments just as some Indians do in Potlatches, have scrimped themselves and their families in order to make these investments and even embezzled from their employers to buy stocks and have lost everything, even their liberty, but still in civilized countries they are allowed to invest."[47] Even Franz Boas, after some thirty years' observation of the southern Kwakiutl, echoed his colleagues' comments, describing the ceremony as "a return on an interest-bearing investment,"[48] and suggested that "a policy might be developed in which the values invested in the potlatch might be administered more efficiently and wisely by what might be called a tribal bank."[49] By drawing analogies between the potlatch and capitalist behaviour, these anthropologists offered a way to make sense of an alien ritual. But in choosing capitalist economic behaviour as constituting the familiar, they revealed the assumptions of their own culture; their sense of what was "natural" and hence powerful.[50]

The problem with and the significance of the ceremony to white society lay in the distributive aspect of the ceremony. Accumulation was laudable, but the way Indians disposed of their goods stood as a radical counterpoint to the existing material order in white society.[51] When Dan Cranmer handed out jewellery, blankets, sacks of flour, pool tables, and gas launches, or simply gave away hundreds of dollars in envelopes, he and countless others who did the same thing up and down the coast displayed an attitude towards material goods that was simultaneously familiar and alien to white society. Working to consume and accumulate was intelligible behaviour, but when Indians gave away or destroyed all they had worked for they debased the very commodity—property—around which white society was constructed. Little wonder Gilbert Malcolm Sproat called the potlatch a "huge incubus."[52]

Potlatching also provoked a reaction from white British Columbians because it was the subject of law. As the DIA and those directly involved in enforcing the law against the potlatch discovered, the law's power was double-edged, a characteristic that made it an unwieldy tool of control. By designating the potlatch illegal, the Indian Act sharpened an old and ongoing conflict between Europeans and Indians. Articulating the conflict between them in the form of law made it harder to ignore, live with, or resolve disputes informally.[53] Bringing certain kinds of behaviour under the formal gaze of the law meant that violations could not be ignored, because if they were, the effectiveness of those who administered it would be undercut. The DIA and its officers had a law they had to enforce but were afraid to, because if enforcement did not result in convictions, Indians would lose all respect for them. If enforcement were not even attempted, however, the same thing would occur. Frustrated with the double-edged nature of the law, the Rev. Dr Sutherland, head of the Methodist missionary organization—whose missionaries had been among those who lobbied for the potlatch law in the first place—told the superintendent-general in 1897 that he would rather do without it. "I would be quite willing, so far as the Indians are concerned, to meet the evil of the Potlatch entirely by moral force and without asking any aid from legal enactments," he insisted,

> but since the Government has seen fit to put a law upon the Statute Book prohibiting the Potlatch ceremony, the very existence of that law, when not in force, is a hindrance in our way, and the appeals and exhortations of the missionary are met by sneering reference to the fact, or what seemed to the Indian to be a fact, that the government is not really opposed to Potlatching.[54]

Sutherland's remarks were motivated by more than twenty years of ineffectual enforcement. In fact, with the exception of the burst of activity shortly before and after the Cranmer potlatch, neither the Department of Indian Affairs nor the province pursued the enforcement of the potlatch provision of the Indian Act particularly vigorously. Very little of the charged atmosphere of moral indignation that led to criminalization of the ceremony translated into real action. Between 1884 and 1895 it appears that only two people were tried for violating the potlatch law and only one was convicted. Even after the 1895 amendment, indictments do not appear to have increased very much. Seventeen people were indicted for potlatching from 1895 to 1918. It was not until 1918 (when the offence was made a summary one) that the act was enforced with any real effect. In the four years from 1918 to 1922, 135 individuals were charged with violations of the potlatch law. The crackdown reached its peak with the Village Island arrests and fell off again (from 1922 to 1935 only ten individuals were indicted), even though potlatching continued, and perhaps even enjoyed a renaissance.[55] The statute remained on the books until 1951.

Initially, a jurisdictional dispute between federal and provincial authorities over who was responsible for enforcement hindered the efforts of the department's agents in prosecuting offenders. Though Indians were wards of the federal government, the enforcement of criminal law was a provincial jurisdiction. With neither level of government willing to assume responsibility—that is, willing to underwrite the costs of enforcement—

agents like Harry Guillod of Ucluelet on Vancouver Island's west coast felt their hands were tied. Without a lockup or a constable to aid him in 1886, Guillod found it difficult, if not impossible, to enforce the law. Ottawa told him to petition Victoria, and the province referred him back to Ottawa.[56] Not only was Victoria unwilling to provide funds for enforcement, but it also refused "to allow their jails to be occupied by prisoners convicted of infractions of the *Indian Act* before Indian Agents, or use their constables in making arrests of such prisoners."[57] Under the circumstances, it was scarcely surprising that there were no prosecutions in the years immediately following the amendment's passage.[58]

There were, however, deeper problems. Even after the jurisdictional dispute was resolved, judges were reluctant to convict, and when they did convict they were reluctant to bring the full brunt of the law to bear on the guilty. County Court Judge W.W.F. MacInnes told Indian agent William Halliday "that a penalty for potlatching would not be popular . . . and he doubted very much if any Judge in BC would do anything but give suspended sentences."[59] Fifteen years later Halliday was still complaining. "You are aware," he told BC Superintendent of Indian Affairs Ditchburn, "that our Judges are inclined to deal very leniently in affairs of this kind."[60]

The reluctance of the courts to convict and their leniency in dealing with offenders reflected a degree of popular sympathy towards the Indians and the potlatch that stemmed from the ceremony's ambiguous nature. The law seemed to be drawing distinctions where none existed. Like the anthropologists, many other British Columbians saw nothing wrong with a ceremony that was, in many ways, similar to some of their own rituals. "The Indian, who is always having the white man held up to him as a worthy example, argues that the white man calls his friends at Christmas time & feasts them & has Xmas trees & gives presents & he dresses up a man & calls him Father Xmas & says he brings presents, etc." West Coast Agency agent A.W. Neill pointed out to Vowell in 1904. "Where is the justice in forbidding them the same species of amusements?"[61] Five years later he registered another observation to the same effect:

> When we cease to dress a man up as Santa Claus and tell our children it is he who brings them presents (down a chimney) it will be time to object to an Indian who dresses himself up and tells his child he is a wolf. . . . At the same time this wolf dance took place there was a ball masque held in Alberni and the prize for the best portrayed character was given to a gentleman who personated, and very ably, a Monkey.[62]

Fisheries officer J. Crichton compared his own family traditions to those of the province's aboriginal peoples. "People howl at the barbarism of a Totem Pole because they don't know what it means, each allegorical figure represents a man's crest," he wrote. "Well, I have the honour to be a member of a noble family, . . . Earl of Carne, Viscount Crichton being the head of the tribe. Our crest is a darned old Dragon's head spitting out flame like the devil himself and yet we are not considered barbaric when we use it as an ornament on our plates, knives and forks."[63]

In addition to sentiments like these that reflected a certain empathy towards the Indians, there was a great deal of resistance to enforcing the potlatch law from the non-Native residents of the locales where the ceremony was practised—the people one might expect to be most opposed to the potlatch. Their opposition was rooted in a pragmatic concern with economy and order. Quite simply, the potlatch meant business for many local merchants. The blankets, bolts of cloth, sacks of flour, and other items that were given away had to be obtained somewhere, and, despite the accusations of the missionaries to the contrary, Indians usually purchased them at the local general store.[64] In fact, missionaries and agents commonly complained, as Cornelius Bryant did, that "the good intentions of the Government, in seeking to suppress so pernicious a practice . . . [are] discouraged and opposed simply for the purpose of selling a few hundred dollars worth of goods."[65]

Other than this material consideration, non-Native residents were also concerned with the issue of order. Their concept of order differed, however, from that of the missionaries who had spearheaded the campaign for the potlatch law. These people were not so much concerned about the moral degradation and the future progress of the Indians, and the threat this posed to creating a Christian social order; instead, they were preoccupied with avoiding violent conflict.[66] If the potlatch law were enforced rigidly, they felt, there was a chance that the local Indians might rise up, and they would pay the consequences. The threat of violent resistance seemed much more tangible than the moral and ethical danger posed by allowing the potlatch to continue.

The sympathy towards the potlatch and the resistance to enforcement from those who stood to gain materially and in terms of safety made securing convictions uncertain and created problems for the Department of Indian Affairs. Amending the law would have little effect if the courts were reluctant to enforce it. In fact, changes could do more harm than good. The department was unwilling to undertake any amendments or to consider repeal. Any alteration, they thought, would be construed by the Indians as a sign of weakness and would thus undermine the authority of the "Queen's Law" as a whole. As A.W. Vowell, BC's superintendent of Indian affairs, told Ottawa, when it came to Indians and the law, "vacillation always produces disrespect and a thorough want of confidence in the source from which it emanates."[67] Acquittals were potentially even more damaging than any "vacillation" in enforcing the potlatch law. If convictions were not secured, the department informed a missionary who had complained about the lack of enforcement, "more harm than good [may] result from prosecution, as it would give the Indians more courage to go on with their practices."[68] Agent William Halliday reported that a quashed conviction gave Alert Bay "offenders great jubilation and a decided moral victory."[69]

In fact, it was this "moral victory" that disturbed whites the most. Not only did it lead Indians to think that the law was "as weak as a baby," as they told Napoleon Fitzstubbs, but it also raised doubts in white minds about the distinction the law had drawn between civilization and savagery—about the validity of the social boundaries that gave meaning and coherence to white society.[70] The potlatch provoked concern because it was a focal point of the law—the other cultural system that, along with economics, shapes the ways whites see. Though the two are conflated somewhat in this paper, the function of the law consists of more than direct control through punishments and sanctions: the law also plays an important symbolic role. Laws express the rules that limit and shape behaviour and expectation, but they are also expressions of ethical norms. Thus, not only are we ruled by law, but law also embodies and articulates the broad ideas around which we are constituted as a society. In an important sense, the function of the potlatch provision of the Indian Act can be considered separately from its coercive effects. This law was a public articulation by white society of its own social norms and boundaries. In this formulation, the act of legislation becomes a symbolic act of self-determination, not one of control.

This argument for the symbolic function of the law is particularly compelling in the context of British Columbia. In other societies, the job of setting out social boundaries—the job of defining a group identity—is done by religious and educational institutions, to name two, over a long period of time. But the province was still a young place in the late nineteenth and early twentieth centuries, very much on the frontier, experiencing rapid and telescoped growth, and possessed of a culturally diverse population ("white" obscures that diversity) and few established institutions that could claim to speak for and define this amorphous "European" group. In a context like this, it might be possible that the law—or perhaps the act of making law—played a central role in adumbrating the social and ethical boundaries of white British Columbia.

The symbolic aspect of the law is not completely independent of its coercive effect, however. Enforcement does matter, as the law against the potlatch so graphically shows. The ambiguity surrounding the ceremony was manifested in a reluctance to prosecute violations fully and, as a result, enforcement was problematic. This not only weakened the authority of the Indian Act and those charged with administering it, but also compromised the authority of the law as a whole and the social order it symbolized and upheld. Given this, Sproat's "huge incubus" appeared even more threatening.

Enforcing the law against the potlatch proved problematic not only because white British Columbians were divided in their attitudes about the ceremony, but also because of the way the law works. The power of the law rests in its ability to define issues, set the terms of the debate and resolution, and provide the measures for assessing the fairness of the outcome.[71] Though some scholars consider that the law and the "legal method"—the way in which cases are decided—are closed systems that tend to perpetuate the status quo under the guise of real, objective enquiry and neutrality, this does not always have to be the case. Both prosecutor and prosecuted had to work on the same narrow terrain, and in the case of the potlatch trials it was those on the side of the prosecution—the so-called powerful—who found themselves at a disadvantage.

The potlatch prosecutions reveal how the power of the law lay in its capacity to set the terms of debate by selectively limiting the terrain of the inquiry. From 1884 on what was at issue in these cases was the interpretation of words like *potlatch, participation, festival,* and *ceremony.* What did these words mean and did the specific instance of behaviour under scrutiny by the court conform to the actions defined by these words?

If the original legislation had failed to specify just what sort of behaviour constituted a potlatch (in *Hemasak*), those charged with enforcing the law or defending Indians indicted for violations of it felt that the amended legislation was the opposite: it was too inclusive. "It would seem," wrote Dickie and DeBeck, the lawyers for the Alert Bay Kwakiutl in 1922, "that the word 'Indian' does not limit the dance, festival or other ceremony to something which is peculiarly Indian, but might include any ceremony participated in by Indians."

> The assumption is a direct inference from the last part of section 149, which excludes from the operation of the statute any "agricultural show or exhibition." An agricultural show or exhibition is not a ceremony which is peculiar to Indians[;] in fact it is not an Indian ceremony at all in the sense that if it was necessary to exclude it from the Act the only conclusion that can be drawn is that an agricultural show or exhibition, if participated in by Indians, would otherwise come within the section; consequently, any other ceremony would. . . .
>
> It will thus be seen that the scope of the law is extremely wide and not only is it a complete prohibition to carry on any of their tribal customs, but also they are technically liable if they take part in any transaction of a ceremonious nature, whether the transaction is of Indian origin or not, should such transaction involve a gift or payment of kind.

"It is respectfully submitted," the solicitors concluded, "that no blue law was ever so wide in its scope, or so oppressive."[72] Dickie and DeBeck's interpretation was supported by Chief Justice Hunter of the provincial Supreme Court in *R. v. George Scow et al.*, another potlatching case originating in the

Kwawkewlth Agency that was heard by the superior court on appeal. Though Hunter sustained the convictions of Scow and his four compatriots, he noted that "'dance' and 'festival' were not words describing a class which would limit 'ceremonies' to events of a like nature, but that 'other ceremonies' might include any ceremonies whatever."[73]

Equally troublesome was the ambiguity surrounding three words in the statute: *participation, festival,* and *ceremony*. William Halliday considered the interpretation given to *participation* by the courts of central importance in putting down the potlatch, and asked Ottawa for a definition. "In our courts in British Columbia, unfortunately, we are overstocked with lawyers who are addicted to what is commonly called hair-splitting on the meaning of the word."

> I take it that the wording of the Act means that any Indian who is present at an Indian dance off his own reserve is guilty of an offense, but I also feel sure that if a conviction were entered that it would be upset on appeal, unless the offenders actually danced themselves. . . .
>
> The Indians are taking subterfuge under the dance question for attending what I believe are potlatches, but I hesitate to have any prosecutions made in this section. . . . If the word "participation" does not mean "is present at" may I humbly recommend that these words be added[?][74]

Halliday's successor, M.S. Todd, also considered the meaning of *participation* given by the courts an obstacle to enforcement. Several Indians he had convicted for potlatching retained a lawyer and filed for appeal on the interpretation of *participation*. In Todd's opinion, however, "any Indian in a Community Indian dance hall with a blanket or regalia on is participating in that dance. . . . It is not necessary to be dancing on the floor to be participating. The definition of community is participation and to be present in the [community] hall with regalia on must be participating."[75]

If *participation* was unclear, defining an illegal *festival* or *ceremony* was even more problematic, as Agent Neill pointed out. "Half a dozen men joined together and invited a few of a neighbouring band," he reported: "They came, spent a few days, got small presents, mostly in food, had dancing and feasting at night but went about their business in the day & in less than a week it was over. Had it been called . . . 'a few friends for Xmas' no one could have found much fault."[76] The problem Neill described was brought into sharp focus several years later in the Cariboo. When Chief Isadore and Thomas and Mary Ketlo were arrested and convicted for holding an "Easter potlatch" in May 1928, they appealed and were granted a *de novo* hearing before the Cariboo District County Court in June. Their counsel asked that the case be dismissed, arguing that the section of the Indian Act dealing with the potlatch criminalized an "'*Indian* festival,' an '*Indian* dance,' or 'other *Indian* ceremony,'" and that the Crown had not established that what had occurred fell under any of these categories. For its part, the Crown held that what Isadore and the Ketlos had staged could be designated an "other ceremony." H.E.A. Robertson did not clarify the act's wording, but ruled in the appellants' favour, noting that the Indians' "supper followed by a 'white man's dance' did not constitute a ceremony."[77]

In other cases, however, the debate was even narrower, and cases were decided on the basis of "technicalities." For instance, Begbie quashed the conviction in *Hemasak* because the accused was incarcerated on an improper warrant of committal.[78] Johnny Moon and his father Chief Harry had the charges against them dropped because of "informalities in the information and the warrant."[79] Six Indians of the Nakwakto band at Blunden Harbour had their convictions overturned on appeal because Agent Halliday had filled out the warrants of committal and conviction improperly, neglecting to state the jurisdiction of his court and the fact he was acting as a justice of the peace.[80]

In none of these cases did the legal debate revolve around the larger social issues of justice or equity. Because there was an implicit acceptance of the law as it was, trials centred on determining whether the action in question constituted the illegal behaviour outlined in the statute. Although the system of argument employed by the law narrowed the terms of debate, it did not determine the outcome of trials. The wording of statutes and legal "technicalities" had a strategic potential that could be exploited by Indians as well as whites. When Indians did appeal to the law in the case of the potlatch prosecutions, they were often successful in securing suspended sentences or in having their convictions overturned on appeal. They showed themselves to be skilled legal players: they employed counsel,[81] certainly were not over-awed by the law's magisterial qualities, and knew its subtleties well enough to take advantage of it.

In the fall of 1913 Halliday informed Ottawa that he expected "some difficulty shortly with regard to the Potlatch as the Indians have determined to put the matter to the test. . . . [T]he man who is giving the potlatch stated at a meeting of the Indians that . . . someone must test the matter and he would be the Agent by which it would be tested."[82] Far from shying away from confrontation, the Indians involved—Johnny Bagwany and Ned Harris—sought to test the law on its own terms.[83] If the exchange between Halliday and one Kwakiutl is any indication, some Native people had a well-developed sense of those terms. In relation to some recent arrests of Cape Mudge Indians for potlatching Halliday wanted to know "what the chances would be if some of the most reputable men of the Cape Mudge Indians . . . should be called as witnesses . . . would they tell the truth?" The Indian's reply was highly suggestive. "I do not think they would lie. I think they would not tell anything at all," he said.

> You know they would have a lawyer to defend them, and the lawyer would not allow anyone to ask them "were you present at the dance given by this man, or did you receive anything from him?" This

would be a leading question, and the lawyer for the defence would not allow it to be asked. They would be hostile witnesses, and it would be a matter of very great difficulty to get any of them to give evidence.[84]

His familiarity with the legal process and its terminology ("leading question" and "hostile witness") demonstrates a degree of skill that could easily be used to resist the law. And it was.

Nowhere was this familiarity with the law put to better effect than in the wake of the Cranmer arrests. Apparently, on the advice of a Vancouver lawyer named W.R. Vaughan, the Alert Bay Indians broke the potlatch into two parts to avoid prosecution. They would have the dancing and ceremonial part publicly, as usual, but dispense the gifts later (sometimes six months later), privately, and often door-to-door. Harry Speck, or Spike, chief of the Klowitsis band, did just this when he held a potlatch on Turnour Island in 1931. "He told the Indians that acting on the advice of his lawyer he did not intend to give anything away for at least six months after the dance and then his lawyer advised him he would be free of prosecution."[85] The six-month period was in reference to the criminal code provision that prohibited prosecutions for summary offences if six months had elapsed after the commission of the illegal act.[86]

The "disjointed"[87] or "bootleg"[88] potlatch was one strategy Indians used to get around the law. Another technique that was employed on at least one occasion was to have the agent distribute the goods. One Billy McDuff presented himself before the agent and asked for permission to distribute some 300 sacks of flour he had purchased from the Sointula Co-operative Store to the Kingcome Inlet Indians. Indian agent Todd refused, at which time McDuff "stated he did not wish to have anything further to do with it and asked if I would not take the flour over and make distribution myself." Todd agreed. It was only later that he found out that Duff "had already distributed to four other tribes and Kingcome was the last, which would have completed this part of the potlatch. In view of this, it appears that I would be placing myself in this position—I would complete the potlatch by distributing to these Indians . . . and by doing so would help him evade the penalty of the law yet fulfil his obligations."[89]

Though both the Department of Indian Affairs and the Native people who were charged with violating the Indian Act by potlatching were forced to frame their arguments within the very circumscribed boundaries provided by the law, it was the prosecution who found themselves disadvantaged. In confining both sides to addressing very narrow issues—to addressing the meaning of words and "technicalities"—the system of argument used by the court removed the potlatch from much of the social context that gave it meaning. The rules of legal rhetoric resolved conflict by reducing disputes to their bare bones; by "skeletonizing" them. In the case of the potlatch prosecutions, the bare bones amounted to ascertaining whether a ceremony at which goods or money were distributed had occurred. However, those who opposed the practice did not base their opposition on a skeleton but on a complete body. The potlatch was not just a "ceremony" or a "festival" where goods and money were exchanged by the "participants": it was emblematic of all that white British Columbians were not. However, much of this larger meaning was lost in the course of the trials, pared away by a system of argument that resolved disputes by reducing them to a set of technical questions. Rather than ascertaining the meaning of what happened, which was embedded in the larger social relationship between the disputing parties, these questions were designed primarily to reconstruct what happened and to compare it to the illegal behaviour outlined in the statute. Reduced in this way to its skeleton, the potlatch and the Indians who practised it did not seem so alien and threatening, or worthy of prosecution.

Decontextualizing actions from their larger social context, as the system of argument used by the courts does, distorts the picture of the relationship between the disputing parties. In cases of sexual assault, doing so can inflict very real harm and injustice on women. However, the potlatch prosecutions show that the distortion created by narrowing the terms of debate and by removing actions from their context can empower those we traditionally think of as powerless. Skeletonizing disputes had the effect of making Indians and their ceremony less alien. Confronted with actions that were now recognizable and even familiar, the courts found it difficult to punish them.

The fact that the same legal process had two very different effects— disempowering women and empowering Indians—suggests two things. First, the system of argument that characterizes the law cannot determine the outcomes of trials; all it does is open up possibilities for them. Second, and more broadly, the different experiences of women and Indians illustrates the relationship between law and justice. In sexual assault cases, the system of argument used by the courts results in injustice because it fails to acknowledge, respect, and act upon the differences between men and women, mainly the differences in power, that surround, shape, and give meaning to heterosexual relationships. However, in the potlatch prosecutions, the same failure to acknowledge differences worked in favour of the Indians. These two results were possible because achieving justice through the law is done in two ways: by treating everyone similarly or by recognizing the differences in each case and acting upon them. There is a constant tension between these two kinds of justice, and because of this there is always the possibility for the "powerless" to triumph over the "powerful."

Strong legal arguments do not depend only on successfully addressing the issues raised by the law and on being fluent in its language. Strong legal arguments also have to be strong arguments; that is, they, like other arguments, have to evoke in the audience certain sensibilities that make them see the accused's actions in a particular way. Many Indians tried for potlatching were successful in making arguments that resonated with both the judges and the British Columbia public. Those arguments reveal much about how the law works; but equally importantly they reveal which sensibilities had power, and shed light on what "made sense" to white British Columbians. More broadly, these arguments give us insight into how they saw the world.

There appear to be three "logics of dispute" at work in the hearings.[90] The first involved invoking tradition, not as a defence of guilt or innocence, but as a way of saying that Indians and their culture were not justiciable; that, in fact, their actions, because they were time-honoured traditions, could not be prosecuted legitimately. The Kwakiutl considered the potlatch a customary practice, and as such it was one that was legitimate simply by virtue of its history.

Second, the Kwakiutl drew analogies between their ceremony and the ones Europeans practised. "A strict law bids us dance," they told Franz Boas. "It is a strict law that bids us distribute our property among our friends and neighbours. It is a good law. Let the White man observe his law, we shall observe ours."[91] To the Kwakiutl, the potlatch was law—a customary law, but a law nonetheless that was as binding and legitimate as the white man's. They also argued that the potlatch was the same as Christmas; both were social and spiritual ceremonies that linked the present with the past and marked that link with gift-giving. So why was one illegal and the other not? "We observe that white people have great feasts, Dances and giving away of presents annually or periodically," Charles Nowell wrote in 1915. "Why therefore should our Feasts, Dances and charity be treated as a crime while you teach us that the white race consider their acts ones [of] virtue[?]"[92] In evoking tradition and using the analogy with "white man's law" and Christmas, Indians attempted to make the alien familiar. Given that many white British Columbians used similar logic to protest the enforcement of the potlatch law, such an argument did have a certain amount of resonance and power.

The third logic of dispute was quite different. Rather than arguing that the potlatch was a traditional social ceremony and thus outside the ambit of the law, the Kwakiutl, through their lawyers, argued that it was an economic transaction and thus subject to law. The potlatch was an occasion for paying back debts or for consummating a contractual obligation; consequently, the law against the potlatch, to put this argument most baldly, interfered with and was in direct contradiction to the laws of obligation (specifically, the laws of contract and debt). This was an effective tactic. As Edward Sapir told Duncan Campbell Scott, "the economic argument is naturally the weightiest" for abolishing the potlatch provision of the Indian Act.[93] It also demonstrates how legal arguments are constructed and suggests what made them successful. In the potlatch prosecutions, lawyers played a central role in framing arguments. Their success lay, as James Boyd White argues, in their ability to "translate" their clients' stories into effective accounts—accounts that are intelligible to the court.[94] These accounts are intelligible and effective if they utilize idioms familiar to the people sitting in judgment. In the case of the potlatch prosecutions, that idiom was economic. The language and logic of economics and the law were so closely allied and reinforcing that a sound economic argument could very well be an effective legal one. The lawyers for the Kwakiutl, particularly Dickie and DeBeck, were able to take their clients' vernacular descriptions and rationales for potlatching and translate them into another more articulate (within the confines of the law) idiom. Thus, in the hands of a lawyer, Chief Lohah's assertion that "it cannot be wrong to pay back what we owe"[95] and George Scow's attempt "to make a pillow,"[96] or down-payment for the purchase of a copper, became "investments or loans to be returned with interest" and "the formal consummation of a contract for the sale and purchase of a copper."[97]

The lawyers for the Kwakiutl had managed to find and exploit the points of intersection between two cultures of argument: one rooted in a Native social and economic organization that stressed mutuality and hierarchy in the context of an organic whole, and the other anchored in the possessive individualism of Western capitalism. Phrases like "pay back what I owe" and words like "debt" had resonance in both. The double meaning of these words bridged two cultures of argument and opened up new and potentially revolutionary possibilities for resistance. Like puns, the language Indians used to describe the potlatch had the potential to subvert the domination of the law.

The power the law represented—the power of argument—was thus a creative force, not simply a repressive one. The system of domination the law was part of did not just happen: prosecutors and the prosecuted had to make strong arguments in order to succeed, and in making those arguments both parties had to abide by rules of legal rhetoric that constrained and empowered each of them. Quite apart from resisting attempts to make them stop potlatching, some Native people recognized that the law's power was creative and used it to further their own interests. There are suggestions that Natives used the creative potential of the law against each other to resolve their own internal disputes and to subvert the constraints of their own culture. These were not a backward people constricted by their own primitive ways. In fact, they were as likely to defend their actions by invoking tradition as they were to use the "Queen's law" to escape the obligations imposed by tradition. Custom and law were matters of "strategy and choice."[98] Some Alert Bay Natives supported the potlatch law and sought its sanction to avoid paying back the social debts they incurred as guests at other potlatches. After the arrests of Johnny Bagwany and Ned Harris, Halliday noted that few Kwakiutl were willing to hold potlatches. "Those who owe money in the potlatch are loathe to pay . . . as they think if the prosecutions hold good and the potlatch is stopped they will escape payment."[99] Certainly, one of the "inducements" held out to the province's Indians to convince them to join the church was "that they need not afterwards repay the amounts they have received in that way [through the potlatch]." The chief of the upper Nass complained to Powell that "many Indians joined the mission so they might repudiate their debts."[100]

Material considerations were not the only ones that motivated Indians to support the potlatch law. The agents' reports suggest that some Indians used the law to overthrow the entrenched hereditary system of rank and privilege that existed within some Native communities. It was the younger members of a band or those who had converted to Christianity who tended to support enforcement, seeing the ceremony as the centre-piece of "the old 'Indian Chief' form of government."[101] The Nishga'a were among the most vocal supporters of the law against the potlatch. "Amongst us Nishkas more than two-thirds of all our people are against it and we want it ended," they told Minister of the Interior Clifford Sifton in an 1899 petition:

> We want to follow the Queen's Law and the Indian Act, but the pot-latch law [the customs surrounding the potlatch] will not agree to the Queen's Law.
> The whiteman's law declares that when a man dies his house and property must go to his widow and children. But the potlatch law says no, but his brothers and nephews may take all. . . . [T]he pot-latch gives him the power. The white man's law says no man may be chief unless he bears good character, but the Potlatch law is that any bad man may become chief if he gives a big potlatch.[102]

For the Nishga'a, the "Queen's law" offered the possibility of an alternate social order. By refusing to participate and by using the law to buttress that refusal, those with less status could challenge the existing social structures and better their own position.

Some Kwakiutl like Jane Cook, Kenneth Hunt, and Dave Shaughnessy went further, and took an active role in suppressing the potlatch. These three provided the information that made the arrests that followed Dan Cranmer's potlatch possible. Their motives are difficult to recover, buried as they are within the complex face-to-face relationships among Indians and between Indians and whites. We do, however, know a little about Gah-uk-sta-lus, or Jane Cook, which is at least suggestive of her social alliances and her possible motivations. She was the daughter of a Kwakiutl mother and a white father and was brought up by Anglican minister A.J. Hall and his wife in Alert Bay.[103] She developed a close working relationship with Indian Agent Halliday, acting as his court interpreter and sometimes travel-ling to Vancouver with him in that capacity. Her role in the Cranmer pros-ecutions was not her first involvement in a potlatch case. A year earlier, in December 1920, she alerted Sergeant Angermann of the RCMP's Alert Bay Detachment that one Munday was about to "buy" fifteen-year-old Jennie MacDougall for $2000. The marriage was to be celebrated with a potlatch on the seventeenth. On the basis of her story, Munday and Mrs Mac-Dougall were arrested.[104] Actions like this did not make her popular, and they appear motivated out of a sense of frustration and marginalization within Indian society. "There is no liberty in the potlatch, no choice whatever," she told Duncan Campbell Scott: "they are all bound and have to pratice [sic] all the different features of the system or they will lose their caste. Those who have left the Potlatch are looked upon not as Indians, or Have no standing or voice in any matters affecting their tribe or band. They are practically Outcasts."[105]

Whatever her motives and those of Hunt and Shaughnessy, the fact of their behaviour suggests that racial boundaries did not create common interest. There was a degree of dissent among the Alert Bay Kwakiutl that must have existed among the aboriginal peoples of the province as a whole. Though the extent of this dissent should not be overestimated, we should recognize that the law stood as a potential means of empowering this minority, and that its potential was occasionally realized. For both Natives and whites, using the law opened up new, unexpected, and potentially dangerous possibilities—new cultural futures—for action.

The creation and enforcement of the law against the potlatch reveal both the nature of the law's power and how it works. The statute embodied certain interests—mainly those of British Columbia's missionaries and some of its Indian agents—and was an attempt to impose a certain kind of moral order on the province's Native peoples. As a law, however, the potlatch provision of the Indian Act also had an important symbolic dimension and served an ideological function. Though its passage was the manifestation of the efforts of a particular group of people, the potlatch law embodied broader interests. It was as much a statement of the social and ethical boundaries of white society—of what they were not—as it was an attempt at regulation and control. Thus, when enforcement proved problematic, questions were raised in the minds of many whites about the validity of the distinction the law had drawn between Indians and whites.

While the potlatch law had coercive and ideological dimensions, its enforcement also revealed that the law was a way of arguing, that it was a rhetorical system. Legal arguments had to follow rules of rhetoric that narrowed the terms of debate and required the person arguing a case to address the issues raised by the law. This ability to limit debate, to shape the questions asked and the line of inquiry that is pursued, is where the true power of the law lies. Strong legal arguments were still dependent, however, on the teller's ability to forge a connection with the audience to whom they were directed. Good arguments make the audience see things the teller's way; they make her alien world and experience familiar. Making arguments resonate in this way involves using analogy: the potlatch was like the white man's law; it was like Christmas. But they must do more than make the alien familiar: arguments must offer the audience a way of seeing the teller's actions as rational, natural, and normal. In the potlatch prosecutions this was accomplished by using economic language to describe the ceremony. Cast in those terms, the potlatch ceased to be the profligate practice its detractors thought it was, and instead was transformed into the embodiment of rational capitalist behaviour.

Looking at the law as a way of arguing reveals a level of complexity and ambiguity in the exercise of its power that is not as apparent when we focus on the law's coercive and ideological nature. Though the system of argument characterized by the law narrows debate, it does not determine its resolution: it simply creates certain possibilities. The power of argument is creative. People have to make arguments—they have a degree of agency—and in making them they can exploit the strategic potential embedded in the way the law works. As a way of arguing, the law not only allows the powerless to resist the oppression of the powerful, but it also gives them a means to transform their own relationships.[106]

• Notes

1 Sergeant D. Angermann, Alert Bay Detachment, to "E" Division, RCMP, Vancouver, 1 March 1922. Canada, Department of Indian Affairs (hereafter DIA), National Archives of Canada (hereafter NAC), RG 10, Black (Western) Series, vol. 3630, f. 6244-4 pt 2.

2 Recollections of Herbert (Mecha) Martin, in Daisy Sewid-Smith, Prosecution or Persecution (Campbell River, BC, 1979), 57.

3 W.M. Halliday to secretary, DIA n.d. (Monthly Report for April 1922), RG 10, vol. 3630, f. 6244-4; also see Halliday to secretary, DIA, 24 Jan. 1922, ibid.; Halliday to Scott, 1 March 1922, ibid.; Angermann to "E" Division, RCMP, Vancouver, 1 March 1922, ibid.; Halliday to Scott, 10 April 1922, ibid.; and Angermann to "E" Division, RCMP, Vancouver, 19 April 1922, ibid.

4 A note on terminology is in order here. Following Douglas Cole and Ira Chaikin, authors of the most recent treatment of the potlatch law, An Iron Hand upon the People: The Law Against the Potlatch on the Northwest Coast (Vancouver, 1990), I will use the term Kwakiutl to describe the 21 tribal

groups that speak the Kwak'wala language and were the chief subjects (along with a number of other Northwest Coast tribal groups) of the law against the potlatch. Today, these peoples prefer to be called the Kwakwa ka'wakw, but because they were referred to as the Kwakiutl in the period dealt with, I will use Kwakiutl.

5 Paul Tennant, Aboriginal Peoples and Politics: The Indian Land Question in British Columbia, 1849–1989 (Vancouver, 1990), 256, n17.

6 Sewid-Smith, Prosecution or Persecution, 1–4.

7 Tennant argues that a series of arrests for potlatching that occurred in the Kawawkewlth Agency in January 1920 was directly responsible for the Kwakiutl joining the Allied Tribes of British Columbia, a province-wide association of aboriginal peoples founded in 1916 for the purpose of taking land claims to court. Aboriginal Peoples and Politics, 94–95, 101.

8 Sewid-Smith, Prosecution or Persecution, 2–3.

9 The law against the potlatch is treated in Forrest LaViolette, The Struggle for Survival: Indian Cultures and the

Protestant Ethic in British Columbia (Toronto, 1973); Robin Fisher, *Contact and Conflict: Indian–European Relations in British Columbia, 1770–1890* (Vancouver, 1977); Peter Macnair, "From Kwakiutl to Kwakwa ka'wakw" in *Native Peoples: The Canadian Experience*, ed. R. Bruce Morrison and C. Roderick Wilson (Toronto, 1986); and Cole and Chaikin, *An Iron Hand upon the People.*

10 An Act to amend and consolidate the laws respecting Indians (Indian Act), 39 Vic., c.18, s.12, 86 (1876).

11 Ibid., s.93.

12 The literature dealing with the bias of the law and the interests it upholds is vast. This list is necessarily selective. On the law as representing class interests see, for instance, Douglas Hay et al., eds., *Albion's Fatal Tree: Crime and Society in Eighteenth-Century England* (London, 1975). On the law and the construction of racial discrimination see Robert A. Williams, *The American Indian in Western Legal Thought: The Discourses of Conquest* (New York, 1990), and Charles Wilkinson, *American Indians, Time and the Law: Native Societies in a Modern Constitutional Democracy* (New Haven, 1987), on Indians. On law and sexuality see Sheila Jeffries, *The Spinster and Her Enemies: Feminism and Sexuality, 1880–1913* (London, 1985); Kathy Peiss and Christina Simmons, *Passion and Power: Sexuality and History* (Philadelphia, 1989); M. Leopold and W. King, "Compulsory Heterosexuality, Lesbians and the Law," *Canadian Journal of Women and the Law* 1 (1985): 163–75; and Judith Walkowitz, "Male Vice and Female Virtue: Feminism and the Politics of Prostitution in Nineteenth Century Britain" in *Powers of Desire: The Politics of Sexuality*, ed. A. Snitow, C. Stansell, and S. Thompson (New York, 1983). On law and sexuality and other aspects of women and the law, see Constance Backhouse, *Petticoats and Prejudice: Women and the Law in Nineteenth-Century Canada* (Toronto,

1991), and Lee Holcombe, *Wives and Property: Reform of the Married Women's Property Law in Nineteenth-Century England* (Toronto, 1983).

13 Backhouse, *Petticoats and Prejudice*, ch. 1, 6, and 7, or see her articles, which are somewhat more "technical," dealing more narrowly with the laws: "'Pure Patriarchy': Nineteenth-Century Canadian Marriage," *McGill Law Journal* 31 (1986): 264–312, and "Shifting Patterns in Nineteenth-Century Canadian Custody Law" in *Essays in the History of Canadian Law*, vol. 1, ed. David H. Flaherty (Toronto 1981), 212–48.

14 Constance Backhouse, "Nineteenth-Century Canadian Rape Law, 1800–1892" in *Essays in the History of Canadian Law*, vol. 2, ed. David H. Flaherty (Toronto 1984), 200–247, or her *Petticoats and Prejudice*, ch. 2; Mary Jane Mossman, "Feminism and the Legal Method: The Difference It Makes," *Australian Journal of Law and Society* 30 (1986): 30–52; and Catharine A. MacKinnon, "Feminism, Marxism, Method and the State: An Agenda for Theory," *Signs* 7 (1982): 227–56.

15 Douglas Hay, "Property, Authority and the Criminal Law" in *Albion's Fatal Tree*, 17–63, and E.P. Thompson, *Whigs and Hunters: The Origins of the Black Act* (London, 1975).

16 Thompson, *Whigs and Hunters*, "Conclusions and Consequences."

17 The law as a system of rhetoric is discussed most directly and fully in James Boyd White, *Heracles' Bow: Essays on the Rhetoric and Poetics of the Law* (Madison, 1985). However, it intersects with a larger literature on legal narrative or legal storytelling. For an introduction to this literature see the special issue of the *Michigan Law Review* 87 (1989). Also of interest in understanding how stories create a way of seeing and thus a way of acting for criminals, see Jack Katz, *Seductions of Crime: Moral and Sensual Attractions in Doing Evil* (New York, 1988).

18 For instance, in criminal trials evidence of the accused's past record is only admissible under certain narrowly defined circumstances. As well, the rules of evidence provide judges and jurors with a set of standards with which to weigh different kinds of testimony. In the 1991 Gitksan and Wet'suwet'en land claims decision (*Delgamuukw v. Attorney-General of BC*), Chief Justice Allan MacEachern revealed the standards he used to assess the testimony of the many expert witnesses who participated in the trial. He dismissed the testimony of the plaintiffs' anthropologists, noting that "apart from urging total acceptance of all Gitksan and Wet'suwet'en [the other tribal group involved in the case] cultural values, the anthropologists add little to the important questions that must be decided in this case" because, in part, in the course of their field work, they had become "too closely associated with the plaintiffs" (50). In contrast, MacEachern had this to say about the historians employed by the plaintiffs: "Generally speaking, I accept just about everything they put before me because they were largely collectors of archival, historical documents" (52). In assessing expert evidence, MacEachern gave more weight to the written word than the lived experience. Both these examples show that not only does the law determine what information counts as evidence, it also assigns a value to the evidence it does deem admissible.

19 Carol Smart, *Feminism and the Power of Law* (London, 1989), ch. 2.

20 Catharine MacKinnon contends it is very difficult to differentiate between rape and sex because all "(hetero)-sex" involves coercion. Thus, the distinction the law makes between rape and sex—a distinction that centres on consent—is a false one. In fact, all the law does is draw an arbitrary line between acceptable and unacceptable levels of force. This is yet another example of how, as she notes, "the law sees and treats women the way men see and treat women." See her *Feminism Unmodified: Discourses on Life and Law* (Cambridge, 1987), 86–88. Her view is shared by L. Kelly, "The Continuum of Sexual Violence" in *Women, Violence and Social Control*, ed. J. Hanmer and M. Maynard (London, 1987).

21 White, *Heracles' Bow*, 98.

22 Smart, *Feminism and the Power of Law*, 9.

23 Sewid-Smith, *Prosecution or Persecution*, 61.

24 Cole and Chaikin, *An Iron Hand upon the People*, 119.

25 Philip Drucker and Robert F. Heizer, *To Make My Name Good: A Re-examination of the Kwakiutl Potlatch* (Berkeley, 1967), 8; and Helen Codere, *Fighting with Property: A Study of Kwakiutl Potlatching and Warfare, 1792–1930* (Seattle, 1950), 63.

26 Homer Barnett, cited in Drucker and Heizer, *To Make My Name Good*, 8.

27 Drucker and Heizer, *To Make My Name Good*, 26. Franz Boas disagreed, contending that the potlatch was a means of "acquiring status." See his *Kwakiutl Ethnography*, ed. Helen Codere (Chicago, 1966), 77.

28 Drucker and Heizer, *To Make My Name Good*, 133.

29 Codere, *Fighting with Property*, ch. 4, and Drucker and Heizer, *To Make My Name Good*, 35ff.

30 Codere, *Fighting with Property*, 94; Drucker and Heizer, *To Make My Name Good*, 13.

31 Codere, *Fighting with Property*, 94.

32 Codere, ibid., 49, notes that "British Columbia was undergoing an enormous industrial expansion in these years [1900–20 approximately]. . . . It is not surprising, in view of the Kwakiutl occupational and financial situation, to see them benefitting from the expansion of the British Columbia economy as it became more and more integrated with the world monetary economy." She also notes

that the per capita income of the Kwakiutl quadrupled between 1903 and 1921 from $54 to $244 (43). As well, Fisher, *Contact and Conflict*, 45–46, discussed the effects the fur trade had on the potlatch and other aspects of Native culture. Rolf Knight, *Indians at Work: An Informal History of Native Indian Labour in British Columbia, 1858–1930* (Vancouver, 1978), discusses the successful integration of Indians into the BC economy, taking issue with Fisher's contention that the Native population was marginalized after the end of the fur trade and the beginning of permanent European settlement.

33 Powell to Macdonald, 15 Aug. 1883, RG 10, vol. 3628, f. 6244-1.

34 Donckele to Lomas, 2 Feb. 1884, RG 10, vol. 3628, f. 62440-1.

35 Lomas to Powell, 5 Feb. 1884, RG 10, vol. 3628, f. 6244-1.

36 Bryant to the superintendent-general of Indian affairs, 30 Jan. 1884, RG 10, vol. 3628, f. 6244-1.

37 Sproat to the superintendent-general of Indian affairs, 27 Oct. 1879, RG 10, vol. 3669, f. 10961.

38 Ibid.

39 Deputy superintendent-general of Indian affairs to the Privy Council, 19 June 1883, RG 10, vol. 3628, f. 6244-1, cited in Cole and Chaikin, *An Iron Hand upon the People*, 21.

40 47 Vic., c.27, s.3 (1884).

41 Judgment of M.B. Begbie, judge in *R. v. Hemasak*, n.d., included in Moffat to Vankoughnet, 30 Aug. 1889, RG 10, vol. 3628, f. 6244-1.

42 58 & 59 Vic., c.35, s.6 (1895). The amendment was framed with Prairie dancing principally in mind.

43 4 & 5 Geo. V, c.35, s.8 (1914).

44 Circular to all Indian agents in British Columbia from Duncan Campbell Scott, 21 Oct. 1918, RG 10, vol. 3629, f. 6244-3. There was a final, unsuccessful attempt to amend the act in 1935–36; Todd to deputy superinten-dent-general of Indian affairs, 27 March 1935, RG 10, vol. 8481, f. 1/24-3 part 1; Mackenzie to Perry, 4 May 1936, ibid.; Cole and Chaikin, *An Iron Hand upon the People*, 147–50.

45 As Gilbert Malcolm Sproat argued, "it is not possible that Indians can acquire property or can become industrious with any good result, while under the influence of this mania." Sproat to the superintendent-general of Indian affairs, 27 Oct. 1879, RG 10, vol. 3669, f. 10691. And Gustave Donckele agreed. Educating Indians to the habits of industry was impossible while potlatching went on because "having squandered their summer earnings potlatching they are compelled to leave their homes and roam about in their canoes in search of food, and thus neglect cultivating their lands and sending their children to school." Donckele to Lomas, 2 Feb. 1884, RG 10, vol. 3628, f. 6244-1.

46 Sapir to Scott, 11 Feb. 1915, RG 10, vol. 3629, f. 6244-3. A copper is literally a piece of copper, shaped like a shield, which represents a large amount of wealth. Coppers were given, bought, or broken as a sign of the giver's or the recipient's wealth.

47 Smith to Sapir, 16 Feb. 1915, RG 10, vol. 3629, f. 6244-3.

48 Boas, *Kwakiutl Ethnography*, 77. Boas first visited the Kwakiutl in 1886 and did his final work in the fall and early winter of 1930 when he was seventy-two (xxiii).

49 Boas to Sapir, 18 Feb. 1915, RG 10, vol. 3629, f. 6244-3.

50 James Clifford and G.E. Marcus, eds., *Writing Culture: The Poetics and Politics of Ethnography* (Berkeley, 1986), looks at ethnographies as texts that reveal more about the people who wrote them than the putative subjects of the anthropological enquiry. On the usefulness of arguments as cultural artifacts that can reveal the sensibilities of a particular time and place see White, *Heracles' Bow*, 175.

51 The comments of the president and the secretary of the Rock Bay Conservative Association indicate that the accumulative aspect of the potlatch was looked on favourably: "Like any other celebration . . . the Potlatch is a stimulation to trade and incites the younger men to ambition," they told their MP in a letter calling for the law's repeal. See Hanson and Milm to Clements, 14 Feb. 1914, RG 10, vol. 3629, f. 6244-2.

52 Sproat to the superintendent-general of Indian affairs, 27 Oct. 1879, RG 10, vol. 3669, f. 10961.

53 Anthropologist Simon Roberts discusses this in *Order and Dispute: An Introduction to Legal Anthropology* (London 1979), as does sociologist Austin Turk, in "Law as a Weapon in Social Conflict," *Social Problems* 23 (1976): 276–91.

54 Sutherland to the superintendent-general of Indian affairs, 12 May 1897, RG 10, vol. 3628, f. 6244-1.

55 Cole and Chaikin, *An Iron Hand upon the People*, ch. 9.

56 Guillod to [Powell], 7 July 1886, RG 10, vol. 3628, f. 6244-1.

57 Vankoughnet to Macdonald, 22 Nov. 1886, RG 10, vol. 3628, f. 6244-1.

58 The jurisdictional dispute was cleared up in 1887 when Ottawa agreed to remit the fines collected in enforcing the Indian Act's liquor restrictions to the province in exchange for "mutual co-operation" in prosecuting violations of the potlatch provision. See Powell to the provincial secretary, 23 March 1887, RG 10, vol. 3628, f. 6244-1; and Powell to superintendent-general of Indian affairs, 5 April 1887, ibid.

59 Halliday to McLean, 20 Feb. 1915, RG 10, vol. 3629, f. 6244-2.

60 Halliday to Ditchburn, 10 June 1930, RG 10, vol. 3631, f. 6244-5.

61 Neill to Vowell, 12 Feb. 1904, RG 10, vol. 3629, f. 6244-5.

62 Neill to Vowell, 14 April 1909, RG 10, vol. 3629, f. 6244-2.

63 Crichton to Clements, 5 March 1915, RG 10, vol. 3629, f. 6244-3.

64 Frank Devlin, the agent at New Westminster, noted that "storekeepers throughout this District give considerable credit to the Indians. They do not give indiscriminant credit. I have continuously advised the storekeepers not to run up a Bill with the Indians. There are times however when it cannot be avoided. As a rule the Indians always try to pay up." Devlin to Vowell, 18 Jan. 1896, RG 10, vol. 3628, f. 6244-1.

65 Bryant to ?, 30 Jan. 1884, RG 10, vol. 3628, f. 6244-1; also see Donckele to Lomas, 2 Feb. 1884, ibid.; Lomas to Powell, 5 Feb. 1884, ibid. I.W. Powell told Ottawa that, given the profits local merchants made through the potlatch, local government officials could lose votes if the act were enforced with any vigour. "The clause prohibiting potlatches is undoubtedly a good one," he wrote, "but it is objected to by White traders who sell large quantities of goods on account of them, and as these people have votes, the Indian Act in this and other respects is not likely to have the sympathy or the assistance of the local government." Powell to the superintendent-general of Indian affairs, 20 April 1885, RG 10, vol. 3628, f. 6244-1.

66 Keith Wrightson, "Two Concepts of Order: Justices, Constables and Jurymen in Seventeenth-Century England," discusses this very notion in *An Ungovernable People: The English and Their Law in the Seventeenth and Eighteenth Centuries*, ed. John Brewer and John Styles (London, 1980).

67 Vowell to the deputy superintendent-general of Indian affairs, 1 June 1897, RG 10, vol. 3628, f. 6244-1; similar sentiments were expressed by the Privy Council after it investigated the potlatch. See Extract from the Report of the Privy Council . . . 22 Feb. 1897, ibid.

68 McLean to Ross, 8 Oct. 1913, RG 10, vol. 3629, f. 6244-2.

69 Halliday to secretary DIA, 1 March 1921, RG 10, vol. 3630, f. 6244-4 pt 1.

70 Pocock to Fitzstubbs, 12 March 1890, RG 10, vol. 3628, f. 6244-1.

71 Interesting work in feminist legal scholarship has demonstrated this with great clarity. See Smart, *Feminism and the Power of Law*, and Mossman, "Feminism and the Legal Method." The inspiration for much of this work springs from Foucault's writings on "power/knowledge." See Michel Foucault, *Power/Knowledge: Selected Interviews and Other Writings, 1972–1977* (New York, 1980), 93.

72 Petition from the Indians of BC by their Solicitors, Dickie and DeBeck, to Scott, 27 Feb. 1922, RG 10, vol. 3630, f. 6244-4.

73 Ibid. Tennant contends that the "definition was so broad that it could apply to virtually any gathering organized by Indians themselves, including not only the traditional potlatch but also, in the hands of zealous missionaries or Indian agents, meetings to discuss land claims" (101). Although the act certainly had this potential, there is no evidence that the department intended to use the act in this way or that it actually did.

74 Halliday to secretary DIA, 1 March 1921, RG 10, vol. 3630, f. 6244-4. DIA legal opinion held that "in order to succeed in the prosecution of a person for participating in such a dance it would have to be shown that the person charged took some active part in connection with the dance." Williams to Moffat, 16 March 1921, ibid.

75 Todd to the deputy superintendent-general of Indian affairs, n.d., Monthly Report, Jan. 1935, RG 10, vol. 8482, f. 1/24-3 pt 1.

76 Neill to Vowell, 12 Feb. 1904, RG 10, vol. 3629, f. 6244-2.

77 Constable A.M. Brien, Prince George Detachment, to "E" Division, RCMP, Vancouver, 26 June 1928, RG 10, vol. 3631, f. 6244-5.

78 Reasons for Judgment, *R. v. Hemasak*, Matthew Begbie, CJ, included in Moffat to Vankoughnet, 30 Aug. 1889, RG 10, vol. 3628, f. 6244-1.

79 Vowell to deputy superintendent-general of Indian affairs, 16 Jan. 1897, RG 10, vol. 3628, f. 6244-1. The case was tried before Judge Harrison in the County Court at Nanaimo. The Crown entered a *nolle prosequi*. See Vowell to deputy superintendent-general of Indian affairs, 5 Feb. 1897, ibid.

80 Indians almost always retained counsel and had some very good ones represent them. Joseph Martin, KC, and Mr Ellis of McTaggart and Ellis represented the people prosecuted as a result of Dan Cranmer's potlatch. Halliday to Scott, 1 March 1922, RG 10, vol. 3630, f. 6244-4 pt 2. J.A. Findlay appeared for Mrs Dick Mountain, an Alert Bay Indian charged with potlatching in February 1922. Angermann to "E" Division, RCMP, Vancouver, 19 April 1922, ibid.; E.K. DeBeck did much work for the Kwakiutl before and after the Cranmer prosecutions (DeBeck to Scott, 4 March 1921, RG 10, vol. 3630, f. 6244-4 pt 1), as did his partner, E.A. Dickie (Todd to Mackenzie, 11 Feb. 1936, RG 10, vol. 8481, f. 1/24-3 pt 1). Halliday considered that "the Indians have had many lawyers advise them and much of the opposition to the enforcement of the potlatch law has been owing to the attitude of the lawyers." Halliday to Scott, 1 March 1922, RG 10, vol. 3630, f. 6244-2 pt 2. M.S. Todd thought that the Indians "employed the best lawyers they can to defend them." Todd to Mackenzie, 11 Feb. 1936, RG 10, vol. 8481, f. 1/24-3 pt 1. This emphasis on the influence "white agitators" wielded over Indians is one that continues today, particularly in relation to land-claims activity. See Tennant, *Aboriginal Peoples and Politics*, 106, 111, 229.

82 Halliday to McLean, 30 Oct. 1913, RG 10, vol. 3629, f. 6244-2.

83 They got suspended sentences. See Maitland, Hunter & Maitland to [the

superintendent-general of Indian affairs?], 8 May 1914, RG 10, vol. 3629, f. 6244-4.

84 Halliday to Scott, 26 Feb. 1931, RG 10, vol. 3631, f. 6244-5.

85 Halliday to Scott, 27 Feb. 1931, RG 10, vol. 3631, f. 6244-5.

86 Ditchburn to Scott, 2 April 1931, RG 10, vol. 3631, f. 6244-5. It was the opinion of the minister of justice that the six-month statutory limitation did not apply to the potlatch law. Edwards to Scott, 18 April 1931, ibid.

87 Ditchburn to Scott, 2 April 1931, RG 10, vol. 3631, f. 6244-5.

88 Halliday to Scott, 27 Feb. 1931, RG 10, vol. 3631, f. 6244-5.

89 Todd to secretary, DIA, 10 March 1934, RG 10, vol. 3631, f. 6244-5.

90 On "logics of dispute" see John L. Comaroff and Simon Roberts, *Rules and Processes: The Cultural Logic of Dispute in an African Context* (Chicago, 1981), and Lawrence Rosen, "Islamic 'Case Law' and the Logic of Consequence" in June Starr and Jane F. Collier, eds., *History and Power in the Study of Law: New Directions in Legal Anthropology* (Ithaca, NY, 1989).

91 From the film *Potlatch! A Strict Law Bids Us Dance*, 16mm, 53 min, Alert Bay: U'mista Cultural Society, 1975.

92 Nowell to ?, n.d., enclosed in Crichton to [secretary, DIA], 30 March 1915, RG 10, vol. 3629, f. 6244-3.

93 Sapir to Scott, 11 Feb. 1915, RG 10, vol. 3629, f. 6244-3.

94 James Boyd White, *Justice as Translation* (Chicago, 1991).

95 Cowichan Chiefs in regard to the Potlatch Act to [Lomas], 8 April 1885, RG 10, vol. 3628, f. 6244-1.

96 Angermann to "E" Division, RCMP, Vancouver, 28 Dec. 1921, RG 10, vol. 3631, f. 6244-5.

97 Indians of BC by their Solicitors, Dickie and DeBeck, to Scott, 27 Feb. 1922, RG 10, vol. 3630, f. 6244-4 pt 2.

98 On this theme see Sally Falk Moore, "History and the Redefinition of Custom on Kilimanjaro" in *History and Power in the Study of Law*.

99 Halliday to McLean, 16 Feb. 1914, RG 10, vol. 3629, f. 6244-2.

100 Fragment of a letter [Powell to the superintendent-general of Indian affairs?], n.d., following superintendent-general of Indian affairs to Green, 18 June 1886, RG 10, vol. 3628, f. 6244-1.

101 Loring to Vowell, 16 July 1897, RG 10, vol. 3628, f. 6244-2.

102 Nishka chiefs to Sifton, 1 July 1899, RG 10, vol. 3629, f. 6244-2.

103 Cole and Chaikin, *An Iron Hand upon the People*, 132. Helen Codere described Jane Cook as "a formidable super-missionized woman who was matriarch of a large household, lay preacher and interpreter of the Bible, a person of great influence among the Indian women of Alert Bay. She was deadset against all Indian ways, none of which she knew much about." Boas, *Kwakiutl Ethnography*, xxvii.

104 Crime Report submitted by D. Angermann, Sgt., Alert Bay Detachment, to "E" Division, RCMP, Vancouver, 31 Jan. 1921, RG 10, vol. 3630, f. 6244-4 pt 1. The case was dismissed for insufficient evidence.

105 Mrs S. Cook to Scott, 1 Feb. 1919, RG 10, vol. 84841, f. 1/24-3 pt 1. Jane Cook was not the only one affected. Because "she had never been 'paid for' [i.e., married in the Kwakiutl manner] [her sons] were seen as illegitimate and boycotted from any work in the district by their own tribe." Cole and Chaikin, *An Iron Hand upon the People*, 178.

106 Throughout this paper I have tried to emphasize the ambiguity and complexity of the power of the law. The law's power, as revealed by the potlatch law and prosecutions, demonstrated some of the more general characteristics of power discussed by a large theoretical literature centred on the work of Michel Foucault. In his most explicit exploration of power, Foucault criticized scholars who con-

ceptualized power as a commodity—a thing possessed and controlled by a single individual or group. Instead, Foucault argues that power was immanent and "decentred." Power surrounds us like a net, and because it does, it has no centre, no single locus. No individual class or group can possess it completely, but each can try to make it work for them, though doing so could and did have unforeseen consequences. . . .

Ascertaining how power is exercised, and what happens when it is, can only be done effectively by examining specific incidents rooted in a particular social and cultural milieu—by looking at what Foucault called "the capillary level of power."

Only in discrete incidents like Dan Cranmer's potlatch does the ambiguity of power—its decentred, intentional, yet non-subjective, transforming, and transformative nature—become apparent. From the shores of Village Island, its repressive effect recedes somewhat and its creative and strategic potential comes into focus. At the same time, the boundary and meaning of distinctions we previously made so easily—distinctions between the powerful and the powerless, for instance—are blurred. See Foucault, "Two Lectures" in *Power/Knowledge*. The two definitions of a net come from Julian Barnes, who uses them to discuss the dual nature of biography. See *Flaubert's Parrot* (London, 1985), 38.

Baseball, Class, and Community in the Maritime Provinces, 1870–1910*

Colin D. Howell

In the past few years, historical writing on the history of sport has concentrated upon the relationship of sport to society, rather than merely chronicling the accomplishments of great athletes or celebrating sport as a form of character building. Serious academic work, such as Tony Mason's history of association football, Wray Vamplew's analysis of professional sport in Victorian Britain, or Alan Metcalfe's study of the emergence of a disciplined and organized sporting culture in Canada, has drawn widely upon the insights of the "new" social history to understand how sport shaped community identities and, yet, was shaped itself by class, ethnic, and gender rivalries.[1] This analysis of the early history of baseball in the Maritime provinces and New England looks at how the development of the game was linked to Victorian notions of respectability and to the growing discourse that emerged with respect to the public organization of play and leisure.[2] In so doing, it investigates the subtle and often unpredictable ways in which reformers, entrepreneurs, gamblers, working people, athletes, and spectators shaped the game to meet their own needs. Seen in this light, the history of baseball involves what Raymond Williams refers to as the "social

*Histoire sociale/Social History 22, 44 (Nov. 1989): 265–86. Reprinted with the permission of the journal.

relations of cultural production," social processes actively shaped by human agents, neither fully determined by nor independent of the capitalist mode of production.[3]

The study of baseball provides a useful window into the continuing redefinition of class relations, gender roles, and community identity that accompanied the industrial transformation of the Maritimes in the last third of the nineteenth century.[4] Baseball's early development was closely linked to the expansion of urban centres in the region in the industrial age. Some historians have suggested that the game's appeal lay in its ability to evoke images of rural simplicity in an age of industrial dislocation;[5] others argue that the game replicated the attitudes of the industrial workplace in its emphasis on organization, precision, and discipline.[6] Whatever its appeal, baseball originated and flourished in urban centres and small towns. Promoted by a group of middle- and upper-class reformers who regarded sport as a powerful antidote to crime, rowdiness, and class hatred, the game was played primarily by adolescents and young men who had only recently entered the world of work. But the interests of reformers and players did not always coincide. If reformers prized baseball for its blending of teamwork and individual initiative, its cultivation of the "manly virtues" and its uplifting character, they also remained suspicious of the way in which players, spectators, and speculators approached the sport.

Baseball first came to the Maritimes during the 1860s and, over the next two decades, grew rapidly in popularity, spreading from the larger metropolitan centres such as Saint John, Halifax, and Moncton to smaller communities like Woodstock, St Stephen, Fredericton, New Glasgow, Westville, and Kentville. Although a number of Saint John residents had earlier played pick-up games of "rounders"—a precursor of the modern game of baseball—it was not until 1869 that Mr P.A. Melville, a prominent newspaperman, introduced baseball to Saint John. Within five years, a number of local club teams, including the Invincibles, the Mutuals, the St Johns, the Shamrocks, the Athletes, and the Royals, were playing each other and occasionally challenging teams from St Croix, Fredericton, and Bangor, Maine. Organized largely along occupational, ethnic, and religious lines, the teams were still exclusively amateur. As of yet, the promoters of the game thought more of its civilizing influence than its profit potential. There was little gate money, and given the limited provision for field security, spectators often crawled over and under fences to escape admission.[7]

Baseball came to Halifax at about the same time it originated in Saint John. In May 1868, the Halifax *Reporter* announced a meeting of the Halifax Baseball Club at Doran's Hotel, followed a few days later by an announcement of an organizational meeting at the Masonic Hall of another independent club and the election of the team's officers.[8] The Halifax club's first president was Dr A.C. Cogswell, a long-time proponent of organized recreation in Halifax. Like many of his contemporaries, Cogswell saw sport as a remedy to youthful idleness and indolence, and a force contributing to mental well-being and physical health. A few years earlier, Cogswell had led a campaign for a public gymnasium, which, the *Acadian Recorder* predicted, would rescue Halifax youth from "gawking lazily at street corners to stare at passers-by, lounging about drinking saloons, smoking and guzzling" and partaking of "other irrational modes of getting over life."[9] Another of Cogswell's contemporaries, Superintendent John Grierson of the Halifax Protestant Boys' Industrial School, shared this faith in the uplifting character of organized recreation. "The necessity of providing recreation for lads of this class," wrote Grierson about the boys in his charge, "is now universally admitted."[10] The Industrial School sported a gymnasium and playing ground for cricket and baseball, and the boys played challenge matches against the Young Atlantas and Young Oxfords of Halifax.[11]

Baseball was particularly attractive to reformers because it brought into play the so-called "manly virtues": courage, strength, agility, teamwork, decision making, and foresight. It was inexpensive and took little time to play or witness, so that "a busy man can gain in two hours on the ball field rest and relaxation that elsewhere he would seek in vain."[12] Another virtue, from the reformer's perspective, was that it appealed in particular to working-class youth. A sample of players whose names appeared in newspaper box scores in Halifax, between 1874 and 1888, makes this clear. Of the 133 players whose occupation can be traced through census records and city directories, the vast majority came from working-class backgrounds. Clerks, labourers, and unskilled workers made up 45.8 percent of the sample; tradesmen such as cabinetmakers, carpenters, tailors, blacksmiths, machinists, brass finishers, gasfitters, printers, bakers, plumbers, coopers, and bricklayers constituted another 31.5 percent; and merchants, students, and professionals made up the remaining 22.7 percent (see table 1).

Table 1: OCCUPATION OF HALIFAX BASEBALL PLAYERS, 1874–88

	Number	Percent
Clerks (including bookkeepers and accountants)	29	21.8
Labourers (including teamsters, janitors, messengers, seamen, porters, and stable boys)	32	24.0
Tradesmen	42	31.5
Students, merchants, and professionals	30	22.7

If baseball was basically a workingman's sport, it was also a young man's game. The ages of those who appeared in box scores for the first time ranged from a twelve-year-old student to a forty-six-year-old physician, Chandler Crane. Most players, however, began their careers in their late teens or early twenties and few continued to play into their thirties. The average age of those appearing in box scores for the first time was 22.6

years. Given that some continued to play after that, it is reasonable to assume that the average age of those who played the sport was somewhat higher, but did not exceed twenty-five years.

Data available with respect to the ethnic origin and religious preference of 153 players also reveals a heavy concentration of Irish Catholics on Halifax's ball diamonds. Irish and black players made up 59.4 percent of the sample; those of English origin 20.9 percent; Scots and Germans 7.8 percent each. With respect to religious denominations, Catholics made up 60.7 percent of players (compared to slightly more than 40 percent of the total population), Anglicans 15.7 percent, Baptists (including African Baptists) 11.1 percent, and Presbyterians 7.8 percent.

Workingmen also made up a substantial portion of the audience for baseball games. At the end of the 1877 season in Halifax, for example, Thomas Lambert, a well-known labour leader and employee at Taylor's Boot and Shoe Factory, presented a silver ball and bat to the city champion, Atlantas, on behalf of the mechanics of Halifax. (The *Acadian Recorder* reported that the prize was offered by the mechanics of the city alone, in recognition of their dedication to the game.)[13] Lambert's involvement in baseball is intriguing. A major figure in the working-class movement, he had come to Halifax in 1865 with the 2nd Battalion of the Leicestershire regiment.[14] Soon after, he took up employment at Taylor's factory and became one of the first trade unionists in Halifax to attain international prominence. In 1869, he was elected an international officer of the Knights of St Crispin and he became First Grand Trustee of the International Lodge in 1872.[15] Although there is no evidence that Lambert ever played baseball, he was instrumental in organizing a team at Taylor's after the company defeated the shoemakers in a bitter strike at the factory. Subsequently, in September 1877, Lambert appears as scorekeeper in a game between the Crispin Club of Taylor & Company and a team representing W.C. Brennan & Co. Later in the same month, two teams from Taylor's—"Lambert's Nine" and "Baldwin's Nine"—squared off, with the Lambert's playing to a 28–18 victory.[16]

Workers, then, were involved in the game as organizers, players, and spectators. As spectators, they seemed more than willing to pay the standard twenty-five cents admission fee for competitive club or intercity matches. Although not much is yet known about the impact of industrialization on the real wages of working men and women in the urban centres of the Maritimes, or upon the family wage, it is likely that factory workers such as Lambert were enjoying an increasing real income, similar to workers elsewhere in Britain and North America at this time.[17] The gradual tightening of workplace discipline, the growing separation of work and leisure, and the concomitant shortening of the workday, moreover, nurtured an increased demand for organized leisure by working people and bourgeois proponents of rational recreation alike.[18] The movement of women into industrial and clerical work also led them to seek out ways to fill their leisure time, one of which was attendance at sporting events.[19] In the last quarter of the nineteenth century, therefore, the changes wrought by industrialization had engineered the basic prerequisite for the commercialization of baseball—the creation of an audience.

For spectators and players alike, class, ethnic, and community identities and rivalries provided an important impetus to the game. In Halifax, for example, challenge matches between the "Mechanics" and the "Laborers," the "Barkers" and the "Growlers," the "Southends" and the "Northends," the "Young Atlantas" and the "Young Oxfords," the "True Blues" and the "Greenstockings" involved rivalries based upon occupation, location, ethnicity, and age. In addition, teams representing various employers such as the "Heralds," the "Recorders," the "Chronicles," the "Dolphins" (for Dolphin's Factory), and Taylor's Factory, sometimes served to secure an identity to the firm and, in other cases, encouraged worker solidarity. While the Taylor Factory teams seem to have been made up exclusively of workingmen, the Dolphins had a lineup which in addition to factory hands included manager K.J. Dolphin.[20] Now and then, novelty games attracted sizeable crowds, as was true of the match in July 1878 between the Fat-Men—Dolphin was suited up here as well—and the Atlantas, a competitive team who agreed to pitch, bat, and throw left-handed in order to give their obese opponents a chance at victory. "The match . . . was a complete success," reported the *Acadian Recorder,* "and the crowd assembled, numbering nearly 500 persons, was kept in continual roars of laughter by the blunders and exertions of the Fat Men."[21]

The rivalries that attracted the greatest spectator interest were those between teams representing various towns and cities throughout the Maritimes and New England. Particularly significant here was the impetus to the game provided by the completion of the Intercolonial Railway to Halifax in 1876. The Intercolonial linked the major urban centres of the region and allowed for dependability in the scheduling of challenge matches. Railway service made it possible for barnstorming New England club and college teams to tour the region during the summer, while telegraph communication allowed promoters to schedule games with touring teams in return for expenses and a guaranteed portion of the gate. By the last half of the 1870s, regional championships were being held annually. In 1875, for example, the Halifax Atlantas travelled to Saint John and defeated the Mutuals and Shamrocks of that city and, in the following year, the Moncton Invincibles travelled to Halifax to play the Atlantas and Resolutes to determine the Maritime champion. The Atlantas prepared for the match by enclosing their grounds and charging an admission fee, and before a large crowd defeated Moncton 15 to 12.

By the 1880s, interurban contests had become regular fare. Indeed, when pioneer baseball player James Pender announced his retirement in 1888, after fourteen years on the most competitive Halifax teams, he could count among his appearances victories over the Saint John Mutuals and

Shamrocks, the Moncton Redstockings, and various other teams from Londonderry, Fredericton, Houlton, St Stephen, Bangor, and Boston.[22] By this time, too, the baseball culture of the Maritimes was becoming more intimately linked with that of New England, a hardly surprising development considering the significant exodus of young Maritimers during the seventies and eighties to the "Boston States."[23]

The gradual integration of Maritime and New England baseball during the 1880s brought a number of changes in the nature of the sport in this region. During the 1885 season, baseball promoters in Saint John contracted with the Queen City team of Bangor, Maine, to play a challenge match in Saint John. Although this was an error-filled match (17 errors on one side and 28 on the other), the lopsided 17–5 victory for Bangor provided an impetus for Maritime teams to import coaches and players from the United States. During the 1888 season, the Saint John Nationals imported two college ball players, Wagg and Larabee, from Colby College, and in so doing, ushered in an era of professional baseball. The following year, three more imports, Small, Rogerse, and Parsons, were added to the team and the Shamrocks secured the services of Edward Kelly of Portland, Maine, and William Donovan of Bangor. In 1890, Fredericton and Moncton established professional teams, and a four-team New Brunswick professional league was established relying heavily upon imported players. The Nationals (now called the Saint John Athletic Association) discarded Rogers and signed Jack Priest, Billy Pushor, Billy Merritt, and pitcher "Harvard" Howe. The Shamrocks cut Kelly and added Jim and Joe Sullivan, Abel Lezotte, Jack Griffin, and John "Chewing Gum" O'Brien.[24]

The development of professional baseball during the late 1880s contributed to the sharpening of metropolitan rivalries that accompanied the coming of industrial capitalism to the region. This was particularly true of the region's two largest urban centres, Saint John and Halifax, neither of which could establish a commercial or industrial hegemony over the entire region. Whenever it could, the Saint John press contrasted the bustling exuberance of the New Brunswick centre to that of somnolent Halifax. A dispatch from the Saint John *Telegraph,* carried in Halifax newspapers on 31 July 1888, described games between the Nationals of Saint John and the Atlantas of Halifax as a "very easy contract" and suggested that if Halifax remained uncompetitive, the Nats would have to go south of the border to find better competition. "The Atlantas play good ball in the quiet town of Halifax," the *Telegraph* concluded, "but when they come to a great city like Saint John, the noise and bustle and excitement seem to unnerve them."[25] In the following year, when the Socials travelled to Saint John to play a challenge match during the Saint John city carnival, they were treated to a city parade which routinely burlesqued Halifax. One float was a replica of the mail steamer *Atlas* detained in fog eighty hours outside Halifax Harbour. Another was adorned with a banner "Little Sister Halifax. Haligonian Specialties. Fog in summer, harbour skating in Winter." When the Socials were subsequently defeated by the Saint John Club, one newspaper wrote that "bright, active, energetic Saint John scored one against her old and unprogressive rival yesterday, and she did not require the assistance of . . . [the umpire] to make that score either."[26]

Halifax held its own summer carnival in early August 1889. The roster of activities included a match between a New York cricket team and the Garrison team, single scull races, a Labrador whaler boat challenge, fencing and gymnastic displays, wrestling, and even a mock military battle at Point Pleasant Park. The highlight of the carnival, however, was a series of baseball games between the Halifax Socials and the John P. Lovell Arms Company and Woven Hose teams of Boston. These teams were made up of players signed and paid to advertise the companies' wares, and were probably the strongest teams in the United States outside of organized baseball. The Socials fared well against high-calibre competition such as this. During the 1889 season, the Socials played twenty-one matches against teams from other cities, winning eleven. In addition to the two teams from Boston, their opponents, in 1889, included Portland, Bath, Gardner, and Bangor, Maine; Bates College—as "gentlemanly a set of fellows as ever graced a diamond"—and the Boston St Stephens. In the following season, the Holy Cross Collegians, the Worcester professionals, and a regular assortment of teams from Maritime centres provided Halifax with stiff competition.[27]

Although the establishment of professional baseball enhanced the calibre of competition in the Maritimes, it also raised questions about the essential purpose of sport itself. Initially, sport advocates hoped that baseball would serve, as cricket and rugby had done, to enhance "gentlemanly" values.[28] Bedecked in uniforms that occasionally included high sneakers and bow-ties, players were often admonished against uttering derogatory remarks about their opponents and the umpire. Newspaper accounts of games regularly criticized the practice of "kicking," or disputing an umpire's decision, and derided those players who would not accede to the arbiter's authority. Protests of calls were seen to be the responsibility of the team captain, and individual players were urged to defer to the captain's authority. The extent to which "kicking" was criticized, however, reveals that the players themselves did not conform easily to the "gentlemanly code" that others wished to bring to the game.

Nor were umpires always the neutral officials that they were supposed to be. Poorly trained and often not completely cognizant of the rules, umpires were frequently biased in favour of their home teams during inter-urban matches. After a game between the Saint John Nationals and the Halifax Socials in 1888, for example, the Saint John press charged umpire William Pickering, who regularly played second base with the Socials, with "barefaced cheating," and also alleged that a Mr F. Robinson of Halifax had bribed the umpire. Robinson admitted boasting to friends in a local hotel that he had bought Pickering, but denied actually having done so.[29] In the following year, Pickering was again the subject of criticism for his partisanship during a double-header between the Socials and a team from South Portland, Maine. Both games, said the Halifax *Acadian Recorder,* featured obviously partisan umpiring and, in the second, Pickering was calling strikes against Portland batters that were nowhere near the plate.[30]

Despite these instances of favouritism, it was generally conceded that the authority of the umpire was an essential component of the game. This was a common theme in the columns of F.J. Power, sporting editor for both the *Acadian Recorder* and the Halifax *Daily Echo,* and a well-respected umpire whose career behind the plate spanned four decades. Power's career began during the 1870s as a player for the Atlantas, but he soon turned to umpiring on a regular basis. As an umpire, Power was an authoritarian figure, respected for his integrity and decisiveness in dealing both with players and unruly fans. Even spectators came to recognize his authority. At one point, for example, Power demanded the ejection of a spectator for joking that the umpire had a glass eye. "He simply raised his arm," said the *Acadian Recorder,* "and a big policeman escorted . . . [the fan] out."[31]

Incidents such as these reveal the hope of many sports reformers that baseball would encourage cultivated behaviour and respect for authority. Players were expected to approach the game in a mannerly and respectable fashion, playing for the love of the sport and avoiding disparaging remarks about their opponents. But the importation of professional players from the United States during the late 1880s raised doubts that these goals could be achieved. In July 1888, a crowd of 1200 Haligonians, including a "large gathering of the fair sex,"[32] turned out to see the Saint John Nationals and their star import player named Wagg. A pitcher from Colby College, playing under an assumed name in order to maintain his eligibility for college baseball, Wagg struck one newspaperman as resembling "the lecturer outside a side-show at the circus." In the sixth inning, a number of "hoodlums" tried to stop Wagg's "continual prattle by endeavouring to irritate him . . . , but it was useless." The same reporter criticized William Pickering, the second baseman and notorious umpire, for loud and uncontrolled language and chided Fitzgerald of the Atlantas for talking too much while guarding his base.[33]

Now and then, games degenerated into actual violence. During one game involving two Saint John teams in September 1901, pitcher Webber of the Alerts was "grossly insulted" by first baseman Friars of the Roses, caught hold of him by the neck and shook him. There was immediate confusion, the bleacherites swarmed on the field, and fisticuffs broke out between Protestant and Catholic spectators. The second-baseman, Bill O'Neil, called for the cops. "It was not nice for the people present, especially the ladies, and players should restrain themselves no matter how great the insult," said the Saint John *Globe.* "If a player makes a habit of using nasty, insulting epithets to opposing players, he should certainly be suppressed. There is some excuse for a man who in the heat of passion shows a disposition to administer bodily punishment, but nothing but contemptuous loathing for one who prefers to waggle an unguarded and insulting tongue."[34]

The concern of most sports reformers was that undisciplined behaviour by the players would encourage similar rowdiness amongst the audience. Promoters of the game especially feared the effect of unruly behaviour and "bad manners" upon women spectators. Women, of course, were important to the future of the game, not only as patrons, but also as symbols of respectability; their attendance provided the game with the hallmark of gentility that reformers wished to establish. Boorish behaviour by male spectators, of course, undermined the quest for respectability. Aware of this, the Saint John *Progress* of 11 August 1888 apologized for the behaviour of a few boors who crowded in the press box and smoked persistently, even though ladies were present. The columnist took further pains to assure female spectators that the perpetrators of this "crudeness" were not pressmen.[35] The *Acadian Recorder* was equally concerned about "hoodlums," "toughs," and "persons of a similar character," many of whom snuck into the grandstands and took the seats of paying patrons.[36] Soldiers from the Garrison at Halifax were another source of displeasure. During a game between Saint Mary's and the Garrison, before a crowd of 1200 spectators, about a hundred men of the ranks "shouted, jeered, hooted and made all sorts of remarks about the opposing players." Noting a similar occurrence in a recent match in the United States, the columnist judged the incident in Halifax to be particularly unsavoury. In the American game, "the language was of a more humorous nature, and there were no remarks unfit for ladies to hear as in this instance. It is said that such actions take place in Montreal, the reporter concluded, but he found no reason for them to occur in Halifax.[37]

Unruly crowd behaviour obviously contradicted the conception of baseball as a "gentleman's game" played before a respectable audience. Bourgeois sport reformers, many of them medical doctors, educators, ministers, or journalists, hoped that the extension of organized sport to working people would help create a common culture that transcended class interest, and dreamt of a world of play where class distinctions would be eradicated. The editor of the Sydney *Record*, for example, believed that sport and physical exercise would help empty prisons, asylums, and workhouses and relieve unemployment. With more recreation, he concluded, "a good half of our social problems might disappear."[38] When the reality fell short of the ideal, these bourgeois sportsmen blamed the subversion of the game upon professionalism. The commercialization and professionalization of team sport, they argued, attracted less dignified members of the working class who put financial reward above the values of self-discipline, self-sacrifice, and teamwork, and who indulged in various forms of desultory and unsavoury behaviour. These attitudes were no doubt confirmed when the off-field activities of two of the early imports to Saint John, James Guthrie and Edward Kelly, blossomed into a public scandal in September

1889. These two Irish-American ball players had arrived in Saint John from Maine, in the summer of 1889, accompanied by a number of young girls destined for employment in a bordello run by Mattie Perry, sometimes known as "French Mattie." One of the girls was a young teenager from Bangor named Annie Tuttle who had been recruited by Guthrie's companion Lizzie Duffy. When Annie Tuttle's mother travelled to Saint John in search of her daughter and reported her disappearance to the authorities, the police raided Mattie's Brittain Street house and found the young girl there. Mattie was told to leave the city at once and, accompanied by Kelly, "one of her boon companions in Saint John for some weeks," left that night on the American Express for Presque Isle, Maine. Guthrie, also "well known in baseball circles" in both Bangor and Saint John, left on the same train with Lizzie Duffy.[39]

Of greater concern to reformers than this connection between the world's oldest and youngest profession was the increasing influence that betting men seemed to exercise upon the sport. Critics of professionalism noted the greater likelihood of corruption, gambling, and match-fixing among professional players, no doubt sympathizing with the Toronto *Mail's* description of a professional as a "double cross athlete who would cut his throat to keep his reputation as crooked if he thought that anyone was betting that he would live."[40] Indeed, gambling was widespread and substantial sums of money changed hands, particularly in matches involving urban rivals or barnstorming clubs from the United States. Players were by no means immune from the lure of quick money and, when the odds warranted, occasionally had friends place bets against them. One such incident took place in Halifax in September 1890, when a number of Saint John players threw a game against the Halifax Socials. Beginning in the third inning, a number of curious incidents raised the suspicion of many in the crowd of over 1000. It was in that inning that a Saint John man whose money was being wagered on the Socials walked across the field to the Saint John players' bench. Shortly thereafter, the umpire, himself from Saint John, began to make calls that favoured Halifax, giving bases on balls to the Socials on obvious strikes. For Saint John, Priest the pitcher struck out by swing at balls nowhere near the plate, and third-baseman Parsons, after hitting safely, removed his hand from the base and allowed a Socials player to tag him out.[41] This transparently fixed match, said the *Daily Echo*, provided an indication of the depth that professional players could sink to when betting men were interested.[42]

A number of reasons were given to explain the fix. In the first place, the Socials were going to Saint John the following week and a victory for the Halifax team would ensure Saint John promoters a big crowd. It was also widely believed that revenge was the motive, because the better who had fixed the match had been taken advantage of by a Halifax gambler who bet $300 on the Saint John team at two-to-one odds during the first game of the series. Haligonians were further outraged when a correspondent of the Moncton *Times* reported that upon returning home, a banquet was held for the Saint John players, despite their acknowledged throwing of the game. Seven of the nine men, the *Times* correspondent reported, were involved in the fix and they "openly avow and boast of it." At the dinner, an MPP from Saint John chaired the festivities, which included a succession of speeches glorifying the players. "This barefaced outrage on public morals," the correspondent concluded, "will perhaps bring a gulled public to some sense of the honour involved in professional baseball."[43]

The thrown match at the end of the 1890 season had a devastating impact upon professional baseball in the region. Prior to that time, the elevated standard of play that accompanied the importation and payment of athletes had attracted a growing clientele. Players were performing before crowds that averaged about 1200 in Halifax and Moncton, and about three times that number in Saint John. In the latter city, fan interest was so great that the King Street merchants installed a telephone at the baseball grounds, in August 1888, so that after each inning, the score of the game in progress could be telephoned to the DeForest and March store, at the corner of King and Germane Streets, and placed on a large blackboard which could be seen from a considerable distance.[44] This enthusiasm for the game attracted sports entrepreneurs, who with admission prices of 25 cents and an extra 10 cents for admission to the grandstand and prize purses that sometimes were as high as $500, could bring in as much as $1500 for a single match in Saint John, or $1000 in Halifax or Moncton.

During the 1890s, fan interest waned. In the wake of the discrediting of the game's integrity, the Halifax Socials disbanded and, through the 1890s, baseball in Halifax was played on a decidedly amateur level. Rivalries between employees at manufacturing or commercial establishments, or between ethnic groups or recreational clubs, provided the community with interesting but not outstanding baseball. Matches with other city clubs or touring teams were rare, and although there were sporadic attempts to revive competitive baseball in the City, there was little enthusiasm for the professional game. In Saint John, the nineties saw the emergence of a great rivalry between two city teams, the Alerts and the Roses, the former supported largely by the Irish Catholic community and the latter appealing to an Anglo-Protestant constituency.

The collapse of professional baseball in the 1890s accompanied the diffusion of the amateur game throughout the Maritimes. In Pictou County, Nova Scotia, baseball originated as a result of the efforts of newspaperman R.S. Theakston.[45] The 1890s also saw the flourishing of the game in the coal-towns of Joggins, Westville, and Springhill, where baseball was an important cultural component of worker solidarity, and in "busy Amherst," one of the most rapidly growing industrial towns in the region. "The baseball craze has struck Springhill," said the *Springhill News and Advertiser* of 13 August 1896, "there are about three teams at Miller's Corner ranging from 6 years of age to 60, also two teams on Herritt Road and two or three in town."[46] Springhill was by no means unique. Rivalries based both upon propinquity and shared occupational and cultural identities invigorated matches between Joggins, Springhill, and Westville. Before long, towns from Truro to Annapolis were playing each other and accepting American challenges. Similar rivalries emerged in the western counties of Nova Scotia between Windsor, Kentville, and Middleton; further south in Digby and Yarmouth; across the Bay of Fundy in Macadam and Woodstock; and in a number of border towns in Maine.

If the 1890s witnessed the diffusion of the sport beyond the large metropolitan centres to the smaller towns of the region, the absence of high-level interurban competition in Halifax, Moncton, and Saint John provided a boon to the development of baseball for women and racial minorities during the 1890s. In 1891, a touring ladies' team from the United States caused great excitement, playing in a number of towns in the region. In Nova Scotia, the women defeated all-male clubs in Amherst, Annapolis, and Middleton and, before a crowd of 3000, beat a Halifax amateur club by an 18–15 score. Tours of this sort helped secure the legitimacy of female participation in organized team sport, much to the delight of feminists such as Grace Ritchie of Halifax, who regularly advocated women's greater involvement in sporting activity. The reaction to the entrance of women into baseball's male domain, however, was mixed. Those who feared the emergence of the "new woman" were concerned that participation in sports such as baseball contradicted the ideal feminine personality, while others regarded physical training for women an antidote to nervous exhaustion or "neurasthenia." Prevailing notions of biology emphasized woman's nurturing character, her physical frailty, and her nervous irritability, and suggested that women were particularly susceptible to an imbalance of physical and mental faculties.[47] Involvement in competitive sport and physical exercise still had its critics, but by the 1890s, there was a growing acceptance of female athleticism because it compensated for nervous debilitation.[48]

The tour of the "Chicago Ladies," in 1891, brought the debate over women and sport to centre stage. The Truro *Daily News* reported that a clergyman in New Glasgow had spoken strongly against the tour at a local prayer meeting, while in Truro, a delegation of citizens unsuccessfully lobbied the Mayor to prevent the team from playing.[49] On the day of the game, the Truro newspaper noted that "many people, doubtless, will be there to witness the antics of the girls, but if all reports be true, the propriety of attending is very questionable."[50] After the games in Truro and New Glasgow, the local press criticized the women as frauds who could not compete on equal terms with men although they presumed to do so. "They are nothing better than a lot of hoodlums from a crowded city," said the New Glasgow *Eastern Chronicle*, "they are frauds of the first order."[51]

Despite these criticisms, a few days later, a crowd of 3000 assembled at the Wanders Grounds, in Halifax, to watch the women. In addition to the paying patrons, boys climbed electric light poles and trees outside the grounds and a crowd "containing people of all classes of life" assembled on Citadel Hill, overlooking the field.[52] In Halifax, there was little of the hostility that accompanied the team's visit to New Glasgow and Truro. The women were popular as well in Amherst, where the victory of the girls over the local boys' team was "both interesting and exciting." In the opinion of the Amherst *Evening News,* there was "nothing, whatever, here which would warrant their being refused the privilege or opportunity of playing."[53] The Moncton *Transcript* agreed and announced the intention of local officials to invite the women to play another match in the city on their return from Nova Scotia.[54]

The tour of the Chicago team provided an important impetus to the organization of women's baseball teams throughout the region. Women were playing baseball in most of the major urban centres before 1900 and even in smaller communities such as Bocabec, New Brunswick, and Oxford, Nova Scotia, teams of women baseballists risked the wrath of the churches as they pushed forward into a formerly male sporting domain. This activity seems to suggest that the idea of maternal feminism and the doctrine of "separate spheres" were by no means universally accepted by turn-of-the-century Maritime women.[55]

Black teams also flourished in a number of Maritime communities during the 1890s. The most powerful of these was the Halifax-based Eurekas who during the 1890s lost only one match, that to the Amherst Royals in 1897. Other black teams active in this period were the Fredericton Celestials, the Truro Victorians, the Dartmouth Stanleys and Seasides and the Independent Stars and North Ends of Halifax. For the black minority in the region, baseball and other sports provided an avenue to respectability and relative acceptance by the white majority. Involvement in athletics created local heroes and encouraged black pride, but also offered a chance for black athletes to visit other communities in the region and demonstrate their skills. While black teams rarely played against their white counterparts, they nonetheless contributed to the more organized character of nineteenth-century sporting life, establishing regional championships and attracting sizeable paid gates. Although the press was inclined to emphasize the "ludicrous incidents" that took place in black baseball, it is fair to say that the coverage of black sporting activity was one of the more positive elements in the press's treatment of the black community in the nineteenth-century Maritimes.[56]

If the 1890s saw the diffusion of the sport throughout the region and the emergence of women and blacks on the baseball diamond, the opening of the new century witnessed the renewed ascendancy of professional baseball in the Maritimes. Professional teams once again graced the diamonds of Halifax, Fredericton, Saint John, and Moncton, and smaller communities also began importing players. Many of these imports were college students from American universities such as "Colby Jack" Coombs, a

Moncton pitcher who would later star in the major leagues and ultimately be inducted into the Hall of Fame. Others, who would play or had at one time played in the big leagues, were Bill O'Neil, the Saint John native and starting leftfielder for the Chicago White Sox in the 1906 World Series, Larry McLean of the Halifax Resolutes, and Bill Hallman, a former second-baseman for the Philadelphia Athletics turned thespian, who played on the touring Volunteer-Organist baseball and theatre company team.[57]

The opening decade of the twentieth century also witnessed the first connections between organized baseball activity on the mainland and on Cape Breton Island. Baseball was slow to arrive in Cape Breton, but by 1905, teams in Sydney, Sydney Mines, Reserve Mines, and Glace Bay were importing players. The Sydney *Record* of 21 August 1905 reported that better baseball than had ever been witnessed on the Island was now being played, "though the results are getting to depend too much on which team can import the most and best men."[58] The Dominion No. 1 team was the only team in this colliery district league that chose not to import men. Crowds of 800 per game were common in Cape Breton during the 1905 season, and seeing the potential for lucrative gates, sports promoters like M.J. Dryden of Sydney began to call for a strictly professional baseball operation for the 1906 season.

Although there were those who regarded the provision of recreation to the colliers of Cape Breton as a valuable antidote to class antagonism, not everyone supported the introduction of professional baseball. The editor of the Sydney *Record* regarded it warily, thinking it a scheme of unscrupulous promoters who, in preying upon the mining districts, would encourage idle habits amongst the working class. The summer months, the editor continued, were already busy with sports, picnics, excursions, and holidays which took people away from the workplace. "We should be the last to deny to anybody a reasonable amount of recreation and a reasonable amount of holidays," the editor wrote, "but this taking a day or a half day off at frequent intervals disorganizes the working man. England today is suffering from an excess of the sporting and holidaying spirit and she is in consequence feeling the competition of the steadier and more industrious continental nations."[59] In taking this stand, the newspaper was echoing the position of the operators of the Dominion Coal Company who complained that the scheduling of games before 5:00 resulted in "a considerable number leaving work early in the day, three or four times a week."[60]

Another concern was that the commercialization of baseball undermined respect for the sanctity of contract. Contract jumping was widespread in the early years of baseball, and without a rigorous governing body for the sport, there were few prohibitions against athletes selling their services to teams on a game-by-game basis. In a game between the Saint John Roses and Fredericton Tartars, in August 1890, for example, the Roses were without four of their players. Friars and Shannon abandoned the club to play a game for Eastport against Calais, Maine. Cunningham was in Houlton playing for the Alerts, while Bill O'Neil was at Black River training for a race for a money purse.[61]

During the same season, the Halifax Resolutes offered a sizeable sum to Fredericton's pitcher "Harvard" Howe to pitch a single challenge match against Moncton. Due to the expense, ladies, who had earlier been admitted free, now were required to pay a fee of fifteen cents.[62] The Resolutes followed a similar course later in the 1900 season, securing a pitcher by the name of Holland from the Saint John Roses to pitch against the Alerts.[63] The inability or unwillingness of clubs to enforce player contracts encouraged widespread player raiding between teams. During the 1901 season, for example, trainer John J. Mack, a professional athletic coach of the Wanderer's Amateur Athletic Club in Halifax, was implicated in an attempt to induce the star battery of the Alerts (Webber and Dolan) to jump the club and sign with the Halifax Resolutes. The Saint John *Globe* noted that Mack and Mr. Nevill, who was attached to the Resolutes club, offered the players salaries higher than those presently offered in the fast New England League. "All this goes to show," said the *Globe,* "how the baseball craze is taking hold of Halifax; how the ring of sporting men, whose sole idea of sport is to gamble on it, are getting in their fine work and are turning the game into a money making speculation, robbing it of all that is genuine and lowering its standard to those of cock-fighting or pugilism."[64] Without an effective regulatory body that could tighten up these loopholes, there was little hope of overcoming the problems of contract jumping. If clubs tried to enforce their contracts, the players would simply play for a release. League officials also found that the lax administration of contracts left them unable to discipline players who broke league regulations. They could only shake their heads in annoyance when players like first-baseman Joe Donnelly, suspended from the Maine–New Brunswick League one week, became a regular in the lineup of the Halifax Socials the next.[65]

By the middle of the first decade of this century, then, the contradictions professional baseball presented to the dream of recreational respectability were abundantly clear. Rather than encouraging a oneness of sentiment that transcended class lines, the development of baseball seemed to reveal the worst influences of commercialism, a flagrant disrespect for the sanctity of contract, an encouragement of reckless gambling, and unruly crowd activity. Competitive baseball also undermined the participatory character of amateur athletics. Rather than playing themselves, spectators preferred "to watch a few experts whose business it is to play for the public amusement," and, in turn, while neighbouring provinces were scoured for ball players in return for "a good salary, a lazy time and the small boys idol," local amateur sport withered.[66]

There were other problems. On the field of play, the workingmen who played alongside college students seemed not to be uplifted to respectability, but in the eyes of sports reformers, posed a threat to the respectable character of young college men. This concern was by no means confined to critics of professionalism in the Maritimes. Dr E.H. Nichols of Harvard University opposed college students playing alongside professionals in summer leagues and voiced the increasingly widespread belief that the longer a person stays in pro-ball "the worse he becomes."[67] Between the turn of the century and World War I, therefore, reformers made a concerted effort to separate amateur and professional sport and to define new standards of play that would distinguish professional baseball from the "gentlemanly amateurism" of the college game. In the United States, the NCAA took steps towards this end, striking a committee, in 1913, to rid college baseball of objectionable practices. Reporting in the following year, the committee made a number of suggestions for changes in the game. The committee recommended:

1. strict adherence to base-coaching rules, especially those prohibiting coaches from inciting or gesticulating to the crowd or using defamatory language;

2. enforcement of rules against blocking the runner, prying runners off base, or other forms of trickery, in order to bring a decorum to the game;

3. prohibition of verbal coaching from the bench;

4. prohibition of encouragement of the pitcher from outfielders. "Remarks of endless iteration" were deemed disagreeable to spectators, thus, encouragement should only come from the infield;

5. prohibition of catchers talking to batters; and

6. restriction of indecorous or unseemly behaviour.

The report concluded that "a college baseball game is a splendid contest of skill between two opposing nines before an academic throng of spectators. It is not a contest between a visiting team and a local team assisted by a disorderly rabble."[68]

The debate over amateurism was equally energetic in the Maritimes by 1910. In that year, the Halifax *Herald* ran a series of fifty columns on amateurism and professionalism in regional sporting life. Much of the debate centred upon the rapid growth of professionalism in hockey, but baseball was also a matter of lively concern. The *Herald's* position was clear. The main evil was not payment, but the system of amateurs and professionals playing alongside each other. What justification was there for promoters paying one athlete while exploiting another? This inequality of treatment encouraged amateurs to turn professional, many of whom would still be playing for the love of the game, except that someone was "getting the green on the side."[69] At the same time, the *Herald* admitted that working-class athletes needed compensation for lost wages and the sacrifice of time, noting the argument of a well-known Maritime catcher who pointed out that he could not afford to play ball on a Saturday afternoon without compensation for docked wages. But the same player's suggestion that the Maritime Provinces Amateur Athletic Association (MPAAA) give up its jurisdiction over baseball and let amateurs and pros play side by side was given a hasty rejection. "Amateurs and Pros Mix," said a headline of 25 February, "No! No! Say All in chorus!"[70]

The growing support for a clearer demarcation of amateur and professional sport led the Maritime Provinces Amateur Athletic Association to tighten its regulations with respect to amateur standing. Critical here was the resignation of James G. Lithgow as President of the MPAAA and his replacement, in 1909, by a new president, Dr H.D. Johnson of Charlottetown. Lithgow, actively involved in sporting organizations in the region and at one time president of the Nova Scotia Amateur Hockey league, had often turned a blind eye to violations of amateur standing. He must have been naive, the Halifax *Herald* concluded, not to know that professionalism was widespread, particularly after a lawsuit involving a Fredericton hockey club revealed that all its players, in the 1908 season, were under salary and that many of them were playing in Nova Scotia during the 1909–10 season.[71] As incoming president of the MPAAA, Johnson took immediate steps to separate amateur and professional play and instituted a tighter transfer rule to discourage player raiding in both hockey and baseball. Johnson's position on amateurism was to let bygones be bygones; subsequent violations of amateur standing, however would be severely dealt with. In the future, Johnson declared, there would be no reprieve. "Once a professional, always a professional" now served as the ruling maxim of the MPAAA.[72]

Ironically, these new regulations tended not to encourage the development of competitive amateur baseball in the region, but led to a more thoroughgoing system of importing professionals, some of whom were on option from major league teams, others who continued to play ball in the summer, while attending American universities in the off-season. In 1911, a professional New Brunswick–Maine baseball league was formed which, though not formally part of organized baseball, relied heavily on players from major league organizations. A four-team professional league followed in Nova Scotia, in 1912, with teams in Stellarton, Westville, and Halifax. Other independent professional teams operated in Cape Breton, Yarmouth, and the coal-mining town of Springhill. The success of these leagues—in August 1912, over 8000 spectators attended a game between the Saint John Marathons and Houlton, Maine—quickly attracted American promoters such as Frank J. Leonard of the Lynn Baseball Club of the New England league who envisaged a prosperous new league in Maine and the Maritimes.[73]

Although Leonard's initial attempt to create a regional professional league ended in failure, it was taken up once again in the spring of 1914. The new organizer was Montrealer Joe Page, sports agent for the Canadian Pacific Railway. Operating on behalf of officials of the Saint John baseball teams, Page hoped to spearhead a new professional league in the Maritimes. This league, slated to operate as a Class "D" circuit within organized baseball, was to include teams in Halifax, Saint John, Moncton, Stellarton, and New Glasgow. Page, who also envisaged his trains transporting players and fans to and from matches, helped secure a number of name players for the new circuit, including former Boston, Detroit, and Cleveland player Cy Ferry. Unfortunately for Page, when Moncton and New Glasgow demanded guarantees of $2745 for thirty-eight appearances in Halifax and an equal amount from Saint John, yet offered none in return to the other clubs, the scheme was scuttled.[74] With the coming of the war in Europe, the prospects of reviving the experiment were permanently dashed. In future years, the distinctions between amateur and professional were strictly maintained. The Depression of the twenties and thirties ensured that professional play would no longer be the widespread phenomenon that it had been before 1914.

Between the origins of Maritime baseball in the late 1860s and the outbreak of World War One, then, life on the region's sandlots changed drastically. Emerging out of the transformation of the region that accompanied the development of industrial capitalism in the 1870s and 1880s, baseball appealed initially to bourgeois reformers intent upon establishing appropriate standards of respectability and gentlemanly play. But the gamblers, promoters, players, spectators, ethnic groups, and women athletes who also played a role in shaping the game brought their own needs to the sport. By the turn of the century, therefore, most reformers recognized their inability to use baseball as a means of social control, and were beginning to demand the separation of amateur and professional play.

The results of the drive to separate amateurism and professionalism were somewhat ironic. Although successful in encouraging a clearer demarcation between amateur and professional sport, reformers such as Dr Johnson and F.J. Power were faced with the growing public acceptance of professional athletics. Yet, in the longer run, the triumph of professionalism over amateurism served the interests of the bourgeoisie just as well.[75] The period between 1870 and 1914 was one in which baseball was transformed from a cultural struggle involving reformers and "rowdies" to a more manageable form of organized mass leisure. And, if the transformation of baseball from an instrument of socialization to that of a marketable spectacle failed to eradicate class conflict as reformers had hoped, baseball gradually became one of the unifying enthusiasms that bridged class divisions and encouraged community solidarity.[76] The roots that baseball sank in the towns and cities of the region prior to World War I, in fact, were so deep that they would nurture the sport for another half-century. Only in recent years, with the coming of television and the increasing sophistication of the consumer marketplace, has baseball become essentially commodified and detached from its community roots. The result has been the withering of community baseball in the Maritimes and the incorporation of the region into a modern baseball culture of mass-produced Toronto Blue Jays caps and Montreal Expos sweatshirts. That, however, is another story altogether.

• Notes

1 Tony Mason, *Association Football and English Society, 1863–1915* (Brighton, 1980); Alan Metcalfe, *Canada Learns to Play: The Emergence of Organized Sport, 1807–1914* (Toronto, 1987); Wray Vamplew, *Pay Up and Play the Game: Professional Sport in Britain, 1875–1914* (Cambridge, England, 1988). See also James Walvin, *The People's Game: A Social History of British Football* (Bristol, 1975).

2 On the centrality of the idea of respectability in Victorian thought, see F.M.L. Thompson, *The Rise of Respectable Society: A Social History of Victorian Britain, 1830–1900* (Cambridge, MA, 1988). For an appreciation of the relationship of respectability to the reform of leisure and recreation, see Peter Bailey, *Leisure and Class in Victorian England: Rational Recreation and the Contest for Control* (London, 1978), and Eileen Yeo and Stephen Yeo, *Popular Culture and Class Conflict: Explorations in the History of Labour and Leisure* (Sussex, 1981).

3 Raymond Williams, *Culture* (Glasgow, 1981), 67.

4 The literature on the industrialization of the Maritimes is extensive. See in particular T.W. Acheson, "The National Policy and the Industrialization of the Maritimes, 1880–1910," *Acadiensis* 1, 2 (Spring 1972): 3–28; L.D. McCann, "The Mercantile-Industrial Transition in the Metal Towns of Pictou County, 1857–1931," *Acadiensis* 10, 2 (Spring 1981): 29–64.

5 Allan Guttmann, *From Ritual to Record: The Nature of Modern Sports* (New York, 1978), 29–64.

6 Steven M. Gelber, "Working at Playing: The Culture of the Workplace and the Rise of Baseball," *Journal of*

Social History 16, 4 (Summer 1983): 3–22.

7 *The Globe* (Saint John), 14 Dec. 1901, sec. 4, p. 7.

8 *Reporter* (Halifax), 9, 12 May 1868.

9 *Acadian Recorder*, 18 July 1857.

10 First *Annual Report*, Halifax Industrial Boys' School, 1864. See in particular the section entitled "Amusements."

11 See, for example, *Acadian Recorder*, 15 Oct. 1877.

12 Ibid., 11 Aug. 1888.

13 Ibid., 11 Sept. 1877.

14 Ibid., 7 March 1891.

15 Knights of St Crispin, *Proceedings of the 5th Annual Meeting of Grand Lodge, April 1872* (New York: Journeymen Printer's Cooperative Association, 1872).

16 *Acadian Recorder*, 6, 18 Sept. 1877.

17 For Great Britain, see E. Hopkins, "Working Hours and Conditions During the Industrial Revolution: A Reappraisal," *Economic History Review* 35 (1982). For the United States, see John Modell, "Patterns of Consumption, Acculturation and Family Income Strategy in Late Nineteenth-Century America" in *Family and Population in Nineteenth-Century America*, ed. Tamara K. Hareven and Maris Vinovskis (Princeton, 1978); Clarence Long, *Wages and Earnings in the United States, 1860–1890* (Princeton, 1960).

18 Ray Rosenzweig, *Eight Hours for What We Will: Workers and Leisure in an Industrial City* (London, 1983). The development of organized sport, amateur athletic associations, and the YMCA also provided alternatives to the tavern as the focus of leisure activity. See, for example, Peter Delottinville, "Joe Beef of Montreal:

Working-Class Culture and the Tavern, 1869–1889," *Labour/Le Travailleur* 8 (1981): 34–35.

19 Kathy Peiss, *Cheap Amusements: Working Women and Leisure in Turn-of-the-Century New York* (Philadelphia, 1986).

20 *Acadian Recorder*, 8 July 1881.

21 Ibid., 11 July 1878.

22 Ibid., 27 Sept. 1888.

23 Alan A. Brookes, "Outmigration from the Maritime Provinces, 1860–1900: Some Preliminary Considerations," *Acadiensis* 5, 2 (Spring 1976): 26–55.

24 *Globe* (Saint John), 14 Dec. 1901.

25 Quoted in *Acadian Recorder*, 27 July 1889. See also ibid., 3 Oct. 1889.

26 Ibid., 27 July 1889.

27 Ibid., 5 Aug. 1889. On the Bates College nine, see ibid., 8 June 1889.

28 On the relationship between team sport and Victorian notions of manliness and the inculcation of ideals of teamwork, patriotism, courage, and respectability, see Morris Mott, "The British Protestant Pioneers and the Establishment of Manly Sports in Manitoba," *Journal of Sport History* 7, 3 (Winter 1980): 25–26; "One Solution to the Urban Crisis: Manly Sports and Winnipegers, 1890–1914," *Urban History Review* 22, 2 (Oct. 1983): 57–70; Norman Vance, *The Sinews of the Spirit: The Ideal of Manliness in Victorian Literature and Religious Thought* (Cambridge, 1985); Brian Dobbs, *Edwardians at Play* (London, 1973); S.F. Wise, "Sport and Class Values in Old Ontario and Quebec" in *His Own Man: Essays in Honour of A.R.M. Lower*, ed. W. Heick and R. Graham (Montreal, 1974). For a contemporary view, see J. Castell Hopkins, "Youthful Canada and the Boys' Brigade," *Canadian Magazine* 4, 6: 551–66. On working-class opposition to bourgeois reformism, see Joe Maguire, "Images of Manliness and Competing Ways of Living in Late Edwardian Britain," *British Journal of Sports History* 3 (Dec. 1986): 256–87.

29 *Acadian Recorder*, 20, 21 Sept. 1888.

30 Ibid., 30 May 1889.

31 *Acadian Recorder*, 24 July 1990. During the 1870s Power had played and umpired games for money, but this was "when the distinction between amateur and professional athletics was unknown in this city." Despite subsequent protests that his earlier actions violated his amateur standing, Power was reinstated as an amateur by the Maritime Provinces Amateur Athletic Association's Executive Committee in 1888. Ibid., 23 May 1888.

32 Ibid., 3 July 1888.

33 Ibid.

34 *Globe* (Saint John), 12 Sept. 1901.

35 *Progress* (Saint John), 11 Aug. 1888.

36 *Acadian Recorder*, 25 May 1900.

37 Ibid.

38 *Record* (Sydney), 19 July 1905.

39 *Acadian Recorder*, 18 Sept. 1889.

40 Quoted in Frank Cosentino, "Ned Hanlan—Canada's Premier Oarsman—A Case Study in Nineteenth-Century Professionalism," *Canadian Journal of the History of Sport and Physical Education* 5, 2 (Dec. 1974): 7.

41 *Acadian Recorder*, 8 Sept. 1890.

42 *Daily Echo* (Halifax), 11 Sept. 1890.

43 *Acadian Recorder*, 8 Sept. 1890.

44 Ibid., 4 Aug. 1888.

45 *Chronicle Herald* (Halifax), 16 Aug. 1951.

46 *News and Advertiser* (Springhill), 13 Aug. 1896.

47 Carole Smith Rosenberg and Charles Rosenberg, "The Female Animal: Medical and Biological Views of Woman and Her Role in Nineteenth-Century America," *Journal of American History* 60 (Sept. 1973): 332–56.

48 Michael J.E. Smith, "Graceful Athleticism or Robust Womanhood: The Sporting Culture of Women in Victorian Nova Scotia, 1870–1914," *Journal of Canadian Studies* 23, 1–2 (Spring–Summer 1988): 120–37; Helen Lenskyj, *Out of Bounds: Women, Sport, and Sexuality* (Toronto, 1986);

Kathleen E. McCrone, *Playing the Game: Sport and the Physical Emancipation of English Women, 1870–1891* (Lexington, KY, 1988).

49 *Daily News* (Truro), 18 Aug. 1891.

50 Ibid., 19 Aug. 1891.

51 *Eastern Chronicle* (New Glasgow), 21 Aug. 1891.

52 *Acadian Recorder*, 24 Aug. 1891.

53 *Evening News* (Amherst), 20 Aug. 1891.

54 Quoted in *Acadian Recorder*, 20 Aug. 1891.

55 Cf. Michael J.E. Smith, "Female Reformers in Victorian Nova Scotia: Architects of a New Womanhood" (MA thesis, St Mary's University, 1984).

56 On the propensity to comment upon ludicrous incidents, see the *Acadian Recorder*, 14 Aug. 1900, for a game between the Eurekas and Seasides before an audience of 250. Black baseball originated in the 1800s, and by the end of the century, there was an annual regional championship, ibid., 28 Aug., 11, 18 Sept. 1900.

57 Joseph Reischler, *The Encyclopedia of Baseball*, 5th ed. (New York, 1983); *Record* (Sydney), 8 Aug. 1906.

58 *Record* (Sydney), 30 July, 21 Aug. 1906.

59 Ibid., 2 Aug. 1906.

60 *Acadian Recorder*, 4 Aug. 1906. The coal operators argued that the scheduling of baseball before 5:00 seriously embarrassed the company's and diminished output. "Picnics have also contributed their share of adverse influence," said the *Recorder*, "but baseball is the principal sinner." The company prevailed upon the league to move the starting time to 5:00 from 3:30 PM, but this proved inconvenient. The company also proposed that all games be held on Sunday, but the miners refused this interference in their leisure and opposed Sunday baseball on religious grounds. See also *Record* (Sydney), 23 July 1906.

61 *Acadian Recorder*, 27 Aug. 1900.

62 Ibid., 18 July 1900.

63 Ibid., 24 July 1900.

64 *Globe* (Saint John), 25 June 1901. Born in 1870 in Chelsea, England, Mack was an accomplished coach, athletic director at Columbia College, New York, in the 1899–1900 term and trainer for the Wanderer's Amateur Athletic Club in the summer season for a number of years. Mack denied allegations of unfair practice but admitted writing to Webber who was "under his care in the University of Maine all last winter and spring" and who contacted Mack expressing his desire to play in Halifax. *Herald* (Halifax), 26 June 1901. In 1905, Mack was hired as Yale's athletic director. *Acadiensis Recorder*, 15 Aug. 1905.

65 *Globe* (Saint John), 11 Aug. 1911.

66 *Record* (Sydney), 23 July 1906.

67 Dr. E.H. Nichols, "Discussion of Summer Baseball," American *Physical Education Review* 19, 4 (April 1914): 292–300.

68 "Committee on Ridding College Baseball of Its Objectionable Features," *American Physical Education Review* 19, 4 (April 1914): 313–14.

69 *Herald* (Halifax), 11, 14 Jan. 1910.

70 Ibid., 25 Feb. 1910.

71 Ibid., 11, 22 Jan. 1910.

72 Ibid., 6, 7 Jan. 1910.

73 *Acadian Recorder*, 14, 30 Aug. 1912.

74 Ibid., 18 April, 6, 15 May 1914.

75 The separation of amateurism and professionalism in athletics may be seen as part of a broader sorting out of high-brow and low-brow culture at the end of the nineteenth century. In this regard, see Lawrence W. Levine, *Highbrow/Lowbrow: The Emergence of Cultural Hierarchy in America* (Cambridge, MA, 1988).

76 Ian McKay, "Industry, Work, and Community in the Cumberland Coalfields, 1848–1927" (PhD thesis, Dalhousie University, 1983), 370–73. McKay makes a similar argument with respect to baseball in the town of Springhill.

RACE AND RECRUITMENT
IN WORLD WAR I:
Enlistment of Visible Minorities in the Canadian Expeditionary Force*

JAMES W. ST G. WALKER

Contemporaries called it "the war to end all wars" and "the war to make the world safe for democracy." During it, women throughout the North Atlantic world stepped forcefully into public affairs; subject populations in Central Europe emerged into national self-determination; the proletariat triumphed beyond the Eastern front. But if World War I has thus been deemed "progressive," whatever its horrible cost, it was not intended as a liberal social instrument. For example, the relations between categories of people termed "races" were regarded as immutable, and therefore expected to emerge from the war intact. Science and public opinion accepted that certain identifiable groups lacked the valour, discipline, and intelligence to fight a modern war. Since those same groups were also the subjects of the European overseas empires, prudence warned that a taste of killing white men might serve as appetizer should they be enlisted against a European enemy. The obvious conclusion was that this must be "a white man's war."

This decision was reached by virtually all the protagonists, but it was modified by an admission that since the subject races would clearly benefit

*Canadian Historical Review 70, 1 (March 1989): 1–26. Reprinted with the permission of University of Toronto Press.

from the victory of their own masters, they might be allowed to do their bit for the cause as appropriate to their own perceived abilities. Early in the war, when they constituted the empire's largest reserve of trained men, British Indian troops from the "martial races" of the subcontinent were committed to France. But when the nature of the conflict became evident, and British forces available, it was discovered that Indian combat troops were unsuitable for Europe. Most were diverted to the Middle Eastern campaigns, where their targets were non-Europeans, though thousands of Indian labourers remained in Europe. Similarly New Zealand sent a Maori infantry unit to Gallipoli, and a Maori labour unit to Belgium and France. Even sensitive South Africa agreed, when labour shortages were most pressing in 1916, to enlist blacks for non-combat duties in Europe. China's contribution as an ally was to provide 50 000 "coolies" to labour behind the lines in France. Typically contrary, France itself began the war using its "force noire" only at Gallipoli and as garrison troops in the French colonies but the huge losses of men on the Western Front overcame the doubts of the high command and in 1916 African troops appeared in the European trenches. When the Americans entered the war in 1917, black volunteers were at first rejected. Though later recruited and conscripted in large numbers, fewer than 10 percent ever fired a rifle in the direction of a German; the overwhelming majority were consigned to non-combat service battalions.[1]

Canada shared the Western ideology of "race," and Canadian wartime practice generally was in step with the allies: until manpower needs at the front surmounted the obvious objections, killing Germans was the privilege of white troops. Even when called upon, members of Canada's "visible" minorities were accompanied overseas by a set of presumptions about their abilities which dictated the role they were to play and which limited the rewards they were to derive.[2] An examination of policy towards them and of their participation in the war offers a temporary opening in the curtain which typically covers Canadian racism, revealing some details from the set of stereotypes applied to certain minorities. The curtain also lifts upon the determination and self-confidence of Canadian minorities, and their struggle to be accorded equal responsibilities as well as equal opportunities. The struggle is further revealed, in many instances, as a community effort: communities encouraged, organized, and financed the enlistment of their young men, and those men volunteered in order to gain group recognition and to further the rights of whole communities.

In August 1914 a surge of patriotism, assisted by severe unemployment, prompted the enlistment of more than the 25 000 volunteers initially required for the first CEF contingent. For over a year, in fact, the supply of men exceeded demand: recruiting officers could afford to be selective, and one of the selection criteria was the "race" of the applicant. Under the terms of the minister of militia's "call to arms," existing militia units enrolled volunteers directly, and the local militia officers had complete discretion over whom to accept.[3] There was one exception, however: within days of the first shots in Europe, the Militia Council forbade the enlistment of native Indians on the reasoning that "Germans might refuse to extend to them the privileges of civilized warfare." This directive was not, however, made public, and some recruiting officers remained ignorant of it. Indian youth, like their white counterparts, were anxious to participate and presented themselves to their local units. Many were enlisted only to be turned away when their Indian status was discovered. Some were able to slip through undetected, with or without the collusion of their commanders, so that the early contingents did contain some native soldiers despite the official policy.[4]

Members of other "visible" groups were less successful. Individual unit discretion appears to have kept East Indians entirely outside the Canadian forces, and in British Columbia, where most of them lived, Japanese were rejected completely. The fate of Chinese Canadians is less clear, but if any were accepted in the early years of the war their numbers must have been extremely small.[5] In a memo of November 1914 responding to a query on "coloured enlistment," the militia would only refer to the established policy that personnel selection was a matter for each commanding officer, though the chief of general staff offered the prevailing opinion: "Would Canadian Negroes make good fighting men? I do not think so."[6] One Cape Breton black volunteer, who decided that "Its a job that I'll like killing germans," was told he was ineligible to join any white unit; a group of about fifty blacks from Sydney, who went to enlist together, were advised: "This is not for you fellows, this is a white man's war."[7]

The Canadian volunteers rejected by this policy were not content to accept either their exclusion or the reasoning that went with it. They sought enlistment in large numbers, and insisted on knowing why their offer was not accepted. As early as November 1914 the black community of North Buxton was complaining to Ottawa and seeking corrective action; from Hamilton blacks came the charge that it was "beneath the dignity of the Government to make racial or color distinction in an issue of this kind"; blacks in Saint John condemned recruitment discrimination and added for the record an account of the discrimination they met daily in their home city.[8] Saint John MP William Pugsley, at the request of Ontario and New Brunswick black representatives, raised the issue in the House of Commons. The government insisted that "there is no Dominion legislation authorizing discrimination against coloured people," and the militia was able to state that "no regulations or restrictions" prevented "enrollment of coloured men who possess the necessary qualifications," but no remedies were offered or comment made upon clear evidence of exclusion for "racial" reasons.[9] And yet the urge to enlist persisted. A group of Cape Croker Indians applied to four different recruitment centres and were rejected from each one; Japanese in British Columbia made repeated attempts to enlist; blacks in Nova Scotia travelled from one unit to another hoping to find acceptance.[10] To some extent this persistence must have been prompted by young men's sense of adventure and patriotism, but they were moved as well by a consciousness that a contribution to the war effort could help to overcome the disadvantages faced by their communities. The Japanese believed that war participation would earn them the franchise, a hope that was shared by some Indian groups. Blacks maintained that a war for justice must have an impact on "the progress of our race" in Canada.[11]

White intransigence was not overcome by these efforts, but a compromise seemed possible: if whites and non-whites could not stand shoulder to shoulder in defence of the empire, perhaps they could stand separately. "Coloured candidates are becoming insistent," a Vancouver recruiter complained, and his superior advised that "as white men will not serve in the same ranks with negros or coloured persons," the only solution was to create a separate unit.[12] Because of the numerous black applications in Nova Scotia, several similar suggestions were made, and one commanding officer, though rejecting individual blacks, agreed to accept an entire platoon if one were formed.[13] On the "reliable information" that 10 000 blacks inhabited Edmonton region from whom 1000 could easily be recruited, Alberta district commander Cruikshank, with the support of the lieutenant governor, offered to create a black battalion since a racially integrated Alberta regiment "would not be advisable." On the same principle General Cruikshank proposed that a "Half-Breed Battalion" be recruited in Alberta.[14] More insistent and widespread were suggestions to raise distinct regiments of Native Indians. Every province from Ontario west produced proposals to enlist Natives in segregated units where, under careful supervision of white officers, their "natural" talents as fighters and marksmen could best be utilized.[15] Some of these suggestions were enthusiastically endorsed by the affected groups, believing that as a recognizable unit they could gain more attention for their communal cause,[16] but none were more energetic than the Japanese. In August 1915 the Canadian Japanese Association of Vancouver offered to raise an exclusively Japanese unit. Receiving a polite reply, the association began to enlist volunteers, eventually 227 of them, who were supported at Japanese community expense and practised their drill under British veteran and militia captain R.S. Colquhoun. With one company thus trained, the association made a formal offer to the government in March 1916 of a full battalion.[17]

The Japanese offer, like every other proposal to create a racially defined battalion, was rejected by Militia Headquarters. Officials doubted that enough volunteers from any group could be found to create and maintain a unit as large as a battalion, and furthermore its members could not be used as reinforcements in other battalions, as was frequently required in trench warfare, if integration should prove difficult. Privately, the combat abilities of blacks and Indians were considered questionable, and although Japanese were regarded as "desirable soldiers," their enlistment was feared as a step towards enfranchisement. Individual "half-breeds," blacks, and Japanese were theoretically admissible into all militia units. "There is no colour line," insisted the adjutant general, but commanding officers were free to accept or reject any volunteer for any reason.[18] One incident more than any other provoked this statement. In November 1915 twenty black volunteers from Saint John were sent to Camp Sussex, where they were told to go instead to Ontario where a "Coloured Corps" was being formed. Protesting that this action was "shameful and insulting to the Race," the Saint John blacks pressed their case with the governor-general and militia minister Sir Sam Hughes. Apparently outraged, Hughes ordered a full investigation into the incident and promised that there would be no racial barriers and no segregated units in his army. When the Sussex commanding officer complained that it was not "fair" to expect white troops "to mingle with negroes," a sentiment supported by all the commanding officers in the Maritime district, militia officials quickly explained that local commanders retained their discretionary powers: "it is not thought desirable, either in the interests of such men themselves or of the Canadian Forces, that Commanding Officers should be forced to take them."[19] Whatever Hughes's intentions, the statement reinforced the status quo. It remained a white man's war.

At the outbreak of the war a surplus of volunteers had afforded considerable latitude in selecting recruits. By the spring of 1915, when the second Canadian Contingent sailed, trench warfare had eroded all hopes for a short and glorious war, and casualty rates were horrifying. Domestic production competed with the armed services for manpower, just as more and more men were required for the trenches. Selectivity became less rigid, as height, medical, and marital requirements were relaxed, and the recruitment method itself came under scrutiny. In the fall of 1915 a new policy was substituted, enabling any patriotic person or group to form a battalion. This "patriotic phase," distinguished from the earlier "militia phase," led to the proliferation of new units and to rivalries among them for the available manpower. Since the fighting regiments were not being reinforced directly by new recruitment, the "patriotic" policy also meant that the units thus raised almost inevitably had to be broken up on arrival in Europe to be used to fill the gaps caused by casualties in the existing regiments. The entire situation was compounded by Prime Minister Borden's announcement that, as of 1 January 1916, Canada would pledge 500 000 troops to Europe. With prevailing casualty rates, it would require 300 000 new recruits per year to maintain this figure in the field.[20]

All these developments—the scramble for men, the raising of special regiments, and their use as reinforcements for fighting units overseas—had implications for recruiting "visible" minorities. First to fall was the restriction against Indian enlistment. Certain regiments had been discreetly recruiting Indians since 1914, but when Ontario's new 114th Battalion was being formed in November 1915 its commander hoped to enlist four companies of Brantford and region Indians. His superior, the Toronto district commander, lent support to the plan on the understanding that all Indians recruited in his division would be transferred to the 114th. It was apparently this limited plan, consistent with the "special units" policy, that was at first approved by the militia minister; Indians already in other regiments were invited to transfer to the 114th, and the new battalion was permitted to recruit Indians outside its own geographical territory.[21] The memo that went out to commanding officers, however, stated that Indian enlistment was henceforth authorized "in the various Units for Overseas Service," and this impression was reinforced in individual letters to commanders permitting Indian enlistment. The confusion amongst recruiting officers was shared by the chief of general staff, Willoughby Gwatkin, who confessed that he did not know whether open enlistment was now the rule or whether Indian battalions were to be formed.[22] Meanwhile, the 114th was advertising itself, even in the public press, as *the* Indian unit, and at least a dozen regiments transferred their Indian recruits to the 114th.[23] In the event, pressure from other battalion commanders convinced divisional headquarters to cease transferring Indians to the 114th, which was therefore unable to fill more than two Indian companies. The result was a concentration of Indians in the 114th, but others were scattered individually throughout the battalions willing to accept them.[24]

It was perhaps this reigning confusion over special units, coupled with the pressure to find a half million men, that led to one of the war's most discouraging episodes for black Canadians. In November 1915 J.R.B. Whitney, editor of a Toronto black newspaper, the *Canadian Observer,* wrote to Hughes asking if the minister would accept a platoon of 150 black men provided it would be maintained at that strength throughout the war. Hughes warmly replied that "these people can form a platoon in any Battalion, now. There is nothing in the world to stop them."[25] On this basis Whitney began to advertise through the *Observer,* and enlisted volunteers in the projected platoon. Early in January 1916 he was able to report to Hughes that he had enlisted a number of Toronto recruits, adding a request to second a black enlisted man for a recruitment tour of southwestern Ontario. Hughes passed this on to the adjutant general, W.E. Hodgins, for action, and this latter official was forced to return to Whitney for an explanation of what was meant by all this. In the process Hodgins discovered that no arrangement had been made with any battalion commander to receive a black platoon. In fact, advised Toronto's General Logie, it was doubtful if any commander would accept "a coloured platoon" into "a white man's Battalion." Hodgins therefore decided that permission to recruit a black unit could not be granted, and he asked Toronto division so to inform Mr Whitney. On 15 March Whitney received a blunt letter from the Toronto recruiting officer stating that as no commanding officer was willing to enlist them, the plan must be abandoned.[26]

A very hurt Whitney asked for a reconsideration; he had already gathered forty volunteers and could not now tell them to disband. An embarrassed Hodgins begged Logie to find some unit prepared to admit Whitney's platoon, and Logie diligently conducted a canvas of his district. The responses from battalion commanders dramatically revealed the prevailing feelings among the military leadership in 1916. Most rejected the idea without explanation, stating simply their unwillingness to accept blacks. Several acknowledged that white recruitment would be discouraged, and dissatisfaction aroused amongst men already enlisted. Some confirmed that they had already rejected numbers of black volunteers. The most ambiguous answer came from the 48th Highlanders, whose adjutant stated that "we have, being a kilted regiment, always drawn the line at taking coloured men." No one apologized or offered any positive suggestions. No one seemed to think his prejudices would not be understood, and shared, in headquarters. Logie replied to Hodgins that the situation was obviously hopeless. Whitney's personal appeal to Hughes provoked sympathy and some furious cables, but the result could not be changed. Even with a half million soldiers to find, Ontario's military establishment could not "stoop" to the recruitment of blacks.[27]

But Ottawa desks had been shaken, and General Gwatkin was ordered to write a report on "the enlistment of negroes in the Canadian Expeditionary Force." Besides Whitney's experience, overtures from black Nova Scotians had become more difficult to ignore, since they were supported by several influential Conservative politicians.[28] Gwatkin's memorandum was scarcely complimentary, but it did offer an opportunity for blacks to join the war. "Nothing is to be gained by blinking facts," Gwatkin began:

> The civilized negro is vain and imitative; in Canada he is not being impelled to enlist by a high sense of duty; in the trenches he is not likely to make a good fighter; and the average white man will not associate with him on terms of equality. Not a single commanding officer in Military District No. 2 is willing to accept a coloured platoon as part of his battalion; and it would be humiliating to the coloured men themselves to serve in a battalion where they were not wanted.
>
> In France, in the firing line, there would be no place for a black battalion, CEF. It would be eyed askance; it would crowd out a white battalion; it would be difficult to reinforce.
>
> Nor could it be left in England and used as a draft-giving depot; for there would be trouble if negroes were sent to the front for the purpose of reinforcing white battalions; and, if they are good men at all, they would resent being kept in Canada for the purpose of finding guards &c.

Gwatkin concluded with the recommendation that blacks could be enlisted, as at present, in any battalion willing to accept them, and that a labour battalion could additionally be formed exclusively for them.[29] On 19 April 1916, with Prime Minister Borden presiding, the Militia Council decided to form a black labour battalion headquartered in Nova Scotia, provided the British command would agree. This approval was received three weeks later.[30]

"It is a somewhat peculiar command," admitted Adjutant General Hodgins, after some difficulty was experienced in finding a qualified officer willing to head a black battalion. But Prime Minister Borden, himself a Halifax politician, took a personal interest in the new project and suggested the name of a potential commander, Daniel H. Sutherland. On 5 July, the day after Sutherland's acceptance, the Nova Scotia No. 2 Construction Battalion (Coloured) was formally announced. Officered by whites, the unit was authorized to recruit blacks from all across Canada.[31] The black community in Nova Scotia heartily welcomed the formation of the No. 2. "Considerable joy and happiness" erupted, particularly among the young men, for the No. 2 seemed to recognize that "they were men the same as everybody else." The African Baptist Association, at its 1916 annual meeting, expressed the view that through the No. 2 "the African race was making history," and pledged to do all in its power to encourage enlistment.[32] Although the all-white No. 1 Construction Battalion complained bitterly about its name, fearing association with "work which might be done by the negro race,"[33] no doubts seem to have been uttered by black representatives at the nature of the work or the fact of segregation.

By the summer of 1916 Canadian blacks, Indians, and Japanese were all being actively recruited into the services. Following the rejection of the Canadian Japanese Association's offer to form a full battalion, militia authorities encouraged other battalions to accept the volunteers who had already received basic training through their private efforts. The association itself promoted this policy, appealing to Alberta's General Cruikshank to permit Japanese to enlist in his district, since BC commanders remained adamantly opposed. On his return trip to Vancouver from Ottawa, where he had gone to present the case for a Japanese battalion, association president Yasuchi Yamazaki met with Cruikshank in Calgary, and the general immediately wrote to battalion commanders with the offer of up to 200 Japanese recruits.[34] The response was overwhelmingly positive. The 192nd Battalion offered to receive all 200, and the 191st asked for 250 but this was vetoed from headquarters as "there is no objection to the enlistment of odd men, but large numbers are not to be enlisted." Advertisements from Alberta recruiters appeared in Vancouver's Japanese-language press, and temporary recruiting offices were established in British Columbia, though this latter practice was contrary to regulations. Battalions from other provinces, too, sought Japanese recruits. Eventually 185 served overseas in eleven different battalions, mainly in the 10th, 50th, and 52nd infantry battalions. It was undoubtedly at this time that individual Chinese were being enlisted by under-strength battalions.[35]

The rivalry to recruit Japanese was being reflected in the much larger campaign to enlist native Indians. The 114th began with the advantage of being identified as an Indian battalion, and confusion continued for several months over whether all Indians, recruited before or since December 1915, were to be transferred to it. Some Indians who had enlisted in other regiments applied to transfer to the 114th; others asked not to be transferred because they preferred not to serve with "Mohawks."[36] The Department of Indian Affairs lent its official support to the 114th recruitment drive, and seconded Charles Cooke to the regiment with the honorary rank of lieutenant. Described as "the only male Indian employed in the Service at Ottawa," Cooke toured the Ontario reserves on behalf of the 114th, sometimes in the company of an Indian commissioned officer, stressing the pride and the opportunity derived from serving in an identifiably Indian unit. Although by this time it had been determined that only two companies, that is half the battalion, would in fact consist of Indians, the 114th stressed its Indian connection. The regimental badge contained two crossed tomahawks, and its band, composed mostly of Brantford reserve Iroquois, gave concerts which included Indian war dances.[37]

Other battalions were not slow to enter the recruitment race. Hodgins's attempt to settle the 114th's jurisdiction, by giving it authority to recruit Indians beyond its regimental territory but not *exclusive* authority, seems merely to have stimulated rivalries. Other commanding officers sought to entice Charles Cooke into their service; one battalion allegedly was offering a $5 recruitment bonus to Indians plus a free trip to Europe in case the war ended before they went overseas; others were reportedly recruiting young boys from the residential schools. In July 1916, when Colonel Mewburn called for a report on Indians enlisted in Military District 2, headquartered in Toronto, the 114th had 348, including five officers, and 211 others were arrayed across fifteen different units. This did not include the 107th battalion, raised in Winnipeg and commanded by G.L. Campbell, a senior Indian Affairs official. At first intended as an all-Indian battalion, the 107th shared the experience of Ontario's 114th and eventually enlisted approximately one-half its membership among Indians.[38]

Although these numbers were all recruited, at least ostensibly, into infantry battalions, there were parallel efforts to enlist Indians in noncombatant labour and construction units, particularly for forestry. Duncan Campbell Scott, the senior Indian Affairs official, urged this movement through Indian agents across Canada. When white officers and recruits in forestry units, primarily on the west coast, objected to working amongst "Indians and Half-breeds," authority was granted to establish separate Native companies and platoons.[39] One of the construction units to recruit amongst Indians was none other than the No. 2, from Nova Scotia. Five Indians joined the No. 2 at Windsor, Ontario, allegedly on the promise of becoming non-commissioned officers. Once enlisted they claimed to be disgusted by the fighting, gambling, and drinking going on in the No. 2. camp, and they called for a transfer. When Colonel Sutherland's response was slow, Chief Thunderwater of the Great Council of the Tribes took up the Indians' case, claiming "a natural dislike of association with negroes on the part of Indians." The adjutant general in Ottawa and General Logie in Toronto had to become involved before this entanglement could be settled and the Indians moved to the 256th Railway Construction Battalion, which had a large Indian component. Chief Thunderwater admonished the adjutant general "that you so arrange that Indians and negroes are kept from the same Battalions."[40]

The reason the No. 2 was in Windsor, Ontario, was that Sutherland had been given authority to recruit nationally, though this clearly meant that he could recruit blacks, for whom there was no interregimental competition. Information was sent to every commanding officer in the country authorizing "any of the coloured men in Canada, now serving in units of the CEF, to transfer to the No. 2 Construction Battalion, should they so wish." Several black volunteers did transfer from other units, at least some with the overt encouragement of their officers.[41] Within Nova Scotia a regimental band was organized, holding recruiting concerts in churches and halls wherever a black audience might be attracted. In the larger black communities, Citizens Recruiting Committees were formed to encourage enlistment, the Rev. W.A. White of the African Baptist Church in Truro gave "stirring" speeches, and black church elders lent moral support.[42] Early recruiting reports were satisfying, but by November 1916 Sutherland felt it necessary to undertake a more active campaign outside Nova Scotia. His request to recruit in the West Indies was turned down, but funds were authorized in January 1917 to take the band on a tour to Montreal and Toronto, and black centres in southwestern Ontario. After a decline between October and December, recruitment picked up again in January, most of it in Windsor, Ontario, where many American blacks joined the Canadian unit.[43] In Western Canada Captain Gayfer established a recruiting office in Edmonton, from which he too conducted tours and spoke in black churches. He later moved his headquarters to Winnipeg, leaving a black enlisted man in charge of the Edmonton office while a white lieutenant visited British Columbia. All across Canada young black men were being advised that "the need of the day" was for pioneers and construction workers whose contribution to the movement forward to victory was vital.[44]

Two years into the war, recruitment policy towards "visible" minorities had been reversed completely. But during those two years, the ardour to join their white brethren in the defence of Canadian democracy had been somewhat dampened among the minority youth. Japanese recruitment never remotely approached the thousand men projected by Yamazaki, perhaps because they were not allowed to serve in recognizable units as they believed was essential to win rights for their community. Native Indians did have the opportunity to enlist in concentrated units, but where such units existed they never recruited up to their authorized strength. The fact was that the invitation to serve was coming too late, and after a discouraging demonstration of majority attitudes towards their potential contribution. The Six Nations, who had offered their assistance as allies to the King in

1914, now opposed recruiters on the ground that they were an independent people and would enlist only upon the personal appeal of the governor-general and recognition of their special status.[45] Other Indian groups complained that "We are not citizens and have no votes, as free men"; anti-recruiters followed recruiters around the reserves, speaking out against Indian enlistment during "Patriotic" meetings, reminding Indians of their grievances and the many government promises made to them which had been broken throughout history.[46] Other factors interfered as well. There was resentment against recruitment methods including reports of intimidating tactics and the enrolment of underage boys. Indignation followed a rumour that overseas the Indians would be disguised as Italians, thus preventing any recognition for their accomplishments. Complaints from Indians already enlisted, alleging racial discrimination and inferior treatment in the forces, filtered back to the reserves. Other letters from Indians at the front described "the awfulness of war" and "openly advised the Indians not to think of enlisting."[47]

Nor did black Canadians fail to register scepticism at the recruitment campaign. In Nova Scotia, where black community leadership was won over, many individuals "were feeling keenly that their Loyal offers of service were refused in so many instances," and were reluctant now to join the No. 2. Blacks in the west told recruiters the same thing.[48] Resentment at previous insult was reinforced by continued insult: in Winnipeg black recruits were derided and called "nigger" by medical staff assigned to examine them. When Colonel Sutherland decided to move his headquarters from Pictou to Truro, he rented a suitable building and had begun furnishing it when the owner suddenly cancelled the contract. The same thing happened to Captain Gayfer when the owner of his recruiting office cancelled the contract "on account of color of recruits." Eventually established in Truro, black recruits met segregation in the local theatre. Rumours percolated through the black communities as well, for example that they were to be used only as trench diggers in France.[49] Although several prominent whites, notably Nova Scotian MPs Fleming McCurdy and John Stanfield and businessman H. Falconer McLean, assisted in the formation and recruitment of the No. 2, the military hierarchy itself was less than enthusiastic, perhaps feeling that the black battalion had been imposed on them for political reasons. The chief of general staff regarded the unit as "troublesome." It took Sutherland two months to gain approval for his tour beyond Nova Scotia, and then only with the strictest admonitions to economize. Western recruiter Gayfer was denied office supplies, had his transport warrants delayed, and received no rations or barrack accommodation for his recruits.[50] And yet Sutherland received constant memos and cables asking him when his unit would be ready for overseas service. The first target was three months; after seven months, Sutherland was told to prepare the men already recruited for sailing, and new recruits could follow later; eventually it was in March 1917, nine months after recruitment began, that the No. 2 embarked for England, and with only 603 men enlisted of an authorized strength of 1033 other ranks.[51] Because it arrived in Britain below battalion strength, the No. 2 was converted to a labour company of 500 men, and Sutherland was reduced in rank to major.[52]

It was not only "visible" minority youth who had developed a reluctance to volunteer. In July 1916 recruitment in general plummetted, from monthly peaks near 30 000 earlier in the year to fewer than 8000, and continued to fall to around 3000 a month. Not a single battalion raised after July 1916 reached its full strength, from any part of Canada. Employment in domestic war production, and increasing awareness of the carnage at the front, caused the virtual collapse of the voluntary system just at the time when the push was being made to enlist "visible" minorities. In May 1917, when casualty rates in Europe were more than double new recruitment, Prime Minister Borden announced his intention to introduce conscription with the cry that "the battle for Canadian liberty and autonomy is being fought today on the plains of France and Belgium." The Military Service Act, when effected later that year, was less than a popular success among those liable to its call. Over 90 percent of them applied for exemption.[53]

Canada's Indians were immediate and outspoken in denying the legality of their conscription. "Indians refuse to report," cabled one anxious Indian agent. More sophisticated responses referred to the fact that Indians were "wards of the government," legally "minors" and treated as children: surely children were not being called to defend the empire? Since they had no vote, and no voice in the conduct of the war or of the councils of state, it was unfair to expect them to participate now in the war. "We cannot say that we are fighting for our liberty, freedom and other privileges dear to all nations, for we have none," stated an Ontario Indian declaration. BC Indians considered "that the government attitude towards us in respect to our land troubles and in refusing to extend to us the position of citizens of Canada are unreasonable, and until we receive just treatment . . . we should not be subject to conscription." Still others quoted the treaties made in the 1870s, and the negotiations surrounding those treaties, during which Indians were assured that they would never be called to war. Petitions flowed to Ottawa, and even to the King: if they were not to have the rights of citizens, they must not be forced to perform a citizen's duty.[54] Similar petitions came from BC Japanese, pointing out that although they were naturalized Canadians they lacked the franchise and other citizenship privileges, and they claimed exemption from obligatory military service.[55] In these objections to conscription there was a scarcely submerged articulation of the "war aims" of Canadian minorities: if it was to be their war, it must result in the extension of equality to their people.

The government hesitated. Indians were first granted an extension of the time required to register; then they were advised officially to seek exemption under some existing regulation, such as agricultural employment.[56] Finally, on 17 January 1918, an order in council exempted Indians and Japanese, on the grounds of their limited citizenship rights and, for the former, the treaty promises. The order also referred to the War Time Elections Act which had deprived certain naturalized Canadians of the franchise and at the same time relieved them of military service. In March the regulations were amended so that any British subject disqualified from voting at a federal election was exempted from conscription. Despite the fact that they would already have been covered by this regulation, East Indians were granted a special exemption order three months later.[57]

This did not of course apply to black Canadians, who already enjoyed the franchise and therefore remained liable to conscription. The No. 2, still smarting from its demotion to a labour company, immediately requested that all blacks conscripted across Canada be sent to it, so that it could be restored to battalion status. The No. 2 proposal was promoted by Nova Scotian MP Fleming McCurdy, among others, and was received sympathetically by the new militia minister, General Mewburn, who confessed that "The whole problem of knowing how to handle coloured troops has been a big one for some years back." A collection depot was established in London, Ontario, where No. 2 reinforcements could be made ready for overseas, and orders were sent to commanding officers to transfer all "coloured men" to the London depot. The wording of the order did not appear to leave the commanders with any choice in keeping black conscripts in their own units.[58] In March, when it began to seem that black numbers were lower than anticipated, No. 2 recruiters travelled to Detroit to attract black Canadians living there, but this was squelched by Ottawa on the grounds that "we are not hunting for coloured recruits but merely making a place for them as they come in under the Military Service Act." Again, when the British-Canadian Recruiting Mission in New York announced that "about two thousand colored British subjects have registered," some or all of whom could be sent to reinforce the No. 2, Ottawa's answer was a terse "none required."[59] Deciding that the number of black conscripts coming in, directly or by transfer, was not worth the effort, Ottawa ordered the abandonment of the London reception centre in May. Sutherland was informed that his company would not be restored to battalion strength after all.[60]

There was one more try. The Rev. William White, chaplain to the No. 2 and as an honorary captain "the only colored officer in our forces," wrote an impassioned letter to the prime minister. "The coloured people are proud that they have at least one definite Unit representing them in France," he stated, requesting that the conscripted blacks be sent to strengthen the No. 2.[61] As a consequence Major Bristol, secretary to the Canadian overseas militia minister in London, was asked to make a report. In a response labelled "personal," Bristol admitted that "these Niggers do well in a Forestry Corps and other Labour units," but since numbers were so limited "the prospects of maintaining a battalion are not very bright." Following a survey of district commanders, it appeared that scarcely more than 100 identified black conscripts were already enlisted, and "on this showing it would hardly be possible to carry out the suggestion made" to use them to enhance the No. 2. The plan was dropped once and for all.[62] Fifty-five black conscripts already gathered in Halifax were trained in Canada as infantrymen, together with white conscripts, but on arrival in England they were placed in a segregated labour unit. They were eventually assigned to the 85th Battalion, but the Armistice intervened before they could leave Britain.[63]

The ambivalence and the frankly racist confusion surrounding their recruitment was reflected in the overseas experiences of the enlisted minorities. The Japanese, it appears, were consistently used as combat troops, which was their purpose in volunteering.[64] The Indians had a mixed reception. The 114th, recruited with such pride as an Indian unit, was broken up on arrival in England and the men assigned to different battalions, many for labour duties. The 107th, also recruited with an Indian identity and as a fighting unit, was converted to a pioneer battalion in France, where the men dug trenches and built roads and muletracks under direct enemy fire, with heavy casualties. Some Indians did go to the front as combatants, but a sizeable contingent served in forestry work, chiefly within Britain itself.[65] Those blacks who served individually in combat regiments, since their admission had been entirely voluntary on the part of their officers, apparently met few problems. When the 106th Battalion was broken up, for example, its black members went to the Royal Canadian Regiment as reinforcements on the front lines, where they were welcomed. Undoubtedly there were many more where blacks served without incident.[66] But the No. 2 itself, as a separate unit with its own administration and records, leaves a different trail. To avoid "offending the susceptibility of other troops," it was suggested that the black battalion be sent overseas in a separate transport ship, without escort. Since their sailing occurred during the war's worst period for German submarine attacks, it is fortunate that this suggestion was rejected by the Royal Navy.[67] The battalion arrived in England under strength, and the decision was made not to absorb the men into different units where whites might object, but to keep them together as a labour company attached to the Forestry Corps in French territory. Working as loggers and in lumber mills, and performing related construction and shipping work, the men of the No. 2 were established near La Joux, in the Jura region of France, with smaller detachments at Cartigny and Alençon. Although they laboured side by side with white units, the black soldiers were segregated in their non-working activities. Remote from any means of amusement, they had to await the creation of a separate "coloured" YMCA for their evenings' entertainment. When ill, they were treated in a separate "Coloured Wing" of the La Joux hospital. Those who strayed from military discipline were similarly confined in a segregated punishment compound. An extra Protestant chaplain had to be sent into Jura district "as the Negro Chaplain is not acceptable to the White

Units." Always regarded as a problem and never seriously appreciated, the No. 2 was disbanded with almost unseemly haste soon after the Armistice was announced, though the demand for forestry products remained high, and they were among the earliest Canadian units to leave France.[68]

The treatment received by "visible" Canadians did not originate with the military; recruitment policy and overseas employment were entirely consistent with domestic stereotypes of "race" characteristics and with general social practice in Canada. And Canadian attitudes themselves were merely a reflection of accepted and respected Western thought in the early twentieth century. Racial perceptions were derived, not from personal experience, but from the example of Canada's great mentors, Britain and the United States, supported by scientific explanations.[69] In these circumstances it is notable that the Canadian military, while by no means avoiding the influence of prevailing ideology, at least had the independence to be less restricting than most of the allies. For example, General Headquarters advised the Forestry Corps to reorganize the No. 2 to conform to imperial standards, as were applied to South African, Chinese, and Egyptian "coloured labour" units. This would have affected their pay and privileges, and for black non-commissioned officers it would mean a reduction to private. Colonel J.B. White, Forestry's La Joux commander, rejected this directive because "the men of this Unit are engaged in exactly the same work as the white labour with whom they are employed . . . and it is recommended that no change be made." Headquarters withdrew the order and the men of the No. 2 continued to be treated as other Canadian forestry units.[70] One reason for assigning the No. 2 to French territory was to avoid contact and comparison with other British "coloured labour" units "who are kept in compounds, and not permitted the customary liberties of white troops."[71] Black American troops in France were completely segregated, forbidden to leave their bases without supervision, and barred from cafés and other public places. Friendly relations with French civilians led to the strictest measures, including the arrest of blacks who conversed with white women, and to an official American request to the French military beseeching their co-operation in keeping the races separate. British East Indian troops were restricted in their off-base activities and were liable to a dozen lashes for "seeking romance" from white women. Senior army officials objected to East Indian sick and wounded being treated by white nurses. South African black labourers were kept in guarded compounds. Throughout the ranks of the Allies with the partial exception of the French, non-white soldiers and workers were humiliated, restricted, and exploited. It was simply not their war.[72]

Generally speaking, the efforts of "visible" enlisted men did not gain recognition for themselves or for their communities at home. Postwar race riots in the United States generated the worst violence experienced by black Americans since slavery. Attempts by Punjabi veterans to gain moderate political reforms led to the infamous Amritsar Massacre in April 1919, where 379 peaceful demonstrators were killed and 1208 wounded while trapped in a box-like park. French use of African troops to occupy defeated Germany led to condemnation by the Allies and to international censure for subjecting white Germans to the horrors of black authority.[73] Respect, evidently, had not been won by four years in defence of Western ideals. There was even a Canadian incident to illustrate this situation: on 7 January 1919 at Kinmel Park Camp in Britain, white Canadian soldiers rioted and attacked the No. 2 ranks on parade after a black sergeant arrested a white man and placed him in the charge of a "coloured" escort.[74] Far from expressing gratitude for their services, the militia minister in 1919 seemed unaware that the No. 2 had even existed.[75] It is true that individual Japanese veterans were granted the franchise, belatedly and grudgingly, in 1931 by a one-vote margin in the BC legislature, and Native Indians actually serving in the forces were enfranchised by the War Time Elections Act and its successors, but their families and other members of their communities remained as only partial Canadian citizens.[76] Especially indicative of their failure to attain genuine acceptance was the fact that at the outset of World War II, "visible" volunteers would again be rejected altogether or directed towards support and service functions consistent with their peacetime stereotypes.[77]

During World War I about 3500 Indians, over 1000 blacks, and several hundred Chinese and Japanese enlisted in the Canadian forces. To their number must be added the many who tried to enlist and were rejected. Though there was an understandable resistance to later attempts to recruit and conscript them, still the numbers in uniform were impressive, a demonstration of loyalty and a confidence that accepting equal responsibilities would win the advantages of Canadian citizenship. Individual exceptions occurred, but as a group they were denied that equal opportunity to defend their country and empire. Stereotypes which at first excluded them continued to restrict their military role, and even survived the war. In 1919 respect and equality remained beyond reach. Lessons which could and should have been learned in the first war had to be taught all over again in a second global conflict.

The experience of "visible" minorities in World War I illustrates the nature of Canadian race sentiment early in this century. Most abruptly, it demonstrates that white Canadians participated in the Western ideology of racism. This was true not only in the general sense of accepting white superiority, but in the particular image assigned to certain peoples which labelled them as militarily incompetent. Canadian history itself should have suggested the contrary—blacks and Indians, for example, had a proud record of military service prior to Confederation—but the stereotypes derived from Britain and the United States were more powerful than domestic experience. Some degree of cynicism is discernible in the rejection of "visible" volunteers, for example, the fear that military duty would enable them to demand political equality, yet it is not possible to read the entire record without concluding that most white Canadians, including the military hierarchy, were convinced by the international stereotypes and their supporting scientific explanations. This was carried to the point where Canada's war effort was impeded by prejudices for which there were no Canadian foundations.

Equally interesting is what the World War I experience reveals about the minorities themselves. Their persistence in volunteering, their insistence upon the "right" to serve, their urgent demand to know the reasons for their rejection, all suggest that "visible" Canadians had not been defeated by the racism of white society, had not accepted its rationalizations, and were not prepared quietly to accept inferior status. They retained a confidence in themselves, most obviously that they could achieve a glorious war record if given the opportunity. While recognizing the restrictions imposed on themselves and their communities, they were convinced that by their own efforts and the good will of white Canada they could remove those restrictions. Their appeals to Parliament and the Crown reveal as well that they had not lost faith in British/Canadian justice. The minority campaigns during World War I, for recruitment and later against conscription, were only possible for persons convinced that they were equal and could achieve recognition of their equality. Their loyalty to Canada and the empire included loyalty to an ideal which the dominant majority had forgotten.

• Notes

[1] For example, see Jeffrey Greenhut, "The Imperial Reserve: The Indian Corps on the Western Front, 1914–15," *Journal of Imperial and Commonwealth History* 11 (1983): 54–73, and "Sahib and Sepoy: An Inquiry into the Relationship Between the British Officers and Native Soldiers of the British Indian Army," *Military Affairs* 48 (1984): 15–18; Keith L. Nelson, "The Black Horror on the Rhine: Race as a Factor in Post–World War I Diplomacy," *Journal of Modern History* 62 (1970): 606–8; Fred Gaffen, *Forgotten Soldiers* (Penticton, BC, 1985), 24, 74–75; B.P. Willan, "The South African Native Labour Contingent, 1916–1918," *Journal of African History* 19 (1978): 61–86; C.J. Balesi, *From Adversaries to Comrades in Arms: West Africa and the French Military, 1885–1918* (Waltham, MA, 1979), 112–13, 120–21; C.M. Andrew and A.S. Kanya-Forstner, "France, Africa, and the First World War," *Journal of*

African History 19 (1978): 11–23; A.E. Barbeau and F. Henri, *The Unknown Soldiers: Black American Troops in World War II* (Philadelphia, 1974); J.D. Foner, *Blacks and the Military in American History: A New Perspective* (New York, 1974), 109–32. Black combat troops remained an American embarrassment. The all-black 93rd Division, for example, was first offered to the British army, and upon refusal was eventually attached to the French army for its combat service. The Chinese "coolies" were shipped across Canada, en route to and from France, in sealed railway carriages. There are voluminous files on this episode in the Directorate of History, Department of National Defence (hereafter DND, DH), Ottawa, and in RG 24 at the National Archives of Canada (hereafter NAC).

[2] A small but growing literature is available on the subject of minority

Canadian participation in the world wars. Pioneering chapters on black Nova Scotians in M. Stuart Hunt, *Nova Scotia's Part in the Great War* (Halifax, 1920), 148–53, and Ontario blacks and Indians in Barbara M. Wilson, *Ontario and the First World War, 1914–1918: A Collection of Documents* (Toronto, 1977), cviii–cxiv, 166–75, are being supplemented with more detailed studies. Gaffen's *Forgotten Soldiers* is a colourful description of Native Indian soldiers in both world wars, a welcome addition to James Dempsey's brief account, "The Indians and World War I," *Alberta History* 31 (1983): 1–8, and a useful corrective to Duncan Campbell Scott, "The Canadian Indian and the Great World War" in *Canada and the Great World War* (Toronto, 1919), 3: 285–328. Calvin W. Ruck, *Canada's Black Battalion: No. 2 Construction 1916–1920* (Halifax, 1986), is anecdotal and illustrative, with portraits and quotations from several of the black veterans themselves. The first scholarly treatment of the No. 2 is Major John G. Armstrong's "The Unwelcome Sacrifice: A Black Unit in the Canadian Expeditionary Force, 1917–1919," unpublished paper presented at RMC Military History Symposium, March 1986. Roy Ito, *We Went to War: The Story of the Japanese Canadians who Served During the First and Second World Wars* (Stittsville, ON, 1984), is a valuable combination of scholarship and reminiscence, though most of the attention is paid to the Second World War. Further detail on World War II can be found in Patricia Roy, "The Soldiers Canada Didn't Want: Her Chinese and Japanese Citizens," *Canadian Historical Review* (hereafter *CHR*) 59 (1978): 341–58.

3 Robert Craig Brown and Donald Loveridge, "Unrequited Faith: Recruiting the CEF 1914–1918," *Revue internationale d'histoire militaire* 51 (1982): 46; Desmond Morton, *A Military History of Canada* (Edmonton, 1985), 130; G.W.L. Nicholson, *Canadian Expedi-*

tionary Force, 1914–1919 (Ottawa, 1962), 18, 19, 212, 213.

4 NAC, RG 24, vol. 1221, file 593-1-7, vol. 1, telegram, 8 Aug. 1914; Scott to Hughes, 16 June 1915, and reply, 23 June; Nethercott to Hughes, 11 Oct. 1915; Armstrong to Hughes, 10 Oct. 1915, and replies, 18 Oct. 1915; Brown to Hodgins, 9 Oct. 1915, and reply, 22 Oct. 1915. Gaffen, *Forgotten Soldiers*, 20, points out correctly that since "race" was not recorded on recruitment documents, it is not possible to give precise numbers on Indian volunteers. The same caveat should apply to the other minority groups discussed here as well.

5 After the war, the minister of militia and defence, Hugh Guthrie, told the House of Commons that the CEF had enlisted "something like twelve" Chinese and no East Indians; *Debates*, 29 April 1920, 1812. Several sources refer to larger numbers of Chinese veterans in postwar Canada, for example, Jin Tan and Patricia Roy, *The Chinese in Canada* (Ottawa, 1985), 15; Edgar Wickberg et al., *From China to Canada: History of the Chinese Community in Canada* (Toronto, 1982), 200; and Carol F. Lee, "The Road to Enfranchisement: Chinese and Japanese in British Columbia," *IBC Studies* 30 (1976): 57–58. A search of the records in the National Archives of Canada and the Directorate of History, Department of National Defence, failed to identify these men. Some could have served as British "coolies" rather than as Canadian soldiers. Guthrie's comment does suggest that a small number were enlisted as regular soldiers, an impression confirmed by Professors Graham Johnson and Edgar Wickberg who report in a personal communication, 31 Oct. 1987, having seen photographs of Chinese in the uniform of the CEF. A separate Sikh regiment has been suggested as early as 1911, apparently with favourable comment from Sam Hughes, but no action was ever taken; Norman Buchignani, personal com-

munication, 14 Oct. 1987. On British Columbia's rejection of all Japanese volunteers see NAC, RG 24, vol. 4740, file 448-14-262, vol. 1, Cruikshank, circular letter, 26 April 1916.

6 NAC, RG 24, vol. 1206, file 297-1-21, memo, 13 Nov. 1914, Gwatkin to Christie, 30 Sept. 1915.

7 NAC, RG 24, vol. 4562, file 133-7-1, Bramah to Rutherford, 4 Oct. 1915, and reply, 6 Oct.; Ruck, *Black Battalion*, 58, quoting interview with Robert Shepard. Despite these obstacles, some Nova Scotia blacks are reported to have been in the first contingent, which left Canada in October 1914. Ibid., 11.

8 NAC, RG 24, vol. 1206, file 297-1-21, Alexander to Hughes, 13 Nov. 1914; Morton to Hughes, 7 Sept. 1915; Richards to Duke of Connaught, 4 Oct. 1915; Hamilton to Duke of Connaught, 29 Dec. 1915.

9 House of Commons, *Debates*, 24 March 1916, 2114–15; NAC, RG 24, vol. 1206, file 297-2-21, Edwards to Stanton, 31 Jan. 1916; Hodgins to Stewart, 16 Oct. 1915.

10 NAC, RG 24, vol. 1221, file 593-1-7, Duncan to Scott, 19 Nov. 1915; RG 24, vol. 1860, file 54; RG 24, vol. 4740, file 44-14-262, vol. 1; RG 24, vol. 4562, file 133-17-1, Bramah to Rutherford, 4 Oct. 1915.

11 Ito, *We Went to War*, 8ff; NAC, RG 10, vol. 2640, file 129690-3, Jacobs, circular letter, 17 Aug. 1917; RG 24, vol. 1206, file 297-1-21, *Canadian Observer*, 8 Jan. 1916.

12 NAC, RG 24, vol. 1206, file 297-1-21, Henshaw to Ogilvie, 7 Dec. 1915; Ogilvie to Hodgins, 9 Dec. 1915.

13 Ibid., Tupper to Hughes, 11 Nov. 1915; Allen to Rutherford, 14 Dec.; NAC, RG 24, vol. 4562, file 133-17-1, Langford to Rutherford, 23 Sept. 1915; Borden to Rutherford, 23 March 1916.

14 NAC, RG 24, vol. 4739, file 448-14-259, McLeod to Cruikshank, 25 Nov. 1915 and 20 Jan. 1916; Munton to

Cruikshank, received 11 March 1916; Cruikshank to Hodgins, 11 March 1916; Brett to Cruikshank, 13 March 1916; Martin to Cruikshank, 17 March 1916; RG 24, vol. 4739, file 448-14-256, "Half Breed Battalion," 1915.

15 NAC, RG 24, vol. 1221, file 593-1-7, vol. 1, inspector of Indian agencies, Vancouver, to Fiset, 23 Dec. 1915; Jackson to Ruttan, 20 Dec. 1915; McKay to Hodgins, 3 Jan. 1916; Donaldson to Hughes, 26 Nov. 1915; Read to Militia Council, 3 Feb. 1916; Rendle to Department of Indian Affairs, 17 Feb. 1916; Henderson to Hughes, 18 March 1916.

16 For example, see *Canadian Observer*, 8 and 15 Jan. 1916; NAC, RG 24, vol. 1221, file 593-1-7, vol. 1, Chief Thunderwater, on behalf of the Council of the Tribes, to Hodgins, 29 May 1916; RG 24, vol. 1469, file 600-10-35, White to McCurdy, n.d.; RG 24, vol. 4662, file 99-256, resolution, BC Indian Peoples, 1 Feb. 1916.

17 NAC, RG 24, vol. 1860, file 54, "Recruiting—Special Units and Aliens," numerous letters and telegrams, Jan.–April 1916; Roy Ito, personal communication, 18 Nov. 1987. An overseas battalion in the CEF consisted of approximately 1000 men grouped in 4 companies each with 2 platoons.

18 NAC, RG 24, vol. 1860, file 54, Gwatkin to Yamazaki, 21 April 1916; RG 24, vol. 1206, file 297-1-21, Gwatkin to Christie, 30 Sept. 1915; Hodgins to Tupper, 11 Nov. 1915; Hodgins to Armstrong, 19 Nov. 1915; Gwatkin to Hodgins, 22 Dec. 1915; Hodgins to Ogilvie, 23 Dec. 1915; Hodgins to Gwatkin, 21 March 1916; MacInnes to Hodgins, 25 March 1916; RG 24, vol. 1221, file 593-1-7, vol. 1, Fiset to inspector of Indian agencies, Vancouver, 29 Dec. 1915; Hodgins to McKay, 3 Jan. 1916; Gwatkin, memo, 12 Feb. 1916; Ogilvie to Hodgins, 23 March 1916; RG 24, vol. 4599, file 133-17-1, Hodgins to Rutherford, 29 Oct. 1915; RG 24, vol. 4739, file 448-14-256, Hodgins to Campbell, 15 July

1915; Hodgins to Cruikshank, 20 Nov. 1915; file 448-14-259, Hodgins to Cruikshank, 9 Dec. 1915 and 23 March 1916; Cruikshank to Martin, 27 March 1916; Ito, *We Went to War*, 25.

[19] NAC, RG 24, vol. 1206, file 297-1-21, Richards to governor-general, 20 Nov. 1915; *Saint John Standard*, 20 Nov. 1915; Hughes to Richards, 25 Nov. 1915, Fowler to GOC Halifax, 25 Nov. 1915; Hodgins to GOC Halifax, 29 Nov. 1915, and reply, 10 Dec.; Hodgins to GOC Halifax, 22 Dec. 1915; Gwatkin to Hodgins, 22 Dec. 1915; MacInnes to Hodgins, 25 March 1916. Interestingly, at least one commanding officer interpreted the minister's statement as a direct instruction. Lt Col. W.H. Allen of the 106th Battalion, Halifax, accepted 16 black Nova Scotians into his unit, though he reported that it discouraged white volunteers, since "word has come from Ottawa that there is to be no distinction of colour for enlistments." Allen to GOC Halifax, 14 Dec. 1915.

[20] Brown and Loveridge, "Unrequited Faith," 59, 60; Morton, *Military History of Canada*, 135–41, 147; Nicholson, *Canadian Expeditionary Force*, 212–15, 223; J.L. Granatstein and J.M. Hitsman, *Broken Promises: A History of Conscription in Canada* (Toronto, 1977), 22–59.

[21] NAC, RG 14, vol. 1221, file 593-1-7, Logie to Hodgins, 23 Nov. 1915, and reply, 26 Nov., Logie to Hodgins, 27 Nov. 1915, and replies, 6 Dec. and 10 Dec.; RG 24, vol. 4383, file 34-7-109, transfer order, 11 Dec. 1915.

[22] NAC, RG 24, vol. 1221, file 593-1-7, Hughes to Donaldson, 4 Dec. 1915; Hodgins to McLean, 9 Dec. 1915; Hodgins, circular letter, 10 Dec. 1915; Gwatkin to Hodgins, 6 Jan. and 5 May 1916.

[23] NAC, RG 24, vol. 4383, file 34-7-109, "Enlistment of Indians in CEF," numerous reports, OC 44th Regiment to Logie, 17 Jan. 1916; Scott to Logie, 19 Jan. 1916, and reply, 21 Jan.; OC 114th Battalion to Logie, 27 Jan. 1916.

[24] Ibid., Logie to OC 114th Battalion, 22 Jan. and 28 Jan. 1916; Hodgins to Logie, 31 Jan. 1916; Hodgins to Baxter, 8 Feb. 1916.

[25] NAC, RG 24, vol. 1206, file 297-1-21, Whitney to Hughes, 24 Nov. 1915, and reply, 3 Dec. A platoon would contain about 125 men in a standard CEF overseas battalion.

[26] Ibid., *Canadian Observer*, 8 and 15 Jan. 1916; Whitney to Hughes, 19 Jan. 1916, and reply, 26 Jan.; Hodgins to Logie, 3 Feb., 8 and 13 March 1916; Logie to Hodgins, 4 and 10 March 1916; Trump to Whitney, 15 March 1916.

[27] Ibid., Whitney to Logie, 24 March 1916, to Kemp, 29 March 1916; Hodgins to Logie, 31 March 1916; Logie to commanding officers, 3 April 1916; Logie to Hodgins, 10 April 1916; Whitney to Hughes, 18 April 1916; Hughes to Logie, 3 May 1916, and reply, 4 May. Battalion replies to Logie's appeal of 3 April 1916 are found in NAC, RG 24, vol. 4387, file 34-7-141, as are copies of much of the correspondence cited from file 297-1-21.

[28] NAC, RG 24, vol. 1206, file 297-1-21, Christie to Gwatkin, 29 Sept. 1915; Allen to GOC Halifax, 14 Dec. 1915; RG 24, vol. 4562, file 133-17-1, Langford to Rutherford, 23 Sept. 1915; RG 9, 111, vol. 81, file 10-99-40, McCurdy to Harrington, 16 July 1919.

[29] NAC, RG 24, vol. 1206, file 297-1-21, "Memorandum on the enlistment of negroes in Canadian Expeditionary Force," 13 April 1916.

[30] Ibid., Militia Council minutes, 19 April 1916; cable to War Office, 19 April 1916, and reply, 11 May.

[31] Ibid., Militia Council, memo, 2 June 1916; RG 24, vol. 1469, file 600-10-35, Hodgins to Gwatkin, 5 June 1916, and reply, 11 June; Hodgins to Sutherland, 13 June 1916, and reply, 4 July.

[32] Ruck, *Canada's Black Battalion*, 27, quoting interview with Mrs Mabel

Saunders; African Baptist Association, annual meeting, minutes, 1916.

33 NAC, RG 24, vol. 1469, file 600-10-35, Ripley to Hodgins, 7 and 15 July 1916, Hodgins to Ripley, 10, 19, and 21 July 1916.

34 NAC, RG 24, vol. 1860, file 54, "Recruiting—Special Units and Aliens"; RG 24, vol. 4740, file 448-14-262, Ityama to Cruikshank, 24 April 1916; Cruikshank, circular letter, 26 April 1916.

35 Ibid., OC 192nd Battalion to Cruikshank, 28 April, 19 May, 4 Aug. 1916; Cruikshank to OC 192nd Battalion, 16 and 20 May and 1 Aug. 1916; Cruikshank to Hodgins, cable, 4 May 1916, and reply, same date; Cruikshank to Yamazaki, 5 May 1916; Ito, We Went to War, 34, 70, and appendix 3, and personal communication, 18 Nov. 1987. RG 24, vol. 1860, file 54, gives the number of Japanese Canadians enlisted as 166, while the militia minister reported 194 Japanese enlistments; House of Commons, Debates, 29 April 1920, 1812. On Chinese recruits see note 5.

36 NAC, RG 14, vol. 1221, file 593-1-7, vol. 1, Chief Thunderwater to Hodgins, 29 May and 20 June 1916; RG 24, vol. 4383, file 34-7-109, Mewburn to OC 119th Battalion, 26 April 1916; OC 227th Battalion to Mewburn, 4 May 1916. Although the adjutant general directed in February that Indian transfers should thereafter be carried out only when "special circumstances exist, as in the case of brothers," Col. Mewburn was still writing in April demanding the transfer of Indians to the 114th. See Hodgins to Baxter, 8 Feb. 1916.

37 NAC, RG 24, vol. 1221, file 597-1-7, vol. 1, Cooke to minister of militia, 15 Dec. 1916; RG 24, vol. 4383, file 34-7-109, Hodgins to Logie, 31 Jan. 1916; Baxter to Hodgins, 2 Feb. 1916; Scott to Logie, 22 Jan. 1916; Logie to Hodgins, 22 Feb. 1916; Thompson to Mewburn, 13 April 1916; Gaffen, Forgotten Soldiers, 23.

38 NAC, RG 24, vol. 4383, file 34-7-109, Hodgins to Logie, 22 Feb. 1916; Thompson to OIC Divisional Recruiting, 1 March 1916; Thompson to Mewburn, 20 April 1916; Mewburn to OC 227th Battalion, 10 April 1916, and reply, 26 April; various regimental reports to Mewburn, July 1916; Gaffen, Forgotten Soldiers, 23.

39 NAC, RG 10, vol. 6766, file 452-13, Scott to Renison, 15 Jan. 1917; cables to Indian agents, 15 Jan. 1917; Militia Department to Tyson, 5 April 1917; RG 24, vol. 1221, file 597-1-7, vol. 1, Scott to Fiset, 15 Jan. 1917; vol. 2, Ogilvie to Hodgins, cable, 22 March 1917; RG 24, vol. 4662, file 99-256, Ogilvie to Hodgins, 23 March 1916; Reynolds to Ogilvie, 20 March 1917; Tyson to Scott, 21 March 1917; Ogilvie to Hodgins, 22 March 1917.

40 NAC, RG 24, vol. 1221, file 593-1-7, vol. 1, Chief Thunderwater to Hodgins, 30 Dec. 1916, 2 Jan. 1917; Hodgins to Logie, 8 Jan. 1917; vol. 2, John to Thunderwater, 19 Feb. 1917; Mrs. Maracle to Thunderwater, 17 Feb. 1917; Thunderwater to Hodgins, 23 Feb. 1917; Hodgins to Logie, 9 and 22 March 1917; Logie to Hodgins, 15 and 24 March 1917. Colonel Thompson of the 114th Battalion had rejected the offer of Whitney's Toronto black volunteers by explaining, "the introduction of a coloured platoon into our Battalion would undoubtedly cause serious friction and discontent." RG 24, vol. 4387, file 34-7-141, Thompson to Logie, 4 April 1916.

41 Ibid., Wright to Logie, 4 April 1916; RG 24, vol. 4680, file 18-25-2, Adjutant General's Office to district commanding officers, circular letter, 16 Aug. 1916; RG 24, vol. 4486, file 47-8-1, transfer order, 28 Aug. 1916.

42 NAC, RG 24, vol. 1469, file 600-10-35, Sutherland to McCurdy, 7 Aug. 1916; Hodgins to Sutherland, 8 Aug. 1916; RG 24, vol. 1550, file 683-124-2, Sutherland to Hodgins, 27 Nov. 1916, to McCurdy, same date.

43 NAC, RG 24, vol. 1469, file 600-10-35, Sutherland to Hodgins, 25 Aug. 1916; Elliott to Hodgins, 19 Oct. 1916; Hodgins to Sutherland, 1 Dec. 1916; RG 24, vol. 1550, file 683-124-2, Sutherland to Hodgins, 27 Nov. 1916 and 4 Jan. 1917; memorandum, Minister's Office, 5 Jan. 1917; adjutant general to GOC Halifax, 23 Jan. 1917; RG 24, vol. 4486, file 47-8-1, Morrison, memo, 31 Aug. 1916. The Sailing List of the No. 2 Construction Battalion, 28 March 1917, contains information on the birth place, recruitment place, and date for each man, so that monthly and regional totals can be compiled.

44 NAC, RG 24, vol. 4739, file 448-14-259, Duclos to Cruikshank, 8 Sept. 1916, Gayfer to Cruikshank, 6 and 18 Sept. 1916, 9 and 15 Oct. 1916; No. 2 Recruitment Poster, Ruck, *Canada's Black Battalion*, appendix, 126.

45 NAC, RG 10, vol. 6765, file 452-7, Cooke to Scott, 12 Feb. and 4 March 1916; minutes of the Six Nations Council, 15 Sept. 1914, in Wilson, *Ontario and the First World War*, 174.

46 NAC, RG 24, vol. 1221, file 593-1-7, vol. 1, Chief George Fisher to Gray, 19 Feb. 1916; RG 24, vol. 4383, file 34-7-109, Baxter to Williams, 18 Dec. 1915; Whitelaw to Baxter, 31 Dec. 1915; RG 10, vol. 6765, file 452-7, Cooke to Scott, 4 April 1916.

47 NAC, RG 24, vol. 1221, file 593-1-7, vol. 1, Chief Thunderwater to Hodgins, 20 June and 29 Nov. 1916; Indian Mothers from Saugeen Reserve to Sir Robert Borden, 12 Oct. 1916; Smith to Scott, 1 Oct. 1916; RG 10, vol. 6765, file 452-7, Cooke to Scott, 28 Feb. 1916.

48 NAC, RG 24, vol. 1469, file 600-10-35, Sutherland to Hodgins, 18 Dec. 1916; RG 24, vol. 4599, file 20-10-52, Gayfer to Gray, 22 Nov. 1916; RG 9 III, vol. 81, file 19-9-40, Sutherland to Perley, 27 April 1917.

49 NAC, RG 24, vol. 4599, file 20-10-52, Gayfer to GOC Winnipeg, 23 Oct. 1916, to Gray, 22 Nov. 1916; RG 24,

vol. 1469, file 600-10-35, Stackford to McCurdy, 7 Sept. 1916; Sutherland to Hodgins, 17 Jan. 1917, to Kemp, 18 Jan. 1917; RG 24, vol. 4558, file 132-11-1, GOC Halifax to Sutherland, 5, 8, and 10 Sept. 1916; Ruck, *Canada's Black Battalion*, 24, and appendix interviews.

50 NAC, RG 24, vol. 1469, file 600-10-35, Gwatkin to Hodgins, 18 Sept. 1916; RG 24, vol. 1550, file 683-124-2, Militia Ottawa to GOC Halifax, 23 Jan. 1917; RG 24, vol. 4739, file 448-14-259, Gayfer to Cruikshank, 6 Sept., 18 Sept., 4 Oct., and 7 Nov. 1916, and replies, 9 Sept., 19 Sept., 10 Oct.; Cruikshank to Grant, 6 Nov. 1916; Aitken to Cruikshank, 9 Nov. 1916.

51 NAC, RG 24, vol. 4558, file 132-11-1, Hodgins to GOC Halifax, 31 July 1916, to Sutherland, 22 Dec. 1916. Sailing List, No. 2 Construction Battalion, 28 March 1917. Of the 603 enlisted men and non-commissioned officers (not including white officers), 342 were Canadian-born, 72 were West Indian, 169 American, and 20 of various other nationalities. Nova Scotia supplied 296, Ontario 207, and the West 33.

52 NAC, RG 9 III, vol. 81, file 10-9-40, Sutherland to Perley, 27 April 1917; McCurdy to Perley, 1 Oct. 1917, and reply, 1 Nov.; White to Stanfield, 18 Oct. 1917.

53 Brown and Loveridge, "Unrequited Faith," 55–56, 60–64, 67, appendix D, 76; Nicholson, *Canadian Expeditionary Force*, 344, 347, 350, appendix C, 546; Morton, *Military History of Canada*, 153, 156–58; Granatstein and Hitsman, *Broken Promises*, 60–104; A.M. Williams, "Conscription 1917: A Brief for the Defence," *CHR* 37 (1956): 338–51.

54 NAC, RG 10, vol. 6768, file 452-20, Mississauga of New Credit to Scott, 22 Oct. 1917, Nishga to prime minister, Nov. 1917; Chief Peter Angus to the King, 13 Nov. 1917; Committee of Allied Tribes to prime minister, 17 Nov. 1917; BC Indian agent to

department, 26 Nov. 1917; Chief John Prince to Scott, 27 Nov. 1917; Garden River Reserve to governor general, 4 Dec. 1917; Katzelash band to Department of Indian Affairs, 4 Dec. 1917; Kitzumkalwee band to department, 24 Dec. 1917; Michipicoten band to department, 5 Dec. 1917; Edmundston, NB, Reserve to department, 15 Dec. 1917; Manitoba Rapids Reserve to department, 24 Dec. 1917; Hurons of Lorette to governor-general, 10 Jan. 1918; RG 24, vol. 1221, file 593-1-7, vol. 2, Military Sub-committee to Chisholm, 28 Nov. 1917, and reply, 29 Nov.

55 DND, DH, minister of justice to Governor-General in Council, 31 Dec. 1917.

56 NAC, RG 10, vol. 6768, file 452-20, Scott to Ditchburn, 1 Dec. 1917, to Anaham Reserve, 14 Dec. 1917.

57 PC 111, 17 Jan. 1918; Military Service Regulations, sec. 12 and 16 as amended, 2 March 1918; PC 1459, 12 June 1918.

58 NAC, RG 24, vol. 1469, file 600-10-35, McLean to McCurdy, 10 Oct. 1917; McCurdy to Perley, 14 Nov. 1917; White to McCurdy, n.d.; Gwatkin to adjutant general, 21 Oct. 1917; Shannon to adjutant general, 16 Jan. 1918; McCurdy to Mewburn, 17 Jan. 1918, and reply, 21 Jan.; adjutant general to Shannon, 5 Feb. 1918; Shannon to adjutant general, 13 and 21 Feb. 1918; adjutant general, circular letter to commanding officers, Feb. 1918; White to Sir Robert Borden, 11 Aug. 1918.

59 Ibid., Young to Milligan, 13 March 1918; Shannon to adjutant general, 19 April 1918; adjutant general to Shannon, 24 and 30 April 1918; British-Canadian Recruiting Mission, New York, to adjutant general, 1 May 1918, and reply, 2 May.

60 Ibid., adjutant general to Brown, 8 May 1918, to Sutherland, 22 May 1918.

61 Ibid., White to Sir Robert Borden, 11 Aug. 1918.

62 Ibid., Bristol to Creighton, personal, 26 Aug. 1918; Creighton to AG Mobilization, 14 Sept. 1918; cable to commanding officers, 17 Sept. 1918, and replies; Creighton to Bristol, personal, 28 Sept. 1918. The record of black conscripts provided by commanding officers showed London, Ontario, 23, Toronto 10, Kingston 4, Halifax 55, Saint John 13. The Military Service Council asserted, however, that it had "no record of coloured men who are liable to draft, as all men are shown according to Nationality regardless of colour." Ibid., Captain Newcombe, memo, 25 Sept. 1918.

63 Ruck, *Canada's Black Battalion*, 37–39, and interview with Isaac Phills, 57.

64 Ito, *We Went to War*, 70 and appendix 3. Of 185 volunteers, 54 were killed and 119 wounded.

65 NAC, RG 9 III, vol. 5010, War Diaries, 107th Pioneer Battalion. In 1918 the 107th was disbanded and the men absorbed into an engineering brigade. See also Gaffen, *Forgotten Soldiers*, passim.

66 Ruck, *Canada's Black Battalion*, 65, interview with Sydney Jones of the 106th. At a black veterans' reunion in 1982, reference was made to 8 different units, besides the No. 2, in which the survivors had enlisted; ibid., ch. 6, Reunion and Recognition Banquet. Mr Thamis Gale of Montreal, himself a World War II veteran and whose father was in the No. 2, has been assiduously tracking down every black to serve in the CEF. From his as-yet unpublished results it appears that there may have been more than 1200 blacks in the CEF, which would mean over 600 distributed in various units outside the No. 2; personal communications, 16 and 24 June 1986 and 14 Feb. 1988.

67 NAC, RG 24, vol. 1469, file 600-10-35, Mobilization to Gwatkin, 19 Feb. 1917, and reply, n.d.; memo to naval secretary, 21 Feb. 1917 and reply, 23 Feb.; Hunt, *Nova Scotia's Part in the Great War*, 149–50.

68 NAC, RG 24, vol. 1469, file 600-10-35, Morrison to Bristol, 20 Dec. 1917; RG 9 III, vol. 1608, file E-186-9, director of forestry to YMCA, 9 June 1917; OC No. 12 District to Timber Operations, 17 Jan. 1918; OC No. 9 District to Timber Operations, 19 Aug. 1918; director of timber operations to General Headquarters, 28 Nov. 1918, and signal, 30 Nov. 1918; RG 9 III, vol. 4616, file C-B-8, assistant director to director, Chaplain Services, 20 Feb. 1918; RG 9 III, vol. 4645, folder 747, War Diaries, 2nd Canadian Construction Coy (Colored), vol. 11: 10, 13, and 22 March 1918, vol. 12: 14 and 17 April 1918, vol. 13: 18 and 12 May 1918.

69 There is of course a huge literature on the nature and extent of Western racist thought, and it is not considered necessary to recount its features here. Studies that explicitly set Canadian developments within a broader context, usually imperial or continental, include Carol Bacchi, "Race Regeneration and Social Purity: A Study of the Social Attitudes of Canada's English-Speaking Suffragists," *Histoire sociale/Social History* 11 (1978): 460–74; Carl Berger, *The Sense of Power: Studies in the Ideas of Canadian Imperialism, 1867–1914* (Toronto, 1970), and *Science, God, and Nature in Victorian Canada* (Toronto, 1983); Douglas Cole, "The Origins of Canadian Anthropology, 1850–1910," *Journal of Canadian Studies* 8 (1973): 33–45; Terry Cook, "George R. Parkin and the Concept of Britannic Idealism," *Journal of Canadian Studies* 10 (1975): 15–31; Robert A. Huttenback, *Racism and Empire: White Settlers and Colored Immigrants in the British Self-Governing Colonies, 1830–1910* (Ithaca, 1976); and Howard Palmer, "Mosaic Versus Melting Pot? Immigration and Ethnicity in Canada and the United States," *International Journal* 31 (1976): 488–528.

70 NAC, RG 9 III, vol., 1608, file E-186-9, Provisional Mobilization Store Table for a Labour Company, White to GHQ, 10 Jan. 1918, and reply, 14 Jan.

71 NAC, RG 9III, vol. 81, file 10-9-40, Morrison to Bristol, 20 Dec. 1917.

72 DND, DH, "Secret Information Concerning Black American Troops"; Foner, *Blacks and the Military*, 121–22; Balesi, "From Adversaries to Comrades," 112–13; Jeffrey Greenhut, "Race, Sex and War: The Impact of Race and Sex on Morale and Health Services for the Indian Corps on the Western Front, 1914," *Military Affairs* 45 (1981): 72–73; Willan, "South African Native Labour Contingent," 71–73.

73 Nelson, "Black Horror on the Rhine," passim; Robert C. Reinders, "Radicalism on the Left: E.D. Morel and the Black Horror on the Rhine," *International Review of Social History* 13 (1968): 1–28; John C. Cairns, "A Nation of Shopkeepers in Search of a Suitable France," *American Historical Review* 79 (1974): 718; Bernard Shaw, *What I Really Wrote About the War* (New York, 1932), 322–23; Robert A. Huttenback, *The British Imperial Experience* (New York, 1966), 175–89.

74 NAC, RG 9, III, vol. 1709, file D-3-13, Collier to OC Canadian Troops, 10 Jan. 1919; Ruck, *Canada's Black Battalion*, 58–60, interviews with Robert Shepard and A. Benjamin Elms. See also Desmond Morton, "Kicking and Complaining: Demobilization Riots in the Canadian Expeditionary Force, 1918–19," *CHR* 61 (1980): 341, 343, 356.

75 House of Commons, *Debates*, 20 June 1919, 3741.

76 Ito, *We Went to War*, 73; Roy, "Soldiers Canada Didn't Want," 343; Provincial Elections Act Amendment Act, *Statutes of British Columbia*, 1931, c. 21; War Time Elections Act, *Statutes of Canada*, 1917, c. 39.

77 See, for example, NAC, RG 24, vol. 2765, file 6615-4-A, vol. 6, secret memorandum no. 1, to all chairmen and divisional registrars, 20 Nov. 1941,

and order from adjutant general to all district commanders, 12 July 1943; RG 27, vol. 130, file 601-3-4, "Conscription of East Indians for Canadian Army"; DND DH, "Sorting out Coloured Soldiers" and "Organization and Administration: Enlistment of Chinese"; *The King's Regulations and Orders for the Royal Canadian Air Force*, 1924, amended 1943; *Regulations and Instructions for the Royal Canadian Navy*, amended by PC 4950, 30 June 1944. Ito and Roy give considerable detail on Chinese- and Japanese-Canadian efforts to enlist during World War II.

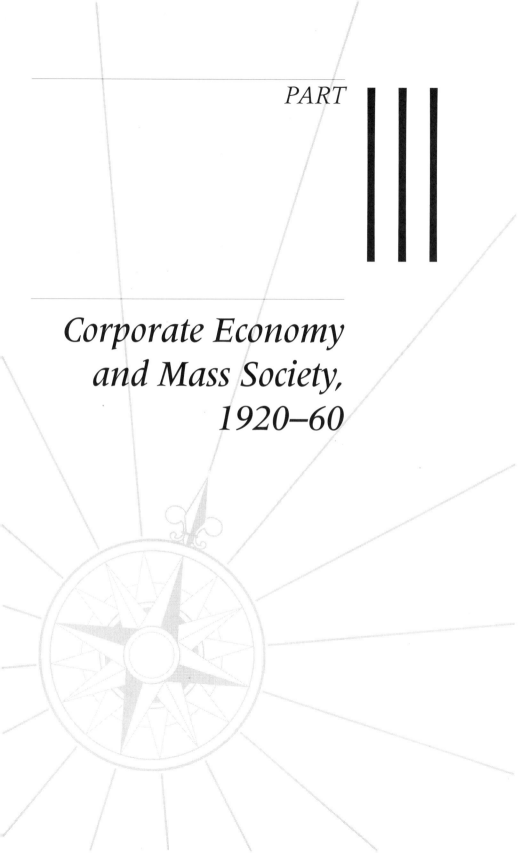

PART

III

*Corporate Economy
and Mass Society,
1920–60*

In studying the period beginning after World War I and ending with the 1950s, historians have recently placed a great deal of emphasis on the changing relationships among individuals, families, and the larger society. The first three readings in this section examine different aspects of the perceptions and experience of women and men in the context of a developing corporate economy and consumer society. The ambition of this research is to understand the actual meaning for specific people of the large-scale transformations of the twentieth century.

Cynthia Wright uses the history of Canada's best-known department store to explore the ways in which the history of women is a central theme in the creation of a national market in Canada. By focussing on Eaton's strategies for attracting consumers, Wright shows how department stores targeted women in order to transform shopping routines. More importantly, though, Wright also considers the consumer preferences of the women themselves, according to social class and cultural traditions. She argues for the importance of viewing shopping in terms of "gendered space" in which the spatial organization of society reflects the character of relations between men and women. Wright's article connects directly to Keith Walden's earlier study of grocery store window displays.

In recent years, researchers have taken a new interest in the method of oral history to reconstruct the everyday experiences of men and women. As Joy Parr and Mark Rosenfeld show in their accounts of work in small-town Ontario, memories can add substantially to our understanding of other forms of historical documentation. Parr's study benefits from the recollections of men who knew first-hand the meaning of working with wood, and of women who remembered their work with textiles as teenagers. She emphasizes the ways in which waged work was gendered and thereby played different roles in the construction of masculine and feminine identity. Rosenfeld addresses similar themes in the case of a railway town where, in most families, husbands were breadwinners and wives were homemakers. Like Parr, Rosenfeld uses a micro-historical approach in the belief that "analysing the historical constitution and reconstitution of class and gender relations within a specific community can help contribute to a better understanding of the way in which these relationships generally developed and changed over time." In other words, his ambition, like Parr's, is not simply to learn about one small town but rather to learn about large-scale social change in Canada.

The article by Ernest Forbes addresses aspects of Canada's political history during the Second World War. Forbes uses a regional focus to examine how federal policies contributed to regional disparity in Canada. Forbes's work reflects a growing tendency among historians to view national political history with considerable scepticism; from this perspective, federal policies are often seen as representing the best interests of only Central Canada.

The final article in this group of readings explores the relationship between political history and the social history of families. By studying the impact of family allowance policy on Canadian families, Dominique Marshall illustrates the ways in which a social historical perspective can contribute to a better understanding of high-level politics. The key difference between Marshall's approach and that of earlier researchers is her attention to the views and experience of both politicians and the ordinary families who affected and were affected by the politicians' actions. Her research reveals a "dialectic relationship between families and the state" and, thereby, emphasizes the connection between everyday life and parliamentary debate.

The readings in this section are thus important for the ways in which they distinguish between ambition and achievement. By studying the perspectives and experience of consumers as well as advertisers, workers as well as owners, voters as well as politicians, and families as well as legislation, historians are now reinterpreting the making of a corporate economy and mass society in twentieth-century Canada.

"*F*EMININE TRIFLES OF VAST IMPORTANCE": Writing Gender into the History of Consumption*

CYNTHIA WRIGHT

In 1928 the T. Eaton Company Limited began construction of Eaton's College Street, a major new store located at the southwest corner of Yonge and College streets in downtown Toronto.[1] Devoted largely to home furnishings, it was the first attempt to build a modern, city-oriented department store in Toronto. The College Street store was conceived as the culmination of a new merchandising strategy for Eaton's. Under the management of John Craig Eaton, founder Timothy's youngest son and successor, Eaton's began to go after the so-called carriage trade, Toronto's upscale market. In this regard, Eaton's was influenced by similar changes in retailing initiated by leading department stores in New York and London.[2] Not coincidentally, this was the same period in which the Eaton family, socially and financially, became the equivalent of a local Canadian aristocracy, particularly after John Craig Eaton was knighted in 1915 for his contribution to the war effort.[3]

While planned as early as 1910, the first stage of Eaton's College did not open until 1930.[4] Because of the Depression and certain building problems, the other stages were never built: only seven storeys were actually

*Franca Iacovetta and Mariana Valverde, eds., *Gender Conflicts: New Essays in Women's History* (Toronto: University of Toronto Press, 1992), 229–60. Reprinted with the permission of the publisher.

constructed, and the skyscraper remained an architect's dream.[5] Yet, whatever the difficulties of its conception, the opening of Eaton's College Street resulted in a tremendous amount of fanfare in the press, with such headlines as "Imposing New Store of Eaton Company Acclaimed by Public." The *Star* referred to Eaton's College Street as a "symphony in silver,"[7] and *Canadian Homes and Gardens* declared it "one of the few great stores of the world."[8] Eaton's College Street would operate for years as *the* arbiter of distinction and correctness for urban bourgeois women. This article will use Eaton's College Street as a case study from which to reflect on the historiographical and theoretical problems of writing about consumption, specifically shopping, in a gender-critical manner.

The department store has traditionally been the territory of the business historian. However, business-oriented studies of department stores have been narrowly defined and preoccupied with the question of entrepreneurship.[9] Recently, breaking with the constraints of business history, new writing by American and British social historians has identified the department store as a key bourgeois cultural institution.[10] These historians have pointed to some of the ways in which the department store can be understood as a business whose concern precisely was the dissemination of a class-defined taste and culture. Benson, for example, argues that "Department stores were . . . the agencies of a class-based culture, carrying the gospel of good taste, gentility, and propriety to those who could afford its wares."[11] Understanding the department store as a bourgeois cultural institution also enables us to see the gendered character of middle-class consumption, a perspective that the business history approach misses altogether.

The history of mass consumption is arguably central to an analysis of class and gender relations in twentieth-century Canada. Remarkably little Canadian work has been done, whether by labour, social, or feminist historians, to research and to theorize the impact of consumer culture.[12] This is striking given that Bryan Palmer, for example, argues strenuously in *Working-Class Experience* that by the 1920s a mass commercial culture had supplanted many aspects of local working-class culture, including the political traditions of the working class.[13] Along with some American writers, Palmer sees the development of mass consumer culture as an effective brake on the class struggle.[14]

Yet Canadian labour and working-class historians have concentrated for the most part on the productive sphere of social relations, investigating the history of factory and shop, the labour process, and the structure of labour relations. By contrast, as American historian Jean-Christopher Agnew argues, writing on consumer culture remains a "conspicuous absence" within historical scholarship.[15]

A history of consumer culture is necessary for an understanding of the specific experience of women. With industrialization, women were excluded from many areas of paid production, while consumption increasingly became a particular responsibility of women. By the twentieth century, shopping had come to form a major part of most women's lives.[16]

This article will begin by surveying some of the theoretical and methodological issues in the history of consumer culture, including some feminist perspectives. I will then turn to the Canadian context to explore how Eaton's department stores and mail-order catalogues were central to the formation of a national market. Along with national advertising, particularly for the new brand names, and the media, Eaton's reorganized local retailing practices and transformed women's shopping routines. Finally, drawing on my own work on the history of the Eaton's College Street store in Toronto, I will suggest how an account of mass consumption demands a rethinking of traditional approaches to source material.

• The Politics of Longing: Gender, Class, and Consumption

Theoretical work on mass culture is often burdened with elitist or conspiratorial assumptions. There has been a tendency in some analysis to focus on the irrationality of the consumer rather than on the irrationality of the way consumption is organized under capitalism.[17] Feminists have tended to be hostile to elitist formulations of consumer culture. In an early feminist polemic, "Consumerism and Women," for example, Ellen Willis scathingly attacked the sexist assumptions in a lot of what passed for cultural critiques, both radical and conservative, of postwar American affluence. "Consumer-as-idiot" theory, she argued, was essentially "woman-as-idiot" theory.[18]

Meg Luxton acknowledges the influence of Willis's essay on her own analysis of consumption as women's work.[19] Indeed, the dominant tendency within existing work on women and consumption has been to reject the popular, sexist construction of women's shopping as self-indulgence and to call attention to the fact that consumption management is an important, and socially unrecognized, aspect of women's domestic labour.[20]

Both Willis and Luxton were in explicit disagreement with the argument put forward by Betty Friedan in the early feminist text, *The Feminine Mystique*. Friedan basically posits women as the dupes of "the manipulators"—of advertisers and motivational researchers. For her, consumerism is nothing less than the mass deception of the middle-class American housewife, and certainly Luxton is correct to reject the behaviourism of this simplistic model of women and consumption.[21]

Luxton's own model of the housewife as ever-rational consumer in the face of the demands placed upon her by permanently dissatisfied household members is, however, not entirely convincing. For one thing, how is it that the housewife is able to remain impervious to the lure of advertising at the same time that the rest of the household, according to her analysis, is enthralled by it? Luxton does argue that wage levels in working-class households set real limits on the housewife: financial considerations, and her responsibility as consumption manager, force her to be "rational" in a way that other household members need not be.[22]

Luxton's approach assumes that consumption in the working-class household can be understood by what the woman actually buys. This assumption is shared by historians who, for the most part, have thought about consumption in terms of goods produced or the standard of living. One problem with this approach is that it interprets consumption as a series of *completed* acts.[23] It does not encompass window-shopping, consumer desire, or what Agnew refers to as "mental consumption."[24] From the point of view of experience, it may be just as important to understand what a woman desired but could never afford to buy.

For the working-class woman, the privileged object of desire was frequently fashionable clothing.[25] Social historian Carolyn Steedman's biographical account, *Landscape for a Good Woman*, details the structuring of one woman's unfulfilled desire for a single stylish item. Her working-class mother's longing for a Dior skirt runs powerfully throughout the text; indeed, Steedman writes, it "symbolizes the content of my mother's desire."[26] Steedman's mother, a weaver's daughter from the north of England, "came away wanting: fine clothes, glamour, money: to be what she wasn't."[27] Despite her roots in "a traditional Labour background," she became a working-class Conservative, "for the left could not embody her desire for things to be *really* fair, for a full skirt that took twenty yards of cloth."[28]

What are we to make of Steedman's account of her mother's longing? Should we see her mother as a victim of false consciousness, or as "bought off" by consumerism, despite the fact that she was never able to afford any of its benefits? Should we see her as a woman who, after her move to South London, was cut off from her working-class kin and the political culture of industrial Lancashire, and therefore susceptible to all the distractions of clothing and glamour? Such an approach is suggested by Palmer, who dismisses the mass culture of the 1920s as lacking the redeeming political value of the entertainments put on by the Knights of Labor.[29]

Steedman herself rejects these suggestions, arguing instead that in a curious way her mother's longing was an extension of her class traditions rather than an abandonment of them. Indeed, her class background shaped her longing in particular ways. As Steedman writes of the political culture out of which her mother came:

> The legacy of this culture may have been her later search, in the mid-twentieth century, for a public language that allowed her to want. . . . But within the framework of conventional political understanding, the desire for a New Look skirt cannot be seen as a political want, let alone a proper one. We have no better ways of understanding such manifestations of political culture than they

did in Burnley in 1908, when they used to say dismissively that "a motor car or carriage would buy a woman's vote . . . at any time."[30]

Steedman's discussion might apply to a brief account of working-class women and their longing for clothes that appeared in the Canadian left journal the *Woman Worker* in the 1920s:

> Two working women walked out of a big departmental store. Passing the big store front, one of the women stopped. She gazed enraptured at the window. Then she exclaimed with great fervour in her voice, "I do like that!"
>
> "That" meant a beautiful evening dress made of a delicate soft yellow material and highly bespangled. Of course she pictured herself in it—what woman wouldn't? But this is as far as working women get. They see the clothes they like always on wax models waiting for the woman who has the money.[31]

One of the things that is noteworthy about this passage is that it assumes that all women, regardless of class, want such things as diaphanous yellow evening dresses, an item of clothing every bit as extravagant as a Dior skirt. There is a kind of democracy of desire here, but class position sets clear limits on who will have access to the objects of desire.

I am not here arguing for a politics of consumption in which window-shopping and consumption are seen as acts of resistance on the part of working-class women. Rather, I want to suggest that the intersection between the world of clothing and working-class women was far more complex than any of the existing theoretical models can suggest. To date, most existing historical work on gender and consumption has concentrated on middle-class women, in part because they were at the centre of a key institution of late nineteenth-century consumption, the department store.

• Go Out and Buy: Middle-Class Women and the Department Store

In any account of modern, mass consumption, the department store and the middle-class woman shopper must figure prominently. Yet women have generally been absent in accounts written from a business history perspective. When women were studied at all, it generally was as department store workers.

Yet, historically, department stores have been a site *par excellence* of pleasure and social life for women, and, above all, middle-class women. As historian William Leach comments: "Feminization so marked the life of the stores that a twentieth-century historian of Macy's could write in 1943 that a department store was not a department store unless it 'catered primarily to women.'"[32] This observation is echoed by the 1969 popular history of Eaton's, *The Store That Timothy Built*, which declares: "A department store is . . . a woman's world, where she reigns supreme."[33]

Indeed, the first department stores were a new kind of public space for bourgeois women. In addition to selling goods, many stores featured reading rooms, art galleries, and lounges where women could rest and socialize with friends. Benson suggests that department stores operated as the equivalent for women of the downtown men's club, and included many of the features of the bourgeois home.[34] For this reason, some middle-class, nineteenth-century feminists celebrated the department store as an arena of freedom for women.[35]

Give The Lady What She Wants! a popular history of Marshall Field's first published in 1952, in an era committed to the gospel of freedom through consumption, is explicit about the links between department stores, shopping, and feminism, for the nineteenth century: "An offshoot of the Feminist movement was a vast buying spree in the early 1850s, led not only by the radicals but by the more numerous conservatives who wore crinoline hoop skirts."[36] The authors attribute this to the fact that no other places but the dry-goods and department stores would receive women and allow them to linger for hours: "Here an unescorted woman was received with deference, catered to, waited upon. Few other such retreats existed, even in Chicago. No lady would dare venture without an escort into a downtown restaurant, for she would not be served. There were no beauty shops, tearooms, clubrooms."[37] The ultimate goal of feminism, the pinnacle of freedom for women, is the right to buy without interference from husbands and fathers.

Give The Lady What She Wants! extols leading suffragist Elizabeth Cady Stanton for her militant defence of women's "right to buy for themselves, their children, and their households." The account of Stanton's story of "The Congressman's Wife" is worth quoting at length:

> To dramatize her appeal that women were partners in the family and should have the privilege of sharing the family purse, Mrs. Stanton invariably told her audiences her tremulous tale of "The Congressman's Wife." This unfortunate lady, she related, had an ill-equipped kitchen, with a faulty stove. Whenever her husband returned from Washington, he chided her about her poor cooking and miserable meals. The woman had been hysterical when she asked Mrs. Stanton for advice. "Of course you can't cook here!" Mrs. Stanton shrilled as she replayed the scene before avid crowds. "Go out and buy a new stove! Buy what you need! Buy while he's in Washington!"
>
> The housewife was horrified, Mrs. Stanton declared. It would never do! Her husband would be enraged! He bought everything, even her clothes! He might beat her!
>
> At this point Mrs. Stanton always paused to pierce the nearest male in her audience with an angry stare. Then she cried, "I told her—and I tell this to you women—'Go out and buy! When he returns and flies into a rage, you sit in a corner and weep. That will soften him! Then, when he tastes his food from the new stove, he

will know you did the wise thing. When he sees you so much fresher, happier in your new kitchen, he will be delighted and the bills will be paid.' I repeat—GO OUT AND BUY!"[38]

A similar set of links is made in the official history of Eaton's, *The Store that Timothy Built*, where we read that "the fact that the largest stores developed in North America was due to a singular phenomenon: the earlier emergence of American and Canadian women from the bondage which afflicted their sex in other parts of the world."[39] Again, women's freedom from "bondage" is measured in terms *of freedom to consume.* It is taken for granted that cultures that do not offer women many shopping opportunities are not only backward but patriarchal.

At least some first-wave feminists did indeed become enthralled by the possibilities of consumption as a yardstick of freedom. The nineteenth-century American dress-reform movement countered what was seen as the sexual enslavement of women by fashion with a rationalist commitment to physical hygiene and natural simplicity in clothing. But that critique proved no match for the allure fashion continued to hold for some feminists. Nor did it seem creditable in the face of the department store's promise of freedom for the middle-class woman and employment for her working-class counterpart.[40]

If the late nineteenth century had already seen the emergence of consumption as the definition of middle-class femininity and freedom for women, it was probably not until the 1920s that these sets of links became more widely circulated. There is now a substantial body of work which establishes that, by the 1920s, advertisers targeted women as the shoppers at the centre of the world of consumption.[41] "The proper study of mankind is *man,*" declared a journal of the American advertising industry in 1929, "but the proper study of market is *woman.*"[42] Advertisers were able to translate and rechannel early twentieth-century demands for more freedom and choice for women into a consumerist model of choice. An advertisement from a 1930 edition of the *Chicago Tribune* makes this link explicit: "Today's woman gets what she wants. The vote. Slim sheaths of silk to replace voluminous petticoats. Glassware in sapphire blue or glowing amber. The right to a career. Soap to match her bathroom's colour scheme."[43] As a number of feminist historians have argued, we need to understand the rise of consumerism in the 1920s within the context of the defeat after the First World War of feminist visions of collective housekeeping.[44]

This is not simply a feminist variant of Palmer's argument that consumerism was a brake on working-class militancy. Palmer argues, as have others, that the expansion of consumption in the 1920s resulted in the withdrawal of workers from their immediate community and their preoccupation with the narrower unit of consumption represented by the family.[45] Certainly, in many respects he is correct, as the middle-class craze for ideal homes and interior decorating testifies. But again, we need to pay attention to the contradictions and class differences in this process, for consumerism also gave women "public definition as consumers."[46]

Canadian feminist historians have pointed to the many ways in which both working- and middle-class women were involved in political activism from their position as consumers.[47] Moreover, for working-class women, and single women in particular, the allure of commercial culture was precisely that it was a route out of the confines of the household.[48] For some middle-class women with the means, the prospect of exercising some power within the arena of consumption was appealing. The department store setting catered to the middle-class woman's "sense of her class position and personal attractiveness"; as a result, some women used that class position to make what were frequently interpreted as unreasonable demands upon both saleswomen and male managers.[49]

Other middle-class women pursued careers as consumer experts; they advised manufacturers, retailers, and advertisers on how to appeal to women, but also acted as ambassadors for better living through consumption. By the late 1920s, "efficiency expert" Christine Frederick, who had written on the application of Taylorism to domestic labour, argued that the problem with scientific management was that it couldn't give women the "thrills" that shopping could. In her *Selling Mrs Consumer* (1929), she wrote: "One reason why so many women have failed to get a thrill out of scientific training in home economics or budget-keeping is because it is too strictly logical."[50] The new route to feminine fulfilment was via consumption. Frederick's women wanted "more kinds of food, more leisure, more athletics and sport, more education, more travel, more art, more entertainment, more music, more civic improvement, better landscaping and city planning, more literature, more social graces, more social freedom and more cosmopolitan polish and smartness."[51] In Canada, the store that tried to embody all these aspirations was Eaton's College Street, the "palace of consumption"[52] which opened in Toronto in 1930.

The College Street store was the culmination of a set of changes that had overtaken the Canadian retailing landscape in the decades before the store opened. In this next section, I will outline the role that department stores and mail-order catalogues played both in transforming retail practices and in the formation of a national market. From there, we will return to the College Street store.

•The Canadian Department Store and the Formation of a National Market

Daniel Horowitz has argued for the American context that "department stores and catalogues turned a series of local markets into integrated, national ones."[53] Although Canada's first department store opened in

1866, and Eaton's launched a mail-order catalogue in 1884, it was not until the 1920s that we can speak of a national market in Canada.[54] The 1920s saw a major enlargement in Eaton's mail-order organization, with the opening of one hundred order offices that enabled customers to walk in, make their selection from the catalogue, and have the order sent in by the sales staff.[55] Eaton's first French-language catalogue was produced in 1927.[56] By the end of the decade, Eaton's had forty-seven department stores and a nationwide catalogue sales system.[57]

The process of creating a national market was uneven and not without conflict. For settlers in isolated areas of Canada, the catalogue was a lifeline; however, it was also part of a set of changes in the organization of distribution and retailing. Nellie McClung recalls in her 1945 autobiography: "I remember very well the first ready-made dress I saw. A daring woman, Mrs. Bill Johnston, sent to Montreal for it and sent the money, fifteen dollars, mind you, and the neighbours cheerfully prophesied that she would never see the money again or the dress either. But the dress came and even the doubters had to admit it was a good-looking dress."[58] McClung adopts here her familiar tone of gentle satire, inviting us to be amused by the "backwardness" of Mrs Johnston's neighbours, but this should not distract us from noticing some of the changes in shopping routines and practices to which this passage points.[59]

These changes include, among others, a greater trend towards the buying of ready-made clothing, with the result that clothing made at home frequently came to signal poor or immigrant status;[60] the practice of paying a fixed price and cash only for purchases, rather than relying on combinations of credit, barter, and bargaining; and an increasing orientation towards national retailers instead of, or in addition to, local ones. Sending away for goods, with one's scarce cash, required trust in the process of buying goods not produced locally by people one knew.[61]

These incursions by national retailers into local markets were strongly resisted. As in the United States, where in some communities catalogues were publicly burned, there were those who thought department stores and their mail-order catalogues pernicious.[62] With less commercial development in Canada, one retail firm could quite conceivably monopolize the market. Newspapers refused advertisements from Eaton's to avoid the anger of local merchants. In small towns, where the general merchant was often the postmaster, mail-order catalogues would disappear or meet with destruction. For this reason, catalogues were sometimes mailed in plain wrappers. Ordering from a mail-order catalogue could provoke economic sanctions, particularly in the Maritime provinces.[63]

Mail-order catalogues were strongly resented by rural merchants, but the urban department store came under fire as well. In the late nineteenth century, department stores were vilified in tracts that accused them of feeding on the blood of women and children.[64] Referring to Eaton's, a writer in *Saturday Night* magazine declared: "It is not necessary for me to give some recital of the shame practised by this or other department stores."[65] Another issue of *Saturday Night* carried a mock department store advertisement that savaged department store retailing practices such as saturation advertising and constant bargain sales. The ad put the blame squarely on the gullibility of the woman shopper: "Thousands of ladies visit our store every day, brought here by our cunning advertisements. . . . The ladies— bless 'em—are our game. If it wasn't for them we couldn't make the thing work at all. Men are not so easily caught, but the women just fall into our trap by the thousand. . . . Darling woman! It is you that makes the department graft a possibility."[66] *Saturday Night* gave its support to the campaign by the Retail Merchants' Association of Canada for legislative restrictions on department stores, a campaign that met with little success.[67]

In the 1930s, at the height of the Depression, department stores would again come under fire when the Royal Commission on Price Spreads carried out an investigation of the chain-store phenomenon in Canada.[68] While the big stores continued to be heavily criticized by small retailers, the fact is that the large retail stores had undercut their critics by building an empire on a firm foundation: the newly created mass buying public.

The 1920s, particularly the latter half of the decade, were a period of major expansion for the department store in Canada. This was remarked upon at the time in an article in the Canadian architectural magazine, *Construction.* The article noted that expansion was noticeable in two ways. First, smaller communities were being pulled into the orbit of the department store:

> To the observer of building and business developments of today it is obvious that the department store, even in communities of modest magnitude . . . is taking a continually larger and actually present place in their business life. This is occurring in a large number of centres. Even in the prairie cities such as Calgary, Saskatoon and Edmonton, to name no others, points which in the personal experience of men not over the threshold of middle age were little more than Hudson bay trading posts with a few satellite smaller stores and business establishments about them, the trend is evident.[69]

Second, in the city centres in which department stores had long been established, the big retail stores were "extending their premises, and the scale and variety of their mercantile operations and services."[70]

This expansion brought concentration: by 1929, three department stores (Eaton's, Simpson's, and the Bay) commanded 80 percent of all department store sales and some 10 percent of the retail market.[71] (There were an estimated twenty to twenty-five different department stores in Canada in 1930.)[72] After 1931, when they cornered a peak 12.6 percent of the Canadian retail market[73] (12.8 percent in Ontario[74]), department stores never again enjoyed a bigger share of the retail pie. Eaton's College Street was the last major store to be built before the department store began to lose ground, as the combined effects of the Depression and competition from discount chain stores such as Kresge's (particularly noticeable in Ontario and British Columbia) took their toll.[75] While the *Construction* article celebrated "the metropolitan sense of things" that the department store brought to smaller centres, local retailers resented the competition intensely.

Many factors combined to account for the expansion of department stores for this period. Urbanization and population growth were certainly important. The Canadian population grew by 63.6 percent (3.4 million people) between 1901 and 1921, and by 16.2 percent between 1921 and 1930. Changes in transportation, most notably "the production of a gasoline-powered automobile . . . brought about a dramatic increase in the trading area [i.e., the number of potential customers] of department store customers."[76] Certainly, the introduction of instalment buying, available to Eaton's customers beginning in 1926, was a major force for department store growth.[77] The significance of the extension of credit cannot be overemphasized. As Strong-Boag points out, "given average annual wages that in 1929, for example, were $1200, and conservative estimates of the minimum budget required to maintain an average Canadian family, $1430 in the same year, domestic survival often relied on credit."[78]

Although retailers such as Morgan's, Ogilvie's (both of Montreal), Simpson's (Toronto), and the Hudson's Bay Company were all growing in the interwar period, it was Eaton's that was unquestionably in the lead. For example, while the Hudson's Bay Company probably initiated the trend towards the building of branches, Eaton's rapid construction of branches in seven provinces within a space of two decades probably put it ahead of rival stores.[79] Moreover, Eaton's was the department store with the biggest sales in Canada. By 1930, Eaton's had 7 percent of the Canadian retail share, making it the department store with the biggest sales in Canada and the eighth largest retailer in the world.[80]

Of course, Canadian regional differences made for an uneven growth process. For example, Eaton's did not open stores in British Columbia until 1948, when it bought out nine stores from David Spencer Limited.[81] It was not until 1955 that Eaton's had department stores in all ten provinces.[82] However, numbers of retail stores in the various provinces is not the only way of measuring the retail influence of a department store or its percentage of the retail market share, for Eaton's massive mail-order system ensured that sales would be generated even where the company had no department stores.

While I have focussed on the importance of the mail-order catalogue and the department store for the formation of a national market, it would be a serious mistake to ignore other key contributors, among them the growth of a nationally distributed media, the development of saturation advertising, and the coming of nationally advertised name brands. In both the United States and Canada, the advertising agency and the brand name were part of the retail landscape by the last two decades of the nineteenth century. A nationally distributed media, however, lagged behind in Canada.[83]

Again, it was the 1920s that emerge as the decisive decade. For one thing, it was not until the early 1920s that, for the first time, the majority of Canadians lived in cities and towns, thereby providing one of the preconditions for the growth of nationally distributed magazines.[84] This period saw the first publication of new mass-market magazines aimed at women, including *Canadian Homes and Gardens* (1924) and *Chatelaine* (1928).[85] As we shall see, such magazines, together with the city newspapers, were particularly active in organizing relations to the urban department store.

• "A Symphony in Silver": The Eaton's College Street Store

Of all the Canadian department stores, it was Eaton's that best defined a class-based "taste." Herbert Irvine, for example, who began to work in Eaton's College Street's decorating department in 1935, was an arbiter of distinction for the Canadian elite for thirty years. A journalist wrote of Irvine that "his superior taste and feeling for period design were sought after by the cream of the country's architects and matrons ('If you didn't get Herbert Irvine,' says a woman who did, 'you didn't exist')." Another individual commented, "Herbert taught everyone. He started the whole chain of taste in Toronto."[86]

The newspaper account reads as if Irvine was able to influence so many by sheer innate "taste," but his career must be understood in relation to the department store's position as a bourgeois cultural institution. This does not mean that we simply replace an individual source of "taste" and "distinction" (Irvine) with an institutional one (the department store). Rather, it involves situating a store such as Eaton's College Street within a complex set of relations involving advertising, the media, the organization of credit, and the arrangement of space. In what follows, I will look at only two of these factors: Eaton's College Street and the media, specifically the new women's magazines; and the department store's interior design and architecture.

The department store is often studied in relative isolation, even by historians such as Benson who see the department store as a microcosm in which all the class and gender contradictions of the society are reflected and re-enacted.[87] It is also important to be aware of the ways in which the local media, primarily the daily newspapers and mass-circulation magazines, organized relations to Eaton's College Street. In the same way that advertising "naturalizes" the commodity,[88] so the media operated to define and celebrate Eaton's College Street as an important site of social life, excitement, and taste.

While large-circulation women's magazines certainly existed in Canada before the 1920s,[89] it was this decade which saw the founding of important new periodicals, among them *Canadian Homes and Gardens* (1924–62), *Mayfair* (1927–61), and *Chatelaine* (1928–).[90] With the growth of nationally distributed media, magazines began to target particular audiences.[91] For example, while *Chatelaine* aimed for the broad middle class, *Canadian Homes and Gardens* and *Mayfair* both aimed for a more upscale female readership.

Interestingly, editors of both *Canadian Homes and Gardens* and *Chatelaine* had histories of working in department-store advertising. Samuel McIlwaine, editor of *Canadian Homes and Gardens* in the 1940s, had worked for Simpson's.[92] *Chatelaine* had a long-standing history with Eaton's. Bryne Hope Saunders, editor of *Chatelaine* for the years 1929–42 and 1946–51, worked as an advertising copywriter for Eaton's for three years.[93] Mary-Etta Macpherson, who replaced Saunders during the war years, wrote a popular account of Eaton's, *Shopkeepers to a Nation: The Eatons*, which was serialized in *Chatelaine*.[94] Doris Anderson, who became *Chatelaine* editor in the 1950s, was another "graduate" of Eaton's advertising department.[95] But the relationship between the large-circulation women's magazines and the department store was more complex than simply one of overlapping personnel. One example is the relations among Eaton's College Street, upmarket magazines such as *Canadian Homes and Gardens,* and the modernist movement in furniture and design.

In the summer of 1925 the Exposition Internationale des Arts Décoratifs et Industriels Modernes was held in Paris. For the first time, "the domestic interior was the subject of an international exhibition of this size" and all "the latest ideas in furniture and interior decoration" were on display.[96] Eaton's College Street, when it opened five years later, enthusiastically embraced the modernist movement. An advertisement announcing the opening of the store observed: "Nowhere is the newness of the new era more apparent than at home. . . . In the minds of the homemaker and her husband is the common knowledge of decorative values; starched lace curtains and three legged tables could never have happened now."[97] This "common knowledge of decorative values" was located, at least in part, in textual sources.

Canadian Homes and Gardens, for example, devoted a special issue to the modernist movement in interior decoration, and observed in an editorial that "true, Europe has been sending us warnings. . . . Now a thoroughly comprehensive exposition of *art moderne* has been given to us with the T. Eaton Company's enterprising show."[98] A 1930 number of *Canadian Homes and Gardens* devoted several pages to Eaton's College Street's famous period furniture rooms, declaring: "In this 20th Century, stores and their merchandise are news. Because of their definite and daily influence upon the lives and the taste of millions, it is essential that the public's buying centres show leadership and a sense of responsibility. Any shop that makes a sincere effort to lead its patrons along the paths of good taste and good values is worthy of consideration."[99] Magazines such as *Chatelaine* and *Canadian Homes and Gardens* were part of the production of this common knowledge but they also identified Eaton's College Street as *the* site of taste in furniture and interior decoration, the link between Canada and the Paris-based modernist movement in design.

Eaton's, for its part, actively fostered the relationship between the store and American mass women's magazines that also had high circulations in Canada. Speakers from *House Beautiful* and *Ladies' Home Journal* were brought to Eaton's College Street to popularize the new ideas about home decoration.[100] Moreover, Eaton's College Street was itself, spatially and architecturally, a lesson in the modern decorative arts movement, as the advertisements for the store constantly emphasized. Indeed, the spatial organization of the College Street store provides a particularly fruitful source for historical analysis.

• Space and the Department Store

The analysis of space is an important key to department stores, since it suggests a way to understand one of the most interesting of the big stores' structural contradictions: while based on the retail principle of free entry and the freedom to browse without obligation to buy, they are constrained to organize in various ways the thousands of customers who go through their revolving doors each day.[101] While the department store, in theory, was open to all, barriers of class and ethnicity were there. In the first pages of her autobiography, for example, Gabrielle Roy recounts with bitterness the humiliation that often accompanied her mother's attempts to negotiate service in French in the Eaton's store in Winnipeg.[102] Such experiences were no doubt reinforced by the refusal of department stores to hire among certain ethnic groups. "Italians," according to Robert Harney, "knew that one needed to change one's name and hide one's origin to clerk in the big department stores."[103]

The spatial organization of the department store can be understood at a number of levels. One approach is to examine the relationship between the department store and the city. Elizabeth Ewen has argued that department stores in New York City moved progressively uptown away from the downtown working class—that is, the primarily Jewish and Italian garment workers who made the fashionable clothes for the big stores.[104] In broad outlines, the same development occurred with Eaton's in Toronto. Eaton's College Street did not have adjoining factories, as did the earlier Eaton's, located further south on Queen.[105] Interestingly, according to Macpherson, the original plan was that Eaton's would relocate *"in toto* from the old downtown location."[106] Aside from the building problems, Macpherson outlines two other factors which, in the end, went against the centralization of Eaton's at College Street. Both, significantly, related to women's shopping patterns.

Eaton's worried that women in downtown office jobs who shopped at Eaton's Queen Street store on their lunch hours would not transfer their business one mile north to College Street. Second, if Eaton's moved northward, it would be leaving behind the Simpson's store which, since 1872, had always been steps from its biggest competitor. It was "the habit of several generations of Toronto women to visit both the department stores on every shopping-trip."[107] Eaton's did approach Simpson's about sharing the Yonge–College corner but, according to former Simpson's president C.L. Burton, they simply did not have the capital to take advantage of the opportunity.[108]

The architecture of the Eaton's College Street store also set it apart from its sister store on Queen. Timothy Eaton (in contrast to his contemporary, Robert Simpson) had been uninterested in the possibilities of architecture for creating an image for a department store. While the Queen Street store was a "confused collection of buildings of varying dates," the architecture of the College Street premises was planned with a view to "the transformation of the store's image."[109] Or, as a 1930 advertisement for the store put it, "It will be something new in Toronto, won't it, to talk of Eaton's in the architectural terms of Greece and Rome. . . . While building on these noble, eternal principles the architects, withal, have not been unmindful that the store opens in 1930, in the restless age that wants change."[110] Certainly the store was intended to be, in size and commercial terms, the leading Canadian department store of its time. It was also designed, and this was particularly true for the store's spectacular Art Deco interior, with a view to distinguishing it from anything else that had hitherto been the tradition for Canadian retail building.

At the level of the interior space of Eaton's College Street, the store's non-selling space is as central as its counters and cash registers. One of the most interesting arguments made by Benson in her *Counter Cultures* is that the key distinction between department stores and other forms of selling merchandise is in the non-selling arena, "the world of bourgeois gentility and lavish service": "Using an elaborate array of services to create an ethic of consumption that transcended individual sales, the palace of consumption was the department store's peculiar contribution to the consumer society."[111] The non-selling arena was vital to Eaton's College Street. Its famous seventh floor ("the climax and showpiece of the entire store"[112]) consisted of the Eaton Auditorium (one of the most important concert and lecture halls in the city), the elegant Round Room restaurant, and a large foyer or lounge. The Eaton Auditorium was used for concerts, featuring musicians from Glenn Gould to Lady Eaton herself, many of which were broadcast on the radio. It was also the venue for lectures from leading couturiers and decorators.

Indeed, a 1931 advertisement for Eaton's College Street declared that the Eaton Auditorium was not merely a functional hall, but was meant to be an object of study:

> Come to a lecture, if only to see the EATON Auditorium. That alone will amount to a lesson in Interior Decoration. Study its lighting, its colour scheme, the placing of its mirrors, its exquisite simplicity and fine proportion and you'll have gained a good idea of what the modern movement stands for when interpreted by such brilliant exponents as Jacques Carlu, the designer of the Auditorium.[113]

This same advertisement begins with the headline, "No, it isn't enough these days for a man or woman to talk books, art, music—one has got to be up on all the rights and wrongs of INTERIOR DECORATION," and continues, "One of the big purposes of the EATON Auditorium is to popularize this fascinating subject."[114]

This College Street advertisement, interestingly, is one of the very few that addressed both men and women. Most advertisements assume a female audience, and structure the store as "feminine space." An advertisement that appeared in the *Globe* ten days before the opening of the store begins: "Of course, there's a woman in the case. A woman's as essential to a store like this as Helen to the tale of Troy."[115] *Construction* described Eaton's College Street as certain to become "one of the most prominent rendezvous of the feminine Toronto."[116]

"Feminine space" meant not just a place where women might comfortably browse and shop, but a sense that the spatial organization of the store's interior was feminized. A pre-opening advertisement of the Elevator Arcade of Eaton's College Street declared:

> each group of elevators is a different color. . . . How much easier to grasp 'Take the Green Elevators, Madame' than the old befuddling reference to the points of the compass or the right or left hand. Moreover, for the usual mirror of the elevator de luxe has been substituted a clock—a bit of optimism on the part of the designer to the effect that punctuality is a keener instinct than vanity.[117]

In a short description of elevators, this text manages to suggest that women are both vain and unable to orient themselves spatially without the use of colour (rather like elementary school children). Another advertisement from the same period, this time for the small shops within Eaton's College, cries: "Little Specialty Shops—isn't the mere sight of them to the smart woman as the song of the lark to the poet or the scent of the fox to the pack?"[118]

Department store managers have long assumed certain principles of the spatial organization of gender; for example, it is rare to find the men's clothing section above the main floor in major department stores because it is thought that men will not plunge into "feminine territory" much beyond the first floor.[119] Examples such as these from Eaton's College Street suggest that historians must learn to read "against the grain" the spatial dynamics of class and gender in the department store.

• Conclusion

We need a history of consumer culture in Canada, not just because it is a "gap" that urgently needs to be filled, but because it is a key component of understanding the reorganization of class and gender relations in the twentieth century. The existing theories and approaches to consumerism and the department store are inadequate, given the complexity of the material the historian has to analyse. We need to think in some new ways about the sources, in view of the limitations of approaches based largely on quantitative data and archival materials. This is not to suggest that we abandon these two traditional sources since, for one thing, the full holdings of the huge Eaton's archives have never been analysed and, second, we need much more concrete information than we have about real incomes in the 1920s and about who, in fact, was able to afford the consumer goods then available. But we also need to pay attention to evidence such as spatial organization or relations between the store and the media because they enable us to get at the full complexity of gender and class relations within and without the department store.

Finally, for historians of women, the study of consumer culture is a rich site for research into gender relations apart from the more common subject areas of work and family. Not only is consumption gendered in fundamental ways, historically and in the present, but there is a vast diversity in what women subjectively make of that fact, from women who hate shopping to those wearing T-shirts with the slogan, "A woman's place is in the mall." This explicit turnaround of the anti-feminist notion that "a woman's place is in the home" suggests the continued resonance of the nineteenth-century idea that shopping is the ultimate feminine pleasure and liberation.[120] From the first department stores to the contemporary mall, feminist historians of consumer culture have a great deal of fascinating links to uncover.

• Notes

[1] The phrase, "feminine trifles of vast importance," is from an advertisement for Eaton's College Street that appeared in *Canadian Homes and Gardens* 7, 12 (Dec. 1930): 86.

[2] William Dendy, *Lost Toronto* (Toronto: Oxford University Press, 1978), 157.

[3] Mark Starowicz, "Eaton's: An Irreverent History" in *Corporate Canada*, ed. Wallace Clement (Toronto: James, Lewis and Samuels, 1972), 9–13. See also Lady Eaton's memoirs, *Memory's Wall: The Autobiography of Flora McCrea Eaton* (Toronto: Clarke Irwin, 1956).

4 As early as 27 March 1912 the *Toronto World* made the plans for Eaton's College Street front-page news, revealing that Eaton's had been secretly buying up land at the corner of Yonge and College streets for the purpose of building a ten-storey store. The date of 1910 for the first plans for Eaton's College Street is cited by Hilary Russell, "Eaton's College Street Store and Seventh Floor" (unpublished paper, Canadian Parks Service, 1983), 395.

5 Russell, "Eaton's College Street," 395–96.

6 *Globe* (Toronto), 31 Oct. 1930, 13–14.

7 *Toronto Daily Star*, 29 Oct. 1930, 27.

8 *Canadian Homes and Gardens* 7, 12 (Dec. 1930): 85.

9 Michael B. Miller, *The Bon Marché: Bourgeois Culture and the Department Store, 1869–1920* (Princeton: Princeton University Press, 1981), 6.

10 Ibid., 3. For other examples of this recent work see Susan Porter Benson, *Counter Cultures: Saleswomen, Managers, and Customers in American Department Stores 1890–1940* (Urbana: University of Illinois Press, 1986); Rachel Bowlby, *Just Looking: Consumer Culture in Dreiser, Gissing and Zola* (New York: Methuen, 1985); Elaine S. Abelson, *When Ladies Go A-Thieving: Middle-Class Shoplifters in the Victorian Department Store* (New York: Oxford University Press, 1990); William Leach, "Transformations in a Culture of Consumption: Women and Department Stores, 1890–1925," *Journal of American History* 71 (Sept. 1984): 319–42; William Leach, *True Love and Perfect Union: The Feminist Reform of Sex and Society* (London: Routledge and Kegan Paul, 1981), esp. ch. 9. For one of the few studies of consumerism and working-class women see Elizabeth Ewen, *Immigrant Women in the Land of Dollars: Life and Culture on the Lower East Side, 1890–1925* (New York: Monthly Review, 1985).

11 Benson, *Counter Cultures*, 4.

12 For an exception see Veronica Strong-Boag, "Keeping House" in *The New Day Recalled: Lives of Girls and Women in English Canada, 1919–1939* (Toronto: Copp Clark Pitman, 1988).

13 Bryan Palmer, *Working-Class Experience: The Rise and Reconstitution of Canadian Labour, 1800–1980* (Toronto: Butterworths, 1983), 190.

14 For an influential discussion of the impact of consumerism on class relations and political democracy in the United States see Stuart and Elizabeth Ewen, *Channels of Desire: Mass Images and the Shaping of American Consciousness* (New York: McGraw-Hill, 1982). See also Stuart Ewen, *Captains of Consciousness: Advertising and the Social Roots of the Consumer Culture* (New York: McGraw-Hill, 1977), and his *All Consuming Images: The Politics of Style in Contemporary Culture* (New York: Basic Books, 1988). For an overview of theories of popular culture as the end of civilization and democracy see Patrick Brantlinger, *Bread and Circuses: Theories of Mass Culture as Social Decay* (Ithaca: Cornell University Press, 1983).

15 Jean-Christophe Agnew, "The Consuming Vision of Henry James" in *The Culture of Consumption: Critical Essays in American History 1886–1980*, ed. Richard Wightman Fox and T.J. Jackson Lears (New York: Pantheon Books, 1983), 67.

16 For one account of this transformation see "Consumption and the Ideal of the New Woman" in Ewen, *Captains of Consciousness*.

17 Fox and Lears, *Culture of Consumption*, xv–xvi.

18 Ellen Willis, "Consumerism and Women" in *Woman in Sexist Society*, ed. Vivian Gornick and Barbara K. Moran (New York: Basic Books, 1971), 480–84. Compare Fredric Jameson, "Pleasure: A Political Issue" in *Formations of Pleasure* (London: Routledge and Kegan Paul, 1983), 4.

19 Meg Luxton, *More than a Labour of Love: Three Generations of Women's Work in the Home* (Toronto: Women's Press, 1980), 172.

[20] Ibid., 168–73. Daniel Horowitz notes that "in history of women as consumers, housework has received the most concentrated attention." See his *The Morality of Spending: Attitudes Toward the Consumer in America, 1875–1940* (Baltimore: Johns Hopkins University Press, 1985), 200.

[21] Betty Friedan, *The Feminine Mystique* (New York: Dell, 1963), 218; Luxton, *More than a Labour of Love*, 172.

[22] Luxton, *More than a Labour of Love*, 162.

[23] Agnew, "Consuming Vision of Henry James," 69.

[24] Ibid., 73.

[25] Middle-class observers often associated working-class women's love of fashionable clothing with sexual immorality. See Mariana Valverde, "The Love of Finery: Fashion and the Fallen Woman in Nineteenth-Century Social Discourse," *Victorian Studies* 32, 2 (Winter 1989): 169–88; Kathy Peiss, *Cheap Amusements: Working Women and Leisure in Turn-of-the-Century New York* (Philadelphia: Temple University Press, 1986).

[26] Carolyn Steedman, *Landscape for a Good Woman: A Story of Two Lives* (London: Virago, 1986), 24.

[27] Ibid., 6.

[28] Ibid., 47.

[29] Palmer, *Working-Class Experience*, 197–98.

[30] Steedman, *Landscape for a Good Woman*, 121 (second ellipsis is in the original).

[31] "I Do Like That!" *Woman Worker* 1, 10 (April 1927): 6. I am indebted to Janice Newton for referring me to this source.

[32] Leach, *True Love and Perfect Union*, 234.

[33] William Stephenson, *The Store that Timothy Built* (Toronto: McClelland & Stewart, 1969), 142.

[34] Benson, *Counter Cultures*, 83. The construction of the department store as "feminine space" may also be seen at

work in nineteenth-century novels such as Zola's *Au Bonheur des Dames* (1883) and Dreiser's *Sister Carrie* (1900). For a discussion of Zola, Dreiser, and the department store see Bowlby, *Just Looking*, ch. 4 and 5. For more on Zola see Miller, *Bon Marché*, and Rosalind H. Williams, *Dream Worlds: Mass Consumption in Late Nineteenth-Century France* (Berkeley: University of California Press, 1982).

[35] Leach, *True Love and Perfect Union*, 26.

[36] Lloyd Wendt and Herman Kogan, *Give The Lady What She Wants! The Story of Marshall Field and Company* (Chicago: Rand McNally, 1952), 30.

[37] Ibid., 32.

[38] Ibid., 29.

[39] Stephenson, *Store that Timothy Built*, 141–42.

[40] Leach, *True Love and Perfect Union*, 260.

[41] See, for example, Michael Schudson, *Advertising, the Uneasy Persuasion: Its Dubious Impact on American Society* (New York: Basic Books, 1984), 61 and 173; Strong-Boag, *New Day Recalled*, 85 and 116; William Leiss, Stephen Kline, and Sut Jhally, *Social Communication in Advertising: Persons, Products and Images of Well-Being* (Toronto: Methuen, 1986), 112 and 114.

[42] *Printer's Ink*, 7 Nov. 1929, as quoted in Nancy F. Cott, *The Grounding of Modern Feminism* (New Haven: Yale University Press, 1987), 172.

[43] *Chicago Tribune*, 1930, as quoted in Cott, *Grounding of Modern Feminism*, 172.

[44] Strong-Boag, *New Day Recalled*, 117 and 120. Dolores Hayden, *The Grand Domestic Revolution: A History of Feminist Designs for American Homes, Neighborhoods, and Cities* (Cambridge: MIT Press, 1983), esp. 281–89; Rayna Rapp and Ellen Ross, "The Twenties' Backlash: Compulsory Heterosexuality, the Consumer Family, and the Waning of Feminism" in *Class, Race and Sex: The Dynamics of Control*, ed.

Amy Swerdlow and Hanna Lessinger (Boston: G.K. Hull, 1983), 93–107.

45 Palmer, *Working-Class Experience*, 190–92.

46 Leach, *True Love and Perfect Union*, 213.

47 Strong-Boag, *New Day Recalled*, 118; Ruth A. Frager, "Politicized Housewives in the Jewish Communist Movement of Toronto 1923–1933" in *Beyond the Vote: Canadian Women and Politics*, ed. Linda Kealey and Joan Sangster (Toronto: University of Toronto Press, 1989), 258–75; Joan Sangster, *Dreams of Equality: Women on the Canadian Left, 1920–1950* (Toronto: McClelland & Stewart, 1989), 138–40; Christine Foley, "Consumerism, Consumption and Canadian Feminism" (MA thesis, University of Toronto, 1979).

48 Ewen, *Immigrant Women in the Land of Dollars*, 106–7; Peiss, *Cheap Amusements*.

49 Benson, *Counter Cultures*, 5. Other middle-class women used their ready access to department stores as a means to investigate saleswomen's working conditions. See, for example, Ontario Archives, Pamphlet Collection, *The Work of Women and Girls in the Department Stores of Winnipeg. Being the Report of the Civic Committee of the University Women's Club after a Study of the Condition of the Work of Women and Girls in Department Stores*, 1914.

50 Christine Frederick, *Selling Mrs Consumer* (New York: Business Bourse, 1929), 22. For a discussion of Frederick's shift in emphasis from efficient housekeeping to consumption, see Annegret S. Ogden, *The Great American Housewife: From Helpmate to Wage Earner, 1776–1986* (Westport, CT: Greenwood Press, 1986), 158.

51 Frederick, *Selling Mrs Consumer*, 31.

52 The phrase is Benson's. See her *Counter Cultures*, 81.

53 Horowitz, *Morality of Spending*, xxvii.

54 James Bryant cites Morgan's of Montreal as the first Canadian department store. See his *Department Store Disease* (Toronto: McClelland & Stewart, 1977), 17. On the Eaton's mail-order catalogue see "The Scribe," *Golden Jubilee, 1869–1919: A Book to Commemorate the Fiftieth Anniversary of the T. Eaton Co.* (Toronto: T. Eaton Co., 1919), 150–60.

55 Stephenson, *Store that Timothy Built*, 89.

56 Ibid., 186; "as far back as 1899 Eaton's was inviting *Canadiens* to correspond with it in Canada's other official language, assuring them of replies in the same tongue" (192).

57 Simpson's, of course, also began a mail-order business, but Eaton's catalogue dominated from the beginning. See Michael Bliss, *Northern Enterprise: Five Centuries of Canadian Business* (Toronto: McClelland & Stewart, 1987), 292.

58 Nellie L. McClung, *The Stream Runs Fast: My Own Story* (Toronto: Thomas Allen, 1945), 47. I am indebted to Alison Prentice for drawing my attention to this passage.

59 Strong-Boag, *New Day Recalled*, 113 and 114, emphasizes the unevenness of the transformation to consumer society, even for middle-class people, as does Susan Strasser for the American context. See her *Satisfaction Guaranteed: The Making of the American Mass Market* (New York: Pantheon Books, 1989), 110. Barter, for example, remained a reality for many cash-poor Canadians right into the twentieth century. See Enid Mallory, *Over the Counter: The Country Store in Canada* (Toronto: Fitzhenry and Whiteside, 1985), 55, 57.

60 Mary Antin, an Eastern European Jewish immigrant, recalls in her autobiography: "A fairy godmother to us children was she who led us to a wonderful country called 'uptown,' where, in a dazzlingly beautiful palace called a 'department store,' we exchanged

our hateful homemade European costumes, which pointed us out as 'greenhorns' to the children on the street, for real American machine-made garments, and issued forth gloried in each other's eyes." *The Promised Land* (London: William Heinemann, 1912), 187.

61 For a discussion of these changes in the American context, much of which is relevant for Canada, see Strasser, *Satisfaction Guaranteed.* See also Bliss, *Northern Enterprise.*

62 On catalogue burnings see Robert Hendrickson, *The Grand Emporiums: The Illustrated History of America's Great Department Stores* (New York: Stein and Day, 1979), 214. "There were even firebombings of department stores across the country" (32).

63 Stephenson, *Store that Timothy Built,* 48. According to a document probably prepared by the Eaton's Archives, there was far less resentment of mail-order catalogues in Canada than in the United States. City of Toronto Archives, Business Firms (pre-1900) File, Anonymous, "Some Information on the Beginning of Eaton's Catalogue and Mail Order," n.d.

64 One example is an unsigned tract, "Departmental Stores. The Modern Curse to Labor and Capital. They Ruin Cities, Towns, Villages, and the Farming Community." It is undated, but the Canadian Institute for Historical Microreproduction, from which I obtained a microfiche, places it in the 1890s.

65 *Saturday Night,* 31 July 1897, as quoted in Fraser Sutherland, *The Monthly Epic: A History of Canadian Magazines 1789–1989* (Markham, ON: Fitzhenry and Whiteside, 1989), 89.

66 *Saturday Night,* 27 Feb. 1897, as reproduced in Sutherland, ibid., 89.

67 Sutherland, ibid., 89. The final line of "Departmental Stores. The Modern Curse to Labor and Capital," states: "Read the Barnums of Business as to the trickery of Departmental Stores, Published by 'Saturday Night.'" On

the lack of success of the anti-department store campaign see Bliss, *Northern Enterprise,* 363, for Canada, and Strasser, *Satisfaction Guaranteed,* 215, for the United States. Sutherland notes that, by the early years of this century, *Saturday Night* was carrying "numerous ads for the Eaton Company." *Monthly Epic,* 92. This no doubt was interpreted by the anti-department store forces as further proof that department stores controlled the press through massive injections of advertising revenue.

68 There are no book-length or even substantial accounts of the Royal Commission on Price Spreads, although many Canadian social historians mention it in passing. For two brief discussions from different perspectives see Starowicz, "Irreverent History," 13–20, and Bliss, *Northern Enterprise,* 425. Short excerpts from workers' testimony have also been published in various anthologies. See, for example, Irving Abella and David Millar, eds., *The Canadian Worker in the Twentieth Century* (Toronto: Oxford University Press, 1978), 184–94.

69 "Department Store Growth in Canada," *Construction* 21, 12 (Dec. 1928): 401.

70 Ibid.

71 Statistics Canada, Merchandising and Services Division, *Department Stores in Canada, 1923–1976* (Ottawa: Queen's Printer 1976), 9. This was one of the findings of the Royal Commission on Price Spreads.

72 Ibid., 9.

73 Ibid., 25.

74 Ibid., 74 (table 10).

75 Ibid., 17. For evidence that Ontario and British Columbia lost the most ground, see 28.

76 Ibid., 15.

77 Ibid., 16.

78 Strong-Boag, *New Day Recalled,* 114.

79 Statistics Canada, *Department Stores,* 14.

80 Ibid., 16.

81 Stephenson, *Store that Timothy Built*, 106.

82 Ibid., 118.

83 "The first Canadian advertising agency, Ansom McKim, was set up in 1889; others followed to promote the emerging name brands and department stores. But, though there might be national advertising, there was a dearth of nationally distributed media." Sutherland, *Monthly Epic*, 113.

84 Ibid.

85 Indeed, Sutherland suggests that Canadian women's magazines were among the first and most important mass periodicals in the country. *Monthly Epic*, 153. Compare Leiss et al., *Social Communication*, 80.

86 Adele Freedman, "A Master of Tradition: Life for Herbert Irvine Is a Matter of Taste," *Globe and Mail*, 8 Nov. 1986.

87 Benson, *Counter Cultures*, 8.

88 Agnew, "The Consuming Vision," 72.

89 According to Sutherland, *Canadian Home Journal* (1905–59) was "the first modern women's magazine." It later merged with *Chatelaine*. *Monthly Epic*, 156 and 206.

90 Sutherland notes that "Between 1928 and 1933, the circulations of *Canadian Home Journal*, *National Home Monthly*, and *Chatelaine* had all roughly doubled. That the increase and onset of the Depression were simultaneous was one signal that a strongly supportive mass audience was in place." *Monthly Epic*, 160.

91 Leiss et al., *Social Communication*, 79–82.

92 Ibid., 163.

93 Ibid., 160. Sutherland calls her Byrne Hope Sanders, but I believe he has incorrectly spelt her name. Compare Alison Prentice et al., *Canadian Women: A History* (Toronto: Harcourt, Brace, Jovanovich, 1988), 297.

94 Sutherland, *Monthly Epic*, 163; Mary-Etta Macpherson, *Shopkeepers to a Nation: The Eatons* (Toronto: McClel-

land & Stewart, 1963). Macpherson was also an editor with *Mayfair*, *Canadian Homes and Gardens*, and *The Canadian Home Journal*.

95 Sutherland, *Monthly Epic*, 246.

96 Witold Rybczynski, *Home: A Short History of an Idea* (New York: Viking, 1986), 180.

97 *Globe*, 28 Oct. 1930, 18.

98 *Canadian Homes and Gardens* 5, 11 (Nov. 1928): 15.

99 Ibid., 7, 12 (Dec. 1930): 85. For a description of the period rooms see Ellen E. Mackie, "And So to Eaton's—College Street," in the same issue, 85–91, 107.

100 See the Eaton's College Street advertisement of speakers on home decoration, *Globe*, 27 March 1931.

101 Susan Porter Benson, "Palace of Consumption and Machine for Selling: The American Department Store, 1880–1940," *Radical History Review* 21 (Fall 1979): 200–1. This article has been central to my understanding of space as a source for analysing the department store.

102 Gabrielle Roy, *Enchantment and Sorrow: The Autobiography of Gabrielle Roy*, trans. Patricia Claxton (Toronto: Lester and Orpen Dennys, 1987), 3–8.

103 Robert F. Harney, "Ethnicity and Neighbourhoods" in *Gathering Place: Peoples and Neighbourhoods of Toronto, 1834–1945* (Toronto: Multicultural History Society of Ontario, 1985), 15. While working-class and immigrant people often had a conflicted relationship to department stores, this does not mean they did not patronize them. See Varpu Lindström-Best, "Tailor-Maid: The Finnish Immigrant Community of Toronto Before the First World War" in *Gathering Place*, 221.

104 Elizabeth Ewen made this point during the "Women as Department Store Customers, 1870–1940" workshop at the Sixth Berkshire Conference on the History of Women, 1–3 June 1984, Smith College.

105 Indeed, the prospect of Toronto's retail centre of gravity shifting northward particularly animated the *Toronto World*, 27 March 1912: "What The World is most concerned about is telling the people of Toronto that the down town district has been settled as the financial part of Toronto and that there will be, in a very few months, little or no retail business below Richmond-st [sic].... The seat of the retail business of Toronto must go up town with the same forcefulness that it has gone up town in New York, and is now going up town in Montreal."

106 Macpherson, *Shopkeepers to a Nation*, 83.

107 Ibid., 84.

108 C.L. Burton, *A Sense of Urgency: Memoirs of a Canadian Merchant* (Toronto: Clarke, Irwin, 1952), 214–15. Burton was a former president of Simpson's.

109 Dendy, *Lost Toronto*, 157.

110 "Eaton's Daily Store News," *Globe*, 18 Oct. 1930.

111 Benson, *Counter Cultures*, 81.

112 Dendy, *Lost Toronto*, 159.

113 *Globe*, 27 March 1931.

114 Ibid.

115 Ibid., 20 Oct. 1930.

116 Sinaiticus, "Eaton's College Street Store, Toronto," *Construction* 23, 11 (Nov. 1930): 356.

117 *Globe*, 23 Oct. 1930.

118 Ibid., 25 Oct. 1930.

119 Stephenson, *Store that Timothy Built*, 140 and 142–43.

120 For an interesting account of contemporary cultural representations of "feminine" pleasures see Rosalind Coward, *Female Desire: Women's Sexuality Today* (London: Paladin, 1984).

FOR MEN AND GIRLS:
The Politics and Experience
of Gendered Wagework*

JOY PARR

• Men Work Wood

In an essential and visceral way, in their connection to the wage, the men who made furniture in Hanover in 1900 were different from the carpenters and cabinetmakers who had tramped the Garafraxa Road into the new counties of Grey and Bruce. Both in making and in earning they had lost that equivocal but discernible autonomy artisans had claimed. Few had lived or could even recall the craftsman's day, "going out through the snow to a board pile, selecting stuff, carrying it in and after scraping off the snow in winter, or sweeping off the dust in summer, laying of the stuff with a chalk-line . . . dressing it up with a jack plane . . . mortising by hand, cutting tenons and shoulders with a backsaw."[1] Yet to assert that "the working life of the furnituremaker changed from that of skilled craftsman to day labourer"[2] would construe too narrowly what gave the work meaning. In the factory the processes of craft production retained their distinguishable satisfactions. Furniture remained a good appreciated for its beauty as well as its usefulness, still valued most for the careful hand work which made it rare and distinctive. A Canadian poet writing in 1925 captured a continuity that withstood changes in scale and technology.

*The Gender of Breadwinners: Women, Men, and Change in Two Industrial Towns (Toronto: University of Toronto Press, 1990), 165–86. Reprinted with the permission of the publisher.

Each man to his trade. Thank God for mine.
To fashion out of the hearts of trees
Some lasting beauty, from oak or pine . . .
To make the cradle, to shape the chair . . .
Each man to his trade—each is good . . .
But we who work with pungent wood
Are serving mortals and serving art . . .
A greater boon I would never ask
Than curling shavings around my feet,
And the sawdust smell that is always sweet.

The sensual pleasures that came from working in wood, the honour of making something that would endure and be treasured because it had been crafted—the best and right word—with care, infused the tasks in the distinctive departments of the furniture factory with a significance drawn from grounds entirely separate from the wage. A man who had worked in the machine room at Knechtel with his father and his uncles and gone on into public life to work in cabinets of another kind spoke as a craftsman's son of factory-made goods, "I think of the designs they made, those older traditional designs, and the quality. There is something deliciously heavy in wood. You have to have a certain love for the stuff and for what they put into it."[3]

John Richards, thinking about the transformation from workshop to factory production, thought "the wood workmen's occupation . . . greatly changed" but not "like Othello's, gone."[4] The wood workmen's work continued to confer manliness. There was a comforting certainty that making these strong and aromatic materials into beautiful, useful, and timeless goods was fitting work for a man, work that both secured and constituted his manly identity. Perhaps this is why Othello came to Richards's mind. The contrast he wished to draw was not defensive but observing. Neither wage payment—nor steam power and the belts and gears of modern machinery—had severed the vital essence that made masculine the men who fashioned objects from wood, no matter how partial their participation in the process of the making had become.

Woodworking was a vocation that fathers passed to sons, that men learned by watching other men. In its resplendent variety it seems to confound easy attribution by gender. From some it demanded strength, from some the toleration and taste for danger. Amputations were "the woodworker's trademark." From others it called for the most scrupulous discernment, the ability to capture and render the most subtle variation, to work to fine scale with the most delicate of tools. The unity and honour in this diversity made, and was made in, gender. In the noise and danger, the proudly hierarchical work relations of the machine room, in the quiet deliberating equality of the cabinet shop, the heat and rush and vaporous pall of the finishing department—the experience of work was starkly different but the claim to and by the work was the same.[5] Paul Willis has made this point well: "whatever the specific problems of the difficult task, they are always essentially masculine problems, requiring masculine capacities to deal with them." The factory system, the partition of craft skills, and the subordination and vulnerability of the wage had taken away from the significance of the work within class relations. But burnished and cherished as continuity and compensation was the value of this complex of tasks as a way to mark worth between men, as men, and to mark them in their gender as apart from that saliently absent other.[6]

The most hierarchical workplace within a furniture factory was the machine room, where parts were shaped from dimensioned stock, and its antecedent annex, the break-out department, where rough boards were cut and glued into standard sizes. This was where most entry level jobs in the plant were located and where the differentiations between men retained the closest analogies with the relations between fathers and sons in agriculture and masters and apprentices in the crafts. Most men felt indebted to older male kin—fathers, uncles, or elder brothers for intervening to secure them their first place in the plant: "if he knew the foreman, he would maybe say, 'Give him a chance.' That's possibly the only way you would get a chance."[7]

Most began as the junior helper, the "tailer" taking away stock being fed through the machine by a senior worker on the "front end." Evidence of the ladding system which governed work in the machine room emerges clearly in the twin peaks in the age distribution of the department (figure 1). There were exactly as many men in their fifties as men in their twenties at work in the room in 1938, with a scattering of other workers spread in between. Here, too, was the full hierarchy of earnings in the plant most readily apparent. The best paid and the least well paid of Knechtel employees were about equally represented in the department (figure 2).

Progressing through the hierarchy in the machine room was a schooling in patriarchal relations, which young men learned and later reproduced. As boys got their jobs through the interventions of male kin, so later they gained the experience and knowledge they would need to succeed to a machine of their own through their personal relationships with older men in the room. Even after Knechtel tried in the 1920s to install a scientific management regime in the plant, machine operators in practice retained the right to choose their successors. Young men amiably bore a measure of deprecation in token for this dispensation. Henry Gateman, describing events of the late 1930s, remembered:

> Sam Colby. He run the mattison lathes. He was getting older and they wanted somebody to take it over. There was different ones suggested and he said no, they're nice fellows to me, but I'm not teaching them anything. They said, who would you suggest? He said, get Henry down, that's me. . . . I was grateful to him because, I asked him one day, why are you showing me all this. And he said, well, I

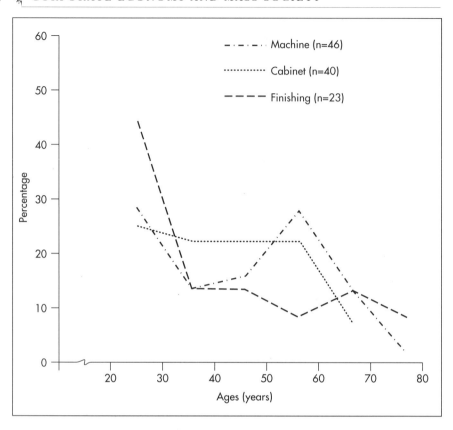

FIGURE 1: *Age Distribution of Employees by Department, Knechtel Main Plant, 1938*

always got along with you and I like you. And he said, one thing about you is you're a little like an elephant—when I teach you something, you never forget.

In later years Gateman confidently replicated this pattern. "If I had a somebody working with me and I didn't care for him, I wouldn't tell him a lot of things they should know. Where if I did, I'd explain it down to as much as I knew about it." A young man could not learn enough to run a machine merely by being present in the room and observing; older men were frugal with their knowledge, their only job security, willing to train only a successor who would acknowledge the teaching as a personal favour and not betray the trust by displaying precocious mastery of the work. In this patriarchal thicket of patronage and deference, by definition the best-placed men were sons with fathers working in the room. Karl Ruhl was candid about the process. Although he benefited by his kin connections, he saw the highly personalized barriers to knowledge about the machines as "one of the big faults" at Knechtel. He recalled as a tailer asking the router operator for whom he worked how to read the design drawing for their

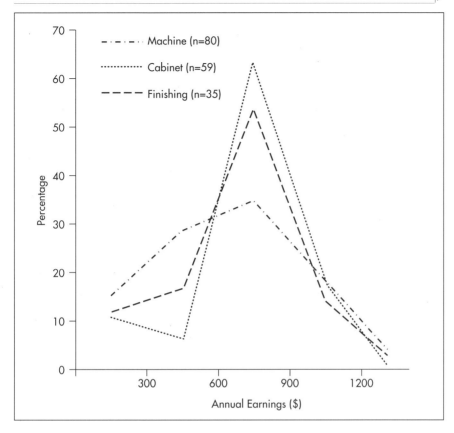

FIGURE 2: *Distribution of Annual Employee Earnings by Department, Knechtel Main Plant, 1938*

machine and being told, "Go ask your Dad." After months of doing what he called "joe boy" work in the veneer room, Ruhl got his first good job in the plant, doing waterfall bending, an intricate process that his father had been the first in the plant to master. Among relatives the passing on of knowledge was a legacy and in practicality a loan. Male kin kept some joint entitlement to whatever earnings the bequeathed information might command.[8]

There was no shift work at Knechtel. Each operator retained exclusive responsibility and control of his machine.[9] Each piece of equipment was demanding in its own way. The highest paid man in the machine room, and in the plant, was the saw filer. His job was to braze, or fashion, and then properly tension band-saws, a task that required many years of study and experience to master. In 1938 when the average Knechtel employee took home $639 for the year, the saw filer, Cameron Peppler, earned $1367. Cameron, age forty-two, had learned this work from his father, Alex, who in 1938 was sixty-seven, and continuing as the only other filer, part time.[10] Next best paid were the men who ran the shaper, the moulder (colloquially the "sticker"), and the router, all of whom earned over $1000 in 1938. These workers had to grind their own knives from small, quarter-inch-thick plates of steel, mounting and balancing the knives in revolving cutter heads to suit the demands of each new design.[11] In each of these cases the capacity of the machine was both limited and extended by the ingenuity and experience of the operator. Much sanding continued to be done manually in the interwar years, but if a firm had an expert belt-sander, one "of those alert inventive men, the kind who is always devising new forms, new hand blocks and new devices for holding and in some cases moving the work," the continuously running band of abrasive on a mould sanding machine could be jigged to do a large proportion of this work. Here too the best worker was a man of long experience who could remember just that wrinkle that had worked once years before.[12]

The workhorse of the machine room was the double-end tenoner, a substantial piece of equipment which could tackle a piece of stock from four sides at once. The tenoner was fitted with multiple cutting heads, powered by separate motors which could be set to run at different speeds. The operator needed considerable facility in interpreting the designer's drawings as well as the ability to grind knives, position heads, and set speeds to achieve the specified effect. The two Knechtel tenoners each earned 50 percent more than the average wage in 1938.[13] Although furniture workers' skills had become more specialized, like craft proficiencies they continued to be regarded as personal attributes, which gave a man worth and allowed him to command authority over other, especially younger, men.

In the machine room men most valued the variety in their work and the sense of control and autonomy they experienced as they appraised the stock and retooled the equipment for each new task.[14] They gained stature among their peers, and extra pay, because their work was dangerous. Cutting speeds were much higher in woodworking than metalworking plants; variations in the density of the stock and shifts in the direction of the grain might cause a board unaccountably to buck back against the operator's body, or the cutting head to explode in a dangerous shower of flying knives. Because the cutters were being repositioned frequently, it was difficult to design effective multi-purpose guards. On the mattison lathe and the shaper, where "the woodworker's trademark" frequently was made, there were no automatic feeds; each piece of stock had to be manhandled into contact with the spinning knives. There could be no "day-dreaming" on the machine room floor and, even in jobs that demanded considerable forward planning from the operator, no "thinking about something other than what you're doing at the time—even though it is pertaining to your work."[15] The danger, both emanant and imminent in the work, lurking hidden in the grain and texture of the fine and fragrant wood, men tolerated, even embraced, for the extra pay such tasks were assigned—but as much, and perhaps more, for the manly character the work demanded and conferred—the toughness, the steely nerve, the hardiness which could be called courage.[16]

Technological change did not alter radically the experience of working in the machine room during the interwar period. In unadjusted dollars, earnings in the department were about the same in 1938 as in 1928, although the dispersion of the income distribution had narrowed.[17] Briefly in the mid-1920s Knechtel experimented with the use of teenaged workers in front of rip saws and jointers. But the picture of Jane Kunsenhauser, the only female employee in the Knechtel machine room, often used in Canada Machinery Company ads was deceptive. The new equipment installed in the main plant in the 1920s and 1930s substituted electric motors for steam power, and ball for babbitt bearings. Higher-speed, steel cutting heads were built into heavier frames. Together these changes meant that each of the eight to ten set-ups an operator installed in a day could be put in place more quickly and accurately and was more likely to hold its tolerance, without adjustment, for the length of the run.[18] Rather than taking experienced operators from work they had mastered, younger men usually were assigned these machines, on the grounds that they had less to unlearn and would be more willing to press the new equipment to its higher production limits.[19] This, and the Depression concern to provide work for men with young families, probably accounts for the decline in the average age of workers in the machine room from forty-eight years to forty-three between 1928 and 1938. Men still read drawings, cut knives and blocks, calibrated set-ups, and scrutinized stock, but the most ornery machines in the room had, in some measure, been tamed. Older skilled workers were not displaced, but the proportion of machine-room operators in the upper tail of the income distribution, those earning over $1200 yearly, declined from 10 percent in 1928 to 4 percent ten years later. There was a certain levelling but not a lowering of earnings in the room, and the key instruments to confer patronage and demand deference among the men remained intact.

Boys grew in manliness as they rose, by favour and deference, through the ranks in the room. But all, from the tailer to the saw filer, were secured alike in their self-respect as men by doing work that was men's alone to do. "I got out of school and I got working, even though I didn't keep my money, I got working with other fellas. And I always liked working with other fellas." For a time during the Second World War, women worked in numbers in the machine room, but the discomfort with their presence was acute on all sides. Accounts of their injuries were made exceptionally graphic and were explicit about gender differences:

> This was in a machine that was about five feet long. A chain that goes right in the knives. She got her hand in there and she run it half way through the machine. I was on the other side of the room and I seen it happen and I run quick and caught it before it got up to the knives and took her hand out. It was just about that thick, just squashed flat. And she fainted, and I grabbed her and carried her to the office.

The coda to this story, "They took her to the hospital. She was back again though. Just crushed," was not meant to matter as much to the listener as was the depiction of the event itself. Men were described as having been carried out of the room unconscious, but never as having fainted. The girl's response was made womanly by the man's diction, and she thereby was defined, whether she came back again or not, as an inappropriate co-worker in the room. Women themselves described the work as unfitting, not because of the danger, but because of the readiness to take charge which being in front of a machine required.

> I worked about five years. Mostly take away. The men had the upper hand there and so they should as far as that goes. We were just their helpers. None of us were trained. We just went in to sweep floors, whatever we could do that we could be hired.
>
> Q: Most men I've talked to weren't trained when they arrived there either.
>
> They were men, so they stepped in and took over.

The dynamic in gender relations here—"The work was for men. For the responsibility, the danger, for everything else"—is very much like that Cynthia Cockburn describes among printers. It mattered terribly that there be a settled understanding of who men and women were, that there be confirmation that this was work women could not do, and that men were superior because they could.[20]

Upstairs in the cabinetmaking shop, work relations were very different from those in the machine room. The age distribution was remarkably even, by comparison with other departments in the factory. In 1938 men in their twenties, thirties, forties, and fifties were about equally represented in the cabinetmaking shop (figure 1). One by one, younger men were taken into the department as, one by one, older men left. The average age in the room remained steady through the interwar period, at about forty-one years.[21] Newcomers worked beside old hands, working with them, rather than for them, in stark distinction from the "tailers" down below. Many had been first employed in the machine room, where the most "first jobs" in the factory were to be had, but they entered the cabinet shop on a footing of relative equality. Despite the broad range of ages working in the room, the earnings of cabinetmakers did not vary greatly from man to man. The majority of the sixty men in the cabinet shop in 1938 earned somewhere around $700; only one earned over $1200; only six took home less than $300 for the year (figure 2).[22]

There was a progression through the range of tasks in the shop, but a man moved from working among men doing one job, on to working among men doing another. There was no ladding in the room. Newcomers began putting together small pieces, usually drawers, and after a time moved on to the case clamps, where they assembled the supporting members, the gables, for cabinets and chests. Those longest in the room worked "on the bench," selecting and trimming parts for each assembled case. The bench hands worked doors and drawers so that they moved smoothly but with a pleasing sensation of solidity in the case, choosing pieces that came together visually and physically into a harmonious whole.

Whereas within the machine room, hierarchy was a sphere of action in which each man played his part—young men worked to form deferential relationships as helpers which would smooth their succession to their own machine, older men appraised and selected among pretenders to their station—in the cabinetmaking shop work histories were recalled in the passive voice: "They moved me along to making drawers. So I was there eleven years making drawers. Then they decided that I should go on bench and hang doors and drawers and fit them. Dining room, bedroom, cellarettes, wine cabinets. Anything on hinges. That's how I got there." The "they" was a single "he," the foreman, but in the cabinet shop he seemed outside, almost marginal to, the significant workplace relationships. He is almost never identified by name. Cabinetmakers recalled exactly who had worked beside them, at the desk clamps, the case clamps, and the bench, but they did not see being put to that task as the product of a personal relationship; they made plural and anonymous the single man who had selected them for the work. The process of succeeding towards and to the bench was described in organic rather than political terms, as a matter of mortality: "They put a newcomer in when one fellow would drop over and die. They mostly died off. They'd put a man right beside you. I had them on either side of me. You'd teach them and do your own work too, you know." Teaching was not a matter of discretion or patronage, but a matter of course.[23]

The emphasis upon horizontal rather than vertical work relations in the cabinet shop emerges clearly in discussions of work pace. Pace and quality were seen as closely related, and necessarily and appropriately within the purview of the cabinetmakers themselves rather than the foreman.

> You'd set a nice little pace to that work and you carried it on day after day. . . . You had an idea of how long it would take you to do this and how long it would take you to do that. You just went along. You could see what the other man was doing . . . the two guys on each side of me, that's Bill Colby and Sam Wise, they worked on each side of me and they were very steady guys [, which made them] very good cabinetmakers.[24]

The setting made it easy for cabinetmakers to observe and confer with one another. The men on the bench line worked at stations set six feet apart along the windows facing the main street on the third floor of the factory. With no machinery, there was "not near the noise in the cabinet shop. Just maybe when they're hammering something together and that's only a few minutes," and no belting or equipment to disrupt lines of sight. Younger men who tried to rush the pace learned by observation rather than instruction that steadiness, the cabinetmaker's highest compliment, and deliberateness and economy of effort yielded the best results.

Q: Is bench a hard job?

I wouldn't say that. It's steady. It's really interesting. That's what I like about it. You always learn something. . . . I know some of the fellows would come up to me and say, I don't know how you do it. You're taking your time and we're going like heck and you're keeping up with us. Well, I said, you have to deal with your common sense. I said, the more you hammer, then the more you have to fix it. That's where they got behind. They were trying to speed up.

When the firm tried an incentive production scheme after the Second World War, the whole bench line opted out for two years. Their settled "steady" pace was rated as 70 percent of a day's work. "We says, no, 70 percent was a day's work. You could make more if you want to. We just worked—70 percent was a day's work so that's what we did. Then you could make your job right, you know, too. If the wood was warped, or something like that, you've got to straighten that out. That's what we did." Even piecework for cabinetmakers was an oddity in the industry. Early on the industrial engineers came to realize that, whatever might apply in the rest of the plant, "one [was] just as far ahead with a crew of reliable cabinet makers working at so much per hour."[25]

In the 1920s the cabinetmakers had been, on average, the least well-paid workers in the factory; by the late 1930s their earnings ranked highest. The "hand skill"[26] that cabinetmakers admired and emulated in one another retained its authority with the employer as well. The bench hand's initials on the back of each cabinet he completed were not only a device by which the quality of his work could be checked, but an affirmation of the standards he espoused. Work relations in the cabinet shop, where a man worked among men rather than for a particular man, where learning was by self-directed observation rather than submission to authority, created a group of men confident in their identities as men and as workers, who would play a leading role in industrial unionism in town in the 1930s and after.

It is possible to say least, and in fact nothing at all, from the point of view of the men themselves, about work in the finishing room. No one who had experience as a finisher in the interwar years survives in Hanover. In retrospect it is plain that the work was the most dangerous in the plant; at the time the finishing department probably was most conspicuous for the rapid rate at which technological change was transforming the finisher's work. The new manner of working was more hazardous than the old, but neither the health implications of the change nor the appropriate remedies were immediately apparent.

Until the First World War most finishes at Knechtel were applied by hand. An experienced man dipping a brush into a pot of oleoresinous varnish, the standard coating at the time, could finish four chairs per hour. After the war, an entirely new technology, borrowed from the automobile industry, was put into place. Finishers now worked with spray guns rather than brushes, applying nitrocellulose lacquers. Because four times as much lacquer was emitted into the air as came to rest on the furniture, each finisher worked inside a booth which confined the dispersion of the spray. The new process was prodigal of materials but, in the strictly technical sense of the word, labour saving. One man with a helper could now process twenty-four chairs per hour.[27] Engineers, aware that naptha gas, seeping down towards the boiler, might cause an explosion and that fumes from fillers and stains escaping from the finishing department would make workers in other parts of the plant nauseated, emphasized the need for proper ventilation. At the time nitrocellulous lacquers were acknowledged as more "capricious" but not as more pernicious than varnishes.[28] Even in 1923 finishing was a young man's job, and it became ever more so as the years went on (figure 1).

Two-thirds of the men in the plant worked in the machine, cabinet, and finishing rooms; the rest were employed in the last stages of the production process, rubbing down finishes, upholstering chair seats, affixing mirrors and trimmings, and preparing the goods for shipping. The only long-term female employees here were Augusta Krug and Elizabeth Wisler, both widows, who ran sewing machines in the upholstery department. Wisler and Jane Kunsenhauser were the only two women working in the factory in 1923; ten years later the number was the same. By tradition, furniture making was men's work, "for the danger, for the responsibility, for everything else." In the interwar years in Hanover the claim was undisputed. In learning the work boys learned to be men; the performance of the task both tested and secured their manly identities. Both for the local political economy and for the dynamics of family life in the community—and indeed for the men themselves—what was essential about the gendering of this work masculine was not its apparent and considerable diversity, but the agreement that by right if not by reason it was men's alone to do.

• Girls Can Work

Women's work in town remained largely outside the market. For a time in the 1890s there was a small woollen and knitting mill in Hanover which employed young women for wages, but the firm was never a thriving enterprise, and by 1901 it had ceased operations.[29] The wives of town manufacturers and merchants hired girls to do light housework; the proprietors of the two town hotels employed diningroom girls and linen maids; but servant keeping was not general in Hanover and most daughters who remained in town worked at home alongside their mothers until they married.[30]

The score or more female artisans in Hanover were dressmakers and milliners. Unlike the wood workman's crafts, those of the women bespoke trades that had not been consolidated into large-scale enterprises. Some female craft workers became proprietors, but their businesses remained small, sustained by the skills of one woman and usually conducted in premises loaned or leased from a man. Milliners were waged employees, engaged spring and fall by the three general merchants in town. Only one local milliner, Miss Barltrop, ran her own fancy-goods shop and engaged her own apprentices.[31] Dressmakers were more commonly proprietors conducting their businesses from rooms above the stores on the main street. They, like the milliners, emphasized the skill and knowledge they had gained by working in larger fashion centres, usually Toronto or Detroit, yet at the turn of the century their new position as independent proprietors retained elements of the itinerant seamstresses' role. Under the heading "Fashionable Dressmaking" Miss L.M. Bricker advertised herself in 1897 as "late of Detroit, now permanently located in Hanover" and willing to "take in or go out sewing by day. Style and satisfaction guaranteed. Rooms above Lorenz store." Other women did millinery or dressmaking work part time, from their own homes, or those of male kin.[32] This craft work, especially millinery, was important in town life, part of rituals to affirm respectability, to distinguish rank, to claim connectedness with the wider world, but in a community of 2000 souls, half of them men, it did not provide employment for many, or financial independence for any more than one or two.

There were glimmerings of the new, white-collar female occupations in town; the furniture factories employed women as stenographers and clerks; the Portland Cement Company engaged a female lab technician in 1899; the manager and chief operator of the telephone exchange was a woman who employed an all-female staff. Most of these salaried workers, however, were not local girls but women who came from away.[33]

There were, of course, many young women in town, not, as in Paris, half as many more women than men, but in the years before the First World War just about as many girls as boys, leaving school and looking toward adulthood. When boys went into the machine rooms at the furniture factories, what did girls do? Plainly there was lots of work at home. Both families and dwellings were large in Hanover, and girls' help in garment making and seasonal food processing made a real difference in the household economy. Farm traditions were not far away in Hanover. There were large gardens and poultry to be tended; some households also kept a cow. A girl who married in her late teens would not have too long to bide her time at home before she had a household of her own to run. Still, the example of the co-operative woollen mill of the 1890s remained. There had once been a payroll in town, collected by daughters and added to the community's store of cash. There might be a social interest at issue concerning how teenaged girls spent their time.

In 1910 a local tailor, Andrew Hamel, construing the absence of waged work for young women as an opportunity, organized a group of town businessmen to build a factory which would "employ girls especially."

Table 1:   **POPULATIONS OF HANOVER AND PARIS, 1901 AND 1911**

	Total population	Women	Men
1901			
Hanover	1392	732	690
Paris	3229	1830	1399
1911			
Hanover	2342	1178	1164
Paris	4098	2274	1824

Source: *Census of Canada 1901,* vol. 1, 56, 62; *1911,* vol. 1, 73, 76.

A firm of shirtmakers used the premises for several years as a branch plant. When the branch closed, many young women from Hanover followed their jobs to the main factory in Kitchener. Through the war years the *Post* carried lists of scores of Hanover girls, often in groups of sisters, returning to their home town for the annual two-week summer plant closing. Recruiting advertisements from out-of-town firms directed particularly at young women who had never before worked for wages appeared with greater frequency in the town paper. Some tried to anticipate the preferences of daughters (and their parents) on neighbourhood farms with offers of "steady work for the winter, at good pay and in a clean, warm mill." Others addressed uncertainties about the transition, both to waged work and life away from home, with promises that beginners would be "paid salaries from commencement," and given "valuable training in agreeable work for the inexperienced" in "clean, airy, sunlit workrooms," with transportation provided and "boarding houses secured."[34] Hamel's plan had tapped a local interest but inadvertently initiated a troubling pattern. Teenaged girls were experimenting in increasing numbers with waged work. Their employment was acceptably different from that of their brothers' and appropriate to their gender in two ways: (1) they worked among women with textiles rather among men with wood, and (2) they worked as girls rather than women—expecting to learn womanliness later in marriage rather than through their work behind a machine. In another way, however, the waged work of young women was unacceptably different from that of their brothers. Against all good sense about how girls and boys should be guided, the new pattern meant that while young men stayed in town under the watchful eyes of male kin, young women left the protecting gaze of the community, to do work their mothers had never done, in places their mothers might never have been.

Thus by 1920 the interests of adult men in town, as ratepayers and as fathers, converged around the question of a "factory for girls." The town now owned the plant Hamel's group had built. In April, by a vote of 367 for to 28 against, the community agreed to give a Toronto firm $30 000 and tax-exempt status to reopen the building as the Hanover Cotton and Woolen Mills, the sum to be raised by issuing twenty-year municipal debentures. The town kept a 6 percent mortgage for $45 000 on the building, but not the equipment, and agreed to forgive $1500 of the principal yearly if the firm maintained a payroll of 200 or more. In two years the Toronto proprietors of the factory, R.G. Long and Company, were gone. By 1926 the plant had opened and closed again. The new holders of the mortgage, Allen Silk Mills of Toronto, sold out to a firm of Wisconsin knitters in 1929, who went bankrupt in 1938. By this time the town mortgage had been repaid. Subsequent manufacturers of hosiery and denim clothing were not seen as creatures of the community will in the same way.[35] But through the rocky interwar years each failure and resurrection of the "factory for girls" reopened the discussion of whether and why the daughters of town ought to work for wages.

Hanover was an unpretentious community, never aspiring to be the county seat, pleased to be known as a "mechanics town," proud of the modestness of its civic buildings, holding fast to a civic creed of spare efficiency. Bringing daughters into the labour force appealed, especially to the Board of Trade, on these grounds, as a way to expand the number of wage earners in town, without expanding the number of residents with claims upon town services. Succeeding occupiers of the "factory for girls" assured council that they would not "bring in an army of outside people" but employ largely local help. In the early 1920s, when times were lean in town, the prospect of a larger and stronger economy provisioning a stable population within the current town limits had great appeal. After several years of short time in the woodworking plants, having "men and boys get work in the furniture factories, while girls work" in the mill, seemed a prudent way to ensure that households would not be left for long stretches without any cash income at all. The crisis of the early 1930s underlined this principle: "every manufacturing centre should have both heavy and light industries, the men of each family being employed in the heavier work, and the girls of the same family in the lighter work," so that the community had some protection from the vagaries of national markets.[36] Female employment, thus, was an economic failsafe for the community as a whole and the individual households within it.

But always the females to be employed were closely specified. They were to be local girls, not strangers. They were to be daughters, not mothers or wives. Parents were not averse to strangers in town; they were averse to having their unmarried daughters hive off to strange places just at a time in their lives when they might get themselves in trouble. The demand put to succeeding mortgagees of the "factory for girls" that they give preference to young women from Hanover, even though they might be inexperienced in the work, was part of the strategy to try to keep daughters in their home town and under scrutiny during the years when they might be sexually active outside marriage, or, to use the phrase of the time, courting. The availability of waged work for young women in town not only reassured parents that their daughters remained under the watchful gaze of neighbours and kin; it also by deft and effective indirectness, by seeming inadvertence, increased the likelihood that local young people of both sexes would marry persons whom their parents knew.[37] Inauspicious as the location proved to be for the first five firms that took up the space, the "factory for girls" served the purposes of the community relatively well.

Some early managers of the factory stepped outside the local consensus and tried to recruit married women for work in the mill. They did not succeed. Unlike the situation in Paris, where women married and stayed on at their jobs, in Hanover all the workplace festivities surrounding marriage were celebrations of parting. The factory was a place for daughters to work, but only until they became wives. The plant was planned to bring more money into the community, by bringing young women into the labour force. But in terms of gender relations in town, it was a conservative measure, a way to protect existing courtship patterns and regulate sexual conduct. It secured the established path towards marriage for the daughters of the town. But the "factory for girls" by design was no place for wives.[38]

• Conclusion

The creation of jobs was a matter of public interest and municipal policy initiative. Both the interest and the initiatives, however, varied as between men and women. The town fathers took steps to safeguard the jobs of working men in the municipality when it became clear, as it did after the fire that destroyed the Knechtel main plant, that town capitalists must be paid to give community needs precedence over their individual class interest. The bounty paid to Knechtel to rebuild in Hanover rather than another town seemed the only way to hold on to the men who both directly and indirectly provided the financial foundation for town life. There was a strong local consensus that town monies should be spent to keep a "factory for girls" employing young women in town, but women's wages were seen not as a foundation, but as a failsafe, for municipal fortunes.

As men's and women's pay packets played different roles in economic relations in town, at the level of both the household and the community, so, in gender relations, waged work took on different meanings for men and women. Through waged work, boys learned manliness; they mastered disciplines and discriminations, ways of appraising their work and one another, which they would practise through their adult lives; varied though these ways of being manly were, they shared one trait: they were lessons males alone might learn. Girls did not learn womanliness through their paid employment. Their experience of waged work in the town-sponsored "factory for girls" was important in their growing into womanhood because it became them to remain under the protection of male kin while they waited for their life's work, in marriage and outside the market, to begin.

• Notes

1 John Richards, *Arrangement, Care and Operation of Woodworking Factories and Machinery* (New York, 1885), xi.

2 W. John McIntyre, "From Workshop to Factory: The Furniture Maker," *Material History Bulletin* 19 (1984): 34; L.A. Koltun, *The Cabinetmaker's Art in Ontario, c 1850–1900* (Ottawa, 1979), 172.

3 The poem "The Woodworker" by Douglas Malloch was published in *Canadian Woodworker and Furniture Manufacturer* (hereafter *CWFM*) (Aug. 1925): 41. On beauty and usefulness see Sudhir Kakar, *Frederick Taylor: A Study in Personality and Innovation* (Cambridge, MA, 1970), 68–69. On hand work see Michael J. Ettema, "Technological Innovation and Design Economics in Furniture Manufacture," *Winterthur Portfolio* 16, 2/3 (Summer/Autumn 1981): 197–224; Kenneth L. Ames, "Grand Rapids Furniture at the Time of the Centennial," *Winterthur Portfolio* (1975): 43; David A. Hounshell, *From the American System to Mass Production 1880–1932* (Baltimore, 1984), 151; Peter Stalker, Hanover Industrial History Project (hereafter HIHP).

4 Richards, *Arrangement, Care and Operation of Woodworking Factories*, xii.

5 On fathers and sons, Clayton Planz, HIHP; *Hanover Post*, 30 June 1898; *CWFM* (Sept. 1919): 37, 38; (March 1928): 71.

6 Paul Willis, "Shop Floor Culture, Masculinity and the Wage Form" in *Working-Class Culture: Studies in History and Theory*, ed. J. Clarke, C. Critcher, and R. Johnson (New York, 1979), 196; Stan Gray, "Sharing the Shop Floor" in *Women and Men*, ed. Greta Hofmann Nemiroff (Toronto, 1987); John H. Gagnon, "Physical Strength, Once of Significance" in *Men and Masculinity*, ed. Joseph H. Pleck and Jack Sawyer (Englewood Cliffs, NJ, 1974).

7 *CWFM* (Feb. 1921): 67; Clyde Dankert, "Autobiography" (typescript, Dartmouth College Library), 35–36; Peter Gateman, Henry Gateman, Clayton Planz, and Karl Ruhl, HIHP. The quote is from Planz.

8 Henry Gateman, Clayton Planz, and Karl Ruhl, HIHP. See similarly Cynthia Cockburn, *Brothers* (London, 1983), 43–46, on male kinship and craft hierarchy in the printing trades.

9 Gordon Peck, Peter Gateman, HIHP.

10 *CWFM* (Jan. 1919), (May 1919), 46. The earnings data are from Queen's University Archives (hereafter QUA), Knechtel papers, payrolls. I have most often used 1938 as the reference year because there is a detailed occupational listing available. Other payrolls can be disaggregated only to the departmental level. The personal data, here and subsequently, are from the Hanover assessment rolls, Hanover town hall.

11 *CWFM* (April 1925): 52; Jacob Krueger, HIHP

13 Wilf Cooper, Clarence Helwig, Ed Fischer, Peter Gateman, Gordon Peck, HIHP. In 1938 Knechtel's lead tenoner, William Ford, a leader in the union, earned $1048 for 2223 hours' work. The second tenoner in the plant, John Huenermoeder, worked 2207 hours and earned $929. QUA, Knechtel papers, 3.

14 *CWFM* (Aug. 1921): 69; (July 1933): 12; (Oct. 1929): 59–60; (Feb. 1934): 17; Ed Fischer, Henry Gateman, Clayton Planz, HIHP.

15 "A Code of Safety Standards for Woodworking-Machine Guards," American Society of Mechanical Engineers *Transactions* (1917): 1191–200; *CWFM* (Oct. 1929): 59–60; Sern Madsen, "New Factors Influencing the Design of Woodworking Machinery," *Mechanical Engineering* 45 (March 1923): 180; *CWFM* (Sept. 1934): 12–14; (Feb. 1919): 38. Karl

Ruhl, Henry Gateman, Clarence Helwig, Gordon Peck, HIHP. The quotation about the concentration demanded by the work is from Dankert, "Autobiography," 37; Richards, *Arrangement, Care and Operation of Woodworking Factories,* 63–71.

16 See similarly Willis, "Shopfloor Culture," 196.

17 Yearly earnings, machine room employees: 1928, mean = $660, standard deviation (sd) = 462; 1938, mean = $661, sd = 312. Calculated from Knechtel wage books, QUA, Knechtel papers 3, 4.

18 C.L. Babcock, "Refinements in Woodworking-Machinery Design," *Mechanical Engineering* 48 (1926): 415–22. *CWFM* (July 1921): 72–73; (May 1923): 63; (July 1928): 96; (March 1930): 53; (Nov. 1931): 31–33; (April 1939): 15-16. Henry Gateman, Gordon Peck, HIHP.

19 *CWFM* (April 1929): 45–46; (March 1936): 10; (April 1936): 12.

20 The quote concerning school leaving and the description of the accident is from Henry Gateman, HIHP 3, 8. Mrs Peter Gateman was recounting her own years in the machine room. Peter Gateman, HIHP. The summation about danger and responsibility is from Clarence Helwig, HIHP. See the analysis by Cynthia Cockburn of the imperative of keeping work sites homogeneous by sex, *Brothers,* 151–53, 179.

21 Average age in the cabinet-making shop: 1923, mean = 40.7, sd 14.2; 1928, mean = 43, sd = 12.0; 1933, mean = 41, sd = 12.3; 1938, mean = 41, sd = 12.9

22 This difference between the machine room and the cabinet shop emerges clearly in a comparison of the dispersion around the means in earnings. Machine room: 1923, mean = 660, sd = 462; 1938, mean = 661, sd = 312; cabinet shop: 1923, mean = 655, sd = 373; 1938, mean = 740, sd = 247.

23 Edward Wilson, Alan Lang, Thomas Schaus, HIHP.

24 Edward Wilson, HIHP.

25 Alan Lang, HIHP; *CWFM* (Jan. 1926): 70.

26 Richards, *Arrangement, Care and Operation of Woodworking Factories,* 147.

27 Frank Edward Ransome, *The City Built on Wood: A History of the Furniture Industry in Grand Rapids, Michigan* (Ann Arbor, MI, 1955), 61; M. Silverstein, "The Technology of Wood Finishes and Their Application," *Mechanical Engineering* 48 (1926): 423–26.

28 *CWFM* (June 1920): 82; F.L. Browne "Wood Finishing—A Glance Ahead," *Mechanical Engineering* 48 (Nov. 1926): 1286–88.

29 *Hanover Post,* 2 Dec. 1897; 3 Feb. and 7 April 1898; 7 June and 5 July 1900.

30 *Hanover Post,* ads for domestic servants: 13 June 1901, 9 Aug. 1900, 7 Dec. 1899, 7 Sept. 1899; for hotel workers, 29 June 1920, 13 June 1901.

31 *Hanover Post,* Barltorp, 25 Aug. 1898; 25 Oct. 1900; ads from general merchants concerning the milliners they employed, 5 Oct. 1899, 16 Sept. 1897, 1 March 1900, 8 March 1900, 8 Sept. 1898, 9 March 1899.

32 *Hanover Post,* Miss Bricker, 11 Nov. 1897; other dressmakers in rented rooms above general merchants 11 May 1899, 31 March 1898; businesses run from home 15 April 1920, 22 Feb. 1900.

33 *Hanover Post,* 1 Feb. 1900, concerning the hiring of Jessie Graham as stenographer at Knechtel (Graham moved to Hanover from London and later became secretary-treasurer of the firm); 23 Nov. 1899, hiring of Miss Mary Gaskell of Owen Sound, as chemist for the cement company; 31 July 1919, retirement summary of the career of Mrs Patchell at the Bell Telephone Office.

34 Josephine Hahn, *Home of My Youth* (Hanover, 1947), 196; *Hanover Post,* 17

March 1937, 25 July 1918, 3 April 1919, 4 Sept. 1919, 11 April 1918, 29 Sept. 1918, 7 Sept. 1922.

35 *Hanover Post*, 1 April 1920, 29 April 1920, 4 May 1922, 16 Nov. 1922, 11 March 1926, 30 Sept. 1926, 13 June 1929; Hahn, *Home of My Youth*, 197; *Hanover Post*, 7 Jan. 1932, 26 Dec. 1935, 7 Jan. 1937.

36 *Hanover Post*, 16 Nov. 1922, 8 March 1923, 30 Sept. 1926, 13 June 1929; 21 Jan. 1932.

37 Ibid., 22 April 1920, 14 July 1921, 12 April 1923.

38 Peter Stalker, Clarence Helwig, Alan Lang, HIHP; *Hanover Post*, 27 May and 14 Oct. 1920; 12 April 1923; 23 Feb., 1 March, and 5 July 1928; 28 Feb. 1929; 22 Sept. 1938.

"*I*T WAS A HARD LIFE":
Class and Gender in the Work and Family Rhythms of a Railway Town, 1920–1950*

MARK ROSENFELD

In December 1939 Ed Walker was hired as a brakeman by the Canadian National Railways Company (CNR) in Allandale, the railway ward of Barrie, Ontario. This event was not an unexpected one for him. Railway work was part of Walker's heritage—his father had been a conductor and his grandfather a section foreman, overseeing the maintenance of railway track. Having celebrated his twenty-third birthday, Walker was anxious finally to be able to carry on a family tradition. The Great Depression had prevented him from getting work "on the road" and, after completing two years of secondary school, he spent the next five years working in a number of temporary jobs. With the outbreak of war and the need for men to operate trains, Walker's prospects of a career on the railroad were now more assured. His work schedule as a brakeman was nonetheless very irregular. For the next two-and-one-half years, Walker was on the "spare board," replacing brakemen who were off work due to injury, sickness, or the need for rest. There was nothing predictable about where he would be working or the time at which he would be called for work. The tensions created by this type of existence, however, were partially offset by the support and fellowship of workmates in a similar position.

*Canadian Historical Association *Historical Papers* (1988): 237–79. Reprinted with the permission of the Canadian Historical Association.

In 1942, Walker left the railway to join the army. Returning home four years later, he resumed his work as a brakeman. That year he also married and bought a house just outside the railway ward. His wife, a nurse, continued working at the Barrie hospital until the birth of their first child a year later. She then left her job as a nurse to assume full-time domestic work in their home. Except for one brief occasion, she stayed out of the paid-labour force until her children were in their teens, and then resumed nursing on a part-time basis. Walker's frequent absences meant that her responsibilities for the welfare of their family greatly increased. Though promoted to a freight conductor in the late 1940s, her husband still had to work at odd hours and was away from home two or three days a week. Only in 1961, twenty-one years after being hired by the CNR, did he begin work on a regularly scheduled passenger train, which permitted him to be with his family most nights of the week until he retired.[1]

For those of the railway community, Walker's experiences were unexceptional. These were the common patterns of existence for the engineers, conductors, brakemen, and firemen who began operating trains during the Second World War, as well as for their families. There were also many features of Walker's life that were experienced by his father's generation. Though unremarkable to the railroaders of Allandale, the circumstances of Walker's and his father's generation reveal a great deal about the way in which the world of work and its rhythms dominated the lives of men and women in the community.[2] Their experiences also reveal much about the way in which working-class women and men developed strategies, drawing upon the resources of family, friends, union, and community to meet the constraints of their lives.

The constraints they faced were those of both class and gender. Attempts to understand the nature of class relations have had a long, if controversial, history of their own.[3] The study of gender relations, however, has been of more recent vintage. Until the past two decades, gender issues received little attention from historians. Moreover, studies from the 1970s and 1980s that have considered such issues have tended to focus on the experience of women.[4] Histories of men have been largely gender-blind. Most depictions of the past that strive to be sensitive to the nuances of class relationships among male workers and employers have not considered the role of gender in shaping class interaction.[5] Yet, as one school of feminist inquiry has convincingly argued, class and gender constitute an integrated system of relations that shapes both the world of women and men and an understanding of that world.[6]

Gender does not simply pertain to the relations between women and men. It plays an important role in class relations among male and among female workers and between workers and employers.[7] The organization of the labour market and the paid (as well as unpaid domestic) work process, definitions of skill, the exercise of workplace authority, wages, and job status—all are affected by gender. If the structure of work is created out of

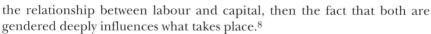

the relationship between labour and capital, then the fact that both are gendered deeply influences what takes place.[8]

Analysing the historical constitution and reconstitution of class and gender relations within a *specific* community can help contribute to a better understanding of the way in which these relationships *generally* developed and changed over time. Such analysis also allows for the affirmation, qualification, or challenge of previously held conceptions of these issues. For example, it is commonly assumed that, within the working class, men have occupied a position of subordination at work and superordination at home. Historians have explored the complexities and contradictions of class domination to a greater degree than those of patriarchal domination, however. It would appear, nonetheless, that complexity and contradiction have characterized gender relations as well. The dimensions of that subordination and superordination need to be portrayed in fine detail. If wives were subordinate to husbands within the working-class family historically, what were the contours of that subordination? How was it enforced? Were there areas where wives could achieve some control and autonomy? If so, why, and to what effect?

Questions might also be asked about the nature of gender identities and bonds, and their influence on the formation of class solidarities. Generally, the literature on male and female bonding argues that ties between men have been typified by individualism, independence, and competition while those between women have exhibited the qualities of interdependence, co-operation, and nurturance.[9] Though it is recognized that the nature of such bonds has varied according to class and age, these characteristics are still viewed as the main distinguishing features. Such simple dichotomies, however, seem to belie the intricacy of ties between men and between women, as recent studies of working-class masculinity, for example, have indicated.[10] The degree to which concepts of masculinity or femininity have prompted or undermined solidarity among workers and struggles against class inequality would also seem to defy any simple generalization. Again, in the case of working-class masculinity, some sociologists and historians have stated that concepts of "manliness" have on the whole undermined unity among workers on the job,[11] while others have suggested that the relationship between class and gender identity has been contradictory and ambiguous. Moreover, the latter observe that gender identities are not immutable; they can shift in emphasis and meaning as the conditions that shape them alter.[12] Such studies also underscore the important cognitive and emotional dimensions of both class and gender identities. To understand the actions of working-class women and men, one needs to know not only the experiences that helped mould their world view, but also the complex of emotions that influenced gender and class interaction.[13]

The following study is an oral history that explores the relationship among work, family, class, and gender in the railway ward of Barrie,

Ontario, as experienced by two generations of engineers, firemen, conductors, and brakemen and their families between the 1920s and the 1950s.[14] It begins with an examination of the structural constraints faced by the men and women of the railroad community, and looks at the world of both paid and domestic unpaid labour. As feminist scholars have emphasized, an examination of the interconnections between these two spheres is essential to an understanding of the forces that shaped the women and men of the working-class community. These interconnections reveal much about working-class reproduction and survival and the social construction of gender.[15] The study considers the implications of such structural constraints for railroaders and their families, and the strategies that were developed in response. It then examines the role of gender identity in shaping relations between husbands and wives, and class relations on the railway, though only certain features of these relationships are investigated. For both the men and women of Allandale, the fact of being working-class was experienced in gender-specific ways. Conceptions of masculinity and femininity and of men's and women's "proper sphere"—all shaped and were derived from those experiences. The study concludes with some general comments on the nature of class and gender relations in Allandale over a forty-year period.

> On the railroad there was no night or day. (Dave Kingston, conductor, born 1892, hired 1913)

> It's a very poor life. I mean layin' in the bunk houses waitin' to go to work. Waitin' to be called. You're away from home more than you're ever home. . . . I was away 300 days out of 365. (Jim Blythe, engineer, born 1913, hired 1940)

> You never knew from one day to the next what you were going to do. . . . I might go to work at five o'clock in the morning or I might go at midnight. (Norman Crane, conductor, born 1914, hired 1942)

Work, family, and community life in Allandale were profoundly influenced by the railway. The historical recollections of the ward's residents were often prefaced by the comment that "this was a railroader's place." Indeed, until after the Second World War, the economies of Allandale and of Barrie itself were dependent on the railroad—a pattern that had existed since the mid-nineteenth century. Allandale was an important divisional point on both the Grand Trunk Railway (GTR) and its successor in 1923, the Canadian National Railways Company. In a town with a relatively small population and few industries, the railroad was well known as the major employer. Its work force comprised some five hundred employees, approximately 40 percent of whom were running-trades workers.[16] These consisted of what were known as "head-end" and "tail-end" crews of men. The "head-end" comprised firemen, responsible for maintaining the steam engine's supply of coal fuel, and engineers who, as former firemen, had gained enough experience and skill to run a locomotive engine. The "tail-end" comprised brakemen, responsible, among other duties, for coupling and uncoupling railway cars and switching trains from one track to another, and conductors who, as former brakemen, had gained enough skill and knowledge to oversee and be accountable for the general operation of a train.

To be employed by the railway as a fireman, engineer, brakeman, or conductor was to enter a world where the rhythms of work were in the main chaotic and unpredictable. The hours were long and the work demanded that these men absent themselves from their homes for days, and sometimes for weeks or months. An engineman or a trainman based in Allandale could be moved to any one of a number of terminals that fell within his union's northern Ontario seniority district. Seniority determined the location, amount, and type of work assigned to employees.[17] Most running-trades crews, however, operated freight trains for the greatest part of their career on the road. These trains ran on a twenty-four-hour schedule. Passenger trains offered steadier and more predictable hours of work, but only towards retirement were most running-trades workers entitled to operate such trains exclusively.[18]

The rhythms of railway labour were also shaped by cyclical changes in the economy. Work patterns for the generation hired before 1920 were disrupted by the massive layoffs of the Great Depression.[19] Men who had over fifteen years' seniority were laid off for months or longer. Some had to leave their families to work out of terminals located in the far reaches of northern Ontario. Those who normally would have been recruited in the 1930s had to wait until the outbreak of World War II before they were given positions. As the most junior workers, they spent the duration of the war in the north while their families, in many cases, remained in Allandale.[20]

Engine and train crews, however, were able to gain some control over their work rhythms. They could use their elaborate and extensive seniority arrangements and union regulations to intensify their workload. Since pensions were based on the best ten years of earnings, many men chose to labour long hours and take any runs to which they were entitled towards the end of their career when their work schedules should have been the least disruptive. Some also manipulated the payment system where wages were based on the number of miles travelled and quotas were set limiting the miles a worker could accumulate in a month.[21] By exceeding his quota, a running-trades worker not only increased his own workload but also decreased that of others. This type of manoeuvring was not regarded favourably: "Fellas would stay up all night tryin' to figure out a goddamn angle till they get another trip or steal a trip off you or some goddamn thing. . . . They just wanted the money."[22]

Union regulations were also applied in an attempt to regulate the intensity of one's workload in a period before paid holidays and vacations. Crews were allowed to book rest after twelve hours on the job. They could also book off sick in order to be with their families. There were, nevertheless, financial limits to such controls. As one engineer commented, "if you felt like being off, you booked off or you booked sick. Usually they let you off. But years ago when you had a family you couldn't book off because you couldn't afford it. You didn't have the money."[23] The high unemployment of the 1930s also had its effect: "In them days [the 1930s] the unions weren't so strong. And very few booked rest which wasn't good. They'd make you stay on and then penalized you if you made a mistake."[24]

Men also devised informal ways of gaining some limited control over their work rhythms. When summoned to work by the call boy, they would arrange to be absent for the call and this resulted in the next available crew member on the seniority list having to go to work. Some had an arrangement with the call boys that allowed them to get runs which were both profitable and relatively short in duration: "I used them call boys pretty good down there and they used me pretty good too. I got a lot of good trips out of them. . . . I never paid the buggers but when they were stuck I always went. . . . You knew when you worked you'd always get somethin' back. You always did."[25] In addition, when the opportunity arose, engine-crew and train-crew members would try to arrange to work with those who were known to be able to "get over the road" as quickly as possible. Running-trades workers were quite aware of the differences in the skill of their workmates and often attempted to avoid those who were slow or unsafe.

Despite these stratagems and regulations, however, a large portion of a fireman's, engineer's, brakeman's, and conductor's employment on the railroad involved uncertain hours, frequent absences from home, and a highly variable supply of work. It was characterized neither by the certainties of industrial shift-work time nor that of "white-collar" work. Often the most predictable feature of this work was its unpredictability. Indeed, though work in the running trades offered more economic security than most working-class occupations, it came with a price. The rhythms of labour in the running trades during these decades essentially constituted a special category of industrial work time, incorporating its most disruptive features. Men had to be at work at the designated time; yet at least in the case of most freight runs there was no set time at which work would be over. One could always book off after twelve hours, but there were limitations in doing so. Furthermore, from one day to the next, many workers would not know when work would begin again.[26] Such rhythms could not but have profound implications for the work and non-work lives of these railwaymen and their families.

The big burden fell on the women, to look after the home and children, and so on. . . . The boys, both of them grew to realize that there were many things dad couldn't participate in, that mother had to fulfil both functions as both parents. (Ed Walker, conductor, born 1916, hired 1939)

They really had to adapt. They had to adapt to not only running the family, the home, and it didn't matter what created [a problem], they had to solve it. So they became, well, real pros. There wasn't anything they didn't do. (Elizabeth Burt, born 1918, daughter of a conductor)

Given the chaotic and often unpredictable work rhythms of engine and train crews, it would have been difficult for trains to operate, and for the families of these men to remain intact, without the existence of a particular configuration of gender relations. In Allandale, as with other railway and non-railway communities of this period, households were constituted and gender divisions shaped according to the predominant twentieth-century pattern. After marriage, husbands were the sole or primary wage earners and their wives were responsible for unpaid domestic labour. There were, however, variations in this pattern between the two generations of families whose husbands or wives were interviewed. The first generation of wives were married by the end of the 1920s, and all worked in the paid labour force or on their family farms before marriage.[27] Upon marriage, they left the paid labour force or farm to assume full-time domestic work in their new homes.[28]

Paid work after marriage was more common for the second generation of wives. As with those of the previous generation, the wives who were married in the late 1930s or early 1940s worked before marriage, in the paid-labour force or on family farms, in occupations that conformed to the sexual division of labour of the time.[29] One-third continued to work outside the home after marriage, before they had their first child. With the arrival of their first child, which was generally within a year or two of marriage, the majority withdrew from the wage-labour force until their children were older.[30] One-third re-entered the paid work force at a later stage of their lives.

There were many interrelated pressures that shaped the after-marriage wagework patterns of these wives. The economy of Barrie offered little opportunity for the wives of the first generation, most of whom were either residents of Allandale or moved there after marriage.[31] The town's female work force was small and concentrated into service, clerical, and retail occupations, all of which were notoriously poorly paid. As a result of the Second World War, there were greater work opportunities in town for the wives of the second generation who were from Allandale or moved there in the late 1930s and early 1940s.[32] By then, however, many already had children for whom they were responsible. Unlike the first generation, the majority of wives of the second generation married before their husbands were able to get a position on the railroad. Fewer than one-third married after their husbands had already taken up railroading.[33]

The rhythms of work in the running trades made it *necessary* that there be a full-time domestic worker in the home after the first child was born. Also, it would have been extremely difficult for a woman to maintain a family on her own income. In view of the fundamental role these women had in providing for their families' well being, there was little economic sense in wives re-entering the wage-labour market while their children were growing up. Re-entry would only have increased the burdens of women already labouring under the time-consuming and often stressful conditions of domestic work.[34]

The ability of engine and train crews to earn enough on their own to support their families for most, if not all, of their career in the running trades allowed wives to assume domestic responsibilities without having to return to the paid work force. Compared to other sections of the railroad labour force, and to most working-class occupations in general, running-trades work was one of the most highly paid. The earnings of these men, however, varied according to occupation and seniority. Firemen and brakemen were paid less per mile than engineers and conductors. The income of junior men improved as they gained seniority and were offered more work and the possibility of promotion.[35]

In spite of these circumstances, earning enough to maintain a family was also at times very difficult for an engineman or trainman, and this made it necessary for a wife to devise strategies to stretch family income in ways that attempted to avoid her re-entry into the paid labour force. For the generation of wives whose husbands began railway work in the 1920s or before, family income was limited by the layoffs of the Great Depression and a reduced work schedule. In families where the husband started railway work in the late 1930s or early 1940s, previous savings were minimal or non-existent. As well, in the experience of both generations, family income was limited by a husband's need to pay for living expenses when he was away from home and working in northern Ontario. As the wife of an engineer recalled, "you were keeping two homes going. I was here and he was up [in] Hornepayne and Nakina and money wasn't like it is today. I can remember that if you got fifty dollars every two weeks you thought you were in heaven."[36]

Despite these fluctuations in family income, employment in the running trades still brought greater financial security than most working-class occupations. For the wives of these workers—the majority of whom came from farming or working-class backgrounds—marriage, and particularly marriage to a railroader, also offered more economic security than that of women forced to subsist on the wages paid to female employees in the labour market.[37] As was the case of work in the running trades, however, labouring as a wife and mother in a railroader's family had its price.

In many ways these women faced a situation similar to that of all working-class wives of the period. Like them, they were primarily responsible for all facets of domestic labour—housework, reproduction, and care of dependent children, and of working and dependent adults. Their labour was essential to the maintenance of the family and its wage earners and, within a larger framework, essential to the maintenance of workers as a class and to the economic conventions of industrial capitalism. Their domestic labour was also shaped by the work schedules of their husbands or, if they re-entered or remained in the paid labour market, by the added demands of the "double day."[38] The rhythms of work in the running trades, however, had unique implications for the wives of engine and train crews.

Wives had to juggle the schedules of their own domestic routines to meet those of their husbands. In many cases this involved getting up at odd hours to prepare the meals that husbands would take to work. Dave Kingston's wife had to tend to the needs not only of her husband but also those of her cousin, who boarded with them for almost ten years: "My wife used to have to maybe get up twice in the night. I might go out at one o'clock in the morning and he'd go out at three or four o'clock in the morning. And she'd have to get up and pack that basket."[39] The demands placed on wives to cater both to husband and children could be especially exhausting.

When husbands were home, the rhythms of domestic labour could be actually more chaotic than when they were away for long periods of time. Not only did wives have to prepare a meal at odd hours, but also the irregular sleeping patterns of their husbands meant that children had to be kept quiet while their fathers rested during the day. The long absence of a husband who had to work in the north was, in one sense, easier for a wife. Domestic routines could be organized in a less chaotic fashion, in accordance with a wife's own preferences. Long separations from husbands, nevertheless, also created difficulties for these women. They had primary responsibility for the financial management of the household and for the care of their children. Most working-class wives also had these responsibilities. However, railway husbands were often not around to offer support in instances where such help might have been given. "We were left with everythin'," recalled a conductor's wife. "It seemed always if there was an emergency come up they were on the other end of the line. You didn't have a husband."[40]

After long separations, and even after frequent short absences, family members had to make emotional adjustments. The need to be away from home often meant that running-trades workers had limited contact with their children. When a man came home and was in a position to take on some child care responsibilities, his priorities could differ from those of his wife. The recollections of Joe Mathews, an engineer, underscored the conflicts that could result: "[My wife] more or less brought the children up. I was never home. She'd say once in a while, oh you have to straighten that guy out, one of the girls out. I said listen, I've been away for four days. . . . I want to hug 'em, I don't want to be fightin' with 'em."[41]

As tension managers, wives were expected to deal with the work frustrations of their spouses and those caused by their husband's inability to participate in family events.[42] A certain degree of understanding about railway operations was necessary in order that a wife be able to co-ordinate her own routines with her husband's needs. This understanding was gained through conversations with spouses and other railroaders' wives and, for those who came from railway families, from having observed their fathers on the job. Despite a wife's knowledge and abilities, however, explosive situations could not always be avoided. The intensity of frustration that at least some women could feel was indicated in one wife's comment: "That's the trouble. We all were for our husbands. He's like number one. Like God himself coming in the door and out the door. . . . I used to think for a long time 'You make me so sick I wish to heck he'd run off the track.' Then I prayed like eff that he wouldn't."[43]

Though sometimes exasperated, a railway wife was also keenly aware of her significance to the family's welfare. Household economic management was particularly important to these women. The most common pattern for both generations was that wives would be given their husbands' pay cheque and then would allocate money for groceries, clothing and material to make clothing, furniture, and other essential items. Husbands would then take an allowance or a small portion of their wages for themselves.[44] When two households had to be maintained or in times of economic crisis, some wives augmented family income by offering room and board to single railroaders, by taking in washing for a fee, or by selling knitted goods. Planting vegetable gardens, doing work that might otherwise be purchased on the market, or putting the needs of other family members ahead of one's own were other ways of making ends meet when family resources were limited.[45]

The financial balancing act wives had to perform was both a source of pride and a cause for anguish. When managing finances, these women had autonomy in determining daily expenditures, though this appeared to be less so concerning the purchase of large items. Their position as financial managers was based on a fundamental dependence on their husband's wages. This dependence could have dire consequences if a husband put his own priorities ahead of his family's, and squandered away his pay cheque in gambling and drinking. Most wives, however, were not faced with such a situation. Decisions about household expenditures were often amicably made. Yet, as the wage earner, a husband could also exercise his prerogative and refuse to sanction certain expenses. Rebecca Crane recalled that "it took a lot of years [to work decisions out] because the first few years the man was the boss. There was no question about it."[46] Her comments were echoed by others.

The wives of running-trades workers found themselves in a situation that could be intensely lonely and sometimes exasperating. Their loneliness was not only a product of being separated from their spouses for long periods of time. It was also the result of the work situation of these women. As others have observed, the domestic labour process is isolated, private, and fragmented, and this contrasts sharply with the socialized and integrated process of industrial capitalist production.[47] Wives were quite aware of the conditions shaping their isolation and loneliness, on the whole more so than their husbands.

Though much of their time was spent doing domestic work in the home, wives also had support networks that played a very significant role in aiding them to deal with the isolation and loneliness of their situation. The most important of these networks was that of kinship. For both generations, family provided the material and emotional support that helped both husbands and wives survive the tensions of railroad life. Many wives decided to remain in Allandale rather than move north to join their husbands because of the support offered by their relatives.[48]

Most railroaders had what would technically be considered nuclear family households. The close proximity of kin, however, made the isolation of the household unit more apparent than real.[49] In addition, at specific periods in the life cycle of a number of running-trades workers, the household was extended to include other close family members. Wilma Laidlaw, a conductor's daughter who married a brakeman in 1920, lived with her parents and her brother in an extended family household after marriage. Even after having children, she continued to live with her parents until her husband bought a house across the road from her mother and father. In her extended family situation, housework was done collectively by the women, though "everyone seemed to go their own way, do their own thing" with regard to social activities. Each component of the household was also financially self-sufficient, though family members shared household expenses and collective management, an arrangement that reduced their living costs. When Wilma's husband went to London, Ontario, to work for seven years during the Great Depression she would see her family daily.[50] Wilma Laidlaw's situation was not unique. After they were married, Catherine Roy lived just up the street from her family, Vera Miller took a place next door to her parents, and Rosemary Sharpe settled only a few houses away from her mother and father.[51]

Allandale railway families not only provided emotional and material support, they were also essential in conditioning future railway workers and future railway workers' wives to running-trades work and its rhythms. In the case of the men interviewed, half of whom came from railway families, it was well known that, with a father or uncle in the railway work force, one not only had an important contact that made it easier for a man to get a job on the road. Having a relative on the railroad also allowed a future worker to acquire rudimentary knowledge of the skills and terminology that he would eventually use when hired by the company. It was this type of exposure that was valued by the CNR and its predecessor.[52]

As with sons, daughters were also exposed to their father's work routines. Furthermore, both sons and daughters had experience with the way a father's work rhythms affected family life. Daughters, however, were more likely to be involved with their mother's domestic labour and to hear a great deal more about the anguish and turmoil that their mothers might feel. "My oldest daughter was my sounding board and I talked to her probably before she knew what I was saying," recalled the wife of a conductor.[53] It was certainly felt that a daughter's exposure to railway life equipped her to handle its pressures should she also marry a railroader. Jim Blythe, an engineer, expressed this common belief succinctly: "It was hard for a woman but not for my wife because she was used to it, being the daughter of an engineer. She adjusted to it, but for the other women it was hard to adjust. . . . Had a lot of trouble. Lots of trouble."[54]

Next to the family support network, that established among friends and neighbours and among fellow church members was most important to the wives of running-trades workers. For the most part, friends were the wives of other railroaders, many but not all of whom had husbands working in the running trades. This was true of both generations. Similarly, fellow church members were also from the railway community.[55] Wives looked upon friends and neighbours as a source of help and comfort, especially in emergencies. They would visit one another with their children, thereby creating an informal arrangement of collective child care. Visiting with other wives was a way of combatting loneliness and a form of entertainment. Card parties, community dances, and other social gatherings were also popular forms of entertainment that were important to the support networks railway wives created. Both husbands and wives might participate in these events, but frequently only wives would be involved.

Indeed, there was a gender division of leisure in the railroad community. Many wives of both generations were members of the church women's auxiliaries and, to a lesser extent, the women's branches of union and fraternal organizations. As with the informal networks women created, these auxiliary committees offered them a forum to share their experiences and to break some of the isolation they might experience, especially for those who did not have family in the town. Their participation in such organizations and in informal arrangements was governed, however, by the demands of their domestic work schedule, and especially by their ability to make arrangements for child care.

While others might depend to various degrees on their support networks to deal with the pressures of their situation, they also devised ways to gain some control over the effects of their husband's work schedule on family life. As one historian has observed, "it is within the private sphere that women could wield the most influence over their families. They made effective use of their capacity to argue, nag, manipulate . . . in order to achieve certain demands."[56] Many wives of running-trades workers refused to move their families to northern Ontario when their husbands were sent there to work. In isolated towns such as Hornepayne, Capreol, and Nakina, living conditions were extremely harsh compared to what existed in

Allandale. Facilities improved in the 1950s, but still compare unfavourably with those available at home. In light of such conditions, wives stood firm in their commitment to remain in Allandale or in other divisional points in southern Ontario. Given a wife's refusal to move, a husband might pass up a better job in the north to remain with his family when he was allowed to do so, as in the case of senior brakemen and conductors. A conductor's daughter vividly remembered her mother's determination to stay in Toronto: "Our dad, he . . . started on a passenger [train as a] conductor. And he wasn't on there very long because he got transferred out to Toronto, from Toronto to North Bay. And my mother says no way would she break her family in Toronto. That was the last thing. So my dad just dropped back to a freight [conductor]."[57] Conversely, some wives insisted that they move up north with their husbands in order to avoid a long separation.

For many wives, a move to northern Ontario would mean the loss of an important family-support network. They were also aware, not only of how conditions in the north would affect their own domestic labour and well-being, but also how such conditions might affect the health of their spouses, especially in the harsh winters when much time would be spent outside in temperatures that could fall to as low as minus 35 degrees Celsius.

Some wives pressured their husbands to take every opportunity to get work in the southern Ontario terminals, if their seniority permitted this. Vera Miller's approach was more direct. She used her knowledge of the seniority system and union regulations to have the Allandale station superintendent bring her husband home, much to her spouse's dismay:

> [I said] why aren't you bringing Peter home? Well, he said, I thought maybe he might just get home and he'd have to go back again. I said that's his worry, not yours. I said, by the way, I said, when Mr. Newton was cut off the railroad, I said, retired, I said that automatically brings a man back. . . . And I said he's still up there. I said what's the point? What did you leave him for? . . . I said you call him back. So he [telephoned the terminal at Hornepayne] and called Peter home. And he never had to go back. Never had to go back. And he could have killed me for it. He said, what did you do that for? I said just because you should have been home, Peter. And I said that's where you should be. And he said, well, I was making good money. I said I don't care how much money you were making. He never had to go back.[58]

Some wives also would meet their husbands at the station on the day they were paid in order to collect their cheques. In certain cases this would provide protection against the spending habits of husbands known for their prowess at drinking and gambling. As the railway would not give the pay cheques directly to the wives, this was one of the few recourses open to women in such situations.[59]

The degree to which women could manoeuvre, however, was still limited. A wife might refuse to move to northern Ontario or to get up at night to make her husband dinner, or she might try to have him come home from the north, but she was in no position to prevent the chaotic and disruptive nature of railway scheduling. Her efforts were directed towards *curtailing* the effects of railway work rhythms on family life. Similarly, a wife might develop ways to manage household finances that met the needs of her family as well as her own needs, but her management was dependent on the wages of her husband.

Running-trades workers were aware of the economic pressures that kept them in the work force as the family breadwinner. These men also derived a certain pride from being able to earn a "family wage."[60] The fact that running-trades workers were the family breadwinners was viewed through a particularly masculine frame of reference. Their situation did not simply reflect economic necessity, but was also a desirable state of affairs. It confirmed their masculinity and underpinned the patriarchal power they might exercise in the family.

As theorists of masculinity have argued, "definitions of masculinity enter into the way work is personally experienced, as a life-long commitment and responsibility. In some respects, work itself is made palatable only through the kinds of compensations masculinity can provide. . . . When work is unpalatable, it is often only his masculinity (his identification with the wage, 'providing for the wife and kids') that keeps a man at work day after day."[61] A male worker views his wages as proof of his ability to endure the harsh working conditions that a woman would supposedly be incapable of surviving. For him, to be the breadwinner of the family is not simply a result of the sexual division of wage labour; it is also a confirmation of his male prowess. It is a prize won "in a masculine mode in confrontation with the 'real' world."[62]

The self-image of running-trades workers as men was bound up in their notion of a wife's place being in the home. For the first generation, this meant after marriage; for the second generation, this meant, if not after marriage, at least after the first child was born. As an engineer's son recalled, "back in those days the women didn't work. If a woman had to go out to work her husband was kinda looked down on because he was supposed to keep her."[63]

A wife working for wages outside the home was, for some men, a threat to the power and privileged position of the male breadwinner in the family, despite the improbability of a wife being able to become economically independent. The comments of one railroader made explicit what others might have also felt but were reluctant to articulate: "My wife never worked outside the house. I don't believe in the woman working. I'm an oldtimer. In the old days that was their place but now it's so much different. A man that starts a little argument [with his wife would be told]: 'Well, I can keep myself. To hell with you.'"[64]

While many railwaymen believed that a woman's place was in the home, their wives did not always concur with this view. Some women, especially of the first generation, resented being told that they had to leave the paid work force upon marriage. Though wives were aware of how wage work for married women reflected badly on their husbands, some were particularly irritated with the way such restrictions were enforced by their employers, and by the railway company itself. To allow married women to work outside the home would give the unwelcome impression that Grand Trunk or CNR wages were insufficient to support a family. Catherine Roy's recollections underscored the irritation that these women felt: "You [were] not allowed [work outside the home after marriage] when you belonged to the CNR in those days. No, you couldn't dare have another job. Your whole life was CNR. . . . The railroad disapproved of it, you see. I don't know how they can run your affairs for you."[65]

Once his wife became a homemaker, a railwayman believed that he was entitled to certain benefits that were compensation for his breadwinning efforts—for example, the right to spend a portion of his time off the job as he pleased. The degree to which a husband might become involved in housework and child care was limited by his own wage-labour schedule and the time necessary to recover from the demands of his job. Domestic labour was not simply assigned to wives as a result of their husband's work schedule, however. For the vast majority, domestic work was allocated on the basis of gender; it was women's work. In certain instances, husbands might "help out." Some intervened to ease their spouse's workload through the acquisition of home appliances.[66] Some husbands also prepared meals, though generally after their retirement. As well, many practised a division of labour in which they were responsible for house repairs and maintenance.

Domestic labour was, nevertheless, a woman's responsibility from which a husband was exempt unless he chose otherwise.[67] This arrangement was somewhat ironic, however. When away from home, running-trades workers would often cook for themselves and be responsible for keeping their living accommodations clean. The peculiar working conditions of engine and train crews legitimized their involvement in specific elements of what might be considered "domestic labour away from home." When a worker returned to Allandale this labour again became his wife's duty.

Patriarchal practices, however, cannot be seen as simply being imposed on these women (or on these men, for that matter), though impositions certainly did occur. As others have observed, such practices are perpetuated "in the main by consent, by identification with the status quo and a belief in common interests or inevitability."[68] While domestic labour for a railway worker's wife could be stressful, frustrating, and burdensome, much of a wife's identity and pride was bound up in the work she did in the home. "I never wanted to go to work once I had my children," commented an engineer's wife. "I don't know how people can do it really. So I was just like a home person. I wanted to be in the house. I wanted to keep my family. And it never bothered me."[69]

A great deal has been written about the "heroic" elements of working-class masculinity, that enabled a man to survive hostile working conditions through "sheer mental and physical bravery."[70] Similarly, there are also "heroic" elements to working-class femininity that enabled a woman to survive the often conflicting and onerous pressures of domestic labour. Wives of both generations spoke with pride of being able to meet the demands of their situation, though often with great difficulty. They were aware of the essential role they had in the family and its importance, from the smallest matter of family care to the largest.

For a woman, not to tend to the needs of family and husband was to call into question her identity as a housewife and mother. It would also call into question the necessity of doing her job well. Wives who drank to excess, or did not provide the "proper care" for children or spouse, or who had extramarital affairs, were viewed unsympathetically.[71] Husbands who were poor providers, alcoholics, or philanderers were also criticized, though elements of a double standard did exist, especially concerning the question of drinking.

Seeing themselves as wives and mothers, the women of the railway community did not challenge the predominant gender relations of the period. According to their ideological conceptions, a wife's (or at least a mother's) place was in the home—but this was also a necessity. As one railway wife and mother stated, in comments that have been already noted: "I never wanted to go to work once I had my children." Yet underlying this view of herself as a non-wage-working mother and wife was the recognition: "I don't know how people can do it"—that is, raise children and do wage-work under conditions in a railway family that would make such a "double day" formidable. In the decades after World War II it became more acceptable for wives without children, or with older children, to work in the paid labour force. Yet this acceptance was not total. Practical and ideological considerations that pointed to the home as the proper sphere for women also remained strong.[72]

> The railroad man is a little different from a lot of people. . . . There was togetherness. . . . The railway man was closer because . . . outside the odd time you'd be off, you'd be together all the time. You'd eat together. You slept together. . . . You'd be together for miles and miles, hours and hours. (Dave Kingston, conductor, born 1892, hired 1913)
>
> We were always brothers. That's what we worked on. (Mike Allen, conductor, born 1915, hired 1941)

The manner in which running-trades workers manoeuvred within the limits of their work and family lives revealed a great deal about their self-image as men. This identity both shaped and was an outgrowth of their work experience. Their view of themselves as breadwinners was conditioned by their class situation, the prevailing gender division of wage labour, and the ideology of patriarchy. As economic providers they persisted in wage labour for the greatest part of their lives and attempted to ensure economic security for their kin through occupational inheritance.[73] When they intensified their labour by taking all the work they could handle, running-trades workers not only indicated the degree to which economic insecurity might guide their actions, they also revealed how concepts of masculinity, with an emphasis on the role of breadwinning and expectations of competitive individualism, could fracture unity among workers. Yet the masculinity they practised was multidimensional and contradictory. It played a role both in promoting and undermining solidarity among workers and opposition to authority at work.

There was much in the lives of enginemen and trainmen to promote a sense of being part of a "brotherhood." Both on and off the job, engineers, firemen, conductors, and brakemen were in close company with fellow workers. When away from their families, married workers returned to the world of single men. Along with their unmarried counterparts, they participated in a bachelor culture of recreation, sanctioned by the particular circumstances of their work.

These men would sleep and eat together in vans or bunkhouses when waiting for a return train, or in hotels or boarding houses when working out of northern Ontario terminals. After rest, and depending on their work schedule, men might go hunting or fishing, if in the north country. Frequently they would play cards, such as poker and "catch"—not the games that were played in the mixed company of card parties at home. The mainstay of conversation was often their work on the railroad. A large part of this recreational culture also involved drinking. As one conductor commented, "booze was mixed up in pretty well every activity they had."[74]

When away from their families, crew members would also go to parties or dances in nearby towns. Freed from the constraints of wife and family and from the view of one's home community, some men threw caution to the wind. "There was a rough old life up there [in the north]," remarked Dave Spalding, an engineer. "A lot of boys got away from their families, you know, and they kinda whooped it up a bit."[75] In the recollections of another railroader, "as soon as the day's work was over it was a hard playin' bunch of fellas."[76]

Wives generally had some knowledge of their husband's recreation away from home, though not necessarily the details. It would appear that these forms of entertainment among men were accepted by wives, except if done to extremes and consequently threatened the security of the family. Tensions did arise at home when workers returned from the world of single men to the world of wife and family and continued to live as if they were still away from home. This was especially true concerning the question of drinking. Some men would spend most of their recreation at home away from the family, drinking in the local bars with their fellow workers. The majority of Allandale's running-trades workers, however, did spend time with their families when at home.

As with their wives, however, there still existed for these workers a gender division of leisure. When in Allandale, engine and train crews by no means completely abandoned the world of men for that of wife and family. Aside from going to a pub with workmates, these men would go together to certain sports events and to monthly union meetings. Many running-trades workers were also members of fraternal organizations in the community. During this period, the Masonic Order was the most popular.[77] In the years before 1930, and especially in the nineteenth century, organizations such as the Sons of England or Scotland, the Oddfellows, and the Orange Order also had a large railway following among Protestant workers.[78] Masonic meetings and events provided these men with the opportunity to get together to discuss lodge affairs as well as events on the railroad. Railroaders became members in order to be with fellow workers and friends, and were often encouraged to join by their supervisors and other workmates.

Participation in such male societies, and in male forms of recreation when at home, was in many respects an extension of the camaraderie that was established at work. Away from home, men spent long hours together both on the job and off. In certain respects, co-operation was necessary not only to get a train over the road but also to avoid intensifying the already-existing strains that came with working long, and often irregular, hours under demanding conditions. The friendships established were valued, and for some were important compensations for the disruptions that were part of running-trades work rhythms.

When speaking of fellow workers in the running trades, or on the railroad in general, men used terms such as "brothers," "brotherhood," and "family." These terms of consanguinity were not simply figurative, given the widespread kinship ties that did exist in the railroad labour force. They did underscore, however, a closeness that was felt among crew members. Upon entering the running trades, a man was essentially initiated into what sociologists have termed an "occupational culture," with its own language, accepted forms of interaction, and set of expectations. This was also a male culture where one's masculinity came under scrutiny by seasoned workers.[79] The ability of a new fireman to maintain the necessary supply of coal for the engine's firebox, or the ability of a new brakeman to couple railway cars and "throw" the proper switches, became a test of one's stamina and endurance. The new recruit's lack of detailed knowledge of railway operations, particularly those who had no early exposure to railway work, also became a source of amusement and sport for "old hands."

In this world of male workers, men were often given nicknames based on their particular idiosyncrasies. These could be terms both of affection and of friendly (or in some cases not-so-friendly) ridicule, and exhibited a degree of creativity by their originators. Among a number of these, the running-trades work force usually had its "Roarer" ("I was always roarin' about some bastard or something"), "Whiskey Face," "Slippery Dick," "Diamond Jim," "Fats," and "Brandy."[80]

Co-operation and close companionship were important not only "to getting the job done" and to surviving the rigours of work, however. They also provided the basis for collective solidarity in resisting or curtailing the authority of railway officials and supervisors. As those who have studied the labour process of mass-production industries have observed, the formal negotiating power of the union provides only a limited challenge to the discipline of production.[81] In the highly organized running trades, union regulations were an important form of protection. Workers did have some recourse to defending themselves against decisions by officials through grievance procedures (which were stronger in the post–World War II period). Nonetheless, in dealing with authority at work, crew members also relied upon informal means of protecting themselves and challenging the structures of discipline that existed.

A sense of responsibility to fellow workers and to one's companions led workers to protect each other from possible discipline when company regulations pertaining to train operations and the conduct of employees were violated. This most frequently took the form of a "conspiracy of silence" regarding rule violations: "If something happened, you never mentioned it. You just kept quiet. Back in the old days [i.e. in the days of the Grand Trunk Railway] the officials, you know, you could be fired for nothing, practically. They were tough in those days. And the railroad men, especially the running trades, they all worked together. Some guy made an error, you didn't say anything about it.[82] In cases where workers were caught violating regulations, men spoke of company officials offering to limit suspensions from work or to reduce or eliminate the demerit points assigned if the person most responsible was turned in by his workmates. To submit to this form of plea bargaining (by turning company's evidence) was particularly insulting to workers and, for those who did, it represented a betrayal of one's fellow workers and the established code of ethics.[83]

While close co-operation and friendship could exist among Allandale running-trades workers, relations among crew members and between them and the rest of the work force were not as unblemished as the recollections of some railroaders would have them. Faced with the threat of company discipline or the needs of an emergency, workers could "pull together" according to their code of ethics. Nevertheless, generational and occupational tensions and infighting also existed in the running-trades work force, and those tarnished the idealized image of co-operation and camaraderie, and revealed another dimension of their working-class masculinity.

For the generation that began work in the 1920s or earlier, relations between junior firemen and brakemen and their more senior engineers and conductors appeared to have been more harmonious than those that existed for the following generation of workers who started during the

Second World War. In the experience of the first generation, most firemen and brakemen were in their late teens or early twenties and unmarried when they began, while engineers and conductors were considerably older, with wives and children. Junior crew members would be treated paternalistically, as sons needing guidance and a firm hand when necessary. Bob Lenard, an engineer, had fond recollections of his early years on the railroad: "A lot of the old men, they more or less adopted me. Like I was only a boy compared with them. That time those men were creatin' a family. They were good to me. I haven't got no complaints about any of them."[84]

Given the extent of the kinship ties that existed in the running-trades work force, a young man's entry into railroad work could be seen as a way of reaffirming a bond between kin, between father and son or nephew and uncle. As a new recruit learned his job, the paternal authority of senior crew members came to bear on these young workers, as a source of support, knowledge, and discipline. In this generation's experience, paternalism characterized relations between younger and older workers, and was both a remnant of historical tradition and an outgrowth of the actual kinship bonds that existed in the work force. The railway company saw these familial ties as a *potential* source of discipline, with the actions of sons or nephews reflecting on the reputation of fathers and uncles. The existence of these bonds could also act as a source of solidarity, in resisting or defending workers against company authority, such as in the case of the "conspiracy of silence" that existed on the railroad.

The existence of family ties and paternalistic practices in the work force could as well lead to a rejection of paternalistic relations, as young men came to resist or challenge the authority of their elders. As this first generation of running-trades workers grew older and attempted to apply aspects of the paternalistic practices of their early days on the railroad to the generation that started work in the late 1920s and early 1940s, they met with resistance. There were several reasons why relations between older and younger workers in the experience of the first generation were unlike those of the second generation.

With the outbreak of World War II, the first generation of railroaders was faced with the responsibility of training new men after not having done so for over a decade. These new recruits were also older—many were married and had children, unlike the teenagers and young adults who began running-trades work in the 1920s and earlier decades. Established patterns of work for the first generation were disrupted not only by the introduction of new men but also by the need for the intensification of labour rhythms to meet wartime requirements. In the case of head-end crews, men who had always been firemen and wished to remain so were now forced to become engineers and had to cope with their new jobs as well as with the training of new recruits who might be more technically competent. These new men were perceived as a threat: they were younger and in some respects could better withstand, or appeared better to withstand, the demands of wartime work. Essentially they came to symbolize the turmoil these older men were experiencing during the war years, and their presence could raise awkward questions about an oldtimer's own masculinity.

Workers of the second generation spoke of being ostracized by engineers and conductors of the first generation when they began on the road. These "oldtimers" often would not associate with the new men or would sometimes refuse to work with them, would provide only minimum training and advice, and would strongly criticize new crew members when they made a mistake. Such behaviour was not simply part of the harsh running-trades initiation rite, for those of the first generation had not experienced this treatment to the same degree themselves. Antagonism was not only directed to unrelated members of the work force, but could involve fathers and sons as well. John Heath, who came from a family of railroaders, remembered such conflicts vividly: "When you first started out you ran into these old [crew members]. My father was one of them. They hated to see these young upstarts coming into their territory, you might say. And boy, you had a rough time with those guys. . . . They hated us."[85]

The reaction of many of these recruits was not a passive one, although they were placed in a difficult position of having to work with the "oldtimers" while learning a new job (sometimes on their own) with its attendant uncertainties and vulnerabilities. In addition, company officials apparently took a dim view of oldtimers' refusal to work with new men, especially if this interfered with the training of new recruits. The fact that there were large numbers of men hired during the war alleviated some of the isolation they might feel. These "teddy bears," as they were called by the "oldtimers," drew closer together in light of the similar circumstances they faced. Workers cited incidents of fighting between junior and senior crew members as well as verbal assaults on "oldtimers" who attempted to browbeat the new men. The interaction between crew members could take a very masculine form of confrontation, and was recalled in such terms: "For about two years there used to be fire and hell to pay. Because the young fellas comin' up wouldn't take the BS that was bein' handed to 'em. There was a lot of trouble. Once the older men realized what was goin' on, that they weren't goin' to be the little god any more, then things changed."[86]

It would appear that relations between these generations of workers did improve as the new men fought back against the authoritarianism of the oldtimers and became proficient in their jobs. In addition, in the postwar period, particularly in the 1950s, many of the oldtimers retired, thereby removing a source of conflict. There could also be tensions, however, between engine crews and train crews as proud engineers and conductors argued with one another about train operations and authority. Such rivalries have been well noted in railway histories and celebrated in literature. In the case of Allandale workers, generational tension between "oldtimers" and "teddy bears" also had elements of occupational rivalry between the head-end and tail-end crews. New firemen would be scorned by conductors and new brakemen would be held in disdain by engineers not only because of generational antagonism but also for reasons of traditional occupational conflict. Workers of the second generation spoke of this conflict being less pronounced among their peer group, in part because of the common hostility all new running-trades workers felt from the "oldtimers." Nonetheless, within this generation, as with the previous one, occupational rivalries could still occur.

Rivalry between the "head end" and "tail end" in certain respects was part of a masculine style of interaction, characterized by playful ridicule and insults that did not necessarily indicate any genuine feeling of antagonism. Engine and train crews could be very friendly with one another and, while some spoke of enginemen having nothing to do with trainmen, many others, especially of the second generation, recalled spending leisure time together both at home and away. There were also instances where junior crew members informally switched jobs among themselves for a period while on a run, though this was against company regulations. A brakeman assigned to the "head end" would "fire" (i.e., shovel coal into the firebox) while the fireman would either take a rest or perform the duties of the brakeman.

A difference in technical knowledge and the meaning these men attached to the concept of skill also underpinned the rivalry between engine and train crews. As theorists of the labour process have argued, skill is not only a technical category but is also an ideological construct that is highly gendered. Definitions of skill are bound up with masculine identities and play an important part in defining the skill level of work performed.[87] Not only has the process of skill definition served to devalue the labour done by women in predominantly female occupations but it has also had an important influence on relations between male workers. To be less skilled was to a certain degree to be less of a man, given the way in which the notion of skill has been infused with the supposed masculine qualities of technical proficiency and competence.

The conflicts that arose between enginemen and trainmen—for example, over speed limits—could become intense when an engineer asserted his belief in the superiority of his technical skills and judgment. That a conductor had jurisdiction over the operation of the entire train could be particularly galling. In the words of one engineer, "[conductors] ran the train, allright. But that engine. Bomb the goddamn train on them. You were in charge of the engine. They could do whatever they liked with that train."[88] Some engineers also were not inhibited in presenting their views to conductors or brakemen: "[Conductors] were largely referred to as the messenger boy. That was the extent of the love between the head end and the tail end. . . . You see some of these fellas [i.e. conductors] come in here on the last trip and oh, are they important. I don't know how they kept the buttons on their coats."[89] This dynamic also played a role in the sectionalism evident between running-trades workers and those who worked in other railway occupations. Engineers, firemen, conductors, and brakemen, who had the most prestigious and autonomous of jobs in the railway labour force, could be accused by those working in the car shop, the roundhouse, or the bridge and building department of forming a self-important elite that would have little to do with other railroaders. More than a few engine- and train-crew members apparently did little to dispel this accusation.[90]

The nature of the work itself contributed much to both the masculine self-image and practices of these workers. The labour of engine and train crews demanded a great deal of physical effort and endurance. These men had to brave temperatures of extreme heat and cold. Long hours, often limited rest, the uncertainty of weather and track conditions, and the ever-present prospect of accidents that could be fatal—all were an integral part of the job. As theorists of masculinity have argued, the harsh physical demands and mental strains of a working-class occupation can lead men to view their work in terms of "a heroic exercise of manly confrontation with 'the task.' Difficult, uncomfortable or dangerous conditions are seen not for themselves, but for their appropriateness to a masculine readiness and hardiness."[91]

For engine and train crews, a sense of "manly confrontation" with the elements was confirmed by the rhythms and conditions of their labour as well as by the technology they had to operate. Brakemen and conductors noted the skill and physical exertion required to "pull" switches and to couple or uncouple cars, as well as the dangers they courted when doing so. Engineers and firemen proudly spoke of mastering huge locomotive engines and of "breathing life" into inanimate objects. To run an engine at high speeds while pulling a long line of freight or passenger cars gave these men a sense of enormous power. One engineer captured the perspective of many others when he stated: "I loved the engines. I loved power, when I handled power."[92] When diesel engines replaced coal-fired ones in the 1950s, engine crews felt not only a loss of skill but also of some of the qualities of their labour that for them made it a specifically masculine calling. The dirt and sweat involved in feeding coal to a hot firebox, the physical exertion and co-ordination required to operate the steam engine, and the sometimes deafening noise in the cab, were gone.[93]

Paul Willis among others has observed the way in which male workers' "mechanical, sensuous, and concrete familiarity with the tools of production" can mediate both the experience and understanding of the labour process.[94] An engineman might be tired by the demands of needing to be constantly on the move and feel harassed by a supervisor or dispatcher keeping track of his performance or the movement of his engine from a distance. At the same time he could feel exhilarated and be fascinated by the massive and intricate piece of technology he was controlling. For many workers, there was a close identification with the power of the technology they operated. Engineers spoke of this power as an extension of themselves. When discussing the operation of their locomotives they would say that "I got up enough power to make the steep grade" or "I was losing power so I had to cut and run [i.e., disconnect the engine from the rest of the train and go to the nearest coal- or water-storage facility on the line]." It was no coincidence that their descriptions of railway technology and the terminology of train operations were often invested with sexual or gender-specific metaphors and allusions that underscored the close relationship between work and gender identity that existed for engine and train crews. In the lexicon of the railroader an "old girl" was a locomotive, which was always given a title of female gender. When operating his engine an engineer, who would be called a "hogger," "hog jockey," "hoghead," or "whistle pig," might "beat her on the back [i.e., maintain high speed using full engine power]" or "maul his pig [i.e., run an engine at full stroke and throttle]." He would have to "get up steam" in his locomotive until "she was hot [i.e., with enough 'steam up' to run the engine]." Figures of authority and symbols of privilege associated with authority could be given appellations that were meant to symbolize uselessness and impotence, though these workers were quite aware that supervisors were not particularly impotent in the exercise of authority. Division officials might be referred to as "old men," and their private railway cars as "drone cages."[95]

Metaphors of unequal gender relations—of men's domination of women—figured in railwaymen's working vocabulary, and these were also employed to describe relations with supervisors. In his analysis of contemporary male workplace culture at Westinghouse, Stan Gray has argued that the language of sex and sexual imagery is used by men to express the reality of class relations. The "sex act is conceived fundamentally as one of exploitation. . . . [It] is used as a model for all forms of exploitation and degradation of people, of which that taking place in production is one."[96] When officials exercised their power, the terms of domination that workers might employ to describe their mastery of gender-ascribed technology were now used to indicate their own subordination. They were the ones who were now being "mauled" or "beaten." As with workers elsewhere, railroaders might also use explicitly sexual terms to describe authority relations at work. A worker who was given demerit points, suspended, or otherwise disciplined by a superintendent, trainmaster, or master mechanic might speak of being "screwed" or "fucked over" by an official. Supervisors who had a reputation of being particularly harsh, vindictive, or overly zealous were viewed contemptuously, and spoken of in crude terms that referred to aspects of male or female anatomy. Steve Price graphically conveyed the language and metaphors used when appraising company officials: "That's where we got the pricks. Some of the supervisors . . . Old Pete Marwick was a no-good bitch. Bill North was a hell of a good guy. . . . Ray Cummings was a rotten little son of a bitch. Sneakin' bastard. Sneakin' around seein' what everybody was doin'. . . . Hal Richards wasn't too bad but he done a lot of dirty goddamn tricks too, the son of a bitch."[97]

A mindset that stressed the need to put on a brave front in the face of very difficult or stressful labour conditions was also an important element of these workers' masculinity. Even when admitted, the personal turmoil created by the rhythms of railway labour on work and family life was not discussed at length among fellow workers. This "emotional illiteracy" or inability to express feelings, which was part of a male worker's socialization, was perpetuated by the conventions of work.[98] The fears and insecurities a worker experienced were rarely mentioned, though they might find an acceptable outlet in drinking, arguments, rough play, or fighting. To succumb to such tensions was to be less of a man. Indeed, the pressures of work could be understood as a challenge to one's masculinity rather than as an illustration of the power relations at work, which forced crew members to endure such conditions.[99] Evaluating his work experiences on the railroad, one engineer spoke for many when commenting that he "look[ed] back on things . . . as sort of successful experiences where you master the job and not let the job get the best of you."[100]

Many workers recalled the harsh conditions they survived with pride and, for some, even with a sense of nostalgia. According to these men, the present generation of running-trades workers would be unable, if not unwilling, to tolerate such circumstances. An emphasis on manly endurance could lead an engineman or trainman to persist in his job when it was neither demanded by supervisors nor safe to do so. Often, workers regarded fatalistically the prospect of being in a major accident. The conventional wisdom among crew members was not to worry about what could not be avoided. Others might repress their fear and believe themselves immune from such a possibility. "You just felt like the same as when I worked in the mine," claimed one man. "Christ, we killed a man every day but ya never thought it was gonna be you. Ya never worried."[101]

In light of the frequent accidents which did occur in running-trades work, many of which involved injury and sometimes death, a fatalistic attitude became one of the means of surviving the tensions of the job.[102] Underpinning the masculinity of these workers was an acceptance of limitations, however uneasy or conditional that acceptance might be. One made the best of a situation and endured what could not be changed. "Making do" could become a virtue in itself. Yet, as with the friendships formed among co-workers, a conception of "manliness" could lead enginemen and trainmen not only to accommodate themselves to the conditions of their labour, but also to challenge authority when its exercise by supervisors impinged on a man's dignity. Such challenges are limited in the sense that they did not fundamentally call into question the relations of power at work, though they might be directed towards containing them to some degree. The demands for a grievance system by the railway unions were motivated not only by the very real need to protect workers from the sometimes arbitrary exercise of officials' authority, but also out of a concern that such treatment was offensive to one's masculine pride. It was this manly pride that proscribed kowtowing to officials and could be a reservoir of aggressiveness in confrontations with authority. Glen McPherson's account of one confrontation captures this style of masculine aggressiveness. His comments also underline the rivalries that exist between engineers and conductors and the degree to which confrontations with supervisors could be futile in correcting a perceived injustice:

> The road foreman of engines . . . was criticizing me for pulling this draw bar, [improperly] applying the [engine] brakes at that point. Well, I told him, I was nervy enough to tell him that, "Well, lookit, are you goin' to assess me demerit marks," which he did. He handed me the slip to sign and I wouldn't sign it for him. I says, "I'm not goin' to sign that." I says, "I'm not takin' criticism from you as to how I run an engine. From you, a man who never run an engine." He was a conductor beforehand. . . . The demerit marks went against my record as far as that's concerned.[103]

The nature of a worker's interaction with authority and his willingness or ability to challenge it, however, were also affected by the changing labour conditions of the period. These conditions contributed to what appears to have been a shift in emphasis in the meanings that masculinity had for running-trades workers and a shift in masculine practices themselves. When the sanctions against challenging authority were too great, as was the case during the Great Depression, aggressiveness towards authority was more muted and greater stress was placed on definitions of masculinity that focussed on hard work and endurance. In periods of labour shortage, such as the war years, challenges to authority were less likely to result in dismissal. While a worker's masculinity still emphasized his ability to be "tough," this toughness was also more likely to be practised in relations with senior engineers and conductors (as in the case of new recruits hired during the Second World War) or with officials (as in the case of both generations of workers).[104]

In these "manly" confrontations with supervisors or with each other, workers were not constrained by the presence of women. The work world of the running trades was a male preserve. Historically, women had been excluded from such labour, even during both world wars, when women made limited and temporary inroads into traditionally male occupations. During those wars mainly single women found employment in the railway shops and roundhouses, as well as in the traditional area of office work. They did not work outside the perimeter of the railway station and its maintenance facilities.[105] For the men of the Allandale running-trades labour force, this was both a necessary and preferable state of affairs. Primarily, workers felt that such work would be unfit and unsafe for a woman, married or single: a woman would be unable to withstand the hard physical labour and dangers of the job. Wives also concurred in the view that running-trades occupations were gendered as masculine. Part of the working-class morality of these men and their community was the concept of protecting women from dangerous employment.[106] As one engineman argued, "I wouldn't want any women goin' out when I was runnin'. Their life wouldn't be safe."[107]

Running-trades work could indeed be unsafe, for women or men. The exclusionary arguments of engine and train crews did not, however, simply involve the question of safety and the needs of the family. Aspects of patriarchal privilege would certainly be at stake if women were to enter the running-trades fraternity. Hiring a woman to do a "man's job," particularly a single woman, would deprive a married man of the means to support his family. Aside from the standard defence of the male provider, the nature of running-trades work itself could be invoked in arguing for the exclusion of women. In the running trades, unlike other male occupations into which women were admitted during wartime, it would have been difficult to segregate men and women workers on the job. Given the large amount of time that was spent away from home, separate living facilities would also need to be constructed for female crew members, for reasons of sexual propriety. Such issues had been raised in resisting the entry of women into other areas of the work force; in running-trades work these problems would become especially worrisome and costly to resolve. Moreover it was felt that a woman's own sense of morality would prevent her from seeking employment on the road—no self-respecting woman would do so.[108]

For a woman to become an engineer, fireman, brakeman, or conductor would call into question the ideological conception of these occupations as men's work. Her work in the running trades would make it difficult for a male worker to get a sense of confirmation of his own masculinity. The physical strength and the endurance of harsh and sometimes dangerous conditions demanded by the job could no longer be understood as the unique and special preserve of a man. At the same time, the entry of women into the running trades would constitute an invasion of an important sanctuary of male working-class culture, where men could escape from the constraints of wife and family and be as profane and as rough as they wished, at least when they were not in contact with passengers. It was no coincidence that trainmen stated that the most disagreeable feature of their work on passenger trains was dealing with "the public." While the problems of unruly or dissatisfied passengers were cited as the major source of irritation, it was also the case that these men disliked the constraints placed on their own behaviour, constraints that were absent when working on freight trains. Passenger-train conductors had to wear uniforms that were popularly known as "harnesses," a telling colloquialism that did not refer to the restrictions of a dress code alone.[109]

Theorists of masculinity have argued that male workplace culture can be seen as a form of rebellion "against civilized society's cultural restraints.[110] It was also a domain that had to be protected against representatives of civilizing restraint—women. The presence of women in this world forced men to "clean up their act" and alter the way they behaved with one another. In the presence of women, both on and off the job, running-trades workers did act differently than when just among themselves.[111] Women were not totally closed off from the work-world of engine and train crews. The wives and children of these workers periodically travelled on the trains with their husbands or fathers, and events on the railway were discussed in many running-trades families. Nonetheless, in the presence of women a sanitized image of male work culture would often be conveyed.

The masculinity practised by enginemen and trainmen shared many features with that of other sections of the railway labour force and the male working class in general. As with many workers, these men could be rough and aggressive, "hard drinking" and "hard swearing." In his analysis of contemporary male workplace culture in mass-production industry, Stan Gray has written that male workers worship a self-identity of "vulgar physicalness" where intellectual pursuits and theoretical knowledge are disdained. According to Gray, it is this self-identity that is antithetical to a tradition that spoke of the dignity of labour. The obsessive celebration of physical prowess can be seen as "accepting and then glorifying the middle-class views of manual labour and physical activity as inferior, animalistic and crude."[112] Running-trades workers were certainly proud of their physical capabilities, but their masculinity was not reduced to a simple "self-identity of vulgar physicalness." There was much in the nature of their work—for example, the relative autonomy from direct supervision and the skills demanded of their trade—as well as a rich and proud historical tradition that militated against a view of the labour as inferior or animalistic. These men viewed themselves to be "respectable" and cherished their respectability as did skilled workers within the class as a whole. This was not simple middle-class (or petit-bourgeois) male respectability, though it had many of those features. Its style was too aggressive, direct, and rough for middle-class gentility, nurtured as it was in part at work. Though the exercise of company authority might wound a railwayman's masculine pride and offend his working-class dignity, pride and dignity were also tenacious qualities in the running-trades workers' world.

For the men and women of Allandale, the class and gender conditions and relations of the period set limits to what was available and possible. In most running-trades families, husbands were breadwinners and wives were full-time homemakers. This pattern was the response of railway families to the constraints created by the gender division of wagework, running-trades labour rhythms, the prevailing conditions of reproductive labour, and the ideology of patriarchy. Nonetheless, railroaders and their wives also made choices within the limitations of their lives. Some decided that it was better for a family's welfare if a wife remained in Allandale while a husband worked in the north. Others believed that families should stay united.

Wives consequently moved to northern Ontario with their husbands. Many men chose to remain running-trades workers despite the disruptive and unpredictable rhythms of their labour. Others, however, could not tolerate the work and sought employment elsewhere in order to support their families. These choices had different implications for the men and women of the community.

The strategies railroad families adopted for survival and well-being revealed some striking continuities. Nevertheless, there were changes as well. Married women of the first generation provided for their family's welfare through their labour in the home. A number of second-generation wives, however, also contributed as secondary wage-earners, at least until they became mothers. During the Great Depression, running-trades families had to abandon temporarily their emphasis on occupational inheritance as a means of providing economic security for the next generation. Men whose career on the railroad belatedly began in the early 1940s were even less able to offer their own sons the prospect of occupational inheritance. With the decline of Allandale as the railway centre and the general contraction of the running-trades work force in the 1960s and 1970s, fathers encouraged their sons to pursue other employment. These strategies both altered and were changed by the constraints of the lives of railway-family members.

Conceptions of masculinity and femininity which informed family strategies also shaped and were moulded by the class and gender relations of the time. Especially in the paid work of railroaders, notions of "manliness" had a rather contradictory influence on labour relations. An emphasis on the breadwinning role and elements of competitive individualism could come into conflict with notions of worker solidarity and the established code of ethics on the job. This was evident in instances when men exceeded their mileage limitations, tried to manipulate their seniority standing, or reported a fellow crew-member's violation of company regulations. An emphasis on masculine hardiness could lead enginemen and trainmen to view the difficult and dangerous conditions of their labour as a test of their manhood and played no small role in relations among workers themselves. Officials would also appeal to such manly virtues when supervising their workers. Yet being "tough" could as well lead to the challenge of authority and resistance to managerial intimidation when the sanctions were not too great. While a worker's identity as the family provider might foster a dependence on the railway, it might also lead to demands for better wages and working conditions in order to fulfil that breadwinning role.

Within the running-trades "brotherhood," elements of egalitarian and hierarchical relations co-existed.[113] The experience of railroaders hired during the Second World War highlighted the intensity of the conflicts that could arise as claims of equality came up against the paternalistic practices of an earlier generation. Generational conflict and sectionalism between enginemen and trainmen could threaten the solidarity of the brotherhood; yet these men could also stress a united front against officials. Having come up from the ranks, supervisors might claim to remain a "brother" and use that identity with some effect, but the actual power relations on the railroad also served to undermine such appeals.

Running-trades workers themselves played an important role in shaping their gender and class identities. Breaking the conspiracy of silence when faced with company discipline was actively discouraged as unbecoming to both a worker's and a man's dignity. Those who ran afoul of unwritten codes quickly learned accepted practices or were ostracized. In crafting these practices enginemen and trainmen revealed how the strains of individualism in their socialization as men might be contained. The bonds that were formed between these men also revealed many dimensions. Though putting a premium on "toughness," a worker could be supportive and nurturing with his "brothers," too. Independence and interdependence, competitiveness and co-operation, existed uneasily with one another in the bonds of the brotherhood. As the experience of the two generations of railroaders indicated as well, the shaping of gender identities was an ongoing process.

Relations between husbands and wives could be equally complex. The family wage earned by a running-trades worker allowed his wife to become a full-time homemaker. The rhythms of railway work and the demands of reproductive labour made her presence in the home a necessity as long as her children were still young. Both the family wage and running-trades work rhythms were also central to the construction of working-class masculinity and femininity in Allandale. The spouses of enginemen and trainmen saw themselves primarily as wives and mothers. Their "proper sphere" was in the home, though this began to shift in the post–World War II period. A husband's self-image as a man was bound up in his breadwinning labour. His role as economic provider also formed the basis of the power he could exercise in the family. Yet wives were not simply subordinate to their husbands. They had autonomy in the handling of finances, sanctioned by a husband's frequent absence from home. That autonomy, however, could be undermined when large expenditures were involved. Indeed, the family wage was an arena of conflict and co-operation between men and women.

Wives could also be aggressive with husbands and company officials when the welfare of their family was threatened. At home or in public they challenged the prerogatives of the male breadwinner by refusing to move their families, demanding that their husbands return from the north, and going to the station to take possession of their spouse's pay cheque. By their actions these women called into question notions of passive femininity and confronted husbands whose concept of masculinity emphasized the need to be dominant and tough. The results were sometimes explosive.[114] Notions of respectability, however, constrained some wives to maintain their independence within the confines of the home while in public they tended to bolster the masculine image of the spouses.

In the construction of gender identities, material conditions and ideology reinforced one another. Wives had to become self-reliant due to their husbands' unpredictable work schedule. Nonetheless, this self-reliance did not extend to mothers working outside the home. Aside from the great hardship involved, a mother's wagework would threaten the respectability, not only of her spouse, but of the whole family as well.

Both men and women of the railway community were quite aware of the material and ideological constraints of their lives. Given the class and gender limitations of the period, they worked out a division of labour based on how their families could best survive. Essentially held together by the railway wife, the family could be a forum where all the tensions of conflicting schedules and pressures were expressed. It could also provide a measure of stability and continuity for a worker who was frequently on the move. Indeed, if the family strategies railroaders adopted were essential to their own well-being, they were the linch-pin of railway operations. Railway families provided a major component of the company's future labour force, early exposure to work rhythms and demands, and a potential source of discipline which operated through kinship networks as sons came to recognize that their actions also reflected on their fathers' reputation. The scheduling of trains was based, among other considerations, on the assumption that enginemen and trainmen could look to their wives for the critical emotional and physical support needed to endure the rigours of work.

The arrangement between husbands and wives was a partnership, though not necessarily of equals. While influenced by concepts of working-class masculinity and femininity, family strategies were conceived and carried out as collective endeavours among members involving emotional and physical burdens for men as well as women.[115] Indeed, as both railroaders and their spouses frequently recalled, "it was a hard life."

• Notes

1 Interview with Ed Walker, born 1916, hired by the CNR in 1939.

2 For the most part, Canadian railway histories have been limited to considerations of railway finance, politics, and economic development. When considering railway workers, they generally have been concerned with union activity and industrial relations, or with the men who actually built the railroads. The different labour processes on the railroad have only recently been closely examined, and few studies of the railroad community exist. In those community studies, there is very little analysis of the relationship between the paid-work world of railroaders and the world of unpaid domestic labour maintained by their wives.

3 For example, sample the sometimes heated debates of the past decades that heralded the emergence of the new working-class history in David Bercuson, "Through the Looking Glass of Culture: An Essay on the New Labour History and Working-Class Culture in Recent Canadian Historical Writing," *Labour/Le Travail* 7 (1981): 95–112; Gregory S. Kealey, "H.C.

Pentland and Working Class Studies," *Canadian Journal of Political and Social Theory* 3, 2 (1979): 79–94; "Labour and Working-Class History in Canada: Prospects in the 1980s," *Labour/Le Travail* 7 (1981): 67–94; "Looking Backward: Reflections on the Study of Class in Canada," *History and Social Science Teacher* 16 (Summer 1981): 213–22; Kenneth McNaught, "E.P. Thompson vs Harold Logan: Writing about Labour and the Left in the 1970s," *Canadian Historical Review* 42 (1981): 141–68; Terry Morley, "Canada and the Romantic Left," *Queen's Quarterly* 86 (1979); Bryan D. Palmer, "Working-Class Canada: Recent Historical Writings," *Queen's Quarterly* 86, 4 (Winter 1979/80): 594–616, and "Listening to History Rather than Historians: Reflections on Working-Class History," *Studies in Political Economy* 20 (Summer 1986): 47–84.

4 For example, see the critical comments of Ava Baron in "Technology and the Crisis of Masculinity: The Social Construction of Gender and Skill in the US Printing Industry, 1850–1920" (paper presented at the fifth UMIST-ASTON Conference on the Organisation and Control of the Labour Process, Manchester, England, April 1987).

5 The work of Greg Kealey and Bryan Palmer, for example, does begin to consider such issues. See Kealey, *Toronto Workers Respond to Industrial Capitalism, 1867–1892* (Toronto, 1980); Palmer, *A Culture in Conflict: Skilled Workers and Industrial Capitalism in Hamilton, Ontario, 1860–1914* (Montreal, 1979); Kealey and Palmer, *Dreaming of What Might Be: The Knights of Labor in Ontario, 1880–1900* (Cambridge, 1982). The historical dimensions of class and gender relations for male workers have been explored in some detail in Ava Baron's study of American printers, "Technology and the Crisis of Masculinity," and in Cynthia Cockburn's examination of British

printers, *Brothers* (London, 1983). Most studies that address this concern deal with the present and are often written by sociologists. See, for example, Paul Willis, "Shop-Floor Culture, Masculinity and the Wage Form" in *Working-Class Culture: Studies in History and Theory*, ed. John Clarke, Chas Critcher, and Richard Johnson (London, 1979), 185–98, 281–82; Andrew Tolson, *The Limits of Masculinity* (London, 1982); Jeffrey Weeks, *Sexuality* (London, 1986); Stan Gray, "Sharing the Shop Floor" in *Beyond Patriarchy: Essays by Men on Pleasure, Power, and Change*, ed. Michael Kaufman (Toronto, 1987), 216–34; and Michael Yarrow, "Class and Gender in the Developing Consciousness of Appalachian Coal Miners" (paper presented at the fifth UMIST-ASTON conference on the Organisation and Control of the Labour Process, Manchester, April 1987). It should be noted that the conceptions of masculinity discussed in this paper refer to heterosexual masculinity. See, for example, the comments of Blye Frank on the importance of distinguishing the type of gender identities and practices in "Hegemonic Heterosexual Masculinity," *Studies in Political Economy* 24 (Autumn 1987): 159–70.

6 This approach rejects a "dual systems analysis," which argues that a system of patriarchal gender relations exists apart from that of capitalist class relations. For a sample of the debates that discuss the different conceptualizations of the relationship between class and gender, see, for example, Pat Armstrong and Hugh Armstrong, "Beyond Sexless Class and Classless Sex: Towards Feminist Marxism," *Studies in Political Economy* 10 (Winter 1983): 7–43; Pat Armstrong, *Labour Pains* (Toronto, 1984), 19–48; and Jane Lewis, "The Debate on Sex and Class," *New Left Review* 149 (1985): 108–20.

7 Baron, "Technology and the Crisis of Masculinity," 6–8.

8 For example, the way in which concepts of masculinity have shaped class relations at work is examined in Baron, ibid.; Cockburn, *Brothers*; Yarrow, "Class and Gender in the Consciousness of Appalachian Coal Miners"; Willis, "Shop-Floor Culture"; and Gray, "Sharing the Shop Floor." Whereas Cockburn argues that there is a "sex/gender system" that is separate from the system of class relations, Baron sees class and gender as making up one integrated system and speaks in terms of a "gendered class."

9 For a discussion of this issue's theoretical and empirical literature, which deals primarily with the present, see Lorette K. Woolsey, "Bonds Between Women and Between Men, Part I: A Review of Theory," and "Part II: A Review of Research," *Atlantis* 31, 1 (Fall 1987): 116–36.

10 For example, Yarrow, "Class and Gender in the Consciousness of Appalachian Coal Miners," and Baron, "Technology and the Crisis of Masculinity."

11 This is indicated, for example, in the studies of Willis, "Shop-Floor Culture," Gray, "Sharing the Shop Floor," and Cockburn, *Brothers*. They underline the contradictory features of working-class masculinity while emphasizing the way it has been used to exclude women from the workplace and from working-class organizations in general.

12 The same can be said of identities based on race, ethnicity, and religion. In "Class and Gender," Yarrow has explored the way in which concepts of manliness have figured in the unity of male Appalachian miners against mineowners and contributed to what he has called a "gender specific class conflict consciousness." Baron's "Technology and the Crisis of Masculinity" and Yarrow's work also bring out the contradictory and changing character of male gender identities in their studies.

13 See Yarrow, "Class and Gender in the Consciousness of Appalachian Coal Miners" for a discussion of the emotional and cognitive dimensions of class and gender consciousness.

14 Research for this study is based on a series of interviews with 53 men and women who primarily were either running-trades workers (i.e., engineers, firemen, brakemen, or conductors), their wives, or their children. In a few cases, those interviewed came from other sections of the railroad work force but were long-time residents of the railway community. In total, 21 women and 32 men were consulted. Of the women, 5 were wives of engineers (who had previously been firemen), 7 were wives of conductors (who had previously been brakemen), 4 were daughters of conductors, 1 was a clerk who had worked in the Allandale CNR office, 1 was the daughter of a chief clerk, 2 were daughters of a railway crane operator, and 1 was the wife of a carman. Of the men, 16 were engineers (and former firemen), 11 were conductors (and former brakemen), 2 were railway clerks, 1 was a CNR policeman, 1 was a carman, and 1 was a personnel manager. Those interviewed also made up a total of 32 families of running-trades workers. Eight of those families consisted of husbands and wives who married in the 1920s or earlier. Spouses in the remaining families married mainly in the late 1930s and early 1940s.

The men and women interviewed were not randomly selected, and it cannot be simply stated that they were representative of Barrie's running-trades workers or its railroad families of the period. The majority of Barrie railway families noted in the CNR Pensioners' Club files and on the company's mailing list of pensioners was contacted. Those interviewed had been preselected on the basis that they had chosen to remain in Barrie or to return there. The men interviewed also spent the greatest part of their working lives on the railroad. All had been hired by the CNR before 1948 and remained with the company until their retirement.

15 See, for example, Veronica Strong-Boag, "Keeping House in God's Country: Canadian Women at Work in the Home" in *On The Job*, ed. Craig Heron and Robert Storey (Montreal, 1986), 124–51; Meg Luxton, *More than a Labour of Love* (Toronto, 1980); Bonnie Fox, ed., *Hidden in the Household: Women's Domestic Labour Under Capitalism* (Toronto, 1980); Wally Seccombe, "The Housewife and Her Labour Under Capitalism," *New Left Review* 83 (Jan–Feb. 1974): 3–24; Armstrong and Armstrong, "Beyond Sexless Class"; Armstrong, *Labour Pains*; and Bettina Bradbury, "Women's History and Working-Class History," *Labour/Le Travail* 19 (Spring 1987): 23–43.

16 Except for the Great Depression of the 1930s, the size of the work force seems to have remained stable until the late 1950s. Complete CNR payroll records for the Allandale terminal for this period have not yet been located, and relatively detailed census information for Barrie is only available beginning with the 1951 census. That year it was reported that the CNR had a work force of 380 employees, including express and telegraph workers. These figures might not have included engine and traincrews temporarily working out of different terminals but with a "home base" in Allandale. A number of those interviewed, including the payroll clerk, spoke of a work force of approximately 500 of which a little less than half were running-trades workers. An occupational breakdown of the Barrie work force in the 1951 census indicates a similar proportion of running-trades workers. As well, in 1951 the CNR was still the largest industrial employer in the town. *Census of Canada*, 1941, vol. VII, table 10; 1951, vol. IV, table 4 and table 17; interviews with Steve Williams, clerk, born 1904, hired 1923; Len Stevens, CNR police, born 1892, hired 1920; Tim Armstrong, clerk, born 1915, hired 1946.

The replacement of coal-fired steam engines with diesel-fuelled ones in the late 1950s, in conjunction with the CNR's program of centralization, dramatically reduced the size of the work force in the next decade. Other industries set up after the war, such as Canadian General Electric, replaced the railroad as Barrie's major employer. See Rosemary Spiers, "Technological Change and the Railway Unions, 1945–1972" (PhD thesis, University of Toronto, 1974); Department of Economics and Development, Trade and Industry Branch, Industrial Survey, 1966; John Craig, *Simcoe County: The Recent Past* (Simcoe County, 1977), 231–34; Gail Foster, "Industrial Growth in Barrie and Orillia" (BA thesis, University of Toronto, 1968); Richard LeGear and John Kearns, "History and Development of Industry in Barrie" (unpublished paper (OFY Project 4K2419, 1974), copy in Simcoe County Archives), and interviews.

17 Seniority had been in place since the late nineteenth century, when the Brotherhood of Locomotive Engineers, Brotherhood of Locomotive Firemen and Engineers, Order of Railway Conductors, and the Brotherhood of Railroad Trainmen began organizing engine and train crews; see J.H. Tuck, "The Canadian Railways and the International Brotherhoods" (PhD thesis, University of Western Ontario, 1976), 21 and passim; G.M. Rountree, *The Railway Worker* (Montreal, 1936), 29–30, 216–23, 227–28 and 273; L.A. Wood, *Union Management Cooperation on the Railroad* (New Haven, 1931); Rex Lucas, *Minetown, Milltown, Railtown: Life in Canadian Communities of Single Industry* (Toronto, 1971), 120–23; W.F. Cottrell, *The Railroader* (Stanford, 1940), 42–59.

18 This is a simplification of what was a very complex system of seniority and promotion. Beginning with the

Second World War, firemen and engineers had less control over their promotion and geographic mobility than did, for example, brakemen and conductors. The experience of work rhythms could consequently vary for engine and traincrews. As well, there were regional variations in work rhythms. In the sparsely populated north country, freight and passenger runs were longer and work was steadier and more predictable than in the south.

19 According to G.M. Rountree's calculations, based on annual statistics for all railway lines, road service staff was reduced by more than 40 percent in the five-year period between 1928 and 1933. Out of a total reduction of 62 000 men, 10 000 were involved in the operation of trains; see G.M. Rountree, *The Railway Worker*, table X, 123 and, in general, 103–36.

20 Interviews with Dave Kingston, conductor, born 1892, hired 1913; Bob Lenard, engineer, born 1901, hired 1918; Tim Reilly, conductor, born 1899, hired 1920; Vera Miller, engineer's wife, born 1906, married 1929; Catherine Roy, engineer's wife, born 1900, married 1923; Ed Walker, conductor, born 1916, hired 1939; Glen McPherson, engineer, born 1909, hired 1942; Don Nelson, conductor, born 1915, hired 1939; Mike Allen, conductor, born 1915, hired 1941.

21 Running-trades workers were paid on a mileage rate basis. Passenger service paid less per mile travelled than freight service since one could "get over the road" and earn one's miles more quickly on a passenger run. As well, engineers and conductors were paid more per mile than firemen and brakemen. A worker was allowed to earn a certain quota of miles per month, which increased throughout this period. After reaching that quota one was supposed to stop working for the month and allow others to make up their quota. Rountree, *The Railway Worker*, 74, and interviews.

22 Steve Price, engineer, born 1915, hired 1942.

23 Joe Mathews, engineer, born 1919, hired 1941.

24 Tim Reilly, conductor, born 1899, hired 1920.

25 Steve Price, engineer, born 1915, hired 1942.

26 See, for example, E.P. Thompson's classic statement on the shaping of industrial work time in "Time, Work Discipline and Industrial Capitalism" in *Essays in Social History*, ed. M.W. Flinn and T.C. Smout (Oxford, 1974), 39–77.

27 In my study, 3 of these 8 women had jobs in retail sales, 3 came from farms, 1 worked as an operator for Bell Telephone, and 1 was a nurse.

28 There were 2 exceptions: one woman worked part-time as a nurse before and after her child was born, and another worked in a bakery after her husband retired from the railroad.

29 Of these 24 wives, 4 were in retail or office work, 4 were teachers, 4 worked on family farms, 6 were factory employees, 2 were nurses, 2 were waitresses, 1 was a babysitter, and another a dancer. All but 5 of these women also lived at home before marriage.

30 Only 2 of these 24 wives did not withdraw from the labour force while their children were still young. One worked as a nurse part-time and the other, also a nurse, briefly resumed her job in response to a family financial crisis.

31 This was the case with 6 of the 8 wives interviewed.

32 Nineteen of the 24 wives considered were in this situation.

33 Seven of the 24 wives considered were in this category. Most husbands began railroad work a few years before, or after, marriage.

34 For example, the absence of a state-supported system of child care placed the onus on women to make informal arrangements for the care of their children if they worked outside the

home. As Ruth Pierson has observed, while a state-supported system of child care was created during World War II, it was only a temporary measure to allow mothers to enter the paid work force at a time of wartime labour shortages. Both the provision of child care and tax concessions to married women ended after the war. In the case of the wives of Allandale running-trades workers, there was still little economic incentive for them to take up wartime wagework. See Ruth Pierson, "Women's Emancipation and the Recruitment of Women into the Labour Force in World War II" in *The Neglected Majority*, ed. Susan Mann Trofimenkoff and Alison Prentice (Toronto, 1977), 125–45 and 185–92.

35 Though no complete wage and income data for the Allandale terminal have been located for this period, census figures for Toronto and Hamilton train and engine crews on all railway lines for the period between 1921 to 1951 provide a rough indication of the relatively high earnings of the men. The rate paid per mile was fairly standard in the industry. *Census of Canada*, 1921, vol. III, table 37; 1931, vol. V, table 22 and 23; 1941, vol. VI, table 7; 1951, vol. V, table 23.

36 Vera Miller, engineer's wife, born 1906, married 1929.

37 This is not to say that the motivations for marriage were simply economic, only that the prospects for a woman who remained single and dependent on the wages paid to most women were not very attractive. See, for example, the comments of Luxton, *More than a Labour of Love*, 43–44. Of the 27 wives married to railroaders whose father's occupation is known, 14 came from working-class families, 11 from farming families, and 2 from lower-middle-class families. Of the wives who came from working-class families, 10 had fathers who were skilled workers, and 7 of these were railroaders.

38 These categorizations of domestic labour are taken from Strong-Boag, "Keeping House in God's Country," 126. See also Luxton, *More than a Labour of Love*. The above generalization is not meant to ignore the differences in the experiences of working-class women. Gender was experienced in class-specific ways, and there were differences within the various sections of the working class, for example, concerning the ability of wives "to make ends meet," the frequency of the need to cope with their husbands' unemployment, and the ways of doing so.

39 Dave Kingston, engineer, born 1892, hired 1913.

40 Evelyn Martin, conductor's wife, born 1915, married 1943.

41 Joe Mathews, engineer, born 1919, hired 1941.

42 See also the observations in Cottrell, *The Railroader*, 73–75, concerning the problem of planning family events.

43 Rosemary Sharp, engineer's wife, born 1924, married 1948.

44 Luxton provides a very interesting analysis of the various ways family finances might be handled in *More than a Labour of Love*, 165–68.

45 See also, for example, the observations of Strong-Boag, "Keeping House in God's Country," 143–44, and Luxton, *More than a Labour of Love*, 127 and 173–75.

46 Rebecca Crane, conductor's wife, born 1916, married 1937.

47 For example, Luxton, *More than a Labour of Love*, 201–4.

48 Of the 21 families that stayed in Allandale while the husband worked in the north for long periods of time, more than three-quarters had either the wife's or husband's parents or siblings living in the town or nearby. Only 3 wives with relatives in Allandale moved their families north to join their husbands. The remaining 8 of the 32 families considered did not originally come from Allandale

and only moved there after the husband worked up north for a number of years.

49 The classic, as well as most problematic, examination of household structure is found in the work of Peter Laslett. See, for example, *The World We Have Lost* (New York, 1965), and Peter Laslett and Richard Wall, eds., *Household and Family in Past Time* (Cambridge, 1972).

50 Interview with Wilma Laidlaw, conductor's wife, born 1900, married 1920, and Val Laidlaw Bates, conductor's daughter, born 1934.

51 Interviews with Catherine Roy, engineer's wife, born 1900, married 1923; Vera Miller, engineer's wife, born 1906, married 1929; Rosemary Sharp, engineer's wife, born 1924, married 1948; Mike Allan, conductor, born 1915, hired 1941; Carol Webster, engineer's wife, born 1918, married 1941; Jim Blythe, engineer, born 1913, hired 1940; and Ed Walker, conductor, born 1916, hired 1939.

52 See also, for example, Cottrell, *The Railroader*, 4–11; Lucas, *Minetown, Milltown, Railtown*, 135–37; Alick R. Andrews, "Social Crisis and Labour Mobility: A Study of Economic and Social Change in a New Brunswick Railway Community" (MA thesis, University of New Brunswick, 1967, 72–73).

53 Jill Allen, conductor's wife, born 1920, married 1939.

54 Jim Blythe, engineer, born 1913, hired 1940.

55 Allandale had a United, an Anglican, and a Presbyterian church within half a block of one another. The congregation of each was almost exclusively composed of railroad families.

56 Franca Iacovetta, "From Contadina to Worker: Southern Italian Immigrant Working Women in Toronto, 1947–1962" in *Looking Into My Sister's Eyes: An Exploration of Women's History*, ed. Jean Burnet (Toronto, 1986), 202.

57 Barbara Cruickshank, conductor's daughter, born 1917.

58 Vera Miller, engineer's wife, born 1906, married 1929.

59 Dick Cook, personnel manager, born 1929, hired 1944.

60 The debate over the importance of the "family wage" for working-class survival and for gender relations has been controversial. See, for example, Jane Humphries, "Class Struggle and the Persistence of the Working Class Family," *Cambridge Journal of Economics* 1, 3 (1977): 241–58, and "The Working Class Family, Women's Liberation, and Class Struggle: The Case of Nineteenth Century British History," *Review of Radical Political Economics* 9, 3 (Fall 1977): 25–41; Michele Barrett and Mary McIntosh, "'The Family Wage': Some Problems for Socialists and Feminists," *Capital and Class* 11 (Summer 1980): 51–72, and *Women's Oppression Today: Problems in Marxist Feminist Analysis* (London, 1980); Ruth Milkman, "Organizing the Sexual Division of Labour: Historical Perspectives in 'Women's Work' and the American Labour Movement," *Socialist Review* 10,1 (1980): 95–150; Johanna Brenner and Maria Ramas, "Rethinking Women's Oppression," *New Left Review* 144 (March–April 1984): 33–71; Martha May, "Bread Before Roses: American Workingmen, Labor Unions and the Family Wage" in *Women, Work and Protest: A Century of US Women's Labor History*, ed. Ruth Milkman (London, 1985), 1–21.

61 Tolson, *Limits of Masculinity*, 48.

62 Willis, "Shop-Floor Culture," 196–97. See also, for example, Weeks, *Sexuality*, 38.

63 Tim Armstrong, engineer's son and railway clerk, born 1915, hired 1946.

64 Tim Reilly, conductor, born 1899, hired 1920.

65 Catherine Roy, engineer's wife, born 1900, married 1923.

66 For general observations on the availability of domestic technology and its uneven development and application, see Strong-Boag, "Keeping House in God's Country," 130–35, and Luxton, *More than a Labour of Love*, 128–59.

67 On the allocation of domestic work in the household and the benefits derived from wage labour, see also, for example, Luxton, ibid., 45 and 163; Tolson, *Limits of Masculinity*, 68–70, 81; and Joy Parr, "Rethinking Work and Kinship in a Canadian Hosiery Town, 1910–50," *Feminist Studies* 1 (Spring 1987): 137–62.

68 Cockburn, *Brothers*, 206.

69 Rosemary Sharp, engineer's wife, born 1924, married 1948.

70 For example, Willis, "Shop-Floor Culture," 189.

71 There was, however, little divorce in this period. Those interviewed commented that divorce might have been more prevalent if it had been more culturally acceptable. As well, for a woman divorce was economically prohibitive and legally difficult. In 1921, only 10 men and women in Barrie (out of a population of 6936) were divorced. In 1951, 37 men and women (out of a population of 12 514) were divorced. *Census of Canada*, 1921, vol. II, table 33; 1951, vol. 1, table 29.

72 Rosemary Sharpe, engineer's wife, born 1924, married 1948.

73 This was especially the case for the generation of workers that began in the 1920s or earlier. The pattern of occupational inheritance, at least for Allendale railway families, appeared to have changed for the generation of sons whose fathers began work during the Second World War. Of the 21 families with sons who might have followed in their father's footsteps, only 4 families had sons who made a career out of railroading. The contraction of the railway work force beginning in the 1950s, the greater accessibility to postsecondary educa-

tion beginning in the 1960s, and family encouragement of social mobility directed sons away from a career on the road. It would appear that many, however, did have summer jobs on the railroad.

74 Rusty Brown, conductor, born 1915, hired 1941.

75 Dave Spalding, engineer, born 1911, hired 1941.

76 Rusty Brown, conductor, born 1915, hired 1941.

77 Half of the conductors and two-thirds of the engineers considered in interviews were Masons. The oldest Masonic lodge in Barrie, the Corinthian Lodge, attracted most of the running-trades workers. The few Catholic workers in the running trades belonged to the Knights of Columbus.

78 See, for example, accounts of meetings of these organizations in Allandale in the late nineteenth and early twentieth century in *Northern Advance and Examiner*. While the Orange Order was strong especially in Protestant Simcoe County's rural areas, it appears to have had less of a following among the Allandale running-trades workers who began on the road in the late 1930s and early 1940s. A number of these men recalled, however, that their fathers belonged to the Orange Order.

79 On the masculine aspects of contemporary British male working-class "occupational cultures" in general, see, for example, Tolson, *Limits of Masculinity*, 451–81; see also Cockburn, *Brothers*; Baron, "Technology and the Crisis of Masculinity"; and Yarrow, "Class and Gender in the Consciousness of Appalachian Coal Miners."

80 Herbert Stitt, a former CPR engineer, provides an interesting collection of nicknames of fellow workers in his autobiography, *I Remember* (Toronto, 1983), 99–102.

81 Studies that have examined informal resistance on the factory shop floor

are too numerous to mention more than a few. See, for example, Michael Buraway, *Manufacturing Consent: Changes in the Labour Process Under Monopoly Capitalism* (Chicago, 1979); Richard Edwards, *Contested Terrain: The Transformation of the Workplace in the Twentieth Century* (New York, 1979); Andrew Friedman, *Industry and Labour: Class Struggle at Work and Monopoly Capitalism* (London, 1977); Huw Beynon, *Working for Ford* (London, 1973); Jim Peterson, "'More News From Nowhere': Utopian Notes of a Hamilton Machinist," *Labour/Le Travail* 17 (Spring 1986): 169–223.

82 Tim Armstrong, engineer's son and railway clerk, born 1915, hired 1946.

83 The railways had an elaborate system of rules and regulations governing the operation of trains and the conduct of its employees. This was necessary for the purposes of safety and the protection of property and passengers and as a means of controlling and disciplining the work force. Rule violators were assigned demerit points. A worker could accumulate 60 points before he was fired. The number of points assigned depended on the gravity of the transgression. One of the most serious offences was drinking on the job (Rule G). Good behaviour and work habits could result in a reduction of dermerit points. In certain cases, the company might also suspend a worker for a period of time instead of firing him. As with the seniority system and other union regulations, the operation of the railway company's system of discipline was not etched in stone. There was room for company officials and supervisors to manoeuvre. On the genesis of the demerit system, and on the evolution of different management styles on American railroads in the nineteenth century, see, for example, Walter Licht, *Working for the Railroad* (Princeton, 1983).

84 Bob Lenard, engineer, born 1901, hired 1918.

85 John Heath, conductor, born 1914, hired 1938.

86 Rusty Brown, conductor, born 1915, hired 1941.

87 For example, Cockburn, *Brothers*, and Baron, "Technology and the Crisis of Masculinity."

88 Steve Price, engineer, born 1915, hired 1942.

89 Rodney Davies, engineer, born 1909, hired 1941.

90 At this point it is difficult to measure the dimensions of sectionalism in the railway work force. While running-trades workers themselves professed an absence of sectionalism, and attributed it to a previous generation or to the sentiments of the very few, those from other areas of the work force were more likely to recall the elitism of the running trades. Studies of the railroad work force have also observed this sectionalism and the resentment of running-trades workers' elitism and "aristocratic" self-image; see, for example, Lucas, *Minetown, Milltown, Railtown*, 119–24 and Andrews, "Social Crisis and Labour Mobility," 77–78.

91 Willis, "Shop-Floor Culture, Masculinity and the Wage Form," 196; see also Gray, "Sharing the Shop Floor," 216–34, and Tolson, The Limits of Masculinity, 51–81.

92 Skip Johnson, engineer, born 1914, hired 1941.

93 On the way in which technological change also can call into question a worker's masculinity, see the discussion of the printing industry in Cockburn, *Brothers*, 93–190 and Baron, "Technology and the Crisis of Masculinity." As Baron has observed (9), "deskilling represents a crisis of masculinity, a crisis for men workers simultaneously as men and as workers."

94 Willis, "Shop-Floor Culture," 191.

95 The terminology analysed here is taken from interviews and from the glossary of terms listed in Cottrell, *The Railroader*, 117–39.

96 Stan Gray, "Sharing the Shop Floor," *Canadian Dimension* (June 1984): 25. This is a longer version of the article published in *Beyond Patriarchy*. See also Tolson, *Limits of Masculinity*, 60, and Weeks, *Sexuality*.

97 Steve Price, engineer, born 1915, hired 1942.

98 The term "emotional illiteracy" is taken from Tony Eardley, "Violence and Sexuality" in *The Sexuality of Men*, ed. Andy Metcalf and Martin Humphries (London, 1985), 101. See also Tolson, *Limits of Masculinity*, 71.

99 See also the comments of Willis, "Shop-Floor Culture"; Gray, "Sharing the Shop Floor"; Tolson, *Limits of Masculinity*; and Weeks, *Sexuality*.

100 Glen McPherson, engineer, born 1909, hired 1942.

101 Steve Price, engineer, born 1915, hired 1942.

102 All of the running-trades workers interviewed had been in accidents, at least one of which involved a fatality. While some of these were "head-on" or "back-end" collisions, the most common accident with fatalities was a collision with an automobile at a railway crossing.

103 Glen McPherson, engineer, born 1909, hired 1942.

104 Michael Yarrow has also noted shifts in the masculine practices of Appalachian miners in the 1970s and 1980s that were connected to the changing conditions in the coal mining industry; see Yarrow, "Class and Gender in the Consciousness of Apalachian Coal Miners."

105 On women's work in the railways and in general during World War I, see James Naylor, "The Woman Democrat" (unpublished draft), and Paul Phillips and Erin Phillips, *Women and Work* (Toronto, 1983), 25. On the experience of women during World War II, see Pierson, "Women's Emancipation." On the exclusion of women from running-trades work during the period under study, see interviews and Canada, Bureau of Statistics, *Distribution of Occupations by Industry*, 1931 (Ottawa, 1938), table 2; *Census of Canada*, 1951, vol. IV, table 6, for the Allandale railway work force.

106 Interviews. For an excellent analysis of protective legislation concerning female and child labour in the early decades of the twentieth century, and of male unionists' motivations for excluding women from areas of work traditionally monopolized by men, see Naylor, "The Woman Democrat." See also the position of the American Federation of Labor in Milkman, "Organizing the Sexual Division of Labor."

107 Jim Blythe, engineer, born 1913, hired 1940.

108 In this period the admittance of women into the running trades was never seriously contemplated by the CNR, the railway brotherhoods, or the men and women of Allandale. These issues were forcefully raised when a few women were hired as running-trades workers in the last decade; see interview with Dick Cook, personnel manager, born 1929, hired 1944.

109 Cottrell, *The Railroader*, 128.

110 For example, Gray, "Sharing the Shop Floor," 225.

111 This was also quite noticeable in interview situations. The language and nature of interaction of these men were influenced by the presence of women. When men were alone, or especially in a group with their former co-workers, the rough and boisterous masculine style of conduct was most evident.

112 Gray, "Sharing the Shop Floor," 226.

113 Michael Yarrow has written that "male subordinates tend to experience relations with other men as involving difficult contradictions between competition and solidarity, between expectations to be subordinate to domineering fathers and yet assert their rights as equals among men and as superordinate to wives

and children. Above all is the necessity to maintain membership in good standing in the brotherhood." "Class and Gender in the Consciousness of Appalachian Coal Miners," 5.

[114] An emphasis on masculine toughness and power in a husband's relationship with his wife and other family members could lead to domestic violence. Its magnitude in Allandale railway families, however, was not revealed in interviews. Such a sensitive topic was difficult to pursue, though some men and women referred to a few husbands who were known to have mis-

treated their spouses. While court records might provide an indication of domestic violence, most cases would not have been reported in this period.

[115] On the issues involved in conceptualizing family strategies, see, for example, Laurel Cornell, "Where Can Family Strategies Exist," *Historical Methods* 20, 3 (Summer 1987): 120–23; Nancy Folbre, "Family Strategy, Feminist Theory," ibid.: 115–18; Daniel Scott Smith, "Family Strategy: More than a Metaphor," ibid.: 118–20; Louise Tilley, "Beyond Family Strategies, What?" ibid.: 123–25.

CONSOLIDATING DISPARITY:
The Maritimes and the Industrialization of Canada During the Second World War*

ERNEST R. FORBES

The politicians and bureaucrats who directed Canada's economic development emerged from the Second World War with a profound sense of
accomplishment. The Department of Munitions and Supply arranged for
the writing of its own history so that what C.D. Howe called the "magnitude
of our achievement" would not be forgotten. The accounts not only stress
the quantity of munitions produced but also boast of the government's
contribution to a new industrial base for the nation.[1] These claims have not
been challenged. Howe's biographers credit the minister and his advisers
with having "shaped Canada's war program, renewed Canada's industrial
plant and reconstructed the Canadian economy."[2] But the scholar interested
in the problem of Canadian regional disparity might well ask why, if
Canada's industrial development during the war was so largely a product of
government initiative, it did not include the Maritimes? Indeed, it can be
argued that the policies of Howe and his associates were detrimental not
only to maritime industries but also to Canada's war effort.

The events of the war period help illuminate the process by which
regional disparity is created. They are particularly pertinent to the debate
between "orthodox" scholars who have attributed the growth of regional

Acadiensis 15, 2 (Spring 1986): 3–27. Reprinted with the permission of the journal.

disparity to the forces of the marketplace and "liberal revisionist" and "neo-Marxian" scholars who give greater prominence to political and social factors in the region's decline.[3] The war highlighted the role of government in spectacular fashion and removed much of the illusion that events were controlled by the invisible natural laws of Adam Smith. Prime Minister William Lyon Mackenzie King and his colleagues suspended the law of supply and demand for the duration of the war. They appointed controllers over each major industry to develop and implement plans for industrial expansion. They aided private companies directly through government grants and indirectly through accelerated depreciation of plants and equipment. Firms could not substantially alter patterns of production without the permission of a controller. Those which failed to co-operate or became bogged down in labour problems could be, and sometimes were, expropriated, although co-operation between industry and government for mutual advantage was the more common practice. When private firms proved unable to meet particular war needs, the government created new Crown corporations for the purposes required. Wages and prices were governed by the Wartime Prices and Trade Board. Subsidies were paid to compensate firms for the rising cost of imports, and cost of living bonuses were awarded to workers in lieu of wage increases. Commodity shortages were met with rationing and limits were set on the production of consumer products.[4]

The government's policies regarding coal, steel, shipbuilding, ship repair, and general manufacturing industries in the Maritimes formed a consistent pattern. For more than a year into the war C.D. Howe and his controllers withheld government funds for the modernization and expansion of Maritime industries while labour was drawn to Ontario and Quebec or into the armed forces. With the realization of impending commodity shortages and the growing strategic importance of the region, they finally turned to Maritime industries only to encounter manpower shortages and a limited infrastructure. Their failure to resolve these problems, especially in the matter of ship repair, undermined the effectiveness of the Royal Canadian Navy at a critical point in the war. What government investment the Maritimes did receive tended to be in industries of a temporary nature. It is ironic that the region which received the least wartime investment would later be identified by the Department of Reconstruction as the one which would have the greatest difficulty in adjusting to a peacetime economy.[5]

The motives for bypassing the Maritimes were seldom articulated and not always clear. At the beginning of the war Ontario lobbyists stressed the value of a central location for industry safe from German attack. After the War a Dominion Bureau of Statistics profile on the Maritimes offered "strategic reasons" as one explanation for the location "of much new industrial plant in the Central Provinces."[6] During the war, however, bureaucrats justified their masters' decisions largely in terms of efficiency. The

Maritimes, they claimed, suffered from the fatal flaw of "distance." To what extent efficiency was the actual motive or merely a rationale is difficult to discern. The British Admiralty Technical Mission in Canada, which, after June 1940, depended upon the Department of Munitions and Supply to place their contracts, reported that "political issues weigh heavily" in the decisions taken. Moreover, they raised issues of efficiency which the Canadians seldom mentioned. Specifically, they pointed to the difficulties of building ships in yards which were cut off from the ocean for five months of the year and in the climate where the vessels under construction were often damaged by the deep frosts. They also questioned the practice of requiring vessels to make the long trip up the St Lawrence River for servicing.[7] While the demands of Canada's allies were concerned with immediate efficiency in wartime, C.D. Howe and his controllers often appeared to be following an agenda for industrialization based on their perception of Canada's needs after the war. Their vision of a centralized manufacturing complex closely integrated with the United States apparently did not include the Maritimes in any significant role.

The perception of Maritime industries as peripheral to Canada's needs emerged early in the war. In the summer of 1940 the senior bureaucrats who composed the Economic Advisory Committee prepared a memorandum recommending against transportation subsidies for Maritime and Western coal. It would be better, they argued, to purchase the coal from the United States. The government would gain revenue from tariffs and the surplus miners would be absorbed into other sectors of the war effort. The recommendation was partially implemented by the government when the coal subsidies were reduced by more than one-third.[8] The Steel Control, in planning for shipbuilding and other steel requirements, approved a large new ships' plate mill for the Steel Company of Canada at Hamilton and a new rolling mill for the Algoma Steel Company at Sault Ste Marie, and also assisted both of these and the smaller steel producers to modernize and increase capacity.[9] The Dominion Steel and Coal Corporation, another of Canada's "big three" steel producers and the largest industrial employer in the Maritimes, was conspicuously less fortunate. Efforts to negotiate federal assistance for modernization encountered inexplicable delays. A memorandum from Dosco's assistant manager to company president Arthur Cross detailed a meeting in July 1940 of three senior Dosco executives, including Cross himself, with steel controller Hugh Scully. On the basis of this meeting written proposals were presented to Scully with copies addressed to Howe. Later, however, the controller denied any recollection of the meeting or Dosco's proposals.[10] Prominent in Dosco's plan was a scheme to re-open its ships' plate mill in Sydney, a plant which was built in 1918 but closed after the war. On the advice of W.S. Drysdale, director of production, Dosco obtained an independent engineering study which proved favourable and was duly forwarded to Ottawa. Meanwhile, the controllers approved and Stelco proceeded with the construction of a new ships' plate mill at Hamilton, Ontario. This plant opened in April 1941.[11]

Dosco's manufacturing potential in the Maritimes was finally discovered in the fall of 1940 by an industrial task force which, under the auspices of the Department of Munitions and Supply, toured the country in search of unused manufacturing capacity to develop for British orders. The visitors later recalled that they found industry fully engaged in Ontario and Quebec but that considerable excess capacity remained in the Maritimes and the West.[12] Their recommendations for investment to allow the production of shells and gun-mountings from Dosco's plants at Trenton, Nova Scotia, were accepted by the British government. "The main thing, however, on our entire trip and what impressed us most," one member reported, "was the fact that the large [ships' plate] mill at Sydney is lying idle."[13] They enthusiastically recommended "that immediate arrangements should be made to put this mill into production." It would require much less time and money than the construction of a new one and would be needed to meet "a definite shortage of plate in Canada" which they predicted "by March 1, 1941."[14] Their recommendation ran into trouble in the upper echelons of the Department of Munitions. Frank Ross, director of naval supply and president of the Saint John Dry Dock and Shipbuilding Company, noted the difficulty and urged the naval minister, Angus L. Macdonald, "to discuss this matter" with his colleagues. The task force was overruled. The controllers planned to purchase the balance of their plate needs from the United States.

Dosco itself persevered with a formal offer to open the plate mill and to expand production to meet additional requirements for basic steel at a total cost of $3.5 million, about one million of which would be borne by the corporation.[15] Queried by Maritime politicians, C.D. Howe later explained his rejection of the offer to Parliament on the grounds that it would cost $4.5 million, that Dosco's primary steel was already under long-term contract to Great Britain and that government expenditure to increase basic steel production in the Maritimes could not be justified.[16] Howe's letter of refusal was particularly disquieting to Dosco president Arthur Cross, less perhaps because of the rejection of the specific project than because of the rationale offered. Howe's phrase, "having in mind our needs after the war," seemed to imply that the government was directing investment according to its own plan for postwar development and that steel production in the Maritimes would have a very limited role. Moreover, in the anticipation of future needs the government appeared to be heedless of the impact of its interference on the existing equilibrium among competing industries. Noting the approximately $4 million in federal funds that had gone to each of his competitors, Algoma and Stelco, Cross protested to Howe that this left Dosco "the only primary steel producer in this country which is receiving no government assistance." While Cross was "reluctant to believe that your advisers have deliberately formulated a policy which is bound to discriminate against the post-war future of this corporation and in favour of its central Canadian competitors," a continued failure to grant Dosco "some reasonable measure of assistance" would render such a conclusion "inevitable."[17]

Meanwhile, the government financed two new shipbuilding plants on the Great Lakes and reserved for major naval contracts ten out of the fifteen existing Canadian shipyards capable of producing freighter class vessels.[18] Conspicuously absent were the Halifax Shipyards and the Saint John Dry Dock and Shipbuilding Company. Angus L. Macdonald later defended the government for failing to develop steel shipbuilding at these yards on the grounds that they were needed for repairs and service.[19] This interpretation would appear more plausible had the Department of Munitions effectively developed Maritime ports for repair purposes or directed to them the business required for year-round operation. It did neither.

Both Halifax Shipyards and the Saint John Dry Dock Company were busy with service and repairs in November 1940 when the government appointed D.B. Carswell, formerly manager and vice-president of Canada Vickers Ltd. and vice-president of Montreal Dry Dock Company, as controller of ship repair and salvage. When the ice moved out in the spring of 1941, Carswell, from his office in Montreal, authorized the layoff of skilled workers at the Maritime ports and shifted the repair industry up the St Lawrence River. Thereafter, the controller maintained the same alternate use of summer and winter facilities in the repair yards as had characterized the use of ports in Canada's export trade. Maritime ports would be employed to the extent that Montreal was inaccessible.[20]

Just how little support the Department of Munitions and Supply channelled into the Maritimes for industrial expansion is confirmed in the first report on capital assistance to Canadian industries prepared by the department for the period up to 30 April 1941. Of the $484 299 078 committed to that cause by British and Canadian governments, Prince Edward Island received exactly nothing, New Brunswick the same amount, and Nova Scotia $8 759 430. The region's share of this investment was 1.81 percent. Even disregarding its 9.8 percent of the population and the strategic importance of the region in an Atlantic war, and considering only its 5 percent share of the nation's manufacturing, the discrepancy is still striking. Moreover, of the Maritime portion, about half went to develop the region's service capacity: a Montreal firm received $3 million to build a floating dry dock for Halifax, and another $1 million served to outfit an aircraft depot at Dartmouth. Most of the remainder went to Dosco's Eastern Car Company and Trenton Steelworks as the British government financed the retooling required for its orders of shells and gun mountings.[21] Even this operation was delayed, Arthur Cross complained, as the priority rating initially assigned the two Dosco plants by the Department of Munitions did not allow effective competition with other Canadian firms in the purchase of machinery. In two years the Maritime share of Canada's investment in manufacturing declined from 5.1 to 4.6 percent, and the region's share of the labour force in manufacturing fell from 5.1 to 4.7 percent.[22]

The initial bypassing of the Maritimes for industrial investment would ultimately prove critical for its wartime development. A majority of workers in all the new industries had to be trained, and retooling and expansion were much easier with the surplus labour supply left by the Depression. Maritime industries which failed to gain that initial headstart tried to catch up. Yet their skilled workers had been drawn away, essential commodities were in short supply, and they found themselves in competition with the military services for a dwindling pool of manpower.[23] The labour shortages became the standard excuse for the Department of Munitions' failure to develop industries in the Maritimes which were later recognized as important to Canada's war effort.

By the spring of 1941 the government's economic policies drew vigorous protests from the Maritime press, boards of trade and politicians. In October 1939 the New Brunswick Advisory Board for Economic and Industrial Development joined with the Saint John Board of Trade in lobbying British and Canadian purchasing agents and later maintained a permanent "representative" at Ottawa for that purpose. Meanwhile, New Brunswick's Liberal premier, A.A. Dysart, called upon the federal government for a policy of "decentralization" in industrial development.[24] The following year his successor and former colleague, J.B. McNair, approached the federal cabinet to help his nearly bankrupt province to develop the necessary infrastructure, such as roads and electricity, to participate more effectively in Canada's industrial war effort. McNair's request for $4.5 million was rejected by the cabinet, but King, perhaps mindful of the political implications of McNair's appeal, prevailed upon his colleagues for a grant of $100 000 specifically tied to the upgrading of roads and bridges in northern New Brunswick.[25] Thereafter, the lack of electricity became a factor in, or at least a rationale for, the Department of Munition's failure to invest any money in New Brunswick before the summer of 1941. Saint John Board of Trade President Colin McKay protested that the department's refusal to grant federal funds for hydro development was a method of discrimination in favour of the wealthier provinces. "Our shortage of power is definitely and directly due to our shortage of money," McKay declared. The government, he reported, had missed "a wonderful opportunity" to redress the problems arising from centralization and to redistribute industry more evenly throughout the country.[26]

In Nova Scotia, from early in the war, newspapers complained of the loss of skilled workers, in both metal and wood, to shipbuilders in Central Canada and blamed both levels of government for failing to develop an industry so natural to their region.[27] Through the later months of 1940, Premier A.S. MacMillan of Nova Scotia bombarded the federal cabinet with warnings of the damage which the public criticism was doing to the Liberal Party and called for the construction of steel shipbuilding plants in his province. He offered on behalf of the Nova Scotia government to deliver the electrical power required to any site in the province "as quickly as the plants can be produced." Finally, after a meeting with Howe in May 1941, MacMillan was able to report that the federal government would finance a plant in Nova Scotia provided that local entrepreneurs took the initiative.[28] The expanded program for the construction of civilian shipping, announced in the summer of 1941, included a plant to build a small class of 4700-ton freighters at Pictou, Nova Scotia. The Pictou plant, although federally financed, was operated by a Halifax firm, Foundation Maritime, and constructed 24 freighters before the end of the war.

Angus L. Macdonald and the provincial minister of industry, Harold Connolly, pressed the tiny shipyards of the outports to go after major contracts for the multitude of small wooden vessels needed in Canadian and Allied harbours. A few, such as Clare Shipbuilding of Meteghan, LeBlanc Shipbuilding of Weymouth, and J.A. Urquhart of Parrsboro, were successful. In New Brunswick K.C. Irving at Buctouche and Ashley Colter at Gagetown turned out several million dollars' worth of barges and other wooden vessels.[29] Additional construction came to the Maritimes as an unexpected outgrowth of the problems of inland shipbuilding. The first ten corvettes completed for a British order narrowly escaped being trapped in the winter freeze-up and required substantial work in the Maritimes before they could risk an Atlantic crossing.[30] The Toronto Shipbuilding Company, the Crown corporation which built the large Algerine class of minesweepers, established a subsidiary at Saint John to allow outfitting and sea trials in the winter months.[31] The additional demand exhausted the electricity available from the limited hydro and coal plants and rationing was imposed in 1943.[32]

From an even weaker political base Prince Edward Island, under the leadership of Liberal Premier Thane Campbell, lobbied for a share of shipbuilding and munition plants. When this failed, he argued the need for federal funds to develop food processing plants to increase the Island's contribution to the war effort. From the fall of 1941 lobbying efforts concentrated on procuring a new car ferry, as the *S.S. Charlottetown*, the island's largest and most modern ferry, sank on the Borden–Tormentine run.[33] J.L. Ralston waged a systematic campaign for the ferry and other island causes but only after his resignation from the cabinet in 1944.[34]

Where were the federal Maritime politicians when decisions were taken which were so adverse to regional interests? It cannot be argued that the region lacked a voice at Ottawa. Indeed, the Maritimes had strong representation in the wartime cabinet. After the defeat of the Liberals in Nova Scotia in 1925, a little group of young lawyers or lawyer-academics conspired to remove their party's image as the mouthpiece for "big business" and the foe of progressive legislation.[35] While their electoral success was less than spectacular, their joint activities did establish lasting friendships.

J.L. Ralston, a Halifax lawyer and war veteran originally from Amherst, might be considered the group's leader. He entered Mackenzie King's cabinet in 1926 seeking the implementation of the Duncan Commission Report and the protection of returned servicemen, with whom he strongly identified. After the government's defeat in 1930, Ralston continued as financial critic in the shadow cabinet. Another Amherst native, Norman MacLeod Rogers, whose military endeavours were followed by study in history and law at Oxford University, left a teaching appointment at Acadia to work as King's secretary and later returned to academic life at Queen's University.[36] Angus L. Macdonald, a Scottish Catholic from Inverness County who taught at the Dalhousie law school, became leader of the provincial party in 1930 and in 1933 premier of the province. J.L. Ilsley, a lawyer from Kentville, was one of the few Liberal candidates in Nova Scotia to overcome the Tory tides in the federal elections of 1926 and 1930. When the Liberals returned to power in Ottawa in 1935, Ilsley entered the cabinet in place of Ralston who stayed out, rumour has it, to aid a financially troubled law partner. Rogers, representing Kingston, became minister of labour.

With the outbreak of war Ralston became minister of finance. Rogers died in 1940, but with the expansion of the defence portfolio into three ministries, Ralston, now sitting for Prince County, Prince Edward Island, became minister of national defence. Ilsley took over finance. Angus L. Macdonald was invited to become minister of national defence for naval services.[37] Macdonald's appointment had an additional logic as the strategic emphasis in Canadian naval planning had, near the outbreak of war, shifted from the West to the East Coast.[38] Besides the three Nova Scotians, New Brunswick's J.E. Michaud held the fisheries portfolio from 1935.

Thus, the Maritimes had four representatives in the cabinet and three of them (later four when Michaud shifted to Transport in October 1942) on the powerful nine-member War Committee. This committee, as Macdonald put it, was regarded "more as a cabinet than a committee of the cabinet" in matters relating to the war.[39] The region appeared to enjoy the strongest representation in any cabinet since Confederation. There were some limiting factors, of course. Without previous experience at the federal level, Macdonald faced a formidable challenge in defending the interests of either navy or province. As minister of finance, Ilsley was hardly in a position for overt regional advocacy. Ralston had earlier remarked of that office, that its role of "barring the way to the money bags" left a new minister open to the "accusation . . . of having forgotten the rank and file alongside . . . whom he fought and having become a 'statesman.'" Ilsley did indeed become a statesman—one who became increasingly alarmed at the unprecedented costs of modern warfare.[40] Nevertheless, one would expect that four senior Cabinet ministers could have done more to protect the interests of the Maritimes during the preparations for war. That they failed to do so may be explained in part by the unusual delegation of responsibility within the wartime Cabinet and by the extraordinary power of the Department of Munitions and Supply under the leadership of C.D. Howe.[41]

Howe's appointment as minister of transport in 1935 had initially pleased leaders of the Maritime Board of Trade. In their perpetual battle to defend the region's transportation interests, they had seen the 20 percent regional freight rate reductions recommended by the Duncan Commission negated by a series of special competitive rates to which, the railways argued, the Maritime reductions could not apply.[42] Having lost all confidence in the minister previously responsible they hoped that Howe, who had once taught at Dalhousie University, would understand Maritime problems and appreciate the justice of their case. They were soon disillusioned.

Howe not only failed to sympathize with the Maritimes' representations on freight rates, but supported a series of initiatives which seemed to threaten the future of their ports. These included a bill to terminate the independence of the National Harbours commissions, to which the Maritime provinces had gained access only nine years before, and proposals to regulate freight rates between Atlantic and Great Lakes ports and to standardize wharf charges in Canadian harbours. Against the united representations of Maritime Liberals the latter proposals were not implemented, but the impression remained that Howe favoured the powerful Great Lakes ports lobby.[43] This was hardly a surprising position for someone who had built a business from constructing grain elevators on the Great Lakes and was member of Parliament for Port Arthur.

Howe's regional orientation is further suggested by his close ties with Sir James Dunn, the piratical head of the Algoma Steel Corporation. In a recent account of that corporation, Duncan McDowall notes Dunn's anti-Dosco lobby and his campaign to concentrate manufacturing on the Lakes. McDowall implies that Howe's spectacular support of Dunn's empire, which received more than 80 percent of the government's direct grants to the steel industry during the war, had less to do with lobbying and personal contact than with a shared perspective on continental development and the integration of the Great Lakes economy.[44]

There may have been an element of regional conflict in the occasional confrontations between Howe and the Maritimers. One of these involved the construction in wartime of the St Lawrence Waterway, an international project for hydro development and the enlargement of the St Lawrence canals for major ocean vessels. Howe's proposals, presented to the cabinet early in 1940, drew protests from J.L. Ralston that they would divert funds from the war effort. Ralston was overruled on the grounds that the project was important in retaining the good will of the United States. He objected again several months later at the projected $60 million price tag. According to King, Ralston could see no "corresponding advantage except what would accrue to Ontario for power." King concluded that Ralston "does not seem to regard Ontario as part of the Dominion." King was personally committed to the scheme which in 1941 he predicted would "prove one of the great achievements of the present administration."[45]

In other matters of industrial expansion Howe's views, backed by King, normally prevailed. The industrial controllers were his nominees and his responsibility. In the War Committee, Macdonald, Ralston, or "Chubby" Power, minister of national defence for air, might voice the needs of a service, but they had then to turn to Howe to learn whether the tanks, ships, or aircraft could be built, where they would be built, and when they might be delivered. When Angus L. Macdonald took office in July 1940, he could not hope to affect the decisions taken for the location of naval manufacture for which production lines had already been established. He could, however, propose classes of vessels not yet under construction for which Maritimes yards were available. This may account for his enthusiasm for the building of destroyers in Canada. Howe was sympathetic to the idea, perhaps in part because the principal components other than the hull were to be manufactured by the John Inglis Company of Toronto, a firm whose close relations with the federal government had been the subject of the Bren Gun controversy.[46] In 1941 when Macdonald proposed to the War Committee the building of two Tribal class destroyers at Halifax, Howe endorsed the proposal as a supplement to repair work.[47]

On several other proposed naval projects Macdonald and Howe were far apart. The most serious confrontation involved ship repair. As the British analysed their shipping and supply needs they became concerned with the lack of year-round repair facilities on the Atlantic coast. They regarded Halifax as the logical naval headquarters and terminus for their Canadian convoys and they begrudged the additional time and risk required in sending escorts to Montreal. Early in 1941 they specifically asked the Canadians to consider developing Halifax as a repair centre with multiple graving docks which could, if necessary, hold their largest vessels. Macdonald, supported by Ralston and acting on the advice of the Chiefs of Staff, proposed building a graving dock at Halifax. Citing the shortage of labour, Howe came out strongly against the proposal. He was backed by Mackenzie King who argued against "the dangerous concentration of nearly all naval facilities at Halifax."[48] King's strategic concern may have been political as well as military. Montreal would not surrender lightly the pre-eminent role which it had maintained in the repair industry and Saint John was alarmed at a proposal which would so greatly strengthen its arch-rival. As though on cue, Opposition Leader R.B. Hanson, a New Brunswicker, wrote King expressing concern at the impact of the British plan on the postwar prospects of Saint John.[49]

Unable to create a major centre for ship repair in the Maritimes, Macdonald was reduced to a series of proposals for marine railways to be scattered about the region. When these were delayed by Howe, for whom the manpower barrier in the Maritimes seemed insurmountable, Macdonald successfully proposed a greater role by the three services in the determination of priorities within Howe's department. He also began to move the navy out from under Howe's empire through the recruitment and training of naval ratings for shipbuilding and repair.[50]

In December 1941 Howe objected to Macdonald's request for a second pair of Tribal destroyers on the grounds of a steel shortage. The problem was real enough. The military crisis in Europe had led to a greater urgency in shipbuilding construction. Shortages began to appear even before the United States' entry into the war limited exports of the ships' plate, steel, and coal on which Howe's department had been relying. Certainly the Americans were not ungenerous. Their controllers often gave Canadian producers the same priority rating as their own. But in the general scramble for basic commodities, the Canadians could not expect to expand their supply from the south.[51] Howe withdrew his opposition to the destroyers for Halifax after the War Committee approved a $17 million government investment in a new blast furnace for Algoma at Sault Ste Marie.[52]

The shortages signalled a new crisis stage in Canada's wartime economy as the controllers searched for ways of increasing production. The deficiencies surfaced first in ships' plate. In the summer of 1941 steel controller Fred Kilbourn gave the orders to Stelco to "shoot the works" by changing to a three-shift system and operating its new mill at maximum capacity. Since this operation now consumed all of the primary steel that Stelco could produce, the controller ordered Algoma and Dosco to supply Stelco's traditional customers in Ontario and Quebec. The government picked up the tab for transportation.[53] Howe proposed to meet long-term needs for primary steel with the new blast furnace for Algoma. About the same time the controller finally gave the green light to Dosco to "rehabilitate" its idle ships' plate mill at Sydney. Early in 1942 the cabinet granted Dosco $1.75 million to bring the shell of an old blast furnace purchased in Ontario into production at Sydney. The plate mill began operations early in 1942 and in that year accounted for more than one-third of Canada's output of regular ships' plate.[54]

The shortages also led to a dramatic change in government coal policies. The industry which the mandarins were prepared to discourage at the beginning of the war was now seen as critical to steel production and domestic fuel needs. The coal industry did not thrive under the arbitrary control of the bureaucrats. Although the miners heeded the call of patriotism to enlist, many rejected the same call as a reason to accept lower wages than paid elsewhere in Canada. In 1941 the miners staged a five-month slowdown strike to protest the regional wage differential.[55] A year later the industry suffered a net loss of nearly 4000 workers. Those who remained drew the ire of the controllers for persistent "absenteeism" as they closed the mines for traditional holidays, to protest specific grievances, and to attend the funerals of those killed in accidents.[56] But the key to the slump in coal production during the war was the loss of the "contract men," those workers at the coal face who actually mined the coal and were paid on the basis of output. It was this vital group of skilled miners which had responded most enthusiastically to the call for enlistment. Early in 1943 the cabinet declared coal production to be critical to the entire war effort, forbade further enlistment by skilled miners and ordered those who had done so to return to the mines. A disproportionate number of those returning appeared to be "datal men," and as production continued to decline, an investigator in 1944 reported that the "main trouble" was "a shortage of producers."[57]

Intensification of the war brought the predictable crisis in ship repair and harbour facilities in Maritime ports. Having failed in their efforts to interest the Canadian government in developing Halifax, the British turned to the United States for the North American refit of their larger vessels. The Americans too were surprised by Canadian nonchalance at the state of their repair facilities. In the spring of 1942 they completed their own survey of the port of Halifax and were strongly critical of facilities in general and the scarcity of repair berths in particular. The investigators recommended that the American government send tugboats to Halifax to rescue "vessels of all nationalities . . . detained for an unreasonable length of time in Canadian waters awaiting repairs."[58] C.D. Howe took umbrage at the Americans for undertaking the survey without his knowledge or permission. While the War Committee supported Howe in his indignation, its members also wanted assurance that the criticism was unfounded or that the deficiencies were being repaired. Howe advised them that the American survey was inaccurate and outlined new construction then in progress.[59]

In fact, despite Halifax's strategic location as convoy headquarters, Howe's department had continued to treat the port as secondary to Montreal. The Maritimes' shortage of repair berths and machinery was, at least in part, the result of priority decisions taken within the Department of Munitions and Supply. Confronted with shortages in the spring of 1941, Howe promised to "move heaven and earth to make sure that adequate repair facilities are available on the Atlantic coast before the St. Lawrence closes this year." But even specific commitments failed to materialize. In January 1942 Dosco president Arthur Cross reported to Howe that less than 13 percent of the half-million dollars' worth of repair machinery, which the government had authorized for Halifax Shipyards, had been delivered by Citadel Company, the Montreal-based Crown corporation responsible, and the harbour renovations announced the previous spring were incomplete or not even begun.[60] Moreover, the government's willingness to direct repair work to Montreal for half of the year made it difficult for Maritime firms to staff what facilities they had. After the layoffs in the Maritimes in the spring of 1941, D.B. Carswell reported great difficulty in recruiting skilled workers for the Maritime industry for the following winter.[61]

With repairs falling behind and the department seeking to train new workers, a worse crisis was avoided when naval authorities, short of both escorts and the facilities to service them, decided to forgo their normally scheduled refits.[62] Yet in February 1942, at a meeting of the Advisory Committee on Ship Repair, Controller Carswell treated the approaching seasonal shift in repair work to Montreal as inevitable. In May he reported that volunteer workers recruited in Ontario and Quebec had been let go and expressed fear that the smaller plants would lose local workers in the slack period to follow.[63]

To Carswell's surprise the slack period did not materialize even after the St Lawrence re-opened. There was a back-log from the winter, damage from U-boats continued high, and still impending were the overdue naval refits. In the late summer another American investigator reported that, at Halifax, repair facilities were "taxed far beyond their capacity, causing great delays to vessels in need of drydockage and major repairs."[64] Severe additional pressure on all Canadian facilities came with the order in April 1942 to outfit the naval escorts with modern submarine detection equipment. The conversion involved reconstruction of the corvettes to receive the new equipment. Until this was completed the effectiveness of the Canadian navy for convoy protection—its principal responsibility in the war—was seriously impaired. Yet November of 1943 found the modifications completed on only twenty-two out of seventy-four corvettes. The navy was reduced to the desperate expedients of leaving some vessels frozen in St Lawrence ports for the winter, routing others to British Columbia and sending still others on the dubious gamble of breaking into refit schedules at American ports.[65] Marc Milner's *North Atlantic Run: The Royal Canadian Navy and the Battle for the Convoys* shows the cost in naval efficiency of Canada's failure to develop an adequate repair service. The Canadian navy was forced to watch "from the sidelines" while the better-equipped British escorts brought victory to the allies in the Battle of the North Atlantic.[66]

Conditions were rendered even more chaotic at Maritime ports late in the summer of 1942 when the St Lawrence suddenly closed three months early. British and Canadian naval authorities had noted the greater risks and strain on the escort system resulting from the dependence on Montreal. But the government failed to direct shipping or ship repair to the Maritimes until forced to do so by the activities of the German U-boats lurking within the narrow confines of the River and entrances to the Gulf. From the opening of the shipping season in 1942 U-boats sank twenty-three vessels. In August the Cabinet ordered the St Lawrence closed to all but local traffic, for which convoys would be maintained.[67]

With the additional traffic and naval refit priorities, the repair facilities in Halifax and Saint John were in difficulty even before the freeze-up. Although the navy opened new repair facilities at Shelburne and Point Edward, it required time to "break in" the new operations. In the first six months they completed only four refits, although their combined capacity was projected to be 145 vessels a year. The naval authorities found that servicing in the little naval repair yards invariably seemed to require a further stop at Halifax for additional parts or expertise.[68] The construction of the tribal destroyers, which was intended to occupy workers in the summer months, became an embarrassment. Labour was diverted in order to rush completion of the hulls to free additional berths for repair purposes. The destroyers themselves would not be completed until after the war.

The shortage of facilities at Halifax and Saint John created a hopeless bottleneck for civilian shipping requiring maintenance or repair. By the spring of 1943 Carswell's desperation was reflected in instructions to port surveyors that dry docks limit repairs to problems which "seriously affect the sea-worthiness" of vessels. This order was sharply queried by the surveyors who informed him that a vessel is "either seaworthy or not seaworthy."[69] In his reports to Howe, Carswell was hard-pressed to find explanations for his problems which did not imply criticism of the department. He blamed the National Selective Service for failing to provide the skilled labour required, and in 1944 he attributed the shortage of berths in the repair yards to "Acts of God and perils of the sea." If the damaged vessels had only arrived "in reasonable numbers and at regular intervals," his yards might have coped, but they tended to come "in batches."[70]

In the spring of 1943, with Carswell, the navy and local port administrators all complaining of the labour shortage in Halifax, the government appointed a committee of interested parties to investigate. A survey of shipyard firms in the region reported a deficit of 4872 workers. Discussion on how to meet the problem brought to light overcrowded conditions in the city which made temporary solutions difficult. As the navy expanded operations at Halifax, it tended to expropriate existing buildings. Overcrowding was aggravated by the congregation in the city of the dependants of service personnel who were stationed there or who had left from there to go overseas.[71] A local official complained of shortages in food and commodities which were still distributed on the basis of a census population of 65 000 at a time when 115 000 ration cards were issued exclusive of service personnel. He also protested the inability of the municipality to provide the transportation, hospital, and other services required by military activity and the increased population. His complaint was confirmed by Carswell, who reported "good food . . . difficult to procure, sleeping space . . . not available . . . [and] transportation . . . inadequate."[72] Their complaints resulted in a cabinet decision to place Halifax under the control of the harbour director who had the authority to restrict access and remove from it those deemed non-essential to the war effort. Nine months after the appointment of the committee, a naval memorandum complained that "Despite warnings and recommendations . . . no apparent action has been taken to move large bodies of skilled men . . . to . . . Nova Scotia where the demand has not only been urgent but has been long foreseen."[73]

The intensification of the war brought some industrial expansion, including plant renovation, to the Maritimes. These investments, however, tended to be limited in scope and featured types of industry which had very little chance of continuation after the war. None of the 28 Crown corporations was located in the region. The Department of Munitions and Supply reported a total investment of $1.6 billion in the expansion of Canadian industry as of the end of December 1943, of which $823 million could be identified as located in particular provinces. The Maritimes' share of this, exclusive of housing, was a bit more than $27 million or 3.7 percent. This was less than either British Columbia or the Prairies. Prince Edward Island received nothing, New Brunswick $6.5 million, and Nova Scotia $20.8 million. New Brunswick obtained $1.5 million for aircraft repair, $1 million for naval construction, and $2.7 million for ship repair. In Nova Scotia $5 million went to ship repair, $3.8 to the repair of aircraft, $3 million to steel and coal production, and $4.6 million to the manufacture of gun parts and ammunition. Shipbuilding totals also give an indication of the region's share of that industry: the Maritimes accounted for 6.2 percent of the value of total contracts issued compared with 50 percent for British Columbia, 28.6 percent for Quebec, and 15.1 percent for Ontario. Within the region Nova Scotia's shipbuilding contracts totalled $62 million, New Brunswick's $9.8, and Prince Edward Island's $0.4 million.[74]

The regional inequities of the federal government's wartime industrial investments were amplified in a reconstruction policy of channelling more money into the same industries to enable them to make the transition to peacetime production. The depreciation formula ensured that only profitable companies which were in a position to make the conversion would receive assistance. By 1 July 1945, 48 percent of the funds had gone to Ontario, 32 percent to Quebec, and 15 percent to British Columbia. The other 5 percent was divided among the remaining six provinces. The authors of a report to the Department of Reconstruction giving these figures observed that "the problems of the transition period" will be "most acute in the Maritimes . . . where wartime dislocations have been superimposed on the special problems of a depressed area."[75]

The transfer of shipping and ship repair to Maritime ports proved temporary and did not survive the crisis stage in the war. In justifying their return to the St Lawrence, the controllers had ample evidence of the inability of Maritime ports to handle Canada's trade. The number of vessels travelling in the emergency convoys, supposedly for local needs on the St Lawrence, tripled as exceptions were made in the ban on through traffic. By the winter of 1945 Howe reported an enormous quantity of stores backed up at Maritime ports and 13 000 Canadian railway cars stranded in the United States, a result of other attempts to bypass the Maritime bottleneck. The shipping directors called for the reopening of the St Lawrence regardless of the U-boat threat or the strain on the escorts.[76] By early summer Carswell was able to report business as usual with the port of Montreal back in full service and two-thirds of the ship repair activity shifted to the St Lawrence. At the end of July, he reported repairs to be proceeding "at full capacity" in Montreal and "fallen off substantially in the Maritimes." This was two months before the government officially lifted its controls on ship repair.[77]

The steel controller also began to emphasize the inefficiencies of the steel industry in the Maritimes. Dosco had suffered losses during the war as coal carriers were sunk in the St Lawrence and ore carriers torpedoed on their way from Brazil. Like many firms it operated on a cost-plus basis, with the profits to be determined by a subsequent audit. In a firm as complex as Dosco, determining overall costs of operation was no mean feat and open to controversy. In 1944 the controller employed the costing of steel plate production derived from the audit—68 cents for Dosco compared to 57 cents for Stelco—to record different prices in the books of the Crown corporations buying it. As the demand for ships' plate declined, the difference in cost became the rationale for directing all domestic orders to Hamilton. With the decline in foreign orders, in February 1945 the Sydney plate mill closed down.[78]

The cost of producing steel, however, could not be separated from the pattern of previous government investment. Early in 1944 the steel controller sent T.F. Rahilly, a former general manager of Algoma, to report on the Sydney plant and its postwar prospects. Relentlessly, Rahilly compared the performance of each section with that of the new government-funded plants in other corporations. The Dosco coke ovens, for example, produced 100 tons of coke while the new ovens at Algoma could produce 160 tons. The blast furnaces were less efficient—one should be closed down immediately—and the iron ore was of a lower grade. But his conclusion was a surprising one and probably not welcome to Howe and his controllers. Rahilly argued that if the plant now had problems it was because "acts of the government have placed it in its present position." Dosco would "come out of the war period with less new plant than any of its competitors." Dosco was less efficient because of the government's intervention. In Rahilly's view the government had a clear responsibility to assist the company to re-establish itself in a peacetime economy.[79]

This view was not shared by Howe. Indeed Dosco's own efforts at survival proved embarrassing. Discouraged by the Maritimes' bleak postwar industrial prospects, the corporation turned to plants in Central Canada to provide captive markets for its primary products. Late in December 1943, having recently acquired the Canadian Tube and Steel Products Company of Montreal with its "extensive bolt and nut manufacturing plant," Dosco set out to close the bolt and nut department at Trenton and to lay off approximately 800 workers. A brief meeting of Arthur Cross with Howe sufficed to gain the minister's permission. To the surprise of both, this apparently routine shift in operations aroused extensive protest in the Maritimes. Maritimers were not strangers to the closure of their industries in periods of depression. But this closure, coming in wartime when business was booming, was recognized for what it was, a deliberate and conscious attempt to shift operations to a more promising location and, as the Dosco announcement proclaimed, to "consolidate operations now being conducted in the Montreal area."[80]

Pushed by a public outcry led by the trade unions, Premier A.S. MacMillan appeared before the federal cabinet to urge that the government deny the corporation permission to close the Nova Scotia plant.[81] MacMillan did not accept the cabinet's rejection of his request but appointed a royal commission conducted by Judge W.F. Carroll to investigate. The hearings, which lasted from December 1943 to May 1944, kept the issue before the public. The unions accused the corporation of employing public funds to facilitate its shift from the region and its abandonment of its responsibilities to dependent communities. Clearly implied was a criticism of the government, and in particular the minister who originally gave permission for the plant's closure.[82] Nor was the criticism effectively rebutted by Howe's lame explanation that he "was not told" that the products of the Trenton plant were used for war purposes.[83]

Howe may not have forgiven either Dosco or the Nova Scotia government for this public embarrassment. In 1944, as Duncan McDowall records, Howe advised the steel controllers to use Dosco "to the minimum extent possible even if we have to buy the steel from the United States."[84] Howe's animus towards Dosco may have had even greater repercussions for the Maritime region. In 1943 the federal government invited the provinces to co-operate in appointing commissions to investigate each province's needs in adjusting to a postwar economy. The three Maritime provinces did so. Nova Scotia, as part of its study, retained the firm of Arthur McKee and Company of Cleveland, Ohio, to investigate the Nova Scotia steel industry. Its report in the spring of 1944 proposed a sheet steel mill as a basic requirement for both Dosco and the manufacturing industries in the Maritimes. The McKee proposal included the results of a tentative market survey and diagram of the plant. In the same year Howe's department assisted Stelco to develop a mill for the production of sheet steel and invited other companies to submit proposals for a second mill to meet anticipated postwar needs. Dosco was not included in the invitation.[85]

The long-term impact of the government's wartime policies on the Maritimes was largely negative. While the government did generate economic activity, it created relatively little new industry in the region and even less of a permanent nature. It harmed existing industries which survived the war only to discover, as did Dosco, that their relative position in the country had been eroded by the expansion and modernization of their competitors. Even the service or repair industries did not escape damage from the increased capacity at the centre. The Canadian National Railways' repair shops in Moncton, for example, found their position undermined by a big new machine shop in Montreal which, at Howe's suggestion, the railway built as a munitions plant and then converted at the war's end.[86] Maritime manufacturers who sought to develop lines of consumer products for the postwar era faced long odds in importing their sheet steel from

Ontario while attempting to sell their products nation-wide. Companies which did so, such as Enterprise Stoves and the Enamel and Heating Products of Sackville, New Brunswick, found themselves doubly vulnerable to freight rate increases and a rate structure which increasingly favoured the central producers.[87]

By the pattern of its wartime investment, the federal government appeared to be telling businessmen that the Maritimes would have little part to play in Canada's new postwar industrial complex. Dosco responded to that message at first by vigorous protest and later by the transfer of secondary operations to Montreal. Meanwhile, with the taxable resources of the country now hived more than ever within the boundaries of Ontario and Quebec, provincial governments in the Maritimes were in no position to themselves finance the steps towards the re-industrialization of the region which their royal commission studies often suggested.[88]

While one can outline with precision the negative impact of the federal government's role, its motives remain open to controversy. There was, of course, no conspiracy to de-industrialize the Maritimes. Little more plausible is the suggestion that Howe and his controllers avoided the Maritimes in their investments from fear of German attack. It is true that Dosco was vulnerable to submarines in the acquisition of ores, and the corporation in 1942 went so far as to open emergency reserves of iron ore near Bathurst, New Brunswick, although these were never employed. Yet the strategic threat was not cited as a problem in the use of Maritime industry by the controllers at the time nor does it seem to have been a matter of discussion among their military advisers. The efficiency argument cannot so easily be dismissed, for it was the explanation most frequently offered by the bureaucrats in their industrial memoranda. But this rationale rings hollow when applied to the location of shipbuilding and ship repair industries or to the unnecessary delay in opening the Sydney plate mill.

The suggestion by officials of the British Admiralty Technical Mission, who were intimately involved in Canadian industry in an advisory capacity, that locational decisions were "heavily" political seems more plausible. Indeed the political hypothesis goes far in accounting for the entire pattern of economic development. The beginning of the war at the end of the Depression found Canadian industries starved for business and lobbying actively for the contracts anticipated from the war. Federal and provincial politicians were keenly interested. The earliest and biggest contracts went to the largest centres in the most influential provinces and with them went the federal assistance for industrial development.

The controllers' tacit respect for the political power of the Montreal metropolis also appeared obvious in their willingness to allow that city to dominate the lucrative ship repair industry. They persisted in this policy regardless of the inconvenience to convoys or the impediment to developing a stable industry, accessible during the winter months. Montreal's influence was also reflected in the discussions of the War Committee of the cabinet, which apparently found it easier to contemplate building destroyers at Halifax to provide off-season employment than to divert repair business from the St Lawrence. Certainly the decision to locate one shipbuilding plant in Nova Scotia appeared to be largely a response to public protest. It should come as no surprise that politicians act from political motives.

One suspects, nevertheless, that there was more than the consideration of immediate political gain in the behaviour of C.D. Howe and his controllers. Howe's personal motives in decisions affecting the Maritimes cannot be shown conclusively at this stage of research. Letters and memoranda on controversial decisions involving the Maritimes are absent from his papers, and his public statements often appear as simplistic rationales. Howe's extraordinary support for Algoma and his apparent hostility towards Dosco, its most direct competitor, suggest that his friendship with Sir James Dunn might have been an influencing factor. His subsequent attempt to deny this relationship and his admission to destroying portions of their correspondence also point in that direction.[89] Yet his apparent preference for Algoma should not be exaggerated. Assistance to that corporation appeared outstanding largely because, unlike Stelco, its profit margin was too low to allow government investment to be hidden as depreciation.

Howe's general policies and occasional comments suggest that he was more than merely reacting to the hectic events of the period. Repeated references by Howe and his controllers to Canada's postwar needs, even during periods of crisis, suggest that they were working from a plan for the long-term industrial development of the country. Their blueprint included a continued industrial integration with the United States—a relationship which effectively undermined Dosco's claim to virtue as the only steel company not dependent on the Americans for primary materials. It also anticipated the St Lawrence Waterway, an international project which promised to turn the cities of the Great Lakes into ocean ports. This scheme was abandoned by the Canadian government only after the Canadian–American treaty, signed in March 1941, failed to pass the United States Congress.[90]

From Howe's perspective, it may have appeared a more efficient use of Canada's resources to develop ports and concentrate industry on the Great Lakes and St Lawrence rather than the coast. Moreover, such a plan had the practical advantage of meeting the long-term aspirations of the two politically powerful central provinces and their metropolises. Such an approach served the interests and regional prejudices of Howe, his controllers, and his influential friends. It even appeared to conform to the conventional wisdom of Canadian economists. If the weakness of Maritime industry in the twentieth century was a natural outcome of the free interplay of the forces of the marketplace, as studies by S.A. Saunders and W.A. Mackintosh seemed to suggest, then it logically followed that government investment to develop industry there might be wasted in the long term. B.S. Keirstead probably reflected the thinking of many of his contemporaries when his studies in 1944 and 1948 set out the classic interpretation of the decline of manufacturing in the Maritimes as the inevitable result of economies of scale and agglomeration in Central Canada.[91]

One should not blame Howe, the politician, for responding to the political pressures of his day. He was not responsible for the structure of Confederation, which some have aptly called an "unequal union." But neither the political pressures nor Howe's industrial blueprint served the interests of Canada's war effort in the Maritimes. Not only did Howe's department fail to develop the industrial potential of the region for the war, but hindsight also reveals the negative impact of spectacular errors in particular industries. The long delay in reopening the plate mill at Sydney contributed to severe shortages in ships' plate in Canada in 1941 and 1942. Howe and his controllers failed to develop in Eastern Canada a major centre for the production of naval vessels. The construction of escorts on the lakes led to battles against frost and freeze-up, a loss of flexibility in shifting to larger vessels, and the lack of support capacity in refit and ship repair. Their failure to heed the advice of major allies on developing a repair centre at Halifax and their persistence in maintaining that industry at Montreal seriously impaired the effectiveness of the Canadian navy.

Meanwhile, their policies, far from helping to overcome trends towards regional disparity of which some Canadians were conscious, served rather to accentuate and consolidate them. Howe may have sincerely believed, given his vision of Canada's future development, that the decline of industry in the Maritimes was inevitable. If so, with the mobilized resources of the Canadian state at his disposal, including billions of dollars in direct investment, his was a powerfully self-fulfilling prophecy.

• Notes

1 J. de N. Kennedy, *History of the Department of Munitions and Supply: Canada in the Second World War* (Ottawa, 1951), 1:v. See also Canada, Department of Reconstruction and Supply, "Canada's Industrial War Effort, 1939–1945," unpublished manuscript, 1947, vol. 264, B2–B8, Records of the Department of Munitions and Supply (RG28), Public Archives of Canada (hereafter PAC).

2 Robert Bothwell and William Kilbourn, *C.D. Howe: A Biography* (Toronto, 1979), 350.

3 Michael Clow, "Politics and Uneven Capitalist Development: The Maritime Challenge to the Study of Canadian Political Economy," *Studies in Political Economy* 14 (Summer 1984): 117–40, and "Situating a Classic: Saunders Revisited," *Acadiensis* 15, 1 (Autumn 1985): 145–52. See also T.W. Acheson's "Introduction" to S.A. Saunders, *The Economic History of the Maritime Provinces* (Fredericton, 1984 [1939]) and the bibliography in J.B. Cannon, "Explaining Regional Development in Atlantic Canada: A

Review Essay," *Journal of Canadian Studies* 19, 3 (Fall 1984): 81–86.

4 C.R. Waddell, "The Wartime Prices and Trade Board: Price Control in Canada in World War II" (PhD thesis, York University, 1981). See also Robert Cuff and J.L. Granatstein, *War and Society in North America* (Toronto, 1971); C.P. Stacey, *Arms, Men and Governments* (Ottawa, 1970); J.L. Granatstein, *The Ottawa Men: The Civil Service Mandarins, 1935–57* (Toronto, 1982); James Eayrs, *In Defence of Canada: Peacemaking and Deterrence* (Toronto, 1972); Robert Bothwell, Ian Drummond, John English, *Canada Since 1945: Power, Politics, and Provincialism* (Toronto, 1981); and Donald Creighton, *The Forked Road: Canada 1939–1957* (Toronto, 1976).

5 Canada, Department of Reconstruction, Economic Research Branch, "Area Study Tables," 30 Sept. 1945, vol. 264, B2–B8, RG28, PAC.

6 Dominion Bureau of Statistics, *The Maritime Provinces in Their Relation to the National Economy of Canada* (Ottawa, 1948), 97.

7 "History of the British Admiralty Technical Mission in Canada," 30 April 1946, esp. 3, 57, 72–73, vol. 29, RG28, PAC.

8 "Report of the Economic Advisory Committee on Wartime Organization regarding policies relating to Canadian coal," July 1940, C246240, W.L. Mackenzie King Papers, PAC; F.G. Neat, "Report of the Activities of the Dominion Fuel Board," 11 Oct. 1945, vol. 1, 31–3, file 50-1-1, vol. 45, Records of the Dominion Coal Board (RG81), PAC; PC 3969, file 91-3-3, vol. 138, RG81, PAC.

9 "Report on the Activities of Steel Control from its establishment ... June 24th, 1940, to October 1st, 1943," 1943, 48, file 176-2-15, vol. 205, RG28, PAC.

10 C.M. Anson, "Memorandum for Mr A. Cross," 21 Sept. 1940, F1157 #6, Angus L. Macdonald papers, Public Archives of Nova Scotia (hereafter PANS).

11 The historical sketch of the first three years of Steel Control implied that work on the Hamilton plant had begun before the war. This was corrected in the survey of the next three years, as someone specifically recalled approving the project in 1940: "Report on the Activities of Steel Control from October 1st, 1943 until its termination November 1st 1945," 1946, 48, file 196-14-13, vol. 261, RG28, PAC. See also Canada, House of Commons, *Debates*, 1941, 6928–29.

12 Kennedy, *History of the Department of Munitions*, 1:229.

13 F.M. Ross to A.L. Macdonald, 24 Oct. 1940, F1157 #1, Macdonald papers, PANS.

14 The task force consisted of W.F. Drysdale (director of production), F.M. Ross (director of naval supply), Commander E. Watson, R.N. (British Admiralty technical mission) and James Crone (adviser to the Department of Munitions and Supply): "Memorandum Covering the Visit of Representatives of the Department of Munitions and Supply...," 7 Oct. 1940, F1157 #7, Macdonald papers, PANS.

15 Arthur Cross to C.D. Howe, 29 Jan. 1941, F1157 #4, Macdonald papers, PANS.

16 Commons *Debates*, 1941, 2104. See also *Halifax Chronicle*, 19 May 1941. According to the figures given by Dosco representatives before the Carroll Commission, the Sydney plate mill when later opened cost just more than $3 million: "Statement Showing Additions and Reductions, Property Account Covering Period January 1st, 1939 to December 31, 1942," loose sheet inserted in Dosco's brief to the Carroll Commission, Box 15 #11, Records of Royal Commissions and Reports (RG 44), PANS.

17 Arthur Cross to C.D. Howe, 12 March 1941, F1157 #5, Macdonald papers, PANS.

18 "History of the British Admiralty Technical Mission in Canada," 6; "Naval Construction Programme, 1942, 1943, 1944," vol. 42, C.D. Howe papers, PAC; "Branch History, Shipbuilding Branch, Department of Munitions and Supply," 31 Oct. 1945, 5–6, file 5 of 12, vol. 29, RG28, PAC; Commons *Debates*, 1941, 1629. The concentration of production in Ontario became particularly embarrassing for the Canadians when frigates were required for escort duty which were too long to go through the locks of the St Lawrence canals. The Quebec yards began the production of frigates in 1941, but the Ontario yards could not make the transition. See G.N. Tucker, *The Naval Service of Canada* (Ottawa, 1952), 2:66.

19 Commons *Debates*, 1941, 1666. See also Tucker, *The Naval Service of Canada*, 2:39. The Saint John Dry Dock and Shipbuilding Company did build three corvettes during the first three years of the war.

20 See the order-in-council appointing a separate controller for ship repairs, 17 Nov. 1940, file 196-38-1, vol. 30, RG28, PAC, and D.B. Carswell's, "Reports on Ship Repairs and Salvage," esp. 4 Nov. 1941, file 196-13-3, vol. 256, RG28, PAC.

21 Department of Munitions and Supply, "Digest of Canadian and British Programme of Capital Assistance to Industry . . . corrected as of April 30th 1941," vol. 42, Howe papers, PAC.

22 Arthur Cross to C.D. Howe, 7 Jan. 1942, F1222 #54, Macdonald papers, PANS; *Maritime Provinces in Relation to the National Economy*, 98.

23 By 1943 Maritime industries were prominent among those trying to receive labour from Newfoundland. See Peter Neary, "Canada and the Newfoundland Labour Market, 1939–45," *Canadian Historical Review* 62, 4 (Dec. 1981): 470–95.

24 *Telegraph-Journal* (Saint John), 14, 17 Oct. 1939, and "Report . . . of the New Brunswick Advisory Board for Economic and Industrial Development," Sept. 1940, Box 14, RS 415, J.B. McNair papers, Provincial Archives of New Brunswick.

25 Minutes of the Cabinet War Committee, 17 July 1940, vol. 424, King papers, PAC.

26 President's Report, Minutes, Saint John Board of Trade, 20 Jan. 1942, New Brunswick Museum, Saint John.

27 See for examples *Halifax Herald*, 19 Feb., 21, 22 March, 12 June 1941, *Post-Record* (Sydney), 29 April 1941.

28 See files on shipbuilding F1121 and F1222, especially A.S. MacMillan to A.L. Macdonald, 9 Aug. 1940, 2 Dec. 1940, and 16 May 1941, Macdonald papers, PANS.

29 "Contracts for the Construction of Ships and Small Craft, Nova Scotia," file 5 of 12, vol. 29, RG28, PAC.

30 C.D. Howe to Admiral B.A. Fraser, 6 Jan. 1941, file S9-25 (2), vol. 339, RG28, PAC.

31 Kennedy, *History of the Department of Munitions and Supply*, 1:455.

32 *Annual Reports of the New Brunswick Electric Power Commission*, 1942, 4; 1943, 9; 1944, 8.

33 Scrapbook of reports of Prince Edward Island legislative debates, 14 April 1941, vol. 102, Records of the Department of Education (RG10), Public Archives of Prince Edward Island (hereafter PAPEI). See also reports for 17 March 1942 and 11 and 13 March 1943.

34 See J.E. Michaud to J.L. Ralston, 8 Feb. 1945, J.L. Ralston papers, PAC, and the *Summerside Journal*, 14 June 1945.

35 H.J. Logan to W.L.M. King, 16 Feb. 1926, 113864, King papers, PAC; E.R. Forbes, "The Rise and Fall of the Conservative Party in the Provincial Politics of Nova Scotia, 1925–1933" (MA thesis, Dalhousie University, 1967), ch. 3.

36 J.R. Rowell, "An Intellectual in Politics: Norman Rogers as an

Intellectual and Minister of Labour, 1929–1939" (MA thesis, Queen's University, 1978).

37 J.W. Pickersgill, *The Mackenzie King Record* (Toronto, 1960), 1:100–101.

38 R.F. Sarty, "Silent Sentry: A Military and Political History of Canadian Coast Defence, 1860–1945" (PhD thesis, University of Toronto, 1982), 455.

39 A.L. Macdonald, "Memorandum re Cabinet and War Committee of the Cabinet," 4 Feb. 1943, F277 #2, Macdonald papers, PANS.

40 J.L. Ralston to J.J. Cox, 22 Feb. 1936, file "C" Miscellaneous, vol. 18, J.L. Ralston papers, PAC. See also H.M. Mackenzie, "Sinews of War: Aspects of Canadian Decisions to Finance British Requirements in Canada During the Second World War" (paper presented to the Canadian Historical Association, June 1984).

41 Leslie Roberts, *C.D.: The Life and Times of Clarence Decatur Howe* (Toronto, 1957), ch. 5–10.

42 E.R. Forbes, "Misguided Symmetry: The Destruction of Regional Transportation Policy for the Maritimes" in *Canada and the Burden of Unity*, ed. D.J. Bercuson (Toronto, 1977), 75–76.

43 C.J. Burchell to J.L. Ralston, 12 March 1937, R.L. Matheson and F.M. Sclanders to J.L. Ilsley, 10 March 1937, file "B" Miscellaneous, vol. 16, Ralston papers, PAC; J.D. McKenna to T.A. Campbell, 29 July 1937, Rand Matheson to T.A. Campbell, 6 March 1938, T.A. Campbell papers, Premier's Office Records, RG25, PAPEI.

44 Duncan McDowall, *Steel at the Sault: Francis H. Clergue, Sir James Dunn, and the Algoma Steel Corporation, 1901–1956* (Toronto, 1984), 169–71 and ch. 8.

45 J.W. Pickersgill, *The Mackenzie King Record*, 1:61–62, 77, 165.

46 Roberts, *C.D.*, 52, 59–61.

47 Minutes of the Cabinet War Committee, 7 Nov. 1940, 21 May 1941, vol. 424, King papers, PAC.

48 W.C. Hankinson to N.A. Robertson, 15 May 1941, file S-9-26, vol. 42, Howe papers, PAC; Minutes of the Cabinet War Committee, 27 May 1941; "Appreciation . . . Canadian Military Effort as of May 28, 1941," file S 14, vol. 51, Howe papers, PAC.

49 Minutes of the Cabinet War Committee, 27 July, 29 Oct. and 12 Nov. 1941.

50 Minutes of the Cabinet War Committee, 12 Nov., 17 Dec. 1941; J.C. Mitchell, Memorandum to G.C.C., 26 May 1942, file NSS 830-2-9, vol. 5619, Department of National Defence Records (RG24), PAC.

51 See also R.D. Cuff and J.L. Granatstein, *American Dollars—Canadian Prosperity: Canadian–American Economic Relations, 1945–1950* (Toronto, 1978), 11.

52 Minutes of the Cabinet War Committee, 19 Nov., 17 Dec. 1941; 28 Jan. 1942.

53 M.A. Hoey to J.B. Carswell, 2 Feb. 1943, file 196-14, vol. 3, 257, RG28, PAC.

54 See PC 6 and PC 85, 6 and 8 Jan. 1942, file 196-14-1, vol. 258, RG28, PAC; "Report on the Activities of Steel Control 1940 to 1943," 50 and "Report on the Activities of Steel Control 1943 until 1945," 51.

55 Minutes of the Cabinet War Committee, 28 July 1941. See also Paul MacEwan, *Miners and Steelworkers* (Toronto, 1976), 265.

56 "Towards a Background for Solid Fuel Control," 29 March 1943, 9–12, file 50-1-5A, vol. 45, RG81, PAC, and G.A. Vissac, "Emergency Coal Production Board Report on the Dominion Coal Co. Ltd.," Sept. 1944, 114, file 196-37-6-1, vol. 328, RG28, PAC.

57 Minutes of the Cabinet War Committee, 5 May, 15 April 1943; G.A. Vissac to E.J. Brunning, 12 Sept. 1944, file 196-37-6-1, vol. 328, RG28, PAC.

58 Captain N. Nicholson, A.J. Sullivan and C.G. Graham, "Report on Conditions in Halifax, Nova Scotia,

and Saint John's, Newfoundland," 30 March 1942, file #111-45, Records of the United States Maritime Commission and the War Shipping Administration, Washington National Records Center, Suitland, Maryland. This and other interoffice memoranda were made available to the author by the Freedom of Information Officer for the United States Maritime Administration.

59 Minutes of the Cabinet War Committee, 7 May 1942.

60 Commons *Debates*, 1941, 1631; Arthur Cross to C.D. Howe, 6 Jan. 1942, F1222 #54, Macdonald papers, PANS.

61 See "Report on Ship Repairs and Salvage for the period ending, 31 October 1941." (Note that two different reports bear the same date. This reference is to the one near the end of the file.) See also reports for 28 Jan. and 28 Feb. 1942, file 196-13-3, vol. 256, RG28, PAC.

62 G.L. Stephens to ACNS, 9 June 1943, file NSC 1057-1-35, vol. 1, vol. 3996, RG24, PAC.

63 "Minutes of the Advisory Committee on Ship Repairs," 23 Feb. 1942, file 196-13 "General Correspondence," vol. 1, vol. 256, RG28, PAC; "Report on Ship Repairs and Salvage for the period ending 31 May 1942."

64 "Memorandum," A.T. Cluff to C.G. Graham, 8 Sept. 1942, file #111-45, Records of the United States Maritime Commission and the War Shipping Administration.

65 G.L. Stephens to CNS, 11 Nov. 1943, F276 #37, Macdonald papers, PANS; J.W. Keohane, memorandum to CNEC, 19 Feb. 1944, file 35, vol. 2, vol. 3996.

66 Marc Milner, *North Atlantic Run: The Royal Canadian Navy and the Battle for the Convoys* (Toronto, 1985), ch. 9, and "Royal Canadian Navy Participation in the Battle of the Atlantic Crisis of 1943" in *The RCN in Retrospect, 1910–1968*, ed. J.A. Boutilier (Vancouver, 1982), 158–74.

67 "Minutes of the Saint Lawrence Operations Conference," 22–24 Feb. 1943, Appendix "G," file NSS 8280-166/16 vol. 3, 6789, RG24, PAC. See also M.L. Hadley, *U-Boats Against Canada: German Submarines in Canadian Waters* (Toronto, 1985).

68 G.L. Stephens to A/CNS, 9 June 1943, file NSC 1057-1-35 vol. 1, vol. 3996, RG24, PAC.

69 D.B. Carswell to W. Bennett, 7 June 1943, A.R. Riddell to the Principal Surveyor, 21 June 1943, file 19-6-13 vol. 2, vol. 256, RG24, PAC.

70 "Report on Ship Repairs and Salvage for the period ending 31 March 1944." Howe did not readily forgive anything which might be construed as criticism by subordinates. See *On the Bridge of Time: Memories of Hugh L. Keenleyside*, vol. 2 (Toronto, 1982), 79–81.

71 "Minutes of the third meeting of naval and merchant ship maintenance committee on man power," 29 April 1943, file 196-13-8, vol. 257, RG28, PAC. See also Kay Piersdorf, "Anybody Here from the West," *Nova Scotia Historical Review* 5, 1 (June 1985), 5–14, Jay White, "'Sleepless and Veiled Am I': An East Coast Canadian Port Revisited," ibid., 15–29, and Jay White, "The Ajax Affair: Citizens and Sailors in Wartime Halifax, 1939–1945" (MA thesis, Dalhousie University, 1984).

72 J.A. Hanway to Henry Borden, 22 June 1943, D.B. Carswell to C.D. Howe, 8 May 1943, file S-14 (2), vol. 51, Howe papers, PAC. It is remarkable how casually the federal authorities appeared willing to discriminate against the Maritimes in the distribution of commodities. An oil shortage in 1941 resulted in a federal directive that ration coupons for gasoline would allow only two gallons in the Maritimes while continuing to yield five in the rest of the country: *Halifax Herald*, 19, 21, 23 May 1942, and interview with R.A. Tweedie of Fredericton, 26 Feb. 1985.

73 Minutes of the Cabinet War Committee, 22 Sept. 1943; K.F. Adams, "Inadequacy of Refitting Facilities on the East Coast of Canada," Memorandum to ACNS, 7 Dec. 1943, file NSC 1057-1-35 vol. 2, vol. 3996, RG24, PAC.

74 Department of Munitions and Supply, Economics and Statistics Branch, "Report on the Government-Financed Expansion of the Industrial Capacity in Canada as at December 31, 1943," summary table 2, vol. 184, RG28, PAC; Shipbuilding summaries, file 5 of 12, vol. 29, RG28, PAC.

75 Department of Reconstruction, Economic Research Branch, "Area Study Tables," 30 Sept., 11 July 1945, vols. 263, 264, B2–B8, RG28, PAC; "The transformation of the Canadian economy from a peacetime to a wartime basis and the machinery developed for that purpose," vol. 262, B2, RG28, PAC. For the role of the federal government in the problems of two primary industries adjusting to the postwar economy, see Margaret Conrad, "Apple Blossom Time in the Annapolis Valley, 1880–1957," *Acadiensis* 9, 2 (Spring 1980): 14–39, and David Alexander, *The Decay of Trade: An Economic History of the Newfoundland Saltfish Trade, 1935–65* (St John's, 1977).

76 "Convoys in the Gulf of St Lawrence," Memorandum from Deputy Secretary of the Naval Board to Commander-in-Chief, Canadian Northwest Atlantic, 28 Aug. 1944, file NSS 8280-166 vol. 4, 6789, RG24, PAC; Minutes of the Cabinet War Committee, 17 March 1945; E.S. Brand to W.G. Hynard, 2 Feb. 1945, file NSS 8280-166 vol. 4, vol. 6789, RG24, PAC.

77 "Report on Ship Repairs and Salvage" for the periods ending 31 May, 31 July, and 30 Sept. 1945.

78 F.H. Brown to C.L. Dewar, 22 Sept. 1944, file 196-2D-2, vol. 195, RG28, PAC.

79 T.F. Rahilly to F.B. Kilbourn, 5 Sept. 1944, file 196-2D-2, vol. 195, RG28, PAC.

80 "Proceedings of the Carroll Commission re. Trenton Steel Works Ltd.," vol. VI, 406, 421–22, Box 15 #4, RG44, PANS.

81 Minutes of the Cabinet War Committee, 1 and 16 Dec. 1943.

82 "Submission of J.L. Cohen on behalf of United Steelworkers of America and District #26, United Mineworkers of America in the matter of . . . the curtailment of operations at DOSCO Trenton Steel Works . . . ," 24 June 1944, Box 15 #2, RG44, PANS.

83 Province of Nova Scotia, *Report of the Commissioner on Trenton Steel Works* (Halifax, 1944), 26.

84 Quoted in McDowall, *Steel at the Sault*, 200.

85 A.G. McKee & Company, "Report on the Steel Industry" in *Report of the Royal Commission on Provincial Development and Rehabilitation* (Halifax, 1944), part 11, 19. This consulting firm had acted as consultants to Steel Control at the beginning of the war: M.A. Hoey to J.G. Godsoe, 10 May 1944, file 196-14-4, vol. 257, RG28, PAC.

86 See draft history of "National Railways Munitions Ltd.," file 3 of 12, vol. 29, RG28, PAC.

87 See their statements in "Submission of the Transportation Commission of the Maritime Board of Trade to the Royal Commission on Transportation," vol. 1, 119, Box 9, RG34, PAPEI. Appendix 46 in volume 2 suggests that competitive rates led to decreases of 10 to 35 percent on basic steel to manufacturers in Central Canada, with the differential against the Maritime manufacturer increasing sharply after each rate increase.

88 Nova Scotia, *Report of the Royal Commission on Provincial Development and Rehabilitation*; New Brunswick, *Report of the New Brunswick Committee on Reconstruction* (Fredericton, 1944); Prince Edward Island, *The Interim Report of the Prince Edward Island Advisory Reconstruction Committee* (Charlottetown, 1945); J.R. Petrie, *The*

Regional Economy of New Brunswick: A Study Prepared for the Committee on Reconstruction (Fredericton, 1944) and J.M. Beck, *The Government of Nova Scotia* (Toronto, 1957), 341.

89 McDowall, *Steel at the Sault*, 205. See also S.R. Howe, "C.D. Howe and the Americans, 1940–1957" (PhD thesis, University of Maine, 1977), 251–52.

90 T.L. Hills, *The St Lawrence Seaway* (London, 1959), 66–67. The files of press clippings on this subject in Howe's papers suggest the enthusiasm of Great Lakes harbour communities at the prospects of becoming ocean ports.

91 Saunders, *The Economic History of the Maritime Provinces*, 84–85, and W.A. Mackintosh, *The Economic Background*

to Dominion-Provincial Relations (Ottawa, 1939), 43–45. See also *Report of the Royal Commission on Dominion-Provincial Relations* (Ottawa, 1940), book 1, 119; B.S. Keirstead, *Theory of Economic Change* (Toronto, 1948), 267–310, and *The Economic Effects of the War on the Maritime Provinces of Canada* (Halifax, 1944). W.Y. Smith pointed out, however, that although Howe and his adviser W.A. Mackintosh borrowed heavily from the work of British economist J.M. Keynes for their *White Paper on Employment and Income* (Ottawa, 1945), they conspicuously ignored his strictures on regional development: "Recognition of Regional Balance," *Policy Options* 2, 5 (Nov./Dec. 1981): 41–44.

FAMILY ALLOWANCES AND FAMILY AUTONOMY: Quebec Families Encounter the Welfare State, 1945–1955*

DOMINIQUE MARSHALL

Among the many transformations affecting Western families during the twentieth century, historians agree that the advent of the welfare state is of major importance. Yet the impact of new social policies has been difficult to isolate from the general movement towards a better standard of living or from the changing demands of the economy upon families. This paper seeks to assess the impact of one major policy of the postwar welfare state— family allowances—on the economic and social autonomy of Canadian families. It is based largely on analysis of the rich array of documents existing in the archives of the government departments in charge of implementing the program. These allow a reconstitution of the process of policy formation, shed some light on the diverse interests involved, and allow a critical reading of the declared intentions of politicians. Furthermore, studies conducted by the agents of the welfare state combined with written exchanges between the state and its "clients" allow us to describe the enforcement of welfare measures and to assess the economic and political impact of the program on Canadian families.

The study of the family allowances inaugurated in 1945 offers an interesting window into the history of Canadian families and their relation

*Originally published by Dominique Jean in *Canadian Family History: Selected Readings*, ed. Bettina Bradbury (Toronto: Copp Clark Pitman, 1992), 401–37.

with the welfare state, because they were the first universal measure of social security in the country. On one hand, state agents and social workers were particularly curious about the impact of such a novelty, so they undertook many investigations of the impact and the use made of the allowances. On the other hand, families were especially conscious of this new intervention of the state in their lives. The first part of this paper outlines the major goals articulated by politicians and the various social groups that promoted family allowances. The second part focusses on the ideology of the family that pervaded the program. Next, I analyse the educational campaign, which was the main public tool of intervention in family consumption patterns, and contrast these intentions with the program's effects on the incomes and expenditure patterns of rural and urban families. Finally, I describe the struggle for the indexation of allowances, an episode that helps to explain family practices and the political leverage of poor clients of the welfare state. The first sections of the paper address Canada as a whole, while the discussion of the effects of family allowances on families focusses on the province of Quebec.

• Why Were Family Allowances Enacted in 1944?

A convergence of factors prompted the passage of family allowances legislation in Canada at the end of the Second World War. While Canadian scholars still debate their relative importance, they agree on four major influences. First, there were immediate political objectives. The approach of a federal election hastened the Liberal government's adoption of this politically potent policy. During the war years many proposals for comprehensive social security had been drafted in Canada, and their endorsement by the CCF considerably threatened the Liberal government. By launching the program just before the elections, the government could send money into 1 400 000 households, thus proving that it sought to avoid the return of harsh prewar economic conditions. Mackenzie King could also remain vague as to the adoption of other measures popularized by the *Report on Social Security for Canada* of 1943, particularly health insurance and a comprehensive employment policy. This strategy placed the opposition Conservatives in the difficult situation of denouncing the electioneering character of the measure while voting unanimously in favour of it.[1]

Politicians also expected the program to reinforce the popularity of the federal state among citizens, particularly in postconscription Quebec. Cheques and educational pamphlets repeatedly reminded beneficiaries that "Family allowances are paid by the federal government."[2] At the same time, the allowances program was one of the many means by which the federal government tried to widen its jurisdiction. By making family allowances non-contributory, Mackenzie King used federal spending power to circumvent the provincial responsibility for welfare. The program, once implemented, gave the prime minister strong bargaining power in postwar federal–provincial meetings. He justified his proposal of federal appropriation of income taxes by citing the costs of national public welfare programs. Quebec Premier Maurice Duplessis, a promoter of provincial autonomy, fully appreciated the threat of centralization brought by federal family allowances. However, his opposition was launched too late and soon decreased as the political danger of fighting such a popular measure became clear.[3]

A source of conflict between French and English MPs was the decreasing size of the benefits after the fourth child, a feature unique in the history of family allowances. French-Canadian MPs were especially anxious to enhance the links between family allowances and fertility, which had already been suggested in the 1931 census monograph on the family. They relied on two decades of Catholic campaigns for family allowances in the name of the *"famille nombreuse."* This made it easy for English Canadians to accuse Mackenzie King of paying "baby bonuses" to the French-speaking electorate. To prevent the debate over family allowances from dividing along ethnic lines, the government reduced the allowance paid after the fourth child. Yet, perhaps in the face of declining fertility rates in Quebec and the widespread satisfaction with the program, objections to equal allowances for all children did not last long. The decreasing rate was abandoned in 1949 without any debate.[4]

A second goal of family allowances was to stimulate the postwar Canadian economy. The government wanted to avoid an unemployment and production backlash similar to the postwar crisis of 1919–22. Ministers assumed that family allowances would promote consumption, fuelling a sustained demand for goods, stabilizing the national economy, and preventing the national revenue from dropping. Giving families money to spend for clothes, shoes, and food for their children would stimulate the most vulnerable Canadian enterprises, especially factories that had been fully mobilized for soldiers' needs during the war. Certainly the program responded to requests of the Canadian Manufacturers Association to increase citizens' purchasing power. In this way, family allowances would indirectly contribute to raising the level of employment.[5]

The promoters of family allowances promised additional economic advantages. They would free other social programs from the dilemma of having to adjust rates to family size and would ensure a regular income for children, independent of fluctuations in a father's earnings.[6] This was all the more important since other contemporary reforms concerning children, including compulsory schooling in Quebec and new limitations on child labour, conflicted with the working-class practice of supplementing a father's wage through children's earnings.[7]

From the government's point of view, the allowances also appeared to solve the problem of inadequate wages for urban workers, especially those with large families. In Quebec, many members of the Catholic Church had long proposed family allowances, both because of their advantages for large families and their concordance with the concept of a "fair wage" elaborated in the encyclicals *Rerum Novarum* (1891) and *Quadragesimo Anno* (1931).[8] Most Canadian unions, in contrast, opposed allowances, fearing they would allow employers to maintain salaries below the level necessary to raise a family.[9] Indeed, during the war a committee of the National Labour Board had investigated industrial conflicts and had suggested the introduction of family allowances as a way of maintaining low salaries. Prime Minister Mackenzie King clearly had this advantage in mind. In public, however, he preferred to argue that allowances could provide workers with the material base for greater negotiating power.[10]

Family allowances, according to at least some liberal rhetoric, represented "a step towards the eradication of misery and fear."[11] Some liberal MPs proclaimed that the number of children in families was the major cause of poverty. For Minister of National Health and Welfare Brooke Claxton, the size of families was the primary cause of want:

> The greatest single factor in creating differences between one family in Montreal and another family in Montreal—or even between one family in Montreal and one family in Toronto—is neither their wages nor their health; it is the number of their children. Taken by and large across the great bulk of the population, nothing so much affects the relative economic position of the family than the number of their children. This is why this measure is introduced at this time; it is an endeavour to correct that disparity by attempting, in part of course, to bridge the gap between wages and the number of children.[12]

The allowances could provide a minimum of welfare to everybody, "equal advantages in the battle of life," in the words of the 1944 speech from the throne.[13] In doing so they would ease the economic pressure of raising a family so that children—all too often seen as a burden—would instead become a source of pleasure.[14]

In 1945, politicians had to answer the mood of a hopeful electorate for whom the idea of universality was becoming popular, thanks to the sense of community generated by the war effort and the campaigns for a "social minimum," "social security," and "freedom from want" that were then being launched in many Western societies. Until 1945, Canada had never embarked on a universal program of assistance. Relief programs to the poor had required investigation of the recipients' need. The old-age pension scheme of 1927 was a means-tested measure. So were the numerous provincial relief schemes of the Depression, which had been partly funded by the federal government, and the various provincial programs of allowances for needy mothers.[15]

The third purpose, a concern for children's welfare, combined with these political and economic goals to shape the family allowances policy.

The program addressed families as agents of social reproduction who had to be maintained and encouraged, in part to ensure Canada's defence as well as supply an adequate labour force. Social surveys conducted during the Depression and medical examinations of soldiers during the war had awakened the authorities to the poor physical condition of many young people. In 1942 the armed forces had rejected 28 percent of volunteers and conscripts because of their physical unsuitability. Two years later, the proportion had risen to 52 percent.[16] The government expressed its concern clearly: Canada's three and a half million children were the most important component of the country's future wealth. The Liberals compared state intervention through family allowances to the more generally accepted subsidies to private enterprises. Only a few conservative thinkers denounced this equation of children with human capital. To Montreal economist François-Albert Angers, it was nothing less than fascism.[17]

The fourth immediate purpose of the government in launching family allowances was to promote the return of married women workers to their homes after the war. Early in the conflict, the government had attempted to attract married women into the labour market. The proportion of wives in the female labour force increased from 10 percent in 1939 to 35 percent in 1944. But the cabinet feared that returning soldiers would glut the labour market. By stressing the importance of their domestic role, the government not only encouraged married women to leave the labour force, it also appeared to meet the demands of feminists and reformers for recognition of women's domestic labour. Indeed, Paul Martin stated that family allowances were "a long overdue tribute to the mothers of Canada."[18] But payment to mothers was a matter of some contention, especially in Quebec where it was opposed by the conservative elite. A group of social scientists, asked by the provincial government in 1944 to write a report on the desirability of allowances in Quebec, had proposed to send the cheque to both parents, to acknowledge both the patriarchal character of the Quebec Civil Code and the democratic evolution of families. But the feminist leader of the struggle to have the cheques made out with the name of the mother, Thérèse Casgrain, recalled that she "knew perfectly well that by tacit agreement it was generally the wife who handled the family budget." She was backed in her victorious fight by the Catholic Union of Agricultural Producers and the Canadian and Catholic Confederation of Labour.[19]

In sum, the Liberal cabinet invested family allowances with all the expectations generated by larger reconstruction schemes popular during the war. Not only were the allowances to help families with children, they were supposed to maintain a high level of employment in the country and enhance the health of its citizens. The program was launched with the promise of ensuring equality of opportunity for all children and of freeing Canadians from a major cause of poverty.

• The Thin Line Between Promoting Family Autonomy and Supervising Family Spending

Beyond these immediate economic, political, and demographic objectives, politicians harboured ideals of family life that shaped the content of family allowances legislation. By attempting to solve the problem of poverty with family allowances, the government placed families at the centre of its welfare interventions. The family, according to King's speech from the throne, was the basis of national life, and children within it were entitled to a minimum of welfare. When the material basis to which families were entitled was threatened by an economic system in which most depended on salaries to survive, the state had a responsibility to help. King affirmed that "if it is want that has been brought about through no fault of the individual himself, but because of an existing industrial system, which the state permits to exist, then that want should be met in some way by the agency of the state itself."[20] In Canada, as in many other Western countries, increased consciousness of the family problems posed by dependence on wages was crucial in the development of a more active welfare state.[21]

Yet most politicians still believed strongly in individual responsibility. The debate over what form allowances were to take highlighted the conflicting visions about individual and state responsibilities. Conservatives questioned the wisdom of making cash payments to families, arguing that because the government could not be assured that these benefits would be spent for the welfare of children, the money would be better used for the improvement of welfare services to children.

Liberal MPs insisted that families were a better agency to take care of children than any services the federal government could fund. To prove that parents were dependable, these politicians invoked, among other things, maternal instinct, parental love, and scientific studies of the quality of nutrition according to level of income. They argued that mothers had proven their reliability during the war mobilization on the home front and by their good management of federal allocations to soldiers' dependants.[22] Such reasoning was in line with the spirit of the Marsh Report, which had stated that:

> Canadians believe not only in the family, but in a strong measure of individuality. There must be reasonable leeway for parents' decision in the expenditure of the budget for their children. It is an impossible situation to imagine that all guidance and all services should be provided by non-family authorities. The virtue of a standard endowment of benefit in cash is that it becomes part of the normal family income, which is left to the parent to expend.[23]

Similarly, in 1944 in Quebec, the report on allowances prepared by social scientists for the short-lived Liberal government of Adélard Godbout, had supported payments in cash because they fostered initiative and upheld the superiority of family services to children over state services.[24]

By promoting cash payments, Liberal MPs could argue that their confidence in parents' autonomy was greater than that of their opponents. They used the same weapon to dismiss Conservative MPs' suggestions of allowances in kind. Liberals proclaimed that they meant to break away from such degrading practices. According to Brooke Claxton, choosing payments in kind would involve

> going back to such set-up as was adopted by a former administration during the worst period of the depression. It led to every kind of effort to get around the regulations; it reduced the self-respect of the recipients; it was a reversion to the days when the rich man took a basket of necessaries to the poorer people in his city. . . . [This] will not be accepted by the people in Canada."[25]

Yet there were real limits to the Liberals' professed confidence in parents' sense of responsibility for the welfare of their children. Promoters of allowances believed that parents had to assume some of the economic responsibility for their offspring. Thus, rates of allowances were set at a level under the actual cost of raising children. During the war the government estimated this cost at $14 to $20 a month per child in Canadian urban areas, but the actual family allowances ranged from $6 to $9 according to the child's age.[26] Higher payments, the government thought, might deter parents from working or, worse, encourage procreation "for gain." One reassured civil servant proclaimed that the low purchasing power of the monthly cheque would ensure production of children for "pleasure, rather than profit."[27]

Although ministers had argued against too much supervision of family spending, they did want to ensure that allowances were spent for their intended purpose. Even CCF members such as House Leader J.W. Colwell admitted the necessity of accounting for the effects of public spending and of ensuring that the allowances would be used for food, clothes, and other important items.[28] In this they were supported by the Canadian Council of Welfare for whom supervision constituted the condition of success of family allowances.[29] Similarly, Brooke Claxton declared that "it is not enough just to pay this money out"; the government had to convince parents "to spend it in the best possible way for the benefit of their children."[30] To that end, the law specified that parents had to spend these sums exclusively for their children, and it allowed the minister and his department to stop payments in cases of misuse.[31] In order to monitor the efficiency of the program, the government initiated a series of studies into the uses people made of their allowances.[32]

Most MPs saw education as the most acceptable way of ensuring that the allowances were spent for the welfare of children. For Liberals, publicity was a preventive measure. Educational material sent with the monthly cheque would influence parents who were, in their view, not ill-intentioned but ill-informed. Middle-class women's groups had long emphasized the advantages of a campaign of education aimed at poor mothers, and many commented on the benefits of sending educational literature along with cheques.[33] Conservative MP Ellen Louks Fairclough's description of working-class families is typical of the faith placed in education:

> Today, there are families living in two and three rooms in many municipalities in this country. Under the conditions which prevail in housing, they are living in quarters in which there is no adequate provision for food storage so it is necessary for them to live from hand to mouth. . . . Owing to this situation, the money which is going into these homes, ostensibly for the care of these children, is being spent on the most expensive type of food that the homemaker can buy. It is being spent on that food because, in many instances, the mother of the family does not realize there is a better way in which to spend that money.[34]

The 1944 Quebec report on family allowances also stressed the necessity of popular education, as did many social workers. Montreal businessman Gérard Parizeau even suggested that the church join the government in the educational campaign.[35]

Some Liberal MPs showed a lack of confidence in parents' spending habits, not unlike the mistrust displayed by Conservative proponents of payment in services. Manitoba Liberal J.P. Howden, for instance, warned his colleagues that a family might save the money while depriving children of necessary goods. In the end, the law would reflect this element of mistrust. When misuse was suspected, officials could investigate families. Conservative MP Gordon Graydon pointed in vain to the contradiction between this clause and Liberals' statements about family autonomy over expenses. The conservative economist François-Albert Angers also opposed investigation in the name of the very principle of family independence the Liberals had defended during the debate over cash payments. Angers saw no more reason to tell parents how to spend their allowances than to tell them how to spend their salaries.[36]

The government's mistrust was the product of many biases, which quickly compromised the initial message of universality. Opposition MPs were quick to point out that rich families had not been subjected to such public scrutiny when tax deductions for children were established in 1919. King's answer was that rich citizens who paid income taxes deserved more privileges than citizens who did not. Suspicion was directed more at poor fathers than poor mothers. One reason for promoting payment of the allowances to the mother was to keep the money out of the hands of unemployed or drinking husbands. When it came to native parents, politicians showed their lack of confidence in a series of strict regulations. True, for selected native groups the economic autonomy of the families remained a strong government goal: family allowances entitlements could be converted into "rifles, boats and other hunting and fishing equipment . . . in these cases where a reasonably large credit has accumulated . . . , thus increasing the capacity of self-reliance." Administrators of family allowances and at the Department of Indian Affairs initiated a plan whereby allowances could be used to finance up to 80 percent of the price of fishing boats. A minority of "Indians" (21 percent in 1949) and the majority of "Eskimos" received allowances in kind. Families could choose from a list of eligible items prepared in collaboration with the Department of Indian Affairs. Public ideals regarding the well-being of children were clearly those of mainstream, white society. The program made powdered milk and cereals for babies semi-mandatory and gradually introduced other nutritive foods, and, later, children's clothing.[37]

In summary, new parameters were to shape the relationship between the state and families over the welfare of children. Cash payments symbolized the end of a particularly degrading form of relief. Universal allowances also marked the advent of a type of assistance that was not means tested. But the government kept some measure of control over the beneficiaries through its right to suspend misused payments and through the promotion of specific forms of spending. Only a close study of the reality of such aspects of the program can help to evaluate the extent of government control and whether the anti-poverty goals of the legislators were realistic.

• The Many Messages of the Educational Campaign

The task of devising the content of the educational campaign fell to the civil servants. Between 1945 and 1955, the Information Division of the Department of National Health and Welfare disseminated propaganda proclaiming the benefits and the desirable uses of family allowances. In the literature that arrived with their cheques, parents were invited to consider images of ideal family spending patterns, roles, and attitudes promoted by their government. In both scale and means this educational campaign recalled the war propaganda on the home front. This was no coincidence. The Wartime Commission of Information contributed to the launching publicity.

The literature makes clear that, from the bureaucrat's point of view, the main agent of the domestic economy was the mother and wife, "a wise woman [who] regards housekeeping as a profession and prepares and follows plans as carefully as an engineer draws and follows his blueprints for a bridge. . . . She is not only the planner but the purchasing agent and the maintenance man." Mothering was represented as a full-time occupation, a message consistent with the government's desire to return married women workers to their homes after the war. While the distribution of power over the decisions within the family was not explicitly prescribed, husbands were depicted as sole breadwinners whose involvement with the program was limited to tasks like filling in the application form or planning long-term expenses.[38]

In keeping with the program's major concern, children were at the centre of the family activities and choices depicted in the literature. Unlike earlier pamphlets produced by Social Catholics promoting family allowances in Quebec, campaign illustrations seldom showed more than two children.[39] Spending the allowances to prolong children's education and dependency was encouraged, but parents were also advised to avoid spoiling their offspring. Giving them an allowance as they grew up or encouraging them to save for their own bicycles were presented as good ways to make them "self-reliant and responsible about money." Government officials saw this lesson as the key to the reproduction of values in a subsequent generation. Young citizens would be ready to raise progeny of their own in a responsible fashion, having themselves learned that "things have value and that dolls' carriages and baseball bats, chesterfields and motor cars do not grow on trees. . . . Someone has to earn them." In this way propagandists reconciled the two roles of the family: protecting children while training them for independence.[40]

The ambivalence exhibited in pamphlets regarding the ideal way to spend allowances indicated there was some recognition of the socio-economic diversity of families. Some pamphlets seemed to address families with economic difficulties, showing "how to get the most value from the food you buy with your family allowance," how to spend the cheque wisely, or "how to get more for your money." For this group the literature emphasized "necessities" as well as occasional crucial expenses like medicine or visits to the doctor or dentist. The campaign also addressed comfortable families by promoting the investment of this "extra" money in a "fuller life": piano lessons, bicycles, sports equipment, summer camps. The dual rhetoric echoes the politicians' hesitations about the vocation of the family allowances as a "minimum" or a "supplement."[41]

The booklet *You and Your Family* made explicit the distinction between families of the "lower income brackets" and others. Another government booklet, *Speaking of Family Allowances*, portrayed three imaginary families in different socioeconomic positions. It invited the reader to meet the Gagniers, who used their allowances for vaccinations, vitamin D, skates for the son Jean, and a journey to the countryside for Suzanne, the daughter. Their neighbour, a widow by the name of Mme Leduc, needed "each cent of her son's allowance; when the cheque does not arrive, things become complicated." She used most of the allowances for clothes. Finally, it introduced her friends, the Sauvés. They "couldn't allocate a large part of the allowances to these things [that exclusively concern the development of children], and would preferably spend them on more milk, school supplies for the eldest girl, visits to the dentist and exceptionally on the piano lesson of their son who was gifted."[42]

Yet this occasional tendency to make a distinction between families according to their socioeconomic level was more than offset by the more widespread tendency to confuse them. The government's literature emphasized budgeting and saving. All families were equally exhorted to adopt these practices, whatever the amount, whatever the period of saving. Comfortable families were warned to save for periods of illness or economic difficulty. *You and Your Family* extolled planning as a remedy for poverty:

> It may mean that you do without new shoes for another month, or that the family eat more baked beans and less meat, but somehow find the money within your means for entertainment and do not let the children do without something they really need just to make this extravagance possible.[43]

Poorer families were depicted as capable of imitating their richer neighbours' spending on matters that meant a lot to them, if "they consciously save[d] in order to do it." Similarly, the farmers' weekly, *La Terre de Chez Nous*, encouraged its readers to save the allowances. Families were already accustomed to wartime propaganda exhorting them to save. The war finished, the new objective of delayed spending for consumer goods reflected the government's preoccupation with a smooth transition towards a peacetime economy.[44]

In publishing pamphlets that tended to show all families sharing similar economic problems, civil servants of the Information Division acted as if they confused the promises of equality attached to family allowances with the realities of Canadian life. In the meantime, other branches of the Department of National Health and Welfare were conducting studies into the efficiency of the program. They were discovering unexpected levels of poverty. These studies began to paint a picture of poor families that made the educational campaign look irrelevant and that called into question the feasibility of the initial objectives of family allowance legislation.

• Unravelling of the Real Impact of Allowances on Families

When the first cheques were distributed in the summer of 1945, prognoses were still oscillating between the likes of conservative nationalist François-Albert Angers, who feared that an "esprit de lucre" would penetrate the households of the beneficiaries of family allowances, and of Communist MP Fred Rose, who sardonically predicted that beneficiaries would not deposit the cheques in a bank or spend them on luxury goods or overseas travel: "They will bring them to the store."[45] The Department of National Health and Welfare was eager to know how the money was being used, and it initiated investigations in various areas of the country. The social policy makers and high civil servants of the 1940s were influenced by the general development of social science in Canada. Even when they had not trained in social science departments themselves, they hired many prominent scholars to conduct studies of family allowances. Policy makers and civil servants hoped such studies would improve their knowledge about the Canadian family, thus increasing their own power and legitimizing Liberal intervention in family welfare with proof of the positive impact of the legislation.[46]

These surveys unexpectedly uncovered a significant proportion of Canadian families living in poverty. On the average, as predicted, the allowances represented a small part of family incomes. From 1945 to 1957, benefits amounted to $5 to $8 per child, depending on his or her age; Canadian families received an average allowance of $16.07 per month during these years. In 1945–46, the net total of payments in the province of Quebec amounted to a minimum of 3.5 percent of family income. However, these averages hid a diversity of situations. For some, the allowances brought an improvement in economic conditions. As table 1 reveals, rural families, large families, and low-income urban families saw major proportional gains in their income.[47]

The aggregated results of four studies of the effects of the program are reported in table 1 and form the basis of this section. None of the studies observed rigorous methods of sampling. To be representative, they would have had to consider family size, income level, ethnic origins, and distribution by age and sex. Yet, when interpreted with care, they clearly demonstrate the different ways in which family allowances modified the family economy and family strategies among rural families, and among poor and more comfortable urban families.[48]

To the Liberal leaders, who had believed that state help was necessary mainly to correct the inadequacies of the industrial wage system, the level of relief that family allowances brought to rural families might have come as a surprise. Families in rural areas spent most of their funds on essential goods like food and clothing, as table 2 shows. This was true in the grain-growing Prairies, in the Quebec dairy farming area of Nicolet, and in the mixed lumbering and farming area of North Gaspé. The level of relief brought to rural areas equalled that in poor urban sections. Because of the scarcity of cash income in farming households, the ideals of budget planning and delayed spending were even less attainable for rural parents than for their urban counterparts. Rural families were less likely than urban ones to save their allowances or to invest them in insurance. Rural income depended on fluctuating staples prices, which bred constant insecurity.

In some cases, the addition of new cash income could even change the working patterns of a family, bringing it closer to the nuclear ideal envisaged by the Department of National Health and Welfare. Not used to having much monetary income, farming, fishing, and lumbering families interviewed by social workers saw their cash income rise by 16 percent to 18 percent. In some areas, the regular payment lowered farmers' reliance on lumbering, if the testimony of this manager of a forestry enterprise is credible:

the program is interfering with the recruitment of labour. It is the practice of the Canadian lumber industry in Quebec and Ontario to hire men for logging in the northern woods for the winter season. In the past, farmers have been available for this work in their off seasons and have been willing to leave their homes to get the needed cash income. The eastern lumber industry found it difficult in the winter of 1945–46 to obtain their seasonal labour supply and believes that this is because the cash income received through the family allowances eliminated the incentive for these men to leave their families during the winter months for employment in the "bush."[49]

The use of, and perhaps the need for, child labour could similarly decrease. Family allowances pushed farming communities to send children to school, as payments were suspended when the compulsory school attendance law was not respected. They gave parents some means to dispense with child labour. When American anthropologist Horace Miner examined

Table 1:   FAMILY ALLOWANCES AS A PERCENTAGE OF TOTAL FAMILY INCOME

Area	Family allowances as % of family income	Number of families in sample	Character of families in the sample

Montreal 1947[a]
Families with
  2 children
Families with
  3 children
	
	7
	
	12.0
		79
		
		(49)
		
		(30)
			Helped by the child welfare agency of South-West Montreal; nuclear** with 2 or 3 children.

Montreal 1948[b]	19	30	Working-class fathers; poor ward; nuclear.
Gaspé-Nord 1945–46[c]	18	115	Diversified sources of income; nuclear; reachable by means of regular transportation.
Nicolet 1947–48[d]	16	66	Distant from large urban market, areas with francophone majority; randomly selected; derive at least half of their income from farm.

Prairies 1947[e]
Northern
  Saskatchewan
West-central
  Saskatchewan
West-central
  Alberta
	
	20
	
	14
	
	14
		416	Distant from large urban market; randomly selected; derive at least half of their income from farm.

Table 1, *continued*

Area	Family allow-ances as % of family income	Number of families in sample	Character of families in the sample
Maritimes 1947[f]			
Families with		114	From 1 to 5 children;
1 child	3*		Mother, father, and
Families with			maximum of one
5 children	13*		boarder; annual
			income: $650–$3000.
Income of $2800 and			
over	6*		
Income between			
$1600 and $1999	5*		

* When income tax is excluded from the income, these four proportions are lowered respectively to 0.9, 12.5, 1.6, and 6 percent.

** In the table, "nuclear" means husband and wife present and nuclear family without the presence of extended kin.

Source:

a R. Blishen, J. Cawley, and J.E. Pearson, "Family Allowances in Montreal: A Study of their Uses and Meaning in a Selected Group of Wage Earning Families" (MA thesis, McGill University, 1948), 52. The survey calculated income from "take-home pay" (i.e., salary minus income tax and other taxes).

b Thérèse Roy, "Influence économique et sociale des allocations familiales" (MA thesis, Université de Montréal, 1948), 35.

c Thérèse Légaré, *Conditions économiques et sociales des familles de Gaspé-Nord, Québec* (Faculté des sciences sociales, Université Laval, May 1947), 129–32.

d M.A. Macnaughton and G. Laflèche, *Preliminary Report on Distribution and Use of Family Allowances Payment in Nicolet County, Québec, 1947–48* (Ottawa: Economic Division, Marketing Service, Department of Agriculture, 1936, NAC, RG 29, R233/105–13/5), 12. The "cash living expenses" considered here do not include the part of the income devoted to capital investments and repayment of debt.

e M.A. Macnaughton and J.M. Mann, *Distribution and Use of Family Allowances Payments in Three Areas of the Prairie Provinces,* supplement to M.A. Macnaughton and M.E. Andal, *Changes in Farm Family Living in Three Areas of the Prairie Provinces from 1942–43 to 1947* (Ottawa: Economic Division, Marketing Service, Department of Agriculture and Department of National Health and Welfare in co-operation with the Universities of Alberta and Saskatchewan, King's Printer, 1949, publication 815, Technical Bulletin 69), 85. The cash living expenses considered here do not include the part of the income devoted to capital investments and repayment of debt. When the whole income is considered, the proportions are lowered to 4.6 and 8 percent respectively. Areas are listed from the poorest (Saskatchewan north) to the wealthiest (Alberta centre-west).

f Derek Griffin, *Family Budgets of Wage-Earners in Four Maritime Communities, 1947* (Halifax: Institute of Public Affairs, Dalhousie University, 1952), 81, 83, 84. Only extreme cases of income and number of children were precise in the original table.

the rural parish of St-Denis de Kamouraska at the end of the 1940s he observed that family allowances, together with new sources of cash income, rising agricultural prices, and other government programs, had allowed farmers to buy their first agricultural machines. This had freed children from farm labour.[50] Increased cash income and the greater need for capital expenditures may explain in part why rural families were more likely to spend the allowance for the whole family than were their urban counterparts (see table 3).

Table 2: PATTERNS OF EXPENDITURE OF FAMILY ALLOWANCES
(Percentage of Families Mentioning Each Type of Expenditure)

Sample	Clothing	Food	Education	Recreation	Insurance	Savings	Medical care	Number
Quebec City[a]	63	30	29	12	35	19	33	172
Montreal 1947[b]								
Total	89	42	—4—		19	24	39	79
Income below $1800	87	53	—2—		—30—		45	53
Income $1800 and above	92	19	—8—	—31—			27	26
Montreal 1948[c]	80	63	7			17	23	30
Gaspé-Nord[d]	62	34	10		—6—		20	115
Nicolet[e]	72	54	31		—26—		18	65
Prairies[f]								
Total	77	59	20	19		16	22	277
Northern Saskatchewan	85	71	22	22		8	23	
West-central Saskatchewan	68	72	12	16		25	28	
West-central Alberta	77	53	25	20		18	17	

Table 2, *continued*

Sample	Clothing	Food	Education	Recreation	Insurance	Savings	Medical care	Number
Canada[g]								
Families with 1 to 2 children	39	14	——10——		20	16	14	1749
Families with 3 to 4 children	42	24	——18——		13	8	21	
Families with more than 5 children	49	32	——23——		12	3	30	
Canada[h]	66	37	——23——		10	15	16	319

Source:

a Maurice Tremblay, Albert Faucher, and J.-C. Falardeau, *Family Allowances in Quebec City. Report of a Study in the Faculty of Social Sciences of Laval University*, trans. Department of National Health and Welfare (Quebec, 1951, NAC, RG 29, R233/100-63-2), 42.

b Blishen, Cawley, and Pearson, "Family Allowances in Montreal," 64, 93. Unfortunately, results on insurance and savings are not consistent from one page to the other.

c Roy, "Influence économique et sociale des allocations familiales," 45.

d Légaré, *Conditions économiques et sociales des familles de Gaspé-Nord*, 133–34.

e Macnaughton and Lalleche, *Preliminary Report on Distribution and Use of Family Allowances Payment in Nicolet County*, 10.

f Macnaughton and Mann, *Distribution and Use of Family Allowances Payments in Three Areas of the Prairie Provinces*, 82.

g Research Division, Department of National Health and Welfare, "The Use of Family Allowances Payments by Canadian Families" (Ottawa, unpublished), quoted by J.C. Vadakin, *Children, Poverty and Family Allowances* (New York: Basic Books, 1968), 104.

h NAC, RG 29, 1934, R233/110/13. Results of the "Ten Families Surveys" conducted by civil servants of the regional offices of family allowances in various cities of the country. I could not get a precise idea of their methodology.

Table 3: PERCENTAGE DISTRIBUTION OF FAMILIES ACCORDING TO THEIR USE OF FAMILY ALLOWANCES

Area	Exclusively for children under 16	Into general family budget	Partly for children under 16, partly for other members of family	Undefined	Total	Number
Quebec City[a]	65	24	11	–	100	213
Montreal[b]						
Total	46	20	34	–	100	79
Income below $1800	42	21	38	–	100	53
Income above $1800	54	19	27	–	100	
Gaspé-Nord[c]	63	34	–	3	100	115
Nicolet[d]	33	50	5	12	100	65
Prairies[e]						
Total	38	34	24	4	100	277
Northern Saskatchewan	34	41	23	2	100	
West-central Saskatchewan	40	33	25	3	100	
West-central Alberta	40	26	26	8	100	

Table 3, continued

Area	Exclusively for children under 16	Into general family budget	Partly for children under 16, partly for other members of family	Undefined	Total	Number
Canada[f]						1749
Families with 1 or 2 children	43	38	19	-	100	
Families with 3 or 4 children	34	45	21	-	100	
Families with more than 5 children	28	46	26	-	100	

Sources:

[a] Tremblay, Faucher, and Falardeau, *Family Allowances in Quebec City*, 37.

[b] Blishen, Cawley, and Pearson, "Family Allowances in Montreal," 56.

[c] Légaré, *Conditions économiques et sociales des familles de Gaspé-Nord*, 133–34.

[d] Macnaughton and Laflèche, *Preliminary Report on Distribution and Use of Family Allowances Payment in Nicolet County*, 8.

[e] Macnaughton and Mann, *Distribution and Use of Family Allowances Payments in Three Areas of the Prairie Provinces*, 81.

[f] Research Division, Department of Health and Welfare, "The Use of Family Allowances Payments by Canadian Families," 104.

Rural children clearly benefited a good deal from family allowances. Yet the results of the program fell far short of politicians' expectations, largely because they had counted on a level of economic autonomy that was absent from many households. In the elaboration of social policies, Canadian governments had long considered that the mythical self-sufficiency of families in rural areas was available to all citizens. The Montpetit Commission, established by the Quebec government during the Depression to consider the question of social insurance, had used this argument to justify the rejection of a family allowance policy. Its rationalization had been that rural families did not need allowances and that allowances to urban parents would encourage rural depopulation.[51]

To be fair, some promoters of family allowances had taken a step away from these assumptions. A long-time promoter of the allowances, Jesuit Léon Lebel, stated in 1927 that "one has to be blind not to realize that the majority is far from benefitting from a living standard superior to the conditions of urban workers. Only poets, now, can celebrate the charm of country living." In the House, during the debates of 1944, MP G.E. Wood had proclaimed: "I am inclined to think that this is one of the first measures in which the farmer has been permitted to share alike with urban folks." Wood hoped allowances would enable farm families to afford better and more varied diets and that increased nutrition would promote the growth of robust children. One year before, Leonard Marsh had proposed that family allowances would maintain rural families in agriculture and compensate them for their disadvantages in schooling, job placement, and health-care institutions. Similarly, Prime Minister Mackenzie King had alluded to the lack of social services in rural areas, but he had hoped that rural families would be comfortable enough to use the allowances for more than the basic needs: "Combined with the floor under farm prices, family allowances will give real social security to rural Canadians for the first time in [their] history."[52]

In reality, family allowances were used mostly for more immediate needs. One-fifth of rural families reported using their benefits for basic medical and dental care, a proportion comparable to that among workers' families in poor sections of Montreal. Yet, in more than three-fifths of the families interviewed by Légaré in rural Gaspésie in 1946 neither the mother nor the children had ever received medical care. In 60 percent of the cases, no doctor had delivered the children. The educational literature may have improved hygiene in some families even in the absence of medical care. Mothers in Saint-Octave, a newly settled community in Gaspésie with poor medical services, began to use the government booklet *The Canadian Mother and Child*, which was advertised in the family allowances educational campaign.[53] In the Beauce region, allowances enabled mothers to afford food and medical care that was better for the health of their progeny, as their MP, Dr Poulin, explained to the Commons:

In the practice of my profession, in the country, I have been able to see . . . the way this money is used. Often, in my office, mothers bring their small children of every age, and ask me to examine them, even if they don't consider them to be sick, to know if there was not something they could do to better their health. After an examination, and a prescription if need be, these mothers are proud to take from their purse their family allowances cheque and to tell me that it allows them to take good care of their children.[54]

Poulin was so enthusiastic about these effects of the allowances that he suggested raising them to replace proposed public health insurance.

Allowances also permitted mothers in rural areas north of Montreal to diversify the diet of their families. One merchant reported that his clients were able for the first time to buy oranges for their children: "Yesterday, oranges were golden fruits for rich people, rare fruits that children only discovered once a year in their Christmas sock . . . if their bad behaviour had not transformed it into a potato!" These were not isolated occurrences. Social workers across Canada reported that rural children fared better as a result of improved diet.[55]

Family allowances represented the first form of public social assistance many Canadian rural families encountered. The program fulfilled many of its promises to rural children: better health, a closer family life, and a prolonged dependency. However, these improvements were far from sufficient to improve their standard of living to the level of the majority of the country. Their parents soon discovered that universality did not mean economic equality for children, or the end of poverty.

Another new clientele of the universal welfare state was the middle class. Unfortunately, the aggregate data of most of the studies don't allow for an analysis weighted by levels of income. However, examination of interviews conducted for the "Ten Families Surveys" in Montreal and Quebec City permits some economic analysis.[56]

Many well-off parents came to see the program as insurance, and this was in line with the expectations of the government. They were already receiving a tax deduction for dependants, so the new program didn't have much effect on their total income. They "hesitated to apply . . . and finally decided to in case of possible sickness or unemployment." Thus, they got a monthly payment that the federal government recovered, in whole or in part, through income tax.[57]

Some wealthy parents chose not to apply to the program. Among those interviewed, several mentioned their disappointment at having to return part of the allowances in taxes; one family opposed allowances altogether on this ground. They "consider[ed] Family Allowances a nuisance for families having an income over $3000.00." Journalist Jeanne Grisé-Allard of the Jesuit monthly *Relations* discovered that some middle-class parents felt embittered by the lack of consideration the federal government showed for the hardships of raising children. These parents may well have felt there was a stigma attached to accepting state benefits. Others considered their own acceptance of a universal measure a necessary step for the benefit of poorer classes, "a good reform for poor families."[58] In January 1947, the government began to encourage richer families to apply by deducting $100 of their taxable income for each child eligible for family allowances, and registrations increased accordingly.[59]

While allowances did not significantly enrich such relatively comfortable families, they could provoke a slight realignment of economic power from fathers to mothers, an unintended consequence of the government's campaign to bring mothers who had held jobs during the war back to their families. Middle-class women had more control over the allowances than over tax deductions from their husbands' incomes. The McGill enquiry discovered that as family incomes rose, so did the husband's degree of control over spending.[60] For some of these men, the transfer of power that accompanied family allowances constituted a governmental interference in their affairs. One angry father of four, earning $3491 annually, wrote to a Quebec City newspaper in 1949 challenging the right of any representative of the federal government to usurp the right of a father to decide which part of surplus salary should be dedicated to his children's advantage.[61] The divergent interests of mothers and fathers in wealthier families may explain why it was a middle-class woman, Thérèse Casgrain, who led the campaign in Quebec for the payment to the mother and why it was a group of middle-class men who opposed the idea in the name of paternal authority.

In urban areas, the allowances had the greatest impact on families where the father's income was inadequate or non-existent. The widow Leduc presented in the governmental education campaign accurately depicted a lived reality. Nineteen of the 116 families interviewed in the "Ten Families Surveys" had no father–husband breadwinner. An even larger proportion of those families benefiting from the salary of the father at the time of the enquiry had faced this situation previously when the breadwinner had been sick or unemployed, or had deserted them. In one case, the father had returned to school using the privileges offered to veterans. Like Mme Leduc, each of these families "needed every cent of the allowance. . . . " For the family of a sick inspector and a mason who was only employed periodically, allowances were sometimes the only source of income. In one-quarter of the "Ten Families Survey" sample, the federal program supplied more than one-third of the monthly income.[62] Housekeepers described the allowances as "very welcome" for they gave "a new sense of security." In this context the program truly realized one of its goals: ensuring a minimum family income.

Family allowances were not the only welfare support available to families without a male breadwinner. But those interviewed compared the new benefit favourably with older types of help they had received, such as needy mothers' allowances and private charities. The rigid conditions surrounding needy mothers' allowances excluded many families. One woman "applied for Needy Mothers' Allowances but the uncertainty of [her husband's] illness made her ineligible. . . . Family Allowance of $24.00 was the only income of which she was certain. As she discussed a budget, the fact that she had it, and had a right to it, seemed to restore some of her self-assurance."[63] Needy mothers' allowances were too low to raise children. Thus the family allowances represented 35 percent of the income of one needy Montreal mother who had four children under sixteen.[64] Some families interviewed were receiving income benefits from contributory welfare schemes, available to the members of the most stable sectors of the work force. These included unemployment insurance for the breadwinner, or for older children, a father's private pension scheme, and a veterans' allocation. When such families had many children, family allowances made a crucial difference. One family with six children under the age of sixteen received almost $40 from the allowances, a major complement to the $60 the father was receiving in unemployment insurance. Another family with five children under sixteen lived on the monthly salary of $39 earned by one older son and the $27 family allowance cheque.

Family allowances alone were not sufficient to allow all families without a male breadwinner to attain the life promoted in the publications of the Department of National Health and Welfare. Many families without an earning father could not offer children the prolonged dependency and the constant care of a mother at home. Most relied on the work of older children or of the mother outside the home.[65] Many of these families shared their living quarters with other people, either by taking in lodgers, living in the house of the grandmother without paying rent, or living in a boarding-house. Their domestic arrangements were often far from the ideal. An extreme example was that of the wife of a mason who worked irregularly. She was planning to move to a smaller, cheaper flat and to place her seven children in institutions. Had the McGill survey not been so restrictive in the selection of its sample, its investigators would also have met many families who took in lodgers or lived with in-laws. Nearly one-half of the 3331 families under the care of the Child Welfare Association of Montreal in 1947 (the association from which subjects were chosen) had such living arrangements.[66]

The government had predicted that allowances would help families purchase essential goods, and at least two-thirds of the families interviewed did spend their allowance on clothes. Clothing dealers were quick to grasp the opportunity. Dalfen's of Montreal advertised prices reduced by 10 percent for all goods bought with a family allowance cheque. One-tenth of the families interviewed in south-west Montreal had a department store account that was financed by the allowances. Some salespeople even scheduled their monthly collection according to the rhythm of the allowance cheques. And a few zealots among them threatened to report mothers to the government if they did not continue to buy their products. The Regional Office of family allowances countered by asking the Quebec bishops to have a letter read in every church warning the public about these tactics.[67] Increased ability to purchase clothes for children had an indirect impact on family roles. Firstly, spending for ready-made clothes relieved some mothers of domestic production, even though many still knitted and sewed new clothes or altered old ones to save money. Grandmothers, sisters, and even more fortunate neighbours could assist them in this task. Secondly, clothes could make the difference between regular and sporadic school attendance. Finally, clothes meant more than comfort. They symbolized one's economic background, often a source of shame or pride. The McGill investigation found that 37 percent of the families believed the allowances had improved the quantity or quality of their clothing.

The studies also showed that legislators' expectations of the relief allowances would bring to children in large families were too high. In such families, allowances were not sufficient to improve clothing for all members. Thérèse Roy wrote after her interviews with the wives of French-Canadian workers that in families of seven or more children it was often still impossible for mothers to provide adequate winter clothing for all the school children or even the most basic of clothes for preschoolers. She concluded her report by recommending the abolition of the decreasing rate of allowances for fifth and subsequent children. Countering the prime minister's justifications for the reduced rate, she contended that "it is difficult to believe that the clothes of the first four children can still be of use when the thirteenth and the fourteenth children are born." Clearly the political goal of muting ethnic conflict had prevailed over the socioeconomic goal of alleviating poverty.[68]

Food expenditure figured second among the uses that families reported making of the allowances. Actually, the use of some or all of the allowances for food was probably greater than reported if we consider that some women may well have been ashamed of mentioning it. The food purchased was not the kind that would add surplus vitamins to the children's diet but was the essential staples of the family meal. Purchase of food was mentioned most often among the lowest-income families, especially in large households.[69]

The government had not predicted that allowances would be used for rent, but one-fifth of the labourers' households studied in the eastern Montreal sample used their allowances either for rent or for repayment of debts. The regularity of the allowance income and the timing of its arrival influenced its allotment. Mothers' spending on rent showed a capacity for planning worthy of the government's propaganda. They "considered that this solution was most practical, because they were always sure to get, usually at mid-month, their cheque of family allowances from which they can immediately take out the amount of the rent." It's worth noting that the monthly allowance exceeded the cost of rent for over half the tenant families for whom the survey listed rents.

Unfortunately, this new ability to buy necessities soon diminished. Rising prices aggravated by the termination of price controls in 1947 rapidly depreciated the value of allowances. As early as 1948, only one-third of those studied in south-western Montreal believed that the quantity or quality of their diets had increased since the beginning of the program. Family allowances might cushion the spiralling cost of living, but they could not offset it. One year later, 90 percent of Montreal women interviewed by Roy testified that, while it had been possible to buy more milk, fruit, and vegetables when allowances were first initiated, at current prices mothers had to be content with diminishing quantities of these foods. In 1951, nine of the 214 families in the Quebec City study mentioned that the allowances did not even pay for milk; half found the allowance insufficient.[70] Macro statistics verify what mothers knew. While the payment levels had stayed the same, the consumer price index had risen by 55.2 percent between 1945 and 1955. The cost of clothing and food had increased even more quickly, by 74 percent and 80 percent respectively. As a result, allowances of $5 and $8 in 1955 were worth only $3.16 and $5.07 respectively in 1951 dollars. To have maintained their initial value, the government would have had to increase these payments to $8 and $13.[71]

About one-third of the urban families receiving allowances used them to pay for medical care. Medical expenditures apparently had more to do with urgent care than with the forms of prevention promoted in the educational campaign. Few parents had anticipated making this a primary use of the fund. In the "Ten Families Surveys," seven of the 116 mothers reported having had to pay for an operation; five purchased medicine or the services of a doctor or a dentist when the children fell sick; eight others used the allowances for health care of an unspecified nature. Only one family made an explicit reference to prevention—the purchase of tonics. Many doctors adjusted their fee instalments to the allowance rates.[72] This practice suggests that the new welfare measure helped stabilize the income of these professionals, many of whom had suffered during the Depression. Indeed, it may have contributed to the decrease in the approval of public health insurance among doctors after the war, yet another way in which family allowances could have delayed the adoption of universal health care in Canada.

In sum, many urban families could not use the allowances "as an extra." For them, consumption of "surplus" goods was impossible however much they tried to plan their spending.[73] The panacea promoted in the government's leaflets was beyond their reach. This does not mean that poorer families were unable to adopt long-term economic strategies, only that their patterns of delayed expenditure differed from those of more comfortable families. The wish parents in general had expressed most clearly was to save their allowances. Findings on actual savings practices are difficult to interpret. In Montreal, labourers' families did not mention saving. In south-western Montreal and Quebec City, where the background of the families interviewed was more varied, one-quarter of parents put at least part of their allowances in the bank. But this doesn't mean that the alternative was possible only for the rich. The Quebec City enquiry suggests almost the opposite. There, "the proportion of families depositing the allowance money in saving accounts was relatively higher in 'poorer' wards."[74] This phenomenon suggests a pattern of small-scale deposits, similar to that found by Paul Johnson in nineteenth-century England. Then, workers' families put away cash on a short-term basis to stabilize consumption and to save for major expenditures.[75] Wealthier families could be more confident in their future capacity to meet large expenditures and needed less short-term planning.

Insurance, another form of saving, was also important for families at all socioeconomic levels. Despite government reluctance, one-third of the Quebec City households and one-fifth of those in Montreal devoted a part of the allowance to insurance policies. In Quebec City, insurance represented the second most important type of expenditure. Monthly payments varied from $1 to $3 per child and thus could consume up to 50 percent of the allowance. In the wake of salespeople and doctors, insurance agents "would call just after the dates when the family allowance cheques were due."[76] Family allowances encouraged the spread of insurance into the poorer parts of eastern Montreal, according to Roy. She commented that "this is a very nice initiative allowed by family allowances and which did not exist before, at least amongst the families whom we have interviewed." Roy expected this practice to enlarge educational opportunities. However, parents did not always gear insurance towards education. In three-fifths of the Quebec cases, they insured the life of their children; only in another fourth did parents buy endowment policies in which the capital could be recovered to pay for the children's schooling. As some life-insurance policies could terminate and be reimbursed in part when the child arrived at a certain age, insurance was used as a form of saving.[77]

The government not only continued to promote ideals more in tune with the spending habits of wealthier families, it also tried to discourage practices like investing allowances in insurance because they jeopardized hopes for immediate consumption. Ministers had relied, after all, on poor people's high propensity for spending. When insurance companies advertising policies for children directly addressed the family allowances beneficiaries, Deputy Minister of Welfare George Davidson warned them that he wished to avoid campaigns,

> either in terms of high-pressure salesmanship of consumer goods or in terms of savings investments, insurance, etc., that will have the effect of diverting the Family Allowances moneys into unwise spendings, or even into unwise savings and hoarding, during the deflationary period of the postwar years when the interest of the country may call for a policy of encouragements to spending rather than encouragements to saving.[78]

Four years later, when the need for increasing consumer demand diminished, the research department of the ministry kindly agreed to a request for information from the Bank of Montreal, which was preparing publicity to encourage the saving of family allowances for children.[79]

Sociologist Maurice Tremblay and his colleagues denounced life insurance on the child's behalf as selfish behaviour on the parents' part, because "in such a case, it is the parents of the child who, if the latter dies, are financially protected."[80] It would be interesting to study the extent to which life-insurance policies for children provided security for mid-twentieth-century Quebeckers. In reality, payments by instalments such as those accepted by doctors, department stores, and itinerant sales agents were convenient ways of budgeting for poor urban families. For these poor families,

> the unpredictability of income and expenditures made some financial provision for the future essential. The way most households chose to cope with the problem was by committing a set portion of income each week to financial planning. . . . Small regular deductions were not missed in the way a lump-sum would be, and they imposed a degree of external discipline on the saving scheme. Willpower was seldom strong enough to permit accumulation in a week when money for food and rent was short, but the power of contract often was.

The debtors saw in the regular family allowances sums that could easily be kept aside for repayment. However, Canadian politicians, bureaucrats and social scientists, like the British middle classes studied by Paul Johnson, did not "appreciate that in small scale borrowing, saving or spending on durable goods, workers were demonstrating not their fecklessness but their true desire for financial stability."[81]

On the whole, social workers painted a picture of the realities of Canadian family life that was darker than the one projected by most MPs during the debates over family allowances. The series of investigations drawn on above, combined with daily contacts with poor families, led many employees of regional offices of the Department of National Health and Welfare to believe that "family allowances were not too much of a good thing. . . . We may safely assume that the monies are currently spent by the parents who, in the great majority, are in need of this 'extra' income."[82] Canadian society numbered more of the Sauvés, the family portrayed in the Speaking of Family Allowances booklet who spent their allowances on the most basic food and supplies for the children, than the Gagniers who spent it on extras. Many families benefited from the program in unexpected ways. Family allowances permitted poor families both rural and urban to buy essential food and pay their rent more easily. Some had the means to pay for emergency medical care for the first time. Mothers both in poor and better-off families gained some economic power and autonomy from this monthly cheque.

These were important gains for individual families. Family allowances did not, however, succeed in realizing the greater socioeconomic promises pronounced at the time of their enactment. Equality of economic opportunities for children, a minimum of welfare for young Canadians, and an end to poverty remained dreams. This was not only because of the conflict between these goals and other immediate political objectives, but also because policy makers' lack of knowledge about or unwillingness to admit the causes and extent of poverty in Canada had led them to invest the program with an illusory potential, and the educational campaign with unattainable ideals.

Politicians and bureaucrats had distinguished realistically between the different uses wealthier and poorer families would make of allowances, but they had underestimated the amount of real poverty. They had underrated the economic instability of rural and urban working-class families. It is difficult to decide which part of this attitude we should attribute to ignorance, and which part we should explain by their unwillingness to question the adequacy of salary levels in Canada and to enact the truly distributive welfare programs proposed in the reconstruction plans drafted during the war. What is certain is that once the results of the inquiries about family allowances were published, it was no longer possible to pretend that the elimination of poverty could be achieved through the allowances alone. Economic autonomy based on the salary of a father obviously remained unattainable for many, and this knowledge probably encouraged politicians to build support for the welfare programs of the years to come.

In the meantime, the unrealistically high expectations that had been so widely broadcast threatened to have a negative impact on the morale of poor parents. At times, the Department of National Health and Welfare's illusory standards could trigger feelings of inadequacy or guilt. McGill social workers reported that some interviewees in south-west Montreal seemed to feel that they were not using the family allowances as they "were supposed to be used." The researchers believed that "this attitude may well have arisen from emphasis in family allowances publicity on the use of money for children specifically while mothers usually bought food for the whole family, rather than separate family members."[83] The educational campaign added another voice to the growing number of directives aimed at parents from both the booming publicity for consumer goods and popular psychology. Family allowance propaganda may have contributed to the blurring of ideas about child raising, increasing some parents' uneasiness about their child-rearing capacities.[84]

• Epilogue: The Struggle for the Indexation of Family Allowances and the Political Role of Families

What does the history of the implementation of family allowances mean for our understanding of the impact of the welfare state on Canadian parents and children? A range of theories has addressed the question of the relationship between families and the state. The "social administration" approach to social policies and the functionalist tradition of family sociology have proposed a bottom-up model that relies on a strong faith in the workings of liberal democracy. According to these approaches, a consensus emerged in the twentieth century in which the state was called upon to assume new tasks, either to fit the new needs of an industrial–urban society or to take over traditional family responsibilities that families could no longer manage.[85] In reaction to this consensus-politics view, which was too uncritical of the rhetoric of policy makers, historians of the "social control" school have crafted a top-down model. They describe an authoritarian and bourgeois state, progressively dispossessing passive families of traditional functions and imposing its morality on them.[86] In the simplest versions of this view, the apparent generosity of the state is an illusion: the economic and political elites of post-industrial societies conceded some measure of social security to maintain their power and control and avoid public disorder.

Family allowance policy can be interpreted using either of these models. In terms of the democratic-liberal idea, the program brought the anticipated electoral rewards, helping King return to power in 1945. The Liberal Party continued to hold the federal majority until 1957. During the decade following the implementation of the allowances, the popularity of the program increased from 49 percent to 90 percent in Quebec public opinion polls, despite the decrease in the real value of allowances.[87] As late as 1971, married women in Quebec viewed more generous family allowances as the most important of six measures proposed to them by demographers to help them with their family responsibilities.[88] Virtually none of the Canadian families interviewed by social workers and government officials on the effects of allowances explicitly opposed state intervention in family matters. Those that did did so either because they felt they could raise their children alone or because they suspected that the public authorities expected something in return.[89] There seemed, then, to be a consensus about the need for such policy, based on the fact that these regular and predictable sums of money responded to real needs, strengthening the economic basis of many families in both rural and urban areas and injecting needed money into the postwar economy.

On the other hand, many elements of social control can be discerned both in the enactment and the enforcement of family allowances. Without question the desire to intervene materially and ideologically in family economies existed among politicians and public servants in the 1940s. And while the forms of control were mild compared to the investigation apparatus brought to bear on those living on relief during the Depression, one family in seven hundred was inspected for alleged misuse of allowances during the first decade of the program. Authorities proposed a change in payment provisions for one-third of those investigated.[90] Moreover, family allowances opened the realm of domestic consumption to state influence. Liberal ministers' ideas on the social role and economic priorities of the family conflicted with the actual values of poor families. They did not endorse poor families' ways of planning or their traditional income strategies. The unrealistic rhetoric promoting ways of spending and the failure to index allowances to the rising cost of living left many poor parents with a sense of disillusionment. Comparison of parents' hopes regarding the use of allowances and of their actual expenditures certainly reveals a lot of frustrations. The government's broken promises renewed poorer parents' sense of economic powerlessness.

There was consensus about the usefulness of family allowances, yet their implementation also involved the desire to control. Thus neither the consensus politics nor the social control theory is adequate to fully understand family allowances.[91] A more recent theoretical trend—a revision of the social control approach—can be of help. Historians of nineteenth-century education have begun to describe families as having their own distinct cultures and beliefs, which led them to resist state intrusions. Such work rehabilitates the concept of family autonomy and focusses attention on families' opposition to government control.[92] This kind of more dialectical approach opens up the possibility of studying the internal dynamic of families and of observing them in interaction with the state.

The history of family allowances suggests we could push this model further and give greater weight to the role of families in policy formation. The idea of family resistance, which may be sufficient to explain nineteenth-century social policies, does not adequately account for the history of a universal program in the mid-twentieth century. There was definitely more to these allowances than electoralism through cash benefits, more than an illusory resolution of the economic problems of the mid-1940s in favour of elites. Family allowances may have been a cheap version of reconstruction plans popular during the war; they may have been an easier way to intervene in the economy than by regulating enterprises. The cabinet felt that the population would not let them get away with less. If Canadians were to lend their support to the Liberals in the 1945 elections, they wanted to be reassured that the party cared for the general economy. Universal child benefits were the necessary minimum the government had to enact to maintain its legitimacy. Means tests would "not be accepted by the people in Canada."[93]

Parents did not vanish from the political arena once allowances became policy. Some of the disillusionment concerning the diminishing purchasing power of the allowances surfaced in the House of Commons in the demands of specific groups. By the end of the 1940s, two major labour councils were among the many groups asking for the indexation of the allowances. In a major campaign held between July 1954 and May 1955, several unions, 327 municipal or school councils and various other associations again requested indexation. Nearly three thousand Canadian citizens signed petitions making the same request. Over subsequent years some opposition MPs also called for indexation. Quebec MP Lionel Bertrand received so many letters asking for a rise in the amount of family allowances that he could not answer them all.[94] In 1951, the tireless Father Léon Lebel deplored that:

> given the actual price of milk—19 cents for a pint—the monthly allowance of $5.00 given for children of less than six years does not even pay for the pint of milk that doctors recommend as the daily requirement for children and adolescents to ensure the normal development of their body. . . . The allowances are ineffective in helping workers' families in large cities.[95]

Concerns about child welfare backed by pressures from recipients were not sufficient in themselves to win the indexation of allowances.[96] By the mid-1950s, the government no longer feared a fall in the demand for goods. Postwar prosperity had been ensured, and ministers shifted their focus to policies of economic management aimed at promoting the health of enterprises rather than of children. The threat of a CCF victory was vanishing, and the "Government Party" could afford to be less sensitive to public demands. Assessing the impact of family allowances in 1955, R.H. Parkinson, chief supervisor of welfare services related to the program, confidently declared that they had accomplished almost everything expected. Liberal ministers countered the mounting pressure for indexation with budgetary arguments largely absent a decade earlier: the government didn't have enough money; family allowances already represented one-fourth of the social security budget; linking the program to the cost of living would threaten the program itself; Canada still offered more than other countries.[97]

But there was more to the unwillingness of the government to index allowances than simple economics. Members of cabinet now feared that their own welfare promises might feed an ever-increasing stream of claims on the state. Ministers began to hint at a new type of abuse of state help. Speaking in the House of Commons, Paul Martin, minister of health and welfare, suggested that it would be regrettable to give people the impression that there was no limit to what the government could do in this domain.[98] Civil servants of the Department of National Health and Welfare, who quickly saw the devastating effects of inflation, dealt with the politicians' lack of willingness by adjusting their propaganda. The annual report in 1947–48 acknowledged that family allowances might only have maintained rather than improved the standard of living, but "the increase in the cost of living would have had a far worse impact without family allowances." In 1951, the draft of a pamphlet of the nutrition division still pretended that for $5 per month per child, "you can be sure that your child receives the two foods that are needed most to improve the diets of Canadian children. 1. Milk: at least one pint daily. 2. Vitamin D. . . . That still leaves some money for other foods." Such blind optimism may explain why the government never printed this pamphlet; instead, a new brochure told families how to get more for their money but refrained from alluding to the purchasing power of the allowances.[99]

To complete an explanation of the impact of family allowances on Canadian families, we need to reject monolithic approaches to the study of the state. The state was and is a diverse and changing institution that is not a simple tool of economic elites but reflects the existing levels of social tension, power, and class conflict within a society, while still maintaining a certain logic of its own.[100] Seeing the state in this way encourages the study of specific state actions or policies, following laws at different stages of their life, and allowing for some autonomy among civil servants, cabinet members, MPs, lobby groups, and electors.[101] From such a point of view, families can be seen not simply as the objects of policy, but also as political agents, able to influence the implementation of some laws by resistance or promotion at the local level and able to shape the larger political process of the country. With this more flexible idea of a dialectic relationship between families and the state, the two institutions can be considered as co-existing actors, as dynamic and complex systems of reproduction that can influence each other.[102]

In the end, the interests of Liberal politicians prevailed. The failure to respond to a widespread demand for improved welfare is sufficient to challenge the model of consensus politics, but our interpretation should not stop at this critique. Parents who had voted for the Liberal Party in 1945 were not the victims of authoritarian bourgeois manipulations. They did not experience economic constraints passively. While the propaganda surrounding the enactment and the distribution of allowances fostered unrealistic expectations and generated a sense of alienation among some poor parents, it also led parents to incorporate the idea of an adequate allowance into their concept of their rights as Canadians. In putting forward the idea that the state had a financial responsibility for the economic welfare of all children, the government had set a new threshold for families' claims in the future. The history of family allowances does not fit the idea that increasing state activity automatically lowered family responsibilities, a concept found in some of the literature. This study shows a more complex history, where a particular program did not automatically dispossess parents from their traditional functions but might lead them to enlarge their concepts of their rights as citizens.[103]

• Notes

[1] J.L. Granatstein, *Canada's War: The Politics of the Mackenzie King Government, 1939–1945* (Toronto: University of Toronto Press, 1990), 397, 406. For the way in which the King government surrounded most proposals of the Marsh report, see Michiel Horn, "Leonard Marsh and the Coming of the Welfare State in Canada: A Review Article," *Histoire sociale/Social History* 9 (1976): 197–204; Frank Breul, "The Genesis of Family Allowances in Canada," *Social Service Review* 27, 3 (1953): 276–77.

[2] See, for instance, Service de l'information, Ministère de la santé nationale et du bien-être social, *En parlant des allocations familiales* (Ottawa: King's Printer, 1950); Quebec Regional Office of Family Allowances (hereinafter ABRQ), 40-13, vol. 1.

[3] Dominique Jean, "Les parents québécois et l'État canadien au début du programme des allocations familiales: 1944–1955," *Revue d'histoire de l'Amérique française* 40, 1 (1986): 89–92.

[4] *Débats de la chambre des communes*, 1944, 5740, 5564. Since this study was conducted in French, most references to the Debates of the House of Commons use the French version, referred to henceforth as *Débats*. Only when a direct quote was involved did I go back to the English version. They were following the lead of the leading British expert on social policy matters, Sir William Beveridge; A.J. Pelletier, "La famille canadienne" in Canada, Bureau fédéral de la statistique, *Recensement du Canada*, 1931, 12: 189–90; *Débats*, 1944, 5564, 5567, 5619, 5569, 5633; 1947, 4451; 1952, 1779. See Léon Lebel, s.j., *Les allocations familiales: solution du problème des familles nombreuses* (Montreal: École sociale populaire, no. 159–60, 1927); Gérard Forcier, o.m.i., *Les allocations familiales: Savez-vous ce qu'elles sont?* (Ottawa: Centre social de l'Université d'Ottawa, 1944); Robert Lévesque and Robert Mignier, *Camilien et les années vingt suivi de Camilien au Goulag, cartographie du Houdisme* (Montreal: Éditions des Brûlés, 1978), 84. Other pro-natalist statements came from some Western MPs of all parties. *Débats*, 1944, 5704, 5633, 2790. See also, from the Maritimes, 5695, 5563. The same ethnic differentials long blocked Canadian measures on family planning. Angus McLaren and Arlene Tigar McLaren, *The Bedroom and the State: The Changing Practices and Politics of Contraception and Abortion in Canada, 1880–1980* (Toronto: McClelland & Stewart, 1986) 13; *Débats*, 1949, 2548. No MP publicly endorsed conservative

social worker Charlotte Whitton's view that allowances punished those with responsible attitudes towards family planning. See "The Family Allowances Controversy in Canada," *Social Service Review* 18, 4:432.

[5] *Débats*, 1944, 5619–20; 1946, 2790, 5333.

[6] Leonard Marsh, *Report on Social Security for Canada* (Toronto: University of Toronto Press, 1975), 201; D.H. Stepler, *Les allocations familiales au Canada* (Montreal: École sociale populaire, no. 362, 1943), 4–5. Jane Lewis, "Dealing with Dependency: State Practices and Social Realities, 1870–1945" in *Women's Welfare: Women's Rights* (London: Croom Helm, 1983), 22.

[7] Dominique Jean, "Le recul du travail des enfants au Québec entre 1940 et 1960: une explication des conflits entre les familles pauvres et l'État providence," *Labour/Le travail* 24 (Fall 1989).

[8] Abbé Émile Cloutier, "Le salaire et la famille" in *Capital et Travail: Semaines sociales du Canada*, IIIe session (Ottawa: Bibliothèque de l'Action française, 1922), 150–74; Lebel, *Les allocations familiales*; Alfred Charpentier, "La question ouvrière" in *Programme de restauration sociale* (Montreal: École sociale populaire, no. 239–240, 1933), 19–39; R.P. Archambault, s.j., *Pour restaurer la famille* (Montreal: École sociale populaire, no. 371, 1944), 25–27; Forcier, *Les allocations familiales*.

[9] Stepler, *Les allocations familiales*, 12; Jacques Rouillard, *Les syndicats nationaux au Québec de 1900 à 1930* (Quebec: Presses de l'Université Laval, 1979), 169, 247; Tremblay, Faucher, and Falardeau, *Family Allowances in Quebec City*, 73, 74.

[10] Brigitte Kitchen, "Wartime Social Reform: The Introduction of Family Allowances," *Revue canadienne d'éducation en service social* 7, 1 (1981): 29–54; Breul, "Genesis of Family Allowances."

[11] *Débats*, 1944, 5559.

12 *Debates of the House of Commons*, 1944, 5726. *Débats* 1944, 5932; see also 1944, 5553, and Stepler, *Les allocations familiales*, 8–12.

13 *Débats*, 1944, 2, 5739, 5531.

14 *Débats*, 1944, 5552, 5740, 5528, 5529, 5603; *Santé et bien-être social Canada*, July 1948.

15 Dennis Guest, *The Emergence of Social Security in Canada* (Vancouver: University of British Columbia Press, 1981), 110.

16 *Débats*, 1944, 11, 5529–30; Guest, *Emergence of Social Security*, 129–31.

17 *Débats*, 1944, 5593, 5603. See also Léon Lebel, *Le problème de la famille nombreuse: Sa solution: les allocations familiales* (Montreal: Le Devoir, 1928), 17; François-Albert Angers, "Les allocations familiales fédérales de 1944," *L'Actualité économique* 21, 3 (1945): 229.

18 Geneviève Auger and Raymonde Lamothe, *De la poêle a frire à la ligne de feu: La vie quotidienne des Québécoises pendant la guerre '39–'45* (Montreal: Boréal Express, 1981), 160; Ruth Roach Pierson, *"They're Still Women After All": The Second World War and Canadian Womanhood* (Toronto: McClelland & Stewart, 1986), 216, 220; *Debates*, 1944, 5402.

19 J.C. Falardeau, Maurice Tremblay, Maurice Lamontagne, Roger Marier, Jean-Pierre Després, "Mémoire sur les allocations familiales" (préparé à la requête d'un comité de la Commission permanente du Conseil supérieur du travail de la province de Québec, mai 1944, manuscript document, Bibliothèque du ministère du Travail), 56–57; Thérèse Casgrain, *A Woman in a Man's World* (Toronto: McClelland & Stewart, 1972), 113.

20 *Debates*, 1944, 5336. For other Liberals, *Débats*, 1944, 5692 and 5565.

21 Eli Zaretsky, "The Place of the Family in the Origins of the Welfare State" in *Rethinking the Family: Some Feminist Questions*, ed. Barrie Thorne and M. Halom (New York: Longman, 1981), 195.

22 *Débats*, 1944, 5692, 5532, 5557, 5628, 5631, 5698, 5600, 5932.

23 Marsh, *Report on Social Security*, 199.

24 Falardeau et al.,"Mémoire sur les allocations familiales," 23–24.

25 *Debates*, 1944, 5726.

26 Marsh, *Report on Social Security*, 201–2.

27 "What They Are Saying about Family Allowances," CBC *This Week* Program, ABRQ, Publicité, 40-15; *Débats*, 1944, 5555; see also Falardeau et al., "Mémoire sur les allocations familiales," 39–40; Brigitte Kitchen, "The Family and Social Policy" in *The Family: Changing Trends in Canada*, ed. Maureen Baker (Toronto: McGraw-Hill Ryerson, 1984), 178–79, 180.

28 *Débats*, 1944, 5636, 5637, 5923; 1946, 2786.

29 *Débats*, 1944, 5600.

30 *Débats*, 1945, 3604.

31 Statuts du Canada, 8 Geo VI, art. 5.

32 See especially the comments on the surveys in Canada, Department of National Health and Welfare, Information Division, *You and Your Family* (Ottawa: King's Printer, 1949), 4. These studies constitute the main source for the last part of this article.

33 *Débats*, 1946, 2787–88.

34 *Débats*, 1946, 2787–88; *Débats*, 1944, 5558, *Debates*, 1950, 3914–15.

35 Falardeau et al.,"Mémoires sur les allocations familiales," 58; Stepler, "Les allocations familiales," 6. Thérèse Roy, "Influence économique et sociale des allocations familiales" (MA thesis, Université de Montréal, 1948), 59, 5–6; Gérard Parizeau, "Fait d'actualité. Les allocations familiales," *Assurances* 12, 2 (1944): 85–87.

36 *Débats*, 1944, 5948, 5538; Angers, "Les allocations familiales," 250.

37 *Débats*, 1944, 5932; Parizeau, "Fait d'actualité," 86; *Débats*, 1944, 5556, 5946; 1946, 2787–88; Research Division 1953, NAC, RG 29, 1932, R233/100, 1–2, pt. 1; Rapport annuel du ministère de la Santé nationale et du Bien-être social 1949–50 (there-

after RAMSNBES), 105–6; 1950–51, 88; A.M. Willms, "Setting Up Family Allowances" (MA thesis, Carleton University, 1962).

38 *You and Your Family*, 27, 10, 19.

39 *En parlant des allocations familiales*, 9; Advertisement for family allowances published in *La Terre de chez nous*, 20 June 1945, 19; Canada, Ministère de la Santé nationale et du bien-être social, *Économisez les vivres*, 1946, NAC, RG 29, Education and Nutrition— Cooperation with F.A. re Inserts, 109, 180-26-15.

40 *You and Your Family*, 26; Hervé Varenne, "Love and Liberty, la famille américaine contemporaine" in *Histoire de la famille*, ed. André Burguière (Paris: Armand Colin, n.d.), 420–21.

41 *Débats*, 1944, 5231, 5233, 5593, 5698, 5740; 1947, 4462.

42 *You and Your Family*, 4, 21; *Speaking of Family Allowances* (Ottawa: King's Printer, 1950).

43 *Speaking of Family Allowances*, 21–22.

44 Roger De Bellefeuille, "Les allocations familiales et la jeunesse agricole," *La Terre de chez nous* 1 (Aug. 1945). See also *Revue Desjardins* 6 (June–July 1945): 102; Economisez les vivres Canada, Ministère de la Santé nationale et du bien-être social, Allocations familiales, Charte de l'enfance, 1945, "What They Are Saying about Family Allowances," 7.

45 Angers, "Les allocations familiales," 234; *Débats*, 1944, 5620.

46 For a similar development in Australia, Rob Watts, "Family Allowances in Canada and Australia 1940–1945: A Comparative Critical Case Study," *Journal of Social Policy* 16, 1 (1987): 44. See also Innes de Neufville, "Production de connaissances et processus de planification," *Revue internationale d'action communautaire* 19, 55 (printemps 1988): 189.

47 Statistiques Canada 1976, 246, 248, 530, 535.

48 Undated Memo to Mr Willard, NAC, RG 29, 1934, R233/100/13; John

Modell, Patterns of Consumption, Acculturation, and Family Income Strategies in Late Nineteenth-Century America" in *Family and Population in Nineteenth-Century America*, ed. Tamara K. Hareven and Maris A. Vinovkis (Princeton: Princeton University Press, 1978), 206–24.

49 Edward Schwartz, "Some Observations on the Canadian Family Allowances Program," *Social Service Review* 20, 4 (1946): 471.

50 Horace Miner, *St-Denis: A French-Canadian Parish* (Chicago: University of Chicago Press, 1963), 258–60, 267–69.

51 Stepler, *Les allocations familiales*, 26–27.

52 Lebel, *Le problème de la famille nombreuse*, Debates, 1944, 5504; Stepler, *Les allocations familales*, 26–27; *Debates*, 1944, 5337.

53 Thérèse Légaré, *Conditions économiques et sociales des familles de Gaspé-Nord, Québec* (Faculté des sciences, Université Laval, May 1947), 83, 74.

54 *Débats*, 1949, deuxième session, 180. My translation.

55 Jeanne Grisé-Allard, "Les allocations familiales: Un chèque bien employé," *Relations* 7, 92 (1948): 240. My translation. Schwartz, "Some Observations," 451–73; Légaré, "Conditions économiques et sociales," 52; Nora Fox, "Family Allowances in Northern Ontario," *The Social Worker* 15, 3 (1947).

56 ABRQ, Surveys and Studies, 40–20, vol. 1. I was able to locate 116 interviews.

57 Ten Family Surveys 1948; R. Blishen, J. Cawley, and J.E. Pearson, "Family Allowances in Montreal: A Study of their Uses and Meaning in a Selected Group of Wage-Earning Families" (MA thesis, McGill University, 1948), 100; Canada, Statutes, 9 Geo VI, c. 23, art. 9; Canada, Department of National Health and Welfare, Information Division, *Family Allowances and Income Tax* (1946).

58 Grisé-Allard, "Les allocations famil-iales," 240; Ten Family Surveys 1946.

59 Canada, Statutes, 10 Geo VI, c. 55.

60 Blishen, Cawley, and Pearson, "Family Allowances in Montreal," 54–55.

61 Donat-C. Noiseux, *L'Action catholique*, 19 April 1949, in ABRQ, 42-8, vol. 1, paper clippings. The newspaper clip-ping itself is not dated.

62 See also Roy, "Influence économique et sociale," 35.

63 Agnes Tennant, "Family Allowances Story," *The Social Worker* 15, 3 (1947): 27–28.

64 Roy, "Influence économique et sociale," 35–39.

65 The surveys found a low proportion of mothers who worked outside the home, but this is not surprising according to Quebec standards. The number may have been influenced by the methods of the inquiries. Mothers were less easy for the inter-viewers to find.

66 Blishen, Cawley, and Pearson, "Family Allowances in Montreal," 41.

67 *La Presse*, 14 Dec. 1950, found in ABRQ, 42-8, vol. 1, paper clippings; Blishen, Cawley, and Pearson, "Family Allowances in Montreal," 74, 75, 92, 93; Rapport annuel du service de bien-être du Bureau régional du Québec 1950–51, NAC, RG 29, Annual Reports. FA Division, 1283, 14.

68 Roy, "Influence économique et sociale," 25, 44.

69 Blishen, Cawley, and Pearson, "Family Allowances in Montreal," 79–82.

70 Ibid., 82–84, 106. At the beginning, the newness of the program and the newness of inflation sheltered the government from criticism. The Ten Families Surveys conducted in 1945–46 suggest that families wel-comed the allowances precisely because they helped meet the high cost of living (10 percent of the mothers interviewed mentioned it);

Roy, "Influence économique et sociale," 53; Maurice Tremblay, Albert Faucher, and J-C Falardeau, *Family Allowances in Quebec City: Report of a Study in the Faculty of Social Sciences of Laval University*, trans. Department of National Health and Welfare (Quebec, 1951).

71 A. Asimakopoulos, "Section J: Prices Indexes," in M.C. Urquhart and K.A.H. Buckley, *Historical Statistics of Canada* (Toronto: Macmillan, 1965), 304, (series J147-152); *Débats*, 1952, 1776; 1951, 2nd session, 220.

72 Blishen, Cawley, and Pearson, "Family Allowances in Montreal," 92.

73 Indeed, only one-fourth of the Quebec City families kept budgets, although the researchers could not link the practice to a particular level of income; Tremblay, Faucher, and Falardeau, *Family Allowances in Quebec City*, 17.

74 Ibid., 17. The reason why poor Montrealers did not mention savings is still puzzling to me. It could be that Légaré's questions did not address this type of savings.

75 Paul Johnson, *Saving and Spending: The Working Class Economy in Britain, 1870–1939* (London: Oxford Univer-sity Press, 1985).

76 Blishen, Cawley, and Pearson, "Family Allowances in Montreal," 93.

77 Roy, "Influence économique et sociale," 47; Tremblay, Faucher, and Falardeau, *Family Allowances in Quebec City*, 45.

78 Letters to the Montreal Board of Trade, the Trust Companies Associ-ation of Ontario, and to a firm in Toronto 1945, NAC, RG 29, Acc. 82-83/152, 260-8-1.

79 Correspondence between Willard and Sheldon 1949, NAC, RG 29, 1934, R233/100/13.

80 Tremblay, Faucher, and Falardeau, *Family Allowances in Quebec City*, 33.

81 Johnson, *Savings and Spending*, 220–21.

82 RABRQ, 1950–51, 12.

83 Blishen, Cawley, and Pearson, "Family Allowances in Montreal," 79–82. Enquirers did not agree on the significance of spending for the whole family or for children specifically. On one hand, Blishen, Cawley, and Pearson believed that poorer families could less easily spend the sums separately, a behaviour they explained by the "pressures of everyday needs" (55). On the other hand, Tremblay, Faucher, and Falardeau found parents in the poorer sections of Quebec City spending allowances specifically for the children. They inferred that meagre incomes prompted a stricter budget allotment among family members (29).

84 Arlene Skolnick, "Public Images and Private Realities: The Family in Popular Culture and Social Sciences" in Changing Images of the Family, ed. Virginia Tufte and Barbara Myeroff (New Haven: Yale University Press, 1979), 297–318.

85 See for instance Serge Mongeau, Évolution de l'assistance au Québec (Montreal: Éditions du Jour, 1967); Guest, Emergence of Social Security; P.T. Rooke and R.L. Schnell, Discarding the Asylum: From Child Rescue to the Welfare State in Canada, 1800–1950 (Boston: University Press of America, 1983), 389–413.

86 Michel Pelletier and Yves Vaillancourt, Les politiques sociales et les travailleurs, Cahier I, Les années 1900–1920 (Montreal, 1974), Cahier II, Les années '30 (Montreal, 1975). Jane Ursel, "The State and the Maintenance of Patriarchy: A Case Study of Family, Labour and Welfare Legislation in Canada" in Family, Economy and the State, ed. J. Dickinson and B. Russel (Toronto: Garamond, 1986), 150–91.

87 Granatstein, Canada's War; Canadian Institute of Public Opinion, "Gallup Poll of Canada. 90 p.c. in Favor of Family Allowances," Toronto Star, 12 March 1955.

88 Jacques Henripin and Evelyne Lapierre Adamcyk, La fin de la revanche des berceaux: qu'en pensent les Québécoises? (Montreal: Presses de l'Université de Montréal, 1974), iii. Collection "Démographie canadienne."

89 Three cases in Blishen, Cawley, and Pearson, "Family Allowances in Montreal," 96–105; six cases in MacNaughton and Mann, Distribution and Use of Family Allowances, 91.

90 Jean "Les parents québécois," 80–81.

91 Sarah Eisenstein, Give Us Bread But Give Us Roses: Working Women's Consciousness in the United States, 1890 to the First World War (London: Routledge and Kegan Paul, 1983), 2–11; Zaretsky, "Place of the Family."

92 Philip Corrigan and Bruce Curtis, "Education, Inspection and State Formation: A Preliminary Statement," Canadian Historical Association Historical Papers (1985): 156–71; Bruce Curtis, Building the Educational State: Canada West, 1836–1871 (London: Falmer Press and Althouse Press, 1988); Maurice Crubellier, L'enfance et la jeunesse dans la société française, 1800–1850 (Paris: Armand Colin, 1979), 223; Louise A. Tilly and Myriam Cohen, "Does the Family Have a History?: A Review of the Theory and Practice of Family History," Social Science History 6, 2 (Spring 1982); Tamara Hareven, "Les grands thèmes de l'histoire de la famille aux États-Unis," Revue d'histoire de l'Amérique française 39, 2 (Fall 1985).

93 Brooke Claxton in Debates, 1944, 5726.

94 Roy, "Influence économique et sociale," 120; See also the secretary of one Confédération des travailleurs catholiques du Canada union mentioned in Eugène L'Heureux, "Allocations familiales," L'événement journal, 18 July 1951, found in ABRQ, 42-8, vol.1, paper clippings; Davidson to Willard, 1955, NAC, RG 29, 1933, R233-100-1-6; Knowles and Lockhard and Jackman in Débats de la Chambre des Communes, 1948, 5488 and 5890–91 respectively; Poulin, ibid., 1949, deuxième session, 180; Poulin, ibid., 1951, première session,

2266–67; Poulin, Argue, and Brown, ibid., 1951, deuxième session, 148–49, 220, and 776 respectively; Dubé, Poulin, and Argue, ibid., 1952, 1983, 3138, 1775–77 respectively; Bertrand and Argue, ibid., 1953, 2959, and 1182–204 respectively; Argue, Girard, and Dupuis, ibid., 1954, 1354, 328, 352. In 1953, Argue even presented a proposal to raise the family allowances to compensate for the increase in the cost of living.

95 Léon Lebel, "Notre système d'allocations familiales," *Relations* (April 1951): 93. My translation. See also *L'Action catholique*, 8 July 1955, found in ABRQ, 42-8, vol. 1, paper clippings.

96 This invalidates Bernice Madison's thesis about the program ("during the following decade, the economic objectives receded, and the social welfare objectives emerged which have since been the predominant ones") in "Canadian Family Allowances and Their Major Social Implications," *Journal of Marriage and the Family* 26, 2 (May 1962): 140. See John MacNicol's analysis of the same problem in *Great Britain: The Movement for Family Allowances, 1918-1945: A Study in Social Policy Development* (London: Heinemann, 1980).

97 "Ten Years of Family Allowances," *Canadian Welfare* 31, 4 (1955): 199.

98 *Débats*, 1952, 1783, my translation. See also 1948, 5488; 1954, 1371, 1378.

99 RAMSNBES, 1947–48, 96; 1946–47, 76, my translation; NAC, RG 29, 109, 180-26-15.

100 Kenneth Finegold and Theda Skocpol, "State, Party, and Industry: From Business Recovery to the Wagner Act in America's New Deal" in *State Making and Social Movements: Essays in History and Theory*, ed. C.

Bright and S. Harding (Ann Arbor: University of Michigan Press, 1984), 152–92; James Struthers, *No Fault of Their Own: Unemployment and the Canadian Welfare State, 1914–1941* (Toronto: University of Toronto Press, 1983); Alvin Finkel, "Origins of the Welfare State in Canada" in *The Canadian State: Political Economy and Political Power*, ed. Leo Panitch (Toronto: University of Toronto Press, 1977), 344–70.

101 John Carrier and Ian Kendall, "Social Policy and Social Change: Explanations of the Development of Social Policy," *Journal of Social Policy* 2, 3 (1973): 209–24, and "The Development of Welfare States: The Production of Plausible Accounts," *Journal of Social Policy* 6, 3 (1977): 271–90; Elwood Jones, "Dependency and Social Welfare," *Journal of Canadian Studies/ Revue d'études canadiennes* 14, 1 (1979): 1.

102 Martine Segalen, "La révolution industrielle: du prolétaire au bourgeois" in *Histoire de la famille*, ed. André Burguière et al. (Paris: Armand Colin, 1986), 411; Asa Briggs, "The Welfare State in Historical Perspective" in *The Collected Essays of Asa Briggs*, vol. 2 (Urbana: University of Illinois Press, 1985), 177–211 (the article was first published in 1961); John Carrier and Ian Kendall, "Categories, Categorizations and the Political Economy of Welfare," *Journal of Social Policy* 15, 3 (1986): 315–32; James Dickinson and Bob Russel, "The Structure of Reproduction in Capitalist Society" in *Family, Economy and the State*, 1–20; Brigitte Kitchen, "The Family and Social Policy" in *The Family*, 178–97.

103 See also the warnings of Segalen, "La révolution industrielle," 411.

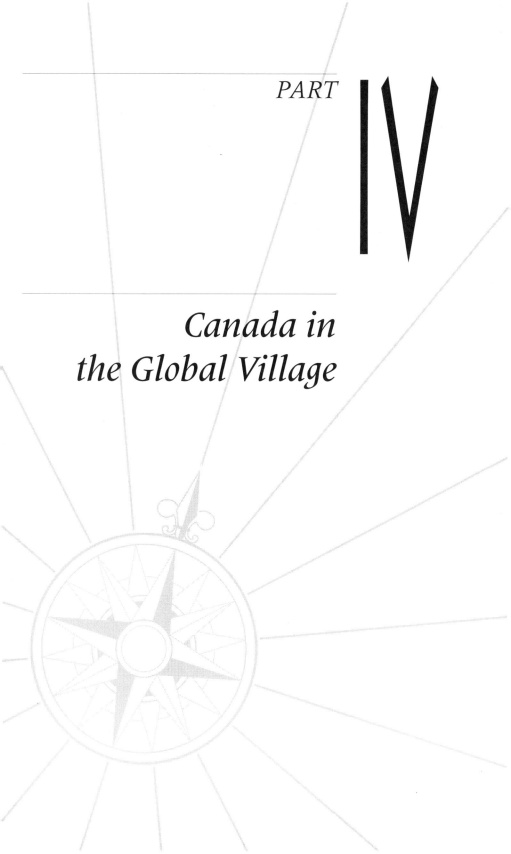

PART IV

Canada in
the Global Village

The title of this section, "Canada in the Global Village," emphasizes that our recent history has been closely tied to international developments. In some ways, this emphasis would be appropriate for any period of Canadian history but, in other ways, the extent and diversity of Canada's relationships with external places is specific to recent years. These readings address new questions as well as analysing the continuing importance of certain topics examined in previous parts of this book.

The first article discusses the complex issues raised for Canada by the increasing interest of many countries in the circumpolar world. As Robert Page explains, these issues include the environment, sovereignty, energy policy, and defence. Page analyses the perspectives of different countries and groups, with special attention to the relationship between Canada and the United States. This reading stresses that the definition and meaning of political boundaries have reached a new level of debate. For example, the aboriginal claims of the Inuit of Greenland, Alaska, and Canada have exposed the fact that international law is having great difficulty keeping pace with the changing world of the late twentieth century.

One of the most visible daily reminders of globalization is the multi-national fast-food chains that are now penetrating all corners of the world. In a previous article in this book, Cynthia Wright described the Eaton's department stores' role in the creation of a national market in Canada early in the twentieth century. Ester Reiter examines this theme in recent decades by showing how restaurants such as McDonald's and Burger King have sought to establish an international market. Like Joy Parr in her examination of the workplace, Reiter studies the actual meaning of employment in a fast-food outlet. Her approach shows how everyday experience is closely connected to global trends. A distinguishing feature of this study is the fact that Reiter uses her own year-long employment in a Burger King restaurant as evidence for her analysis. More than examining documents or interviewing participants, Reiter draws directly upon her own insights and knowledge of the fast-food industry.

The proliferation of fast-food chains has many causes, but there is no doubt that such restaurants are often associated with the shopping strips and malls that dot the suburban landscape. Veronica Strong-Boag explains the development of this landscape in terms of a gendered space in which residential suburbs became the symbolic feminine opposite of the male urban world. Strong-Boag's analysis brings together a wide variety of themes from recent socio-historical work, including the relationship between demographic change and the ideology presented in sources such as magazines and self-help books. Like many other social historians of twentieth-century Canada, Strong-Boag also depends on people's memories to help understand her topic; her strategy involves the use of a questionnaire sent to suburbanites in different regions of the country.

The final four readings explore questions of identity and power that will undoubtedly remain at the forefront of debate in Canada for years to come. Pierre Fortin emphasizes the connection between political attitudes and economic trends in his assessment of Quebec and the constitutional question. Rather than linking politics to cultural issues, Fortin argues that Quebeckers will make political choices based on financial calculations. In his mind, the political question is straightforward: is separation from Canada a wise economic decision for Quebec? This approach stands in sharp contrast to the focus of Gerald Friesen on the changing psychological and cultural attachments of residents on the Prairies. Like Fortin, Friesen uses the word "crisis" to describe the state of federalism, but he analyses the question of identity in terms of an "imagined community" that includes, but is not defined by, formal boundaries. Friesen examines the aspects of politics related to cultural expressions and loyalties. While the evidence he examines supports the concept of a prairie-wide region, Friesen concludes by wondering if "any imagined community smaller than the continent can prevail in the days of globalization." Clearly, this question could also be posed with respect to Fortin's analysis of Quebec.

Robert F. Harney does not emphasize the word "crisis," but he does raise the question of the "survival of the Canadian polity." In order to explain the development of an immigrant society with multicultural policies, Harney studies in detail the racist assumptions of government thinking, the power of lobby groups, and the labour requirements of an expanding society. His research points to another way in which family and kinship relations have helped construct, often quietly and unofficially, modern Canada. Harney's juxtaposition of official racism with the reality of ethnic diversity in an immigrant society harkens back to James W. St G. Walker's reading on visible minorities and World War I. In a similar way, Tony Hall raises questions about the future of Canada's identity by focussing on one of the most bitter battles involving aboriginal land claims. Hall's overview of the Temagami case relates directly to Tina Loo's study of the relationship between Native groups and Canadian law. Along with Page's study of the circumpolar North, these readings point to the importance of aboriginal history throughout twentieth-century Canada.

THE CANADIAN NORTH IN THE CIRCUMPOLAR WORLD*

ROBERT PAGE

In this article the Canadian Arctic will be seen in a broad international set-ting, which Canadians have been reluctant to recognize in spite of its grow-ing importance. Included in this analysis are a number of difficult issues that complicate greatly our relations with the United States and are part of the explanation for the growing tensions between Ottawa and Washington in the early 1980s. These tensions involve the intricate interrelationship among the environment, sovereignty, energy policy, and defence.

This bilateral relationship must now be fitted into a wider scenario. The existing alliance system is faced by the logical need for circumpolar co-operation. We are only slowly coming to recognize the ecological interde-pendency of the nations facing the Arctic Ocean, while our closest military ally is also our greatest challenge in terms of sovereignty and national econ-omic goals in the North. The traditional stereotypes of the "True North Strong and Free" collide with the realities of world politics in the 1980s. Canadians may resent these circumstances but they cannot ignore them. . . . We must return to the theme [of] viewing the Canadian North as an extension of the northern frontier of Europe to understand properly the current scene.

The first problem we face is our own perception of the Arctic world, which has been conditioned by traditional southern maps that are "open at

*From *Northern Development* by Robert Page. Used by permission of the Canadian Publishers, McClelland & Stewart, Toronto.

the top"; yet all the circumpolar nations face each other around the Arctic Ocean. This body of water is nearly landlocked by the territory of the Soviet Union, Alaska, Canada, Greenland, and Norway. The activities of each of these nations interact, the environmental impacts from one area inevitably creating consequences for the surrounding territories. Under these circumstances the only effective means of environmental protection is through international law, diplomacy, and co-operation. Yet the international community was slow to recognize the significance of the scientific research and the overall threat posed for marine ecosystems, including the Arctic. The great powers were reluctant to see coastal states allowed to interfere with the historic principles of the freedom of the seas that their own commercial and military vessels enjoyed.

In the North the need for new regulation became evident in the 1970s when advances in marine technology allowed commercial shipping to penetrate the frozen seas for the first time. In the 1980s and 1990s intense economic development will occur in many areas of the Arctic. Major offshore drilling programs are underway or planned for the Barents Sea (USSR), the Svalbard Archipelago and the Norwegian Sea (Norway and the USSR), the Davis Strait (Canada and Greenland), the Sverdrup Basin (Canada), and the Beaufort Sea (United States and Canada). With all these efforts the urgency for international environmental co-operation is clearly evident, in order to avoid but if not at least to contain and to clean up major oil spills in the difficult Arctic conditions.

In the 1960s Canadian fears about its jurisdiction over Arctic waters were limited by the belief that the Northwest Passage would never be used by commercial vessels. These concerns, however, were brought to a focus by the *Manhattan* and *Polar Sea* voyages and the clear refusal of the United States to recognize Canadian claims to these waters. The fears in Canada revolved around two interrelated issues—sovereignty and environmental regulation. The potential damage of an oil spill was brought to public attention in February 1970, when the tanker *Arrow* sank in Nova Scotia waters, polluting a long stretch of the coastline. There was strong political pressure on Ottawa to take counter-measures to protect Canadian sovereignty as well as the pristine northern wilderness from poorly maintained "flag of convenience" tankers under charter to the Prudhoe Bay producers. Because Canada at this time had never formally claimed the waters through the establishment of baselines around the islands or by proclaiming the sector theory drawn on most Canadian government maps, the American challenge tended to produce bureaucratic confusion and political embarrassment in Ottawa. In the end Canada swallowed its pride and co-operated with the *Manhattan* in 1969 and 1970 while planning future moves to consolidate its position.[1]

The American position on the *Manhattan* was founded on two assumptions basic to the traditional philosophy of maritime powers. The United States maintained that the Northwest Passage was an "international

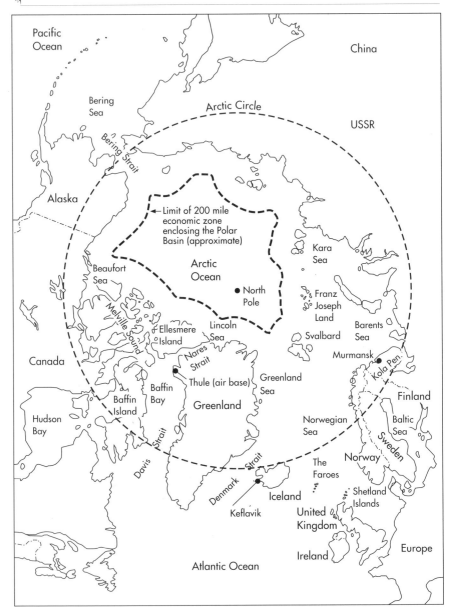

FIGURE 1: *The Circumpolar North*

strait" where the shipping of all nations enjoyed the rights of "innocent passage," stressing that these principles were enshrined in international law and the historic traditions of the freedom of the seas. As a major world shipping power, the Americans were concerned not only about commercial and military access to Canadian waters but about the effect the Canadian action might have in promoting jurisdictional claims by island nations such as Indonesia and the Philippines. The State Department thus chose to take a hard line with Canada even though the Americans knew that Ottawa had no intention of excluding Arctic-class American vessels like the *Manhattan*. It was the principle of having to apply for permission they wished to eliminate, and they were prepared to accept the necessary damage to Canadian–American relations to establish the point. If the Canadian initiative was allowed to go unchallenged it could become an embarrassing precedent that other nations might seek to follow. With many coastal states around the world seeking to extend their jurisdiction, Washington was highly sensitive about any changes in its own backyard.

Canada chose to respond to the American position by adopting an approach that would achieve its political goals without directly challenging the practices of international law, calling its position a "constructive and functional approach whereby Canada will exercise only the jurisdiction required to achieve this specific and vital purpose of environmental protection."[2] Ottawa justified its action on the basis of the pressing need for environmental protection while avoiding any claim to expanded sovereignty. As international law did not recognize the need for coastal states to intervene to protect the environment, Canada had to act unilaterally at once as a precondition for wider multilateral efforts to mobilize international support. Many nations at the UN recognized the shortcomings of international law as it is related to marine pollution but there was no consensus as to the best means of regulation. With the "Limits to Growth" debate ranging around the world, there was growing concern about the long-term viability of the world's oceans as a food source. Canada used this intellectual climate to wrap its own Arctic plans in a wider idealism that many nations would support. However, some of the principles espoused so eloquently in foreign affairs statements were only faintly evident in federal and provincial efforts at environmental regulation.

At many international gatherings Canadian officials argued that the doctrine of "innocent passage" was not appropriate for Arctic conditions because it failed to allow Ottawa sufficient authority to safeguard the northern environment. Normal tankers could be holed or sunk in the tough multi-year ice of the Northwest Passage. Yet under the traditions of innocent passage Canada had no right to interfere to enforce adequate Arctic standards and to refuse entry when these were not met, even though the food supply and the way of life of the local Inuit could be destroyed by a major oil spill. The Canadians argued that environmental integrity was every bit as valid as territorial integrity and coastal states had a duty to intervene to protect the environment on which so many of their citizens depended. These arguments were challenged continually by representatives of the major marine powers, such as Britain and the United States.

As a first step towards achieving its goal, the Trudeau government in 1970 pushed through Parliament the Arctic Waters Pollution Prevention

Act (AWPPA), which established a hundred-mile environmental control zone around the Canadian Arctic islands. The regulations included standards of construction and navigation procedures; they applied to through-transit vessels as well as local resource exploitation and development. Sixteen Shipping Safety Control Zones were set up, which reflected the differing levels of ice danger. Vessels failing to meet the required standards could be banned by pollution prevention officers and their cargo seized by cabinet order. Any dispute emerging from the application of the Arctic Waters Pollution Prevention Bill was excluded from reference to the International Court of Justice, which showed the Canadian worries about the status of its legislation under international law. The bill was passed in 1970 but not proclaimed for two years while Ottawa tried without success to negotiate American compliance. The response of the Nixon administration was to cut the Canadian oil import quota and to threaten further retaliation if the act was put into force. Congress approved funds for the "most powerful ice-breaker fleet in the world" so future Arctic voyages by American shipping would not require any contact or assistance from Canadian authorities. These actions aroused indignation in Canada, evoking media comparisons to the American action on the Panama Canal.

The final vote in the House of Commons on the AWPPA was unanimous, with the only criticism being that it might not be enough to protect the national interest and the northern environment.[3] The act was coupled with amendments to the Territorial Seas and Fisheries Acts to extend the limits of Canadian territorial waters from three to twelve miles, which brought the eastern and western "gates" of the Northwest Passage within Canadian territorial waters. Canada's move to a twelve-mile limit followed that of a number of other coastal states. However, it would have little practical significance if the American contention that the Northwest Passage was an international strait was generally accepted and there were no changes in the prevailing assumptions regarding the freedom of the seas within international law. These were serious barriers to acceptance of the Canadian position.

Internationally, the Arctic Waters Pollution Prevention Act was recognized as a significant unilateral attempt to create separate environmental regulations for Arctic waters and as addressing the general issue of expanding the jurisdiction of coastal states to protect the marine environment. Prime Minister Trudeau, a former law professor, attempted to explain some of the thinking behind his government's initiative. He argued that the action would strengthen international law in an important new way. It was "an assertion of the importance of the environment, of the sanctity of life on this planet, of the need for the recognition of the principle of clean seas, which is in all respects as vital a principle for the world of today and tomorrow as the principle of free seas for the world of yesterday." Canada had an international obligation to protect the northern environment.

The Arctic ice-pack has been described as the most significant surface area of the globe, for it controls the temperature of much of
the Northern Hemisphere. Its continued existence in unspoiled
form is vital to all mankind. The single most imminent threat to the
Arctic at this time is that of a large oil spill. Not only are the hazards
of Arctic navigation much greater than are found elsewhere, making the risk of breakup or sinking one of constant concern, but any
maritime tragedy there would have disastrous and irreversible consequences. . . . Involved here, in short, are issues which even the
most conservative of environmental scientists do not hesitate to
describe as being of a magnitude which is capable of affecting the
quality, and perhaps the continued existence, of human and animal
life in vast regions of North America and elsewhere.[4]

This apocalyptic vision helped to entrench the government's position
with northern environmentalists and reassure native groups, who rightly
assumed that they would be the principal losers in the event of a major
Arctic oil spill in their area. American protests achieved little except that
the compensation provisions were broadened to allow claims from beyond
Canadian territory, which made perfect sense given the pattern of northern winds and currents. The basic policy, however, was non-negotiable for
it constituted the central feature of Canada's functional approach to
extending its marine jurisdiction. Although it tried to avoid international
sensitivities on sovereignty, it was an important initiative in the area of the
law of the sea. An article in a Canadian law journal reflected Canadian
pride when it claimed that the law was "the most significant unilateral
action on the marine environment ever taken."[5] Within Canada it was
clearly a political success, which helped to ease the frustrations generated
by the *Manhattan* voyages that Ottawa was only an impotent spectator to
events in the North.

The AWPPA was a unilateral step, so Canada now began efforts to
promote multilateral acceptance of its Arctic legislation. Negotiations continued in Washington, although without success. President Nixon personally
phoned the Canadian Prime Minister, and, when the Canadians refused to
back down, the United States State Department released a diplomatic note
stressing that "international law provides no basis for these proposed
unilateral extensions of jurisdiction on the high seas," which the American government "can neither accept nor acquiesce [to]."[6] At the United
Nations, however, Canada got a better response for its efforts. The
Canadian government played an influential role in the events leading to
and the proceedings of the Stockholm Conference on the Human Environment held in 1972. Here, Canada promoted its concept of "regulation
based upon scientific principles," which would give new powers to coastal
states. In its proposed "Third Principle," Canada outlined the jurisdictional
changes it sought.

The basis on which a state should exercise rights or powers, in addition to its sovereign rights and powers, pursuant to its special authority in areas adjacent to its territorial waters, is that such rights or powers should be deemed to be delegated to that state by the world community on behalf of humanity as a whole. The rights and powers exercised must be consistent with the coastal state's primary responsibility for marine environmental protection in the areas concerned: they should be subject to international rules and standards and to review before an appropriate international tribunal.[7]

These efforts were strongly opposed by the major shipping powers, but the proposals were passed on for consideration to the Third United Nations Law of the Sea Conference (UNCLOS III), which opened in Caracas in 1973 and continued for nearly a decade.

There is not scope in this chapter for detailed analysis of all the complex negotiations at the Law of the Sea Conference. Canada, however, did achieve partial success in the final version of the Convention through the acceptance of Article 234, the so-called "Arctic clause."

Coastal states have the right to adopt and enforce non-discriminatory laws and regulations for the prevention, reduction and control of marine pollution from vessels in ice-covered areas within the limits of the exclusive economic zone, where particularly severe climatic conditions and the presence of ice covering such areas for most of the year create obstructions or exceptional hazards to navigation, and pollution of the marine environment could cause major harm to or irreversible disturbance of the ecological balance. Such laws and regulations shall have due regard to navigation and the preservation of the marine environment based upon the best available scientific evidence.[8]

Enforcement of such national laws would normally be limited to the coastal state seeking redress through the courts of the flag state. "Monetary penalties only may be imposed" on the offending vessels "except in the case of a willful and serious act of pollution in the territorial sea" (section 230). Thus there is still some legal uncertainty with regard to Canada's jurisdiction to enforce the provisions of the AWPPA outside Canadian territorial seas but within its pollution control zone. Flag states must provide recourse through their courts "for prompt and adequate compensation or other relief" for acts of pollution caused by "natural or juridical persons under their jurisdiction" (Article 235). However, these provisions do not include airplanes, warships, or other vessels owned or operated by a state and involved in "government non-commercial service" (article 236). Thus, Canada has no jurisdiction over foreign vessels operating for their governments for military or research purposes or for the supplying of these vessels. Canada has hailed the Law of the Sea Treaty as formal international recognition of its jurisdiction over Arctic waters as provided under AWPPA.

Unfortunately, the United States' refusal to sign the treaty greatly weakens the importance of the document for Canadian Arctic environmental regulation.

In the 1980s there is still confusion regarding international acceptance of the AWPPA and the United Nations Law of the Sea Convention. Canada maintains that the waters of the Northwest Passage are internal waters subject to complete Canadian sovereignty and regulation. Outside of the waters between the Arctic islands but within the Exclusive Economic Zone, Canada claims the right to enforce the Arctic Waters Pollution Prevention Act equally on all shipping under the terms of the Arctic clause of the Law of the Sea Convention. The rights of innocent passage are qualified by the requirement to meet Canadian environmental standards. The United States rejects Canadian jurisdiction, refuses to sign the Law of the Sea Convention, and declares the Northwest Passage an international strait where nations have the right to unhindered innocent passage. Canada has now drawn baselines around the islands and its claim is founded on the amorphous concept of historic title, that the waters historically have been assumed to be Canadian.

In this scenario, a number of problems are on the horizon. Enforcement of the AWPPA would be difficult in any instance where an American vessel chose to defy Canadian jurisdiction as did the *Manhattan*. The Canadian government presence in the North is so limited that Ottawa might not even be aware of the violation. Also, it is difficult to challenge the American claim that the Northwest Passage is an international strait when there appears to be no internationally recognized definition of what that term means. Canadian arguments have been presented that, as large parts of the passage are locked in land-fast ice for so much of the year, the normal meaning of high seas and straits cannot be applied to it. In this case ice assumes a separate legal status from either land or water. Also, as Professor Donat Pharand had argued, "by no stretch of the imagination could the few foreign American crossings constitute sufficient use for commercial navigation to turn the Northwest Passage into an international strait."[9] Yet all these arguments remain an academic exercise given the American position in the world and the determination in Washington to defend vigorously its own interests. The voyage of the *Polar Sea* in the summer of 1985 is one example.

One of the strongest pressure groups for more stringent environmental regulation is the Inuit Circumpolar Conference, linking the Inuit of Greenland, Alaska, and Canada. Their aboriginal claims include the right to continue their traditional hunting on the sea ice in areas like the Northwest Passage where commercial shipping would chew up the ice. This is a unique problem for international law in determining the legitimacy of these competing claims to the sea lanes. To my knowledge there is no basis or precedent in international law for recognition of these traditional rights. Also, even if Canada or Greenland were to recognize their claims, could they enforce compliance by foreign ships when there is no basis for such claims in the wording of the Law of the Sea Convention? In the last decade the Inuit Circumpolar Conference has been steadily raising its political profile, which was clearly evident in the international media attention accorded the third conference at Frobisher Bay in July 1983. Their strong views on the environment dominate the thinking of the newly autonomous government of Greenland, which achieved "home rule" in 1979. Although foreign and defence policy is reserved to Copenhagen under the new constitution, Greenland has not hesitated to come to Ottawa to lobby directly to stop projects like the Arctic Pilot Project when it opposes them. The Greenland officials stress that current international practices are totally inadequate and the tankers heading for the Northwest Passage will skirt the ice-free coastal waters of Greenland. They are much more radical than the Canadian government in their proposals for protecting the environment. Thus, the Canadian AWPPA is attacked by the United States from one direction and by Greenland from the opposite. The final land claims settlement with the Inuit of Canada will almost certainly have provisions to protect the sea ice and the marine environment, which will be added costs for international resource companies as well as further annoyance to the American State Department.

In regard to the eastern Arctic, Canadian officials have had far fewer contacts with officials from Greenland than is the case in the west with their Alaskan counterparts. Canadian concerns were aroused in 1975 when the Danish government authorized a drilling program off the west coast of Greenland with only a very cursory regulatory structure in place. Danish policy placed full responsibility to plan for and to control a blowout or spill on the drilling company or partnership involved. However, under Danish law, the operator was responsible only as long as he remained on site. When he left, his liability ended. Canadian officials were relieved when the drilling program lapsed without incident and then proceeded to approve permits for drilling on the Canadian side of the Davis Strait. In August 1977, an interim Canada–Denmark Marine Pollution Contingency Plan was signed covering the waters of the Labrador Sea, Davis Strait, Baffin Bay, and Nares Strait. However, without any local coast guard on the Greenland side, the prime responsibility for immediate action would lie with Canadian men and equipment.

Many Inuit in Greenland fear that a major spill from the Canadian side would seriously harm their traditional hunting grounds. Canada has offered a liability regime with a ceiling of $20 million for compensation to Danish nationals for the results of any accidents originating in Canadian waters. In February 1979, Canada agreed to finance the cleanup of spills within its waters, to recover funds for any direct damages, and to allow access to Canadian courts for the recovery of indirect costs (such as to fishermen).[10] While this agreement met with approval in Copenhagen, there is far less enthusiasm in Greenland, where the issue is not compensation but opposition in principle to the idea of drilling. Greenland is upset with the potential environmental impacts of marine drilling or even tanker traffic through its waters or those of Lancaster Sound. Its suspicion of the Canadian government is all the greater because of Canada's key role in northern oil exploration through the Crown corporation, Petro-Canada.

Another controversial area of the Arctic environment has been the Beaufort Sea, where in 1976 Canada became the first nation to attempt exploratory offshore oil drilling in the pack ice of the Arctic Ocean. When cabinet approval was given on 15 April 1976, for drilling that summer, a formal U.S. State Department note requested a delay: there had not been formal public Environmental Impact Assessment (EIA) of the exploratory drilling; there was no adequate contingency planning in the event of a spill; and there was no liability regime for potential American claimants. Ironically, after the rhetoric of the *Manhattan* incident, Canada now appeared to be neglecting the environment. Canada proceeded with drilling in 1976 and in each year since. Joint contingency planning was in place by 1977 with Canada establishing a response centre at Inuvik. But if a major oil spill or well blowout occurred during the short summer drilling season, it is impossible to know if containment and cleanup could be achieved *before* the return of the pack ice in October. The oil would pour out under the ice and be carried by the currents and the movement of the ice westward along the Yukon coast and then into Alaskan waters. Government structures are in place on both sides of the border to react to any oil spills and there has been good co-operation between officials in both countries. However, the physical problems of containment and cleanup are great, for existing booms, skimmers, and dispersants require open water free of pack ice.

A further complication for drilling and environmental regulation in the Beaufort Sea remains the disputed offshore boundary. Canada claims that the land boundary between the Yukon and Alaska along the 141st meridian extends due north from the coast, reflecting the sector theory that appears to have influenced so much of Canadian thinking. The line proposed by the United States follows an arc further east, thus cutting into the area claimed by Canada and creating a disputed zone. The American contention is based on the principle of equidistance and therefore reflects the contours of the coast. As the coast angles northward and westward at the border, the American line swings eastward (into territory claimed by Canada) until the influence of Banks Island comes into play and the line then swings westward, crossing the 141st meridian approximately 200 miles offshore. By this point the area is covered by permanent pack ice and is currently of little economic significance.[11]

In proclaiming the Exclusive Economic Zone and the Arctic Waters Pollution Prevention Act, Canada had assumed that its case would be accepted and that its jurisdiction went right to the 141st meridian; Ottawa even issued leases for petroleum drilling in the disputed zone to companies, including its own Petro-Canada.[12] Some Canadians have implied that their case is based on the Anglo-Russian Treaty of 1825, which the United States assumed through its purchase of Alaska in 1867. This point is of dubious historic validity given that there was no concept of jurisdiction over the continental shelf in 1825, let alone any interest in it by either party. The 1977 International Court decision on the North Sea Continental Shelf Cases noted that one of the four possible methods for delimiting the jurisdictional boundaries involved was "the continuation in the seaward direction of the land frontier."[13] Yet the basic fact is that the sector theory has never been recognized in international law. One of the leading Canadian authorities in international law put it bluntly: "the sector theory has no validity as a legal root of title, whether it be in respect of land or water, and Canada would be well advised to abandon any hope of gaining legal support from the theory . . . with respect to jurisdictional claims in the arctic."[14]

At this point in mid-1985 there does not appear to be any resolution of the Beaufort Sea boundary dispute in sight, even though the principle of equidistance has been employed by Canada in negotiations with Greenland and in the Gulf of Maine, where the United States has rejected it. The current Canadian Beaufort drilling may help to show whether or not there is any chance of oil in the disputed zone. Also, if Canada successfully develops the costly technology required for offshore oil production, it will be of immense benefit to the Americans for future marine production off Prudhoe Bay. If, however, there is a massive oil spill in Canadian waters it will trigger environmental controversy in the United States that will make it all the more difficult for any American administration to proceed further with its own offshore plans. Initially, the Arctic Waters Pollution Prevention Act did not provide any means for Americans to be compensated in the event of a Canadian blowout, but Ottawa has now made changes to try to meet these concerns.

In the eastern Arctic the marine boundary with Greenland has been almost completely defined on the principles of equidistance. The two exceptions involve the northern extension of the line out into the Lincoln Sea (which has still to be negotiated) and Hans Island, lying at latitude 80° 49' north in the Nares Strait, perfectly on the median line between Ellesmere Island and Greenland. This small uninhabited island about one mile long was claimed by both countries, so the decision was made to draw the boundary up to the low water mark at the south end of the island and recommence it at the low water mark at the north end. Hans Island thus remains in dispute, the only example of disputed land sovereignty in the Canadian Arctic.[15]

Inevitably, marine boundary issues have increased greatly in political importance with the recent growing realization of the mineral and petroleum potential. Coupled with these issues has been the rising controversy in Washington about the drive to Canadianize the oil industry that emerged with the announcement of the National Energy Program (NEP) in October 1980. This was the most radical change in the history of Canadian energy policy. The NEP was designed to divert oil and gas exploration to the northern and offshore frontiers; to increase the level of Canadian ownership and control; and to divert significant economic rents from the producing provinces and the corporations to the federal coffers. It was bitterly attacked by western provinces and the multinational oil companies, the full discussion of which lies outside the scope of this volume. But the NEP northern incentives became a serious irritant in Canadian–American relations, which is central to this chapter. The Reagan administration viewed it as a deliberate attack on American-owned interests in Canada, which, along with the Foreign Investment Review Agency (FIRA), was the focus for American attacks. Washington demanded that Canada revert to its traditional open-door policy that had allowed the foreign-owned majors to capture such a dominant position in the Canadian industry. The Trudeau administration viewed this pressure as an open challenge to Canadian economic sovereignty and its own moderate goal of 50 percent Canadian ownership of the petroleum industry by 1990.

When the new Republican administration took over in Washington in January 1981, it injected a new ideological intensity into foreign policy as well as a dogmatic support for American economic interests around the world and a free-enterprise fundamentalism. Within the inner group, no individual showed close knowledge of the Canadian scene such as Vice-President Walter Mondale had shown within the Carter administration. Many of the oil companies who had financed the Reagan victory now expected action to defend their vested interests in Canada. At the same time, several United States oil companies were facing takeovers at home from Canadian interests financed by the Canadian banks operating under regulations not allowed in the United States, which only increased the levels of controversy. At a time when the foreign ownership of the American oil industry stood at about 18 percent and yet Americans were very sensitive about Canadian takeovers, Ottawa could not understand the American opposition to its own goal of 50 percent domestic ownership. But the Americans saw the NEP as part of a worldwide pattern of attack on American interests that must be boldly confronted, especially in their own backyard north of the border.[16]

The specific provisions of the NEP were clearly designed to discriminate in favour of Canadian companies and to promote exploration on federal lands north of 60° or the East Coast offshore. Under the PIP grants, a company with 65 percent or more Canadian ownership would qualify for government support totalling 80 percent of its exploration costs on federal land while a foreign-owned firm could only recover 25 percent of its approved costs. These new grants were to replace the depletion allowances, which were a deduction from corporate income taxes. The previous system of fiscal incentives had greater tax advantages for the large, integrated oil companies with extensive downstream profits in refining and marketing as opposed to the smaller Canadian exploration firms. The NEP also included a variety of other regulatory features to achieve the 50 percent goal. In the event of a major oil discovery the Crown retained the right to a 25 percent working interest in the field and could exercise this option right up until the field went into production. Although this "back-in" provision was denounced as anti-American and confiscatory in Washington, it applied equally to all companies; in fact, it had the most serious implications for Dome Petroleum with its Beaufort discoveries. The result of the American protests was that Ottawa modified its policy, agreeing to make *ex gratia* payments when exercising its option. In turn, these were denounced as merely token payments unrelated to the asset value of the discovery. Ottawa, however, replied that as the owner of the resource and the provider of the PIP grants, the Canadian public had a right to a share of the production revenue. Also, once in, Petro-Canada would be responsible for its full share of the heavy capital costs of the production facilities, which were normally too great in the Beaufort for any one company to shoulder alone.

When a company wished to convert an exploration lease into a production agreement, the new regulations required that the company or joint venture have a minimum of 50 percent Canadian ownership. Under the new Canadian Oil and Gas Lands Administration (COGLA) all companies had to renegotiate their existing leases, returning 50 percent of the land to the Crown. This was designed to open up the huge areas of the North already under lease to the majors but not being actively explored. New regulations were established to require high levels of Canadian content for future Arctic mega-projects while Canadian-owned firms were promised preferential treatment in the awarding of new gas export contracts, an important source for cash flow to finance frontier exploration. Finally, a special tax was placed at the wellhead (the Petroleum and Gas Revenue Tax) to tap production revenues at the source, thus funding the PIP grants and other federal initiatives. A consumer products tax on gasoline and fuel oil helped to finance the takeovers of Petrofina and BP assets by Petro-Canada.

Although none of the large American companies were subject to public-sector takeovers, they objected vigorously to the whole system of increased public ownership and government regulation, claiming that the asset value of their companies decreased under the NEP and that with time they might be forced to sell out at "fire-sale" prices to Canadian buyers. In fact, the takeovers that did take place were all accomplished at a heavy cost to the Canadian purchasers, for the value of the shares was bid up to premium levels by the market forces on the stock exchange. When the world oil prices declined in the following months, the asset value of the properties purchased declined while the revenues declined for both industry and government. The net result of the new fiscal incentives was that foreign-controlled companies like Imperial Oil now sought "farm-outs" or joint ventures with smaller Canadian companies.[17] Many of these Canadian companies did not have the financial resources or the land position (leases) to allow them to participate on their own in the Arctic.

Another factor in the Canadian–American feud on the NEP was the issue of Canadian content in the large northern mega-projects such as the Alaska Highway Pipeline and the Arctic Pilot Project. In the past, most of these huge projects had been constructed by American contracting firms such as Bechtel, which had a built-in bias for American suppliers it was used to dealing with.[18] The government was determined that these industrial spinoffs be captured for Canadians as part of its industrial strategy and its battle against rising unemployment. Thus, a Major Projects Task Force of business and labour leaders was established to propose new policy initiatives. Headed up by Bob Blair, president of Nova, and Shirley Carr, executive vice-president of the Canadian Labour Congress, they tackled directly the supply/procurement problem. Their report stressed that out of the $1 trillion Canada would need for capital investment by the year 2000, $440 billion would be required to finance mega-projects. Procurement policies were needed to ensure that Canadian suppliers would achieve their maximum potential in spite of the traditional patterns of supply from the United States. Their recommendations were translated into a series of guidelines in Bill C-48, the Canadian Oil and Gas Act, and the establishment of the Office of Industrial and Regional Benefits to monitor compliance. The United States protested strongly that this bill was a form of disguised protectionism, for the Canadian bids did not even have to be competitive. Ottawa amended the legislation to include the word "competitive" and pointed out the frequency of "Buy America" clauses in American legislation. Washington remained convinced that U.S. companies would lose their traditional position of dominance as suppliers to these large projects and warned the Trudeau government that it would monitor future tendering and procurement practices to ensure that American companies were given equal opportunity in Canada.[19]

In its communications with Canada, the Reagan administration clearly expressed its profound displeasure with Canadian energy policy.

> We cannot, however, continue simply to discuss matters without substantial movement both on the FIRA and on the NEP. . . . We are most concerned about the following discriminatory and inequitable measures associated with the operation of the FIRA and the NEP. . . . It is most important that the first two practices [of FIRA] be eliminated and that the others [of FIRA and NEP] be eliminated or modified as appropriate.

This was exceedingly harsh language to use in a diplomatic note to an ally and trading partner. The specifics of the NEP that Washington demanded to be changed included: exemption from the "back-in"; for existing exploration leases; asset value payments for "back-in"; end of the discrimination in the awarding of PIP grants; end of the 50 percent Canadian ownership requirement for production licences, and Canadian ownership preference for future natural gas export licences. These would have gutted the whole program and Ottawa refused to consider the American position as a legitimate request of one sovereign nation to another. However, Canada did make several small concessions, and in the following months Washington toned down its rhetoric while maintaining the protests. It must have realized that it had badly overplayed its hand.[20]

In June 1983, Secretary of State Shultz returned to the offensive on the NEP with a strongly worded note of protest delivered by American Ambassador Paul Robinson directly to Allan MacEachen, the minister of external affairs. Shultz described the 25 percent back-in as confiscatory and threatened that unless changed it could lead to a "major issue in Canadian–American relations." The Secretary of State went on to claim that this provision was a breach of international law, which the United States might take to the International Court of Justice at the Hague. Shultz included in his communication a thirty-five-page written opinion from a leading Washington lawyer who frequently acted for the majors. Cecil Olmstead's study concluded that the back-in violated international law and unless directly challenged could be followed by similar action by other nations.[21] The Shultz letter worried officials in Ottawa because it appeared that for the first time the American Secretary of State was becoming directly involved in the dispute with Canada, unlike Alexander Haig, his predecessor.[22]

Given the importance of Shultz's position with the President, this was viewed as an escalation of the crisis. It appeared also that the Americans had been encouraged by the events at the Progressive Conservative Party convention two weeks earlier, when Brian Mulroney had attacked the NEP and promised to abolish the back-in provisions to improve relations with the United States. All this was happening at a time when the majors were no longer attacking the back-in provision because it could be replaced by higher royalties or other measures, which in the long term could prove more costly. Petro-Canada was now accepted as a legitimate partner in the costly northern joint ventures; in fact, government involvement helped to reassure the investment community that the project would proceed with all dispatch and with a minimum of government regulatory interference. But this growing pragmatism within industry clashed with the ideological purity of the Reagan administration and some politicians on both sides of the border.

By the summer of 1983 the PIP grants were flowing north to promote petroleum exploration. But the costs of the Beaufort wells were rising so rapidly that danger signs for the program were on the horizon. The issue of inflated costs came out into the open when Canterra (controlled by the federal government) refused to pay its share of a joint venture with Gulf Oil, which was charging its partners very high rates for use of its expensive drilling equipment. Canterra claimed that Canmar (Dome's drilling subsidiary) could do the job for half the price charged by Gulf and had the equipment available to do it. Yet Canterra's involvement was critical to Gulf for it to achieve the necessary Canadian Ownership Rating (COR) to qualify for the PIP grants.

Federal officials had been growing increasingly alarmed at the ever-increasing size of the payments while revenues were eroded by weak oil prices and fiscal concessions to industry.[23] To bring some order and control back into the system, the PIP regulations were changed in the summer of 1983 so that all wells over $50 million required individual ministerial approval to ensure their costs were competitive. After the election of the new Conservative government in 1984, the whole system was reassessed in the light of this experience and of the new government's greater concern for its relations with the United States.

In 1985 the Mulroney government moved to respond to the American protests. The minister of energy, Pat Carney, announced the phasing out of the PIP grants over several years, to be replaced by a return to a system of depletion allowances (tax deductions for exploration work). Also eliminated was the infamous 25 percent back-in clause and some of the other Canadianization features that had provoked the American outrage. The drive for frontier exploration and Canadianization was now put on the back burner; without the huge government PIP grants, exploration plans for the Beaufort were reassessed and in some cases abandoned. Gulf put its new equipment up for sale and Dome tried to rent drillships to American companies operating off Alaska. With weak world oil prices and new priorities in Ottawa the downturn in Beaufort activities is assured for the rest of the 1980s.

During the Trudeau years northern energy policies were a major factor in Canadian–American relations. The National Energy Program was designed to Canadianize the oil industry, and the Reagan administration was determined to stop it. With southern conventional oil reserves declining since 1972, it was Ottawa's great hope that "elephants" would be found in the Beaufort and the eastern offshore to replace the Alberta conventional reserves. The Trudeau government was determined to see the production from these new fields largely in the hands of Canadian companies, and this would have a profound impact on the whole ownership structure of the industry. If Canadians were to pay the bulk of the costs of Arctic offshore production through PIP grants, they should have a majority stake in the profits and control of the patents in the event they could be used under licence by the Americans or the Russians. The NEP was a tough game of power politics where there was clear and deliberate discrimination in favour of the Canadian companies.

With the Conservative government, the balance has now fallen back in favour of the majors. But the Mulroney government can only go so far before it will suffer the same kind of political damage as befell C.D. Howe in 1956. The Canadian public does not share the same perception of continentalism as the majors operating in Canada. As one American oil executive explained to the author: "Part of our great annoyance with the NEP is that we have *never* treated Canada as a foreign country." Like Alaska, it was just another northern territory. After working for years to see the expansion of their Canadian operations, they resented the sudden emergence of Dome, Petro-Canada, and other Canadian companies through government intervention. With the overall American economic position in the world declining, many Americans felt they must now fight to protect their vested economic interests, and nowhere more so than in Canada, where they already possess great influence. Many Canadians, however, who see their own policies as much more moderate than such oil producers as Norway, cannot understand or accept the ideological intensity of the American response. Irrespective of the friendly platitudes of Brian Mulroney, sooner or later he will have to come to understand that fundamental Canadian economic interests will have to be sacrificed to continue his present policies. The reality of the Canadian–American relationship is the sharply protectionist forces in Congress who are determined to reverse the American decline. They have no interest in giving anyone "the benefit of the doubt," as Mulroney did as Opposition Leader at the time of the American invasion in Grenada, and they see great opportunities in exploiting the new philosophy in Ottawa.

The military and strategic significance of the Arctic waters has been steadily rising in the last decade. Concern has grown in NATO circles about the increasing naval and military strength of the Soviet forces based in the Kola Peninsula just over 1,000 miles from Ellesmere Island across the Arctic Ocean. In 1981 it was the base for the largest and most powerful Soviet surface fleet, 130 attack submarines (including 70 percent of ballistic missile capability), as well as aircraft and missile installations. It is only 180 miles by sea to the cover of the Arctic ice pack, which allows submarines to roam across the Arctic into Canadian or American waters.[24] The Soviet Union, with its interests in Arctic offshore oil and fisheries, recognized much earlier than the West the strategic significance of the Arctic areas and became the world leader, with nuclear icebreakers and other northern technology. Its current dispute with Norway over their joint activities in the Svalbard Archipelago is one example of Soviet concerns. Fisheries, in fact, have been an explosive issue in the North Atlantic in the last decade, with incidents such as the Cod War between Britain and Iceland, both members of NATO.

Similarly, the US Air Force base at Keflavik, which monitored Soviet naval activities in the North Atlantic, became the centre of political controversy and anti-American feelings within Icelandic politics. Using the threat of closing the American base and withdrawing from NATO, the Icelandic government won its battle to control its offshore fisheries. Here the linkage between resources and essential security services was one that both Britain and the United States were forced to accept. Former Secretary of State Henry Kissinger later remarked bitterly: "That little tableau in the town hall of Reykjavik—the beseeching superpower, the turbulent tiny country threatening to make war against a nation 250 times its size and to leave NATO . . . said volumes about the contemporary world and of the tyranny that the weak can impose upon it."[25] Now, in the 1980s, the American battle to retain its bases may shift from Iceland to Greenland.

As the world's largest island, Greenland has important resource and strategic significance even though most of the land is covered by the massive ice cap. From 1721 to 1953 the island was a Danish colony; then, from 1953 to 1979, it became an integral part of the Danish kingdom; and finally, since 1979, it has enjoyed home rule with a local assembly. Greenland possesses important mineral deposits that are exploited by such foreign companies as Canadian Pacific. Politically, there is some interest in Greenland in withdrawing from the European community, restricting the American use of the base at Thule, and assuming a neutralist position outside of NATO. Yet Greenland's importance to NORAD and NATO cannot be underestimated given the North Atlantic and circumpolar threats. It is the eastern end of the DEW line radar system currently being refurbished as well as of the Ballistic Missile Early Warning System (BMEWS). If, for political reasons, the American military presence faced future limitations, the adjacent areas of the Canadian High Arctic, such as Ellesmere Island, would take on a totally new strategic significance to military planners in Washington.

In addition, with the United States proceeding with its cruise missile program, there will be increased need for manned bomber bases in the Arctic, low-level specialized radar facilities, and training missions by bomber crews learning to hug the northern landscape.[26] There are also increasing American worries about the Soviet submarine threat to North America. The Soviet Typhoon-class submarines are now operational with the capability of lengthy submerged patrols under the Arctic ice pack and of firing long-range nuclear missiles through several metres of ice.[27] Hence, with the increased submarine and low-level missile threats, Greenland and the Canadian High Arctic islands will play a critical role in overall NATO and NORAD strategy. The American pressure for cruise missile testing in northern Canada may be only the first of a whole series of "requests" for increased American military presence in Canada.

These strategic assumptions can be documented from the writings of American security experts. Lincoln Bloomfield, former member of the American National Security Council, explained the changing American interest in the Canadian Arctic:

> U.S. strategic interests in the Canadian north declined in the 1960's when the ICBM's emerged as the chief strategic threat to the U.S. mainland. Even with a suspected refueling capability for the new Soviet Backfire medium bomber, it seems unlikely that Washington

will revive its languishing air defense preparations against potential Soviet bombing attacks. But a new Soviet strategic bomber or Soviet ALCM (air-launched cruise missile) might generate a whole new air defense program. The enormous Canadian Arctic still provides a precious cushion of time and space to deal with incoming hostile objects well before they could reach American cities, substantially enhancing U.S. defense.[28]

The reality of such a Soviet cruise missile is clear as Moscow scrambles to counter the American cruise program. The Pentagon is also concerned to devise naval defence barriers to thwart Soviet submarines from launching missiles from Canadian Arctic waters. Hudson Bay, for instance, is considered to be dangerously close to the industrial heartland of the United States. This fact is likely to cause even greater American pressure to open up our North for the "common" defence of the continent.

These changes in strategic thinking do not mean that Canadian bargaining power with the United States will suddenly increase or that Washington will be more grateful to Canada. To quote Bloomfield again:

> The unhappy recent shift in U.S.-Canadian relations to an abrasive and more openly resented dependency relationship is at least somewhat exacerbated by the U.S. strategic perception of Canada as a useful polar barrier against trajectories of weapons targeted on the United States which cross Canadian territory. Put differently, Americans sometimes seem to look straight through Canada as they peer across the arctic at the USSR.

In fact, security worries may make Washington officials even more determined to get Canada clearly into line through not only the use of territory but financial contributions on a scale as never before. Canada has been taken for granted with its small and ineffective role in NORAD and there is little chance that this attitude will change. Although a few Americans have recognized the problem and are concerned about the future, their writings appear to have evoked no official response: "The fact that only a few Americans are even aware of such sensitivities constitutes the unkindest cut of all for our northern neighbour. Impending developments in the arctic are likely to sharpen rather than dampen Canadian resentment of the perceived American mix of power and indifference."[29] These two factors—American power and indifference—together constitute the essence of the Canadian sense of frustration in dealing with the United States even though they are a natural product of the unequal position of the two nations in much the same fashion as Finland and the Soviet Union.

In the current circumstances there is an acute need for international co-operation in scientific and technological research. Although there have been sporadic efforts for decades, they have been too dependent on the "old boy" network of personal friendships, easily disrupted by government financial restraints or Cold War pressures. Even the co-operation between the United States and Canada has been limited by such factors as American security concerns, which stopped the flow of the *Manhattan* ice data. There is considerable potential here for future expansion, especially with the Nordic countries. Sharing of weather data is one critical area of science with clear pragmatic benefits to all countries involved. Also, out of the research links may come important multilateral agreements such as the Polar Bear Treaty of 1973 signed by the United States, the Soviet Union, Canada, Denmark, and Norway. It would seem that a co-ordinated international research program to develop the technology for oil-spill containment and cleanup is essential now that most of the Arctic nations have begun marine drilling in areas of seasonal pack ice. Canada and the United States have developed excellent bilateral relations among officials involved with the Beaufort Sea,[30] but the techniques are still totally inadequate to cope with the nature of the oil-spill problem in pack ice.[31] International co-operation with the Soviet Union was limited even before the Afghanistan invasion; but since then it has become almost non-existent, certainly in terms of North America. Science, like the Olympics, can be highly politicized.

The last decade has seen the North emerge as a fundamental new component for Canadian foreign policy. With the *Manhattan* and *Polar Sea* voyages Canadians were made aware that their traditional complacency constituted a serious menace, for technological change and resource scarcity were ending the isolation of the Arctic. . . . [T]he North has contributed emotional ingredients to the Canadian identity that are now thrown into doubt. Recently, as Peter Dobell stressed: "The arctic became a kind of test of Canada's resolve to hold onto its birthright."[32] This defensive response must now be channelled into more positive and creative multilateral efforts. We will achieve our goals with the United States only if wider international support can be mobilized, as was done with the Law of the Sea. To our advantage, profound changes are under way right across the Arctic, and these are affecting all nations. We must recognize and seek to mobilize the emerging international concerns that Dosman and others have drawn attention to. "An embryonic international sub-system is in the process of formation in the circumpolar north which requires continuous, rather than sporadic, monitoring. In other words, Canada requires a northern foreign policy and a coherent set of policy instruments for its effective implementation."[33] As a precondition for this initiative, Canada must sort out its own priorities with regard to domestic northern policy. Links to the United States draw us towards a pro-development stance; links to Greenland and the Inuit Circumpolar Conference push us towards a conservationist/environmentalist approach.

In approaching this joint problem of defining a domestic policy to create a foundation for a foreign policy, Canada would be wise to study the efforts of Norway to develop its "Nordpolitik." Norway has jurisdictional disputes with the Soviet Union over the Svalbard Archipelago and the

Barents Sea involving fisheries, minerals, and petroleum exploration. Norway is a member of NATO but has no allied troops or nuclear weapons on its soil. In 1981, Johan Holst, the Norwegian State Secretary for the Ministry of Foreign Affairs, defined his country's position in the following manner:

> The overall objective . . . is to develop a framework for a stable order in the high North based on a balance of power maintained at the lowest possible level of military activity, and a pattern of cooperation which cuts across and reduces the saliency of the military competition. This is the essence of the Norwegian "Nordpolitik" which may become an important element in the broader construction of East-West relations in Europe in the 1980s.[34]

A balance of power at the lowest level of military activity, plus economic, scientific, and environmental co-operation, appears to be central to Canadian interests in the Arctic as well. Ottawa obviously has problems ahead with the United States (marine jurisdiction) and the Soviet Union (defence) so we must build new diplomatic bridges to Greenland, Iceland, and the Nordic countries, which share many of our concerns. Nordic Europe and Iceland have followed a curious combination of alignment and non-alignment policies. Yet all these nations, including Finland, have demonstrated a commitment to regional stability that makes their area unique in the context of postwar East–West tensions. These are traditions Canada must seek to emulate and mobilize for the wider benefit of all other Arctic nations. Canada should take the initiative in hosting a circumpolar conference of the nations bordering on the Arctic Ocean, to include also Finland and Sweden. This would be a regular regional forum where international Arctic agreements could be discussed without the complications of the other 150 members of the United Nations and allowing the middle powers to exert some pressure collectively on the two superpowers.

The above is not meant to imply that the task will be easy, for there have been few past successes like the Polar Bear Treaty. Norway and the Soviet Union have serious differences in their northern seas, just as Canada and the United States have over the Northwest Passage. Canada and Greenland have basic differences over tanker traffic in Baffin Bay and Davis Strait, as do Greenland and Norway on fisheries jurisdiction in the Jan Mayen zone. Over all these disputes hangs the bitter Cold War confrontation between the Soviet Union and the United States with its particular Arctic focus. Yet a joint initiative by Canada and one of the Nordic countries would be hard for Washington and Moscow to ignore. The propaganda value to the other would be too high. While the Brezhnev proposal for an Arctic nuclear-free zone was clearly one-sided, yet there are alternatives that countries such as Norway have explored that are far more balanced. If there is to be progress on this issue it must be now, before the full deployment of the rival fleets of cruise missiles and their launching bombers. It is certainly in Canada's interest to keep these bases out of its Arctic islands; unless some progress is made in arms limitations, though, there is little likelihood of the United States allowing Canada any option on this issue, as was the case with the cruise missile testing. A council of Arctic nations might help to put the bilateral talks between Washington and Moscow into a wider framework of debate and improve the chances of success.

As we move through the 1980s human activity in the Arctic will continue to increase and the flow of events will tend to follow one of two roads. Events will be dominated by the competitive economic and military rivalry of the current scene or by a more co-operative approach such as that illustrated by the Nordic countries. Canada, for the sake of its position in the world and for its own selfish interest, must work to see the success of the second option. We cannot become the armed buffer zone for the two feuding superpowers. That would be no future for the Arctic and its peoples.

• Notes

1 E.J. Dosman, "The Northern Sovereignty Crisis, 1968–1970" in *The Arctic in Question* (Toronto, 1976), 34–57.

2 J.A. Beesley, Department of External Affairs, speech to American Society of International Law, Syracuse, NY, 8 April 1972, 9.

3 House of Commons, *Debates*, April 1970; Dosman, *The National Interest: The Politics of Northern Development, 1968-1978* (Toronto, 1978), 58–59; *Canada Gazette*, pt. 2, vol. 106, no. 16 (23 Sept. 1972); D. Pharand, "Canada's Jurisdiction in the Arctic" in *A Century of Canada's Arctic Islands, 1880–1980,* ed. M. Zaslow (Ottawa, 1981), 111–30.

4 Pierre Trudeau, speech to the Canadian Press Association, 15 April 1970.

5 K.M. M'Gonigle, "Unilateralism and International Law," University of Toronto, *Faculty of Law Review* 34 (1976): 189.

6 House of Commons, *Debates*, 15 April 1970, 5923.

7 Quoted in W. Rowland, *The Plot to Save the World: The Stockholm Conference on the Human Environment* (Toronto, 1973), 107.

8 *United Convention on the Law of the Sea,* A/Conf 62/122.7, Oct. 1982, New York, 103.

9 Donat Pharand, "The Northwest Passage in International Law," *Canadian Yearbook of International Law* 17 (1979): 112. On the basis of the Corfu Channel case of 1949, Pharand argues that the International Court has established that "a strait must have been a useful route for maritime traffic" before being called an international strait.

10 E.J. Dosman and F. Abele, "Offshore Diplomacy in the Canadian Arctic," *Journal of Canadian Studies* 16, 2 (Summer 1981): 11.

11 I.T. Gault, *The International Legal Context of Petroleum Operations in Canadian Arctic Waters* (Calgary, 1983), 66–69.

12 Companies holding exploration leases include Petro-Canada, Canadian Superior, Dome, Amoco, Wainco, and the Alberta/Ontario Group. The Natsek well (dry hole) appears to be just inside the disputed zone. Information from map, *Oilweek,* 14 June 1982.

13 Pharand, "Canada's Jurisdiction in the Arctic," 116.

14 Ibid., 118.

15 L.H. Legault, "Canadian Practice in International Law," *Canadian Yearbook of International Law* 19 (1981): 321.

16 Stephen Clarkson, *Canada and the Reagan Challenge* (Toronto, 1982), 71.

17 Jennifer Lewington, in *Globe and Mail* (Toronto), 17 Feb. 1982.

18 Information from interview with Bruce Willson, former president of Canadian Bechtel Ltd.

19 The Blair–Carr report had suggested a 3 percent preference for Canadian bids, which the cabinet did not adopt. Clarkson, *Canada and the Reagan Challenge*, 111.

20 William Brock to Canadian ambassador, 4 Dec. 1981, quoted ibid., 42–44.

21 The letter was leaked to Richard Gwyn of the *Toronto Star*; see Gwyn article of 25 June 1983.

22 The tradition of little interest in Canadian–American relations is a long one for successive American secretaries of state. For instance, in the Kissinger memoirs there is virtually no analysis of Canadian–American relations and hardly any mention of Canada as a factor in American foreign policy.

23 The scale of PIP grants was: 1981, $608 million; 1982, $1.4 billion; estimate for 1983, $2 billion. In 1982 alone, Dome received $469 million. *Energy Analects*, 12, 19 Aug. 1983.

24 Lincoln P. Bloomfield, "The Arctic: Last Unmanaged Frontier," *Foreign Affairs* 60, 1 (1981): 91. Bloomfield had served on the National Security Council for President Carter.

25 Henry Kissinger, *Years of Upheaval* (New York, 1982), 11, 172.

26 The B-52s have used Northern Canada for training purposes for some years, as the author found out when he was buzzed by one while on a canoe trip in Northern Ontario.

27 C. Archer and D. Scrivener, "Frozen Frontiers and Resource Wrangles," *International Affairs* 59, 1 (Winter 1982–83): 65.

28 Bloomfield, "The Arctic: Last Unmanaged Frontier," 92.

29 Ibid., 94.

30 Dosman and Abele, "Offshore Diplomacy in the Canadian Arctic," 5.

31 R. Page, "The High Arctic: Environmental Concerns, Government Control and Economic Development" in *Century of Canada's Arctic Islands*, 243.

32 P. Dobell, *Canada's Search for New Roles* (Toronto, 1972), 24.

33 Dosman and Abele, "Offshore Diplomacy in the Canadian Arctic," 3.

34 Johan J. Holst, "Norway's Search for a Nordpolitik," *Foreign Affairs* 60, 1 (Fall 1981): 66.

Life in a Fast-Food Factory*

ESTER REITER

The growth of large multinational corporations in the service industries in the post–World War II years has transformed our lives. The needs and tastes of the public are shaped by the huge advertising budgets of a few large corporations. The development of new industries has transformed work, as well as social life. This paper focusses on the technology and the labour process in the fast-food sector of the restaurant industry. Using Marx's description of the transitions from craft to manufacture to large-scale industry, it considers the changes in the restaurant industry brought about by the development of fast-food chains. The description of life in a fast-food factory is based on my experience working in a Burger King outlet in 1980–81.

• The Rise of the Fast-Food Industry

Eating out is big business. The restaurant industry in Canada has grown from some 14 000 establishments in 1951 to nearly 30 000 in 1978.[1] Sales in 1982 were 9.6 billion dollars nationally, which, even taking into account the declining value of the dollar, is still a sixfold increase over the past thirty years.[2] Although people with higher incomes dine out more frequently, *all* Canadians are spending money on food away from home. In 1978, over 32 cents of every food dollar was spent on food outside the home.[3]

*From Craig Heron and Robert Storey, eds., *On the Job: Confronting the Labour Process in Canada* (Montreal: McGill-Queen's University Press, 1986), 309–26. Reprinted with the permission of the publisher.

Since the late 1960s, fast-food restaurants have been growing at a much higher rate than independent restaurants, virtually colonizing the suburbs.[4] Local differences in taste and style are obliterated as each town offers the familiar array of trademarked foods: neat, clean, and orderly, the chains serve up the same goods from Nova Scotia to Vancouver Island. The casualties of this phenomenal growth are the small "mom and pop" establishments, rather than the higher-priced, full-service restaurants. Fast-food outlets all conform to a general pattern. Each has a limited menu, usually featuring hamburger, chicken, or fried fish. Most are part of a chain, and most require customers to pick up their own food at a counter.[5] The common elements are minimum delay in getting the food to the customer (hence "fast food") and prices that are relatively low compared to those at full-service restaurants.

The fast-food industry is an example of what Harry Braverman called the extension of the universal market.[6] That is, the family moves into the sphere of the market. The effect of this "extension" on the family has been varied. Often, new technology applied to some household task at first removes the activity from the home; later, still newer technologies return the activity to the home in an altered form. By the late 1930s, for example, many families had come to send a good part of their laundry to power laundries; later when washing machines were widely available, the laundry was returned to the home—to be washed, most often, by women.[7] Similarly, the development of the movie industry during the first half of the twentieth century drew people out of their homes. After television was developed, however, the market at home proved more lucrative, and now virtually every Canadian family has at least one television set, while the movie industry has been declining since the 1950s.[8]

The entry of capital into the food production and consumption process has had several different effects. In the 1930s, for instance, techniques were developed for the quick freezing of foods. The perfection of these techniques made it possible to purchase increasingly diverse arrays of foods that need only be "heated and served." By the 1950s, the growth of large shopping-plaza supermarkets overwhelmed grocery stores, putting the small, independent corner grocer out of business.[9] Shopping trips can be less frequent when large amounts of frozen and packaged foods are purchased, and the huge increase in families owning automobiles made possible visits to the more distant, large shopping plazas.

Seeking to supplement their sales to the supermarkets, large food processors like Kraft began to market their products to the restaurant industry in the late 1960s. Most food production has been taken over by large corporations, but now different capital interests wrestle with each other to determine whether food consumption is going to take place in public businesses or in the home. Restaurant officials welcomed the new products (such as preportioned jellies, frozen entrees, and canned soups) enthusiastically. In 1967, one restaurant official predicted that "custom-made food will soon be as luxurious as custom-made automobiles or shirts."[10] As these new processed, preportioned foods were introduced into public eating places, franchised restaurants began to appear in Canada. These were usually connected to larger parent companies that had started a few years earlier in the United States. "Franchising" confers the right, on payment of an agreed fee, to sell certain products under a recognized trade name; the items are backed by national advertisements and on-the-spot promotions. The products offered are limited in number and are produced in prescribed ways, using machinery specified by and purchased from the franchisor.[11]

During the early years, fast-food franchising seemed like a bottomless gold mine, and indeed a few western operators became millionaires when Colonel Sanders' Kentucky Fried Chicken was first franchised in Canada. The franchise system seemed to offer the small businessperson the opportunity of a lifetime: permitting a big corporation to dictate how a business should be run promised to minimize risks in this very risky business. By 1970, *Canadian Hotel and Restaurant* magazine estimated that about 75 percent of all fast-food outlets were controlled by franchising companies. Three companies, Kentucky Fried Chicken, A & W, and Chicken Delight—all affiliates of United States corporations—together controlled 60 percent of the 1457 franchised outlets in Canada. The large multinational corporations that produced grocery products extended their interest in the restaurant industry by entering it directly in the late 1960s with the purchase of restaurant chains. For example, Lever Brothers Ltd., a wholly owned subsidiary of Unilever, acquired A & W Food Services of Canada and Shopsy's Foods Ltd. General Foods acquired the White Spots restaurant chain in Western Canada, as well as two other chains: Canterbury Foods (which ran the Crock 'n Block restaurants) and the "1867" restaurants. General Foods is one of the largest processors of packaged groceries, with products ranging from coffee (Maxwell House, Yuban, Sanka, Brim) to breakfast cereals and dessert foods under the "Jell-O," "Bird's Eye," and "Minute Brand" names.[12]

The largest of the fast-food restaurants—McDonald's—entered the Canadian market in 1968. Since May 1983, over 450 of its outlets were operating in Canada, posting $636.5 million in gross annual sales—part of an empire of 6800 stores in 27 countries with more than $25 billion in sales in 1983. The second-largest fast-food chain is Burger King. Founded in 1954 by James McLamore and David Edgerton, Burger King became a wholly owned subsidiary of Pillsbury in 1967, during the first wave of mergers between packaged-food and restaurant chains. The company grew from 257 restaurants at the time of the merger to 3022 by May 1981. About 130 000 people are employed in Burger Kings all over the world. By November 1982, there were 87 Burger King stores in Canada, 40 of them company owned.[13] The Canadian-owned company stores operated at an average gross profit of 60 percent in 1980–81.

• Transforming the Operations of a Kitchen

Until approximately twenty-five years ago, all restaurant work involved an extensive division of labour: a complex hierarchy within the kitchen required workers with varying levels of skill and training. For a restaurant to be successful, all workers had to co-ordinate their efforts. A supervisor's function was not only to ensure that the work was done, but to see that the various parts of the operation were synchronized. William Whyte, who studied the restaurant industry in the United States, described the production process:

> Timing and coordination are the keynotes of the operation. If the customer does not get his food when he wants it, he is upset. If the waitress cannot get it from the service pantry, she chafes at the delay. And so on down into the kitchen. A breakdown anywhere in the chain of production, transfer and service sends repercussions through the entire organization. No one can fail to feel its effects, for the restaurant is an organization made up of highly interdependent parts. If one part fails to function, the organization can no longer operate.
>
> The parts are the people who handle the food and adjust their work to each other. But cooks, pantry girls, waitresses, and other workers are not the only important parts. To keep this delicately adjusted machine functioning requires supervision of a high order. At each important point there must be a supervisor helping to organize the work of the employees and to organize their relations with each other to eliminate the friction and build up the cooperation essential to efficiency.[14]

This production arrangement resembles what Marx called "manufacture." In the restaurant described by William Whyte, the skill of the worker remains central to the production process. The commodity created (the meal served to the customer) is the social product of many workers' efforts. Human beings, using tools to assist them in their work, remain the organs of the productive mechanism.

In the fast-food industry, the machines, or the instruments of labour, assume a central place. Instead of assisting workers in the production of the meal, the machines tended by workers are dominant; we now have an objective organization of machines confronting the worker. Marx described this as the transition from "manufacture" to "large-scale industry."[15] Since the motion of the factory proceeds from the machinery and not from the worker, working personnel can continually be replaced. Frequent change in workers will not disrupt the labour process—a shift in organization applauded by *Harvard Business Review* contributor Theodore Levitt.[16] According to Levitt, this new model is intended to replace the "humanistic concept of service" with the kind of technocratic thinking that in other fields has replaced "the high cost and erratic elegance of the artisan with the low-cost munificence of the manufacturer." McDonald's is a "supreme" example of this kind of thinking.

> The systematic substitution of equipment for people, combined with the carefully planned use and positioning of technology, enables McDonald's to attract and hold patronage in proportions no predecessor or imitator has managed to duplicate. . . . If machinery is to be viewed as a piece of equipment with the capability of producing a predictably standardized customer-satisfying output while minimizing the operating discretion of its attendant, that is what a McDonald's outlet is. It is a machine that produces with the help of totally unskilled machine tenders, a highly polished product. Through painstaking attention to total design and facilities planning, everything is built integrally into the machine itself, into the technology of the system. The only choice available to the attendant is to operate it exactly as the designers intended.

The labour process so admired by Levitt has been adopted by many of the large fast-food companies. In the case of Burger King, the adoption has been a literal one: Donald Smith, the operations executive at McDonald's who developed this system, was hired away in January 1977 to become president of Burger King. There, he initiated a number of projects under the heading "Operation Grand Slam," which changed the system of menu and food preparation in an effort to duplicate McDonald's success.[17]

• Managing a Store

The brain centre of all Burger King outlets, company owned or franchised, lies in Burger King headquarters in Miami, Florida. It is there that the Burger King bible, the *Manual of Operating Data, is* prepared. The procedures laid down in the manual must be followed to the letter by all Burger King stores. To ensure that procedures are indeed followed, each outlet is investigated and graded twice yearly by a team from regional headquarters. Termed a "Restaurant Operations Consultation," the assessment administered by the investigators gives each store a numerical grade according to a detailed forty-three-page list of what to look for and how many points each particular aspect is worth. When a store is being investigated, both managers and workers clean frenetically and work as hard as possible. A great deal depends on these investigations, as a manager could be transferred or demoted, or a franchisee's license withdrawn, if the showing is poor.

The criteria for grading a store give heavy weighting to those items that are crucial to a store's profitability. Profitability rests primarily on the volume of a store's sales and the cost of those sales. Therefore, cleanliness, not only in the food-production area but also in the toilets and the surrounding parking area, is stressed so that customers will be attracted to the store. In order to maximize volume and minimize labour costs, there is tremendous emphasis on what Burger King management calls SOS or speed of service. The demand on an individual unit's production capacity can fluctuate as much as 1000 percent over an hour in the period before a lunch or dinner to the height of the meal rush. Demand is at its peak during the lunch hour, which accounts for about 20 percent of sales for the day; the more people served during the hours of twelve to one, the higher the sales volume in the store.

Up Front, the Burger King publication for store managers, reminds them that "an aware manager understands that maintaining speed of service is like putting money in the bank."[18] Miami studies are referred to that show customers will wait patiently for only three minutes from the moment of entering the store; after that, they will walk away. Ideally, then, service time should never exceed three minutes.[19] Labour costs are also kept down by minimizing the use of full-time workers and by hiring minimum-wage part-time workers. Workers are asked to fill out an availability sheet when they are hired, indicating the hours they can work. Particularly when students are involved, management pressures them to make themselves as available as possible, though no guarantees are provided for how many hours a week work they will be given, or on which days they will be asked to work.

Burger King pushed the common restaurant industry practice of using part-time workers one step further in 1978 with the development of a new labour-scheduling method called the "people game." Under this new system, hourly sales projections are recorded, based upon the previous three weeks' sales. Hourly manning guides are then used to allot labour for each hour's projected sales. Scheduling is done each week for the coming week and workers are expected to come to the store and check the labour schedule each week to see when they are supposed to show up. The *Manual of Operating Data* recommends that as many short shifts as possible be assigned, so that few breaks will be required. This rule, the manual notes, is especially important in areas where labour laws require paid breaks.

Food and paper costs make up about 40 percent of the cost of sales in Burger King outlets. These costs are essentially fixed, owing to company requirements that all Burger King outlets buy their stock from approved distributors. While such a policy offers the advantages of bulk purchasing, it also ties each outlet to costs set by head-office negotiations, leaving little room for purchase-cost reductions. In effect, individual stores have control over food costs in only two areas—"waste" of food and meals provided to employees. Both together make up less than 4 percent of the cost of sales. "Waste" consists of food pre-prepared for lunch and dinner shifts that is not sold in the time limit set for each food (ten minutes for sandwiches, five minutes for fries). The discarded food is carefully counted and recorded after each meal rush. Employees are under pressure to have enough food ready so that customers can be served quickly, but are held responsible for any "waste" that results. A chart on the kitchen wall graphs the waste percentage each day. Employee meals are also monitored, and limits on food items available to workers are imposed. For example, while workers were formerly allowed any sandwich, fries or dessert, and a drink, they are now allowed a meal costing not more than $2.50 in menu prices. A manager must inspect all choices, and initial the meal selection listed by workers on their time cards.

Store operations are designed from head office in Miami. In 1980, this office commissioned a study to find ways of lowering labour costs, increasing workers' productivity, and maintaining the most efficient inventories. The various components of a restaurant's operations were defined: customer arrival patterns, manning or positioning strategies, customer/cashier interactions, order characteristics, production-time standards, stocking rules and inventory. Time-motion reports for making the various menu items, as well as corporate standards for service were also included in the calculation, and the data were all entered into a computer. By late 1981, it was possible to provide store managers not only with a staffing chart for hourly sales—indicating how many people should be on the floor given the predicted volume of business for that hour—but also where they should be positioned, based on the type of kitchen design. Thus, although staffing had been regulated since the late 1970s, what discretion managers formerly had in assigning and utilizing workers has been eliminated. The use of labour is now calculated precisely, as is any other objectively defined component of the system, such as store design, packaging, and inventory.[20]

Having determined precisely what workers are supposed to be doing and how quickly they should be doing it, the only remaining issue is that of getting them to perform to specifications. "Burger King University," located at headquarters in Miami, was set up to achieve this goal. Housed in a remodelled art gallery, the multimillion-dollar facility is staffed by a group of "professors" who have worked their way up in the Burger King system to the rank of district manager. Burger King trains its staff to do things "not well, but right," the Burger King way.[21] Tight control over Burger King restaurants throughout the world rests on standardizing operations—doing things the "right" way—so that outcomes are predictable. The manager of a Burger King outlet does not necessarily need any knowledge of restaurant operations because the company provides it. What Burger King calls "people skills" are required; thus a job description for a manager indicated that he/she

- Must have good verbal communication skills
- Must have patience, tact, fairness, and social sensitivity in dealing with customers and hourly employees
- Must be able to supervise and motivate team of youthful employees and conduct himself/herself in a professional manner
- Must present a neat, well-groomed image
- Must be willing to work nights, weekends and holidays[22]

In 1981, a new crew-training program, designed as an outcome of the computer-simulation study, was developed. The training program is called "The Basics of Our Business" and is meant to "thoroughly train crew members in all areas of operations and to educate them on how Burger King and the restaurant where they work . . . fit into the American free-enterprise system." In addition, the training program involves supervised work at each station, and a new feature that requires every employee to pass a standardized test on appropriate procedures for each station in the store.

Burger King thus operates with a combination of control techniques: technology is used to simplify the work and facilitate centralization, while direct control or coercion is exercised on the floor to make sure the pace of the work remains swift. "If there's time to lean, there's time to clean," is a favourite saying among managers. In fact, workers are expected to be very busy *all* the time they are on shifts, whether or not there are customers in the store. Sitting down is never permissible; in fact, the only chair in the entire kitchen is in the manager's office in a glassed-in cubicle at the rear of the kitchen. From there, the manager can observe the workers at their jobs. The application of these techniques is supported by a legitimizing ideology that calls for "patience, fairness, and social sensitivity" in dealing with customers in order to increase sales and profits "for the betterment of Burger King corporation and its employees."[23]

• Working at Burger King

I did fieldwork on the fast-food industry by working at a Burger King outlet in suburban Toronto in 1980–81. The Burger King at which I worked was opened in 1979, and by 1981 was the highest-volume store in Canada with annual sales of over one million dollars. Everything in the customers' part of the store was new, shiny, and spotlessly clean. Live plants lent a touch of class to the seating area. Muzak wafted through the air, but customers sat on chairs designed to be sufficiently uncomfortable to achieve the desired customer turnover rate of one every twenty minutes. Outside the store, customers could eat at concrete picnic tables and benches in a professionally landscaped setting, weather permitting. Lunches, particularly Thursdays, Fridays, and Saturdays, were the busiest times, and during those periods customers were lined up at all the registers waiting to be served. During the evenings, particularly on Friday nights, families with young children were very much in evidence. Young children, kept amused by the plastic give-away toys provided by the restaurant and sporting Burger King crowns, sat contentedly munching their fries and sipping their carbonated drinks.

Workers use the back entrance at Burger King when reporting for work. Once inside, they go to a small room (about seven by twelve feet), which is almost completely occupied by an oblong table where crew members have their meals. Built-in benches stretch along both sides of the wall,

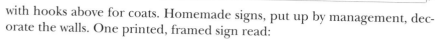

with hooks above for coats. Homemade signs, put up by management, decorate the walls. One printed, framed sign read:

WHY CUSTOMERS QUIT

1% die
2% move away
5% develop other friendships
9% competitive reasons
14% product dissatisfactions
68% quit because of ATTITUDE OF INDIFFERENCE TOWARDS CUSTOMER BY RESTAURANT MANAGER OR SERVICE PERSONNEL

Another sign reminded employees that only $1/3$ ounce of ketchup and $1/9$ ounce of mustard is supposed to go on the hamburgers; a crew member using more is cheating the store, while one using less is not giving customers "value" for their dollar.

The crew room is usually a lively place. An AM/FM radio is tuned to a rock station while the teenage workers coming off or on shift talk about school and weekend activities or flirt with each other. Children and weddings are favourite topics of conversation for the older workers. In the evenings, the talk and horsing around among the younger workers gets quite spirited, and now and then a manager appears to quieten things down. Management initiatives are not all geared to control through discipline; social activities such as skating parties, baseball games, and dances are organized by "production leaders" with the encouragement of the managers—an indication that the potentially beneficial effects for management of channelling the informal social relationships at the workplace are understood. Each worker must punch a time card at the start of a shift. The management urges people to come upstairs five minutes before starting time. The time card, however, is not to be punched until it is time for the scheduled shift to actually begin. A positioning chart, posted near the time clock, lists the crew members who are to work each meal, and indicates where in the kitchen they are to be stationed.

There are no pots and pans in the Burger King kitchen. As almost all foods enter the store ready for the final cooking process, pots and pans are not necessary. Hamburgers arrive in the form of patties; french fries are precut and partially precooked; so are the chicken, fish, and veal to be used in sandwiches. Buns are precut and ready to be toasted, while condiments like pickles and onions arrive in the store presliced. Lettuce comes preshredded; only the tomatoes are sliced on the premises. The major kitchen equipment consists of the broiler/toaster, the fry vats, the milkshake and coke machines, and the microwave ovens. In the near future, new drink machines will be installed in all Burger King outlets that will automatically portion the drinks; the hot-cocoa machine already operates in this way. Even when made from scratch, hamburgers do not require particularly elaborate preparation, and whatever minimal decision making might once have been necessary is now completely eliminated by machines. At Burger King, hamburgers are cooked as they pass through the broiler on a conveyor belt at a rate of 835 patties per hour. Furnished with a pair of tongs, the worker picks up the burgers as they drop off the conveyor belt, puts each on a toasted bun, and places the hamburgers and buns in a steamer. The jobs may be hot and boring, but they can be learned in a matter of minutes.

The more interesting part of the procedure lies in applying condiments and microwaving the hamburgers. The popularity of this task among Burger King employees rests on the fact that it is unmechanized and allows some discretion to the worker. As the instructions for preparing a "Whopper" (the Burger King name for a large hamburger) indicates, however, management is aware of this area of worker freedom and makes strenuous efforts to eliminate it by outlining exactly how this job is to be performed:

- remove preassembled sandwich from steamer
- sandwiches in the steamer are good for 10 minutes maximum— do not take more than 2 sandwiches at one time
- the HEEL which is the lower part of the sandwich is composed of bun heel and meat patty goes in whopper carton
- on the mat we place 4 pickle slices evenly over the meat on each corner
- then we add $1/2$ oz. ketchup evenly in a spiral circular motion, over the pickles, starting from the outside edges of the meat and work your way to centre
- then place $1/2$ oz. of onions evenly over the ketchup in such a way that there will be a bit of onion in every bite of the sandwich . . .

Despite such directives, the "Burger and Whopper Board" positions continue to hold their attraction for the workers, for this station requires two people to work side by side, and thus allows the opportunity for conversation. During busy times, as well, employees at this station also derive some work satisfaction from their ability to "keep up." At peak times, a supply of ready-made sandwiches is placed in chutes ready for the cashiers to pick up; the manager decides how many sandwiches should be in the chutes according to a formula involving sales predictions for that time period. At such times, the challenge is to keep pace with the demand and not leave the cashiers waiting for their orders. The managers will sometimes spur the "Whopper-makers" on with cries of "Come on guys, let's get with it," or "Let's go, team."

As with the production of hamburgers, the cooking of french fries involves virtually no worker discretion. The worker, following directions laid out in the *Manual of Operating Data,* empties the frozen, precut, bagged fries into fry baskets about two hours before they will be needed. When cooked fries are needed, the worker takes a fry basket from the rack and places it on a raised arm above the hot oil, and presses the "on" button. The arm holding the fry basket descends into the oil, and emerges two minutes and twenty seconds later; a buzzer goes off and the worker dumps the fries into the fry station tray where they are kept warm by an overhead light. To ensure that the proper portions are placed into bags, a specially designed tool is used to scoop the fries up from the warming table. Jobs at this station are generally reserved for boys, as the work goes more quickly with a strong wrist. The job can get quite hectic when only one worker is at the station because cooked fries must be on hand when needed. The fry-tender must put new baskets down, take the cooked fries out and bag them, and all the while make certain there are enough partially cooked onion rings ready. At peak periods, the worker seems to be running constantly to keep up with the buzzers. Working near the oil makes one feel slimy; teenagers working at this station commonly complain that they tend to develop pimples.

Even at this station, though, management is concerned about limiting what little worker discretion is possible. Despite the use of a specially designed scoop to control the portions each customer is given, a sign placed in the crew room for a few weeks admonished crew about being too generous with fry portions.

> FRY YIELD Fry yield is the amount of regular portions you get from the total amount of fries used. The ideal amount is 410 portions from each 100 lb. of fries used.
>
> At the moment our fry yield is in the unacceptable range of 365–395 portions of fries for each 100 lb. of fries which is below Burger King standards.

At the cash register, the "counter hostess" takes the order and rings it up on the computerized register. The "documentor" contains eighty-eight colour-coded items, ensuring that all variations of an order are automatically priced. For example, a hamburger with extra tomatoes can be punched in, and the ten-cent charge for the extra tomatoes will appear on the printout. As a menu item is punched in at the counter, it will appear on printers in the appropriate location in the kitchen. In this manner, the worker at sandwiches, for example, can look up at the printer and check what kind of sandwich is required. When the customer hands over the money, the cashier rings in "amount tendered" and the correct amount of change to be returned to the customer is rung up. Thus, cashiers need only remember to smile and ask customers to come again. Although it takes a few days working at the cash register to build up speed, the basics can be learned in a few hours.

The computerized cash register not only simplifies ordering and payment, but is used to monitor sales and thus assist in staffing. If sales are running lower than expected, some workers will be asked to leave early. It is difficult for workers to turn down the managers' request: "Wouldn't you like to go home early today?" But on more than one occasion, workers complained that the cost of bus fare ate up almost their entire earning for that shift. Output at each station is also monitored through the cash register. Finally, the computer at all company stores is linked through a modem to the head office in Miami. Top management has access to information on the performance of each store on a daily basis, and this information is routed back to the Canadian division headquarters in Mississauga.

Unlike the tremendous variation in skills in running the restaurant of the 1940s, skill levels required in a Burger King have been reduced to a common denominator. In a traditional restaurant of the 1940s, there was a wide variation in the levels of skills needed to do each necessary job: a trained chef would have spent many years developing his or her craft, while the dishwasher would have learned the necessary skills in a few days. At Burger King, the goal is to reduce all skills to a common, easily learned level and to provide for crosstraining. At the completion of the ten-hour training program, each worker is able to work at a few stations. Skills for any of the stations can be learned in a matter of hours; the simplest jobs, such as filling cups with drinks, or placing the hamburgers and buns on the conveyor belt, can be learned in minutes. As a result, although labour turnover cuts into the pace of making hamburgers, adequate functioning of the restaurant is never threatened by people leaving. However, if workers are to be as replaceable as possible, they must be taught not only to perform their jobs in the same way, but also to resemble each other in attitudes, disposition, and appearance. Thus, workers are taught not only to perform according to company rules, but also are drilled on personal hygiene, dress (shoes should be brown leather or vinyl, not suede), coiffure (hair tied up for girls and not too long for boys), and personality. Rule 17 of the handout to new employees underlines the importance of smiling: "Smile at all times, your smile is the key to our success."

While management seeks to make workers into interchangeable tools, workers themselves are expected to make a strong commitment to the store. If they wish to keep jobs at Burger King, they must abide by the labour schedule:

> You must be able to close two times a week, that is be available from four o'clock till midnight on weekdays, or 1 A.M. on Friday or Saturday nights. The schedules you fill in apply for the school semester. In the summer we know everybody can work all hours. All part timers (those who work after school) must indicate availability for weekends.[24]

Workers, especially teenagers, are, then, expected to adjust their activities to the requirements of Burger King. For example, workers must apply to their manager two weeks in advance to get time off to study for exams or attend family functions. Parents are seen by management as creating problems for the store, as they do not always appreciate Burger King's demand for priority in their children's schedules. Thus, the manager warns new trainees to "remember, your parents don't work here and don't understand the situation. If you're old enough to ask for a job, you're old enough to be responsible for coming."[25]

• The Workers

One of the results of the transformation of the labour process from one of "manufacture" to that of "large-scale industry" is the emerging market importance of the young worker. While artisans require long training to achieve their skills, a machine-tender's primary characteristics are swiftness and endurance. Thus, young workers become ideal commodities: they are cheap, energetic, and in plentiful supply. As well, they can be used as a marketing tool for the industry: the mass-produced, smiling teenager, serving up the symbols of the good life in North America—hamburgers, cokes, and fries.

Making up about 75 percent of the Burger King work force, the youngsters who worked after school, on weekends, and on holidays were called "part-timers." The teenager workers (about half of them boys, half girls) seemed to vary considerably in background. Some were college-bound youngsters who discussed their latest physics exam while piling on the pickles. Others were marking time until they reached the age of sixteen and could leave school. One brother and sister had a father who was unemployed and ill; they were helping to pay the family's rent and food. Some of the teenagers spent all the money they earned on clothes, food, and entertainment, while others saved a portion of their earnings. Given the low pay, and the erratic scheduling, none of the Burger King workers could depend on their jobs for their total financial support.

The daytime workers—the remaining 25 percent of the work force—were primarily married women of mixed economic backgrounds. Consistent with a recent study of part-time workers in Canada, most of these women contributed their wages to the family budget.[26] Although they were all working primarily because their families needed the money, a few women expressed their relief at getting out of the house, even to come to Burger King. One woman said: "At least when I come here, I'm appreciated. If I do a good job, a manager will say something to me. Here, I feel like a person. I'm sociable and I like being amongst people. At home, I'm always cleaning up after everybody and nobody ever notices!"[27] Many of these women would arrive at work early in order to have a coffee and talk with one another—an interaction denied them in the isolation of their homes, where they are still responsible for all of the domestic labour.

Common to both the teenagers and the housewives was the view that working at Burger King was peripheral to their major commitments and responsibilities; the part-time nature of the work contributed to this attitude. Workers saw the alternative available to them as putting up with the demands of Burger King or leaving; in fact, leaving seemed to be the dominant form of protest. During my period in the store, on average, eleven people out of ninety-four hourly employees quit at each two-week pay period. While a few workers had stayed at Burger King for periods as long as a few years, many did not last through the first two weeks. The need for workers is constant; occasionally even the paper place-mats on the customers' trays invited people to work in the "Burger King family." "If you're enthusiastic and like to learn, this is the opportunity for you. Just complete the application and return it to the counter." At other times, bounties were offered for live workers. A sign that hung in the crew room for a few weeks read:

> Wanna make $10?
> It's easy! All you have to do is refer a friend to me for employment. Your friend must be able to work over lunch (Monday–Friday). If your friend works here for at least one month, you get $20. (And I'm not talking Burger Bucks either.)

Burger King's ability to cope with high staff turnover means that virtually no concessions in pay or working conditions are offered to workers to entice them to remain at Burger King. In fact, more attention is paid to the maintenance of the machinery than to "maintaining" the workers; time is regularly scheduled for cleaning and servicing the equipment, but workers may not leave the kitchen to take a drink or use the bathroom during the lunch and dinner rushes.

The dominant form—in the circumstances, the only easily accessible form—of opposition to the Burger King labour process is, then, the act of quitting. Management attempts to head off any other form of protest by insisting on an appropriate "attitude" on the part of the workers. Crew members must constantly demonstrate their satisfaction with working at Burger King by smiling at all times. However, as one worker remarked, "Why should I smile? There's nothing funny around here. I do my job and that should be good enough for them." It was not, however, and this worker soon quit. Another woman who had worked in the store for over a year also left. A crew member informed me that she had been fired for having a "poor attitude." The same crew member commented: "It's a wonder she wasn't fired a long time ago. She didn't enjoy the work and everybody knew it." I myself was threatened with expulsion from the store for having a "poor attitude" when I obeyed, without sufficient enthusiasm, an order to move from the front counter station to the broiler/steamer station.

Several other incidents underlined the extent to which Burger King could impose its will on workers. One involved the new plan—developed in Miami and introduced into the Toronto outlet in February 1982 at a crew meeting—to cut down labour costs by intensifying work. The new training program made conditions especially difficult for production leaders, who were now expected to give workers tests to make sure they knew their stations (exactly how to make "Whoppers," how long to put them in the microwave oven, etc.) without taking time off from their normal duties. Workers experienced great difficulty in following through on this training scheme because under the new guidelines, fewer people were available to serve the same number of customers; however, there was no organized opposition to the scheme. Nor was there organized opposition when meal allotments were reduced to a $2.50 limit. Although workers grumbled about the change, no one challenged the decision. The one instance in which staff objections forced the outlet to back down involved the right to work: all workers had been told that they were expected to attend the Burger King picnic, and that those normally scheduled to work at that time would have to lose a day's pay. (Crews from another store were to be sent over to keep the outlet running.) Four crew members objected, stating that they could not afford to lose pay by going to the picnic, and management allowed them to work. Such instances were few and far between, however. As one manager informed me, Burger King was careful to dismiss any crew person who was dissatisfied: "One bad apple could ruin the whole barrel."

Management control and lack of worker opposition is further explained by the fact that other jobs open to teenagers are no better, and in some cases are worse, than the jobs at Burger King. The workers at Burger King all agreed that any job that paid the full rather than the student minimum wage would be preferable to a job at Burger King; but they also recognized that their real alternatives would often be worse. Work at a donut shop, for example, also paid student minimum wage, under conditions of greater social isolation; baby sitting was paid poorly; and the hours for a paper route were terrible. Work at Burger King was a first job for many of the teenagers, and they enjoyed their first experience of earning their own money. And at Burger King, these young men and women were in the position of meeting the public, even if the forms of contact were limited by a vocabulary developed in Burger King headquarters: "Hello. Welcome to Burger King. May I take your order?" Interaction with customers, who came in all shapes, sizes, and ages, had some intrinsic interest.

In sum, workers at Burger King are confronted with a labour process that puts management in complete control. Furnished with state-of-the-art restaurant technology, Burger King outlets employ vast numbers of teenagers and married women—a population with few skills and little commitment to working at Burger King. In part, this lack of commitment is understood through reference to a labour process that offers little or no room for work satisfaction. Most jobs can be learned in a very short time (a matter of minutes for some) and workers are required to learn every job, a fact that underlines the interchangeable nature of the jobs and the workers who do them. The work is most interesting when the store is busy; sweeping and mopping already clean floors, or wiping counters that do not really require wiping is not anyone's idea of necessary or interesting work. If the alternative to "leaning" is "cleaning," then it is far preferable to really be busy. Paradoxically, work intensity, Burger King's main form of assault on labour costs, remains the only aspect of the job that can provide any challenge for the worker. Workers would remark with pride how they "didn't fall behind at all," despite a busy lunch or dinner hour.

My findings in the fast-food industry are not very encouraging. In contrast to Michael Burawoy,[28] for example, who found that male workers in a unionized machine shop were able to set quotas and thereby establish some control over the labour process, I found that the women and teenagers at Burger King are under the sway of a labour process that eliminates almost completely the possibility of forming a workplace culture independent of, and in opposition to, management.

It would be reassuring to dismiss the fast-food industry as representing something of an anomaly in the workplace; teenagers will eventually finish school and become "real workers," while housewives with families are actually domestic workers, also not to be compared with adult males in more skilled jobs. Unfortunately, there are indications that the teenagers and women who work in this type of job represent not an anomalous but an increasingly typical kind of worker, in the one area of the economy that continues to grow—the service sector. The fast-food industry represents a model for other industries in which the introduction of technology will permit the employment of low-skilled, cheap, and plentiful workers. In this sense, it is easy to be pessimistic and find agreement with Andre Gorz's depressing formulation of the idea of work:

> The terms "work" and "job" have become interchangeable: work is no longer something that one *does* but something that one has.
> Workers no longer "produce" society through the mediation of the relations of production; instead the machinery of social production as a whole produces "work" and imposes it in a random way upon random, interchangeable individuals.[29]

The Burger King system represents a major triumph for capital: it has established a production unit with constant and variable components that are almost immediately replaceable. However, the reduction of the worker to a simple component of capital requires more than the introduction of a technology; workers' autonomous culture must be eliminated as well, including the relationships among workers, their skills, and their loyalties to one another. The smiling, willing, homogeneous worker must be produced and placed on the Burger King assembly line.

While working at Burger King, I saw for myself the extent to which Burger King has succeeded in reducing its work force to a set of interchangeable pieces. However, I also saw how insistently the liveliness and decency of the workers emerged in the informal interaction that occurred.

Open resistance is made virtually impossible by the difficulty of identifying who is responsible for the rules that govern the workplace: the workers know that managers follow orders coming from higher up. The very high turnover of employees indicates that workers come to understand that their interests and Burger King's are not one and the same. As young people and women begin to realize that their jobs in the fast-food industry are not waystations en route to more promising and fulfilling work, they will perhaps be moved to blow the whistle on the Burger King "team." The mould for the creation of the homogeneous worker assembling the standardized meal for the homogeneous consumer is not quite perfected.

• Notes

1 Dominion Bureau of Statistics (hereafter DBS), *1951 Census* (Ottawa, 1954), vol. 7, table 6; Statistics Canada, *Restaurants, Caterers and Taverns Industry* (Ottawa, 1978), cat. 65-535, tables 1, 14.

2 Statistics Canada, *Market Research Handbook* (Ottawa, 1983), cat. 63-224, tables 3–11, 169.

3 Statistics Canada, *Urban Family Food Expenditure* (Ottawa, 1978), cat. 62-548; Dominion Bureau of Statistics, *Urban Family Food Expenditure* (Ottawa, 1953), cat. 62-511.

4 Foodservice and Hospitality Magazine, *Fact File—Canada's Hospitality Business*, 4th ed. (Toronto, n.d.).

5 This definition comes from the National Restaurant Association and is reprinted in Marc Leepson, "Fast Food, U.S. Growth Industry," *Editorial Research Reports* 7 (1978): 907.

6 See Harry Braverman, *Labor and Monopoly Capital* (New York, 1954), 13.

7 Bonnie Fox, "Women's Domestic Labour and Their Involvement in Wage Work" (PhD thesis, University of Alberta, 1980), table 15-A, 427.

8 M.C. Urquhart and K.H.A. Buckley, *Historical Statistics of Canada*, 2nd ed. (Ottawa, 1983), V410–416.

9 An example of this struggle is in a *Toronto Star* article called "Fast Foods—It's Giving the Supermarkets Indigestion," 25 April 1977, 1. Both fast-food and supermarket entrepreneurs state that they are competing for the same food dollar.

10 *Foodservice and Hospitality*, 23 Oct. 1967, 5.

11 *Foodservice and Hospitality*, Feb. 1981, 38.

12 *Moody's Industrial Manual* (New York, 1981); J.M. Stopard, *World Directory of Multinational Enterprises* (Detroit, 1981–82); and *Who Owns Whom: North America* (London, 1982).

13 Promotional material from Burger King Canada head office in Mississauga, ON.

14 William Foote Whyte, *Human Relations in the Restaurant Industry* (New York, 1948), 3.

15 Karl Marx, *Capital*, vol. 1 (New York, 1977), ch. 15.

16 Theodore Levitt, "Production Line Approach to Service," *Harvard Business Review* 50, 1 (Sept.–Oct. 1972): 51–52.

17 Robert L. Emerson, *Fast Food, the Endless Shakeout* (New York, 1979), 291.

18 *Up Front* 2, 6 (Miami, n.d.): 2.

19 A "Shape Up" campaign instituted at the beginning of 1982 attempted to set a new goal of a 2 $1/2$-minute service time.

20 "Kitchen design—the drive for efficiency," insert in *Nation's Restaurant News*, 31 Aug. 1981.

21 Personal communication, Burger King "professor," 4 Jan. 1982.

22 Job description handout for Burger King managers, 1981.

23 Handouts to Burger King crew members, 1981.

25 Burger King training session in local outlet, July 1981.

26 Labour Canada, Commission of Inquiry into Part-Time Work (Wallace commission) (Ottawa, 1983).

27 Personal communication, Burger King worker, 8 Aug. 1981.

28 Michael Burawoy, *Manufacturing Consent* (Chicago, 1979).

29 Andre Gorz, *Farewell to the Working Class* (Boston, 1982), 71.

HOME DREAMS:
Women and the Suburban Experiment in Canada, 1945–60*

VERONICA STRONG-BOAG

In the years after the Second World War in Canada, residential suburbs provided symbolic female counterparts, "bedrooms" as it were, to the male-dominated, market-oriented world of modern cities.[1] Tracts of new housing embodied a separation of the sexes that held women particularly responsible for home and family and men for economic support and community leadership. Such a gendered landscape was far from new or unusual in Canada. Women and men had long moved in somewhat different worlds, presiding over residential and public space in varying degrees as dictated by custom and, sometimes, by law.[2] After 1945, however, women's, particularly wives', rising labour-force participation might have suggested that spatial segregation on the suburban frontier was ill-timed. Why and how, then, did there occur a massive increase in residential suburbs remote from opportunities for employment, lacking many community resources, and reliant on female labour? What did female residents and contemporary observers make of this investment on the suburban frontier? This article begins to answer these questions by examining the conditions that gave rise to postwar suburbs, the character of housing initiatives, and the nature and meaning of that experience for Canadian women.

---

*Canadian Historical Review 72, 4 (1991): 471–504. Reprinted with the permission of University of Toronto Press.

Historians of the United States have associated postwar housing development not only with technological improvements, gas and oil discoveries, and a massive increase in the number of private automobiles, but also with political conservatism, racism, and domestic roles for women.[3] While scholars studying Canadian suburbs will find much that is useful in American assessments, particularly in their exploration of suburbia's gendered terrain, Paul-André Linteau's question, "Does the border make a difference?"[4] inevitably arises. Works like Michael A. Goldberg and John Mercer's *The Myth of the North American City: Continentalism Challenged* (1986) and Caroline Andrew and Beth Moore Milroy's *Life Spaces: Gender, Household, Employment* (1988) have offered the beginnings of a reply. In particular, Andrew and Milroy point to safer and more livable cities, a long tradition of resource towns, and "the particular institutional and policy framework that exists in Canada,"[5] all of which distinguish Canadian women's lives. Although comparisons with the United States remain peripheral to the study here, my reading of the Canadian suburban "script" suggests that, for all the proliferation of American influences in the years after 1945, life north of the forty-ninth did indeed differ. In particular, Canada's cities, lacking racial divisions comparable with those in the United States, never lost their attraction for citizens of all classes. And just as flight from urban dangers does not seem as influential in Canada, suburbia does not appear as homogeneous as many American commentators have suggested. Communities composed of war veterans, industrial workers, rural emigrants, newcomers to Canada, and the middle-class native- and urban-born contribute to a picture that, as the sociologist S.D. Clark convincingly demonstrated in *The Suburban Society* (1968), seems every bit as complicated as what was happening downtown. While middle-class WASPs were a major presence, they were never alone on the outskirts of cities. Suburbia's meaning is further complicated by the influence of region. The background of residents and the rate of suburbanization in these years varied from one part of the country to the other, distinguishing the experience of Montreal from Toronto and from Halifax, Winnipeg, Edmonton, and Vancouver. Facing as they did a different set of contingencies, Canadian women were not mere reflections of American suburbanites. The nature of their story is set out below.

The postwar experiment with the promise of a spatial segregation that placed Canadian women in suburban homes and men in employment located elsewhere was fuelled by high rates of fertility. During the Second World War and into the 1950s, couples married at ever younger ages. First and second babies came earlier in these marriages and increasing numbers of women gave birth to third children (see table 1). Fewer women had no children. Bigger families increased women's home-based responsibilities. Not surprisingly, women were often preoccupied with their roles as wives and mothers. Housing where children could be cared for comfortably and safely was an urgent priority in many women's lives.

Table 1: AGE-SPECIFIC FERTILITY RATES FOR CANADIAN WOMEN, 1921–60[6]

	Age group of women						
Year	15–19	20–24	25–29	30–34	35–39	40–44	45–49
1960	59.8	233.5	224.4	146.2	84.2	28.5	2.4
1940	29.3	130.3	152.6	122.8	81.7	32.7	3.7
1921	38.0	165.4	186.0	154.6	110.0	46.7	6.6

Whereas their parents had often had to be crowded and uncomfortable, postwar Canadians aspired to something better. Between 1945 and 1960 nearly continuous prosperity, high employment, the extension of the welfare state, and the presumption of a limitless bank of natural resources generated income and hopes for a better life, and, if possible, the lifestyle of comfortable homes and new products advertised since the 1920s in the continent's popular media.[7] Rising car ownership offered unprecedented numbers of citizens the opportunity to search for homes well beyond areas where employment opportunities were concentrated.[8] Many male breadwinners, the most likely both to drive and to control the use of cars,[9] no longer had to rely on walking or public transit to get to work. An increase in the production of oil, gas, and hydroelectric power was available to power both new cars and the central heating characteristic of new homes.[10] Residential suburbs on the periphery were the beneficiaries of these developments.

New housing that enshrined a gendered division of labour also responded to a generation's anxiety about changes in the world about them. The threat of the Cold War and the Korean War encouraged citizens to prize the private consumption and accumulation of products in the nuclear family household as proof of capitalism's success. Stable families, full-time mothers, and the benefits they produced in sound citizenship were to provide the first defence against the "Red Menace" symbolized in Canada by the Gouzenko Affair.[11] Suburban housewives at home in ever-larger houses epitomized the promise that prosperity would guarantee both individual happiness and the final triumph over communism.[12]

The inclination to concentrate on private matters and to cling to the faith in women's particular talent and responsibility for family survival was fostered further in the 1940s and 1950s by the highly publicized predicament of many of the world's citizens. The statelessness of the "Displaced Persons," or "DPs," as the 165 000 who had come to Canada by 1953 were commonly known,[13] like the plight of concentration camp survivors, captured especially poignantly what it meant to lose families and homes. The arrival of 48 000 war brides added to Canadians' consciousness of how much the future depended on the establishment of new households and the persistence of marital bonds.[14] The promise of a renewed family life, secured by all the benefits of a revived capitalist economy, became in some ways the *leit-motif of* the second Elizabethan Age. As one typical enthusiast put it, "the Duke and Duchess of Edinborough [sic] are young, modern parents who, like many other young people, in an anxious and insecure world, find their deepest happiness and satisfaction in the warm circle of family life."[15] In suburban homes and families, Canadians endeavoured modestly to echo the ideals embodied in the domesticated monarchy of the youthful Elizabeth II.

The popular and academic social sciences of the day sanctioned the inclination to believe that collective happiness and well-being were most likely when women concentrated their energies on the home front. Experts' secular sermons, frequently presented in the guise of a celebration of female nature, stressed women's unique qualities. With some few exceptions, assertions of inferiority were out of fashion. As one Toronto psychiatrist observed, "Today we think of marriage as a partnership of equals."[16] To this end, modern fathers were encouraged to take on some care of children.[17] Yet, while up-to-date advisers flattered their female audiences with claims for equality, even superiority, "true" women had normally to demonstrate their authenticity by pursuing roles centred on the private rather than the public sphere. Women's ability to take on a broad range of duties, so well demonstrated during the years of depression and war, was conveniently dismissed as an aberration. In advising Canadians how to live, experts returned to opinions that were reminiscent of the 1920s.[18]

Lives that were gender-specific lay at the heart of a number of influential texts that enjoyed general circulation across Canada in the years after the Second World War. Among the earliest and most influential was Dr Benjamin Spock's best-selling *Common Sense Book of Baby and Child Care* (1947).[19] As one Canadian from the suburb of Lachine, Quebec, recalled, "Dr Spock of course was my 'Bible.'"[20] Although most women consulted the good doctor for practical advice on treating childhood ills, his answers reinforced conventions holding women primarily responsible for the emotional and practical functioning of the household. A veteran of suburbs in Cooksville and North York, Ontario, summed up the conclusions of many of her generation: "I felt quite sure in those days that women who chose to have a family should stay home and raise them! I had worked as a social worker for the Children's Aid Society and had seen the emotional devastation in children separated from mothers."[21]

Spock was far from alone in applauding women who mothered. Ashley Montagu's bestseller, *The Natural Superiority of Women* (1953), celebrated women both for their gentler dispositions and for their biological superiority. Not coincidentally, he concluded that "the most important of women's tasks is the making of human beings . . . [and] because mothers are closer to their children than fathers, they must of necessity play a more basic role in the growth and development of their children."[22] A self-proclaimed women's champion, Montagu applied his reading of modern science to "undermine the age-old belief in feminine inferiority,"[23] but in the process he reasserted the faith that biology was destiny. The capacity for motherhood was, as with both the older anti-feminist and the maternal feminist tradition, identified as the very source of superiority.

Ashley Montagu's fundamentally conservative message appeared in the same year as the publication of *Sexual Behavior in the Human Female* (1953),[24] the second volume on human sexuality by Alfred Kinsey and his colleagues. In the forefront of the "sexology" of its day, this volume documented women's possession of a powerful libido, the physiological equivalent of male sexual response.[25] Under the influence of such scientific authority, an active sexuality became increasingly accepted as the prerequisite of satisfactory personal and marital life.[26] The result could be higher levels of intimacy and equality between the sexes, but women's erotic potential could easily be incorporated into an updated domestic ideal. Kinsey's support for the female libido and his opposition to guilt and shame about sexual acts were closely tied to marital and social stability. His early work was used to justify Canadians' youthful marriage: only then could sexuality find its proper channels.[27] Ultimately, Kinsey's pioneering studies reinforced the tendency to dedicate women to private life.

The assignment of women to roles as wives and mothers was further legitimated by the popularity of the functionalist school of sociology that dominated the discipline as it established itself throughout Canada. The work of the leading American "father" of this tradition, Talcott Parsons, drew on the "anatomy is destiny" psychiatry of Freud and his followers to argue that women and men naturally had different, albeit compatible and equal, roles within society. Women were responsible for expressive functions of mediating and nurturing, men for instrumental functions of struggle and leadership. The first responsibilities directed women to the private sphere and the second legitimated men's domination of public life. Husbands concentrated on the workplace and its values of "rationality, impersonality, self-interest," while wives guided children in the traditional family values of "love, sharing, co-operation."[28] Domestic life might no longer require long hours of hard physical labour, but the unremitting pressure of modern corporate life on men appeared to make women irreplaceable in the home as psycho-sexual managers.[29] The appropriate division of duties was summed up by Bell Telephone's company magazine, *The Bluebell,* which pointed to wives' appropriate role in a short story entitled "WE Were Promoted."[30] Both capitalist prosperity and humanized relationships were to be guaranteed by the functionalist division of labour. Such conclusions became the stock-in-trade of Canadian sociologists like J.R. Seeley, R.A. Sim, and E.W. Loosley, the authors of one of the foremost North American studies of suburban life, *Crestwood Heights* (1956).

Home-grown authorities like the popular gynaecologist Dr Marion Hilliard of Toronto's Women's College Hospital regularly voiced the conservative conclusions of the contemporary social sciences. Speaking to her own patients and countless others through articles in *Chatelaine,* she spread prevailing medical opinion:

The burden of creating a happy marriage falls mainly on the wife. A man's life is much more difficult than a woman's, full of the groaning strain of responsibility and the lonely and often fruitless search for pride in himself. A cheerful and contented woman at home, even one who must often pretend gaiety, gives a man enough confidence to believe he can lick the universe. I'm certain that the woman who enriches her husband with her admiration and her ready response gets her reward on earth, from her husband.[31]

Hilliard and most other Canadian "experts" on home and family joined their American colleagues in arguing that women's most basic satisfactions came through service to others in the domestic sphere.

The verdict of professionals was repeatedly echoed in the dominion's mass media. Typical advertisements credited the housewife with "the recipe for good citizenship . . . for a woman's influence extends far beyond the horizons of housekeeping. She guards the family health by her buying standards; she shares in plans for the family welfare; hers is the opportunity of training her children . . . of promoting good character and good citizenship."[32] Companies readily championed a feminine ideal that offered them real benefits. Corporate profits and male careers alike depended on women's concentrated efforts in the private sphere, more especially in new suburban homes where opportunities for purchases were unsurpassed.

Advertising in these years was only one part of a commercial onslaught hitting Canadians. Newspapers, magazines, radio, films, and, by the 1950s, television entered households with a distinct message about the meaning of the "good life." Radio soap operas such as "Road of Life," "Big Sister," "Lucy Linton," "Life Can Be Beautiful," and "Ma Perkins" offered women escape from isolation and loneliness in dreams of consumption, romance, and improved family life.[33] Television shows like "The Adventures of Ozzie and Harriet," "I Love Lucy," "The Honeymooners," and "Father Knows Best" made it quite clear that good wives and mothers stayed properly at home far from the temptations of employment. Just as importantly, they suggested that women reaped real advantages from this division of duties. Wives may have looked a little foolish in these sitcoms, but audiences were encouraged to join in a conspiracy of good-humoured silence about the real power that they wielded. Housewives after all had the freedom to construct their own routines while spouses were tied to onerous duties as breadwinners.

What the experts and the media largely ignored after World War II was a massive increase in the labour-force participation rate of married women. This increased from 4.5 percent in 1941, to 11.2 percent in 1951, to 22.0 percent in 1961. In the same years, wives rose from 12.7 percent to 30.0 percent to 49.8 percent of all women in paid employment.[34] For all this dramatic change meant in terms of disposable family income and the nature of the labour market, it appears to have done little initially to challenge women's primary identification as labourers in the domestic workplace.³⁵ Many postwar wives accepted periods of employment before childbirth and, sometimes, after children were in high school, as intervals in a modern life cycle that still saw them as chiefly responsible for home and family. In particular, energetic young wives could take pride in establishing families on a sound economic footing. Such was true of a "white-collar wife" in her early twenties employed by Montreal's CIL. Vivian used her salary to purchase new housing and "other rewards: electrical kitchen appliances, bedroom and living room furniture, a small English car." Her husband David paid other expenses. Traditional appearances were maintained when she assumed responsibility for most housework and received an allowance from David. Vivian planned to leave CIL at about the age of twenty-five to have between two and four children.³⁶ Many women hoped to do the same. The same assumptions underlay the "putting hubby through school" phenomenon that first attracted public attention with the return of war veterans to university.³⁷ Women's work in the labour market regularly represented an investment in a more domestic future.

Incentives for female citizens to return home as soon as possible always remained considerable. Never missing were unequal opportunity and wages. Resources in support of female workers were meagre.³⁸ Matters at home were hardly better. Most families could only afford one car, on which the husband had first claim, and few settlements boasted adequate public transportation. Nor was that all. Working wives had to face the "double day of labour." One refugee from a clerical office explained that she had cheerfully given up a schedule that required "twelve hours or more a day, seven days a week."³⁹ Another clerical worker from North Toronto added:

> As a married woman for fourteen years and a working wife for less than one year . . . the two don't go together. You can't be a success at both. So I decided to quit my job to save my marriage.
> You simply can't look after a home and go to the office too. I don't care who you are or how well organized you are, you can't be a good wife and mother, hostess and housekeeper and also do a good job for your employer all at the same time. When you try, someone is bound to get cheated.⁴⁰

Working wives had no right to hope for relief at home. As one writer for the *Star Weekly* insisted: "I don't see how a job gives a woman a legitimate out on housekeeping. She still has the basic responsibility to run a home for the family. . . . [A] man whittles himself down to less of a man by consistently performing woman's work."⁴¹ In the decades after the Second World War, income tax law, the absence of day care, formal and informal bars to female employment,⁴² and school schedules combined with a commercially fuelled celebration of domesticity and maternity and the general reluctance of husbands to assume household responsibilities to confirm the wisdom of staying home, if you had a choice.

Such decisions were applauded by experts who feared the worst. In 1953 a counsellor for Toronto's Family Court and the United Church summed up prevailing opinion, arguing that "where the husband and wife are both working outside the home, very often a dangerous spirit of independence exists. Finally, it is quite impossible to do two jobs well."[43] Women who dismissed such arguments could look forward to being scapegoated for a host of society's problems, blamed for homosexual sons, juvenile delinquents, mental cripples, wandering and alcoholic husbands, and school truants.[44]

When authorities repeatedly insisted that women were needed at home, the corollary often was that men were too weak to have them anywhere else. As the Kinsey reports had documented in detail, sexual orientation was conditional; men were the more vulnerable sex. When men's physical weakness was further disclosed by experts like Ashley Montagu,[45] female discontent or competition appeared enormously threatening. A wife's wages might endanger the very core of the fragile male personality.[46] By the same measure, house-working men challenged the very basis of contemporary masculinity. The Montreal psychiatrist Dr Alastair MacLeod plaintively summed up modern problems for *Chatelaine*'s readers:

> Father no longer has opportunities for pursuing aggressive competitive goals openly at work. Some of his basic masculine needs remain unmet. Mother no longer feels she has a real man for a husband and becomes openly aggressive and competitive herself, even moving out of the home into industry in her efforts to restore the biological balance.
>
> Faced with an increasingly discontented and dominating wife, father becomes even more passive and retiring . . . certain trends in modern industry are theoretically capable of disturbing the biological harmony of family organization. The resulting disharmony can lead to psychological and psychosomatic illnesses.[47]

The message was clear: domestic women guaranteed both their own femininity and their husbands' masculinity.

In the 1940s and 1950s Canadians had many reasons to believe that the gendered division of labour was the most appropriate response to their own and their nation's needs. While some citizens always challenged too narrowly defined roles, many were prepared to accept the fact that women and men had different duties in the family and in society at large. Residential suburbs that enshrined the notion of largely separate spheres for the two sexes proved attractive because most Canadians preferred women at home and out of the labour market.

The recurring housing crisis of the 1940s and 1950s provided the crucial opportunity to fix this preference in space.[48] The dominion entered the postwar years with "a large stock of aging and substandard housing, communities that lacked appropriate municipal services, rural areas that lacked electric power, and with a substantial number of households living in crowded conditions or paying shelter costs they could ill afford."[49] Families with youngsters were particularly hard hit. A boom in babies and immigrants raised the costs of even inferior accommodation.[50] The January 1946 occupation of the old Hotel Vancouver protesting the lack of housing for veterans and their families, like the later seizure of several government buildings in Ottawa by members of the Veterans' Housing League, were only the most visible symptoms of widespread dissatisfaction and rising unrest.[51] The *Star Weekly* summed up popular sentiments: "It must be remembered that the whole situation is charged with an intense emotional desire on the part of veterans and non-veterans alike to have homes of their own. The years of loneliness and being apart, the years of cramped, semi-private living, have created a desire as strong as the migrating instinct in birds to have a home."[52] Not surprisingly, crowded accommodation was regularly cited as contributing to family breakdown and social disarray.[53]

Prime Minister Mackenzie King's postwar government, already alerted by the report of the Advisory Committee on Reconstruction on housing and planning to the magnitude of the housing shortage[54] and fearful of the appeal of the Co-operative Commonwealth Federation, moved to fill the gap. The passage in 1944 of the second National Housing Act (NHA) and the creation of the Central Mortgage and Housing Corporation (CMHC) one year later confirmed the significance of housing for peacetime reconstruction.[55] With some few exceptions, strong anti-public-housing sentiments and official reluctance to interfere with the "free market" sharply limited the reclamation of urban residential cores.[56] Across the dominion, despite the substantial investment in urban infrastructure—sewers, schools, public transportation, sidewalks, churches, and the like—that cities represented, they did not become the focus of government housing initiatives. Attention focussed instead on the construction of new houses in the suburbs.

Despite their neglect by governments, city neighbourhoods continued to attract middle- and working-class Canadians, but many tried to maximize dollars and improve family situations by turning to new residential communities. Not all benefited from state support. In British Columbia's Lower Mainland, poorer citizens made do with little better than squatters' quarters in Bridgeview, a marginal Surrey settlement, without sidewalks and sewers.[57] In Quebec the Montreal working class had to satisfy its land hunger in Ville Jacques Cartier. There the discomfort and distress of life in tarpaper and tin shacks on postage-sized lots bought on the instalment plan helped embitter the future separatist Pierre Vallières.[58] In Newfoundland, the city of St John's was surrounded by "fringe areas . . . characterized by very poor, substandard housing, complete lack of services (piped water and sewer facilities, garbage collection, street-lighting, etc.), poor roads and low family incomes."[59] Few residents in such locations used the provisions of the National Housing Act, since borrowers in the years after World

War II had to earn steadily higher gross family incomes in order to pay rising down payments and interest rates.[60]

Atlantic Canadians, poorer on average than their contemporaries elsewhere, were particularly unlikely to receive federal mortgage help: between 1954 and 1966 only 23.4 percent of all new "dwelling units" in the Atlantic region were completed with CMHC assistance, compared to 51.9 percent in Ontario in the same period.[61] The variability of financing meant that housewives in different regions sometimes confronted dramatically different working conditions. In 1960 and the first five months of 1961, for example, 38.5 percent of new units located in Atlantic Canada lacked flush toilets and 41.9 percent lacked furnace heating, compared with 8.7 percent and 8.2 percent, respectively, in Ontario.[62] Such distinctions helped ensure that accommodation on the urban periphery varied, often tremendously, from one part of the country to the other. In the Maritimes, suburbia would be neither as extensive nor as prosperous as in many other regions of the country.

In contrast to the plight of the poor, the housing predicament of a broad range of Canadians was addressed by federal enthusiasm for subsidizing the construction of single family homes and the desire of private developers, contractors, and mortgage lenders to maximize profits. For those who could meet income requirements, mortgage money, at artificially low rates, was made available to build hundreds of thousands of three-bedroom "residential units."[63] While the foremost scholar of Canadian suburbs, S.D. Clark, has concluded that residents were frequently "middle class in terms of income . . . Canadian born, of British origin, and of Protestant religious affiliation,"[64] suburbs always attracted ambitious working-class and immigrant citizens as well. One daughter remembered that "as refugees from Hungary," her parents "could hardly wait to leave" downtown Toronto "for, to them, lavish splendour of the suburbs," where they settled without regret.[65] In a subdivision of owner-built houses in Cooksville, Ontario, in the 1950s, an English immigrant remembered friendly Italian neighbours whose comfortable homes were constructed by their labouring and small-contractor husbands.[66] The Yugoslav immigrant who began work as a carpenter and plasterer when he arrived after the war and went on to achieve his dream of a suburban bungalow, in his case in Winnipeg's West Kildonan, may not have been in the majority, but he had imitators from one end of the country to the other.[67] The eclectic nature of the suburban community was captured by the comment from a resident who insisted that her modest suburb west of Toronto, whose residents included Olga, Grand Duchess of Russia, was "neither purely WASP nor dull."[68]

Once families moved to suburbia, they often found themselves with people of similar income and in houses of similar price. Neighbours were "all in the same boat."[69] New communities often revealed a distinct class and ethnic character, one that was sometimes legally imposed. Until their overthrow by the Supreme Court in 1951, residential covenants that included race as criteria were commonplace. Drawing on Canadian property law, they were used by land developers to exclude "undesirables" and to set minimum house values.[70] Even after covenants had lost some of their power, homogeneity often survived, a testament to more informal support. In 1957 the new North York suburb of Don Mills, for example, attracted certain occupational groups: 32.1 percent of male homeowners were executives, 23.7 percent professionals, 19.9 percent skilled technicians, 11 percent salesmen, and 3.8 percent teachers and professors, with the remaining 9.5 percent listed as miscellaneous.[71] The hopes of many suburbanites were summed up by one observer in 1945: "It's not just a house, but a way of life that people are seeking. . . . Most people wanted to be part of a community which consisted of congenial people, equality of income—restricted house values."[72] Different suburbs could have distinctive characters, depending on the ability of different groups to afford the cost of houses in their community.

The availability of CMHC mortgages for new homes, relatively low land costs, and builders' incentives, such as that by Saracini Construction in NHA's Glen Park development in Etobicoke in the early 1950s that gave purchasers the "option of taking a lower priced home and completing part of it at a later date,"[73] made a difference to many Canadians. Despite the continuing decline in the rural population, where ownership was most common, the number of owner-occupied houses in Canada increased from 57 percent in 1941 to 65 percent in 1951 to 66 percent in 1961.[74]

Immediately after the Second World War much new housing was constructed either individually, often by "do-it-yourselfers," or as part of developments of a few to several hundred houses. Most early construction took place either within older suburbs like East Vancouver or East York in Toronto or in the first ring of surrounding townships or municipalities, such as British Columbia's Burnaby and Ontario's Etobicoke. By the early 1950s, however, high demand plus the enlarged scale of the development industry increasingly directed growth to more remote areas, many without existing municipal services. There in sites like Halifax's Thornhill Park, Toronto's Don Mills, and Edmonton's Crestwood appeared the suburban, automobile-dependent sprawl that came to characterize the last half of the twentieth century. Between 1951 and 1961 the population in metropolitan areas around city cores grew far more than that in city centres (see table 2).

Table 2: **PERCENTAGE INCREASES IN POPULATION FOR THE CENTRAL CITIES AND REMAINING PARTS OF THE 1961 CENSUS METROPOLITAN AREAS, 1951–61**[75]

Census Metropolitan Area	Central City	Remainder of Metropolitan Area
Canada	23.8	110.7
Atlantic	11.7	70.6
Quebec	27.9	117.7
Ontario	15.5	116.3
Prairies	50.2	133.0
British Columbia	10.9	90.7

These first homes meant a great deal. Coming out of depression and war, couples struggled to become property owners. A team effort was common. As one observer noted of veteran housing: "There is hardly a single case among all these veteran-builders of a wife lounging about. They have been as active in all weathers as their husbands."[76] Such couples had good reason to prize long-awaited houses. Tenants in particular, like one long-time inhabitant of Montreal's Verdun, her husband, and three children, aged five, three, and seven months, were delighted to use CMHC mortgages to move, in their case to Lachine's "Dixie" suburb.[77] Their enthusiasm was matched by the York Township resident in Ontario who remembered being "very poor in the depression—8 people in a 4 room one storey house." She was understandably "really excited—To have a 5 room brick bungalow for the two of us! Such Luxury!!'"[78] A Scottish immigrant expressed the same sense of achievement: "We came from a society where houses were scarce, renting was almost impossible unless one had the proper connections, and from a country which had spent 6 years at war. So owning a house in the suburbs was a dream for us, a dream we achieved after only 6 years in Canada."[79]

While new suburbs varied in many particulars,[80] all shared a commitment to the gendered division of labour. Purchase of a home—whether in a highly planned community like Etobicoke's Thorncrest Village with its provision of a wide range of urban services expected by upper-middle-class buyers[81] or in a mass-produced subdivision like Scarborough's Wishing Well Acres, where the one millionth new house constructed after VE-Day was officially opened[82]—was part of a child-centred strategy for many Canadians. As a study by Vancouver's Lower Mainland Regional Planning Board discovered, "to a young family without much money, faced with the alternative of a small apartment in the city. . . . It is no small thing to be able to look out of the living-room window at one's children playing in relative freedom with fields and woods beyond them."[83] As a mother of two in Toronto's Iondale Heights suburb explained in 1957, "We moved to the suburbs because of the children. We wanted to give them room to romp, where they wouldn't have to worry about street cars and fiend-driven automobiles. True, we have no museums or art galleries. But the children can go outside and see nature as it is."[84] Such commentators took for granted that greater opportunities for children depended ultimately on maternal supervision.

Finally responsible for child care and house maintenance, modern suburban wives were tethered to their communities in ways that few husbands could match. In 1958 one speaker for a Toronto construction company described the suburban home: "A woman is there all the time, she lives there. A man just boards there: he gets his meals there. She is there all day long."[85] A male architect characterized his own experience of gender relations even more vividly: "I spend every day in my Mobile Room [car] going to and from the women at either end [in the office or in his suburban home]."[86] As these remarks suggest, the suburban house remained first of all a workplace for female residents. For husbands, lengthy commutes and long hours at work, not to mention individual preferences, meant that domestic responsibilities were largely subordinated to the demands of waged work.[87] Nor did the suburbs make joint efforts easy. As one husband recalled:

> Like most of my fellow male suburbanites I was the sole auto driver. I also drove a lot in my job. Rushing home to take a child to cubs or brownies, to take my wife to a class in the city, to drive to hockey practice or to a game, or to be shopping driver when required was a daily task. Work pressures made this more difficult. There were the open spaces to cut, cultivate and shovel. Social evenings required a driver to pick up the sitter, drive into town, return home and drive the sitter home. The automobile was a[n] itching appendage needing constant scratching.[88]

To be sure, some suburban wives always joined their husbands in leaving home for employment. As the expansion of Avon's and other door-to-door sales in these years suggested, earning extra money was never far from many residents' minds.[89] So-called "working" wives shored up families' aspirations to a better standard of living; the husband of a young Bank of Commerce clerk, for instance, was reconciled to her job so she could furnish the house they were building in Saskatoon in 1952.[90] Yet women's ideal primary role remained, especially after babies arrived, in the home. As one resident of a Toronto suburb remembered, her husband "didn't want me to work, and I thought that no one could look after my children as well as I could."[91]

While they may not have remained in the labour market, wives regularly contributed to husbands' careers. Women married to professionals or businessmen often functioned as part of a marital "team," spending hours as unpaid assistants, typing, translating, or entertaining. The wife of a successful academic remembered that "in university circles a wife was expected to entertain—often upwards of 50 people."[92] Another academic spouse found her eyes giving out as she typed the manuscripts that advanced her husband in his profession.[93] Acknowledgment of such contributions forms a regular refrain in scholarly prefaces.

The great majority of wives remained crucially dependent on male wages. Women's financial vulnerability was worsened by the fact that many families purchased suburban homes only by rigorous self-denial. More than one investigator discovered that "Baby sitters were done without, food costs reduced, less spent on clothing, and a hundred and one other small ways discovered to save money. 'I'm not going dancing no more' gave expression certainly to the financial plight of more than one suburban housewife."[94] While such careful juggling of finances was not true of all suburbanites, the strains of budgeting, large or small, were likely to be borne unevenly. Not only did male wage-earners usually have prior right of access to what they commonly held to be "their money,"[95] they frequently had to maintain certain standards as conditions of employment. Women and children could dress, eat, and travel much less well without immediately endangering the family economy.[96]

Suburban houses were the stage on which women explored the meaning of separate spheres. That setting varied greatly depending on income and individual preference, but the introduction of CMHC inspections under the 1954 revision of the Housing Act encouraged the giving way of "individual, custom-built homes" to "mass, speculative development" with standardized shapes, sizes, and configurations.[97] In the late 1940s and 1950s master plans and more stringent municipal zoning by-laws across the country, which represented efforts to control errant developers, also contributed to the increasing uniformity of the emerging suburban landscape.[98] CMHC's support of Canadian Small House competitions after the Second World War,[99] like the *Star Weekly*'s sponsorship of the All Canadian Home in 1959,[100] for all their good intentions, had the same effect. In the heady days of easy sales, developers threw up one imitation after another, differing in little but colour and trim. Most models came as Cape Cods, and increasingly, as bungalows or split levels. Like the split-level winner of the first coast-to-coast architectural contest in 1953,[101] almost all boasted three bedrooms, an L-shaped living/dining-room combination, and, in most areas of the country, a full basement. Increasingly, too, a rumpus or recreation room appeared below level, which, together with the proliferation of televisions, encouraged families to spend leisure time more privately. In these homes, more comfortable than many had ever encountered, women were to forge the moral basis for postwar Canada.

Female residents were expected and urged to bring uniqueness to uniformity through a careful attention to decoration and design. As one commentator insisted, "The bugaboo of uniformity bothers her not at all, because every woman knows she can work out her own individual design for living with colors and furnishings and personal touches."[102] Their choice of furniture, appliances, art, and even clothes was to transform the identical into the distinguishable, in the process confirming housewives' skills and status. No wonder that practically every issue of popular Canadian women's magazines like the *Bride's Book, Canadian Home Journal, Canadian Homes and Gardens,* and *Chatelaine,* not to mention their American competitors, offered readers ways, thrifty and otherwise, to personalize suburbia. In a Special Issue in March 1955, for example, *Chatelaine* offered lessons on "How To Live in a Suburb," "A Spring Fashion Bazaar for Suburban Living," and "How To Furnish a New Home without Panic Buying." Subscribers consulted such experts but also prided themselves on developing styles that suited their families best.[103] The mistress of a Rexdale, Ontario, bungalow on "a corner-lot so at least it didn't match everything beside it in either direction, but of course, it matched the house on the corner across the street," spoke for a renovating sisterhood when she reflected that "I almost wrecked it trying to create something unique."[104]

Many women soon found more to concern them in the limitations of the environment at large. Conspicuous in their absence from many new developments in the 1940s and early 1950s, before local governments became more demanding, were public spaces and facilities, such as sidewalks, monuments, parks, and cemeteries. A mother of two children settled in a bungalow on Toronto's outskirts typically remembered that "there were no sidewalks and the road was not paved. The mud and dust were a real pain."[105] For many years developers also counted on the open country that surrounded many subdivisions to provide children with nearby recreational space. In time as the process of urban sprawl accelerated, this resource disappeared, as it did around Scarborough's Wishing Well Acres subdivision in the 1960s, without any provision for its replacement. For women, the presumed mistresses of suburbia, collective provision was almost always curiously lacking. If landscape were any guide, meeting and play were not part of the female mandate.

The location of most commercial shops and services on the periphery or, more occasionally, in the centre of residential development, either in a strip pattern along major roads or in suburban plazas, showed the same lack of attention to women's needs. Patterns of consumption centred increasingly on shopping centres, which first made their appearance in Canada in 1947 in suburban Winnipeg. By 1951, with the construction of Norgate Plaza in Montreal and Park Royal Plaza in West Vancouver, about forty-six shopping centres, all poorly served by public transit and demanding access to a private car,[106] drew buyers from surrounding suburbs.

One Don Mills veteran characterized shopping experiences that were not very different from the majority of her contemporaries, especially those whose husbands didn't have the option of commuting by train to work: "Walked & pushed baby carriage to most places. Never had a second car— poor bus service especially with 3 children! Little co-operation, wives did not own car—walked to local shops. Traffic was hazardous on highway & only route to major shopping centre (suburbs were designed for the car & most of us had only one which husband used)."[107] Once visitors got there, new plazas, lacking free public space and cultural amenities, offered them little beyond a community based on a common commitment to purchase. As a self-satisfied Canadian retailer put it, "Suburban living, by its basic structure, generates wants and brings latent desires more sharply into focus. The not-so-subtle effect of competitive living is also a potent influence in creating an environment that encourages liberal spending for better living."[108] The domestic and individualistic orientation of women, families' major purchasers, was readily reaffirmed.

While plazas were increasingly influential, door-to-door sales and deliveries were commonplace in the 1940s and 1950s. Phone orders were taken by butchers, grocers, and department stores, and trucks with milk and bakery goods made their way among suburban homes. Avon ladies, who might be members of a local church, and Hoover, Electrolux, Fuller Brush, and Watkins salesmen were also occasional visitors. The latter were described by a former client as canvassing a Montreal suburb "once or twice per year and I always kept their wonderful salve, 'Good for Man or Beast.' Very strong, didn't burn and helped heal cut knees very quickly. They also had wonderful flavourings and food colourings."[109]

In Metropolitan Toronto, another purchaser implied advantages beyond mere convenience: "We liked to see a vegetable man come along the street. Ice, milk and bread were delivered as were beer and pop. The Avon lady and the Fuller Brush man provided some new faces."[110] Such sentiments were shared by a resident of Clarkson's Corners (Mississauga) who recalled, with affection, a milk man who "always poked his head in to say good morning and took the children on his van for a ride." She observed, "Obviously these services were very important. I realize, however, that my mother had far more people calling than I. (She even had a Hellicks coffee man, Duggan's bakery, etc.)"[111] Although they grew less in time as the private automobile undermined their viability, such deliveries helped knit new communities together in ways that more modern shopping alternatives rarely did.

Suburbia's households were also connected by schools and churches. Although it often happened that housing sprawled well beyond the capacity of religious groups and municipalities to ensure even minimum services, by the 1950s their institutions were normally included in the initial planning of developments. Even then they might well be strained to their limits or inconvenient to reach, as with schools offering shift classes or located across busy intersections. For all such shortcomings, as well as their tendency to deal with female clients almost solely in their roles as mothers and wives, such institutions constituted important collective resources to a community lacking common habits of working together. Parent–teacher associations, or home and school groups, were the most effective in mobilizing women, from room mothers to fund-raisers and executive officers.[112] Auxiliaries and Sunday schools were critical for some residents who kept suburban churches expanding in these years.[113] Work with local institutions offered more activist and sociable suburbanites the chance to combine domestic duties with a manageable level of public involvement.

As they had done in other Canadian settings, women wove the fabric of day-to-day life. As one observer noted, "For most of the day while the men are away at work the women run the community. After the bulldozers have pulled out, the spadework to make a real community out of your particular collection of houses has to be done by . . . the homemakers."[114] Women commonly moved beyond their homes through contacts with children and "in turn, the fathers get to know their neighbours through their own ubiquitous wives."[115] Casual meetings, dismissed by critics as "coffee klatches," or even encounters between Avon "ladies" and their clients, might be followed by both intimate friendships and formal associations. These ties helped women cope with limited resources and new environments. Since children were rarely far from mothers' minds, much cooperative activity centred on them. After the war women in North Burnaby's new subdivisions established "parent-teacher groups . . . in an endeavour to promote better school conditions and assist in providing hot lunches for the children."[116] In Don Mills, where young children were abundant and teenagers rare, women established baby-sitting co-operatives. In Thornhill, Ontario, mothers formed a community kindergarten and encouraged the fathers, who were "somewhat apathetic at first . . . to contribute some time and energy in making odds and ends of school equipment."[117] In 1955 mothers at North York's York Mills School, alarmed by sexual attacks on local children, created a Parents' Action League.[118] In Etobicoke's Rexdale development, women protested their lack of public transit to local council and to the Toronto Transit Commission. As they explained, "Nearly all of us have children and they have to be taken to the dentist or doctor occasionally. It takes a full day to make the trip and two days to rest up afterwards."[119] Also in 1955, mothers from North York's Livingstone School fought the Board of Education's transfer of pupils to another school.[120] In Clarkson's Corners a Quebecker prompted her neighbours to create French conversation groups and to fund high school scholarships.

Concerns sometimes broadened beyond children to include a variety of community issues. Thorny questions related to sewers, libraries, and garbage disposal provided lessons in collective action and political lobbying. In North York, residents created the North York Women Electors Association on the model of its Toronto counterpart in September 1954.[121] In Etobicoke, a year later, twenty-two mothers with children in tow from Goldwood Heights subdivision "stormed" a council meeting, demanding "action—not answers" to the problem created by their developer's failure to finish sidewalks, sodding, and ditching.[122] In effect, such women were transforming suburbs into good neighbourhoods. As volunteers they facilitated the creation of everything from schools, hospitals, and churches to libraries.

For all the evidence of activism, however, the majority of women were rarely visible on the public stage. For many, suburbia constituted a period of deep engagement in the day-to-day running of the family. Very few had assistance with household duties, particularly on weekdays when most husbands were absent. While a few sometimes found substitutes for their own labour in co-operatives or paid help, others, like a Montreal suburbanite, remembered that "even babysitters were all but unavailable (No Teens, no Grannies)."[123] Questioned about their days as mothers of young children, both happy and unhappy veterans of suburbia remember themselves engrossed in time-consuming duties:

> I had helped my mother in bazaars, tag days, processions, etc. etc.,
> fundraising, church charitable organizations from the time I was
> knee high. However, once married, I was apolitical. I guess, basically,
> because I was so very busy [with nine children].[124]

> I guess there were clubs and political parties but I really didn't have
> much time or energy with four small children to get involved. I've
> always been aware of my own limitations in terms of time and
> energy.[125]

> Not much [leadership from women] in my age group at the time.
> Too busy at home . . . it was a man's world.[126]

> There was no energy or time to do anything about it [feminism].[127]

> I didn't participate in politics when my children were small, I was
> too too too busy. None of my neighbours with children seemed to
> be involved.[128]

Unless they were especially gregarious, such child-rearing women were likely to devote precious free-time moments to private rather than public pursuits.

To the present day, a baleful mythology associated with postwar suburbs and their female residents persists. Suburban women provided a focus for much contemporary debate about the merits of modern life. In particular, in the minds of critics of mass society who flourished in the years after the Second World War,[129] the suburb emerged as the residential and female expression of the moral bankruptcy they identified in society at large, more particularly in giant corporations, big governments, and the "organization men" who served them.

The most famous indictment from North American feminists was provided by Betty Friedan's *The Feminine Mystique*.[130] This soon-to-be classic identification of "The Problem That Has No Name" captured the imagination of a generation no longer satisfied with the restricted options of life in suburbia. As one Canadian reader explained:

> I truly considered my genes disturbed until I read Friedan's book.
> After all, I'd spent my life working to earn and indeed cherishing,
> the one compliment that topped them all—"You think like a man."
>
> But I was afraid of that book. I read it in very small snatches,
> because it stirred me greatly, and I couldn't see any purpose to that.
> There I was, a relatively uneducated woman with two small children
> to raise.[131]

More than anyone else, Friedan helped women challenge the egalitarian claim of North American abundance. Ultimately, she argued, and many readers agreed, the gendered experience of suburbia betrayed women, consigning them to subordination and frustration within society and unhappiness within the family. Limited options for women also meant an immeasurably poorer "Free World," a critical point when winning the Cold War was all-important. In Canada, Friedan's dismissal of modern housekeeping as neither sufficiently dignified nor time-consuming to require full-time dedication by wives and mothers was matched by a barrage of popular articles in the 1950s.[132]

Whatever Friedan's insights, her work concentrated on a privileged minority. Her suburban women, pushed by the forces of a commercialized culture, appeared to have made the "great refusal" in rejecting purposeful and independent lives in the public sphere. A considerable amount of women-blaming goes on in *The Feminine Mystique*. As with many of her Canadian imitators, Friedan associated suburban women with the evils of modern society—its secularism, superficiality, and materialism. Her feminism, with its support for broader interpretations and expressions of female ability, gave her message special meaning, but the message itself, like attacks on suburbia from social critics unconcerned about sexual inequality, finally ignored the complexity of female lives.

Non-feminist critics of modern society routinely targeted female suburbanites. Marshall McLuhan's *The Mechanical Bride: Folklore of Industrial Man* identified "millions of women who live isolated lives from 8:00 to 6:00 PM"[133] in suburbia as part of the dilemma of modern men. In 1956 in "You Take the Suburbs, I Don't Want Them," the novelist Hugh Garner, flexing his muscles as a homegrown literary "bad boy," rejected a world in which men could not make the rules.[134] Suburbia's psychological failings were brutally diagnosed by the assistant director of Montreal's Mental Hygiene Institute. In 1958 Dr Alastair MacLeod warned *Chatelaine*'s readers that "The suburbs give children fresh air, but take away their fathers. They give women efficient kitchens, but are hard on their femininity and gentleness. They give men pride in providing so handsomely, but drive many of them to drink to make up for their watered-down maleness."[135] This psychiatrist damned suburbs as "matriarchies, manless territories where women cannot be feminine because expediency demands that they control the finances and fix drains and where night-returning men cannot be masculine because their traditional function of ruler and protector has been usurped."[136] While Friedan located suburbia's limitations in the domestic definition of womanhood, few psychiatrists acknowledged that many women needed outlets beyond those provided by purely domestic life.

The indictments of social critics were elaborated most fully in *Crestwood Heights*, a case study of Toronto's Forest Hill, an "inner suburb" built before the Second World War. Dissecting the family lives of an upper middle-class sample of WASP and Jewish Torontonians, the authors revealed what many critics of mass society feared. Men concentrated on making money, ignoring families' emotional and spiritual needs. Dissatisfied women wielded power in a community in which they were the dominant adults for the daylight hours. Mothers were preoccupied with their offspring, to the detriment of themselves and their children. Both sexes were overly materialistic. The contribution of women and men to the wider society was intrinsically limited. Despite the lack of comparability of this older suburb to what was happening on the periphery of Canadian cities, Crestwood Heights rapidly became the measure by which modern suburbia was judged.[137]

The Royal Architectural Institute of Canada added to the chorus of dismay. Its 1960 *Report* on the design of the residential environment summed up the views of professional architects and representatives of University Women's Clubs and the National Council of Women in its dislike for "the essential identity of houses, the denial of differentiation, built into new suburbs."[138] The *Report* was alert to suburbia's failure to reflect changing Canadian demography. While new buildings took for granted a father in paid employment and a mother at home with two children, many households were very different.[139] The land-eating sprawl of three-bedroom Cape Cods, bungalows, or split levels dependent on private transportation and reflective of a single style of family life was not what all Canadians needed. Preoccupied with aesthetics, however, the *Report* never confronted the problem embodied in the gendered nature of suburban space.

Arguments about the merits of suburban life were not always restricted to polite discourse. Residents of Scarborough's Highland Creek, which their MPP characterized as "a normal Ontario suburban community,"[140] were outraged in 1956 when S.D. Clark of the University of Toronto was quoted as accusing them of sexual immorality and hard drinking. The leakage of these observations from a private report to a research group forced him to apologize publicly to Scarborough's residents. Even then there were threats of vigilante justice.[141]

Perhaps chastened by this experience, Clark produced a pathbreaking study, *The Suburban Society* (1968), which rejected any simple characterization of suburbia. Dismissing *Crestwood Heights* as unrepresentative in its "culture of a particular urban social class and, in large degree, particular ethnic group,"[142] he championed suburbia's variety and vitality. It was this heterogeneity that Friedan and the other critics of modern life, with their focus on middle-class, highly organized communities, had so largely missed. And yet, ironically enough, for all his stress on suburbia's variety, Clark joined critics of mass society in readily stereotyping women. *The Suburban Society* casually dismissed the female resident as "the suburban housewife seeking amusement or instruction in light reading" and the "lone miserable suburban housewife."[143] Making easy generalizations about the "social waste" of women left behind in suburbia,[144] Clark never applied his insight about the complexity of suburban patterns to any consideration of the role of gender. To a significant degree, women continued to be both victims and authors of their own misfortune, keys to the failings of contemporary family life and thus to much of the imperfection of the modern world.

Suburban women, then and today, have their own contributions to make to this debate. In 1959 *Chatelaine*'s readers responded passionately to the attack on suburban women issued by the assistant director of

Montreal's Mental Hygiene Institute, Dr Alastair MacLeod. In more than 300 letters they captured the complexity of women's lives. In all, 42 percent defended women, men, and suburbia itself, one critic bluntly summing up her rejection of the psychiatrist's misogyny as "Bunk." A further 11 percent of respondents blamed the problems of modern life on something other than suburbia, while 8 percent gave it mixed reviews. The remaining 39 percent agreed, more or less, with MacLeod's criticism of suburban women. Most readers were reluctant to limit women to domestic labour as a solution to the ills of modern society. One woman from Rexdale, Ontario, pointed out that many young wives had more than enough business experience and brains to manage the home and its finances. It didn't make sense to "restrict them to the monotonous unthinking roles of mere cooks and floor waxers."[145] Most suburban women did much more and did it well. A few readers, while admitting something was wrong, refused to blame women. A Regina contributor, for instance, argued that women were feeling frustrated and inadequate because their "opportunity for economic contribution has largely been taken from the four walls of her home."[146] The whole tenor of the published answers to MacLeod's condemnation of suburban womanhood suggested a diversity of opinion and experience.

Suburbia's veterans still remain divided about its meaning. In letters, memos, interviews, and answers to a questionnaire about their experience in the suburbs between 1945 and 1960,[147] women whose families ranged from the well-to-do to the economically marginal reflected on what those years had meant. Many, like one Etobicoke, Ontario, resident, offered a blunt calculation of benefits: "Suburban life was fine. We had an auto so we weren't isolated from the Toronto scene. It also enabled us immigrants to make friends. I'd do it over again. Everyone benefitted. . . . When you live a situation you aren't always analyzing it. The decision was economic. I wasn't buying into an image."[148] Like many others whose satisfaction seemed grounded in happy marriages, this writer argued that suburban life was vital and fulfilling. Helpmate husbands did much to make suburbia a good place for wives.

Favourable assessments also sprang from a recognition that life in the suburbs was a step up in terms of convenience, comfort, and security. Days spent previously as tenants, in too few rooms and without domestic conveniences, could make even modest bungalows feel very good. While not without flaws, suburbs were a good deal better than alternatives. The benefits for children were stressed repeatedly but women, like the two speakers below, were likely to convey a strong sense of their own good fortune as well:

> It was the right choice for us. . . . We did not want to raise our kids on city streets, although I realize now they did miss out on many things such as museums, libraries, etc. . . . I think all who chose the life benefitted from the freer life, the men for a lot of

> companionship with neighbours. . . . It was a happier time because we no longer worried about friends and acquaintances, schoolmates who were overseas and in danger.[149]
>
> Those were good years for us. My husband was getting ahead and I saw myself as a helpmate. . . . For children suburbia really worked. They always had playmates and they had multiple parenting . . . [but] suburbia tended to narrow our vision of the outside world. We thought we had the ideal life. . . . We knew little about the world of poverty, culture, crime and ethnic variety. We were like a brand new primer, "Dick and Jane."[150]

In reflecting on their suburban lives, women who counted them successful firmly rejected any portrait of themselves as conformists and insisted that the suburbs worked best for the independent and self-motivated. An artist noted that she and her friends "were already in charge of our lives and didn't feel abused."[151] Whether they were gregarious and heavily involved in the community or took pleasure in quiet family pastimes, positive commentators revealed a strong sense of achievement. Happy children, rewarding relationships with spouses, and strong communities were their trophies.

Cheerful accounts contrasted markedly with those who remembered the suburbs as "hell." Days spent largely alone with demanding infants and lack of support from friends, relatives, and sometimes husbands were to be endured. The result could be desperation. One Ontario survivor captured her predicament, and that of others as well, when she wrote: "I began to feel as if I were slowly going out of my mind. Each day was completely filled with child and baby care and keeping the house tidy and preparing meals. I felt under constant pressure."[152] Some women recollected feeling guilty about such unhappiness: If families were more prosperous than ever and husbands doing their jobs, what right did they have to be less than content? When a desperately lonely neighbour hanged her three children in the basement, however, one resident of Don Mills put self-doubts aside and set out to create mothers' groups to compensate for the shortcomings of suburban life.[153]

Critics sometimes observed that dissatisfaction extended beyond their sex. Two women explained: "Certainly didn't work for me. I would have been much happier in row housing. . . . It seems to me that everyone loses—Women are isolated. Men don't know their families. Children don't know their fathers."[154] And, "I don't think anybody benefitted, exactly. You could say men, but they benefitted from marriage, suburbs or not. . . . And I think a lot of men were miserable trying to play the part imposed upon them in the wasteland."[155] From the perspective of such veterans, women in particular and society as a whole were the poorer because of the investment on the suburban frontier.

Unlike their contemporaries who relished memories of days nurturing children and husbands, critics yearned for lives that offered them more contact with the wider world, more appreciation of their diverse skills, and more financial independence. For them the suburban landscape entailed an unacceptable restriction on options, a source of frustration, anger, and depression. This group often rejected the domestic ideal embodied in suburbia as soon as possible, ridding themselves of unsatisfactory husbands, moving to more congenial settings, and taking paid employment.

Accounts from suburban women rarely match the image presented by Friedan and the critics of mass society. Their experiences were neither homogeneous nor uncomplicated. They were much more than merely the female counterparts of "organization men." Women were both victims and beneficiaries of a nation's experiment with residential enclaves that celebrated the gendered division of labour. Suburban dreams had captured the hopes of a generation shaken by war and depression, but a domestic landscape that presumed that lives could be reduced to a single ideal inevitably failed to meet the needs of all Canadians after 1945. In the 1960s the daughters of the suburbs, examining their parents' lives, would begin to ask for more.

• Notes

1 See Susan Saegert, "Masculine Cities and Feminine Suburbs: Polarized Ideas, Contradictory Realities" in *Women and the American City*, ed. C. Stimpson, E. Dixler, M. Nelson, and K. Yatrakis (Chicago, 1981), 106. The appeal of the suburbs was not limited to cities. New resources towns, of which 46 appeared between 1945 and 1957, provided numerous instances of "suburbs in the wilderness." See Margaret P. Nunn Bray's useful overview, "'No Life for a Woman': An Examination and Feminist Critique of the Post–World War II Instant Town with Special Reference to Manitouwadge" (MA thesis, Queen's University, 1989), 46. While produced by many of the same forces, the gendered landscape of the resource town is distinctive. This article explores the suburban experience only as it manifested itself around cities.

2 See, for example, the discussion of gendered space in the provocative studies by Joy Parr, *The Gender of Breadwinners: Women, Men, and Change in Two Industrial Towns 1880–1950* (Toronto, 1990), and Peter De

Lottinville, "Joe Beef of Montreal," *Labour/Le Travailleur* 8/9 (1981–82): 9–40.

3 Among the major studies see Kenneth Jackson, *Crabgrass Frontier: The Suburbanization of the United States* (New York, 1985); Robert Fishman, *Bourgeois Utopias: The Rise and Fall of Suburbia* (New York, 1987); Elaine Tyler May, *Homeward Bound: American Families in the Cold War Era* (New York, 1988); Margaret Marsh, *Suburban Lives* (New Brunswick, NJ, 1990); and Dolores Hayden, *Redesigning the American Dream: The Future of Housing, Work and Family Life* (New York, 1984).

4 "Canadian Suburbanization in a North American Context: Does the Border Make a Difference?" *Journal of Urban History* 13, 3 (May 1987): 252–74.

5 Caroline Andrew and Beth Moore Milroy, eds., *Life Spaces: Gender, Household, Employment* (Vancouver, 1988), 4.

6 See John R. Miron, *Housing in Postwar Canada* (Montreal, 1988), from table 3, p. 35. See also ch. 3 for an excellent

discussion of family formation patterns in the years after 1945.

7 See Veronica Strong-Boag, *The New Day Recalled: Lives of Girls and Women in English Canada 1919–1939* (Toronto, 1988).

8 The number of passenger automobiles registered in Canada rose from 1 281 190 in 1941 to 2 105 869 in 1951 to 4 325 682 in 1961. Series T147–194, *Historical Statistics of Canada*, 2nd ed. (Ottawa, 1983).

9 See Charles L. Sanford, "'Women's Place' in American Car Culture," *The Automobile and American Culture*, ed. David L. Lewis and Laurence Goldstein (Ann Arbor, 1983).

10 See Series Q13-18 to Q75-80, *Historical Statistics of Canada*.

11 See, for example, John Thomas, "How to Stay Married," *Canadian Home Journal* (April 1955): 2–3.

12 For a useful discussion of the impact of the Cold War on sex roles in the United States see May, *Homeward Bound*.

13 James Lemon, *Toronto Since 1918* (Toronto, 1985), 94.

14 See Joyce Hibbert, *The War Brides* (Toronto, 1978), for revealing portraits of the brides who came to Canada.

15 Alice Hooper Beck, "Royal Mother," *Chatelaine* (Jan. 1951): 63. See Hector Bolitho, "The Queen's Conflict: How Can One Woman Fulfill the Dual Role of Monarch and of Mother?" ibid. (Feb. 1953): 12–13, 36, 38, 40. See also David Macdonald, "Farewell to the Fifties," *Star Weekly*, 2 Jan. 1960, 10–11, 14, who saw the decade as "frantic . . . an age of anxiety," 24.

16 Dr K.S. Bernhardt, "Happily Ever After," *Bride's Book* (Fall/Winter 1952): 75.

17 See Fred Edge, "Are Fathers Necessary?" *Canadian Home Journal* (Feb. 1953): 24, 63; John Thomas, "Are Fathers Necessary?" ibid. 24, 63–64, and "Father's a Parent, Too," *Canadian Homes and Gardens* (April 1952): 29–31.

18 See Strong-Boag, *New Day Recalled*.

19 See J. Ronald Oakley, *God's Country: America in the Fifties* (New York, 1986).

20 Mildred Grace Baker, "Canadian Women and the Suburban Experience 1945–60: Questionnaire for Residents" (henceforth "Questionnaire"), to author (1991), 8. See also note 147 below.

21 Marjorie Bacon, "Questionnaire," 16.

22 A. Montague, *The Natural Superiority of Women* (New York, 1953), 188. See the favourable assessment in Joan Morris, "The Scientific Truth about 'Male Superiority,'" *Canadian Home Journal* (July 1957): 15, 45.

23 Ibid., 25.

24 See the positive, if cautious, review of Kinsey's work by J.R. Seeley and J. Griffin in *Canadian Welfare*, 15 Oct. 1948; the optimistic assessment of the utility of early marriage for women, based on Kinsey's findings, in Miriam Chapin, "Can Women Combine the BA and the Baby?" *Saturday Night*, 21 Feb. 1948, 24; and the positive attitude to the similarity of male and female sexuality in Eleanor Rumming, "Dr Kinsey and the Human Female," ibid., 15 Aug. 1953, 7–8. See also Gary Kinsman, *The Regulation of Desire: Sexuality in Canada* (Toronto, 1987), 113–15.

25 See Regina Markell Morantz, "The Scientist as Sex Crusader: Alfred C. Kinsey and American Culture" in *Procreation or Pleasure: Sexual Attitudes in American History*, ed. T.L. Altherr (Malabar, 1983).

26 See "Dr Kinsey Talks about Women to Lotta Dempsey," *Chatelaine* (Aug. 1949): 10–11, 59–60, and Claire Halliday, "A New Approach to the Problem of Frigidity," *Canadian Home Journal* (June 1956): 9, 69.

27 See "The Age for Marriage," *Chatelaine* (May 1948): 2.

28 Jan E. Dizard and Howard Gadlin, "Family Life and the Marketplace: Diversity and Change in the American Family" in *Historical Social Psychology*, ed. K.J. Gergen and M.M. Gergen (London, 1984), 10–11.

29 See, for example, Elsieliese Thorpe, "Does He Resent Your Working?" *Star Weekly* (May 1953), who emphasized the husband's right "to have his wife's undivided attentions at times when he needs to unburden himself, the right to have a companion and a friend when he needs one," 7; Charles Cerami, "Are You Jealous of Your Husband's Job?" ibid., 8 Nov. 1958, 30–41; and J.K. Thomas, "If He Lost His Job . . . ," *Canadian Home Journal* (Feb. 1957): 10–11.

30 Ken Johnstone, "How Do You Rate with Your Husband's Boss?" *Chatelaine* (March 1953): 70. See also the fierce rejection of the role of business helpmate in Mrs John Doe, "An Open Letter to My Husband's Boss," *Canadian Home Journal* (May 1954): 10–11, 90, 93.

31 Dr Marion Hilliard, *A Woman Doctor Looks at Love and Life* (Toronto, 1957), 72–73.

32 Full-page ad for Eaton's, *Saturday Night*, 9 Aug. 1949, 19.

33 See the response of 2000 members of *Chatelaine*'s Consumers' Council in Mary Juke, "It Makes Married Life Easier," *Chatelaine* (Sept. 1948): 22–23. On television see Paul Rutherford, *When Television Was Young: Primetime Canada 1952–1967* (Toronto, 1990), 200–201, which includes a useful discussion of the sexism of broadcasting in these years.

34 S.J. Wilson, *Women, the Family and the Economy* (Toronto, 1972), 19.

35 For discussion of this phenomenon see Meg Luxton, Harriet Rosenberg, Sedef Arat-Koe, *Through the Kitchen Window: The Politics of Home and Family*, 2nd ed. (Toronto, 1990).

36 Zoe Bieler, "White-Collar Wife," *Chatelaine* (Aug. 1953): 22–24, 37–40.

37 See, for example, Gwyn Le Capelan, "I Worked My Husband's Way Through College," *Chatelaine* (April 1949): 4–5. See also the discussion in National Archives of Canada (hereafter NAC), MG 31, K 8, Mattie Rotenberg papers, vol. 1, folder 66,

radio broadcast "Changing Patterns" (Jan. 1954).

38 See Ruth Roach Pierson, "Gender and the Unemployment Insurance Debates in Canada, 1934–1960," *Labour/Le Travail* 25 (Spring 1990): 77–103.

39 See Anita A. Birt, "Married Women, You're Fools to Take a Job," *Chatelaine* (Jan. 1960): 41.

40 Dorothy Manning, "I Quit My Job To Save My Marriage," ibid. (June 1955): 16.

41 Jean Libman Block, "Husbands Should Not Do Housework!" *Star Weekly*, 16 Nov. 1957, 6.

42 See the complaint about discrimination against women in Francis Ecker, "Will Married Women Go to War Again?" *Saturday Night*, 30 Jan. 1951, 21–23. For a more extended discussion of the policies of the federal government in this area see Ruth Roach Pierson, *"They're Still Women After All": The Second World War and Canadian Womanhood* (Toronto, 1986), ch. 2.

43 John G. McCulloch, "How To Be Sure of a Happy Marriage," *Bride's Book* (Spring/Summer 1953): 86. See also John K. Thomas, "How To Stay Married: Can Motherhood and Career Mix?" *Canadian Home Journal* (March 1955): 4, 6. For a contemporary assessment of women's own reservations about paid work, especially for mothers with young children, see Department of Labour, "Married Women Workers: The Home Situation" in *Canadian Society: Sociological Perspectives*, ed. B.R. Blishen, F.E. Jones, K.D. Naegele, and J. Porter (New York, 1961), 176.

44 See, for example, John Nash, "It's Time Father Got Back in the Family," *Maclean's*, 12 May 1956, 28; S.R. Laycock, "Homosexuality—A Mental Hygiene Problem," *Canadian Medical Association Journal* (Sept. 1950): 247, as cited in Kinsman, *Regulation of Desire*, 115; Mary Graham, "Mama's Boy," *Canadian Home Journal* (Oct. 1952): 18–19, 37–39; and Hilliard, *Woman Doctor*, passim. The most

famous example of "woman-blaming" in these years was Marynia Farnham and Ferdinand Lundberg, *Modern Woman: The Lost Sex* (1947), with its classic Freudian claim that "anatomy is destiny."

45 Montagu, as cited in Robert McKeown, "Women Are the Stronger Sex," *Weekend Magazine, Vancouver Sun*, 22 Jan. 1955, 2. See also Dr Ashley Montagu, "Why Men Fall in Love with You," *Chatelaine* (Oct. 1958): 23, 58, 99; Joan Morris, "The Scientific Truth about 'Male Superiority,'" *Canadian Home Journal* (July 1957): 15, 45; and Florida Scott-Maxwell, "Do Men Fear Women?" *Chatelaine* (Nov. 1959): 39, 50, 54–55.

46 See the argument by the anonymous author of "Careers and Marriage Don't Mix," *Saturday Night*, 1 Nov. 1949, 32, who concluded that she had been letting her husband down, despite her higher salary of $10 000 a year, by not keeping up the domestic side of their life.

47 *Chatelaine* (March 1959): 214.

48 See J.N. Harris, "One Vacancy!" *Saturday Night*, 15 Nov. 1947, 20; E.L. Chicanot, "Juvenile Immigration Will Help Canada," ibid., 6 Dec. 1947, 24, 37; Benjamin Higgins, "Better Strategy and Tactics To Win the Housing War," ibid., 14 Feb. 1948, 6–7; J. Bhaidlow, "Proper Rentals To Ease Housing Predicament," ibid., 17 April 1948, 17, 32; D. Wilensky, "War's Impact on Family Life," *Canadian Welfare*, 15 Oct. 1945, 8–16.

49 Canada Mortgage and Housing, *Housing in Canada 1945–1986: An Overview and Lessons Learned* (Ottawa, 1987), 6.

50 Ibid., 10.

51 Jill Wade, "'A Palace for the Public': Housing Reform and the 1946 Occupation of the Old Hotel Vancouver," *BC Studies* (Spring/Summer 1986): 288–310; "'Squatter Fever' Spreads to Canada," *The Enterprise* (Lansing, ON), 10 Oct. 1946.

52 John Clare, "Where Are the Houses?" *Star Weekly*, 8 June 1946, 5.

53 See Dorothy Livesay and Dorothy Macdonald, "Why BC Divorces Soar," *Star Weekly*, 15 May 1948, 16, and Marjorie Earl, "Canada's Divorce Headache," ibid., 12 June 1948, section 2, 2.

54 See Canada, Advisory Committee on Reconstruction, Housing and Community Planning, Sub-Committee *Report, No. 4* (Ottawa, 1944).

55 For an excellent review of policy see Albert Rose, *Canadian Housing Policies (1935–1980)* (Toronto, 1980).

56 See John Bacher, "From Study to Reality: The Establishment of Public Housing in Halifax, 1930–1953," *Acadiensis* 18, 1 (Autumn 1988): 120–35, and Albert Rose, *Regent Park: A Study of Slum Clearance* (Toronto, 1958).

57 Graduate Students in Community and Regional Planning, *Bridgeview: A Sub/Urban Renewal Study in Surrey, BC* (University of British Columbia, 1965).

58 See his *White Niggers of America* (Toronto, 1971). For an equally unflattering description of Ville Jacques Cartier see John Gray, "Why Live in the Suburbs?" *Maclean's*, 1 Sept. 1954, 7–11, 50–52.

59 See Project Planning Associates Ltd., *City of St John's Newfoundland: Urban Renewal Study* (Toronto, 1961), 6.

60 See David Bettison, *The Politics of Canadian Urban Development*, vol. 1 (Edmonton, 1975), 110.

61 CMHC mortgage assistance was tied to the earnings of the family head; if earnings were too low, then assistance was denied. In low-income areas such as the Maritimes, CMHC loans were correspondingly fewer. For a discussion of the regional implications of CMHC policy see Atlantic Develop-ment Board, *Urban Centres in the Atlantic Provinces* (Ottawa, 1969), 74.

62 Ibid., 76.

63 For a discussion of the impact of mortgaging by government see Lawrence B. Smith, *The Postwar Canadian Housing and Residential Mortgage Markets and the Role of Government* (Toronto, 1974), ch. 9, and also Rose, *Canadian Housing Policies*, ch. 3. In 1951 single-family construction made up 77.3 percent of all the dominion's housing starts; in 1955, 71.5 percent; and in 1960, 61.7 percent. Smith, *Postwar Canadian Housing*, 22–23.

64 D.S. Clark, *The Suburban Society* (Toronto, 1968), 101.

65 Krisztina Bevilacqua to author, 10 May 1991.

66 Marjorie Bacon, interview with author, 7 June 1991.

67 See John Gray, "A New Life Begins in Winnipeg," *Star Weekly*, 9 July 1960, 2–4, 6–7.

68 Lois Strong to author, 29 May 1991.

69 Montreal suburbanite 1, "Questionnaire," 7.

70 See John Weaver, "From Land Assembly to Social Maturity: The Suburban Way of Life of Westdale (Hamilton), Ontario, 1911–1951," *Histoire sociale/Social History* (Nov. 1978): 437.

71 "More Than Half Don Mills Home Owners Professional Men or Executives Survey Shows," *The Enterprise* (Lansing), 26 May 1957.

72 Dottie Walter, "Homes for Tomorrow," *Canadian Home Journal* (June 1945): 30, 33.

73 "Saracinis Will Build 106 Islington Homes," *Etobicoke Press*, 13 April 1950.

74 Rose, *Housing in Postwar Canada*, 168–71.

75 Peter McGahan, *Urban Sociology in Canada* (Toronto 1986), from table 61.

76 Ronald Hamilton, "You Need a Wife Who Can Saw," *Maclean's* (July 1950): 36.

77 Mildred Grace Baker, "Questionnaire."

78 Helen M. Boneham, "Questionnaire," 5.

79 Catherine Cunningham to author, 14 May 1991.

80 See Clark, *Suburban Society*, 16–18, for his classification of different suburban types.

81 See Collier Stevenson, "City Living in the Country," *Canadian Home Journal* (Nov. 1947): 55–56. For a Scarborough example see "Guildwood Village on the Move," *The Enterprise* (West Hill, ON), 25 Sept. 1958.

82 "All-Canadian Home Designed from Results of Newspaper Survey," *Canadian Builder* (Jan. 1960): 62, and "Million Mark Reached," ibid. (Oct. 1956): 41. See also "Scarborough Has Canada's Millionth New Home," *The Enterprise* (West Hill), 26 July 1956.

83 Lower Mainland Regional Planning Board, *The Urban Frontier*, part 2, *Technical Report* (New Westminster, BC: Oct. 1963), 37.

84 As quoted in William MacEachern, "Suburbia on Trial," *Star Weekly*, 18 May 1957, 2. See also, for a continuation of this preoccupation with children, Isabel Dyck, "Integrating Home and Wage Workplace: Women's Daily Lives in a Canadian Suburb," *Canadian Geographer/Le géographe canadien* 33, 4 (1989): 329–41.

85 Mrs Woods, Saracini Construction, "What the Experts Say About Kitchens," *Canadian Builder* (June 1958): 50.

86 Anthony Adamson, "Where Are the Rooms of Yesteryear?" *Canadian Architect* (June 1958): 74.

87 See, for example, Frank Moritsugu, "Learn How to Relax," *Canadian Homes and Gardens* (Jan. 1955): 7–9, 38–39, 41.

88 Male former resident, Oakridge Acres, London, ON, to author, 10 June 1991.

89 See R.D. Magladry, "Door-to-door Salesmanship Fills the Gap," *Financial Post* 54 (5 March 1960): 13; "Beauty Aid Sales Soar," ibid. (20 Aug. 1960): 1; and J. Schreiner, "Door-to-door is a

Booming Business," ibid. 55 (30 Dec. 1961): 24.

90 "Wife or Working Girl," *Bride's Book* (Fall/Winter 1952): 4, 6.

91 Helen Boneham, "Questionnaire," 14.

92 Alaine Barrett Baines, "Questionnaire," 8.

93 Scarborough suburbanite, interview with author, March 1991.

94 Clark, *Suburban Society*, 121.

95 On this male attitude see Meg Luxton, *More Than a Labour of Love: Three Generations of Women's Work in the Home* (Toronto, 1980), 163–65.

96 On the existence of two standards of living within the family see the bitter observation in Mrs John Doe, "An Open Letter to My Husband's Boss."

97 Bettison, *Politics of Canadian Urban Development*, 110.

98 As a sign of this interest the Community Planning Association of Canada was created in 1946. See Gerald Hodge, *Planning Canadian Communities* (Toronto, 1986).

99 See the bungalow winner for 1947 in *Etobicoke Press*, 17 March 1947.

100 "First All-Canadian Home Completed in Etobicoke," *Star Weekly*, 12 Sept. 1959, 14–18.

101 "Home '53," *Canadian Home Journal* (Aug. 1953): 19, 45, 46, 48, 50, 52–53.

102 Mary-Etta Macpherson, "Postwar Houses," *Chatelaine* (May 1945): 96.

103 See Betty Alice Marrs Naylor, "Questionnaire."

104 Helen Wallis, "Suburban Experience" (typescript), to author, 3.

105 Boneham, "Questionnaire," 5.

106 John Leaning, "The Distribution of Shopping Centres in Canada," *Canadian Builder* (June 1956): 41–45.

107 Marjorie Bacon, "Questionnaire," 9.

108 H.J. Barnun, Jr, executive vice-president, Salada-Shirriff-Horsey, Toronto, as cited in "Calls Suburbs Best Place To Develop Retail Sales," *Style Fortnightly*, 15 Jan. 1958, 35.

109 Mildred Fox Baker, "Questionnaire," 12.

110 Patricia Margaret Zieman Hughes, "Questionnaire," 12.

111 Alaine Barrett Baines, "Questionnaire," 13.

112 See Eileen Morris, "Your Home-and-School Faces a Crisis," *Chatelaine* (Nov. 1955): 11–13.

113 Between 1947 and 1962, for example, the United Church established 2000 new churches. See Mary Anne MacFarlane, "A Tale of Handmaidens: Deaconesses in the United Church of Canada, 1925 to 1964" (MA thesis, OISE, 1987), 80.

114 Doris McCubbin, "How To Live in a Suburb," *Chatelaine* (March 1955): 35.

115 See Frank Moritsugu, "The Amazing Don Mills," *Canadian Homes and Gardens* (Dec. 1954): 13–19, 55–60, 68.

116 *Vancouver Sun*, 6 Jan. 1951.

117 "Thornhill Women Are Proud of Their Flourishing Nursery School," *The Enterprise* (Lansing), 19 April 1951.

118 "Parents Unite To Catch Man Molesting Children," ibid., 28 April 1955.

119 "1000 Families Protest Isolation of Rexdale," *Etobicoke Guardian*, 13 Jan. 1955.

120 "Parents Protest Board Moving School Children," *The Enterprise* (Lansing), 2 June 1955.

121 D. Smith, "Don Mills Memo," ibid., 7 Oct. 1954.

122 "Subdivision Problems Cause Angry Mothers to Storm Council Meeting," *Etobicoke Press*, 19 April 1956.

123 Montreal West suburbanite 1, "Questionnaire," 6.

124 Mildred Fox Baker, "Questionnaire," 14.

125 Surrey, BC, suburbanite 1, "Questionnaire," 14.

126 Betty Marrs Naylor, "Questionnaire," 14.

127 Toronto West suburbanite 1, "Questionnaire," 15.

128 Jasper Place, AB, suburbanite, "Questionnaire," 14.

129 For one of the few discussions of these critics in Canada see Rutherford, *When Television Was Young*, esp. ch. 1. For a provocative assessment of the connection between fears about mass society and the maintenance of masculinity see Barbara Ehrenreich, *The Hearts of Men* (Garden City, NY, 1983).

130 Published in New York in 1963.

131 Wallis, "Suburban Experience," 23.

132 See Richard Roe, "I'm Sending My Wife Back To Work," *Canadian Home Journal* (April 1954): 4–5, 98; Jean Pringle, "How I Broke Out of Solitary Confinement," *Chatelaine* (May 1948): 34; Beverly Gray, "Housewives Are a Sorry Lot," ibid. (March 1950): 26–27, 37; Isabel T. Dingman, "A Widow Writes an Open Letter to Wives," ibid. (June 1954): 20–21, 34–35, 37; Dr Marion Hilliard, "Stop Being Just a Housewife," ibid. (Sept. 1956): 11, 90; Patricia Clark, "Stop Pitying the Underworked Housewife," *Maclean's*, 19 July 1958, 8, 37–38; Jane Hamilton, "Housewives Are Self-Centred Bores," *Star Weekly*, 22 Aug. 1959, 38, 45.

133 Published in New York in 1951. The quote is from page 76.

134 H. Garner, "You Take the Suburbs, I Don't Want Them," *Maclean's*, 10 Nov. 1956, 30.

135 Dr A. MacLeod, "The Sickness of Our Suburbs," *Chatelaine* (Oct. 1958): 23.

136 Ibid., 94–95.

137 See Robert Olson, "What Happened to the Suburb They Called Crestwood Heights?" *Maclean's*, 12 Oct. 1957, 24–25, 34–36, 38. The strength of this legacy can be seen in the incorrect identification of Crestwood Heights as Don Mills in McGahan, *Urban Sociology in Canada*, 187.

138 Committee of Inquiry into the Design of the Residential Environment, *Report* (Ottawa, 1960), *Journal of the Royal Architectural Institute of Canada* (May 1960): 186.

139 Ibid.

140 "R.E. Sutton Censures Story of 'Carefree' Life at H. Creek," *The Enterprise* (West Hill), 25 Oct. 1956.

141 "There Is No Joy in Highland Creek," *Globe and Mail*, 23 Oct. 1956; "Professor's Report Creates Furor," *The Enterprise* (West Hill), 25 Oct. 1956, and "Letters to the Editor," 1 Nov. 1956.

142 Clark, *Suburban Society*, 6.

143 Ibid., 4.

144 Ibid., 224.

145 Ruth Drysdale, "What Our Readers Say About Suburbia," *Chatelaine* (Jan. 1959): 50.

146 Mrs J.M. Telford, ibid., 53.

147 Contacts with these women, 32 as of 15 June 1991, are part of an ongoing effort to get in touch with as many women as possible from different types of suburbs in different regions of the country. These women are asked to specify how they wished to be identified, whether anonymously, by community, or by name, and their choice is reflected in the notes to this article. After the completion of a manuscript now entitled "Home Dreams: Women and Canadian Suburbs 1945–60," these research materials, with certain restrictions on their use, will be deposited in a public archives.

148 Etobicoke suburbanite 1, "Questionnaire," 17.

149 Mildred Fox Baker, "Questionnaire," 17.

150 Metro Toronto suburbanite 1, "Questionnaire," 17.

151 London, Ontario, suburbanite 1, "Questionnaire," 17.

152 Niagara-on-the-Lake suburbanite 1 to author, 10 May 1991.

153 Marjorie Bacon to author, 6 April 1991.

154 Toronto West suburbanite 1, "Questionnaire," 17.

155 Wallis, "Suburban Experience," 27.

How economics is shaping the constitutional debate in Quebec*

PIERRE FORTIN

● Introduction

The current search for a new constitutional order by Quebec is a political reaction to a political event, the rejection of the Meech Lake Accord. However, economic considerations are already playing a crucial role in the political debate, and are likely to exert a major influence on the context of the new constitution. As editorialist Alain Dubuc has recently observed, Quebec has clearly entered the post-romantic era where it is getting down to the practical business of defining exactly what sort of new constitution it wants.

The core of this paper aims at explaining why and how economic events and ideas are in fact shaping the constitutional debate in Quebec. To begin with, in previous rounds of constitutional debate in Quebec, the drive for a greater measure of sovereignty was constantly restrained by the general apprehension that any such occurrence would reduce the province's average standard of living. The main arguments were, first, that Quebec's economy was internally weak and highly dependent on external ownership, finance, labour power, and technology; second, that any unilateral move by the province to appropriate greater constitutional powers

*Robert Young, ed., *Confederation in Crisis* (Toronto: James Lorimer and Company Limited, 1991), 34–44. Reprinted with the permission of the publisher.

would meet with swift trade retaliation from outside; and third, that Quebec drew substantial net economic benefits from its participation in the federation.

Today, all three arguments stand on their heads. First, the perception is spreading that Quebec is not so dependent on the rest of the Canadian economy, and that its dynamic business class and highly educated labour force have allowed it to bridge its traditional productivity gap with Ontario. Second, after the Free Trade Agreement with the United States and the many rounds of GATT negotiations, the point is well understood that trade retaliation against Quebec is no longer a serious possibility under any constitutional option, and that the economic fortunes of countries have become less and less dependent on political size and status. And third, the widespread view now is that Canadian federalism is such an economic failure that it threatens to "Argentinize" Canada in general, and Quebec in particular. I shall examine the three arguments one by one.

• Quebec's Economic Self-Reliance

The first reason why no measure of economic threat is now likely to dissuade Quebec from following the political course it sees best fit to meet its political objectives is that the province now understands it has all the human, technological, and financial bases it needs to generate its own economic development as a mature member of Canada and the world community.

Thirty years ago, francophones in Quebec were poor and illiterate. According to the census of 1961, their relative status in their home province was exactly the same as that of black Americans in the United States. Both earned 64 percent of the national average income. Over half of francophones aged 20 and over had not reached grade 8 in school, and only 2 percent of young people went through university education. In spite of being 80 percent of the Quebec population, francophones owned only 20 percent of Quebec manufacturing and 47 percent of the total commercial sector. Quebec's productivity lagged 15 percent behind Ontario's.

Since then, two-thirds of the productivity gap with Ontario has been closed. Almost all teenagers go through grade 8, and over 20 percent make it to university education. About 40 percent of Quebec university students are in business schools, and they constitute 45 percent of all business students in Canada. The income gap between francophones and others is currently no more than 10 percent. An enterprising, outward-oriented, and pro-free-trade business class has blossomed. They now own 40 percent of manufacturing and 62 percent of the total commercial sector. They run 27 of the 50 fastest-growing companies in Canada, they spend more on research and development than anywhere else in the country, and they have been in the avant-garde of financial innovation in Canada throughout the 1980s. This progress has also been encouraged by strong social cohesion, close co-operation between the provincial government and the private sector, improved business–labour relations, and a more competitive tax system. The provincial government has focussed on supportive economic policies, and is helping to make Quebec opinion and institutions self-reliant, market-oriented, and competitive as well as co-operative.

• Economic and Political Boundaries

The second reason for the greater economic self-confidence in Quebec under any constitutional scenario is the contemporaneous trend towards bilateral and multilateral free trade in goods and capital. Forty years ago, with tariff walls around countries higher than 40 or 50 percent and widespread capital and exchange controls, political and economic boundaries tended to coincide. Nowadays, with world financial deregulation almost complete, and after several rounds of multilateral and bilateral tariff reductions such as GATT and the Canada–U.S. Free Trade Agreement, capital is almost perfectly mobile across countries, the remaining tariff barriers are few, and non-tariff barriers are coming under attack.

There are two major implications. First, economic space is no longer limited by political boundaries, and standards of living are basically independent of population size. For example, in 1985 the correlation coefficient between income per capita and size among OECD countries was −0.10 and statistically insignificant. The size of the Quebec economy is actually equal to or greater than that of Austria, Belgium, Denmark, Finland, Norway, New Zealand, and Switzerland, and not much smaller than that of Sweden. The second implication is that even under the most pessimistic scenario, trade retaliation by Canada against a hypothetically independent Quebec is unlikely and would at any rate not be very effective.

• Economic Failure of Federalism

The third reason why more sovereignty is no longer seen as a threat to standards of living is the widespread conviction that federalism is an economic failure. There are three supporting reasons: (1) the federal debt is out of control; (2) monetary instability is destructive of jobs and competitiveness; and (3) federal development policies have failed. The general presumption is that the situation reflects not merely bad policies, but also a bad system, one which is incapable of correcting its wrong course. Hence the need for constitutional reform.

1. The federal debt is out of control. It has increased from 15 percent of national income in 1981 to 40 percent today. The debt is now $200

billion higher than if this explosion had not occurred. The problem originated from loss of control over program expenditures at the end of the Trudeau era, and it has been inflated further by the record high interest rates of the last few years. In the past decade, we have experienced faster debt accumulation than every other large industrial country except Italy. Applying a hypothetical return of 10 percent per year to these $200 billion of excess debt translates into an annual income shortfall of about $20 billion for Canada, or $2000 per family. The debt makes us all poorer. Furthermore, interest payments on the debt now crowd out federal spending or crowd in federal taxes at the annual rate of over $10 billion just to prevent the problem from getting worse.

The contrast between the failure of the federal government to control its deficit and the success of Quebec government in achieving budget balance is striking. This clearly adds to the relative discredit in which the central government is held in the province.

2. Monetary instability destroys jobs and competitiveness. In Quebec and in other parts of the country, public opinion is also outraged by the high interest rates and exchange rates that are imposed by persistent monetary restriction. In the last year, real interest rates have exceeded 9 percent, and they have been 5 percent higher than in the United States. These high interest rates have been a major factor behind the 25 percent appreciation of the Canadian dollar against the American dollar since 1986. As a result, Canadian manufacturing firms have never been so uncompetitive in North American markets since data on competitiveness began to be collected forty years ago. Monetary policy in this way is delaying and even destroying a substantial proportion of the benefits anticipated from the Free Trade Agreement.

Also hard to take is the fact that in spite of rising unemployment and bankruptcies, inflation is not yet clearly under control. The GST is coming, and another oil crisis looms. Perhaps the monetary authorities will raise the national unemployment rate to 14 or 15 percent, if necessary, to reduce the inflation rate from 4 to 0 percent.

It is hard to convince the average business person that this makes sense. The frustration is not only with the policy itself, but with the seeming inability of the government to realize that the game plan does not work, and that something else should be tried which could keep inflation effectively under control and avoid the astronomical costs of recessions, bankruptcies, and unemployment. The recent Annual Review of the Economic Council of Canada has attempted to face the problem constructively by suggesting that consensus-based inflation control might help solve the quandary. The council's suggestion is probably being laughed out of court as naïve and irrelevant, in disregard of the fact that social cohesion may be one of the major systematic elements associated with good economic performance in modern industrial countries.

3. Federal development policies have failed. The final source of frustration with economic federalism is the perceived failure of development policies, mainly in the areas of manpower, research and development, and financial market regulation. All three are absolutely crucial under the current pressure for global competitiveness, and yet among industrial countries Canada ranks among the worst performers, at least in the first two instances.

One of the reasons may be that under the present constitution the federal government is permitted to spend in almost every area it wants. The constitution allows it to spend in its own areas of exclusive jurisdiction, in areas of shared responsibilities, in all areas not explicitly defined by the BNA Act, and also in areas of exclusive provincial jurisdiction. The result is a monstrous system of competitive government, replete with duplication, contradiction, and waste. Twelve years ago, Senator Arthur Tremblay and two colleagues at ENAP produced evidence showing that out of a total of 465 federal and provincial spending programs in Quebec, 277 (or 60 percent) were directly or indirectly overlapping.

Manpower, research and development, and financial market regulation are just three examples of this absurd administrative mess, which are mentioned here only for their key importance to economic growth. The Quebec business and labour community has long found that in these three areas the provincial government has generally adopted policies which they view as more sensible and better-adapted to the specific Quebec environment than federal policies. Hence the flood of current proposals for constitutional amendments which would give Quebec full control.

These considerations underline the more general principle that the new Canadian constitution should make a major attempt at minimizing the overlaps between jurisdictions. The duplication and waste generated by the current constitution is clearly substantial, and it has certainly contributed to the current financial distress of the federal government to the extent of several billion dollars.

• Conclusion

The economic failure of federalism on the fiscal, monetary, and economic development fronts is the subject of wide consensus in Quebec. One major implication for the constitutional debate is that the traditional defence line of federalism, based on the "obvious" economic benefits of the present system, is in very serious trouble. It is not credible any more. The fear now stems from the fact that the federal government currently operates as a major drag on the economies of Quebec and of the entire country. Hence the reference to Argentina. The prime minister is right to state, as he did ecently in Mont-Sainte-Anne, that "the economic foundations must be completely solid." But this is precisely the point: many in Quebec are so clearly convinced of this truth that they want to change or opt out of the present failing system before it is too late.

Actually, business opinion is even more radical. Earlier this year, a COM-Les Affaires survey of 200 business leaders from the province's 500 largest industrial firms found that those who believed political independence would have a positive impact on the long-term economic development of Quebec outnumbered those who thought the impact would be negative by a 4-to-1 margin. This suggests that no degree of political independence for Quebec is believed economically more dangerous for the province than the way the federal state is now run in Canada.

To summarize, the most important difference between the current constitutional debate and that of ten years ago is that Quebec sovereignty is now more clearly perceived as an economically credible and viable option. Average business opinion goes as far as believing it would enhance the long-term economic prospects of the province. This is reinforced by the view that, even under the worst political scenario, it is unlikely that the Canadian common market will be dismantled. Quebec will obviously want to remain part of the Canadian dollar zone, but it could have its own credible and viable currency if forced out.

The broad political outcome is still uncertain, but the foregoing analysis indicates that the province will want to put an end to the era of competitive government. It will push for a sharp clarification, with minimum overlap, of the legislative and spending responsibilities of the two levels of government, and for wide control over key instruments of economic development such as manpower, immigration, research and development, communications, trade and financial regulation, transportation, regional development, and income security. It will also seek greater control over the Bank of Canada by the regions, and greater exchange rate stability. It may even go as far as asking that constitutional restrictions be imposed on the power of governments to borrow.

Whether this will take place in a much more decentralized federation, in a community of quasi-sovereign regions with delegation of powers to the central government, or in a sovereign Quebec state will depend on interests, but also on emotions, on goodwill, on capacity to communicate, on strategy, and also, obviously, on chance. Needless to say, everything would have been much simpler if Meech had made it through.

THE PRAIRIES AS REGION:
The Contemporary Meaning of an Old Idea*

GERALD FRIESEN

In a period of political crisis, when the accustomed arrangements of the federal state are in question, it is appropriate to review historic grievances and to ask whether a revised constitutional structure might better meet Canada's needs. Canadians would acknowledge that prairie residents have often expressed discontent with Confederation. Today's political discussion—western separatism, western alienation, "the West wants in"—has made the theme familiar. Canadians are aware, too, that the points of dissatisfaction are not new. During the first half of this century, such labels as prairie protest, agrarian revolt, and labour revolt were often applied to similar expressions of discontent. Métis rebellion and aboriginal resistance and provincial rights, all of which might be said to have a regional cast, dominated the last decades of the nineteenth century. Even before Confederation, the Prairies and the western interior were described as a distinct part of the globe. Visitors attributed a special status to the land, a separate identity to this striking expanse that they depicted as one of the noteworthy "wildernesses" on the globe. The talk of a single West, of a prairie region and of prairie regionalism is, therefore, part of Canadian popular expression.

My assignment is to review the idea of prairie region and to provide a context for discussions of the place of prairie residents in Confederation. I

---

*James N. McCrorie and Martha L. MacDonald, eds., *The Constitutional Future of the Prairie and Atlantic Regions of Canada* (Regina: Canadian Plains Research Center, 1992), 1–17. Reprinted with the permission of the publisher.

have interpreted it in the form of several questions: first, how has the concept of prairie region been used and has it been regarded as helpful or appropriate in the interpretation of prairie experience? And, second, when we invoke "prairie regionalism" in our contemporary constitutional discussions, what is the "ism" meant to convey and does it offer a relevant interpretation of contemporary prairie political experience?

There are three main approaches to the phenomenon of region—the formal, the functional, and the imagined. Separately, each has been employed as a means of depicting the Canadian Prairies; together, they present problems. They tend to overlap in popular thinking, mutually to reinforce and, yet, to flee from precise definition. They are often fuzzy when utilized in debates about public policy, so it is as well that we be clear about the concept before we use it in the discussions to follow.

The simplest approach, on the surface, is the formal region: the Prairies *look* like a separate and distinct and homogeneous place—in short, like a region. When Henry Kelsey arrived on the edge of these plains in 1690, he described them as a "barren ground" and said that they offered "Nothing but short Round sticky grass & Buffillo."[1] A century later, David Thompson named this zone "the Great Plains as a general name," said they constituted a "very different formation," and placed the area in continental perspective by suggesting that they stretched from the Gulf of Mexico to the 54th parallel.[2] In the eighteenth century, European Canadian scientific observations having intensified with the extension of national boundaries and surveys into this area, an 1884 geology textbook divided the northern half of the continent in two at the "Laurentian axis extending from Lake of the Woods to the Arctic, arguing that the eastern and western halves were geologically and physically distinct."[3] These generalizations represent the first level of European Canadian regional perceptions. They rely upon land forms and climate and unity of historical experience to define a separate and distinct place on the earth's surface.

The historian Goldwin Smith best encapsulated this phase of thinking about regions in the late nineteenth century. Writing in the era when nation building and national realignment were still transforming the globe, Smith evoked the power of geographical forces to break apart the new transcontinental Canada. He argued in the opening statement of his *Canada and the Canadian Question* that, if one wished to understand Canada's national dilemma, one must turn "from the political to the physical map," from an image of a united land to one that featured "four separate projections of the cultivable and habitable part of the Continent into arctic waste," each separated from the others "by great barriers of nature, wide and irreclaimable wildernesses or manifold chains of mountains" and each "closely connected by nature, physically and economically" with the adjoining American region.[4] Such perceptions represent the physical interpretation of the western interior as a formal region. They underlie all the perspectives that follow, and they *will* linger in our minds, despite our best efforts to rid ourselves of such apparently simple interpretations of human society.[5]

The developing literature on the Prairies, whether in fiction or the social sciences, offered further variations on this interpretation of regional difference—of formal region—in the late nineteenth and early twentieth centuries. Environment, in this view, affected and perhaps even determined human character or social behaviour. Thus, Roger Pocock, a novelist of the 1880s, described mounted police returning from patrol, "their eyes bright with the reflected breadth and freedom of the plains. . . . [They] have no flavour of the old tiresome life of the umbrella and the table-cloth."[6] In a novel by the immensely popular Ralph Connor, a character exclaims: "How wonderful the power of this country of yours to transform men!"[7]

These assertions may now appear foolish but they represent a significant strain in Canadian thought early in the twentieth century. Scholars shared with novelists this preoccupation with the power of the land. The geographer Griffith Taylor, for example, built a career on his environmentalist interpretations. His major work on Canada, published in 1947, distinguished twenty Canadian regions, including the Winnipeg basin and the western prairie, and forecast remarkable population growth for both on the basis of his assessment of the future of world agricultural and energy production.[8] The great prairie historian of that era, Arthur Silver Morton, invoked similar assumptions when, in describing the crucial shift of aboriginal groups from parkland to plains in the 1700s, he wrote that the "Crees wandered over into the prairies and adopted the very different manner of living which characterized the buffalo country." In such works an implied environmental determinism assumed as much as it explained but it also offered an explanation for the presence of formal regions.[9]

The foregoing versions of the western interior, whether depicting the area as a natural product of physical geography (David Thompson and Goldwin Smith), or as a social phenomenon introduced by environmental forces (Ralph Connor and Griffith Taylor), asserted that the Canadian Prairies constituted a definable portion of the earth's surface. No reference to other places was necessary to establish the region's character. The prairie region stood on its own, distinctive and clearly demarcated, as a "formal region" that occupied an unmistakable physical place on the map. Its boundaries would not change significantly as long as the physical environment remained unaltered. It was relatively consistent internally as measured by certain self-evident and allegedly objective characteristics. The link in this analysis between formal region and environmental interpretations of human affairs will be unmistakable.

Environmentalism, pure and simple, has since fallen into disrepute but recognition of environmental *influence* in human affairs can hardly be disputed. Ronald Rees's recent volume on the Canadian plains examines such difficult matters as the impact of an environment devoid of trees and other physical relief upon human well-being.[10] The careers of many Canadian scholars, including W.L. Morton and Harold Innis, were devoted to understanding the interplay between environment and human endeavour. Thus, environmentalism need not become determinism and emphasis upon landscape and resource differences in regional analysis must not be dismissed today as the musing of fanatics. As students of society, we run the danger, ironically, of neglecting environmental influences upon human activity while, because of some atavistic mental reflex, we retain a dogged and simple concept of formal physical region—the Canadian Prairies—that underlies our daily life and thought. My observation is that, no matter how we try, our picture of a prairie region will always retain some degree of this plain and simple thinking, of formal regionalism.

A second kind of regional definition, also important in Canada, employs a relative or relational approach. In order to have one region, in this view, one must have another. Hinterland regions exist because there are also metropolitan regions, frontiers can only be distinguished from densely settled zones, areas of staple exploitation from central markets where consumers and entrepreneurs and, often, cultural and political leadership are located. These places, shaped as much by the coherent whole of which they form a part as by internal consistency or evident boundaries, have been labelled "functional regions." As Janine Brodie has suggested, they are defined by their relationships as well as by their internal characteristics, and by social as much as "natural" elements.[11]

I will offer just two illustrations of how this approach has influenced our thinking about the Prairies. Canadians once were accustomed to describing the West as a frontier. Thus, the Queen's University academic, Adam Shortt, reported that his preconceptions about social organization had been "revolutionized" during his travels in the Northwest in 1894. He found there not the well-defined characteristics of business and social life he was accustomed to in Ontario but, rather, a society "in process of formation."[12] When Isaiah Bowman designed a multivolume scholarly project, the Canadian Frontiers of Settlement series, in the late 1920s, he believed that he was creating a science of settlement that would have international application because "the pioneer belts of the world are regions of experiment—'experimental zones' we might call them."[13] Similarly, the distinguished economist W.A. Mackintosh argued that "Sectionalism is always characteristic of a new and expanding country. There is always division between the frontier and the old settlements, whether exemplified in Jacksonian democracy, or in conflict between Halifax and York currencies and between established churches and Methodism, or in farmers' movements."[14] The sociologist S.D. Clark employed comparable arguments in linking the Seven Oaks incident, the two Métis resistances, the One Big Union, the People's Church, the wheat pools, and Social Credit as "western movements of revolt," the expressions of "a separate people," that would recur in cycles as the predecessor movements lost their bite.[15] Each of these examples distinguishes the prairie West from more settled zones in the rest of North America. Each is an example of a functional region.[16]

Another influential approach to the prairie region has been the so-called staples or Laurentian school of Canadian history. As Janine Brodie has noted, Harold Innis's work on cod, fur, timber, and wheat implies a spatial distribution of economic activity consequent upon the export of particular staples to a metropolis. Unfortunately, the staples thesis lends itself to a simplistic, dualist interpretation of Canadian experience that Innis himself would have rejected. Thus, the so-called metropolis–hinterland, centre–periphery, and regional-disparity models, so familiar among social scientists in the 1970s, are abstractions that convey sharp images of Canadian regions while simplifying the very complex circumstances in which regional differences developed. One point of Brodie's work, indeed, is to recover some of the crucial economic and social forces that have been lost in the model building. By returning to the economic foundations of functional regions, she is restoring strength to an approach that has lacked it. Her emphasis on the uneven spatial development in capitalist economies must be treated seriously and her revival of V.C. Fowke's concern for the spatial biases of government policies must, similarly, be acknowledged as sound.[17]

Both the frontier and staple approaches to prairie history entail the use of a functional definition of region. Each assumes a relationship between at least two entities and, consequently, a larger system, one that encompasses these component parts, that can change over time. In some cases, the boundaries between the communities—and thus the identity of previously distinct regions—may actually vanish. The Prairies need not always be the Prairies, or at least need not be distinguished as a separate place and society.

The third approach to region assumes that a place must be imagined before it can be. This approach grew out of the environmentalism associated with such early novelists as Ralph Connor. It was consolidated in the late 1940s by the critic and novelist Edward McCourt, who argued that prairie literature was distinctive because of the author's association with the landscape.[18] Of course, this environmentalism has been superseded by more precise analysis in later decades, but McCourt's convictions about prairie cultural differences have not been contradicted. Rather, one could argue that more convincing articulations of the same perception have won the attention of cultural scholars.

Eli Mandel, who has written of these matters in the 1970s and 1980s, views region as "a mental construct . . . a myth." He argues that there is a "certain coherence or unity or identity" in the poetry and prose that we describe as *prairie* literature. This coherence is expressed through elements common to regional literatures: a local landscape pictured with startling clarity; a child's view of the world and of home—home being the place where one realizes one's *first* and most memorable vision of things; a grotesque storyteller; a regional dialect; and stories of the past. Thus, in Mandel's view, there is a distinctive regional prairie literature that creates a mythicized prairie world. Prairie storytellers project onto the land their chosen images of the environment—images of the land's redemptive powers (in the figure of a child) and of its demonic tyranny (a hostile father)—and in that choice they adapt their images to a pattern that belongs to all humankind. What images do prairie writers choose? Mandel replies that they are "images of a search for home and therefore a search for the self."[19] Mandel's conceptual language is, we would say today, more convincing, more subtle, than the environmentalism of McCourt. The conviction that drives him, and perhaps even his conclusion, may be little different, but Mandel's understanding of human society and his articulation of the processes of the human imagination convince us that something about this place warrants a distinct category in the company of international social orders or, at the least, in the list of Canadian communities.

There are three fundamental approaches to region—formal, functional, and imagined. Each has been used to distinguish a prairie social order. Together, over the past two centuries, these approaches have sustained an abiding belief that something marked off the prairie place or the prairie experience or the prairie expression from other places, experiences, and expressions. Whether observers were describing a landscape that shaped one's interests and one's mind, or minds that shaped a landscape, or political and economic interests that dominated one's outlook, the cumulative weight of thinking, illustrating, and writing about "the Prairies" asserted the distinctiveness of life on this portion of the globe. There is something here that cannot be ignored. Thus, to my first questions, how has the concept of region been used and has it been regarded as helpful, my answer is that region has been applied to the Prairies in three overlapping ways and that, yes, it has been regarded as helpful, even necessary, in discussing the prairie experience.

The second issue concerns the term *regionalism*—what has the idea of prairie regionalism conveyed to observers and does it offer fundamental insights into *contemporary political* experience?

To this point, I have been discussing the region as a place and a proper noun. One cannot have regionalism without a region or regions, presumably, but the analysis of a popular sentiment or political movement distinguished by the term "regionalism" must be different from the relatively abstract discussions about formal and functional and imagined regions. Regionalism implies protest. It speaks of injustice, of neglect, perhaps even of one community's alleged superiority or power over another. Regionalism demands that the student pay simultaneous attention to community consciousness and community behaviour; that is, regionalism speaks of outlook, on the one hand, and self-interest or needs, on the other. The term "regionalism" presumes a larger administrative, economic, and political entity, of which our special "region" is a part. Regionalism, in

Canada at least, also raises the problem of federalism, meaning such specialized topics as the distribution of powers, revenue sharing, and mechanisms for resolving constitutional disagreements between levels of government. As Northrop Frye once commented, it also raises the issue of national survival. Indeed, regionalism is often used to describe an alternate nationalism, a loyalty to place and people that is built upon the same foundations of sentiment as the nation. In short, regionalism is a messy concept.

Because of the overlap between region and province, between economic and social definitions of a community on the one hand, and political units on the other, such scholars as Donald Smiley and Ramsay Cook have called for an end to talk of regionalism and a focus on province in Canadian scholarly discourse concerning territory-based loyalties. Alan Cairns's landmark article, "The Governments and Societies of Canadian Federalism," probably did much to sustain this approach in contemporary political studies.[20] Nor should one underestimate the fear of national disintegration as a force in proscribing talk of regionalism from the late 1970s on.[21]

Garth Stevenson, Ralph Matthews, Raymond Breton, and Janine Brodie have rejected this conclusion. Stevenson defines region as a "natural and organic unity and community of interests that is independent of political and administrative barriers."[22] Matthews asserts the existence of "a socio-psychological factor that involves identification with and commitment to a territorial unit."[23] Breton has argued that regionalism is a political phenomenon in which other interests are articulated in spatial terms—that is, "an interpretation of social relations that gives political priority to the condition of the territorial entity" rather than to such nonterritorial conditions as gender, class, and race.[24] Brodie, too, emphasizes the political and material foundation of regions, which she defines as *political creations* that state development strategies cumulatively impose upon the geographic landscape."[25] These scholars share a conviction that regions and regionalism exist in Canada, that they are not merely arbitrary intellectual constructs, that their origins lie primarily in material factors (associated especially with the distribution of resources and with economic development policies), and that, in the final analysis, reference to them in public discourse is a significant part of Canadian life. In the case of the Canadian Prairies, I think it is possible to reconcile the views of advocates of regional analysis and those who believe it should be jettisoned.

The case for prairie regionalism is usually made by reference to moments of significant public protest: the Métis resistances of 1869–70 and 1885, the farm and labour and religious outbursts after 1918, the rise of third parties in the 1930s and 1940s, the emergence of provincial rights and secessionist sentiments in the 1970s and early 1980s.[26] What do these expressions tell us about prairie regionalism?

The aboriginal unrest of the late nineteenth century, whether Métis or Indian, is better described as the expression of profound cultural conflict. Moments of violence were not, in the first instance, "regional" protests but rather incidents in the painful adjustment of very different cultures. I am aware that the conflicts arose in part because of Ottawa's failure to communicate effectively and to reconsider particular policies. Seen from the aboriginal perspective, however (and they were the people engaged in the uprisings), the refusal of the government to understand the needs of the First Nations was evidence of a failure of European Canadian cultural imagination. Moreover, the aboriginal cultures did not divide along territorial (east–west) lines. The distinction between resistance by military action and resistance by other means was less significant, in the aboriginal view, than it was in the eyes of European Canadians.

By an unusual reversal, ironically, the aboriginal discontents have been included in the tradition of western grievance. Given this contemporary confusion, it is important that we support W.L. Morton's perspective on the initial bias of prairie politics and reject S.D. Clark's inclusion of Métis uprisings in the tradition of western regional protests. Incoming settlers, mostly Ontarians, who had very little sympathy for the aboriginal cause when the spectre of violence arose in the 1880s, had no difficulty separating their grievances against Ottawa and central Canada from those of the Métis and Indians. The newcomers, often transplanted Ontarians, complained about federal control of lands and resources, the tariffs, freight rates, federal subsidies to the provinces, and the Manitoba school question. They even sustained a revisionist, western-based school of historical interpretation. They did not endorse Big Bear or Riel after the shooting started. The causes of the incoming settlers, as W.L. Morton pointed out, arose from the initial bias of Confederation, the political imbalance established by the Manitoba and North-West Territories Acts and by the economic policies that followed. It was only many decades later, the precise issues having been forgotten, that aboriginal leaders became the heroes of western protest and representatives of the initial "bias" of prairie politics, as W.L. Morton named it.[27]

The second source of prairie bias, in Morton's interpretation, was the agrarian protest that peaked during the opening decades of this century. The agrarian campaign, driven by western unhappiness over tariffs, freight rates, and many other farm-related matters, consolidated the local and national conclusion that a distinctive prairie region had come into being. We have already noted that this is a complicated conclusion. To understand how difficult, we must return to the thorny question of territory-based loyalties.

In the decades between 1900 and 1930, Canadians came to believe that a new community had crystallized in the prairie West. A formal region, a variety of functional regions, and an imagined region had coalesced into a single image. Its characteristics, aside from the all-important lines on the political map, included frontier vitality and economic grievance and political protest. The evidence for the existence of such a regional community is incontrovertible: the secession of western members of the Presbyterian

Church in such numbers that the Church (or most of it) was propelled into the United Church of Canada in 1925; the secession of many trade unions from the Canadian Trades and Labor Congress and their American craft headquarters in the events surrounding the Winnipeg General Strike and the One Big Union; the secessions from the old-line political parties that launched the Progressives; and the secessions from the grain handling and marketing system that produced the co-operatives and the wheat pools. Regionalism was the term applied to this shift in the locus of power and in the requirements placed upon certain national institutions. It was a term coined to explain the apparently collective assault upon Canada's fabric by western residents in these heady decades. A model of "the Canadian region," and an assumption about both the Prairies and all the other parts of Canada had crystallized.

Phillips, Conway, and Brodie follow Morton, Fowke, Mallory, Macpherson, and a host of writers on farm protest in arguing that the manifestations of regional protest during the era of the so-called first National Policy were reactions to that very body of policies.[28] This interpretation of prairie voting patterns from 1918 to 1926 is reasonable, as far as it goes. It does not explain, however, why the One Big Union should have been founded on a regional secession from Canadian and American unions, or why western newspaper editors seceded from the Canadian Press syndicate in favour of the Western Associated Press, or why the establishment of the United Church should have been driven by western needs, attitudes, and individuals. In each case, I believe, the assumption that regions existed, and that regional interests were primary interests in community life, and that regionalism was a fundamental interpretation of social organization, underlay their dissent. This cultural perspective, a supplement to the economic and political analysis, is pivotal to our appreciation of the regional "imagined community" that had just taken shape. Not surprisingly, these "regional" characteristics coincided with the formal prairie region.

Why did the consolidation of the prairie "imagined community" occur between 1900 and 1930 and why within these boundaries? The lines on the map help to explain the boundaries. Such cultural icons shape the way we think. So, too, does the administration of the territory; boundaries are made real by the activity of civil servants who work within the map's boundaries. In prairie Canada, to a degree now forgotten, the administration was the work of the federal government and thus was a unifying force. Ottawa treated the West, especially through the Department of the Interior, as a single administrative unit for lands and forests. Ottawa established policies, too, for naturalization and tariffs and police and Indians and transportation. Another explanation of the regional boundary rests upon the work of Winnipeg, the metropolis of the Prairies in that period, which sent its decrees from the grain exchange and stock yard and newspaper print shop (the boiler plate or "patent insides" that accompanied many prairie weeklies), and by means of an army of travelling salesmen.

These metropolitan forces, too, generated a sense of a single community. The prairieness of this era was also sustained by the intellectual climate, a climate composed of equal parts frontier theory, staple thesis, environmentalism, and simple boosterism, which reinforced the perception that the Prairies constituted a new society, one truly in tune with the times.

Political innovations in the 1930s and 1940s, socialism and Social Credit, have also been attributed to a distinctive prairie regional behaviour. W.L. Morton described the 1930s and 1940s as the era of utopianism and suggested the rise of the two parties was the culmination of the previous biases in prairie politics. In other words, he linked these phenomena to the National Policy era that preceded 1930. No one would wish to deny the presence of East-bashing in some of the platform rhetoric of the 1930s but, by the same measure, CCF and Social Credit owed their electoral successes to far more than regional sentiments.

V.C. Fowke introduced a different perspective by arguing that the first National Policy had been completed by 1930 and that a second was struggling into life in these decades, commencing with the introduction of "social net" or wealth redistribution measures as part of a new Keynesian approach to economic planning.[29] How could the second National Policy be interpreted as a regional phenomenon? One might argue that the devastating prairie experience of depression, unique in its impact, drove Bracken and Dafoe and Douglas and Aberhart, unlike other political leaders, to adopt distinctive approaches to political economy, including social democratic and redistributive measures. Janine Brodie takes another tack by suggesting that the Prairies, whether or not they may have contributed to the introduction of Keynesian approaches, actually were the creation of them, in the sense that the second National Policy, like its predecessor, reinforced regional interests. Indeed, by targeting regional disparities as a primary concern of national politics, according to Brodie, the second National Policy contributed a significant new source of regionalism to Canadian public life. To me, this approach seems viable, especially if we link it to events in the 1960s and 1970s. However, the arguments in favour of a sharp divide in prairie history around 1930 and of prairie continuity during the next half-century will require further elaboration.

Prairie unrest during the Trudeau era was focussed especially on federal government policies. Agricultural issues such as grain sales and freight rates and the temporary LIFT program to reduce crop production, control of such resources as oil and potash—indeed energy policy in general—bilingualism, metric measures, diversification of the prairie economy into secondary and tertiary sectors, multiculturalism, all could be said to have fuelled prairie protest between the late 1960s and the mid-1980s. Of course, Trudeau was held to be responsible for everything.[30] What was especially galling to prairie residents, as David Smith has suggested, was that many of these Liberal policies denied longstanding prairie conclusions. One official language, continuity on the family farm, the Crow's Nest

Pass freight rate agreement, and provincial control of natural resources belonged in the category of sacred trusts in prairie political life. Thus, "prairie regionalism" in this era was a means of describing the prairie revolt against federal policies and against the Liberal party.

The regionalism of the 1970s, indeed the regionalism that had been developing from the 1930s through the 1970s, differed from its predecessor. Though it inherited the causes and the fervour of the 1870–1930 model, this next phase of prairie regionalism was actually expressed through the province. As Roger Gibbins has demonstrated, prairie society became more like Ontario society in these decades. And, as Alan Cairns has argued so effectively, provincial governments assumed an increasingly prominent part in defining their communities. Moreover, Ottawa no longer ruled a fiefdom but, rather, treated all the provinces more or less equally. Winnipeg's economic leadership was superseded by provincial metropolises and by increasingly national and international trade flows. This was the generation of province building. Prairie regionalism in the 1970s simply reinforced the prevailing "provincialism."

What does such an historical review demonstrate? Popular outbursts occurred often in the Prairies during the century after 1870. Some of these expressions of discontent had their roots in aboriginal culture and in European Canadian blindness to the imperatives of that culture; such expressions should not be described as regionalism. The later protests targeted Macdonald's National Policy and probably were reinforced by the second National Policy. The protests demonstrated the ways in which the federal structure of government and the electoral system sustained territory-based loyalties in preference to those of class, gender, or ethnicity. Changes in prairie Canada's relations with the international economy, as in the 1880s and after World War I and again in the 1930s and 1970s, also lay behind the conflict. Rather than enter a debate about the relative merits of regionalism and provincialism, I would prefer to argue that both are territory-based loyalties, both can be plausibly invoked in discussions of prairie history, and one is the heir of the other.[31] The key question, in my view, is the vehicle that carries and simultaneously diffuses the prairie political protest—before 1930, that vehicle was the federal party system; increasingly, after 1930, it was the system of federal–provincial relations.[32]

Our problem is not just to decide whether regionalism, based on the formal region or on the various provinces, has existed but to estimate how important the sentiment is. Does it play a role in public opinion in 1991 comparable to its role in 1941? 1921? 1901? 1881? How much does it really matter? One way to tackle such a difficult question is to approach it from the perspective of nation and nationalism.

In Canada, discussion of region often has provoked concern about nation, especially the unity of the nation, and often is said to contradict national identity. Northrop Frye was not happy with this concatenation of the two sentiments, love of nation and love of region, and preferred to separate them. He argued that they arose out of two very different concepts, unity and identity. In this view, "unity is national in reference, international in perspective, and rooted in a political feeling" whereas "identity is local and regional, rooted in the imagination and in works of culture."[33] Frye's perspective is interesting because it distinguishes between types of feeling. He suggests that sentiments concerning political loyalty—what might be called community subjects—can be separated from sentiments concerning personal identity. If Frye is correct, Mandel's work on prairie literature and prairie region must be revisited. Mandel posits that region in literature is an expression of personal identity. However, if the discussion of "identity questions" is separated from political feelings and other such territory-based loyalties, then we must redefine the cultural or "imagined" region. In this task, some recent work on nationalism might offer assistance.

The nation offers a helpful perspective upon smaller, territory-based, community loyalties (region, province, city, neighbourhood), because, in the last two centuries, it has become the essence of community. As Benedict Anderson has suggested, "nation-ness is the most universally legitimate value in the political life of our time." The nation, in Anderson's definition, is a limited, sovereign, imagined community: limited, in that it does not, in any single instance, cover all of humankind; sovereign within the boundaries of a given state; and a community in the sense that it is "imagined" as "a deep, horizontal comradeship."[34] The strengths of this recent and, I think, fruitful approach are that it treats communities as political places and that it distinguishes these political communities by "the style in which they are imagined." It takes no great leap of imagination to place the region and the province in the same scale as nation. We all possess a hierarchy of political or civic values associated with the imagined communities in which we live. Moreover, the standings within this hierarchy and the reasons for the ranking are probably subject to investigation. If region were profoundly important in the outlook of citizens resident in the Canadian Prairies, then it would tend towards nation; if province were paramount, then it would acquire nation-like attributes; if neither was as important as nation, or some other national alternative such as continental union, then it would not constitute an alternate nationalism. What is the relative importance of the various imagined communities in prairie society? Put another way, what is the cultural context of the Canadian prairie community?[35]

"Culture" is a very difficult word these days. Many cultural scholars now assert that their subject is just as likely to be primary—and important—as economics or technology. Their purpose is to subvert the customary assumption that "base," defined as material reality, determines superstructure; instead, they assert that "the representations of the social world themselves are the constituents of social reality." One of these advocates has written that "Economic and social relations are not prior to or determinants of cultural relations—they are themselves fields of cultural practice and cultural production."[36] Culture, in this perspective, is larger than the arts or the cultural industries, smaller than an entire way of life.[37] When we discuss culture, we are discussing the sense we make of our "selves" and situating that sense within our social order.

Little has been written on prairie culture from this perspective. Let us assume, for argument's sake, that the region, whether in its 1920-era prairiewide boundaries or its 1980-era provincial boundaries, might coincide with an imagined community. Where would it find its definition or rationale? One potential source of an imagined community is kinship.[38] National identity may also be expressed through language and religion. Of course, prairie Canada and its constituent provinces do not possess such genealogical continuity nor do they share a unique religion. On the other hand, the experience of prairie citizens during the preceding hundred years constitutes a relevant and important claim to a common prairie linguistic and religious heritage, one based on shared experience of linguistic assimilation and lost or, to put it more positively, redefined faith. These historical matters that prairie citizens experienced in common might constitute a foundation for a separate nationhood and, perhaps, could work in favour of a more powerful regional identity. This argument might be built on the contention that history, appropriately interpreted, has sustained many nationalisms in the Americas. The argument might be plausible but the fact that it has not been made suggests that it simply does not hold water.

Another foundation of the imagined community is a network of communications, originally based on print but now also on electronic means, that establishes a feeling of simultaneity, or of shared political experience, across space, time, and household. Yet another foundation is the network of functionaries in the modern state whose pilgrimages and very existence outline the boundaries and educate the imaginations of the citizenry. The communications networks did develop in the late nineteenth century on the Prairies. As we have seen, they helped to sustain a prairie regional consciousness between 1880 and 1930. Thereafter, they declined in favour of continental, national, and provincial empires. The professions linked by this communications web, including lawmakers, mapmakers, museum builders, archivists, census takers, and government administrators, also shifted from a prairiewide to a provincial constituency in this century. The Hudson's Bay Company and the Department of the Interior, two pivotal "inventors of tradition" before 1870 and 1930 respectively, gave way to provincial and city leaders in the later decades of the twentieth century. All this would suggest that a prairiewide nationalism is a little less likely in the present than is a province-based alternate nation. But it offers little guidance about the relative power of the regional perspective.

The province-based communications networks and the inventors of provincial traditions have not received a great deal of attention in prairie scholarship. The failure of any single newspaper to sustain a regionwide circulation after World War I might be seen as evidence of provincial pre-eminence in post-1920 cultural networks. This same trend is reflected in the absence of prairiewide electronic media. Significantly, when the CBC entered the Prairies in 1939 and 1945–46 with its own stations, it set up provincial superstations of 50 000 watts. Language and schools issues were fundamental in prairie cultural history; again, it is noteworthy that ethnic cultural distinctiveness capsized on the rocks of provincial education policy. After 1945 and especially after 1970, prairie cultural history is noteworthy for the rise of provincial museums and heritage departments and cultural policies. Thus, we might find two phases in twentieth-century prairie cultural history: the first illustrates the force of prairiewide regional conscious-ness before, roughly, the 1920s and 1930s, and the second is marked by the ascendancy of provincial consciousness in the next half-century.[39] Indeed, David Smith has argued that the cultural shift could be discerned even in the twenty-five years between Saskatchewan's fiftieth jubilee celebration in 1955 and its seventy-fifth in 1980. Thus, by 1980, "when federal policies, including even cultural ones, were perceived as a threat to provincial integrity, the diamond jubilee identified the province as a distinct society. In the 1950s the emphasis was on overcoming isolation, in the 1980s it was on maintaining or developing separateness."[40]

Territory-based loyalty has long been important to residents of the Canadian Prairies. Geography and policy choices and cultural expressions have ensured its continuity. This loyalty was once expressed in terms of a prairiewide imagined community, and later through the province, but there is no law that requires the continuation of such a cultural consensus. If the Confederation of Regions Party created a single prairie province, as it claims it would do, the formal, prairiewide region and the imagined regional community would soon coincide. The power of politics, govern-ment, and the communications media that feed off them would ensure this result. But whether such loyalties really matter in the 1990s is not as clear; and whether any imagined community smaller than the continent can pre-vail in the days of globalization is even less certain. So much will depend on the power and ability of Canadians to establish as strong an imagined com-munity as their forebears were able to do in the preceding 125 years.

• Notes

[1] Cited in B. Kaye and D.W. Moodie, "Geographical Perspectives on the Canadian Plains" in *A Region of the Mind: Interpreting the Western Canadian Plains*, ed. Richard Allen (Regina: Canadian Plains Research Center, 1973), 18.

[2] J.B. Tyrell, ed., *David Thompson's Narrative of His Explorations in Western*

America 1784–1812 (Toronto: Cham-plain Society, 1916), 183.

[3] A.R.C. Selwyn and G.M. Dawson, *Descriptive Sketch of the Physical Geography and Geology of the Dominion of Canada* (Montreal: n.p., 1884). John Warkentin employs an earlier moment in this same generation to define the West. He contends that the exploring

parties of Palliser and Dawson and Hind between 1857 and 1860 laid "the basic conceptual framework for our present interpretation of the physical geography of Western Interior Canada." See John Warkentin, *The Western Interior of Canada: A Record of Geographical Study, 1612–1917* (Toronto: McClelland & Stewart, 1964), 147.

4   G. Smith, *Canada and the Canadian Question* (Toronto: Hunter Rose, 1891), 1–3.

5   They are not, as I will argue later, entirely "wrong." See Donald F. Putnam, ed., *Canadian Regions: A Geography of Canada* (Toronto: J.W. Dent, 1952), and William C. Wonders, "Canadian Regions and Regionalism: National Enrichment or National Disintegration?" in *A Passion for Identity: Introduction to Canadian Studies*, ed. Eli Mandel and David Taras (Toronto: Methuen, 1987), 239–62.

6   H.R.A. Pocock, *Tales of Western Life, Lake Superior and the Canadian Prairie* (Ottawa: n.p., 1888), 56, 62.

7   Ralph Connor, *The Foreigner: A Tale of Saskatchewan* (Toronto: Westminster, 1909), 378.

8   Griffith Taylor, *Canada: A Study of Cool, Continental Environments and Their Effect on British and French Settlement* (London: Methuen, 1947).

9   Arthur S. Morton, *A History of the Canadian West to 1870–71* (Toronto: University of Toronto Press, 1973; first published 1939).

10 Ronald Rees, *New and Naked Land: Making the Prairies Home* (Saskatoon: Western Producer Prairie Books, 1988).

11 Janine Brodie, "The Concept of Region in Canadian Politics" in *Federalism and Political Community: Essays in Honour of Donald Smiley*, ed. David P. Shugarman and Reg Whitaker (Peterborough, ON: Broadview Press, 1989), 42, also William Westfall, "On the Concept of Region in Canadian History and Literature,"

Journal of Canadian Studies 15, 2 (1980): 3–15.

12 Adam Shortt, "Some Observations on the Great North-West," *Queen's Quarterly* 2 (1894–95): 184.

13 Isaiah Bowman, *The Pioneer Fringe* (New York: Books for Libraries, 1931), v.

14 W.A. Mackintosh, "Current Events," *Queen's Quarterly* 29 (1921–22): 312.

15 S.D. Clark, "Foreword" in W.L. Morton, *The Progressive Party in Canada* (Toronto: University of Toronto Press, 1950), vii–xi.

16 For most North American historians, the shorthand version of this approach to region, an approach that assumes one can distinguish stages of social formation, has been the frontier hypothesis of Frederick Jackson Turner. After all, it is no accident that Turner spent much of his career working on sections and sectionalism in American history. See Frederick Jackson Turner, *The Frontier in American History* (New York: Holt, Rinehart and Winston, 1962; first published 1920); Michael C. Steiner, "The Significance of Turner's Sectional Thesis," *Western Historical Quarterly* 10 (1979): 437–66. However, because the distinction between "frontier as place" and "frontier as process" has never been clear, the implications of the frontier hypothesis for analysis of prairie regionalism have been uncertain. Moreover, the idea that American theories might have relevance for Canadians has also raised the hackles of some Canadian scholars. Neither objection need detain us. Canada, like the United States, is a North American nation, after all, and the frontier is, or was in Turner's thought, both a place and a process. In our terms, Canadian scholars who relied upon frontier characteristics to distinguish the prairie West were thinking in terms of a functional region.

Though not often remembered today, the "frontier" assumption was once a commonplace in Canadian discussion. Clifford Sifton observed in 1898 that party loyalty, an important basis of the Canadian community, did not prevail automatically in the newly settled regions: "one of the difficulties in politics in the west," he told Walter Scott in 1898, "is that matters do not run in well settled grooves which exist in the older communities. There is therefore extra need for friendliness on all hands." Saskatchewan Archives Board, Scott papers, Sifton to Scott, 20 Sept. 1898. The region, in this view, was "the West," and was defined in relation to older communities, for which one might read "the East." The West was different—it constituted a region—because it was a "frontier." Such attitudes became a reflex in Canadian public life between the 1880s and 1930s. The West occupied a distinct and obviously different stage of social development. See Henry Nash Smith, *Virgin Land: The American West in Symbol and Myth* (New York: Vintage Books, 1959), 267.

17 Janine Brodie, *The Political Economy of Canadian Regionalism* (Toronto: Harcourt Brace Jovanovich, 1990).

18 Edward A. McCourt, *The Canadian West in Fiction* (Toronto: Ryerson, 1970), 125.

19 Eli Mandel, "Images of Prairie Man" in *A Region of the Mind*, 201–9; also Gerald Friesen, "Three Generations of Fiction: An Introduction to Prairie Cultural History" in *Eastern and Western Perspectives*, ed. D.J. Bercuson and P.A. Bucker (Toronto: University of Toronto Press, 1981), 183–96.

20 Alan Cairns, "The Government and Societies of Canadian Federalism," *Canadian Journal of Political Science* (Dec. 1977); Ramsay Cook, "Regionalism Unmasked," *Acadiensis* 13, 1 (1983); Donald Smiley, *The Federal Condition in Canada* (Toronto: McGraw-Hill Ryerson, 1986), 23.

21 Lovell Clark, "Regionalism? or Irrationalism?" *Journal of Canadian Studies* (Summer 1978): 119–24; J.M.S. Careless, "Limited Identities—

Ten Years Later," *Manitoba History* 1 (1980): 3–9.

22 Garth Stevenson, "Canadian Regionalism in Continental Perspective," *Journal of Canadian Studies* (Summer 1980): 3–9.

23 See Brodie, *Political Economy of Canadian Regionalism*, 12, summarizing Ralph Matthews, *The Creation of Regional Dependency* (Toronto: University of Toronto Press, 1983), 22.

24 This summary is taken from Brodie, *Political Economy of Canadian Regionalism*; she is citing Raymond Breton, "Regionalism in Canada" in *Regionalism and Supranationalism*, ed. D. Cameron (Montreal: Institute for Research on Public Policy and Policy Studies Institute, 1981), 19.

25 Brodie, *Political Economy of Canadian Regionalism*, 77.

26 It is a little early to decide about the impact on the Reform Party phenomenon of the early 1990s.

27 W.L. Morton, "The Bias of Prairie Politics," Royal Society of Canada, *Proceedings and Transactions*, 3rd series, vol. 49 (1955); Doug Owram, "The Myth of Louis Riel," *Canadian Historical Review* 53, 3 (1982), and Owram, *Promise of Eden: The Canadian Expansionist Movement and the Idea of the West 1856–1900* (Toronto: University of Toronto Press, 1980).

28 Paul Phillips, *Regional Disparities* (Toronto: Lorimer, 1978); John Conway, *The West: The History of a Region in Confederation* (Toronto: Lorimer, 1983); Brodie surveys this literature in *Political Economy of Canadian Regionalism*, ch. 5.

29 V.C. Fowke, "The National Policy—Old and New," *Canadian Journal of Economics and Political Science* (1952); Donald Smiley, "Canada and the Quest for a National Policy," *Canadian Journal of Political Science* (1975).

30 David Smith, *The Regional Decline of a National Party: Liberals on the Prairies* (Toronto: University of Toronto Press, 1981).

31 Frederick Jackson Turner preferred the term *sectionalism*; Michael C. Steiner, "The Significance of Turner's Sectional Thesis," *Western Historical Quarterly* 19 (1979): 437–66.

32 Roger Gibbins, *Prairie Politics and Society: Regionalism in Decline* (Toronto: Butterworths, 1980); Cairns, "Governments and Societies."

33 Northrop Frye, *The Bush Garden: Essays on the Canadian Imagination* (Toronto: Anansi, 1971), i–iii.

34 Benedict Anderson, *Imagined Communities: Reflections on the Origin and Spread of Nationalism* (London: Routledge Chapman and Hall, 1991), 4.

35 Culture has become a point of convergence in the human disciplines. As social history has matured and displaced politics and economics as the central organizing principle of historical inquiry, it has simultaneously grown so complex and varied that its organized principles—history from below, the story of an entire society, limited identities of class, ethnicity, and gender—have lost the shock of the new. Its variety of approaches ensures that social history no longer constitutes an automatic challenge to power relations. In addition, the struggle for control in society has moved on. In a world built on service and knowledge, the wage nexus is less influential in life than is communication itself.

Culture has become a scholarly battleground. I am not using the word in the anthropological sense of all aspects of a whole and distinctive way of life. Nor am I equating culture with the arts, especially the high arts, as one would in describing a cultured individual, or the low arts, as we might in pointing to a television show as popular culture. Rather, I wish to follow a line between the two in defining culture as "the ways in which people perceive, make intelligible and organize their being." See Maria Tippett, "The Writing of English-Canadian Cultural History 1970–1985," *Canadian Historical Review* 67, 4 (Dec. 1986): 548.

To follow Raymond Williams, culture in this sense should be seen as "the signifying system through which necessarily (though among other means) a social order is communicated, reproduced, experienced and explored." Williams, *Culture* (Glasgow: Fontana, 1981), 13. As John Fiske says, culture takes "the meanings we make of our social experience, . . . the sense we have of our 'selves' and "situates those meanings within the social system." See Fiske, *Television Culture* (London: Methuen, 1987), 20.

36 Lynn Hunt, "Introduction: History, Culture, and Text" in *The New Cultural History*, ed. Lynn Hunt (Berkeley: University of California Press, 1989), 7, also Roger Chartier, ibid.

37 The fact that such an elaborate introduction is necessary demonstrates how irrelevant the present constitutional restrictions on Quebec's distinct society clause must necessarily be.

38 Perry Anderson, "Nation-States and National Identity," *London Review of Books* 13, 9 (9 May 1991).

39 *Prairie Forum* 15, 2 (Fall 1990), devoted an entire issue to "Heritage Conservation." It contains two articles by Jean Friesen entitled "Introduction: Heritage Futures" and "Heritage: The Manitoba Experience," Don Kerr's "In Defence of the Past: A History of Saskatchewan Heritage Preservation, 1922–1983," and Mark Rasmussen's "The Heritage Boom: Evolution of Historical Resource Conservation in Alberta," each of which sustains this emphasis on the rise of provincial consciousness. Also see Gerald Friesen, "The Manitoba Historical Society: A Centennial History," *Manitoba History* 4 (1982): 2–9.

40 David Smith, "Celebrations and History on the Prairies," *Journal of Canadian Studies* 17, 3 (Fall 1982): 55.

"SO GREAT A HERITAGE AS OURS":
Immigration and the Survival of the Canadian Polity*

ROBERT F. HARNEY

In 1947 Prime Minister Mackenzie King called for a revival of the mass immigration to Canada that had been curtailed during the Depression and World War II. "The objective of Canada's immigration policy," he wrote, "must be to enlarge the population of the country. It would be dangerous for a small population to attempt to hold so great a heritage as ours."[1]

At the time of Mackenzie King's pronouncement, 50 percent of Canada's twelve million people claimed descent from the British Isles and 30 percent from France. Seen regionally, the homogeneity of the population was even more striking. In Ontario, the most populous province, three out of four residents could trace their origins to the United Kingdom or Ireland. In Toronto 80 percent were of British descent. At the same time, 90 percent of the country's francophones were in Quebec and the adjoining French corridors of northern Ontario and northern New Brunswick.

The polity that Mackenzie King initiated has changed the face of Canada. In the four decades since the end of World War II, the country's population has more than doubled. Over 5.5 million of Canada's 26 million people are immigrants. They and their children have settled heavily in Canada's largest cities. Since the war, many of the immigrants have been

---

*"So Great a Heritage as Ours': Immigration and the Survival of the Canadian Polity," reprinted by permission of *Daedulus*, Journal of the American Academy of Arts and Sciences, from the issue entitled "In Search of Canada," Fall 1988, Volume 117, Number 4.

non-British and non-French, and since the late 1960s, non-European. They represent not only an expanding urban work force but also an enormous and highly visible increase in the country's cultural diversity. Today the effects of forty years of mass immigration, tensions between francophones and anglophones, the unresolved issue of the rights of the indigenous people, the disruptive pseudoethnogenesis lurking in the regionalism of the West and the Maritimes, and the traditional fear of absorption by the United States interact to make survival of the Canadian polity a recurring theme in public discourse.

Conversations about Canadian politics, society, and culture, if not saccharine accounts of the joys of multiculturalism, are full of complaint about the divisive nature of certain policies; they seem to begin and end as a "lament for a slain chieftain," the postcolonial dream of a unified, perhaps dualist, Canadian nation felled by the intrigue or ambitions of warring clans—the "French," the "ethnics," the "westerners," the "Anglo-Celts." Of course maintaining a viable political state and achieving a successful (i.e., integrative) nationalism as an ideology and an identity for those who live within that state are two different issues, but they rarely appear so in Canada. Questions about cultural diversity, population, and government policy combine as a single national obsession, a state of affairs that can be characterized as a polity in search of a nation.

"In a state of affairs," writes the philosopher Wittgenstein, "objects fit into one another like the links of a chain. In a state of affairs objects stand in a determinate relationship to one another." Both Canada's "state of affairs" and the debates born of differing perceptions of it are best understood against the backdrop of complex, unexpected ways in which the aspirations of the francophones, the effects of mass immigration, and the imperatives of the anglophone hegemony have since World War II interplayed with the drive to ensure the state's survival.

Immigration policy has always reflected a dialectic between the desired population increase and the impact of immigration on Canadian ways or on the racial and ethnocultural composition of the country. In the 1890s, when the energetic minister of the interior of the day, Clifford Sifton, initiated a policy of peopling "Canada's empty prairies" through an aggressive recruitment of settlers and the importation of migrant labour to build the railroad and industrial infrastructure, preference was shown for British and American settlers or for other "good" (i.e., northwest European) stock. The realities of the British and Scottish economy and of anti-immigrant recruitment laws in Germany meant that Sifton had to find his largest bloc of settlers not in the United Kingdom or Nordic Europe but in the Slavs of the Austro-Hungarian Empire. With remarkable resilience, the minister came to see the "stalwart [Slavic] peasant in a sheepskin coat, born on the soil, whose forefathers have been farmers for ten generations, with a stout wife and a half-dozen children" as "good quality" for the task of defending the prairie from American incursion.[2]

Five purposes of Canadian immigration policy, appearing under changing flags of convenience and employing different idioms, have remained relatively constant over the century from the 1890s to the present. Canada has needed immigrants to:

1. Occupy the country in sufficient numbers to discourage the expansionary tendencies of the American colossus.

2. Protect the Pacific Rim from heavy Asian immigration.

3. Create economies of scale and a rational East–West axis for an independent polity and a viable economy.

4. Maintain a British hegemony by combating separatism, whether in its Prairie Métis and Indian form of the last century or in its Québécois form in this one, and to counter the *revanche des berceaux* of the *Canadiens* against the British conquest.

5. Foster the image of Canada as a new place of opportunity, a country of potential greatness, and "a land of second chance," characterized by the fairness of British institutions and now by the civility of state-sponsored democratic pluralism in the form of official multiculturalism.

The idea of using immigrants as part of a strategy to ensure the state's survival and to create a nation from former French and British colonies has two corollaries—first, a preoccupation with the country's "absorptive power," and second, a sense that the migration phenomenon exists to serve the host country, not the migrants, and that not only the flow of immigration but its sources and character are matters that Canadian authorities can and should manipulate. In 1909 J.S. Woodsworth warned his compatriots that all Canada's other problems "dwindle into insignificance before the one great commanding, overwhelming problem of immigration." Woodsworth, a well-known evangelist and later one of the founders of the Co-operative Commonwealth Federation (the forerunner of the New Democratic Party), went on to state, under the heading "Racial Effects," that the mass migration Sifton had encouraged would have its impact on Canadians: "Canada will not remain Canadian," he wrote.[3]

Mackenzie King's views on what peoples might best serve Canada's need to expand its populace without causing a "fundamental alteration in the character" of the country remained remarkably consistent over his long and influential career. Barely a decade after Sifton had encouraged mass migration from the continent, King, as a deputy minister of labour, advocated keeping out those "belonging to nationalities unlikely to assimilate and who consequently prevent the building up of a united nation of people of similar customs and ideals." His preferred list included American, British, French, Belgian, Dutch, Swiss, German, Scandinavian, and Icelandic settlers.[4] If the argument was not always made overtly from racialist premises about North European stock having more proclivity to orderly society and free parliamentary institutions, such premises, along with those about the compatibility of Northwest Europeans—in terms of complexion, mores, and religion—lay behind the assumption that migrants from the countries King mentioned were the most easily assimilated.

Another prime minister, R.B. Bennett, expressed this way of thinking succinctly in the 1930s: "The people [Continental Europeans] have made excellent settlers . . . but it cannot be that we must draw upon them to shape our civilization. We must still maintain that measure of British civilization which enables us to assimilate these people to British institutions rather than assimilate our civilization to theirs."[5]

King himself observed in his May 1947 statement that "it is of the utmost importance to relate immigration to absorptive capacity" and added his well-known line that "the people of Canada do not wish to make a fundamental alteration in the character of their population through mass immigration."

Within five years of King's statement, an article in *Maclean's*, one of Canada's most influential magazines, suggested that something was awry with the new mass immigration. In an article entitled "What Kind of Canadians Are We Getting?" the alarm was sounded: "The British share of immigration to Canada has been drying up. Until 1924 it was 62 percent. By 1948 it was down to 38 percent. Now it's 17 percent. Meanwhile the proportion of immigrants from continental Europe has climbed from an inconsequential 20 percent to more than 75 percent." A former commissioner of immigration for the Canadian Pacific Railway was quoted as saying that a "slow but certain change in the racial composition of the Canadian people is inevitable unless the trend is arrested."[6] The process begun by King ran afoul of the old dialectic.

Over time, the use of language has become more circumspect. "Founding nations" replaces "founding races" as a label for the French and British. Immigrants are categorized by their assimilability or place within a multicultural mosaic rather than in terms of their "stock." Interethnic and interracial antagonism are given the pseudodistance of social science. Immigrants of certain groups are not undesirable because of their distance from the racial and cultural core but because of the impact they may have on those already in Canada, those "somewhat nervous about rapid ethnic change." As the report of the Canadian Immigration and Population Study had it in 1975, people were "concerned about the consequences for national identity that might follow significant change in the ethnic composition of the population."[7]

By the 1980s, Canada was caught between a potential for zero population growth early in the next century and the prospect of continuing policies that seemed to promise a "fundamental alteration" of her populace, her cultural ways, and her public ethos and justification of nationhood. The central objective of Canada's immigration policy had always been the growth of Canada through the importation of foreign labour and talent.

The policy's secondary purposes had to do with the disposition of the displaced and the allied after World War II and with the imperatives of the Cold War and then of good citizenship in the United Nations and the Commonwealth, especially concerning refugees and the struggle for human rights and against racism. In effect, Canada's current search for a principle of collective national identity can be traced to the impact of the postwar decision to grow through immigration and the ways that an immigration policy escapes the state's control to become an instrument of migration strategies. Canada's state of affairs today derives from what John Stuart Mill once described to Henry George as

> two of the most difficult and embarrassing questions of political morality—the extent and limits of the rights of those who have first taken possession of the unoccupied portion of the earth's surface to exclude the remainder of mankind from inhabiting it, and the means which can be legitimately used by the more improved branches of the human species to protect themselves from being hurtfully encroached upon by those of a lower grade of civilization.[8]

When Mackenzie King and the Senate of Canada spoke to the need for a new age of mass migration policy in the late 1940s, they did so impelled by two traditions of Canadian immigration policy. First, the Canadian population needed to grow in order to defend the space it had inherited from the colonial period. Second, an expanding population was necessary for the development of a healthy economy. King had noted in his diary that all the cabinet was agreed "that in the long range view, Canada would certainly need to have a large population if she hoped to hold the country for herself against the ambitions of other countries and build her strength." Among his colleagues there were some who believed that Canada faced the possibility of a postwar economic boom that would lead her to her postcolonial destiny as a great power. That boom would be thwarted by an absence of manpower.

By 1947, representatives of Canadian industries such as mining, agriculture, and forestry had approached the government for help in finding new sources of cheap and pliable workers. Australia had already begun to tap the Continent's displaced peoples for migrants, and Canada would be remiss if she did not follow suit. When King made his views public in May, he spoke of Canada bringing over immigrants at a rate that would be compatible with the country's absorptive powers. Although the surface of his remarks dealt with this issue of absorption in terms of economics, full employment, and industrial expansion, the usual subtext about finding suitable ethnic and racial stock that would be assimilable broke through the text, especially in the explicit call for exclusion of Asian immigrants. It is clear that his colleagues and the opposition were aware of the subtext since he was asked immediately in the House of Commons whether he had begun negotiations with the governments of the United Kingdom, France, and the Netherlands about recruiting immigrants there officially.

By appeasing anti-Asian racism in Western Canada (King made his remarks in the same year that the new Canadian Citizenship Act finally gave Asians the vote in British Columbia) and paying lip service to an ancillary flow of French-speaking immigrants ("born in France" was given equal footing as a category of admission with "British subject"), the government freed itself to act. In the aftermath of the war, there seemed to be pools of prospective immigrants from Europe who could fulfil long-range demographic needs while nicely satisfying, or at least not antagonizing, the constituencies in Canada. Within the atmosphere of the allies' goodwill, thousands of veterans of the Polish army in exile began arriving in Canada after 1946. The specific terms of payment for their ship's passage, even with the not entirely altruistic help of the British government in dispersing them through the Empire, often led to a period of what amounted to indenture in the Canadian North or in specific industries in need of workers. Canadian Jews and Ukrainians lobbied the government to help their kinsmen who had either survived death camps or were in displaced-person (DP) camps. Such lobbies would prove that in a democracy, existing groups must be heard, but immigration officials were often more interested in developing systematic recruitment in Holland, Scandinavia, and the United Kingdom.[9]

The four forces shaping recruitment choice, then, were: (1) the racialist or cultural assumptions of officials and many politicians, (2) the ethnic lobbies in Canada, (3) the availability of potential migrants of certain nationalities because of wartime and aftermath displacement, and (4) the voracious hunger of Canadian heavy industry for workers who could stand up under strenuous, dangerous, and dirty work done in remote and unhealthy places. The competition among those four forces distorted the population policy King initiated. In the collective memory of the 1950s and 1960s, being able to show an immigration inspector calloused hands and a body ready for hard work is remembered as a more essential rite of passage than questions about ethnicity or wartime politics.

At first the DPs provided ideal, almost chattel labour. Moreover, their recruitment satisfied that other goal of Canadian policy, the maintenance of a reputation for high moral purpose among the community of nations and the image of generosity of spirit in providing access to a land of second chance. Bulk labour schemes worked out with the International Relief Organization soon brought large numbers of Balts and other East Europeans to join the displaced Poles. The discourse's subtext, that immigrants should not only fit into the economy but also into the ethnic and racial needs of the country, continued to break through the surface. Of the first thousand women recruited from the DP camps as domestic servants, the recruiters in the field were reminded that "Protestant girls are preferred, possibly Estonians and of the best type available."[10] Only a year after the war, a Canadian Institute of Public Opinion poll showed 49 percent of Canadians against Jewish immigration as opposed to only 34 percent who would have barred Germans.[11] Race clearly mattered more than politics for most Canadians when it came to an immigrant's credentials. However, the Canadian Jewish Congress sought more vigorous screening of those who had fought with the Axis, and the Association of United Ukrainian Canadians had to remind the government that it should give priority to those immigrants who had fought against Nazi Germany and her satellites if it wished to pay honour to the Canadian war dead.[12]

Elements in the primary sector of the economy—mining, timbering, railway work, industrial agriculture such as sugar beet production—some of which had used POWs as labour during the war, were in great need of manpower. Many industries also saw the chance to keep native-born labour off balance and to dilute the power of unions. The representatives of these industries shared King's view that coming to Canada was not "a fundamental human right" but a "privilege," a privilege that desperate men would acknowledge by being grateful and compliant in the workplace. An official of one of Canada's largest sugar companies described how his firm could use the Polish army veterans. They "could be quartered in the existing [POW] camps. . . . These camps could be operated successfully in a manner similar to the former camps but with much less expense and organization since no guards would be needed."[13] In the 1950s, at least 80 percent of the immigrants who were Poles, Ukrainians, Balts, Dutch, Germans, and British had Ontario and Quebec as their targets. They were accompanied, after the lifting of the Enemy Alien Act, which had excluded citizens of Axis countries from Canada, by a growing stream of Italians, and then by Portuguese and Greek immigrants. Over two decades, Ontario's population of 4.5 million was swelled by another half million immigrants.

Efforts to control the flow of migrants once in Canada and to define areas of settlement were difficult in the context of democracy and free enterprise. Although most mining and railway towns in the North had pre-war enclaves of East Europeans, the arrival of large numbers of Polish veterans, displaced Lithuanians, Slovaks, Croats, Ukrainians, Donau-Schwabs, and other German peoples revivified the ethnic collectivities—often, however, with misunderstanding and conflict between the Left and the Right, and the old and the new immigrants. At the same time, many migrants, after an initial stay in the smaller work sites, moved on to Montreal or the megalopolis of the Golden Horseshoe in Southern Ontario. Others joined one of Canada's oldest and strongest migration patterns by seeking entry to the United States. Dutch and German settlers were distributed more evenly by occupation and geography across Ontario and the West. The country received the new immigrants with mixed feelings; the DPs were anti-Communist (usually committed to capitalism) and had a higher percentage of educated people among them than earlier waves of immigrants. Many, especially among the Dutch and the Balts, were of the Nordic physical type idealized in anglophone-Canadian culture. In this respect they were welcome, but the signs of ethnic persistence they showed from the beginning were less so.

By the late 1950s, the numbers of immigrants from northeastern Europe, which the DPs represented, had begun to dwindle, but Canada's need for manpower had not. The coming of Italians in large numbers and the urban pattern of their settlement brought tension between the demographic and the racial goals of the immigration policy. The matter was rarely couched in language quite so bald. Both the lessons of World War II and the United Nations Charter caused civilized nations to give up talk of the right stock. Sentiment changed more slowly, and issues such as sponsored versus independent migration, assimilability and enclaving, and the appropriateness of recruiting more actively in the British mother country were the media within which the Italian question was studied. Ontario had had since the turn of the century its own immigration and colonization department. In keeping with that province's reputation as a loyal outpost of the British Empire, the department focussed on recruiting immigrants from the United Kingdom, but it saw in the Dutch and Scandinavians appropriate surrogates. In 1947 Ontario's premier, George Drew, began a successful effort to airlift 10 000 British immigrants directly to Toronto.[14] As late as 1964, Ontario's deputy director of immigration toured northern Europe in search of settlers who presumably might counterbalance the heavy flow of Southern Europeans.

That tour took place about five years after the moment, startling to some Canadian authorities, when Italians, who had been listed as "non-preferred stock" in prewar immigration department documents, surpassed the British in numbers entering Canada in a year. The Italian flow, although partly induced by renewal of earlier chain migration, had been, in the main, a flow of labour to capital, of migrant brawn to crude workplace. The subtext about their suitability as new Canadians and assimilability was always present. As the Italians, along with the Portuguese and the Greeks, became the engine of the rapid urbanization of much of Southern Ontario, their visibility changed. Massive ethnic enclaves in the city were not the same as a quaint, impoverished Little Italy clinging to the sides of a smelter, mine, or railway yard. Given the traditional assumption that immigration policy was an aspect of population policy and that regulatory manipulation could fix rates of flow that went awry, it is instructive and a fillip to the anarchist to note how completely the Italian immigrants defeated the Canadian "gatekeepers" between 1947 and 1967.

The Immigration Act of 1952 was intended to secure the type of immigrants that Canada's political leadership has sought shortly after World War II. In the discretionary powers accorded the minister and bureaucrats under the act, the imperatives of the subtext on suitability of stock became text but were couched in a manner that would not insult the UN Charter. An immigrant could be prohibited from entering Canada for reason of nationality, geographic origin, peculiarity of custom, unsuitability of climate, and probable inability to "become readily assimilated." A 1952 *Maclean's* piece railed at "Ottawa's zealous publicity men" who were obscuring the impact on the Canadian future that emerges from an honest analysis of the "characteristics, moral fiber, skills and racial composition of the hundreds of thousands of immigrants" then passing through reception centres. The article added that the people in public relations "don't tell you that our most adaptable class of immigrants, the Briton, is an ever declining proportion of our total immigration."[15]

The 1952 act, then, reflected the view of much of the anglophone host society. In 1956 an influential series of articles in the *Globe and Mail* described the virtue of some German, Dutch, and Estonian immigrants. Nonetheless, it added that "people from the British Isles are more rapidly accepted than those from European countries."[16] Although Barbadian Canadians successfully challenged the systematic exclusion of blacks as unassimilable and unsuitable for reasons of climate[17] and even though southern European migrant labourers, with the Italians as bellwethers, shattered Canada's dream of keeping the population northwest European, attempts to control the flow of immigrants from certain backgrounds continued until the late 1960s. A spate of press accounts about illegal Chinese immigration schemes was followed in May of 1960 by concerted Royal Canadian Mounted Police raids on all of Canada's major Chinatowns in search of incriminating evidence. Whatever else the raids signalled, they showed the government still to "be on guard" for white Canada against a change in its "fundamental character."[18]

The impact of the new mass migration has been specifically unsettling for Ontario. In the forty years since the war, the population has gone from three out of four to less than three out of six residents of British descent. (It should be added that such figures beg the question of whether using the census category "British" and the political term WASP, which mask traditional Celtic–English divisions and the generational distance between new immigrants from Brixton and the Midlands and the old stock, are of any value. They lump together people of such diverse cultures and backgrounds.) A polity that had about 100 000 foreign-born in 1951 had more than two million two decades later.

The impact of mass immigration on Quebec was even more unsettling, although it was less a matter of numbers than of the fact and image of non-French-speaking strangers massing in Montreal and the French-Canadian interpretation of that invasion. Between 1946 and 1971, 3.5 million immigrants arrived in Canada. Only about 15 percent of the newcomers settled in Quebec, but fewer than 5 percent of those who did were francophones. Although many of the educated DPs and Italian and Portuguese migrant labourers who reached Montreal could function in French, they seemed to identify with the anglophone culture and with Canada as a polity rather than with *Francophonie* and Quebec. Quebec's nationalist view, and perhaps the French-Canadian view generally, was that "le Ministre de l'Immigration a introduit le cheval de Troie au Canada française" in order to pierce "une muraille imprenable."[19]

Since the number of immigrants coming from France between 1946 and 1986 was not only smaller than the number coming from the United Kingdom but also smaller than the contingents of Italians, Portuguese, Greeks, West Indians, Poles, Germans, and those from Hong Kong and the Indian subcontinent, *la survivance* of the *Canadien* required higher fertility rates among French Canadians and an ability and a willingness to acculturate immigrants. By the 1980s, the Québécois birth rate was among the lowest in Canada; a combination of turning inward to Quebec rather than a pan-French-Canadian strategy and the assimilation, by law if necessary, of all immigrants in the province, recommended itself. Immigrants arriving in Quebec usually had little idea of or interest in the fact that they were entering a cultural and political battle zone. The gallicization of Montreal and the defeat of the anglophone hegemony were the front, and it was not a place for non-combatants.

English as a language had higher status than any other in Canada, in North America, and in the world, and since their strategies required a primary interest in mobility, the immigrants saw the acquisition and use of standard English as crucial. Learning French might help one get work on the telephone exchange or the police force and might be necessary to a small shopkeeper, but it did not open the door to greater North American opportunity. Moreover, the nationalism, not to say racism, of the Québécois enabled the immigrants to claim with some justification (although the same point could certainly have been made about Montreal's anglophones of British descent) that the fault lay with the francophones themselves, "who, as xenophobes, were not inclined to accept the immigrants and who would claim that those same immigrants could neither speak nor learn French correctly."[20]

Something of a self-confirming hypothesis existed on both sides. In 1962–63, 25 percent of the Italian immigrant children were in the French-speaking school system; by 1971–72 the figure was 10 percent. More than that, it is probably true, as some scholars have pointed out, that the initiation price for acculturation into *Anglophonie* is acquiring a certain disdain for "the French fact" and for speaking French in Canada.

Since the perception and reality of the urban Italian communities as potential centres of political power were a major element later in making the "third force" of non-British, non-French descent more than a Prairie-based Slavic movement and in contributing to the assertion of a public policy of multiculturalism, one can say that the failure of the immigration authorities to maintain a flow "consistent with the country's ability to absorb" had serious consequences for the forging of the Canadian nation. One should add that the image of Montreal's Italian immigrants of the 1950s and 1960s choosing *Anglophonie* in preference to assimilation to a sister Latin culture, especially since many prewar Italians had become gallicized, played a significant role in Quebec's separatism as well. It is not as if the authorities did not attempt to manipulate Italian immigration from the beginning. There is even some suggestion that Canada's doors opened to Italians in the late 1940s, not just because of the pressures for family reunification and labour needs but because of the NATO allies' fear that Italy's population problems would improve the chances of the Communist party coming to power there. Canadian officials showed the traditional concern for cutting a good figure among their senior allies. As a dispatch from the Canadian Department of External Affairs had it, "Any increase in emigration to Canada would be of practical help to Italy in tackling her greatest problem. It would also be a small, but distinctly Canadian, contribution to strengthening the present democratic 'western' government."[21]

Canada had always preferred northern to southern Italian immigrants. That preference was couched in terms of skills and adaptability by the 1950s but steeped in assumptions about the "Germanic" roots of the Friulians and other northerners and the Mediterranean ways of the southerners. Some authorities felt that opening recruiting stations south of Milan would not "draw the best class of immigrant." As sociologists have shown about Italian migration to Australia, in the struggle between "the manifest function of bureaucracy" and the "latent function of informal networks," the latter—family strategies, chain and serial migration, and ethnic group networks of assistance—are always faster, more resilient, and smarter than government agencies.[22] As a result, Italians, predominantly from the South, appeared for more than a decade among the top five arriving groups in Canada.

The government estimated with a note of terror that every Italian male labourer who entered Canada in the 1950s was responsible for forty-nine other Italian immigrants. When efforts were made to manipulate the regulations in order to slow the Italian flow, restrictive definitions of who could be sponsored, previously applied only to the Chinese, were tried. "I doubt if we could get away with it but one step worth considering might well be to announce that 50% of the total Unemployment Insurance Commissions claims in the Toronto area . . . are Italians," wrote a deputy minister of citizenship and immigration in 1960, but he knew better: "We must not make the mistake again of letting the story get abroad that anything we may be attempting is designed to cut down Italian immigration."[23] The immigrants had become political clientele, and the conditions for mass immigration to turn to polyethnicity, and for polyethnicity to lead to multicultural politics, had emerged.

There are a number of ways to tell the story of how the visible polyethnicity that accompanied postwar immigration intruded on the exigencies of French–English relations and of how that intrusion led, in the late 1960s and early 1970s, to a revolution of policy and rhetoric, if not of sentiment. As the charter groups sought to define the new Canadian nationhood in terms of bilingualism and biculturalism, a third force emerged demanding multiculturalism rather than biculturalism. Canadians as "the other North Americans" needed an identity that would no longer be subordinate to the British metropole, that would dampen the appeal of separatism in Quebec, and that would continue to sustain political, social, and cultural values assumed to be distinct from those of the United States. The Royal Commission on Bilingualism and Biculturalism, established in the early 1960s, had as its main task the search for that new identity and for an imicable and more equal sharing of power and culture by the two "founding races." The commission was "state intervention to restructure the symbolic order" in Canada.[24] The French–British dualism that had in the past been seen as a tale of mutual antagonism, of exploitation and inequality, as an impediment to the emergence of the Canadian, would now be refurbished as a national virtue.

Along with it came revival of the old saw that *la survivance* of the *Canadien* was a key element in the survival of the Canadian in the face of the American urge to continental imperium and vice versa. Any assessment of recent Canadian history has to include the sense of surprise, sadness, and anger felt by the mainstream when its effort to build national independence on dualism (in the form of an official bilingualism and biculturalism) foundered on the ethnocentrism of some anglophones, the extremism of some Quebec separatists, and an unanticipated demand on the part of those claiming to represent a "third element," or "third force." These were the one-quarter to one-third of the population who were of neither French nor British descent and who wanted to share power and help formulate the country's culture.

Some explanations of the events of the late 1960s and early 1970s may seem more cynical than others, and some have more explanatory power and appeal for one set of players than another, but all have the sort of truth described by the Indian from James Bay who told a Quebec judge that he could not swear to tell the truth but only what he knew. One can view the public policy of multiculturalism that has emerged since 1971 in four different ways—as:

1. A product of the postwar convergence of arriving nationalist DP intellectuals—Poles, Balts, and Ukrainians especially—and a failure of the will to assimilate on the part of Anglo-Canadian officials.

2. An innovative and altruistic civic philosophy of democratic pluralism to replace loyalty to the British Empire as a legitimizing principle for the Canadian state.

3. A device used by anglophones to minimize the uniqueness of the French minority in Canada.

4. A tactic of venal politicians to find a medium of exchange and thus a way of controlling new ethnic and immigrant voting blocs.

Whichever narrative proves most elegant, they all include the same three mythic protagonists: the British (sometimes and not exactly synonymously identified as the anglophones or Anglo-Celts), the French (sometimes and again not synonymously described as *Canadiens*, francophones, and Québécois), and the "other ethnic groups." Moreover, there is in all of the accounts a sense of the intrusion of the ethnic groups into an antique struggle between the real Canadians/*Canadiens*.

For, although some of the spokespersons for the settlers of the Prairies, especially the Ukrainians, spoke as if they were a third founding nation, in the belief, one assumes, that as the first to break the Prairie sod, they met white society's definition of proprietorship through exploitation and settlement, and although later Ukrainian immigrants spoke as if traces of the failed Hapsburg monarchy had crossed the sea with them, no one until the 1960s thought of Canadian history except in terms of the titanic contest between the British and French. Both saw immigrants and Canadians of other backgrounds as potential anglophones and, to paraphrase H.L. Mencken, as "assistant Canadians" brought in to counterbalance *la revanche des berceaux*. They romanticized the presence of the Prairie isolates such as Mennonites, Hutterites, Icelandics, and Galicians. One participant in the second Canadian Conference on Multiculturalism in 1976 recalled the way in which a more diffuse pluralism had always been used to combat dualism: "Ukrainians, Germans, and others could provide a kind of counterweight to the French Canadians." Faced with claims and complaints from the French, the English of western Canada could come back with "What about the Ukrainians?" He added, perhaps giving away too much about the caretaker's reasons for supporting multiculturalism, "More broadly and generally, the tension when two social groups compete within a polity seems likely to be reduced insofar as there are a number of groups."[25]

The 1960s saw the transformation of polyethnicity from a social consequence of recent immigration to its assertion as a permanent feature of the Canadian political landscape. Polyethnicity evolved along with multiculturalism, an idea en route to an ideology fashioned from the rhetoric of ethnocultural impresarios huckstering for the folkloric and visiting British royalty searching for a way to describe the colourfulness of the colonies (no doubt after countless onslaughts by Cree, Blackfoot, and Ukrainians in full ethnic battle dress, herded by red-tunicked guardians of "the Canadian way"). The speed with which the newcomers, in alliance with some older Prairie ethnic elements, managed to become players in the shaping of the new Canada is evident in the last-minute addition to the mandate of the royal commission of a study of the third element. The study is summed up in the fourth volume of the commission's report, entitled *The Contribution of the Other Ethnic Groups*. This title seems less startling when one thinks about the rapid concentration in urban enclaves of the new immigrants: 64 percent of the Greeks, 82 percent of the Chinese, and 75 percent of the

Italians are in cities of more than 500 000 inhabitants. Also important were the revitalization of some ethnic groups engendered by the arrival of large numbers of their countrymen (already mobilized by nationalist sentiment) and the salience that the issues of ethnocultural rights and ethnic identity acquired in Canadian public discourse because of the separatist movement in Quebec. Among the immigrants and the spokespersons for the third element there was a natural uneasiness that "a deal was being cut without them." As the noted Canadian sociologist Raymond Breton has observed, "the name of the Royal Commission [on Bilingualism and Biculturalism] itself was a symbol generating status anxiety [for the third element] as were several other themes permeating the debate: founding peoples, charter groups, the two nation society."[26] Many immigrant intellectuals also lived with a misunderstanding—reinforced by the fact that they first encountered and understood Canada through the medium of the anglophone hegemony or the ethnoverted discourse of their own kind—of Quebec as an *ethnie* overreaching itself rather than as a suppressed nation engaged in a "quiet revolution," or, in the case of the fanatical few, an insurrection.

Several other factors contributed to the rapidity with which immigrants regrouped and underwent the sort of ethnicization that led them to participate aggressively in the debate about Canadian identity under way in the 1960s and 1970s. Some of the groups arriving—especially the Polish army veterans, the Baltic DPs, and the Ukrainians (veterans of war or labour camps)—saw themselves as "saving remnants" of their people, as nuclei of nations in exile. In all cases, they were peoples who, through long stretches of their history, had had to sustain their national identities without having at their disposal the machinery of nation-states of their own. The democratic structure of Canada and the uncertainty of the Canadian host society and government in responding to the tactics of group persistence of the ethnonationalists encouraged the building of ethnies. It is fair to add that among the same DPs and among immigrants from other parts of continental Europe, there were many who advocated democratic pluralism, or multiculturalism, not as a device to facilitate the maintenance of the nation in exile or to forge ethnic groups but rather as a humane and civil form of nationhood to replace the very ethnonationalism they saw as a cause of World War II.

Distortions and ambiguities in the way Canadians think and talk about ethnicity also have contributed to the impact of the immigrants, and of the third force generally. Politicians and the public have confused the fact of polyethnicity with the idea of multiculturalism, and the latter term has generally been used to apply to both.[27] Leaders have generally preferred to think of those they represent as ethnic groups rather than immigrant groups since *immigrant* conjures up the thresholds of acculturation while *ethnic* implies a permanent quality of otherness. However, as we shall see, the penumbra of the Greek meaning of *ethnos* persists in English, so that to be called ethnic in Canada is to be called less, as in "ethnic writer," and marginal, as in "ethnic enclave." The word *ethnic* has, from the beginning, raised the conundrum of whether multiculturalism is "for all Canadians," including "the founding nations," or just for "ethnic Canadians." Avoiding the term leads to lexical monstrosities such as "the multilingual press" and references to "multicultural groups" or "we multiculturals." The increasing diversity of the population was further magnified by the workings of the Canadian census, which until recently required everyone to list patrilinear ethnic origin and rejected "Canadian" or "American" as answers except for Amerindians. This official definition and measurement of ethnic group membership, maintained at the insistence of French Canada (which saw in it a way to assert the size of the *Canadien* nation by descent since the more subtle calibration by mother tongue and home language showed great attrition outside Quebec and the adjoining corridors of northern Ontario and New Brunswick), also served ethnic and immigrant leaders well. They could ignore the workings of acculturation and the question of intensity of participation and feeling within the group. At the very least, reference to the census abetted those who played the numbers game; it also encouraged the impression that phalanxes of like-minded immigrants and ethnics were massing behind their leaders, an image bound to frighten or fascinate elected politicians.

Within a year of the great commission struck by Lester Pearson to "inquire into and report upon the existing state of bilingualism and biculturalism in Canada and to recommend what steps should be taken to develop the Canadian confederation on the basis of an equal partnership between the two founding races," a Ukrainian-Canadian senator from the Prairies— Paul Yuzyk—rose to give his maiden speech in the Senate. The speech was entitled "Canada: A Multicultural Nation," and Yuzyk used the occasion to denounce biculturalism as a misunderstanding of Canadian reality, which, he said, had "changed from paramountly British and French . . . to multicultural."[28] He went on to speak of the third element, to which one-third of Canada's people belonged according to the census data the senator produced. It was one of the first of years of "arguments from the census" to define the Canadian future, a phenomenon that in Canada has always carried the uncomfortable implication that everyone must have a tribe to belong to, that ethnic identity is stamped at birth and is neither volitional nor processual, and that *census group* and *interest group* are synonymous. "Do you know," wrote another ethic leader, "that the 5 764 075 so-called 'others' outnumber the entire population of seven provinces, the Atlantic and Prairie provinces combined . . . and that the 1 317 200 German Canadians are more numerous than the total population of provinces such as Saskatchewan, Manitoba and Nova Scotia," that there are "more Ukrainians [in Canada] than people in Newfoundland?"[29]

Since the spokesmen for the third element rejected the idea of a separate *Canadien* nation, they tended to see the argument over dualism and the commission's bilingual and bicultural mandate as one about power, not history. In this view, ethnic numbers, density, intensity, and perhaps even hints of societal strife were the strategies by which the Québécois, if not the *Canadiens* of other provinces, had forced the British to negotiate. As an exasperated Ukrainian leader put it, "Is it necessary for all these people to establish their own ethnocultural enclaves before their cultural and linguistic aspirations are truly respected and encouraged?" In their speechmaking, the politicians who have advocated multiculturalism have flexed the muscles of the third force as if they were their own. From the beginning, then, the politicians have confused (usually purposely) immigrant first-settlement areas with permanent ethnic enclaves, and immigrant sentiments of "fellow-feeling," as well as the reality of diglossia, with a sense of ethnic community, group maintenance of boundaries, and shared density in Canada. With the French Canadians, some of the ethnoreligious groups of the Prairies, and the Ukrainians as models, the idea of ethnic persistence rather than inevitable anglo conformism could be brandished as both a norm and an ethos to be pursued, even if statistics on language loss and intermarriage over generations suggest that only extreme geographical and religious isolation has slowed the rates of assimilation.

One of the best and most influential examples of the rhetorical uses of immigrant statistics to promote both uniethnic persistence and multiculturalism came from Ontario's minister of citizenship in 1972:

> No other part of the globe, no other country can claim a more culturally diversified society than we have here in this province. . . . But does everyone really grasp that Ontario has more Canadians of German origin than Bonn, more of Italian origin than Florence, more Canadians of Greek origin than Sparta? That we have in our midst, 54 ethnocultural groups, speaking a total of 72 languages . . . ? Just 100 years ago the Canadian identity was moulded in the crucible of nationalism; it is now being tempered, tempered by the dynamics of multiculturalism.
>
> One effect of the postwar boom in third element immigration has been to bolster ethnocultural groups, some of which have been here through four generations. The government has welcomed and encouraged this immigration. We have recognized and helped to foster all our constituent cultural communities. Is it then any wonder that these communities have heightened expectations in many areas?[30]

The commissioners and researchers preparing *The Contribution of the Other Ethnic Groups*, Book IV of the royal commission report, were by the late 1960s operating on vanished premises. On the one hand, a new Québécois identity, based on a geographically, demographically, and institutionally compact and self-contained nation in one province, was rising to challenge the diffuse legal and linguistic ideal of a francophone–anglophone partnership stretching from sea to sea. On the other hand, few spokesmen for the third element—ethnic leaders as opposed to caretakers in support of multiculturalism—were content with this volume. Its authors observed that: (1) it should be "noted immediately that while the terms of reference deal with questions of those of ethnic origin other than British or French, they do so in relation to the basic problem of bilingualism and biculturalism from which they are inseparable"; (2) "that acculturation is inevitable in a multi-ethnic country like Canada"; and (3) that "multiculturalism within a bilingual framework can work, if it is interpreted as it is intended—that is, as encouraging those members of ethnic groups who want to do so to maintain a proud sense of the contribution of their own group to Canadian society. . . . If it is interpreted in a second way—as enabling various peoples to transfer foreign cultures and languages as living wholes into a new place and time—multiculturalism is doomed."[31]

Book IV, then, was the first modern public recognition of the possibility of group cultural rights for minorities and of limits for Anglo conformity and gallicization. The volume clearly set the limits of acceptable diversity as well. The commission envisaged study and celebration of pluralistic origin, and expressed a willingness to tolerate, even to encourage, the maintenance of ethnocultures, especially for immigrants and their children. Neither political nor linguistic pluralism would be possible, however, and the issue of what amounts of public money and what sort of public programs would be directed towards the support of ethnies remained ill defined enough to offend all three players—the British, the French, and the third element.

Looking back now through some of the havoc and bad feelings about ethnic politics and population policy to the 1970 convergence of "apprehended insurrection" of the Front de libération du Québec, through the declaration of a multicultural policy by Prime Minister Pierre Elliott Trudeau and the reaction of anglophones to what many saw as the country "coming unravelled," it is helpful to borrow from the thought of the Italian Marxist anthropologist Ernesto De Martino. He said that groups despairing for the survival of their ways are not likely to feel much generosity of spirit towards the cultural rights of others.[32] In 1970 the two founding nations, the Prairie ethnic blocs, and the new immigrant ethnies all thought their pieces of the pie and the survival of their cultures were threatened. The sense of impending cultural and demographic doom affects the anglophones because of everything from Quebec separatism to the ravages of American cultural imperialism; the sense of survival that has always informed Quebec nationalism is nothing but a prolonged struggle against the apocalypse, the disappearance of the French language and culture from the continent.

It is easy to see how the arrival of masses of French immigrants to their chief city, Montreal, and the apparent anglicization of those newcomers could signal both the impotence of their nation and its imminent destruction. As political scientist Karl Deutsch has observed, the condition of being immigrant is always apocalyptic in that each generation must make reflective and ideological efforts to counter the effects of accultura-tion and slippage.[33] The rhetoric as well as the behaviour of all groups towards one another since the uncertainty of the late 1960s reflects the scars of those times as much as or more than it does the putative cultural arrogance of one group or another.

Only with this point in mind can one make sense of how shrill the debate over immigration and multiculturalism can become. Certainly the policies and programs the government initiated after Trudeau announced the government's response to Book IV in October of 1971 were not so far ranging, expensive, or intrusive as to fire up the opponents of multicultur-alism. "We believe," the prime minister said, "that cultural pluralism is the very essence of Canadian identity. Every ethnic group has the right to pre-serve and develop its own culture and values within the Canadian context. to say we have two official languages is not to say we have two official cul-tures, and no particular culture is more 'official' than another. A policy of multiculturalism must be a policy for all Canadians." Between Trudeau's pronouncement—his first and last parliamentary utterance on the issue—and the Multicultural Act, Bill C-93, brought before the House of Commons in Ottawa late in 1987, there has been no enabling legislation of any kind about multiculturalism or ethnic group rights.

Since 1973, there has been a multiculturalism directorate within the Department of the Secretary of State. Through grants to scholars, the arts, and ethnocommunity organizations, the directorate seeks to carry out the three chief goals of multiculturalism: (1) to help maintain ethnic group life and culture, (2) to foster cross-cultural understanding, and (3) to integrate immigrants through teaching the two official languages. These goals hardly promise balkanization, and the granting structure does not approach the resources available to mainstream cultural activities through the Canada Council and other agencies.

One might suppose that the ethnic and immigrant clientele would lead the hue and cry against the limited and perfunctory implementation of multiculturalism. To a certain extent, it has. Despite the truth of the remark that the "concerns of the non-British, non-French segment of the society were not primarily with cultural maintenance" and were instead with "status anxiety—fear of being defined as second class citizens,"[34] immi-grant and ethnic leaders, even on advisory bodies carefully selected by the government, have protested the degree to which the integrative aspects of multiculturalism have been advanced over programs to sustain their own cultures. These programs, which they see as the government's obligation, are modelled on the federal programs that provide funding to prepare and pay teachers of French outside Quebec. The report of the very first Canadian Consultative Council on Multiculturalism (CCCM) has as its paramount concern the relationship between language retention and the preservation and future development of the ethnic group:

Without language, cultural pluralism (or to use the contemporary term, multiculturalism) emerges as truncated multiculturalism, confined to such aspects as folk dancing, native costumes, special foods, embroidery, instrumental music or even folk songs with words which few can understand or are encouraged to learn.[35]

While Canadian teachers ran "pizza and pysanky" days and educators met to complain that "all too often such organizations [ethnic clubs and halls] plan extensively for the enrichment and enhancement of their own images and unique purpose without appropriate acknowledgement of all other groups," the politicized ethnic clientele of the government's multi-cultural policies saw only trivialization of their ethnocultures. The federally funded community cultural centres and multicultural centres that were to implement these policies were, according to the CCCM, more "compatible with the melting pot concept" than with pluralism. In 1977, the Ukrainian Canadian Committee made its dissent clear: "Any attempt to develop and maintain the various cultures simultaneously as distinct yet intermixed together in a multicultural centre is contradiction, as it leads to one blend or mass."[36]

Perhaps the two charter groups would have thought the demands of "the ethnics" excessive under any circumstances, but the strong, though rarely garish, funding programs and the accompanying "ethnicking" for votes clearly fuelled the conflict. There were dark mutterings of not dis-pensing government funds to help "keep ex-fascists dancing in their church cellars." A guest editor in *Maclean's* described English Canada as being "in danger of having its old, familiar British North American culture half bludgeoned to death by the cast iron balalaikas of multiculturalism," while the helpless Canadian taxpayer watches as "in the name of 'heritage' programs, he pays for Polish and Swahili Canadians to be taught in Polish and Swahili in the supposedly all-Canadian public school."[37]

Multiculturalism as a policy was denounced for many of the same reasons assimilationists have always objected to the maintenance of ethnicity. It would breed "double consciousness"—loyalty to more than one country; it would contribute to turning immigrant quarters into permanent ethnic ghettos; it would slow the process of overcoming the ignorance of English and French that made the immigrants exploitable. Part of most ethnic heri-tages is a traditional enmity for some other group. Was the Canadian gov-ernment intending to contribute to that problem by funding ethnocultural organizations? Among the English-speaking, hostility to multiculturalism ran from the viscerally xenophobic to well-reasoned preference for a laissez-faire approach to liberal meritocracy and an abhorrence of state interven-tion in the issue of group status, even if a hierarchy of privilege based on ethnicity and class was obvious in the economy. Sometimes, of course, the viscerally xenophobic and the apparently reasonable became confused with one another. "You and me and our children have enough to do with the basic problem of hyphenated Canadianism, that is the French and English duality, without enshrining the whole world's diversity within our history and our borders," a well-known journalist and legislator told the Canadian Conference on Multiculturalism, and many well-intentioned Canadians of every ethnic background agreed with him.[38]

The need to involve newcomers and to inject multiculturalism into the effort to encourage the growth of a new postcolonial Canada seemed initially to confuse many mainstream intellectuals, Anglo-Celt in origin or not. Although embracing multiculturalism as an alternative to the hated melting pot practised to the south should have worked as well as paeans to dualism as a basis for a unique history, the mainstream often reacted defensively and a bit meanly. Some, for example, whittled away at the authenticity of the figures that gave "the others" one-third of the population.[39] Failing that, the Anglo-Canadians tended to speak of themselves in the 1970s as a "vanishing breed," to add hastily how nice their ethnic cleaning ladies were, and to point out that anti-British feeling, or the myth of British bigotry in Canada, was too negative a thing upon which to build the new multicultural Canada. The report of the Commission on Canadian Studies, issued seven years after Trudeau had declared the multicultural policy, was entitled *To Know Ourselves*. It contained only one reference to any ethnic group: "The remarkable Celtic contribution to the life of this country for example has received little attention. The British or Anglo-Canadian heritage is in danger of being ignored by scholars who fail to perceive that it, too, is part of the Canadian mosaic."[40]

The French-Canadian response to the declaration of the policy was, if anything, more ferocious and more consistent. Although in the last several years francophones in the Prairie provinces and Ontario have co-operated to gain heritage language rights, no sympathy, to say the least, existed among francophones for multiculturalism during the 1960s and 1970s. The *Canadiens* who resided outside Quebec saw themselves orphaned by the Québécois, who increasingly turned to strategies of seizing control in their own province, or *indépendantisme*. Despite government promises of protection under the Official Languages Act, they also saw multiculturalism as a device directed against them. As a French-Canadian prelate and scholar from Nova Scotia put it, quoting an editorial in *Le Droit*, "We cannot help but see this as an insidious and steady shift away from biculturalism toward a crushing of *Francophonie*'s special needs under the political weight of multiculture."[41] The response from Quebec nationalists like René Lévesque was less civil and circumspect: "Multiculturalism, really, is folklore. It is a 'red herring.' The notion was devised to obscure 'the Quebec business,' to give an impression that we are all ethnics and do not have to worry about special status for Quebec."[42]

It could be argued that the emergence of the multicultural policy was a godsend for Quebec separatism. It offered proof that the thousands of new immigrants who had come to Montreal since World War II were not prepared to become francophones; it seemed to promise that bilingualism on an a national scale would fail and thus confirmed the Quebec nationalists' view that only a core of unilingual francophones could guarantee the future of the French culture in Canada. On the other hand, the French-Canadian reaction guaranteed that most immigrants would see support for multiculturalism as their only refuge from cultural genocide and the English language as their only avenue of socioeconomic mobility. Two headlines in an Italian newspaper in Toronto reflect the tone of the relationship between the immigrants and the advocates of the new Quebec in the 1970s: "É Assurdo Dover Studiare Il Francese" ("It is absurd to be made to study French") and "I Franco-Canadesi Vogliono Francesizzare Gli Italiani Del Quebec" ("The French Canadians want to gallicize the Italians of Quebec").

Two French-Canadian intellectuals, one a professor at the University of Montreal and the other Quebec's ministre d'état au développement culturel, expressed the francophone view of the policy most forcefully. The first, Guy Rocher, had his remarks read to a federal conference on multiculturalism.[43] Rocher saw the policy as a continuation by other means of an anglophone campaign to define the French Canadians as first among the minorities rather than as a second nation within the Canadian polity. He pointed out that without biculturalism, the French language would function within bilingualism as merely an administrative and a government language. Multilingualism would, he believed, eventually appear to be the logical corollary of multiculturalism and then the uniqueness of the French existing in Canada would be lost. "At a time when 90 percent of the ethnic minorities of Quebec are opting for the English language and the *Anglophonie* culture," he wrote, "thereby constituting one of the most serious threats both politically and culturally to the Francophone community of Quebec, the federal government has undertaken to define Canada as a multicultural nation."

A year later the minister, Camille Laurin, lectured the Canadian Ethnic Studies Association, meeting in Quebec City, on the difference between an *ethnie* and a *nation*. An ethnie "renovie à un ensemble de caractéristiques et de traditions dont l'existence ou la persistance peuvent se verifier au niveau des individus et des familles." A nation, however, is "une société globale, une société complète, qui possède ses caractéristiques propres en tant que société, qui a son propre mode d'organisation et de fonctionnement, qui a sa propre continuité historique, une tradition juridique et politique et enfin, un territoire bien identifié." Laurin went on to point out that all nations had the right to make their mother tongues official languages and to expect minorities to learn those languages. Those who "immigrated to a fully formed nation should not expect 'to modify the character and structures' of their adopted land" but rather "accept the nation and share its destiny."[44]

While the larger Canadian state has groped towards a public policy of pluralism, Quebec has sought to acculturate its immigrants. Once French Canada saw immigration as a threatening program of the federal government and immigrants as allies of "les héritiers des conquérants," but because of the decline of the French-Canadian birth rate and the nationalists' and separatists' dreams of nation building Quebec now sees immigration as a way to draw and assimilate newcomers. This is especially so since natalization programs to encourage Quebec women to have more children seem unsuccessful. Provincial legislation in Quebec has clearly been an instrument to use the state to ensure *survivance*, but the terms of such laws have as their target the immigrants, not merely the vestiges of the anglophone hegemony. Loi 63 (1969), "pour promouver la langue français au Québec," was directed towards ensuring the use of French in the workplace; Loi 22 (1974), "sur la langage officielle," had as its purpose forcing non-anglophone immigrant children to attend the French-language school system; Loi 101 (1977), "Charte de la langue française," required the use of French in all domains of social life—public administration, justice, commerce, small business. Its purpose was to make Quebec unilingually French. Although less than 100 000 of the 250 000 immigrants to Quebec spoke French on arrival, the success achieved in gallicizing the instruments of the provincial government seems to have made Quebec society more confident in its dealings with immigrants of every kind. It is not so much that 25 000 Haitians present less challenge to assimilation than the Italians and Portuguese who preceded them but rather, I believe, that great psychological gain has accompanied the rise and success of *indépendantisme* in Quebec, even among those who see it only as a tactic for improving French-Canadian fortunes within confederation. Seeing itself as a colonized majority in its own land, with a small colonialist elite to neutralize and immigrants to acculturate through state mechanisms, rather than as part of a shrinking minority in a vast land, Quebec can act out of confidence that it will survive rather than fear that it will die.

Despite the hostility and cynicism of much of the intelligentsia, which speaks for those born to or acculturated to one of the charter groups, and despite the limited definition of multiculturalism as an instrument of "gentle Canadianization" held by educators and caretakers, the idea has become a political system and an ideology for many. Ambiguities about what *multiculturalism* should mean, what constitutes an *ethnie*, and how this policy affects individuals' negotiation of identity remain and may even facilitate the exchange between the government and its clientele, the citizens. The Canadian mosaic, the rainbow, polyphony, and the symphony orchestra have all been tried as images, and the first governor general of non-British and non-French descent—Edward Schreyer—spoke of Canada as a cathedral. In his installation speech, he quoted Sir Wilfrid Laurier, who at the turn of the century had called for a Canada on the model of a Gothic cathedral of granite, oak, and marble: "It is the image of the nation I wish to see Canada become. For here, I want the granite to remain the granite, the oak to remain the oak, the marble to remain the marble."[45]

The politicians and the intelligentsia have proven more adept at using metaphors for multiculturalism than at drafting legislation and programs to encourage the emergence of a public ethos of pluralism that both the charter groups and the other ethnic groups could share. In response to the programs of Ottawa and the provinces, an ethnic clientele has grown up that politicians and civil servants try to manipulate. It is easy enough to see the political exchange between the two sides, but it is difficult to see in the exchange more than symbolic gestures and partisan politics. Of the four elements of the policy—integration, the right to cultural retention, cross-cultural understanding, and equality of access and opportunity—the ethnic (at least the white) clientele is most interested in the parts of programs that help ethnic groups persist. They wish to see as corollaries access to the mainstream through acquisition of the official languages, the sort of intercultural understanding that affords each group a good status and a distinct identity in Canadian life, and an end to bigotry and discrimination. Most spokespersons and leaders, however, begin from the premise that the numerical and institutional strength of the ethnie and the coherence of its political mobilization are the prerequisites for gaining the government's attention.

The government, in turn, has an interest in dealing with a limited number of effective leaders from well-organized ethnic blocs. The multiculturalism sector of the federal government runs a program to organize advocacy for newer, less demanding, or more fractious ethnic collectivities. One astute social scientist has observed that the associational structures of most Canadian ethnic groups have so many personnel who represent the "organic intelligentsia" of state-sponsored multiculturalism and depend so heavily on government grants to operate that they cannot be considered independent spokesmen for ethnic feeling any longer.[46] Those who are uncomfortable with the low status of the adjective *ethnic* now favour the term *multicultural*, as in "multicultural group" or "multiculturals." To the extent that ethnic groups become the creations of government rather than representatives of the natural sentiment of those of the descent group, this usage, which seems a semantic monstrosity at first, may be sound usage.

The most ambiguous aspect of multicultural politics, and one that makes the policy and ethos suspect to many, can be summed up in a few unanswered questions: What is the relationship between negotiating one's personal ethnic identity and dealing with the politics of the ethnie's status? What is the ethnic interest (which the Québécois might call *un projet social ou national*) of an immigrant ethnie? In other words, what do immigrants or ethnics want, and does the existence of organized ethnic leadership and a multicultural policy provide what they want? How can government recognize the ethnic group except through funding ethnocultural activities and associations? Recognition of ethnies has received an especially bourgeois and hierarchical spin and reminds one of the quip by the great Italian Marxist thinker Antonio Gramsci that in the exercise of hegemony in a parliamentary context, "corruption or fraud stand midway between consensus and force," Since 1972, advisory councils composed of ethnic representatives, always appointed rather than elected, have recommended that "persons of various ethnocultural backgrounds" be named to boards or hired by a great variety of government agencies.

In 1976 the minister responsible for multiculturalism, John Munro, reacted to criticisms of the policy by denying that it was "a cheap political bone" thrown to the so-called professional ethnics. The policy, he said, was for all Canadians. It was not an English plot to subvert official bilingualism and to dilute the French voice in Canada. Nor was it tokenism or a smoke-screen to make the imposition of bilingualism on the third element easier.[47] Despite such disclaimers, largesse for ethnic organizations and activities, whether doled out by Liberals or Progressive Conservatives, whether handled by federal or provincial civil servants, has often had a distinctly partisan appearance and the scent of the patronage pork barrel. The policy has always been linked to the idea that particular parties can control the votes of particular immigrant or ethnic groups by forms of patronage bestowed in the "legal tender" of the day—magistracies, commission seats, and so forth—on the notables from each collectivity. Prominent politicians make visits to the ethnie's central institutions and pay at least lip service to the ethnie's concerns that arise from "double consciousness" (its interest in the homeland of origin and the foreign policy objectives that go with that interest). Especially significant in the exchange between government and the displaced peoples has been public anti-Sovietism and support for the "captive nations," in some ways a less expensive price for politicians to pay than honest responses to later demands for a piece of the pie in Canada.

It is unclear what underlies the apparent convention in Canada that the interests, standing, and amour propre of the ethnie coincide with the personal negotiation of status and identity by certain ethnoverted individuals. Collective status and personal mobility come together in the form of the parcelling out of an appropriate number of appointive offices. An elaborate list of sinecures, honorifics, and appointments has become the medium of exchange between the ethnic groups and the political parties and bureaucracies. There are as well the inevitable new plaques and parks named after notables and ethnonational heroes to compete with older Anglo-Celtic filial pieties.

These activities are accompanied by grants for community-based historical research and ceremonial ethnonational toponymic changes as well. In the belief that history is infinitely malleable to the civic purpose, the government makes funds available for the rewriting of the national history of Canada, with the third element in. Although such programs provided some leaven to the peculiarly ethnocentric and elitist national historiography, their chief result often seems to be an intellectual steeplechase to prove longevity in the land, rather like the "Mayflowerism" that once characterized ethnic history societies in the United States.

The Canadian party system, as well as the colonial inheritance of competent and intrusive public administration, led to a species of ethnic "wardheeling" in which the entire ethnic group rather than that of a single political constituency was seen as a source of votes in return for attention, jobs, and favours. Such ethnicking was highly visible for several reasons.[48] For one thing, until very recently, the third element was underrepresented among both civil servants and elected politicians. "Although these groups comprised a quarter of the population by ethnic origin in the early 1960s, they elected only 4.4% of new members of the House of Commons and controlled an even smaller proportion of Cabinet positions."[49] As a result, the exchange of everything from money for a new ethnic hall or old-age home to funds to teach "ancestral" or "heritage" languages for bloc votes— as portrayed in the media—had a quality of capturing charter group politicians and ethnic leaders *in flagrantis*. Generally, the problem is less the local candidate's ethnicity or networks of influence with the ethnic groups in his riding than the party's relationship with each group on a national scale. If the local politician delivers grants and honours with fanfare, it is the quieter funding of ethnic persistence through civil services controlled by one party or another that can affect political choice. John Kenneth Galbraith, with a disarming ethnocentric fall from grace to absolve his Scots-Canadian kinsmen, has observed the game of ethnic politics where groups are "solicited, by oratory, unconvincing efforts at identification and inspired banality."[50]

Galbraith and others who criticize politicians for mongering for ethnic votes miss an essential point, usually because they hold too simple a view of the ethnics and the dynamics of maintaining an ethnie. At the level of symbolic politics and the forging of the instruments that enable ethnic leaders to promote ethnogenesis and then ethnicization of the immigrants (that is, to mobilize them politically towards group objectives), there is very little gullibility and a perfect understanding of the exchange of gifts. (Anyone who has spent two decades, as I have, watching politicians struggle to say a few words in the heritage language and promising funds for new wings on ethnic halls, as if the money came out of their own pockets rather than the taxpayers', while ethnic leaders lead rounds of applause as proxies for future votes they cannot deliver, learns not to gag on his pasta or cabbage rolls and gains a new understanding of the "social contract" in a pluralist society.) There are in Ontario, Manitoba, and Alberta politicians who are legendary for the number of ethnic groups with which they claim blood ties. One is described derisively by those among whom he "ethnicks" as claiming descent from all the peoples whose homelands touch the Vistula, the Danube, and the Dnieper.

If the claims of politicians on the multicultural stump are suspect, so are the claims of leaders and spokesmen who say they represent coherent ethnies but are more often self-appointed or government-designated than elected. Of course, opponents of the multicultural policy make much of how unrepresentative ethnic leaders are and of what a corrupting and trivializing effect ethnicking has on issue-oriented politics. A more accurate critique of multiculturalism would be that the policy may serve to perpetuate the hegemony of the British as the elite of Canada. By encouraging political loyalties on lines that cut across class and by rewarding leaders and spokesmen whose concerns are ethnoverted rather than class-oriented, multiculturalism softens issues of immigrant exploitation and representation and removes them from the frame of the flow of labour to capital. A 1973 study found members of ethnic groups more concerned with problems of cultural and linguistic retention than with inequality of opportunity and prejudice in the job place.[51] It is unlikely that a survey of members of visible minorities who arrived in Canada after the impact of the relaxing of racialist immigration restrictions in the 1970s would have similar results.

At the same time, equality of access to services, the struggle against bigotry in the host society, and the guarantees of social mobility are added to the multicultural texts. Most of these issues have no intrinsic relationship to group life, and all of them have objectives that could be met by enforceable legislation. These additions may serve both hegemony and the participants in the ethnic discourse who use the idiom of culture rather than that of law, power, and class to define the immigrants' situation.

The problem with a pluralism based on assumptions about ethnic persistence among immigrants is simply that ethnicity is more and less than a biological given or census fact. It is processual. Canada may tolerate or promote ethnies, but, as Camille Laurin warned, they are not nations. Immigrants and their children negotiate their own identities, and the texts of the ethnoverted leadership are but one level of discourse among many. Without renewal through continual heavy migration and without a territorial base, with porous boundaries and the lure of the mainstream culture, with a public school system and intermarriage, the question becomes less whether intermediaries and leaders represent ethnies and more whether the ethnie is merely an epiphenomenon of immigration that will disappear unless regularly funded institutions of ethnic maintenance are legislated. Recently a Ukrainian Canadian observed rather bitterly that he and others had deluded themselves. He had come to realize that the Prairie Ukrainians were the only ethnic group in the third element. The rest were postwar immigrants facing rapid generational slippage and loss of ethno-culture.[52] An informal count of the leadership of most groups as well as of those who serve on the various multicultural advisory boards shows a majority to be foreign-born.

Measuring the differentials among the census categories "ethnic origin," "mother tongue," and "home language" suggests that, despite the declared policy of multiculturalism, the optimistic or obfuscating claims of ethnic spokesmen, and the presence of extensive heritage language programs, immigrants to Canada and their children are acculturating rapidly. *Linguicide,* the label that advocates who believe multiculturalism will be credible only if multilingualism is possible, seems inevitable under current conditions. To the extent that a subculture needs a subsociety in which to embed itself, only geographical, cultural, and institutional isolation could preserve language. The prevailing situation is diglossia—immigrants speaking English as a second language, with all the limits that implies, and at the same time slowly losing their mother tongues. Their children speak English as a first language at school and on the street and are either bilingual or unable to speak their parents' language.

The leading ethnolinguist, Joshua Fishman, has noted that within three generations the language of the street usually becomes the language of the cradle. Only about half of those who describe themselves as Italian Canadians use Italian as their home language. That number is even less than the number of foreign-born in the group. In the 1971 census, only 71 000 Poles spoke Polish at home regularly, although 135 000 claimed Polish as their mother tongue and over 315 000 as their ethnic origin. For the Dutch in Canada, a group for whom assimilation is considerably easier, the figures are 36 000 speaking Dutch at home out of 425 000. The majority of these speakers of Dutch live in fairly isolated rural settings or have religious ties that are strongly ethnoverted. Since it is the Ukrainians who have led the way for the third element and who have made the most concerted effort to join various of their immigrant cohorts in a single "nation in exile," one would expect language retention to be high. Only about half the census group lists Ukrainian as its mother tongue, and only about a third speaks Ukrainian regularly in the home.

There are, of course, bases of ethnic identity, if not of ethnoculture, other than retention of the mother tongue. Generally, however, Canadian ethnic spokespersons, dismissive of what they view as decultured third- and fourth-generation ethnic identity in the United States, emphasize language as the cement of community. (I am aware of ethnic hockey and basketball teams that have collapsed, not for want of athletes of the descent group but because speaking the heritage language was a requirement for making the team.) Studies of the intensity of associational life and commitment to the discourse of ethnoculture are rare, and sophisticated ones are even rarer. A study of the National Congress of Italian Canadians a few years ago showed only about 30 percent of Canadians of Italian descent active in any ethnic institution except the parish.[53] It is such results that cause ethnic leaders to hesitate before analysing the ethnie publicly.

Ethnic leaders have reason then to seek means as quickly as possible to turn living immigrant ethnocultures into ethnies with institutions that can aid group persistence through future generations, even if immigration ceases. The texts that they produce for discourse with both the immigrant community and the government more and more emphasize this Canadian rather than the old-country side of their double consciousness.

Canada's new Constitution, born of the British juridical and political tradition, is a document about individual rather than group rights. Such an approach to rights and freedoms fits ill with political pluralism. One result has been to add group rights to the document; such an attempt is the

Meech Lake Accord, which recognizes Quebec as a "distinct society." The result for ethnic leadership has been disappointment that there are no justiciable multicultural rights in the Charter of Rights and Freedoms. Article 27 speaks of multiculturalism as a quality of Canadian life and promises that all other articles of the Charter will be interpreted in a manner consistent with multiculturalism. It is, then, an affirmation of multicultural ideals but not a statement of ethnic rights or multicultural obligations. No ethnies will be "distinct societies." *Canadien* spokespersons and those of the aboriginal peoples, Indian or Inuit, can write and speak of pluralism of destination, of the right to public funding to create institutions of otherness as part of a permanent status within Canadian confederation. It is not at all unusual or destructive of consensus in the political discourse for such leaders to describe policies that encourage acculturation and assimilation into anglophone Canada as cultural genocide. Very few Canadians would, however, tolerate expressions of a similar kind about the rights of ethnic groups.

After the new Charter of Rights failed to address the ethnic group persistence directly, many hoped that Bill C-93, the Multicultural Act, brought before Parliament in 1987, would offer redress. The bill is also long on affirmation of the polyethnic Canadian reality and the value of a multicultural ethos but short on enforceable programs. Affirming multiculturalism while legislating first bilingualism and then Quebec's right to a "separate way" in Canada puts the government's view of the rights of immigrant and ethnic minorities in perspective. As always, however, the lack of shared definitions of the boundary and content of multiculturalism as well as uncertainty about the nature and life cycle of group ethnicity itself has been as much an impediment to the development of a public policy as its ideological enemies have been. There is disagreement about whether a minister of multiculturalism would ghettoize those he or she served, whether a commissioner of multiculturalism could work as effectively as the commissioner of official languages has functioned in enforcing bilingualism. Could such a public servant enforce sensitivity towards ethnic cultures and a fair distribution of jobs without appearing to be tainted with a species of pluralist McCarthyism? Should the mainstream be multiculturalized rather than vice versa? In other words, should the secretary of state for multiculturalism or the minister of culture and communications take over all funding for the arts, control of the CBC, and allocations for research?[54]

Is this then "the way the world ends, not with a bang but a whimper?" Without the possibility of enforcement through either the Charter or the act, this would be a multiculturalism that would amount to more than the modest statements made in 1969 in Book IV of the royal commission report about "encouraging those members of ethnic groups who want to do so to maintain a proud sense of the contribution of their own group to Canadian society." Both ethnic and panethnic associational spokespersons have suggested tactics for funding ethnic group persistence, from annual group maintenance grants to tithing. One suggestion is that each Canadian taxpayer could assign 1 percent of his or her taxes to an ethnic umbrella organization, presumably one of his or her choice, not one determined by the census. The possibility of extending tax credits of the kind allowed for charitable donations to gifts given to ethnic associations has also received consideration. The vexing questions of how much this would cost the community and whether the mainstream is obligated to supported alternative cultures arise. Politicians usually prefer not to look at them directly.

For those who speak for ethnies formed from the DP experience or from a history of prairie isolation as well as for the immigrant Italian ethnie, numbers are crucial. Ever since Senator Yuzyk raised the census artifact of ethnic origin to forge the third element, both individual ethnic groups and the third element have depended on the threat of bloc votes and the moral suasion of rights by magnitude to press their case. A guest editorial in response to the proposed new Multiculturalism Act recently appeared in the *Ottawa Citizen*. It represents a genre of texts going back to remarks by John Yaremko, Ontario's first minister of citizenship and culture, to Heritage Ontario in 1972, a provincially sponsored forum on multiculturalism. Yaremko assumed, or chose to assume, that census identity and personal ethnocultural sentiment are synonymous, that polyethnicity automatically engenders multiculturalism: "According to the 1986 census, 38% of the Canadian population have origins other than British or French. Cultural diversity is not a fringe factor as was the case at the time of Confederation."[55]

It is in this context that one must understand the politics of census taking in Canada. Changes in census categories that allow the recording of multiple identities and alternatives to a patrilineal definition of ethnic origin and that make the reporting of ethnic origin voluntary threaten to strip the generals of their field forces. According to the assistant statistician of Canada, more and more people "simply refuse to report origins no matter how we attempt to phrase the question. They steadfastly insist that they are Canadian."[56] The census, he added, "is a questionnaire which is completed by the respondent, and the respondent's perception is what determines what the respondent will answer." Such a democratic and volitional approach to ethnic identity can hardly be faulted, but it causes major problems for those who use ethnic origins as an instrument of political power. The assistant statistician went on to observe that his office had many requests for information from ethnic associations. He also showed some of the wisdom that comes from long experience with the ethnic numbers game:

> A related problem stems from what we might call old world conflicts, in which rival groups will object to the inclusion of each other in the census counts. For example, spokespersons for the Armenian community might object to any associations in the enumeration with Turks. Spokespersons for the Greek community may insist that Macedonians not be counted separately, but be included in the

count of Greeks, and spokespersons for the Macedonian community will demand exactly the opposite. There will be complaints that the Irish are included with the British in the summary tables.

For all the concern with ethnic origin statistics and the maintenance of ethnies, there seems remarkably little information about how the public policy affects the quality of life in other than cultural or psychological terms. If immigrants have prospered or remained niched at the bottom of the economy, what role, if any, has the policy had in bringing about such results? It is forty years since the new mass migration began and over twenty years since John Porter published *The Vertical Mosaic*,[57] a study of ethnicity, stratification, and social mobility. His book has proven to be the anti-text to the multicultural canon and a *vade mecum* for those who believe that liberal principles of individualism and meritocracy along with benign (i.e., unbigoted) forms of assimilationism are the only fair and effective policies for an immigrant nation.

Porter contended that Canada's charter groups had remained in terms of wealth, power, and status in a relatively unchanged relationship to the other ethnic groups. He used indices of disproportionate representation in various occupations and strata to show the British group's hegemony and dominance of elite positions in business and other professions, politics, and cultural life. He attributed this dominance more to longevity of residence, networks of influence, and the low "entry status" of many non-British immigrants rather than to systemic racialism operating against Southern Europeans and other minorities. For Porter, a policy of multiculturalism risked enshrining inequality and low social-class niching for certain ethnic groups. After showing that Porter overemphasized the lack of change to fit his central thesis, his followers, both sympathetic and hostile, have attempted to test his views on the increasingly polyethnic Canadian reality.[58] Thus a 1975 study, using measurements similar to those Porter used in the 1960s, found that although the non-British and non-French components in the higher levels of management and the professions had gone from 1 percent to 5 percent, and although French-Canadian access to the elite had grown a bit, the control of elite categories by the British had only declined from 92 percent to 86 percent in a country in which they made up about 50 percent of the population. A study in Toronto at about the same time showed "significant inequality of income opportunity among immigrant men." The kind of choices available to Canadians, with the exception of the Jews, fairly well parallelled earlier immigration department information about what was possible for preferred and non-preferred stocks: opportunity was best for the English and decreased to less and less for the Jews, the Italians, the Slavs, the Greeks, the Portuguese, the Asians, and the blacks, in that order.[59]

Such attempts to relate ethnicity to stratification and social mobility are fraught with risky inferences. The numbers game may be the only way the third element can maintain political clout, but it is not a sufficiently sophisticated way to measure immigrants' life choices, levels of satisfaction, or intensity of ethnic identity. It is clear that Porter and others underestimated the strength of parallel pyramids of opportunity. In the face of the barriers of discrimination and denial of access to mainstream economies and elites, alternate strategies do develop. It is clear that both the Jews and the Italians have prospered from such parallel economic structures or from concentration in occupations less attractive to charter group elites, such as the construction industry and retail or wholesale commerce. Other ethnic groups have found similar, if less profitable, niching in the food services industries and control of airport limousines. New generations of professionals from the children of these immigrant groups find their clientele within the niche but begin to circulate in the larger society and economy as well.

However, among continental European immigrants, especially those from southern Europe, there remains a mixed sense of place in Canada. Books with titles like *Don't Feed Us on Lentils* and *Bastards of the Nation* remind us that immigration has been painful and that the first purpose of all Canadian immigration policy has been to find the labour power the country needs. For all the talk of seeking skilled immigrants, the policy continues to mean, in the words of the most recent annual report of the minister of immigration, finding people to "accept jobs at distant and remote locations" and to "take jobs that are not accepted by residents."[60] The least unionized, lowest-paid, and most unpleasant urban work in Canada is done by immigrants, especially immigrant women. Latin Americans, Middle Easterners, Asians, and East Africans now do what Slavs did in the 1950s, Italians in the 1960s, and Portuguese and Greeks in the 1970s. No number of individual immigrant or ethnic success stories, either heralded by multicultural or ethnic flacks, or splattered across the country's slick magazines with innuendos about organized crime, fraud, and swindling, can obscure the low entry status of most non-British immigrants to Canada. What immigrants have added to the civility and vibrance of Canada's cities, especially as shopkeepers and restaurateurs, testifies to a presence that has enriched the whole economy.

Almost fifty years after the mass migration of the non-British and the non-French began to intrude into the struggle for *Canadien survivance* and for the survival of the Canadian polity, the situation remains inchoate. It is inchoate in Wittgenstein's sense that the determinate relations between subjects and the nature of objects themselves seem only now to be forming. French-Canadian *survivance,* despite recent successful tests in the Prairie provinces of the Charter's guarantee of French language rights, is now condensed into the concept of Quebec as a distinct society or the dream of an independent Quebec. *English Canadian* has increasingly become a linguistic rather than an ethnic or a sentimental designation as the third element has been acculturating and the distance from British roots for all Canadians growing. As a corollary, despite the Charter, the pending

Multiculturalism Act, and highly differentiated ethnic and panethnic organizations, there are many signs that ethnicity is proving itself an epiphenomenon of several postmigrant generations rather than a basis for permanent communal differences.

Meanwhile, the external threat to the polity takes two forms. Canadian fertility rates and those of white immigrants are below replacement level. Canada faces zero growth and, to sustain itself, will have to turn to races and ethnic groups that Mackenzie King, not to say other Canadians, might not welcome. The second external threat to the Canada that King would have recognized comes from attempts to create a North American free-trade zone.

The current public discourse about Canada's state of affairs reminds one of the advice of German Marxist philosopher Walter Benjamin that the only way to understand the times one lives in is to try to catch "the dialectic at a standstill" by observing the contradictions and choices available to men and women in a "present without resolution." Benjamin went on to suggest the writing of a book made up solely of quotations to fulfil this purpose.[61] I will end with something of the sort.

The Saskatchewan Multicultural Association believes that it has found a "determinate relation" of significance: "If free trade in multiculturalism means adopting the concept of the melting pot rather than cultural pluralism, then multicultural organizations must oppose free trade." Importing the myth of the melting pot, it adds, "would be a far more significant threat to multiculturalism than the Meech Lake Accord." Meanwhile, that accord, with both its promise of special status for Quebec and its implication that such a status might include separate Quebec policies on immigration and the maintenance of ethnic groups, leads to a chorus of protest from the third element. The Canadian Jewish Congress and the National Congress of Italian Canadians denounce the idea. Some Prairie Ukrainian leaders offer a smug "I told you so" and dream dreams of a strategy for Alberta like that of Quebec that would create a regional Ukrainian–English bilingualism.[62] They can point to some stunning facts: that the number of bilingual Canadians has not risen much from the 15 percent it was when the Official Languages Act came into force a decade ago; that in 1986 Statistics Canada reported under 5 percent for Ontario and under 3 percent for British Columbia of non-francophone children in French immersion programs; that Quebec nationalists also view a national bilingual policy with suspicion, as a "trojan horse"; and that more often than not, bilingual francophones outside Quebec become unilingual anglophones, usually within a generation.

The effects of Meech Lake are apparent already. The accord establishes the idea that Canada is a dual society, but it does not oblige the English-speaking provinces to increase their bilingualism. A recent revolt of Tory backbenchers, mainly from the West, is attempting to thwart efforts to reconcile the new Charter of Rights with the Official Languages Act. In

1988 the premier of Ontario rejected a call to make Ontario officially bilingual. The call came from a Franco-Ontarian association, which speaks for the province's 500 000 francophones, orphaned by the Quebec nationalist strategy and the Meech Lake Accord. At about the same time they were making their appeal, a witness before the parliamentary standing committee on multiculturalism, meeting in Toronto, told the legislators that "multiculturalism is totally meaningless without multilingualism. The equity envisioned in the act is not possible in our Canadian school communities, unless the languages of the children in the community are used. . . . Song and dance is not enough.[63]

In April 1987 Keith Spicer, a former commissioner of official languages and the influential editor of the *Ottawa Citizen,* spoke out. He saw the matter starkly: "The final question runs deeper—isn't the time coming to stop making a religion of mosaics altogether and to start fostering a national spirit we can all identify with? With constant intermarriage, for how many generations more must an English- or Ukrainian-Canadian revere his presumed roots?"[64] Only a naïf would ask why Spicer did not add French Canadians to his list; that would be to step outside the limits of legitimate discourse. He went on to accuse the government of "making a virtue of a weakness, a glory of a hindrance to nationhood; we pay people to have foreign roots."

One wonders if those engaged in the Canadian discourse about identity and policy now are ready for the next intrusion. With Canadian fertility rates unable to sustain growth, with the natural decline of immigration from Europe because of similar birth rates there, new Canadians will increasingly come from the Third World. This trend began in 1968 with the end of racialism in immigration legislation.[65] In that year 65 percent of the immigrants to Canada came from Europe. By 1984 the figure was down to 24 percent. The Asian share of immigration rose in that same period from 12 percent to 50. In 1961 no Asian country was among the top sending countries; by 1984 five out of ten were. Caribbean and Central American immigration has also risen rapidly since the early 1970s. Those who deal with the dialectic between the need for numbers and the desire to maintain the "right stock" are at work again.

A demographer for the Department of National Health and Welfare recently told the parliamentary standing committee on multiculturalism about the demographic situation of Canada. He reminded them of the decline of European fertility and went on to describe the impact on immigration of "lumpy events" such as the reversion of Hong Kong to China in the near future. One cannot think of the possibility of other lumpy events, in Johannesburg, Belfast, the Punjab, Sri Lanka, and the West Bank, which could change the pools of potential new Canadians. Would large numbers from any of these places, labelled refugee or DP, start the same problems that began in Canada after World War II? How would their coming affect multiculturalism and bilingualism?

If this has been a darkling portrait of Canada's population policies, it should be balanced against some thoughts about the quality of life amid what amounts to a pluralism of pluralisms. Practical acceptance pf poly-ethnicity and the presence of free and fair institutions make daily life in Canada rich, safe, and hopeful. The economy inclines to meritocracy and free flow despite the hold of old elites upon it and the aspirations of those who believe in corporate rights and freedoms to control part of it. It works for most immigrants, although not without the economic struggle and scarring that accompany insertion into a strange, and often hostile, social and cultural environment. It clearly does not work for the native people and some of the native-born poor, who lack the networks and the strategies that the newcomers have developed to carve out patterns of survival and mobility. If Canada can be saved from the full realization of anyone's dream of multiculturalism—that of the ethnic leaders, the "caretakers," or the politicians—we will continue to live in a civil polity between balkanization and assimilation, between petty nationalism and laissez-faire continentalism, between a begrudging, ungenerous dualism and a separated Quebec. Robert Louis Stevenson once remarked that the "pleasure was in the travelling, not the getting there." For Canada, survival lies in the travelling towards an identity, and we will all be better served if that travelling itself remains our identity.

• Notes

1 The text of King's statement appears in Hansard, House of Commons *Debates*, 1 May 1947, 2644–47. It is reproduced as Appendix A of the *Report of the Canadian Immigration and Population Study (CIPS): The Immigration Program* (Ottawa: Information Canada, 1947). There is no general history of Canadian immigration policy and immigration. For the postwar period, see D.C. Corbett, *Canada's Immigration Policy* (Toronto: Canadian Institute of International Affairs, University of Toronto, 1957); F. Hawkins, *Canada and Immigration: Public Policy and Public Concern* (Montreal: McGill-Queen's University Press, 1972); and R. Whitaker, *Double Standard: The Secret History of Canadian Immigration* (Toronto: Lester & Orpen Dennys, 1987).

2 For studies of the earlier mass immigration see D. Avery, *"Dangerous Foreigners": European Immigrant Workers and Labour Radicalism in Canada, 1896–1932* (Toronto: McClelland & Stewart, 1979), and R.C. Brown and R. Cook, *Canada, 1896–1921: A Nation Transformed* (Toronto: McClelland & Stewart, 1974).

3 J.S. Woodsworth, *Strangers Within Our Gates; or, Coming Canadians* (Toronto: F.C. Stephenson, 1909), 162.

4 See King's 1910 report, as quoted in *The Immigration Program*, 9.

5 Quoted in J.S. Frideres, "British Canadian Attitudes Toward Minority Ethnic Groups in Canada," *Attitudes Toward Minority Groups in Canada—Ethnicity, no. 5* (Toronto: Prentice-Hall, 1978). See also H. Palmer, "Reluctant Hosts: Anglo-Canadian Views of Multiculturalism in the Twentieth Century" in *Multiculturalism as State Policy*, conference report of

the Second Biennial Conference of Canadian Consultative Council on Multiculturalism (Ottawa: Ministry of Supply, 1976), 81–118.

6 Bosworth, "What Kind of Canadians Are We Getting?" *Maclean's*, 15 Feb. 1952, 17.

7 *Demography and Immigration in Canada: Challenge and Opportunity* (Ottawa: Employment and Immigration Canada, Nov. 1987): 18–20.

8 John Stuart Mill to Henry George, Oct. 1869, quoted in R. Takaki, *Iron Cages: Race and Culture in Nineteenth-Century America* (New York: Knopf, 1979), 245.

9 I. Abella and H. Troper, *None Is Too Many: Canada and the Jews of Europe, 1937–1948* (Toronto: Lester & Orpen Dennys, 1982), ch. 8.

10 M. Danys, *DP: Lithuanian Immigration to Canada after the Second World War* (Toronto: Multicultural History Society of Ontario, 1986), 134.

11 N. Tienhaara, *Canadian View on Immigration and Population: An Analysis of Postwar Gallup Polls* (Ottawa: Department of Manpower and Immigration, 1974), 59.

12 Brief of Association of United Ukrainian Canadians on immigration submitted to the Senate, 5 June 1947, reprinted in *Anglo-American Perspectives on the Ukrainian Question 1938–1951*, ed. B.S. Kordan and L. Luciuk (Kingston, ON: Limestone Press, 1987).

13 Quoted in M. Danys, *DP*, 84.

14 Hawkins, *Canada and Immigration*, 201–2.

15 Bosworth, "What Kind of Canadians Are We Getting?"

16 "Gateway to a New Life," *Globe and Mail*, 12 Sept. 1956, 7.

17 Corbett, *Canada's Immigration Policy*, 52–53.

18 E. Wickberg, ed., *From China to Canada: A History of the Chinese Communities in Canada* (Toronto: McClelland & Stewart, 1982), 214–15.

19 R. Morin, *L'Immigration au Canada* (Montreal: Éditions de l'action nationale, 1966), introduction.

20 N.E. Assimopoulos and J.E. Humblet, "Les Immigrés et la question nationale: étude comparative des sociétés québecoise et wallonne," *Studi emigrazione/Études migrations* 24, 86 (June 1987): 155–86.

21 Dispatch to the Department of External Affairs (Ottawa), 8 March 1949, in RG 76, pt. 10, Public Archives of Canada (hereafter PAC), as quoted in F. Sturino, "Post–World War II Canadian Immigration Policy Toward Italians," *Polyphony, Bulletin of the Multicultural History Society of Ontario* 7, 2 (Fall/Winter 1985): 68. See also R.F. Harney, "Italophobia: An English-speaking Malady?" *Studi emigrazione/ Études migrations* 22, 77 (March 1985): 6–43.

22 See J.S. Macdonald and L. Macdonald, "Italian Migration to Australia: Manifest Function of Bureaucracy versus Latent Function of Informal Networks," *Journal of Social History* (Spring 1967): 254.

23 "Investigation of Settlement Arrangements," Immigrants from Italy Agenda Item 2 (1961), RG 26, vol. 128, PAC.

24 See R. Breton, "The Production and Allocation of Symbolic Resources: An Analysis of the Linguistic and Ethnocultural Fields in Canada" in *Ethnic Canada: Identities and Inequalities*, ed. L. Driedger (Toronto: Copp Clark Pitman, 1987), 44–64.

25 N. Keyfitz, "How the Descendants of English-Speakers See the Speakers of Other Languages and Their Descendants," *Second Canadian Conference on Multiculturalism Conference Report* (Ottawa: Minister of State, Multiculturalism, 1976), 69.

26 Breton, "The Production and Allocation of Symbolic Resources," 55.

27 E. Kallen, "Multiculturalism: Ideology, Policy and Reality," *Journal of Canadian Studies* 17, 1 (Spring 1982): 51–63.

28 Senator Paul Yuzyk, *For a Better Canada* (Toronto: Ukrainian National Association, 1973). "Canada, a Multicultural Nation" was delivered in the Senate on 3 March 1964.

29 M. Lupul, "Canada's Options in Time of Political Crisis and Their Implications for Multiculturalism," in *Ukrainian Canadians, Multiculturalism, and Separatism: An Assessment* (Edmonton: Canadian Institute of Ukrainian Studies, 1978), 160.

30 Heritage Ontario, *Report* (Toronto: Government of Ontario, 2 June 1972).

31 *Book IV: The Cultural Contribution of the Other Ethnic Groups*, report of the Royal Commission on Bilingualism and Biculturalism (Ottawa: Queen's Printer, 1969), 4–5. These are remarks of one of the chief authors of the report. See J. Burnet, "The Policy of Multiculturalism Within a Bilingual Framework: An Interpretation" in *The Education of Immigrant Children*, ed. A. Wolfgang (Toronto: Ontario Institute for Studies in Education, 1975).

32 E. DeMartino, *La fine del mondo* (Turin: Einaudi, 1978).

33 K. Deutsch, *Nationalism and Social Communication: An Inquiry into the Foundation of Nationality* (Cambridge: MIT Press, 1953).

34 R. Breton, "The Production and Allocation of Symbolic Resources," 58.

35 *Report of the First Conference of the Canadian Consultative Council on Multiculturalism* (Ottawa: Minister of State, Multiculturalism, 1972), 4–5, 18–20.

36 "UCC Slams Multicultural Centres," *Ukrainian Echo* 1, 1 (April 1977): 2.

37 L. Zolf, "Mulling Over Multiculturalism," *Maclean's*, 14 April 1980, 6.

38 D. Fisher, presentation in *Multiculturalism as State Policy* (Ottawa: Minister of State, Multiculturalism, 1976), 15.

39 For a discussion of these matters, see J. Burnet, "Myths and Multiculturalism," *Canadian Journal of Education* 4, 4 (1979): 43–58.

40 The Symons Report, an abridged version of vols. 1, 2 of *To Know Ourselves: The Report of the Commission on Canadian Studies* (Toronto: Association of Universities and Colleges of Canada, 1978), 60.

41 Rev. Léger Comeau, "Multiculturalism—A Francophone Viewpoint" in *Second Canadian Conference on Multiculturalism Conference Report* (Ottawa: Minister of State, Multiculturalism, 1976), 27.

42 R. Lévesque, "Education in a Changing Society, A View from Quebec" in *Canadian Schools and Canadian Identity*, ed. A. Chaiton and N. McDonald (Toronto: Gage, 1977).

43 G. Rocher, "Multiculturalism: The Doubts of a Francophone" in *Second Canadian Conference on Multiculturalism Conference Report* (Ottawa: Minister of State, Multiculturalism, 1976), 47–53.

44 C. Laurin, "Le Sort des minorités ethniques dans un Québec indépendant" in *Frontiers Ethniques on Devenie*, ed. D. Juteau Lee (Ottawa: Éditions de l'Université d'Ottawa, 1979).

45 See the imagery of Yuzyk's 1964 speech. Governor-General Schreyer quoted Laurier in his address at his installation, Ottawa, 22 Jan. 1979.

46 D. Stasiulis, "The Political Structuring of Ethnic Community Action: A Reformulation," *Canadian Ethnic Studies* 12, 3 (1980): 18.

47 Address by the Honorable John Munro, minister responsible for multiculturalism, in *Multiculturalism as State Policy*.

48 "Now I have had experience as a politician, and I recognize the temptation of what I used to call "ethnicking" in John Diefenbaker's day." D. Fisher, presentation in *Multiculturalism as State Policy*, 17. "Today's official multiculturalism leads to the worst of demagogueries: for example, John

Diefenbaker promising to liberate the Ukraine, and all this for a handful of Ukrainian Canadian seats; Joe Clark moving embassies for a fingerful of Jewish seats." L. Zolf, "How Multiculturalism Corrupts," *Maclean's*, 15 Nov. 1982, 21.

49 D. Stasiulis, "Cultural Boundaries and the Cohesion of Canada" in *Cultural Pluralism and Cultural Identity: The Experience of Canada, Finland and Yugoslavia*, ed. R. Rosandric. Final report of the UNESCO Joint Study on Cultural Development in Countries Containing Different National and/or Ethnic Groups (Paris: UNESCO, 1985), 79.

50 J.K. Galbraith, *A Life in Our Times: Memoirs* (New York: Houghton-Mifflin, 1981), 1.

51 Study by K.G. O'Bryan, J. Reitz, and O. Kuplowska published as *Non-Official Languages: A Study in Canadian Multiculturalism* (Ottawa: Multiculturalism Directorate, 1976), cited in Stasiulis, "Cultural Boundaries and the Cohesion of Canada," 78.

52 M.R. Lupul, "The Tragedy of Canada's White Ethnics: A Constitutional Postmortem," *Journal of Ukrainian Studies* 7 (Spring 1982): 5–7.

53 *Italian Canadians: A Cross Section, a National Survey of Italian Canadian Communities* (Ottawa: Congress of Italian Canadians, 1978). It is only fair to add that it took some courage to publish the report and that the research was flawed and the statistical base insufficient. Its result does, however, dovetail with many other informal indicators of low ethnoversion in terms of participation, except world-cup soccer and family and paese rites of passage.

54 J.H. Grey et al., *Multiculturalism and the Charter: A Legal Perspective* (Agincourt, ON: Carswell, 1987); for the debate about the act and what it should include, see especially "Multiculturalism, Building the Canadian Mosaic," report of the Standing Committee on Multicultural-

ism, House of Commons, no. 5, June 1987, in *Minutes of Proceedings and Evidence of the Standing Committee on Multiculturalism* (Ottawa: Queen's Printer, 1987); see other criticisms of the proposed act in *Ethno-Canada: The Newsletter of the Canadian Ethnocultural Council* (Winter 1988), a special issue on the multiculturalism Bill C-93.

55 L.A. Cardozo, "In Defense of the Federal Government's Multicultural Policy," *Ottawa Citizen*, 19 Jan. 1988, C-1. The columnist is the executive director of the Canadian Ethnocultural Council, an organization that receives large annual grants from the multiculturalism sector within the Secretary of State.

56 Testimony of a demographer for the Department of National Health and Welfare and of the assistant archivist of Canada before the Standing Committee on Multiculturalism, *Minutes of the Proceedings and Evidence of the Standing Committee on Multiculturalism*, House of Commons, no. 13, Feb. 1988 (Ottawa: Queen's Printer, 1988), 23.

57 J. Porter, *The Vertical Mosaic: An Analysis of Social Class and Power in Canada* (Toronto: University of Toronto Press, 1965).

58 The most important correctives and confirmations of the truth of Porter's general points are G. Darroch, "Another Look at Ethnicity, Stratification, and Social Mobility in Canada," *Canadian Journal of Sociology* 4 (1979): 1–25; W. Clement, *The Canadian Corporate Elite: An Analysis of Economic Power* (Toronto: McClelland & Stewart, 1975); and various investigations by J. Reitz, conveniently synthesized in his book *The Survival of Ethnic Groups in Canada* (Toronto: McGraw-Hill Ryerson, 1980). In a lighter vein, Peter Newman's book *The Canadian Establishment* (Toronto: McClelland & Stewart, 1976) confirms Porter's view.

59 J. Goldlust and A. Richmond, "A Multivariate Analysis of the Economic Adaptation of Immigrants in Toronto"

(mimeograph, Institute for Behavioral Research, York University, 1973).

60 *Annual Report to Parliament on Future Immigration Levels* (Ottawa: Employment and Immigration Canada, 1987).

61 W. Benjamin, *Reflections, Essays, Aphorisms, Autobiographical Writings* (New York: Schocken, 1986).

62 *Saskatchewan Multicultural Magazine* 6, 3 (Fall 1987): 1; *La Voce del Congress* (Feb. 1988), open letter from National Council of Italian Canadians president to the prime minister expressing misgivings about the Meech Lake Accord; "Meech Threatens Rights, Jewish Group Says," *Toronto Star*, 24 Feb. 1988, A2; "Peterson Rejects Demand for Official Bilingualism," *Toronto Star*, 18 Feb. 1988.

63 Remarks of representative of Ontario Coalition for Language Rights in *Minutes of Proceeding and Evidence of the Standing Committee on Multiculturalism*, House of Commons, no. 11 (Dec. 1987).

64 *Spectator* (Hamilton), 15 April 1987, A7.

65 *Canadian Ethnic Studies*, special issue: The Green Paper on Immigration 7, 1 (1975), esp. P. Cappon, "The Green Paper: Immigration as a Tool for Profit," and G. Singh Paul, "The Green Paper and Third World Immigrants: A Subjective Analysis."

WHERE JUSTICE LIES:
Aboriginal Rights and Wrongs in Temagami*

TONY HALL

There is an undercurrent of polite brutality in most of the courtroom dramas that pit aboriginal groups in argumentative combat with legal officers of the federal and provincial governments in Canada. On the one side sit lawyers for Native communities, communities that by almost any standard have benefited least from Confederation.[1] On the other side sit Crown officers whose duty it is to represent the interests of the general population. Most often this responsibility to give legal articulation to the larger society's political will is channelled into ideological assaults against the assertion by aboriginal groups that they hold aboriginal rights.

In making their arguments, Crown officials return again and again to a few key ideas: aboriginal people were too primitive before the arrival of Europeans to have a legal system and they therefore lacked a basis to exercise any coherent form of land tenure; because aboriginal people were non-Christians, their laws were automatically superseded by those of the representatives of a Christian monarch; aboriginal people were conquered and thereby lost the right of self-determination; the rights of aboriginal people were created by the imperial Crown and these rights can be unilaterally extinguished by officers of the Crown; aboriginal people can exercise

*Reprinted with permission from *Temagami: A Wilderness Debate,* edited by Matt Bray and Ashley Thomson, "Where Justice Lies: Aboriginal Rights and Wrongs in Temagami" by Tony Hall; Dundurn Press, 1990: pp. 223–53. © Institute for Northern Ontario Research and Development, 1990.

their human rights as individual Canadian citizens but not as members of distinct aboriginal collectivities.[2]

In various combinations and permutations, these ideas constitute the essential arsenal of legal theories employed, especially by provincial authorities, to counter the claims of Native people. What links the ideas is a view of humanity that would situate all groups and races along a hierarchy of worth and advancement. A racially inspired paradigm of law is the result, a legal construct supported by legions of Victorian social philosophers who in the nineteenth century went about elaborating a bold edifice of Darwinian theory to justify the apparent ascendancy on the stage of world history of Anglo-Saxons over the perceived lower races of dark-skinned peoples.[3]

Another major theory of legal relations between Native people and newcomers in Crown domains holds that as a basic rule aboriginal peoples had the inherent human right not to be dispossessed of their ancestral lands without their consent and without some reasonable compensation. This approach to the law places emphasis on the Royal Proclamation of 1763 and the line of Indian treaties and land-claim agreements that flows from it. All of these constitutional instruments, it is held, demonstrate that the Crown rule of law in Canada is founded on recognition, however begrudgingly or insufficiently applied, that aboriginal peoples are fully human and therefore the holders of certain inalienable human rights.

These two approaches to history and law have found clear expression in one of the lengthiest and most contentious land-claim disputes ever to develop in the Canadian courts. The case sets the Teme-Augama Anishnabai, sometimes known as the Bear Island band, against the attorney-general of Ontario.[4] The area in dispute, a major portion of Temagami, covers 9000 square kilometres of prime northeastern Ontario land. In 1973 the chief of the Bear Island band, Gary Potts, together with Bruce Clark, a Haileybury lawyer, successfully filed a legal caution on N'Daki Menan, the Teme-Augama people's ancestral territory. The caution was judicially sanctioned in light of the Supreme Court of Canada's finding in 1973 on the land claim of the Nishga people in British Columbia. Although the Nishga technically lost the case, the finding forced on law officers in Canada the recognition that aboriginal title—that is, the interest of aboriginal people in their ancestral land—is not only an ethical principle but also a legal construct within the Crown tradition of common law, legislation, convention, and jurisprudence.[5]

The contention of the several hundred people who make up the Teme-Augama Anishnabai is that their ancestors never ceded away their aboriginal title to their ancestral lands. They maintain that, when the original Indian treaty covering Temagami and adjacent areas was negotiated in Sault Ste Marie in 1850, their leaders were not present to sanction the agreement. As early as 1885 the Temagami Indians convinced the federal government of this fact, a detail of history demonstrated by the reality that the band found itself without a reserve throughout much of the twentieth century. In 1943 the government of Ontario, the claimant of exclusive proprietary interest in the province's Crown lands, finally relented from treating the Temagami people essentially as squatters,[6] but it was not until 1971 that the 285-hectare Bear Island site of the Indians' village was finally granted reserve status. Further, as Chief Potts was later to assert in the courts, the establishment of the Bear Island reserve did not speak to the larger question of his people's unceded aboriginal title to their entire homeland.

The land claim of the Teme-Augama Anishnabai threw legal attention on the need for reconsideration of Ontario's intricately evolved legacy of Crown–Indian relations through the medium of treaties. Ontario officials, who hold that all provincial lands are subject to the outcome of Indian treaty negotiations, found themselves in a position akin to that of provincial authorities in British Columbia. The vastest part of BC's lands, like much of Yukon, Northwest Territories, northern Quebec, and Labrador, have never been covered by Crown treaties with indigenous peoples. Ontario, on the other hand, is the Canadian jurisdiction with both the oldest and newest heritage of Indian treaties. Major treaties were made with Native people of the Ontario area at intervals between 1784 and 1923, a range of history that encompasses many different political regimes of Native–newcomer relations.[7]

• The Royal Proclamation of 1793 and Early Indian Treaties in Historical Perspective

The constitutional status of the Royal Proclamation of 1763 is one of the major issues in the Temagami land dispute. Indeed the Royal Proclamation, which Lord Denning recently titled the Indian Bill of Rights or the Indian Magna Carta,[8] figures centrally in virtually all the controversies in Canada that hinge on the legal interpretation of Indian treaties and of aboriginal title. King George III, on the advice of his Privy Council, issued the proclamation in order to establish several regimes of colonial government in those portions of North America from which France withdrew its claim after having lost the Seven Years' War. A framework of colonial administration was put in place for Quebec, Grenada, East Florida, and West Florida. As well, a fifth legal regime, the Indian territory, was established south of the Hudson's Bay Company lands and west of the watershed running along the crest of the Appalachian mountains. The Indian territory described by the Royal Proclamation included all of present-day Ontario within the Great Lakes–St Lawrence watershed, including much of Temagami.[9]

The Royal Proclamation was imposed by British imperial authorities as a means to enforce a degree of law and order on the western frontiers of the Crown's Thirteen Colonies. The Seven Years' War, concluded by Pontiac's Indian uprising in the Detroit–Michilimackinac area, had confirmed the importance of appeasing Native fighting forces. The affirmation in the Royal Proclamation that the North American interior was reserved to Indian nations for their exclusive use was therefore a reflection of a calculated geopolitical assessment of British imperial self-interest.[10]

While reservation of the continental interior served Indian self-interest and British imperial self-interest, the move infuriated land speculators in the Thirteen Colonies who had their eyes on the speedy commercial exploitation of the rich Ohio valley. When administration of the Indian territory was given to Quebec in 1774, American land speculators, represented by the likes of Benjamin Franklin and George Washington, saw red. It remains to be widely appreciated just how influential in moving forward the agenda of the American rebels was the desire for unobstructed access to Indian lands on the western frontiers of the Thirteen Colonies.[11]

During the American Revolution and in the following years, the British Indian Department became a bastion of Tory resistance against the westward thrust of republicanism.[12] British army officers and leading Indian strategists in the Ohio Valley–Great Lakes area co-operated strategically in opposing the land-grabbing expansionism of the newly liberated colonials.[13] It was in this atmosphere of collaboration between military allies that Crown treaties were negotiated with Indian groups to open new areas for the settlement of United Empire Loyalists and others in the Royal Proclamation lands north of the lower Great Lakes.

Indian groups entered freely into these treaty negotiations, which were conducted in a manner consistent with the terms of the Royal Proclamation. That document had specified: "If at any time any of the said Indians should be inclined to dispose of the said Lands, the same shall be Purchased for Us in our Name, at some public meeting or Assembly of the said Indians to be held for that purpose." A system began to coalesce around the terms of the Royal Proclamation which made the British sovereign the exclusive agent of land transfers between Indians and non-Indian settlers in the continental interior of British North America.[14]

The successful development of the Indian treaty system during the decades following the American revolution was a fundamental factor in the maintenance of Crown dominion over territories north of the Great Lakes. The crucial British takeover of the American post of Detroit at the outset of the War of 1812, which resulted largely because of the early mobilization of Tecumseh's Indian fighting forces, is generally taken as the high point of strategic co-operation during an era when Indian treaties were but one aspect of a well-established ebb and flow of relations between military allies.[15]

This legacy of military co-operation, a legacy most enduringly entrenched in the early genesis of Canadian Indian treaties, remained a vividly recalled aspect of Ontario's heritage until the early twentieth century, especially among some Tories whose cultivated sense of British imperialism retained a vital anti-republican aspect. In 1887, in the famous *St Catherine's Milling* case, Canadian Supreme Court Justice Strong cited this chapter of the country's past in a dissenting judicial opinion. In seeking to clarify the meaning of "Lands reserved for the Indians," the phrase in the British North America Act most in contention in this seminal conflict in federal–provincial relations, Mr Justice Strong looked not to technicalities but rather to the broad sweep of history to find the essential underlying spirit of the new Dominion's primary constitutional document. After noting "the great impolity" of the Old Thirteen Colonies' "frequent frontier wars" with the Indians, he explained:

> From the memorable year 1763, when Detroit was besieged and all the Indian tribes were in revolt, down to the date of Confederation, Indian wars and massacres entirely ceased in the British possessions in North America, although powerful Indian nations still continued for some time after the former date to inhabit those territories. That this peaceful conduct of the Indians is in a great degree to be attributed to the recognition of their rights to lands unsurrendered by them, and to the guarantee of their protection in the possession and enjoyment of such lands given by the crown in the Proclamation of October, 1763 . . . is a well known fact of Canadian history which cannot be controverted. The Indian nations from that time became and have since continued to be the firm and faithful allies of the crown and rendered it important military services in two wars—the War of the Revolution and that of 1812.[16]

• The Convergence of Arguments in the Ontario Supreme Court

There was a circus-like atmosphere in the proceedings that made the Ontario Supreme Court the principal forum of conflict between the Temagami Indians and the province's chief legal officers. The marathon trial covered 119 days at intervals over a two-year period beginning in 1982. The testimony fills 68 volumes. Evidence presented by both sides included 3000 exhibits which fill an entire room at Osgoode Hall in downtown Toronto. Both the Crown and the Teme-Augama Anishnabai made ample use of expert witnesses. One of these, James Morrison, who had worked with Chief Potts since 1974 in developing the historical research to support the Indian case, was on the witness stand for a full 28 days. The sheer magnitude of the proceedings soon elevated the case to almost legendary proportions in Ontario legal circles.

The preparation of the Indian case by Chief Potts, Bruce Clark, and their colleagues can be viewed as a reflection of a more broadly based scholarly movement. The energy channelled into this movement amounts to a virtual rethinking of the nature of the country's past with a view to correcting the propensity of a previous generation of Canadian historians to relegate Native people and the role of Native–newcomer relations to the periphery of the story of national development.[17] The direction of this enterprise in historical reconstruction intersects with a similar trend among some legal scholars, especially in the field of constitutional history. The writing of constitutional history, in turn, has drawn deeply on the resources and intellectual energy generated by the political activity accompanying both the prelude to and aftermath of patriation of Canada's constitution in 1982. The eloquence and effectiveness of aboriginal voices in this political activity—activity which overflowed into the prevailing atmosphere of the courtroom proceedings—helped to reinforce recognition on several academic fronts of the fundamental importance of Crown–Indian relations in the early stages of Canadian constitutional development.

Gary Potts had become Chief of the Bear Island band in 1972, while still in his early twenties.[18] By that time Chief Potts was well prepared for a remarkable career that would see him combine the tasks of scholar, politician, and social activist in his quest to defend his people. As for Bruce Clark, Pott's early partner in his search for justice,[19] he quickly became so completely immersed in the details of the case that he decided to devote his entire professional life to it. He even moved to Bear Island. Following the successful imposition of the legal caution in 1973, Chief Potts and Bruce Clark increasingly spent their time in libraries and archives, and travelling widely, determined to track down the scholars and sources that would provide the pieces they needed for their giant historical jigsaw puzzle. Their research was not confined to Canada. Clark's files on jurisprudence involving aboriginal people burst with documentation on cases from the United States and throughout the Commonwealth.

As the Temagami case evolved, it attracted the attention of a widening circle of researchers with significant contributions to make. One of the first to become involved was Don Smith, who met Gary Potts in the spring of 1973 at a Native studies conference at Trent University. At the time, Smith was an eager PhD candidate in Canadian history at the University of Toronto. He knew something of the historical background of the land dispute in Temagami as a result of his digging into the life of Grey Owl. Grey Owl, or Archie Belaney, was the famous author, conservationist, and Indian impostor who, during the early twentieth century, had gained much of his knowledge about aboriginal life from living among the Native people of the Temagami district.[20] With Smith's usual generosity, he shared what he knew of the documentation of the Temagami dispute with Chief Potts. The latter was beginning to weave together the basic fabric of the evidence he was gaining from his reading and from the oral testimony he had heard from the elders of his community over his lifetime.

Smith was later asked by Bruce Clark to work on the genealogy of the band. At this stage one of Smith's academic supervisors, the late Dr Ed

Rogers of the Royal Ontario Museum, also developed an interest in the case. Rogers would eventually serve as an expert witness for the Teme-Augama Anishnabai during the marathon trial. Other researchers to enter the fray included Craig Macdonald, Thor Conway, and James Morrison. Morrison in particular was to emerge as one of the most effective researchers and tacticians in this pioneering effort to map the emergence of the basic principles of aboriginal rights in the development of Ontario's constitutional landscape.

Morrison's attraction to aboriginal issues drew strength from his friendship with Smith, a contemporary he had first met in a Latin American history course at the University of Toronto. The former's work on the Temagami land claim began when Morrison was employed as a researcher for the Cree and Ojibwa people under the Grand Council of Treaty No. 9. In 1978 he began working full-time for Chief Potts.

Another important figure in developing the primary documentation in support of the Indian case was Professor Bruce Hodgins of Trent University, the site of much informed discourse in the years ahead on the uses and abuses of Temagami lands. On Bear Island several younger band members, including Mary Laronde, were caught up in the mass of documents and ideas that the chief was assembling. As the court date approached, they too contributed to the articulation of their community's collective position, a position channelled to the courts through Chief Potts's testimony.

Much of the development of the Indian position involved meeting the precedent-setting criteria of a legitimate land claim as laid out in 1980 by Mr Justice Mahoney of the Federal Court in the Baker Lake case.[21] In order to justify its assertions, the band had to show that it was a distinct and organized society in exclusive occupation of the Temagami area at the time when Crown dominion was asserted. Similarly, it had to show that it was not connected either by clan or custom to any of the leaders who did sign the treaty in 1850. Finally, the band had to counter the attorney-general's contention that its aboriginal rights had "been extinguished by various statutes and physical affirmative acts of Ontario."[22]

These legal demands required the researchers to delve deeply into clan lineages, archaeology, oral tradition, original eye-witness literature describing Indian life, and the extensive primary documentation associated with the history of Crown–Indian relations throughout the continent. The need to produce empirical evidence to prove the distinct identity of the Teme-Augama Anishnabai made particularly great demands on the innovativeness of Chief Potts and his colleagues. As part of the wide range of evidence they brought forward, they went to the length of assembling nine canoes of various styles in the courtroom to demonstrate the unique design of the vessel traditionally used by Native people in Temagami.

The investment of time and energy in the development of the Indian case was easily matched by the work of the province's legal staff. Blenus

Wright, the assistant deputy attorney-general, directed the preparation of Ontario's case.

There was sympathy among some in Ontario's legal establishment for the task faced by Steele. According to this view, Chief Potts and Bruce Clark failed to confine their arguments to a manageable framework; specifically, they failed to narrow the issues sufficiently to meet the limitations of what can realistically be addressed through the medium of civil litigation. On the other hand, it has been charged that Steele placed an unrealistically burdensome onus of proof on the Teme-Augama Anishnabai. Moreover, it is asserted that he failed to exercise sufficient control over the wide-ranging inquiry and questioning conducted by both Bruce Clark and Blenus Wright.

Steele's finding is a fascinating and important document of broad sociological significance. In rendering explicit so many attitudes that are usually left unarticulated, the judgment suggests much about the dynamics of tension in Canada between Native and non-Native groups in general, and between Native people and the apparatus of the law in particular. Sally Weaver, one of Canada's pre-eminent anthropologists, has termed the finding "antediluvian."[23] Steele's words reveal the persistent force of old evolutionist views that place aboriginal societies near the low end of a hierarchy of peoples. They also reveal a view of the law without the ability to recognize human rights as inherent, flowing from the common attributes of shared humanity, and an attitude that sees Indianness as a static form of human existence fixed firmly in the past—a form of human existence without the inner capacity for adaptation to changing conditions. In short, Steele's judgment gives clear voice to widely held if largely unconfronted assumptions in society that aboriginal groups are essentially anachronistic holdovers from an earlier era of Canadian history who ultimately should and will disappear in the course of "progress."

The attitudes brought by Steele to the adjudication of the case are revealed with particular clarity in the remark he included in his finding concerning the reliability of the expert witnesses who appeared on behalf of the Teme-Augama Anishnabai. The judge indicated that Craig Macdonald, Thor Conway, and James Morrison "were typical of persons who have worked closely with Indians for so many years that they have lost their objectivity when giving opinion evidence."[24] If non-Indians who have lived with Indians thereby lose their "objectivity," one wonders how Steele views the capacity of Indians themselves for "objectivity." Objectivity, he apparently would have us believe, lies more or less exclusively in the realm of non-Indians who have not lived among Indians.

Steele's controversial finding, given in December 1984, followed by and large the main outlines of the case presented by Blenus Wright. His finding came down against the contentions of the Indians on practically every detail. Much space was devoted to his judicial declaration that the Teme-Augama Anishnabai are a band that has coalesced only in relatively recent times, that the community is but a close offshoot of Ojibwa bands who were represented at the treaty negotiations, and that band members had sanctioned the treaty in any case by accepting the four-dollar annuity payments. Yet Steele also looked far beyond the local details of the case to the broader questions of how aboriginal groups are constitutionally and legally situated in relationship to the principal institutions of the Canadian state. His broad generalizations on these matters therefore have wide significance for the future of all Native people throughout the country. Indeed his finding speaks to some of the most fundamental issues concerning the essential values at the root of our shared citizenship.

Steele held that the aboriginal title asserted in the Royal Proclamation of 1763 is "personal and usufructuary and exists solely at the pleasure of the Crown."[25] He selected this often-quoted phrase from the judgment of Lord Watson in the *St Catherine's Milling* case,[26] a dispute between the governments of Ontario and Canada over the constitutional meaning of the phrase "Lands reserved for the Indians" in section 91(24) of the British North America Act of 1867. With some qualifications, Ontario won this pivotal constitutional case in 1888. By arguing for a narrow interpretation of the phrase in question, the provincial government strengthened its claim to control of Crown lands within provincial boundaries.

The province gained victory in 1888 partly by denying the Dominion assertion that Indian rights have been consistently and expansively recognized by the Crown throughout the history of British colonization in North America. Among the theories marshalled by Ontario officials in making the provincial case against aboriginal rights was the idea that Native people before the arrival of Europeans were too primitive and too unorganized to exercise any kind of binding land tenure over the territories they occupied. And even if they had been able to assert some kind of "primitive" ownership of the soil, this ownership was immediately extinguished when their pagan domains were "discovered" by representatives of the higher laws vested in Christian monarchs.[27]

The Ontario government has never renounced the principles its officials expounded when they originally denied the existence of aboriginal title in the *St Catherine's Milling* case. In fact the province's legal officers implicitly renewed their recourse to such retrogressive theories of Indianness when they relied so heavily on the *St Catherine's Milling* judgment in building their case against the Teme-Augama Anishnabai. Rather than questioning the recycling of such obnoxious theories of racial inferiority in contemporary jurisprudence, Steele reinforced the old pattern in his finding.

In Steele's view, the Royal Proclamation created an Indian right where no right had existed before. In other words, Steele saw the proclamation itself as the source of the right rather than as a recognition of a prior right that existed for thousands of years before the arrival of the British in North America. From the proposition that the aboriginal right is created rather than merely confirmed by the Crown, Steele deduced the "limited dependent nature" of this right[28]—a right than can be "unilaterally extinguished"[29] at the Crown's "pleasure."

Steele only vaguely addressed the issue of how the British sovereign gained this tremendous life-or-death authority over the collective existence of aboriginal groups. He alluded, however, to the notion of "conquest."[30] The quelling by British soldiers of the brief protest by those Indians following Chief Pontiac in 1763 was mentioned as an event in the constitutional process that rendered aboriginal rights subject to legal annihilation by authority of the Crown.[31] Steele's perception of this facet of the country's history contrasts sharply with the view expressed by Justice Strong a century earlier. Whereas Steele saw Indians in Ontario as conquered peoples, Strong characterized them as allies of the Crown who had actively resisted the republican conquest of what remained of British North America after 1776.

Steele's decision included a long section where he attempted to explain "the nature" of aboriginal rights.[32] His efforts along these lines bore with particular weight on the new dynamics of jurisprudence that developed with the patriation of the Canadian constitution. Section 35 of the Constitution Act, 1982, recognizes and affirms "existing Aboriginal and treaty rights," although the phrase is not explicitly defined. Steele's finding started the process of fleshing out the technical meaning of a term which of itself is relatively new to legal language even if it speaks to old concepts that are well elaborated in Canadian constitutional tradition.[33]

Steele found that "the essence of Aboriginal rights is the right of Indians to continue to live on their lands as their forefathers lived."[34] Elsewhere he found that "Aboriginal rights are limited by the wording of the Royal Proclamation; aboriginal rights consist of "the uses to which Indians put the lands in 1763."[35] These uses were outlined in some detail: fish, game, berries, and, possibly, maple syrup for food; furs for clothing and trade; birchbark, vegetable fibre, and tree gum for canoes; wood for fire and poles for tents; stone for pipes, arrowheads, lances, scrapers, knives, and axes.[36]

Steele could hardly have given more precise legal expression to the theory that sees true Indianness as a way of life fixed forever in the past. What else is to be derived from a finding which deems that aboriginal rights cannot involve the use of any technology acquired by Indians after 1763? Clearly the suggestion is that aboriginal life cannot continue apart from the stereotypical realm of teepees, canoes, snowshoes, and feathered wardrobe; when Indian people act differently from their ancestors—when they use modern technology, for instance—they lose the right to be respected for their Indianness.

Such a view of aboriginal societies is iniquitous. It holds aboriginal groups to rules and expectations unlike those applied to other ethnic and national collectivities. It denies members of aboriginal groups regard as adaptive partners in the wider human family. It would hold aboriginal communities exclusively to the status of folkloric remnants of Canadian heritage without affording them a place of dignity and security in the modern-day world.

By fixing aboriginal rights exclusively to a static place in Canada's past, then, Steele's finding seems aimed at shutting aboriginal societies out of a constructive role in the country's future. In this way the sweep of his judgment extends far indeed. He even ventures beyond the secular sphere, declaring "there was no strong legal or no spiritual attachment to the lands" on the part of the ancestors of the Teme-Augama Anishnabai."[37]

The whole thrust of Steele's judgment is that aboriginal rights constitute tenuous and vulnerable principles of law. As rights that are derived from the authority of the Crown, they can be unilaterally eliminated, it is argued, by agents of the Crown. In this scheme of interpretation the existence of Indian treaties or the lack of Indian treaties in any given area counts for very little. The judge wrote: "A treaty is not a conveyance of title because title is already in the Crown. A treaty is simple acknowledgement that may be formal or informal in nature."[38]

In these few words Steele cast the entire tradition of treaty making with the Indians in Canada outside the realm of law. Instead he held that the practice should be understood as belonging more to the domain of diplomacy, ritual, and politics. "Where there was no concern about an Indian insurrection, the Crown did not enter into treaties," he wrote. "Whenever the Crown felt it could defend its white citizens, it did not provide for treaties with the Indians. Where it had doubt, it did so provide."[39]

Does the outlook revealed in these passages indicate that Steele's attitude towards the law has much in common with those who see in the apparatus of the state little more than a protector of the most powerful members of society? Does Steele hold the legal system in contempt when he claims that government officials who made treaties were bereft of any consideration of justice, law and order, or constitutional tradition? Does he see their credo as rooted primarily in the balance of terror—in the might-is-right school of human affairs? His characterization of treaties not as legal instruments but rather as mere theatre designed to appease Indians would seem to mock Native people for having taken Crown representations in the negotiations at face value. Moreover, there is the suggestion that today, as in the past, only the threat of "insurrection" is sufficiently compelling to engage government interest in aboriginal claims.

On the one hand, Steele placed treaties outside the realm of the law, but on the other he named treaties as one of the means for the legal extinguishment of aboriginal rights. Those rights, he concluded, "exist at the pleasure of the Crown and they can be extinguished by treaty, legislation or administrative acts."[40] The "opening of land to settlement" is among the legislative or administrative acts that have the effect, according to Steele, of eliminating the aboriginal interest in territory.[41] Such opening, he argued, involves the making of surveys, the building of railways, roads, and hydro-electric works, the issuing of land patents, and the extension of rights to non-Indians to exploit timber, mineral, and wildlife resources. Since all of these developments have taken place in Temagami, Steele held that the Crown—in this case the Crown in Right of the government of Ontario—has effectively extinguished the aboriginal rights of the Teme-Augama Anishnabai regardless of their status with respect to the treaty negotiations of 1850.[42] And he wrote the decision in such a way as to affect throughout Canada the entire legal infrastructure of Crown–Indian relations through the medium of treaties.

Steele's wide-ranging interpretation of the law of Indian treaties and aboriginal rights essentially amounts to an account of the history of Crown dealings with Native people in Ontario. All down the line his view of these dealings portrays Crown authority as essentially hostile to recognition of the fundamental human rights of aboriginal people. The plaintiff, the attorney-general of Ontario, succeeded in persuading the judge that constitutional tradition in this country justifies unilateral dispossession of Native people.

The principles of racial inequality that appear to inform the Steele decision may be attributable to the racism that predominated in the minds of the lawmakers during the eighteenth and nineteenth centuries. Steele himself asserted, for instance, that at the time of the Royal Proclamation "Europeans did not consider Indians to be equal to themselves."[43] Elsewhere he wrote of the attitude of colonial officials in the mid-nineteenth century "that the Indian occupation could not be considered as a true and legal habitation, and that Europeans were lawfully entitled to take possession of the land and to settle it with colonies." He added: "Whether or not this was the proper view, it was the view in 1845 of persons in what is now Ontario."[44]

Steele is on firm ground in suggesting that notions of racial inequality were ubiquitous and deep-rooted among colonial officials with responsibility for dealing with Indians. But there is also in the history of Crown relations with Indians an imperial appreciation of them as useful allies with a role in helping to shield British North America from acquisition by the United States. While this strategic consideration was ultimately self-serving, it nevertheless resulted in the development of a regime of Indian affairs with an undercurrent of acknowledgment of aboriginal rights. The essential legacy of this acknowledgment is to be found in Indian treaties, agreements which could be regarded as the cutting edge of a process that might yet be cultivated to embrace the developing understanding of the importance of respect for human rights in the institutional structuring of political relations between peoples.

Steele was apparently persuaded by lawyers acting for the government of Ontario to disregard our country's earlier recognition of aboriginal rights. Instead he appears to have been persuaded to see Ontario law as flowing out of the racism that is also undeniably an aspect of the Crown's historic dealings with Indians. This apparent legitimization of old racist principles through contemporary jurisprudence raises profound issues for society—issues suggested forcefully by James Youngblood Henderson in his commentary, "The Doctrine of Aboriginal Rights in Western Legal Tradition." Although Henderson wrote his article before Steele came forward with his decision on the Temagami land dispute, the following passage could have been written with that judgment in mind:

> Instead of facing the role of law in society, weak judges rely on legal precedents and the history of imperial racism. The courts become the caretakers of the racism of the late nineteenth and twentieth centuries. Such cowardice incurs an enormous cost. When governments act in a disorderly and lawless way, their courts save face by classifying oppression as justice or confiscation as a political question. Their decisions do not pretend to have any generality or stability, nor can they sensibly speak of fixed entitlements and duties. As a result, aboriginal people are deprived of the rule of law.

The historical fascination of Anglo-American society with terror—combined with the systematic use of violence unlimited by law as a device of social control—has laid the foundation for the destruction of all political and property rights in modern society. In its approach to the rights of native people the law becomes tyranny at worst and ineffective apologist at best. The Canadian government may call it law but it is racism. It is not founded on principles that recognize the supremacy of God and the rule of law.[45]

• More Controversy and Litigation

The partnership between Bruce Clark and Chief Potts broke up shortly following the handing down of the Ontario Supreme Court's judgment. Clark's handling of the case remains controversial. Not only did he lose the trust of his Indian clients but some charge that his argumentative zealousness was a major factor in stimulating Steele to write perhaps the most sweepingly hostile judicial opinion ever directed against Native people in Canada. In a strictly technical sense, the loss was monumental. On the other hand, perhaps over the long run the legal strategy of Chief Potts and Bruce Clark has forced out of the courts a finding so stunningly and explicitly anti-Indian that this increasingly apparent weakness in our judicial system can at last be squarely addressed. Indeed the problem goes far beyond the judiciary. By the end of the 1980s the many inquiries into the relationship between Native people and the apparatus of the law in Canada have made it even yet more clear that racist attitudes on the part of some officials have too often perverted the course of justice in this country.

Renounced by Native and non-Native colleagues alike, Bruce Clark has kept up the struggle, refining his major arguments in graduate school.[46] He continues to maintain that the Royal Proclamation of 1763 constitutes explicit imperial legislation at the constitutional foundation of Canada that has never been erased. If, as Steele finds, officials in the government of Ontario were capable of overriding the proclamation by unilaterally extinguishing the Indian right to remain "unmolested" in unceded Indian territory, it would not have been necessary to patriate the Canadian constitution in 1982. Before 1982 governments in Canada, whose powers were ultimately derived from the higher jurisdiction of the British imperial authority, did not have the legal capacity to supersede the rights of Indians as affirmed by King George in his famous proclamation.

The Teme-Augama Anishnabai appealed the Ontario Supreme Court's decision. As he approaches his third decade as the principal protagonist in this case, Chief Potts continues to vow that he will take his people's grievances as far as he must to receive justice, even if that involves going beyond Canada to international courts.

The decision of the Ontario Court of Appeal was rendered in the spring of 1989. In upholding the Supreme Court of Ontario judgment, the Court of Appeal was as hostile to the Native position as Steele had been. Indeed perhaps the Appeal Court's decision was even worse from a Native point of view. The Appeal Court judges devoted considerable space to their opinion that the Teme-Augama Anishnabai were represented at the treaty negotiations of 1850. The recorded acceptance by a Teme-Augama Anishnabai leader, Peter Nebenegwune, of $25 from the treaty commissioners was cited as evidence of their adhesion. And the Appeal Court judges made much of the role of a treaty participant by the name of Tawgaiwene who was found to have connections with the Native people in the Temagami area.[47]

In a few words the appeal judges found that "the relevant procedural aspects of the Royal Proclamation were repealed by the Quebec Act (1774)."[48] The anti-Indian argument concerning the Quebec Act, imperial legislation which attached the Indian territory to Quebec for administrative purposes, was first articulated by lawyers for Ontario in the *St Catherine's Milling* case. They did not convince the Judicial Committee of the Privy Council. Writing for them in 1888 Lord Watson decided that "there has been no change since the year 1763 in the character of the interest which its Indian inhabitants had in the lands."[49] But the Appeal Court judges simply ignored this decision, which has been used so often against the claims of Indians. All that the judges indicated was that the "relevant procedural aspects" of the Royal Proclamation that have been "repealed" involve the necessity of "some public Meeting or Assembly" for the purchase of Indian rights to land.

If there is one underlying theme that seems to animate the decisions of Mr Justice Steele and the Ontario Court of Appeal, it is the elaboration of a doctrine for the extinguishment of aboriginal rights. The appeal judges added a new dimension to the lower court's doctrine of extinguishment in the concluding portions of their decision. They cited with approval a lengthy passage from the finding in the case of *Idaho versus Coffee*. In 1976 the Idaho Supreme Court held that it did not matter whether or not a band of Kootenai people were represented in the Indian treaty negotiations covering their ancestral lands. The court declared: "Whether the Indians signing the treaty had the power to give the land away is not relevant. The United States did have the power to take the land, and when it said it was receiving the land, the effect was that the land was taken."[50]

The resort to this finding as a precedent for the interpretation of Canadian Indian treaties smacks at the sensibilities of one schooled in the history of Crown–Indian relations. The Royal Proclamation of 1763 marked a major dividing of the ways between those Euro-Americans whose leaders soon rejected the British imperial connection and those who did not.[51] The military alliances between the Crown and Indians, as sometimes expressed in Indian treaties, became a significant strategic and geopolitical feature of government in that portion of the continent that remained under British rule. On the other hand, wars of conquest directed at different Indian groups, interspersed with the making and breaking of dozens of Indian treaties, were a major characteristic of the United States' westward-moving frontier during the decades following the American revolution.[52]

It seems inappropriate, to say the least, for the Ontario Appeal Court to fall back on the well-known American tradition of lawlessness surrounding Indian treaties as justification for its judicial assault on Indian treaties and aboriginal rights in Canada. But that is precisely what happened in the province at the very heart of the outward-reaching web of treaties which once were so instrumental in supporting the Crown's land claim to large portions of the continent *vis-à-vis* the pretensions of Manifest Destiny in the United States. That such a finding was possible in the Ontario courts, then, speaks to issues that go beyond the injustice of one group towards another. The decision hints of a subversive undermining of well-established constitutional principles fundamental to the setting off of the northern portion of North America as a distinct society from the United States.

• Conclusions

It was officials acting for the federal government who brought the Idaho case to the Appeal Court's attention. This intervention by federal law officers raises significant constitutional questions. Since the passing in 1867 of the British North America Act, which stipulated that "Indians and lands reserved for the Indians" fall within the legislative field of the Dominion parliament, it has come to be understood that the federal authority bears the largest part of the responsibility to uphold Crown obligations to protect Indian interests against encroachment by other jurisdictions.[53] In his arguments for Ontario in the *St Catherine's Milling* case, Edward Blake described this Dominion responsibility as one of "protector and vindicator of the Indian rights."[54] In 1984 the Supreme Court of Canada gave renewed vigour to the principle in its finding on the Guerin case involving the land rights of the Musqueam Indians of British Columbia. This major decision indicated that the federal government has a legally enforceable fiduciary duty to safeguard those aboriginal interests in land and resources which are entrusted to its care.[55] In this light, the federal government's intervention against the interests of the Teme-Augama Anishnabai runs counter to its constitutional role as guardian of Indian rights. Indeed a strong case could be made that, by intervening in this way, the federal government has abandoned its fiduciary obligations to Native people.

Moreover, the major thrust of Mr Justice Steele's whole finding, which is founded on the notion that the source of aboriginal rights lies in the Crown, appears to have been completely undermined by the opening passage of the Supreme Court's decision in the Guerin case. There the Supreme Court declared: "The Indians' interest in their land is a pre-existing legal right not created by the Royal Proclamation of 1763, by s. 18 (1) of the Indian Act, or by any other executive order or legislative provision. The nature of the Indians' interest is best characterized by its inalienability, coupled with the fact that the Crown is under an obligation to deal with the land on the Indians' behalf when the interest is surrendered."[56] In an addendum to his decision, Mr Justice Steele argued that the author of the Guerin decision, Supreme Court Justice Brian Dickson, was wrong if the implication of his finding was that the Crown could not unilaterally extinguish Indian title. This rather strange dismissal of the higher court's finding was based further on Steele's suggestion that the Guerin case has application only to British Columbia.[57] The Ontario Appeal Court failed to address directly this especially dubious feature of Steele's decision.

The responsibility for the federal intervention in the Temagami land dispute, of course, lies ultimately with federal politicians. A similar reality holds true for the government of Ontario. It is the provincial attorney-general who bears major responsibility for the arguments developed against the Teme-Augama Anishnabai. A significant intent of this paper has been to demonstrate how fully these provincial arguments run against any enlightened conception of a just regime that respects human rights and abhors racism. Is it overblown rhetoric to suggest that there is a drift towards tyranny in the political assertion of power to extinguish unilaterally the rights of people? Is it unduly alarmist to fear the genocidal or ethnocidal implications of this tendency?

The distance between the provincial government's political policies and the contents of its legal arguments against the Teme-Augama Anishnabai points to the dangers which accompany the employment of adversarial litigation in its present format as a means to address issues involving such basic human rights. New and innovative forums of arbitration are required to adjudicate how the rights and responsibilities of aboriginal groups are to be balanced against the interests of others, especially in disputes involving jurisdiction over land. The day should have passed long ago when it was even thinkable for the chief legal officer of a province or of Canada to oppose aboriginal assertions by making recourse to such discredited old theories of racial hierarchy. It does a grave injustice to the wider citizenry to present such arguments on its behalf. It is a mode of dealing with disputes which ultimately chips away at the very credibility of government as an effective instrument in the protection of the fundamental rights and freedoms of groups and individuals.

What makes Mr Justice Steele's finding such a remarkable document of social history is the extent to which he was won over to the extreme kinds of adversarial positions advanced by Ontario's law officers. Unfortunately, it is difficult not to see in the court's judgment parallels with other instances of marked judicial bias against Native people that came to light in the late 1980s. Both the Manitoba Aboriginal Justice Inquiry and the royal commission which investigated the wrongful conviction for murder of Micmac Donald Marshall Jr point to a bias in the enforcement of Canada's criminal code among Native people.[58] Steele's rigid doctrine of extinguishment seems to reflect a similar application of civil law to the collective human rights of Native people.

To put the matter plainly, it is difficult to avoid the conclusion that the treatment afforded Indians by the Ontario courts was different in kind from that which could be anticipated by almost any other group. Imagine, for instance, the political consequences that would flow from a judicial finding that Roman Catholic rights, Jewish rights, or French-language rights can be unilaterally extinguished. What major religious, ethnic, or linguistic collectivity other than aboriginal people would be expected to rest calm in the face of such a decision? What other group would be expected to remain patient with a judicial system that threatened its identity and collective survival with such a potent legal weapon?

The passage of this important aboriginal-rights case through the Ontario courts was accompanied, especially during the late 1980s, by an increasingly tough struggle between environmentalists and those with an interest in logging what remains of the old-growth forest in Temagami. The primary focus of the confrontations was along the construction site which marked out the extension of the Red Squirrel road into one of the most majestic of the province's remaining wilderness areas. At intervals the Teme-Augama Anishnabai and the Temagami Wilderness Society raised a series of blockades to prevent or slow work on the Red Squirrel road. Over three hundred people were arrested over a period of several months in the fall and early winter of 1989, a show of civil disobedience which by Ontario standards is quite significant. Certainly some of those charged, Indians and non-Indians, based at least part of their decision to break the law on their assessment of the quality of justice handed down by Mr Justice Steele and the Ontario Court of Appeal.

The road nevertheless was completed on schedule, a corresponding demonstration of political will on the part of the Ontario government. Clearly the intent was to stress forcefully that the entrenched way of doing things was not to be put off track by the assertiveness of Indians or by the advocates of wilderness preservation. When pushed to reveal its true priorities, the Liberal government of Premier David Peterson showed itself as unrelenting in the use of police, dynamite, and bulldozers as it was with the use of ideological explosives in the court to remove any barrier which obstructed the realization of a particular vision of economic advancement.

This convergence of aboriginal issues with environmental concerns is part of a worldwide phenomenon. Oftentimes patterns of history, geography, and economics have combined to cast indigenous societies—the peoples with the deepest cultural roots in the ecology of particular places—in roles where they provide the inspirational guidance that is helping to mobilize environmentalism as such an influential political force. Oftentimes these aboriginal groups, whether in the Himalayas of India or in the rainforests of Brazil or in the old-growth stands of Temagami, become in effect the last remaining human barriers standing before the bulldozers in the market-driven assault on what remains of the world's rapidly diminishing treasure of relatively undisturbed forest life.

In 1987 the Brundtland report, the highly esteemed statement by the World Commission on Environment and Development, stressed the importance of respecting the integrity of indigenous societies as an essential component in the formulation of national strategies aimed at sustainable economic development. The commissioners noted:

> These [aboriginal] communities are the repositories of vast accumulations of traditional knowledge and experience that links humanity with its ancient origins. Their disappearance is a loss for the larger society, which could learn a great deal from their traditional skills in sustainably managing very complex ecological systems. It is a terrible irony that as formal development reaches more deeply into rain forests, deserts, and other isolated environments, it tends to destroy the only cultures that have proved able to thrive in these environments.
>
> The starting point for a just and humane policy for such groups is the recognition and protection of their traditional rights to land and other resources that sustain their way of life—rights they may define in terms that do not fit into standard legal systems. These groups' own institutions to regulate rights and obligations are crucial for maintaining the harmony with nature and the environmental awareness characteristic of the traditional way of life. Hence the recognition of traditional rights must go hand in hand with measures to protect the local institutions that enforce responsibility

in resource use. And this recognition must also give local communities a decisive voice in the decisions about resource use in the area. . . .

In terms of sheer numbers, these isolated, vulnerable groups are small. But their marginalization is a symptom of a style of development that tends to neglect both human and environmental considerations. Hence a more careful and sensitive consideration of their interest is a touchstone of sustainable development policy.[59]

Perhaps the most telling manifestation of environmental degradation is the escalating rate at which species are becoming extinct on this planet. Plants and animals are diminishing in variety as pollution and the rapaciousness of the rush to transform nature into capital undermine the genetic building blocks of life itself. The organized effort to protect what remains of the old-growth forest in Temagami is a small but significant part of the world-wide movement to curtail further impoverishment of the earth's genetic resources. Old-growth forests are complex ecosystems that are major storehouses of genetic diversity. When these forests are cut down, their genetic resources are massively lessened, even if replanting takes place. Tree plantations modelled along agricultural lines are more the domain of monocultures. The genetic pluralism in the mass of life forms associated with the old-growth forest is replaced by the genetic uniformity of the tree farm.

Just as human beings are responsible for a diminishment in the diversity of many life forms, so we are experiencing—with the market-driven expansion of mass society—a corresponding loss of cultural and linguistic pluralism among ourselves. Recognition of the connection between the impoverishment of genetic diversity and of the limiting of cultural pluralism is essential to understanding the linkage between environmentalism and the movement to protect and celebrate aboriginality. Alternatively, this connection presents a broader context in which to assess the principle asserted by Mr Justice Steele and others that because nation states have the power they have the right to extinguish the collective existence of aboriginal communities. It makes clear that continuing down this road has suicidal implications for everyone.

Enlightened formulation and interpretation of national constitutions represent an important means of striving to achieve a degree of ecological harmony in relationships between indigenous groups and others in the so-called New World. Such affirmations of equality between peoples and respect for those societies with the deepest roots in the land could both mirror and inspire the broader environmental initiative to halt the assault on life in its full, wonderful complexity of myriad forms.[60] Accordingly, the convergence of forces with a competitive will to exercise power over the use of Temagami lands presents an historic opportunity to develop the discourse we need on a range of crucial issues.

As this is being written, the Teme-Augama Anishnabai are preparing to bring their case before the Supreme Court of Canada. Let there be no delusions about the significance of the principles in question in this effort to arbitrate where justice lies.

• Epilogue

Public concern in Ontario for the fate of Temagami was especially evident during the 1990 Earth Day festivities throughout the province. The following day, 23 April, the government of Ontario announced the creation of a joint-stewardship council to exercise jurisdiction over a 440-square-kilometre section of Temagami, or about one-quarter of the region covered by old-growth forest. Half of the council's membership is to be appointed by the Teme-Augama Anishnabai and half by the government of Ontario.[61]

The creation of this council represents a significant break with tradition for the Ontario government. Rather than gearing the province's legal strategies towards the extinguishment of aboriginal rights, the Peterson government attempted a political innovation to create a new channel for the exercise of aboriginal rights. Rather than treating aboriginal people as awkward remnants of a past era of human development, the stewardship council implicitly recognizes in aboriginal society a rich source of insight and expertise that should be afforded due authority in the making of land-use decisions. This important innovation will almost certainly become a significant model in working towards more enlightened regimes of ordering the ecological relationships between human beings and the other living entities who draw sustenance from our Mother Earth.

While the creation of the stewardship council holds much promise, the initiative remains relatively limited in scope. The decision, for instance, still leaves the largest part of Temagami's old-growth forest firmly under the authority of the Ministry of Natural Resources. And the existence of the stewardship council does nothing in itself to resolve the dispute over land title, which remains at the heart of the legal clash between the Teme-Augama Anishnabai and the government of Ontario. That dispute continues its way towards judgment by the Supreme Court of Canada.

On the other hand, the creation of the joint-stewardship council begins to set in place one of the fixtures that could be incorporated into the "treaty of co-existence" sought by Chief Potts on behalf of the Teme-Augama Anishnabai. Ultimately, the pursuit of this land claim through the courts is intended to create the political requirements for the negotiation of such a treaty, a treaty whose realization no doubt would breath new life into the entire constitutional tradition of Crown relations with Indians as rooted in the Royal Proclamation of 1763. With the breath of new life would come a revitalized sense of integrity and purpose in a government founded on promises that were to last as long as the sun shines, as long as the grass grows, and as long as the rivers flow.

• Notes

1 James S. Frideres, *Native People in Canada: Contemporary Conflicts*, 3rd ed. (Scarborough: Prentice-Hall, 1988), 138–206; Andrew J. Siggner, "The Socio-Demographic Conditions of Registered Indians" in *Arduous Journey: Canadian Indians and Decolonization*, ed. J. Rick Ponting (Toronto: McClelland & Stewart, 1986), 57–83.

2 See Russell Lawrence Barsh, "Behind Land Claims: Rationalizing Dispossession in Anglo-American Law," *Law and Anthropology: Internationales Jahrbuch fur Rechtsanthropologie* 1 (1986): 15–50.

3 See Christine Bolt, *Victorian Attitudes to Race* (Toronto: University of Toronto Press, 1971); Marvin Harris, *The Rise of Anthropological Theory: A History of Theories of Culture* (New York: Thomas Y. Crowell, 1968), 80–215; Robert F. Berkhofer, *The White Man's Indian* (New York: Vintage, 1979), 49–61; Bruce G. Trigger, "Giants and Pygmies: The Professionalization of Canadian Archaeology" in *Towards a History of Archaeology*, ed. Glyn Daniel (London: Thames and Hudson, 1981).

4 See James Cullingham, "Home and Native Land," *Saturday Night* 98, 4 (April 1983): 7–11; Bruce W. Hodgins and Jamie Benidickson, *The Temagami Experience: Recreation, Resources, and Aboriginal Rights in the Northern Ontario Wilderness* (Toronto: University of Toronto Press, 1989), 267–89.

5 See Thomas Berger, "The Nishga Indians and Aboriginal Rights" in *Fragile Freedoms: Human Rights and Dissent in Canada*, ed. Thomas Berger (Toronto: Clarke Irwin, 1982), 219–54.

6 See Bruce W. Hodgins, "The Temagami Indians and Canadian Federalism: 1867–1943," *Laurentian University Review* 11, 2 (Feb. 1979): 71–100.

7 See Tony Hall, "Indian Treaties," in *The Canadian Encyclopedia*, 2nd ed., vol. 2 (Edmonton: Hurtig, 1988), 1056–59.

8 Royal Courts of Justice, *The Queen v. The Secretary of State for Foreign and Commonwealth Affairs ex parte The Indian Association of Alberta, Union of New Brunswick Indians, Union of Nova Scotian Indians, 28 January 1982*, xerox, 7–8.

9 The Royal Proclamation is published in its entirety in Ian A.L. Getty and Antoine Lussier, eds., *As Long as the Sun Shines and Water Flows: A Reader in Canadian Native Studies* (Vancouver: University of British Columbia Press, 1983), 29–36.

10 See Brian Slattery, "The Hidden Constitution: Aboriginal Rights in Canada" in *The Quest for Justice: Aboriginal Peoples and Aboriginal Rights*, ed. Menno Boldt and J. Anthony Long (Toronto: University of Toronto Press, 1985), 114–38.

11 See Clarence Walworth Alvord, *The Mississippi Valley in British Politics: A Study in Trade, Land Speculation and Experiments in Imperialism Culminating in the American Revolution* (Cleveland: Arthur H. Clark, 1917); Jack M. Sosin, *Whitehall and the Wilderness: The Middle West in British Colonial Policy, 1760–1775* (Lincoln: University of Nebraska Press, 1961); Francis Jennings, *Empire of Fortune: Crowns, Colonies and Tribes in the Seven Years' War in America* (New York: Norton, 1988).

12 See Robert S. Allen, "The British Indian Department and the Frontier in North America, 1755–1830," Canadian Historical Sites, *Occasional Papers in Archaeology and History*, no. 14 (Ottawa: 1975), 5–125.

13 See A.L. Burt, *The United States, Great Britain and British North America from the Revolution to the Establishment of Peace after the War of 1812* (New Haven: Yale University Press, 1940); Colin G. Calloway, *Crown and Calumet: British–Indian Relations, 1783–1815* (Norman: University of Oklahoma Press, 1987).

14 See Robert J. Surtees, "Indian Land Cessions in Ontario, 1763–1862: The Evolution of a System" (PhD thesis, Carleton University, 1982); Ian

Johnson, "The Early Mississauga Treaty Process, 1781–1819, in Historical Perspective" (PhD thesis, University of Toronto, 1986).

15 See G.F.G. Stanley, "The Indians and the War of 1812" in *The Defended Border: Upper Canada and the War of 1812*, ed. Morris Zaslow (Toronto: Macmillan, 1964), 174–88; Calloway, *Crown and Calumet*, 193–222; Robert S. Allen, "His Majesty's Indian Allies: Native Peoples, the British Crown and the War of 1812," *Michigan Historical Review* 14, 2 (Fall 1988): 1–24.

16 *Reports of the Supreme Court of Canada*, vol. 13 (Ottawa, 1887), 609–10.

17 See James W. St G. Walker, "The Indian in Canadian Historical Writing," Canadian Historical Association, *Historical Papers* (1971): 21–50; Bruce G. Trigger, "The Historians' Indian: Native Americans in Canadian Historical Writing from Charlevoix to the Present," *Canadian Historical Review* 67, 3 (Sept. 1986): 315–42.

18 I have drawn this account of the early stages of the case primarily from discussions with James Morrison.

19 The relationship between Chief Potts and Bruce Clark is discussed in some detail in John Lorinc, "If God Is on Vacation," *This Magazine* 23, 4 (Nov. 1989): 22–27.

20 See Donald B. Smith, *From the Land of Shadows: The Making of Grey Owl* (Saskatoon: Western Producer Prairie Books, 1990).

21 *Hamlet of Baker Lake et al. v. Minister of Indian Affairs and Northern Development*, 1980. The case is discussed in Bradford W. Morse, ed., *Aboriginal Peoples and the Law: Indian, Métis and Inuit Rights in Canada* (Ottawa: Carleton University Press, 1985), 81–84.

22 *Attorney-General for Ontario v. Bear Island Foundation et al., Potts et al. v. Attorney-General for Ontario*, 11 Dec. 1984 in *Ontario Reports*, 2nd ser., vol. 49, 1985 (hereafter *OR*), 366.

23 She used the phrase in a conversation with Bruce Hodgins at a Native-stud-ies conference at Trent University in 1985.

24 *OR*, 390.

25 Ibid., 381.

26 *Appeal Cases before the House of Lords and the Judicial Committee of the Privy Council*, vol. 14 (London, 1889), 54.

27 Tony Hall, "*The St Catherine's Milling and Lumber Company v. The Queen*: Indian Land Rights as a Factor in Federal-Provincial Relations in Nineteenth-Century Canada" (paper presented in 1988 at a conference at the University of Manitoba). The paper will be published by the University of Manitoba Press in conference proceedings entitled *Aboriginal Resource Use in Canada*, ed. Jean Friesen and Kerry Abel.

28 *OR*, 381.

29 Ibid., 436.

30 Ibid., 381.

31 Ibid., 375. On Pontiac's uprising see Howard H. Peckham, *Pontiac and the Indian Uprising* (Chicago: University of Chicago Press, 1947). On the implications of how Britain's conquest of the French affected Indian land title in North America see W.J. Eccles, "Sovereignty-Association, 1500–1783," *Canadian Historical Review* 65, 4 (Dec. 1984): 475–510.

32 *OR*, 386–92.

33 See Thomas Flanagan, "From Indian Title to Aboriginal Rights" in *Law and Justice in a New Land: Essays in Western Canadian Legal History*, ed. Louis A. Knafla (Toronto: Carswell, 1986), 81–100.

34 *OR*, 386–87.

35 Ibid., 391.

36 Ibid., 387–93.

37 Ibid., 410.

38 Ibid., 441.

39 Ibid., 378–79.

40 Ibid., 466.

41 Ibid., 440.

42 Ibid., 457–66.

43 Ibid., 386.

44 Ibid., 384.

45 James Youngblood Henderson, "The Doctrine of Aboriginal Rights in Western Legal Tradition" in *Quest for Justice*, 220.

46 Bruce Clark's MA thesis, written for the University of Western Ontario, is published as *Indian Title in Canada* (Toronto: Carswell, 1987). His PhD thesis, entitled "The Right of Indian Self-Government in Canada," was written for the University of Aberdeen.

47 *The Attorney General for Ontario v. The Bear Island Foundation et al.*, 27 Feb. 1989, xerox copy of Appeal Court's finding, 14–25 (hereafter cited as AC).

48 Ibid., 29.

49 Appeal Cases before the House of Lords, 14: 54.

50 AC, 34.

51 Jennings, *Empire of Fortune*. In Jennings' concluding volume of his monumental Covenant Chain series, he stresses that the Royal Proclamation of 1763 marks a major watershed in North American history. The proclamation created the essential framework for the clash of interests that eventually exploded in the American Revolution.

52 See Richard Slotkin, *Regeneration Through Violence: The Mythology of the American Frontier, 1600–1860* (Middletown: Wesleyan University Press, 1983); Richard Drinnon, *Facing West: The Metaphysics of Indian-Hating and Empire Building* (New York: Meridian, 1980).

53 Bradford Morse, "Government Obligations, Aboriginal Peoples and Section 91(24) of the Constitution Act, 1867" in *Aboriginal Peoples and Government Responsibility: Exploring Federal and Provincial Roles*, ed. David C. Hawkes (Ottawa: Carleton University Press, 1989), 59–91.

54 *The Ontario Lands Case, Arguments of Mr. Blake Q.C. Before the Privy Council* (Toronto: Press of the Budget, 1988), 18.

55 On the *Guerin* case see R.H. Bartlett, "You Can't Trust the Crown: The Fiduciary Obligation of the Crown to the Indians: *Guerin v. The Queen*," *Saskatchewan Law Review* 49 (1984–85): 367.

56 *Guerin v. The Queen*, Supreme Court of Canada Reports (1984): 335.

57 *OR*, 480–82.

58 See Tony Hall, "What Are We? Chopped Liver? Aboriginal Affairs in the Constitutional Politics of Canada in the 1980s" in *The Meech Lake Primer: Conflicting Views of the 1987 Constitutional Accord*, ed. Michael D. Behiels (Ottawa: University of Ottawa Press, 1989), 447–48.

59 World Commission on Environment and Development, *Our Common Future* (Oxford: Oxford University Press, 1987), 447–48.

60 On the connection between aboriginal issues and environmentalism, see Christopher Vecsey and Robert W. Venables, eds., *American Indian Environments: Ecological Issues in Native American History* (Syracuse: Syracuse University Press, 1980).

61 *Globe and Mail*, 24 April 1990.